EMPOWERED

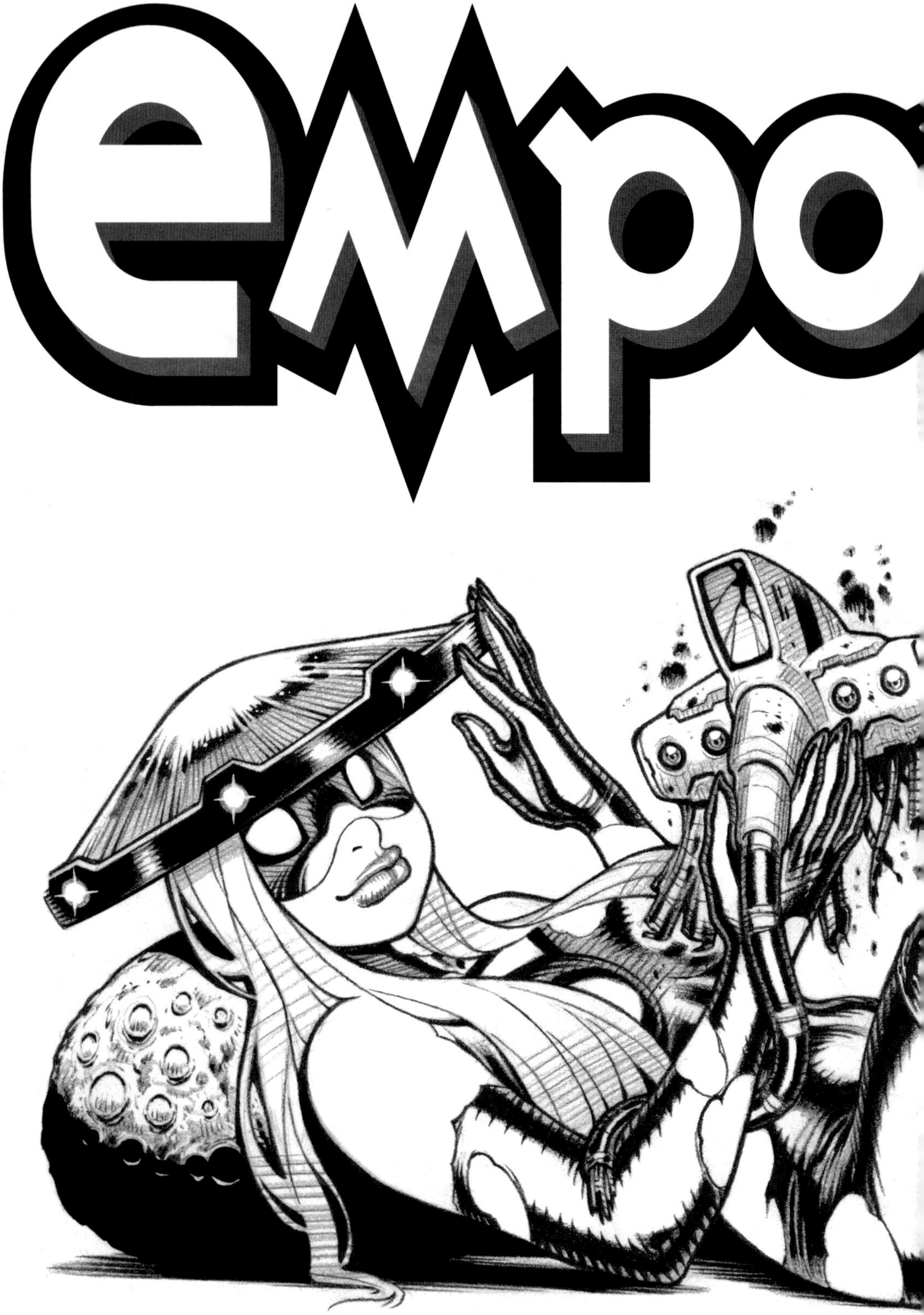
empo

volume **9**

Wered

by ADAM WARREN

(twitter.com/EmpoweredComic adamwarren.deviantart.com
adamwarrencomics.tumblr.com instagram.com/adam_warren_art)

cover colors by ROB "ROBAATO" PORTER   empowered logo by EUGENE WANG

DARK HORSE BOOKS

president and publisher
Mike Richardson

editor
Chris Warner

assistant editor
Everett Patterson

designer
Brennan Thome

digital art and production
Chris Horn

EMPOWERED VOLUME 9

Dark Horse Books
10956 SE Main Street
Milwaukie, OR 97222

DarkHorse.com

To find a comics shop in your area, call the Comic Shop
Locator Service toll-free at 1-888-266-4226

First edition: August 2015
ISBN 978-1-61655-571-9

1 3 5 7 9 10 8 6 4 2

Printed in China

NEIL HANKERSON Executive Vice President • TOM WEDDLE Chief Financial Officer • RANDY STRADLEY Vice President of Publishing • MICHAEL MARTENS Vice President of Book Trade Sales • SCOTT ALLIE Editor in Chief • MATT PARKINSON Vice President of Marketing • DAVID SCROGGY Vice President of Product Development • DALE LaFOUNTAIN Vice President of Information Technology • DARLENE VOGEL Senior Director of Print, Design, and Production • KEN LIZZI General Counsel • DAVEY ESTRADA Editorial Director • CHRIS WARNER Senior Books Editor • DIANA SCHUTZ Executive Editor • CARY GRAZZINI Director of Print and Development • LIA RIBACCHI Art Director • CARA NIECE Director of Scheduling • MARK BERNARDI Director of Digital Publishing

Empowered™

Not a Good Day to Be Empowered

(or, our story's introductory chapter)

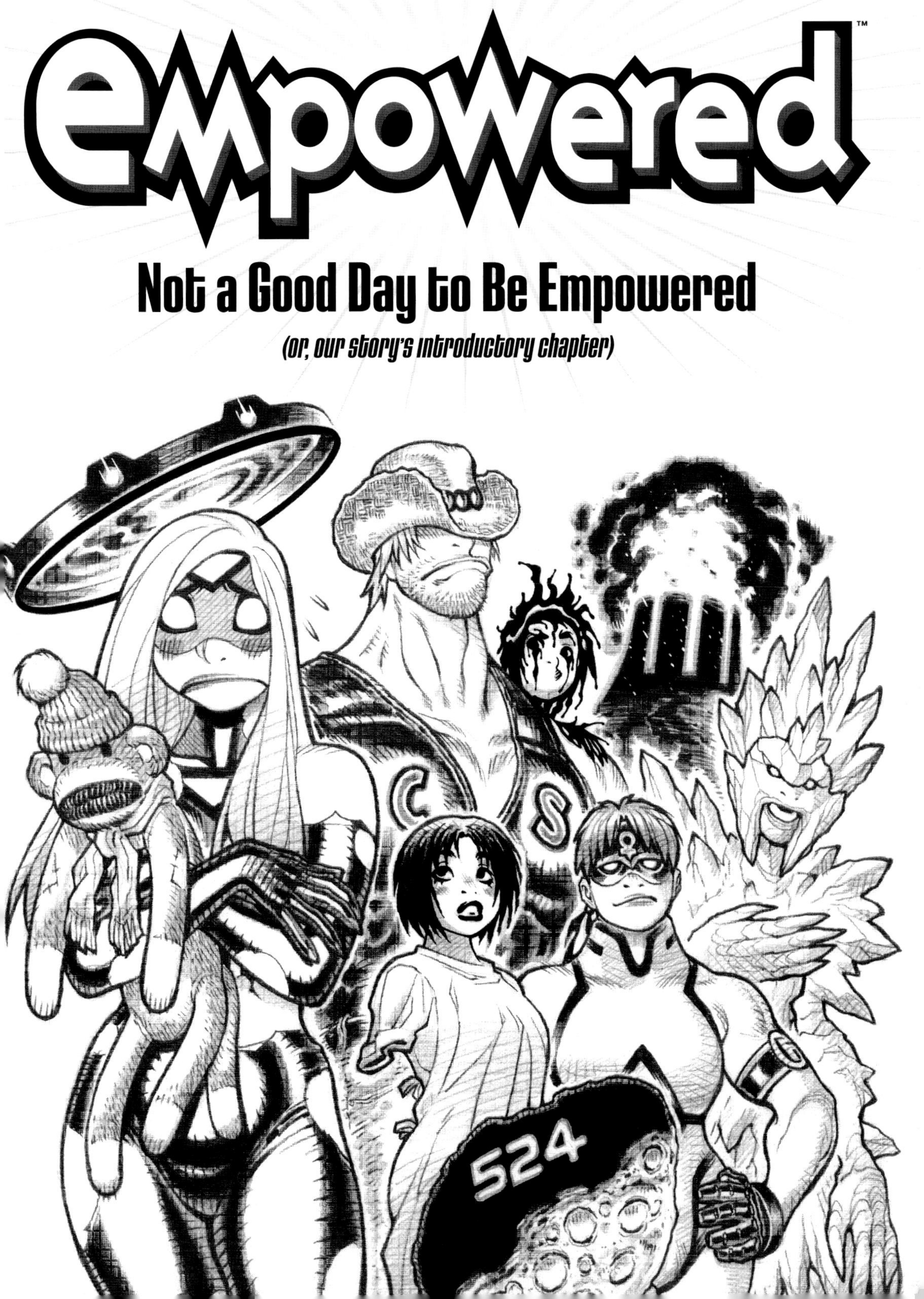
524

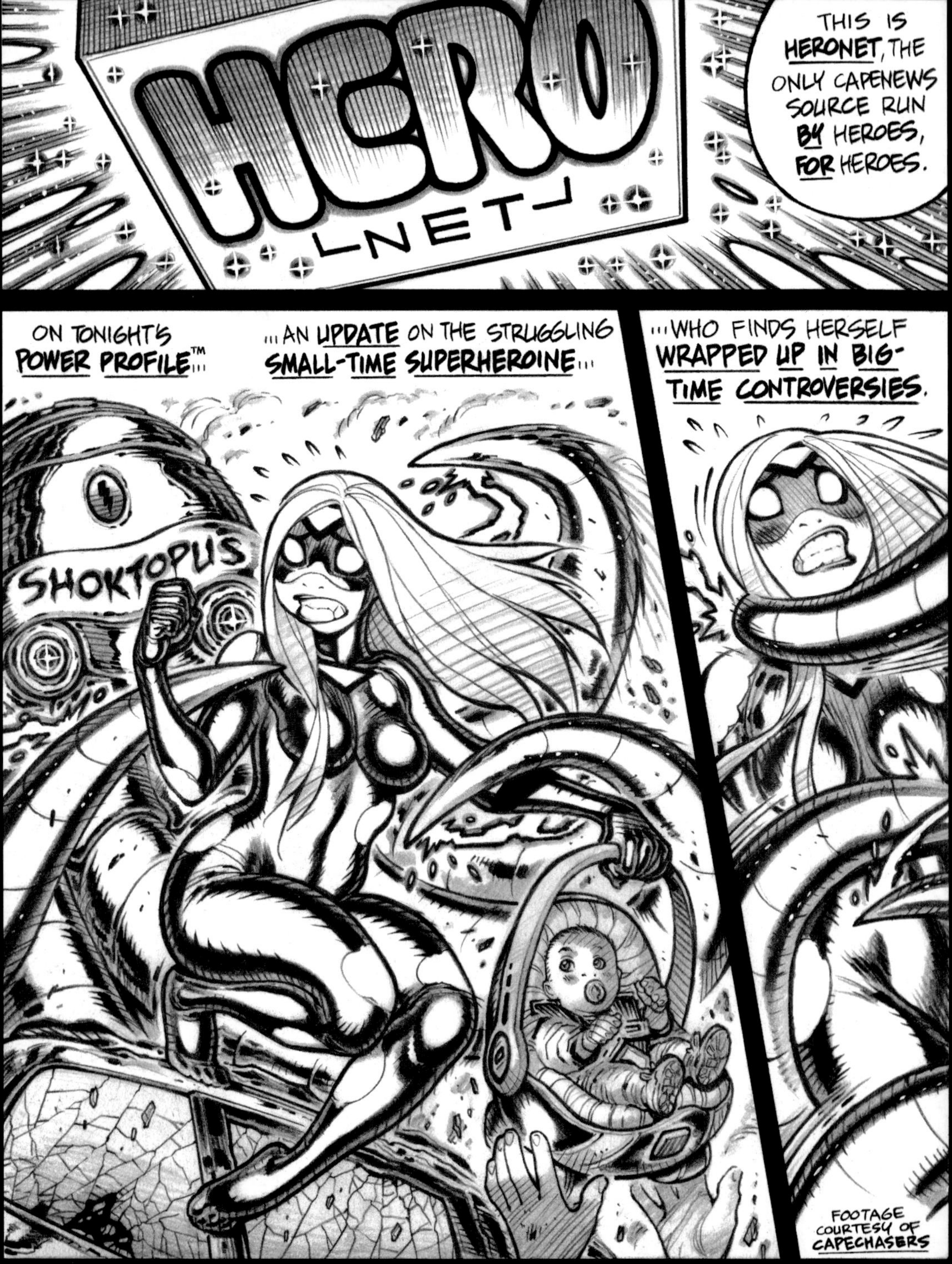
HERO NET
THIS IS HERONET, THE ONLY CAPENEWS SOURCE RUN BY HEROES, FOR HEROES.
ON TONIGHT'S POWER PROFILE™...
...AN UPDATE ON THE STRUGGLING SMALL-TIME SUPERHEROINE...
SHOKTOPUS
...WHO FINDS HERSELF WRAPPED UP IN BIG-TIME CONTROVERSIES.
FOOTAGE COURTESY OF CAPECHASERS

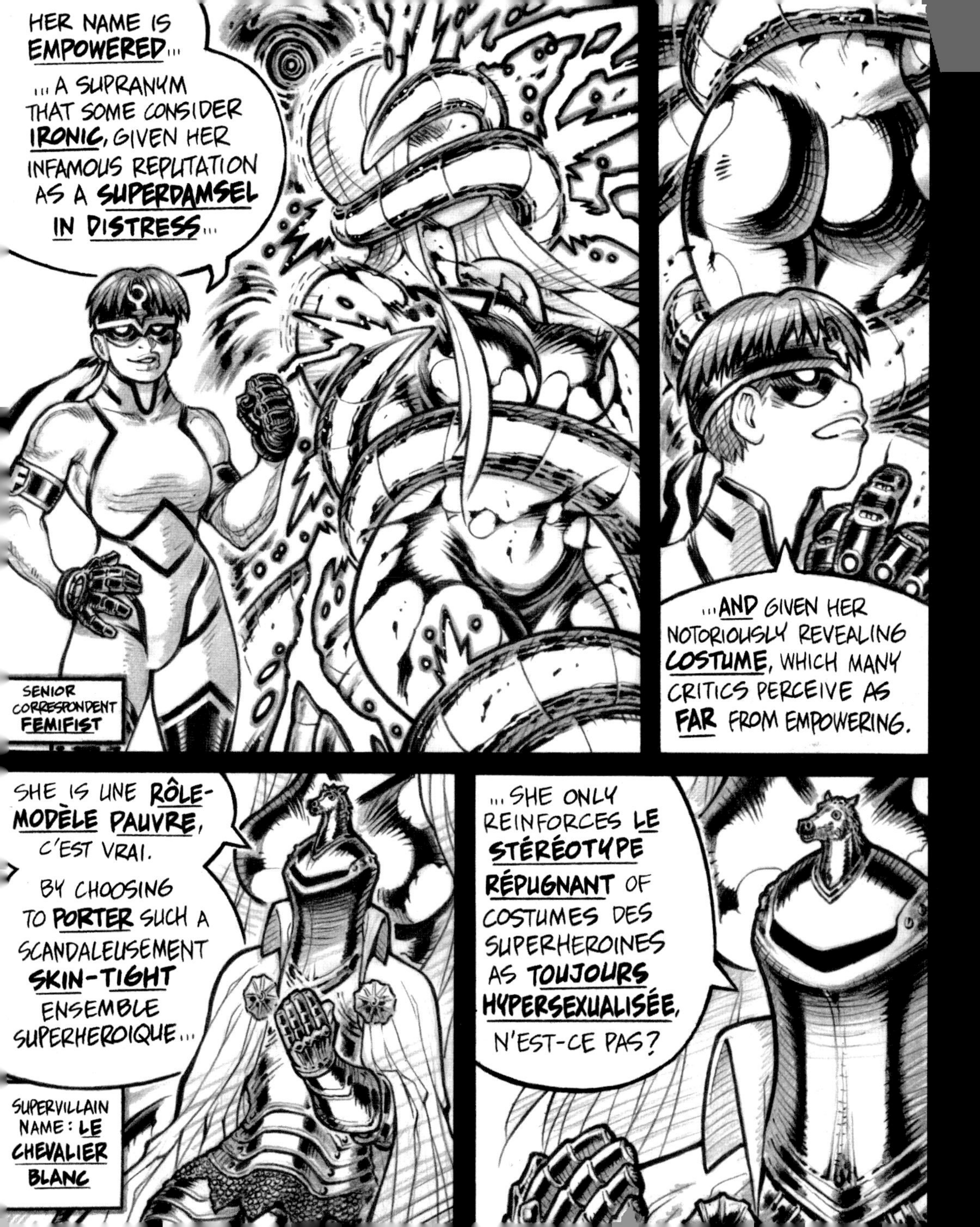
HER NAME IS EMPOWERED...
...A SUPRANYM THAT SOME CONSIDER IRONIC, GIVEN HER INFAMOUS REPUTATION AS A SUPERDAMSEL IN DISTRESS...
SENIOR CORRESPONDENT FEMIFIST
...AND GIVEN HER NOTORIOUSLY REVEALING COSTUME, WHICH MANY CRITICS PERCEIVE AS FAR FROM EMPOWERING.
SHE IS UNE RÔLE-MODÈLE PAUVRE, C'EST VRAI.
BY CHOOSING TO PORTER SUCH A SCANDALEUSEMENT SKIN-TIGHT ENSEMBLE SUPERHEROIQUE...
SUPERVILLAIN NAME: LE CHEVALIER BLANC
...SHE ONLY REINFORCES LE STÉRÉOTYPE RÉPUGNANT OF COSTUMES DES SUPERHEROINES AS TOUJOURS HYPERSEXUALISÉE, N'EST-CE PAS?

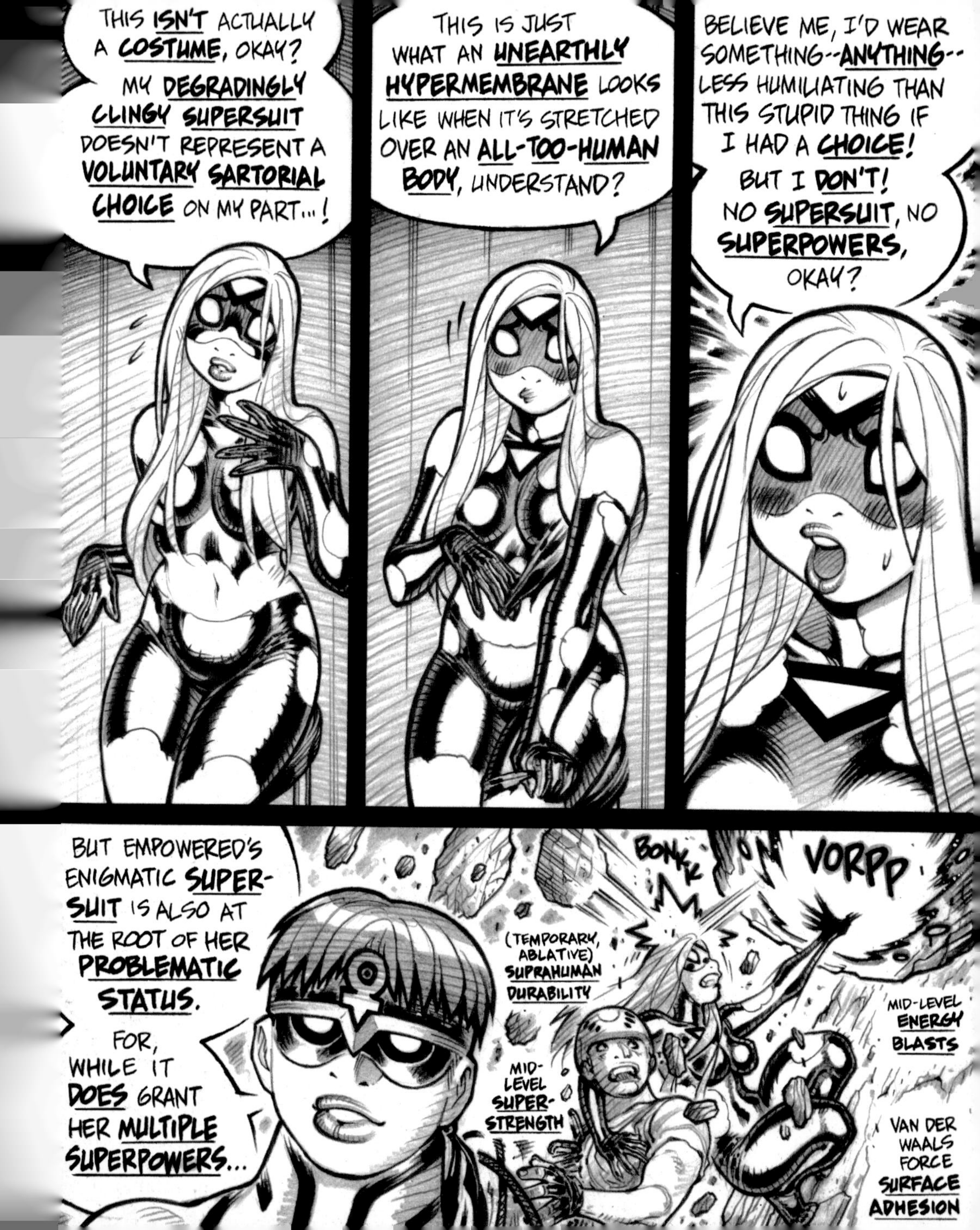
THIS ISN'T ACTUALLY A COSTUME, OKAY? MY DEGRADINGLY CLINGY SUPERSUIT DOESN'T REPRESENT A VOLUNTARY SARTORIAL CHOICE ON MY PART...!
THIS IS JUST WHAT AN UNEARTHLY HYPERMEMBRANE LOOKS LIKE WHEN IT'S STRETCHED OVER AN ALL-TOO-HUMAN BODY, UNDERSTAND?
BELIEVE ME, I'D WEAR SOMETHING--ANYTHING--LESS HUMILIATING THAN THIS STUPID THING IF I HAD A CHOICE! BUT I DON'T! NO SUPERSUIT, NO SUPERPOWERS, OKAY?
BUT EMPOWERED'S ENIGMATIC SUPER-SUIT IS ALSO AT THE ROOT OF HER PROBLEMATIC STATUS.
FOR, WHILE IT DOES GRANT HER MULTIPLE SUPERPOWERS...
BONKK
VORPP
(TEMPORARY, ABLATIVE) SUPRAHUMAN DURABILITY
MID-LEVEL ENERGY BLASTS
MID-LEVEL SUPER-STRENGTH
VAN DER WAALS FORCE SURFACE ADHESION

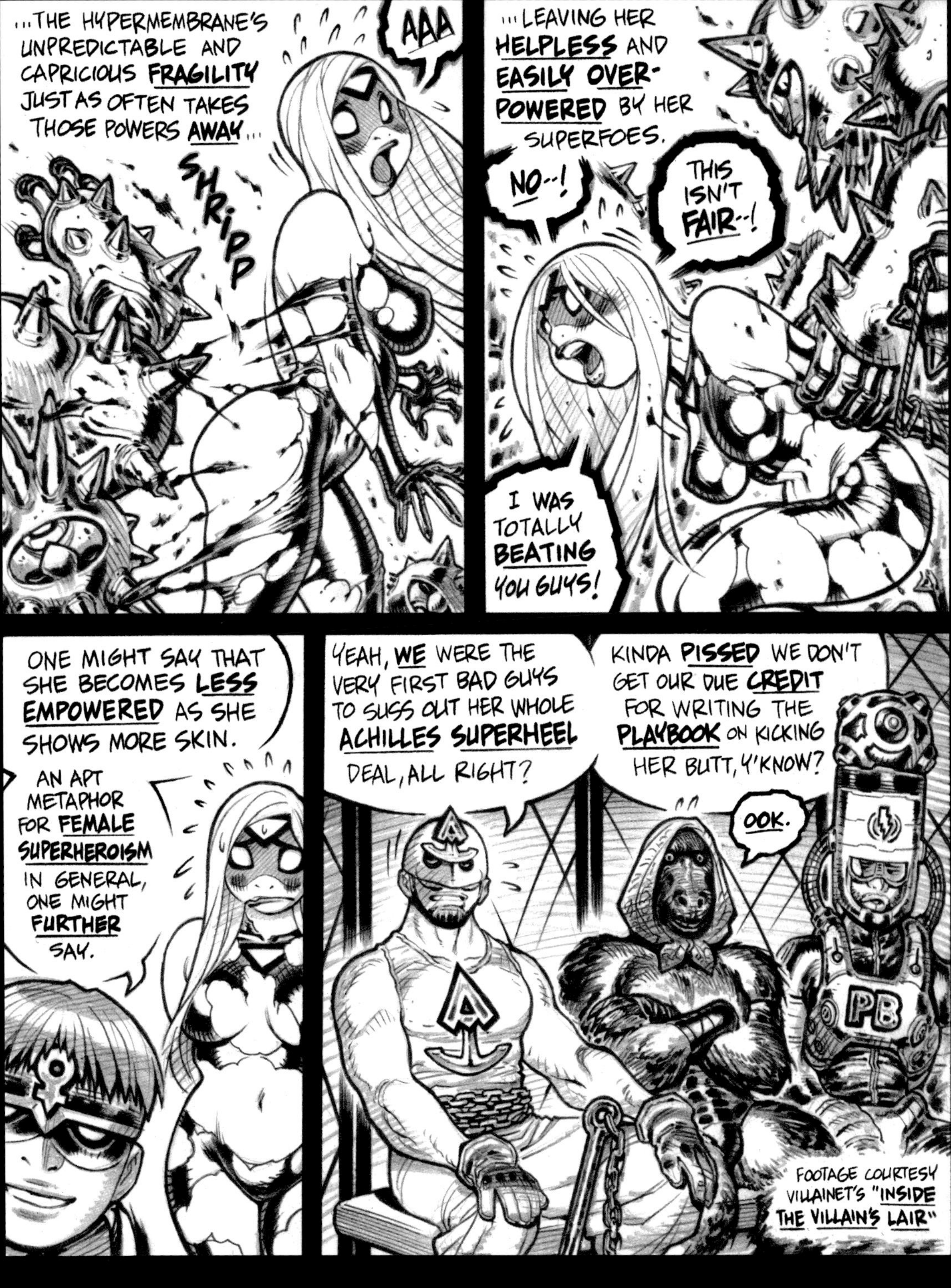
...THE HYPERMEMBRANE'S UNPREDICTABLE AND CAPRICIOUS FRAGILITY JUST AS OFTEN TAKES THOSE POWERS AWAY...
AAA
SHRIPP
...LEAVING HER HELPLESS AND EASILY OVER-POWERED BY HER SUPERFOES.
NO--!
THIS ISN'T FAIR--!
I WAS TOTALLY BEATING YOU GUYS!
ONE MIGHT SAY THAT SHE BECOMES LESS EMPOWERED AS SHE SHOWS MORE SKIN.
AN APT METAPHOR FOR FEMALE SUPERHEROISM IN GENERAL, ONE MIGHT FURTHER SAY.
YEAH, WE WERE THE VERY FIRST BAD GUYS TO SUSS OUT HER WHOLE ACHILLES SUPERHEEL DEAL, ALL RIGHT?
KINDA PISSED WE DON'T GET OUR DUE CREDIT FOR WRITING THE PLAYBOOK ON KICKING HER BUTT, Y'KNOW?
OOK.
PB
FOOTAGE COURTESY VILLAINET'S "INSIDE THE VILLAIN'S LAIR"

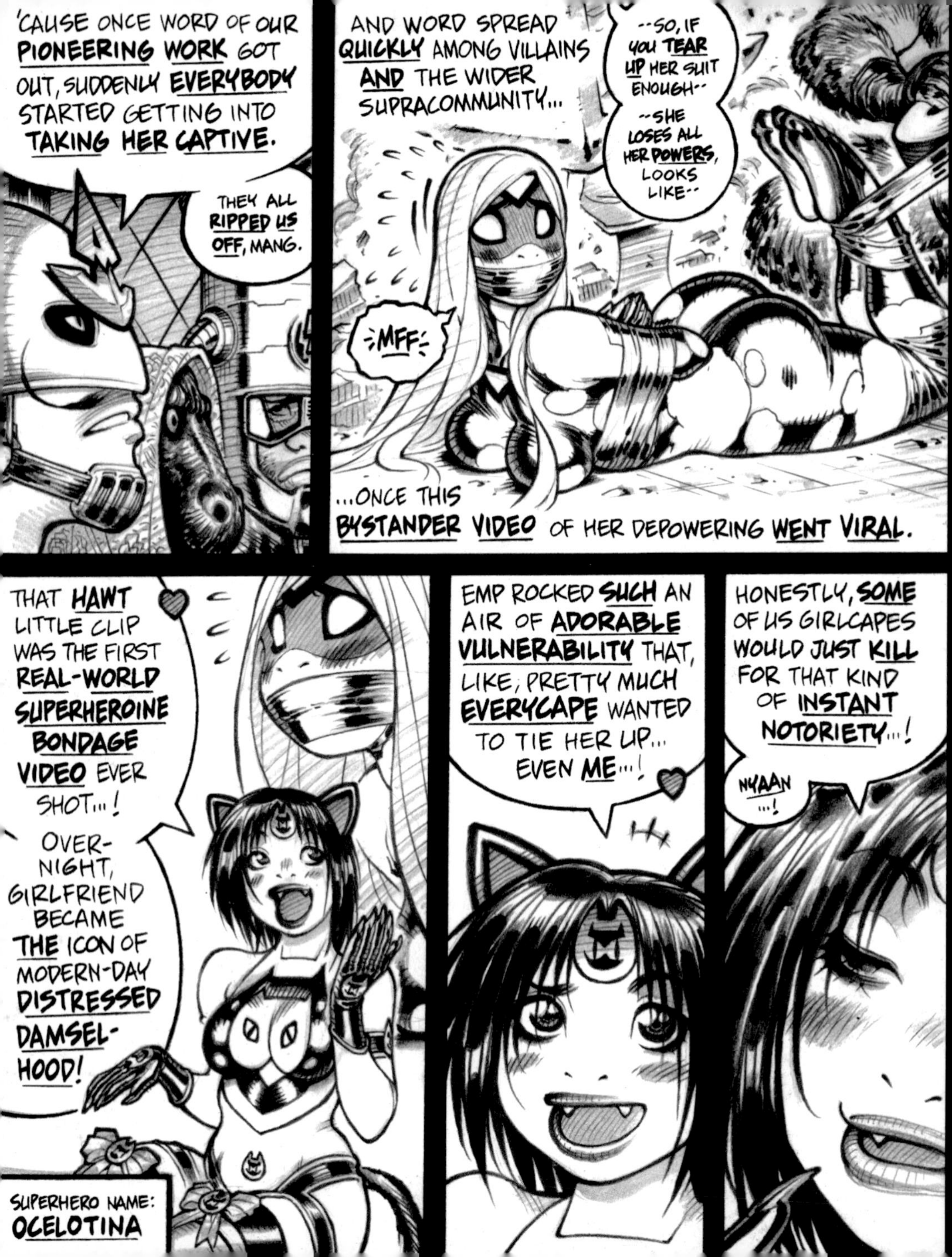
'CAUSE ONCE WORD OF OUR PIONEERING WORK GOT OUT, SUDDENLY EVERYBODY STARTED GETTING INTO TAKING HER CAPTIVE.
THEY ALL RIPPED US OFF, MANG.
AND WORD SPREAD QUICKLY AMONG VILLAINS AND THE WIDER SUPRACOMMUNITY...
--SO, IF YOU TEAR UP HER SUIT ENOUGH--
--SHE LOSES ALL HER POWERS, LOOKS LIKE--
MFF
...ONCE THIS BYSTANDER VIDEO OF HER DEPOWERING WENT VIRAL.
THAT HAWT LITTLE CLIP WAS THE FIRST REAL-WORLD SUPERHEROINE BONDAGE VIDEO EVER SHOT...!
OVER-NIGHT, GIRLFRIEND BECAME THE ICON OF MODERN-DAY DISTRESSED DAMSEL-HOOD!
SUPERHERO NAME: OCELOTINA
EMP ROCKED SUCH AN AIR OF ADORABLE VULNERABILITY THAT, LIKE, PRETTY MUCH EVERYCAPE WANTED TO TIE HER UP... EVEN ME...!
HONESTLY, SOME OF US GIRLCAPES WOULD JUST KILL FOR THAT KIND OF INSTANT NOTORIETY...!
NYAAN...!

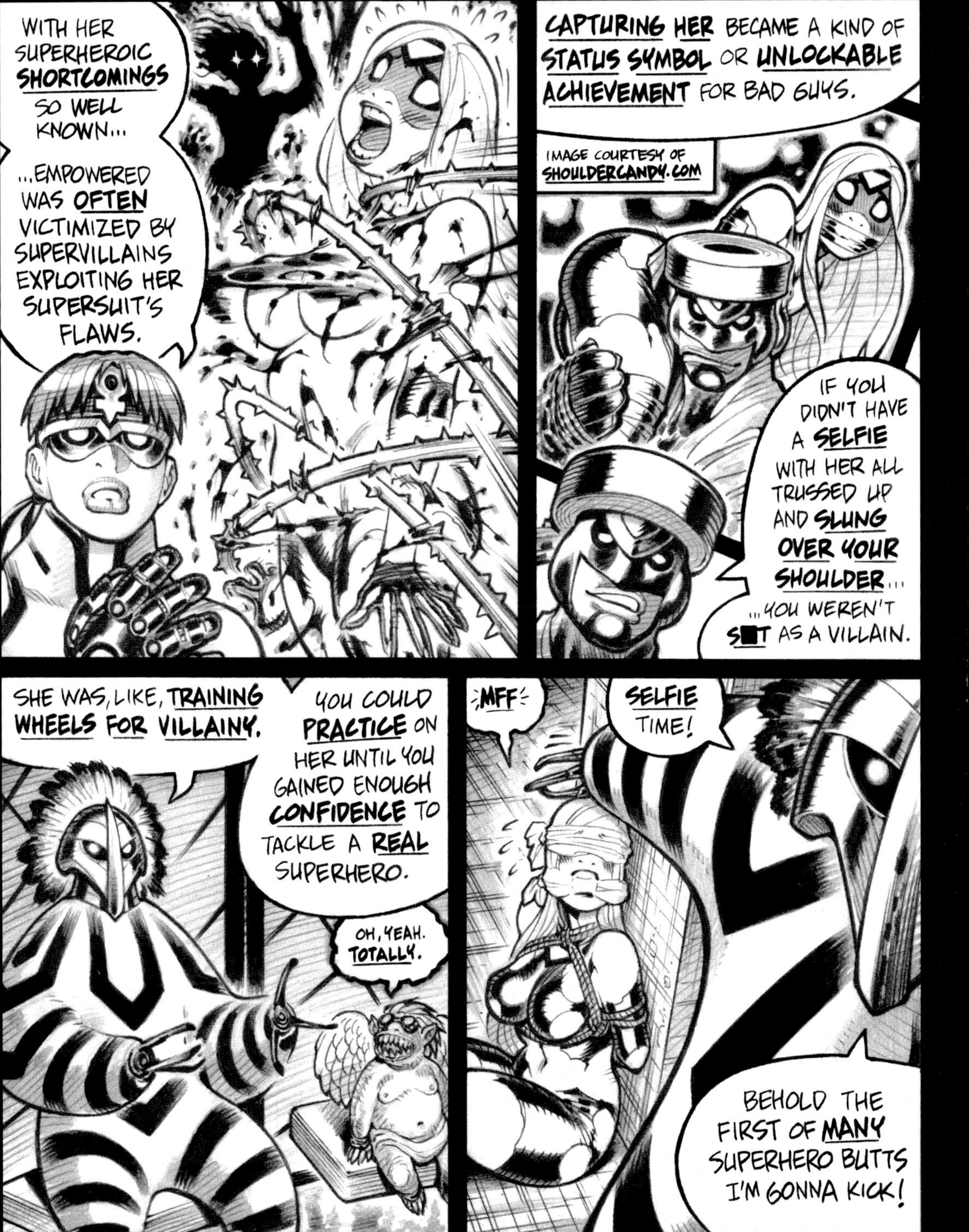
WITH HER SUPERHEROIC SHORTCOMINGS SO WELL KNOWN...
...EMPOWERED WAS OFTEN VICTIMIZED BY SUPERVILLAINS EXPLOITING HER SUPERSUIT'S FLAWS.
CAPTURING HER BECAME A KIND OF STATUS SYMBOL OR UNLOCKABLE ACHIEVEMENT FOR BAD GUYS.
IMAGE COURTESY OF SHOULDERCANDY.COM
IF YOU DIDN'T HAVE A SELFIE WITH HER ALL TRUSSED UP AND SLUNG OVER YOUR SHOULDER...
...YOU WEREN'T S[redacted]T AS A VILLAIN.
SHE WAS, LIKE, TRAINING WHEELS FOR VILLAINY.
YOU COULD PRACTICE ON HER UNTIL YOU GAINED ENOUGH CONFIDENCE TO TACKLE A REAL SUPERHERO.
OH, YEAH. TOTALLY.
MFF
SELFIE TIME!
BEHOLD THE FIRST OF MANY SUPERHERO BUTTS I'M GONNA KICK!

HEY, IF EVERY DUMBASS SUPERVILL IN THE FIELD KNEW THAT, SAY, **CAPTAIN ⊰BEEEP⊱** IS RENDERED POWERLESS BY **ANY** EXPOSURE TO ⊰BEEEP⊱--

--THEN I GUARANTEE THAT **HE** WOULD BE GETTING HIS SORRY BEHIND **TIED UP** ON A REGULAR BASIS, **JUST LIKE ME,** OKAY?

...**WAIT.**

DID I JUST SAY CAPTAIN ⊰**BLEEEP**⊱'S ACHILLES HEEL **OUT LOUD**...?

OH, GOD... CAN WE **EDIT THAT PART OUT**...?

CETTE **PAUVRE FILLE** IS DOOMED TO BE **RIEN** BUT UNE **DÉMOISELLE EN DÉTRESSE,** N'EST-CE PAS?

SHE NEEDS, HOW YOU SAY, **LA DÉLIVRANCE** NOT JUST FROM **LES SUPER-VILLAINS** SINISTRES ET SEXISTES...

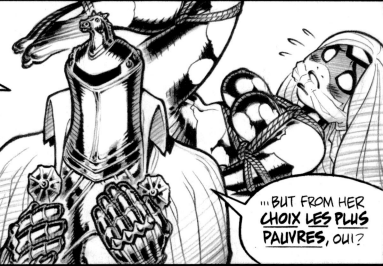

...BUT FROM HER **CHOIX LES PLUS PAUVRES,** OUI?

12

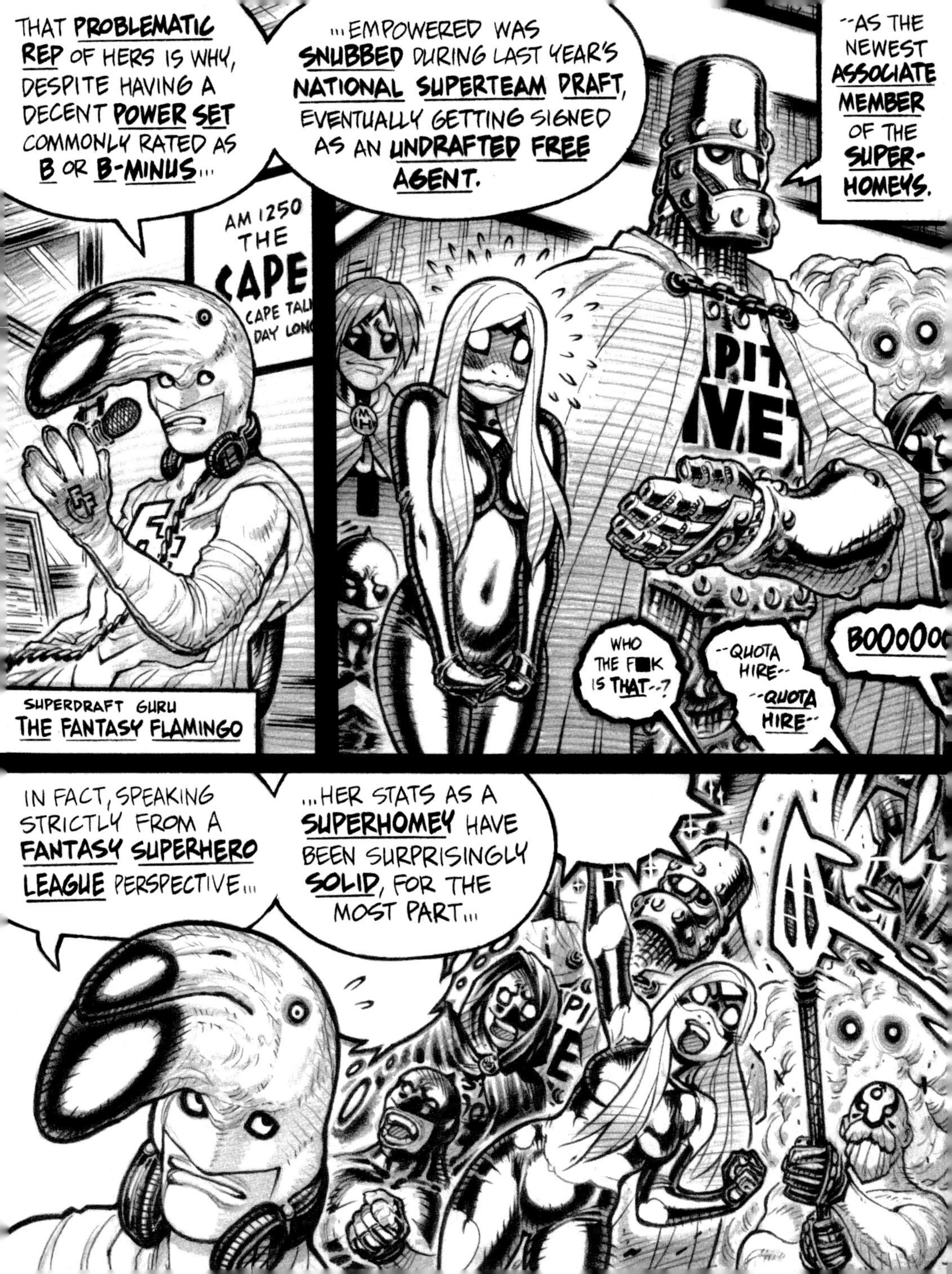

THAT PROBLEMATIC REP OF HERS IS WHY, DESPITE HAVING A DECENT POWER SET COMMONLY RATED AS B OR B-MINUS...
...EMPOWERED WAS SNUBBED DURING LAST YEAR'S NATIONAL SUPERTEAM DRAFT, EVENTUALLY GETTING SIGNED AS AN UNDRAFTED FREE AGENT.
--AS THE NEWEST ASSOCIATE MEMBER OF THE SUPER-HOMEYS.
AM 1250 THE CAPE
SUPERDRAFT GURU THE FANTASY FLAMINGO
WHO THE F[redacted]K IS THAT--?
--QUOTA HIRE--
--QUOTA HIRE--
BOOOOO
IN FACT, SPEAKING STRICTLY FROM A FANTASY SUPERHERO LEAGUE PERSPECTIVE...
...HER STATS AS A SUPERHOMEY HAVE BEEN SURPRISINGLY SOLID, FOR THE MOST PART...

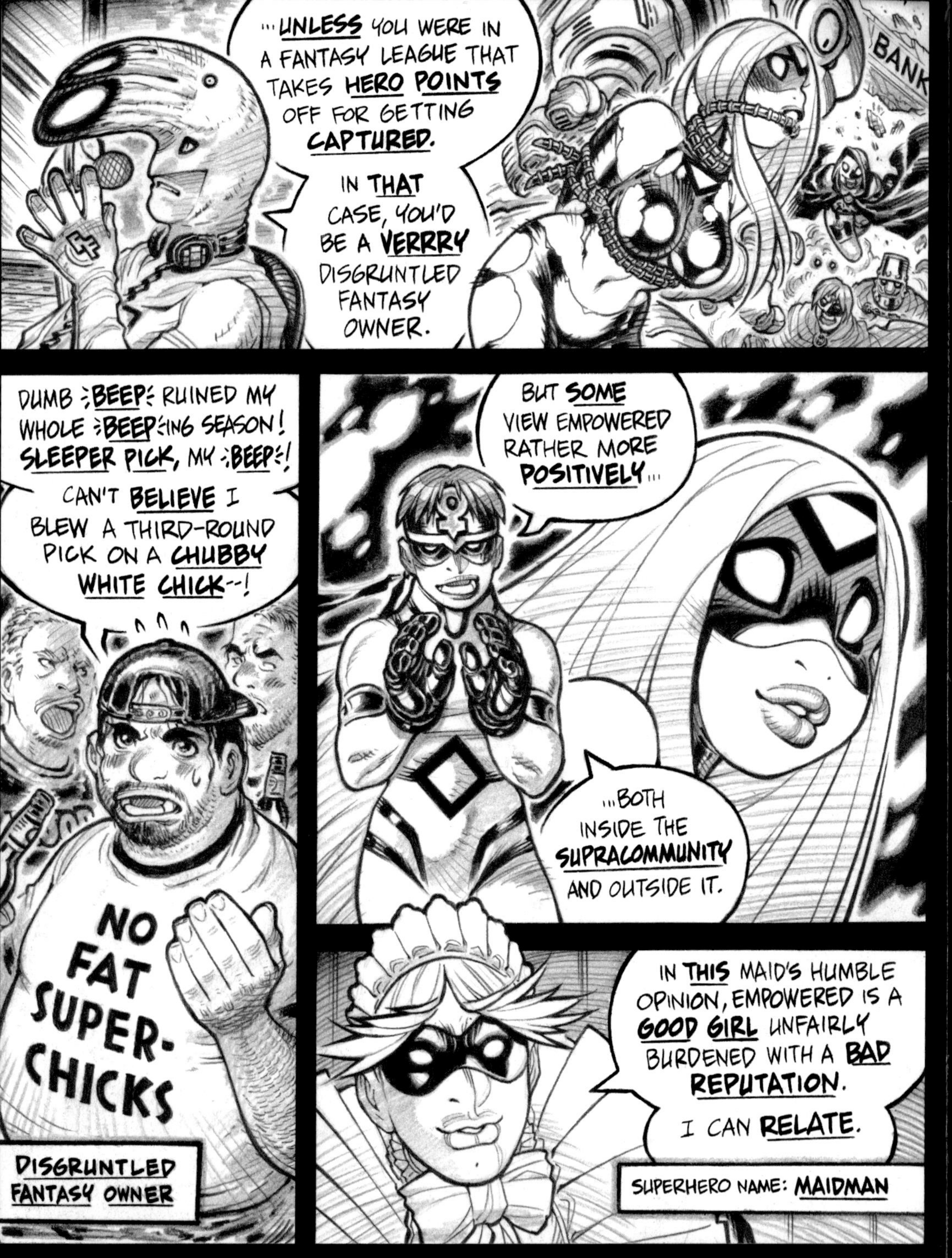
...UNLESS YOU WERE IN A FANTASY LEAGUE THAT TAKES HERO POINTS OFF FOR GETTING CAPTURED.
IN THAT CASE, YOU'D BE A VERRRY DISGRUNTLED FANTASY OWNER.
BANK
DUMB :BEEP: RUINED MY WHOLE :BEEP:ING SEASON! SLEEPER PICK, MY :BEEP:!
CAN'T BELIEVE I BLEW A THIRD-ROUND PICK ON A CHUBBY WHITE CHICK--!
NO FAT SUPER-CHICKS
DISGRUNTLED FANTASY OWNER
BUT SOME VIEW EMPOWERED RATHER MORE POSITIVELY...
...BOTH INSIDE THE SUPRACOMMUNITY AND OUTSIDE IT.
IN THIS MAID'S HUMBLE OPINION, EMPOWERED IS A GOOD GIRL UNFAIRLY BURDENED WITH A BAD REPUTATION.
I CAN RELATE.
SUPERHERO NAME: MAIDMAN

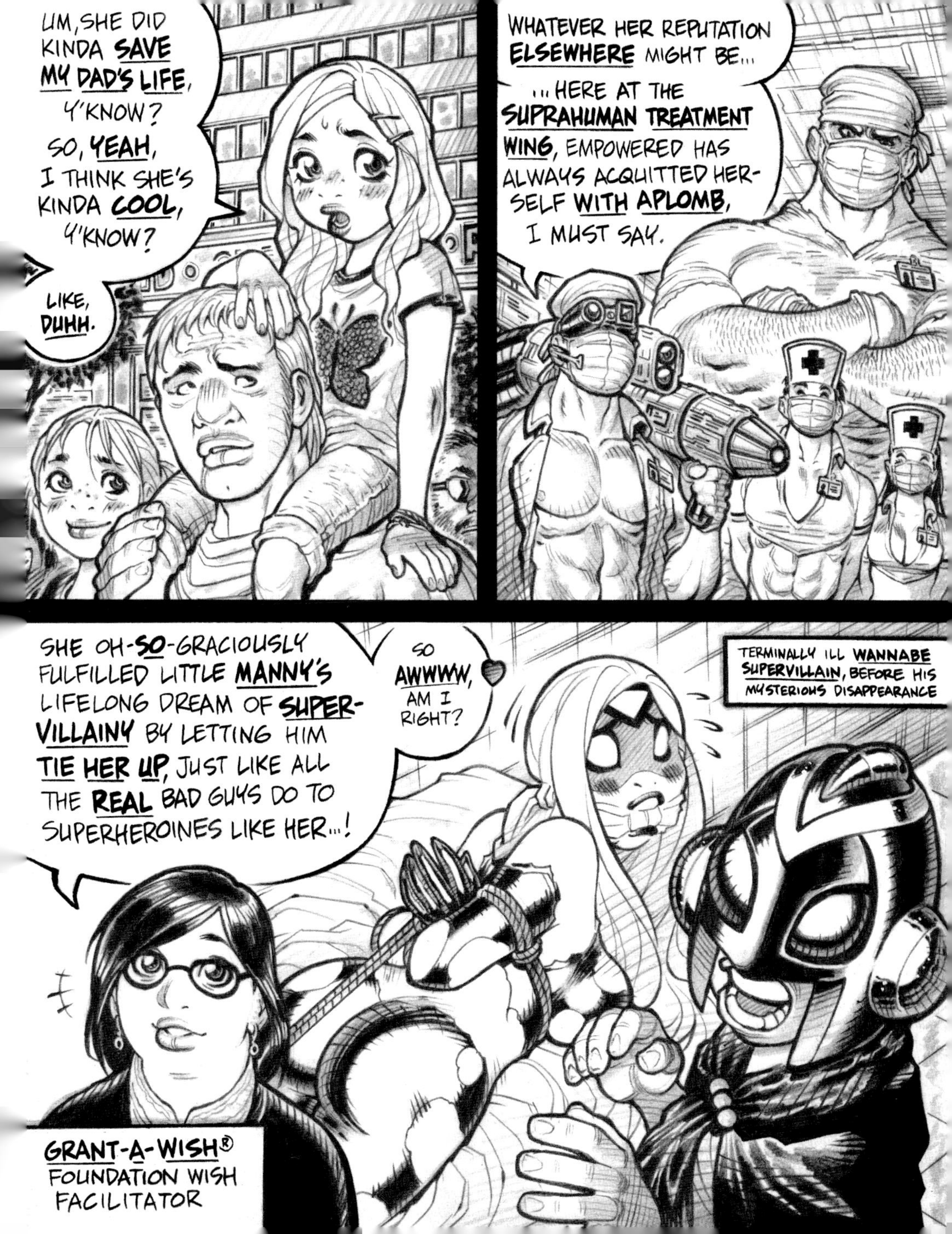
UM, SHE DID KINDA SAVE MY DAD'S LIFE, Y'KNOW?
SO, YEAH, I THINK SHE'S KINDA COOL, Y'KNOW?
LIKE, DUHH.
WHATEVER HER REPUTATION ELSEWHERE MIGHT BE...
...HERE AT THE SUPRAHUMAN TREATMENT WING, EMPOWERED HAS ALWAYS ACQUITTED HER-SELF WITH APLOMB, I MUST SAY.
SHE OH-SO-GRACIOUSLY FULFILLED LITTLE MANNY'S LIFELONG DREAM OF SUPER-VILLAINY BY LETTING HIM TIE HER UP, JUST LIKE ALL THE REAL BAD GUYS DO TO SUPERHEROINES LIKE HER...!
SO AWWWW, AM I RIGHT?
TERMINALLY ILL WANNABE SUPERVILLAIN, BEFORE HIS MYSTERIOUS DISAPPEARANCE
GRANT-A-WISH® FOUNDATION WISH FACILITATOR

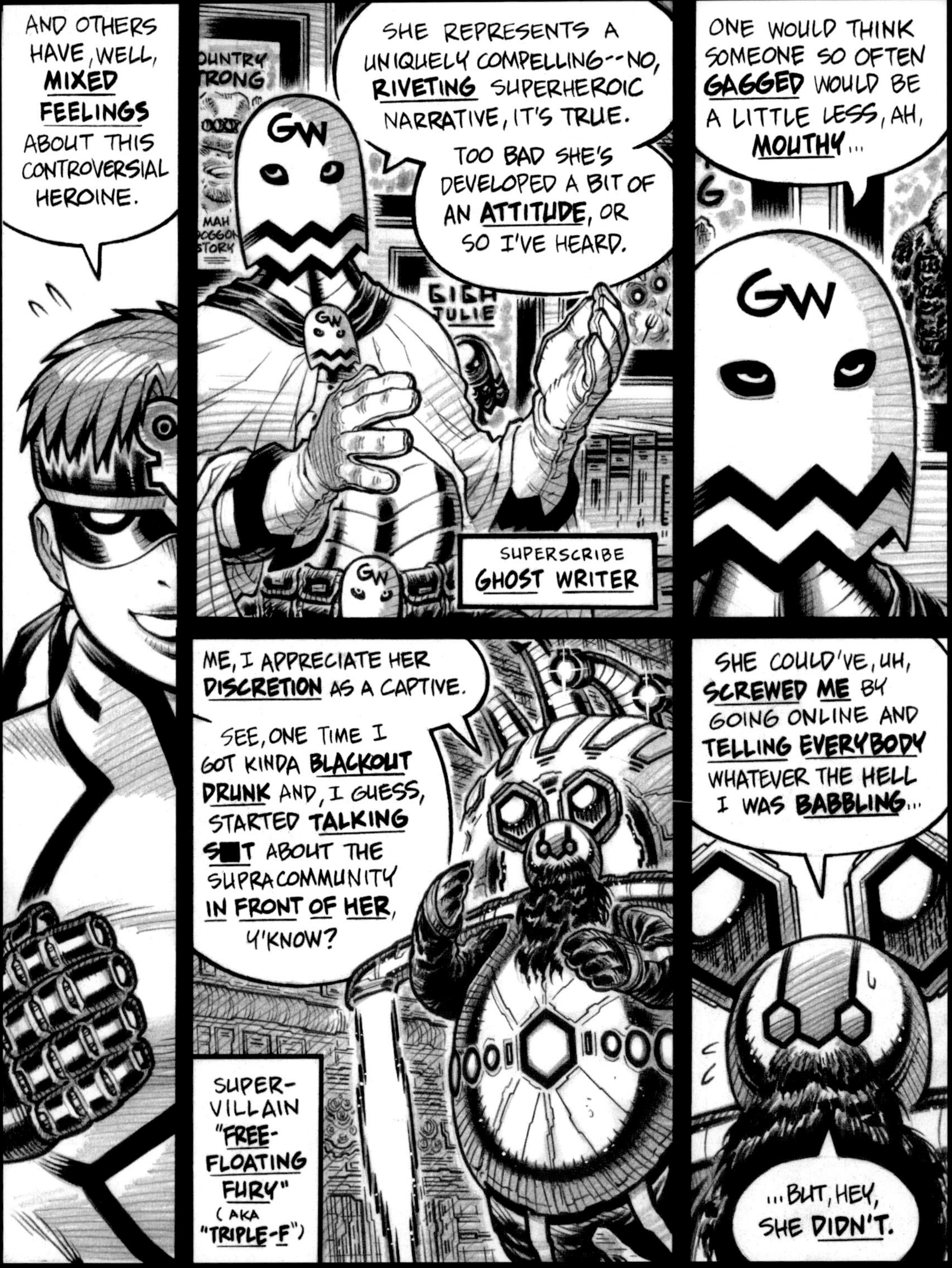

AND OTHERS HAVE, WELL, MIXED FEELINGS ABOUT THIS CONTROVERSIAL HEROINE.
SHE REPRESENTS A UNIQUELY COMPELLING--NO, RIVETING SUPERHEROIC NARRATIVE, IT'S TRUE.
TOO BAD SHE'S DEVELOPED A BIT OF AN ATTITUDE, OR SO I'VE HEARD.
SUPERSCRIBE GHOST WRITER
ONE WOULD THINK SOMEONE SO OFTEN GAGGED WOULD BE A LITTLE LESS, AH, MOUTHY...
ME, I APPRECIATE HER DISCRETION AS A CAPTIVE.
SEE, ONE TIME I GOT KINDA BLACKOUT DRUNK AND, I GUESS, STARTED TALKING S[redacted]T ABOUT THE SUPRACOMMUNITY IN FRONT OF HER, Y'KNOW?
SUPER-VILLAIN "FREE-FLOATING FURY" (AKA "TRIPLE-F")
SHE COULD'VE, UH, SCREWED ME BY GOING ONLINE AND TELLING EVERYBODY WHATEVER THE HELL I WAS BABBLING...
...BUT, HEY, SHE DIDN'T.

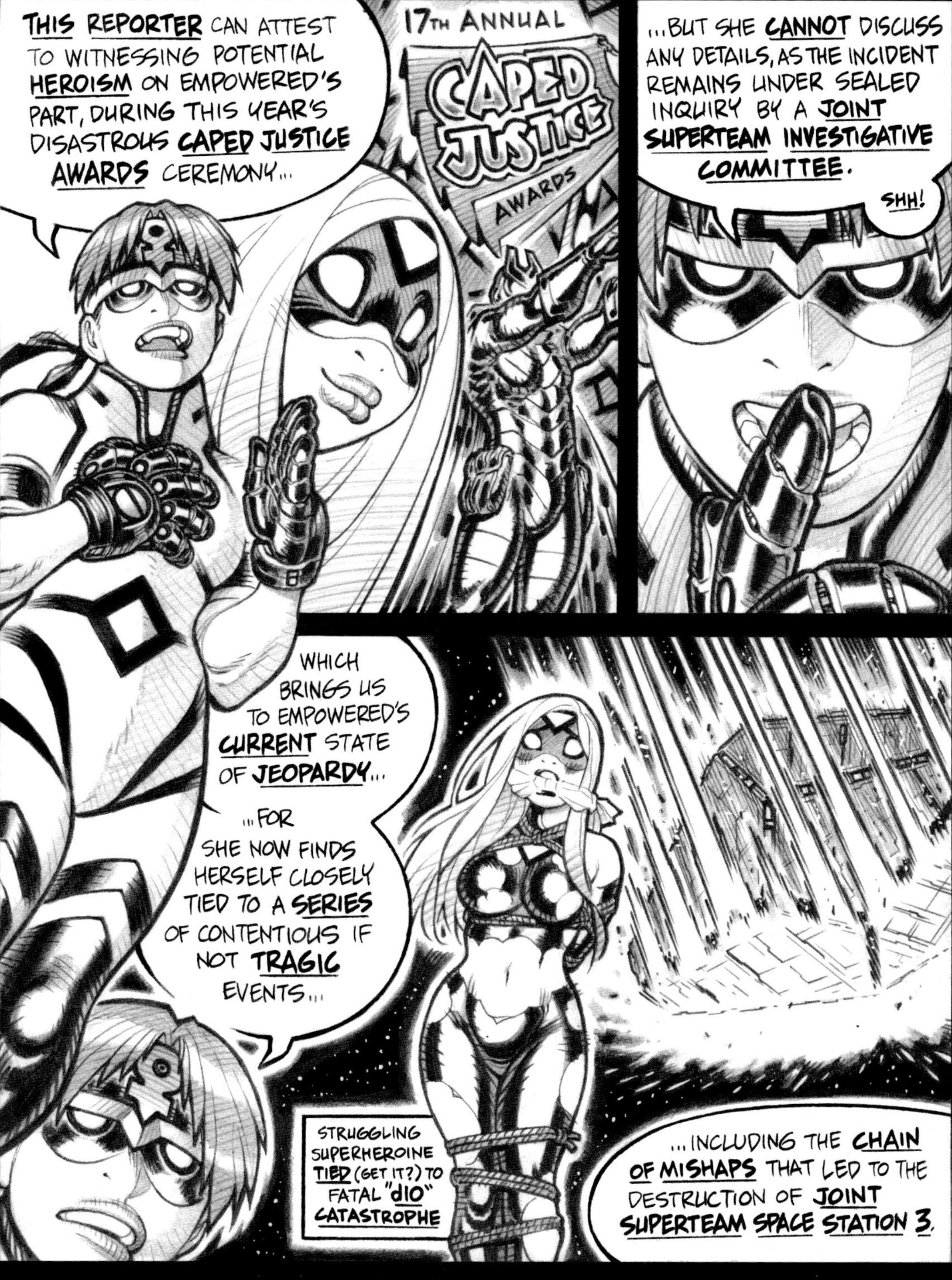
THIS REPORTER CAN ATTEST TO WITNESSING POTENTIAL HEROISM ON EMPOWERED'S PART, DURING THIS YEAR'S DISASTROUS CAPED JUSTICE AWARDS CEREMONY...
17TH ANNUAL CAPED JUSTICE AWARDS
...BUT SHE CANNOT DISCUSS ANY DETAILS, AS THE INCIDENT REMAINS UNDER SEALED INQUIRY BY A JOINT SUPERTEAM INVESTIGATIVE COMMITTEE.
SHH!
WHICH BRINGS US TO EMPOWERED'S CURRENT STATE OF JEOPARDY...
...FOR SHE NOW FINDS HERSELF CLOSELY TIED TO A SERIES OF CONTENTIOUS IF NOT TRAGIC EVENTS...
STRUGGLING SUPERHEROINE TIED (GET IT?) TO FATAL "dIO" CATASTROPHE
...INCLUDING THE CHAIN OF MISHAPS THAT LED TO THE DESTRUCTION OF JOINT SUPERTEAM SPACE STATION 3.

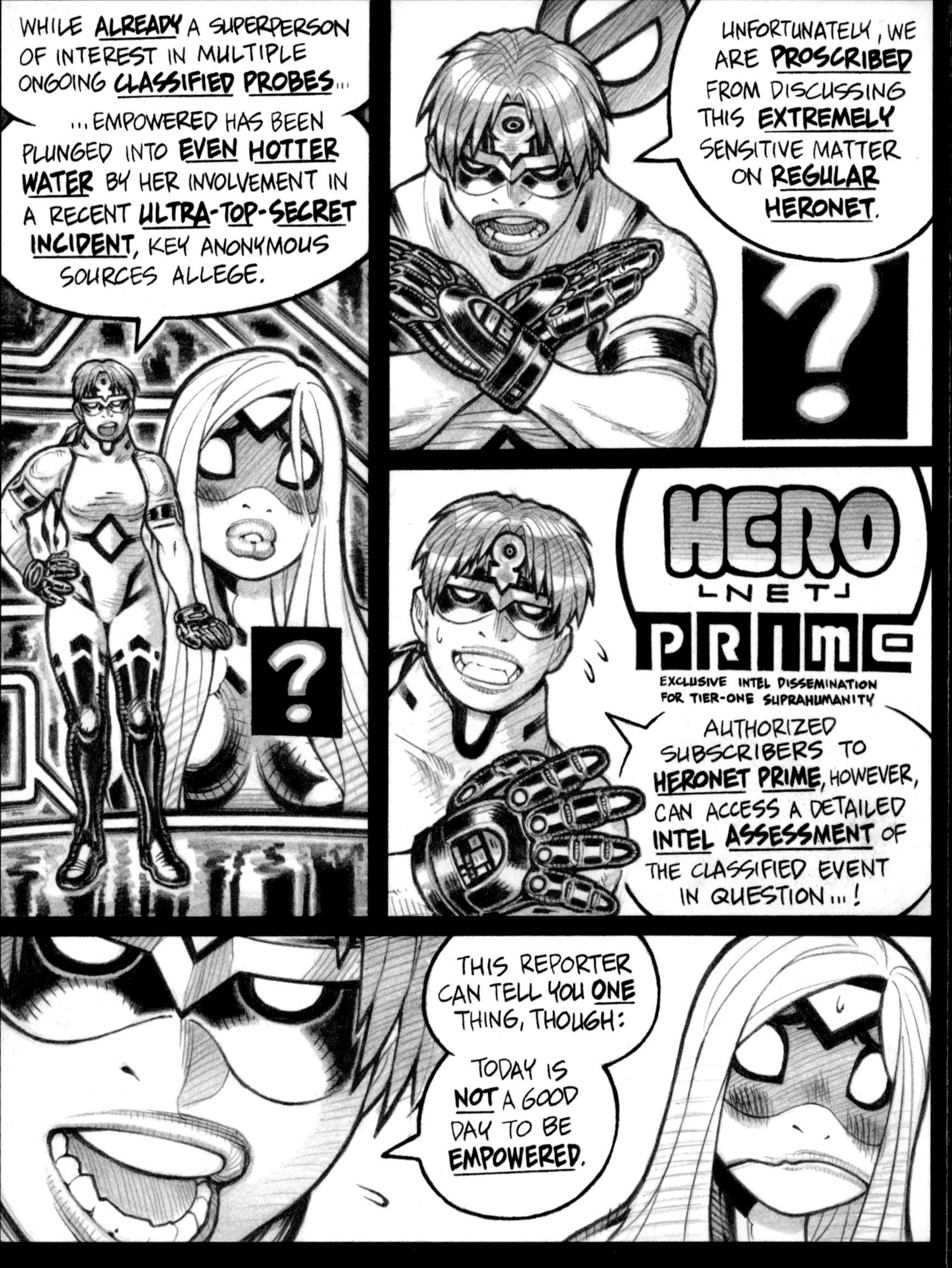

WHILE ALREADY A SUPERPERSON OF INTEREST IN MULTIPLE ONGOING CLASSIFIED PROBES...
...EMPOWERED HAS BEEN PLUNGED INTO EVEN HOTTER WATER BY HER INVOLVEMENT IN A RECENT ULTRA-TOP-SECRET INCIDENT, KEY ANONYMOUS SOURCES ALLEGE.
?
UNFORTUNATELY, WE ARE PROSCRIBED FROM DISCUSSING THIS EXTREMELY SENSITIVE MATTER ON REGULAR HERONET.
?
HERO NET PRIME
EXCLUSIVE INTEL DISSEMINATION FOR TIER-ONE SUPRAHUMANITY
AUTHORIZED SUBSCRIBERS TO HERONET PRIME, HOWEVER, CAN ACCESS A DETAILED INTEL ASSESSMENT OF THE CLASSIFIED EVENT IN QUESTION...!
THIS REPORTER CAN TELL YOU ONE THING, THOUGH:
TODAY IS NOT A GOOD DAY TO BE EMPOWERED.

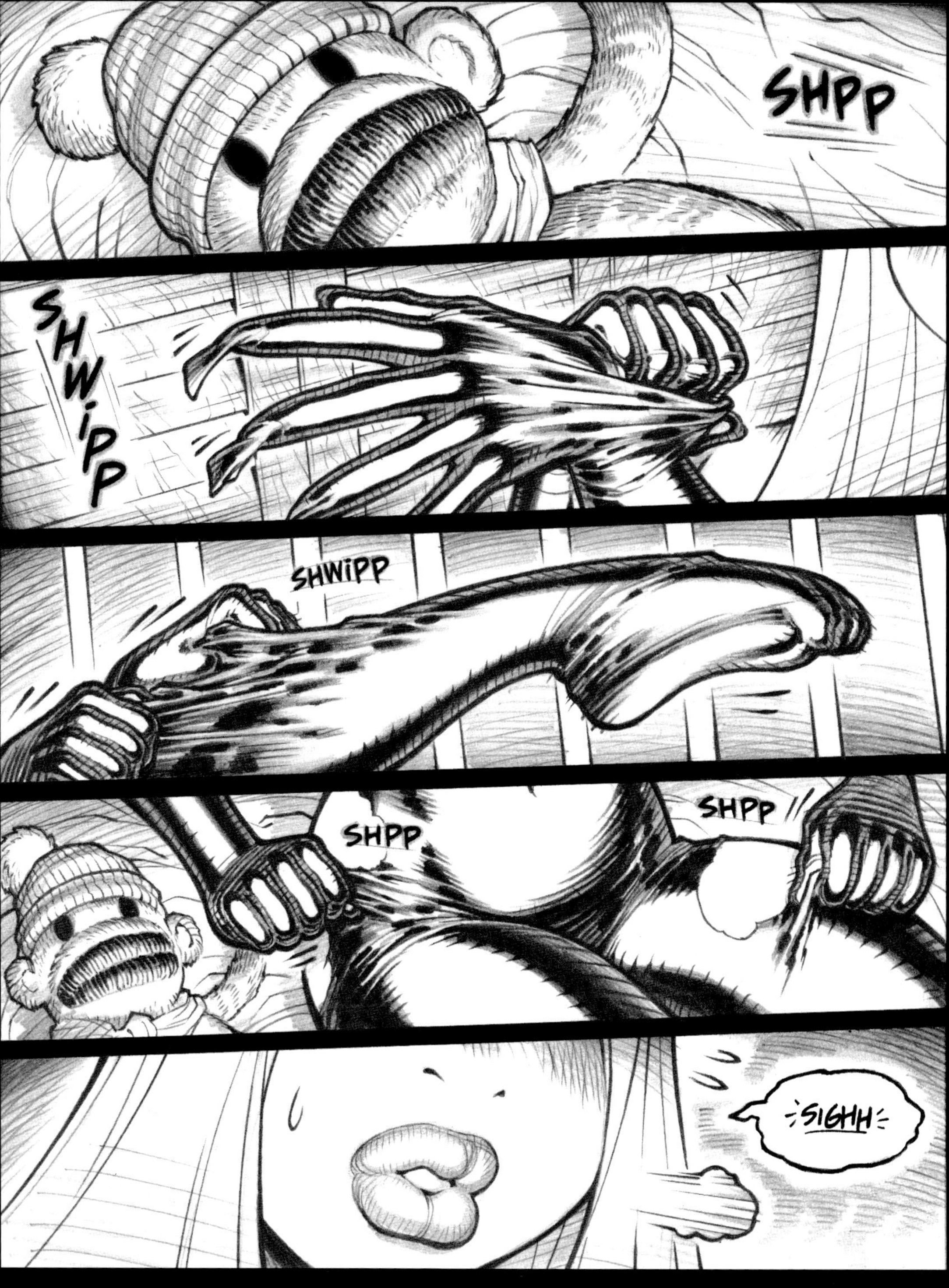
SHPP
SHWiPP
SHWiPP
SHPP
SHPP
SIGHH

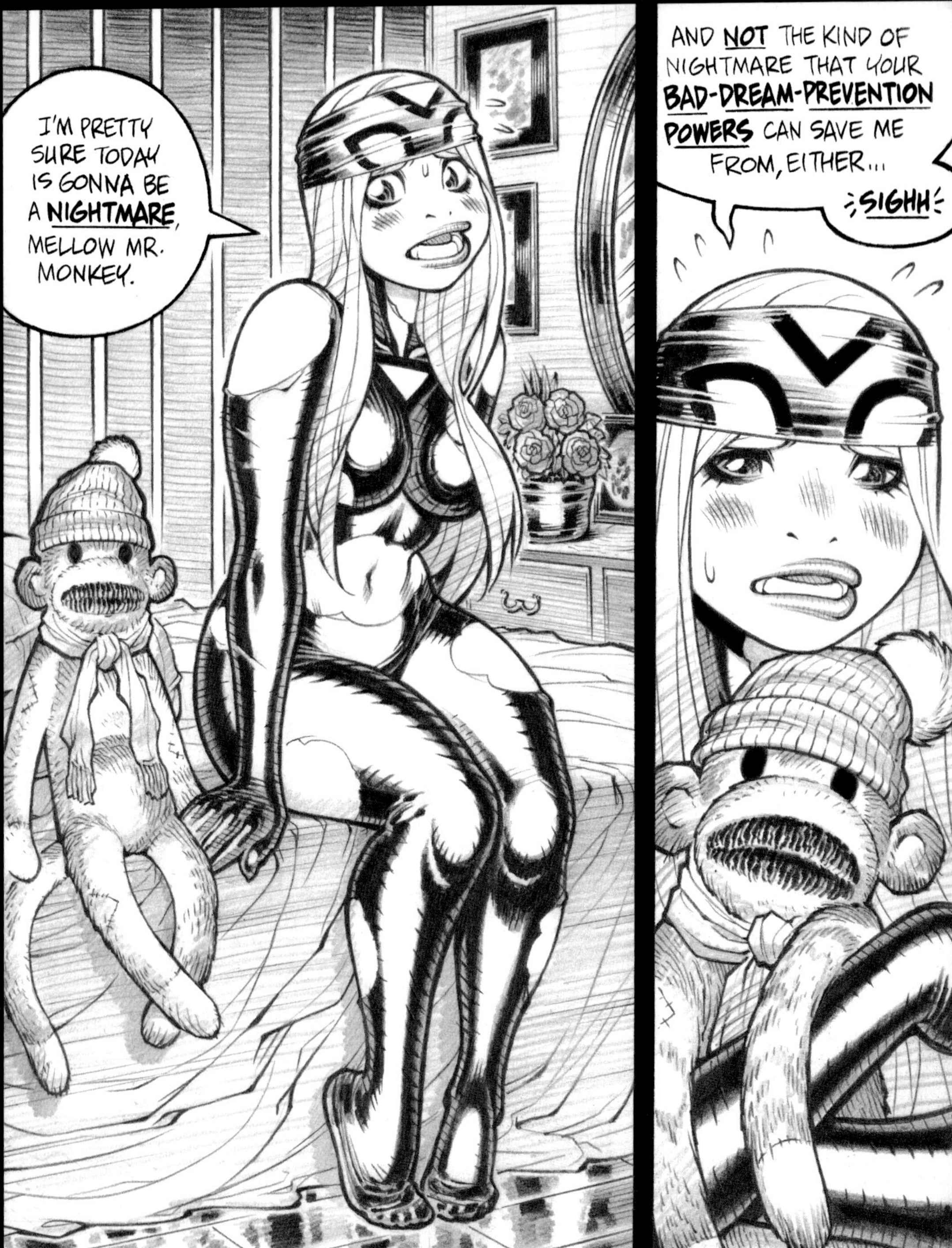
I'M PRETTY SURE TODAY IS GONNA BE A NIGHTMARE, MELLOW MR. MONKEY.
AND NOT THE KIND OF NIGHTMARE THAT YOUR BAD-DREAM-PREVENTION POWERS CAN SAVE ME FROM, EITHER...
SIGHH

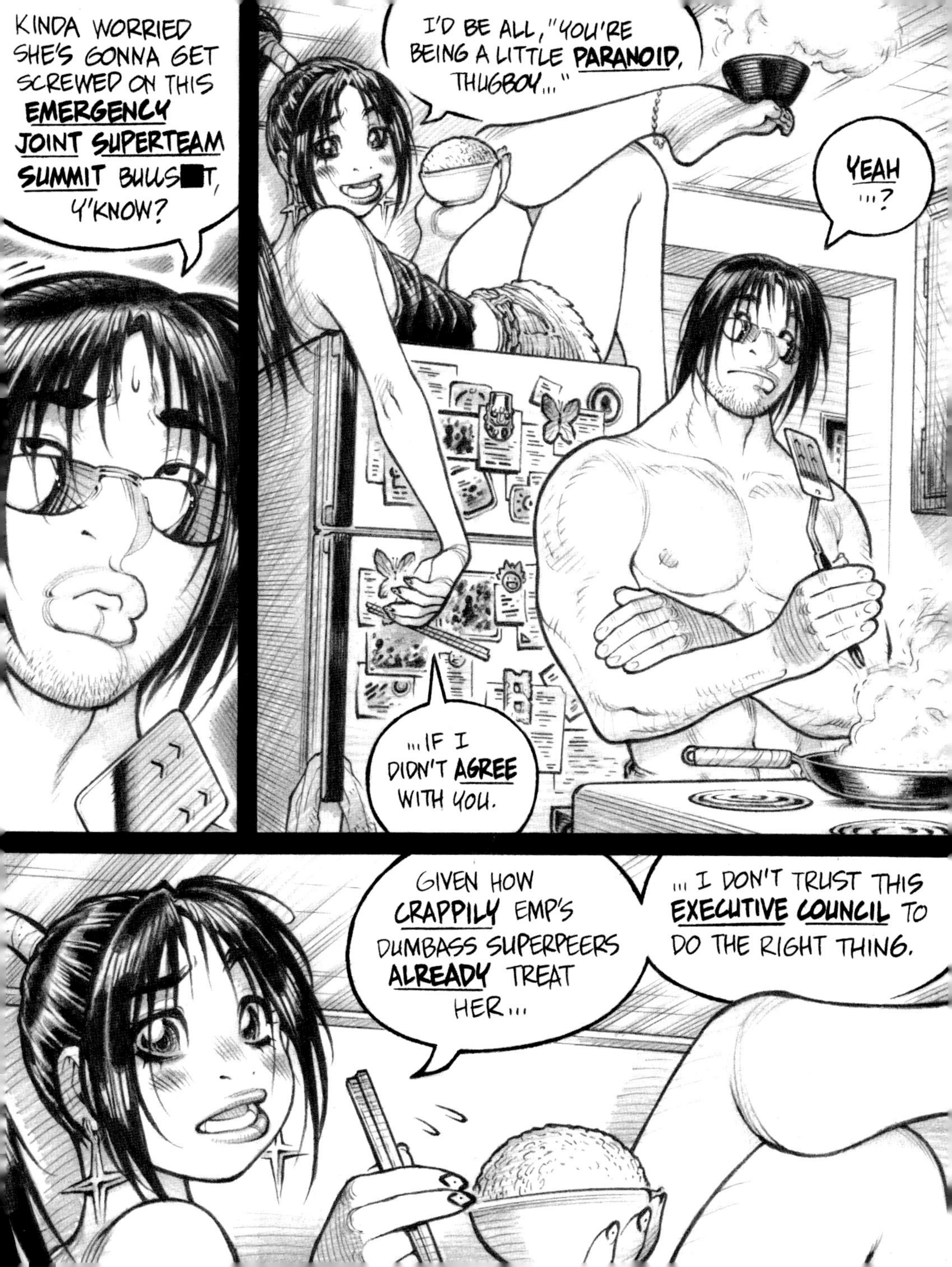
KINDA WORRIED SHE'S GONNA GET SCREWED ON THIS EMERGENCY JOINT SUPERTEAM SUMMIT BULLS[redacted]T, Y'KNOW?
I'D BE ALL, "YOU'RE BEING A LITTLE PARANOID, THUGBOY..."
YEAH ...?
...IF I DIDN'T AGREE WITH YOU.
GIVEN HOW CRAPPILY EMP'S DUMBASS SUPERPEERS ALREADY TREAT HER...
... I DON'T TRUST THIS EXECUTIVE COUNCIL TO DO THE RIGHT THING.

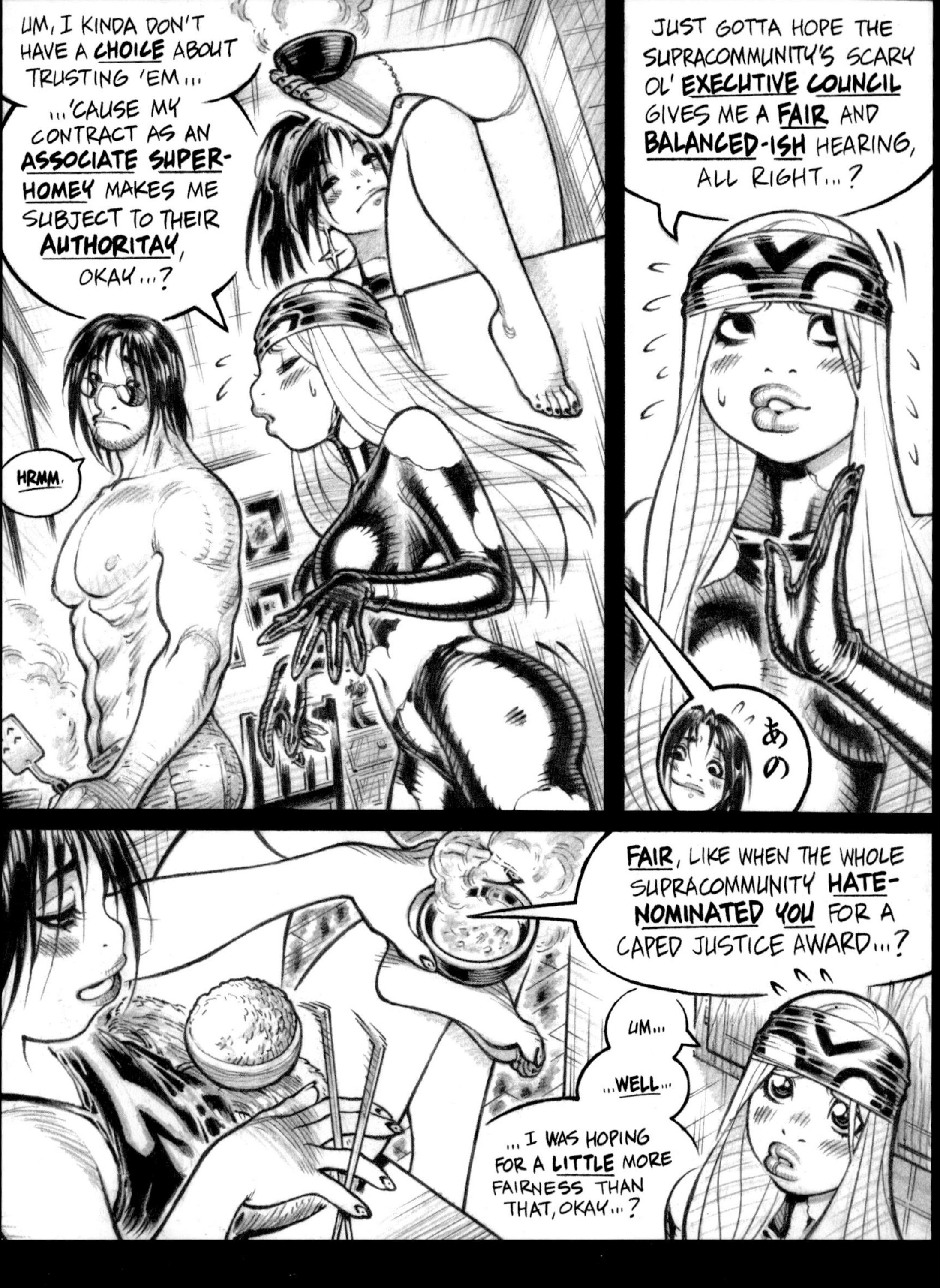
UM, I KINDA DON'T HAVE A CHOICE ABOUT TRUSTING 'EM...
...'CAUSE MY CONTRACT AS AN ASSOCIATE SUPER-HOMEY MAKES ME SUBJECT TO THEIR AUTHORITAY, OKAY...?
HRMM.
JUST GOTTA HOPE THE SUPRACOMMUNITY'S SCARY OL' EXECUTIVE COUNCIL GIVES ME A FAIR AND BALANCED-ISH HEARING, ALL RIGHT...?
あの
FAIR, LIKE WHEN THE WHOLE SUPRACOMMUNITY HATE-NOMINATED YOU FOR A CAPED JUSTICE AWARD...?
UM...
...WELL...
...I WAS HOPING FOR A LITTLE MORE FAIRNESS THAN THAT, OKAY...?

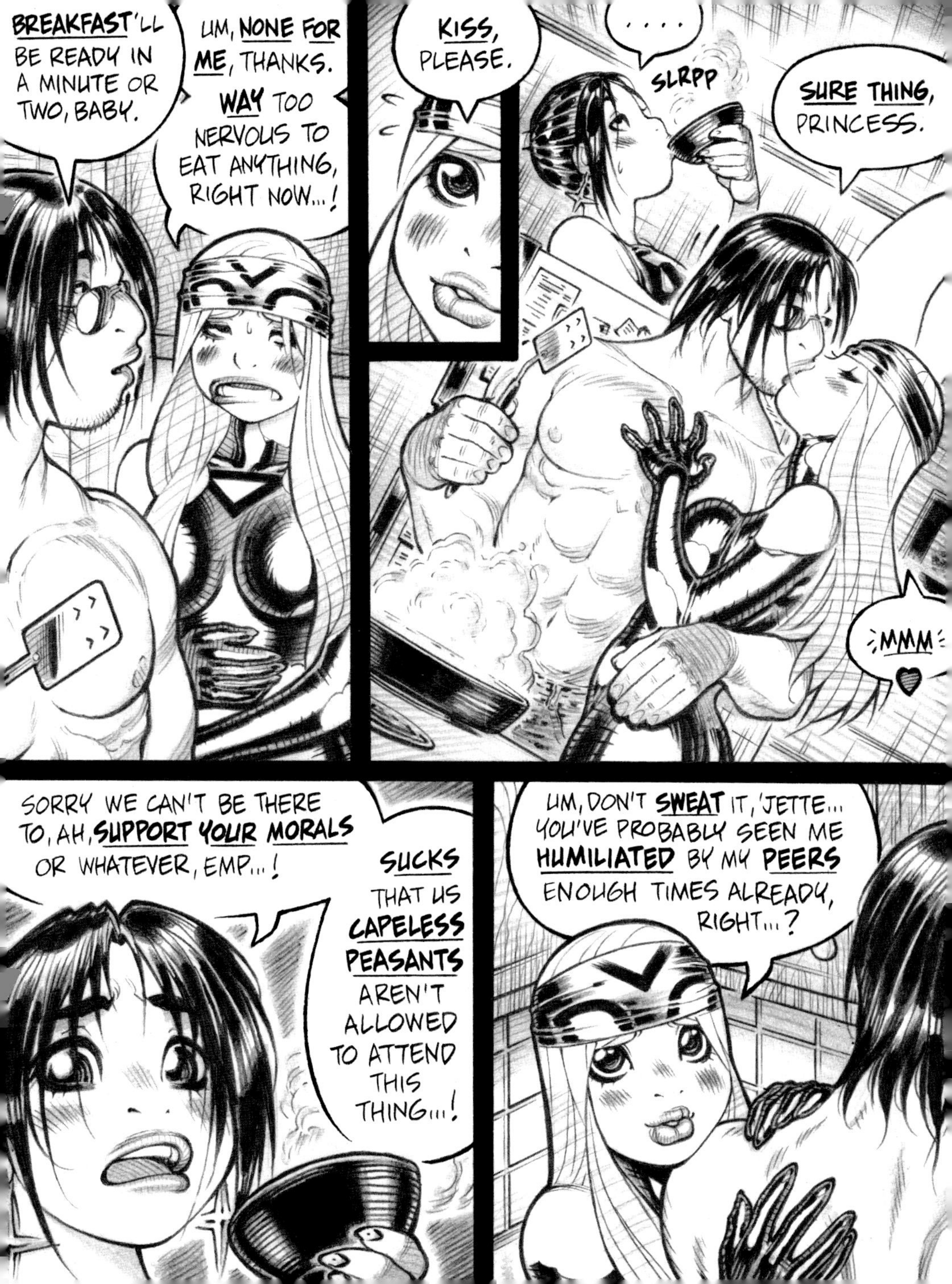
BREAKFAST'LL BE READY IN A MINUTE OR TWO, BABY.
UM, NONE FOR ME, THANKS.
WAY TOO NERVOUS TO EAT ANYTHING, RIGHT NOW...!
KISS, PLEASE.
....
SLRPP
SURE THING, PRINCESS.
MMM
SORRY WE CAN'T BE THERE TO, AH, SUPPORT YOUR MORALS OR WHATEVER, EMP...!
SUCKS THAT US CAPELESS PEASANTS AREN'T ALLOWED TO ATTEND THIS THING...!
UM, DON'T SWEAT IT, 'JETTE... YOU'VE PROBABLY SEEN ME HUMILIATED BY MY PEERS ENOUGH TIMES ALREADY, RIGHT...?

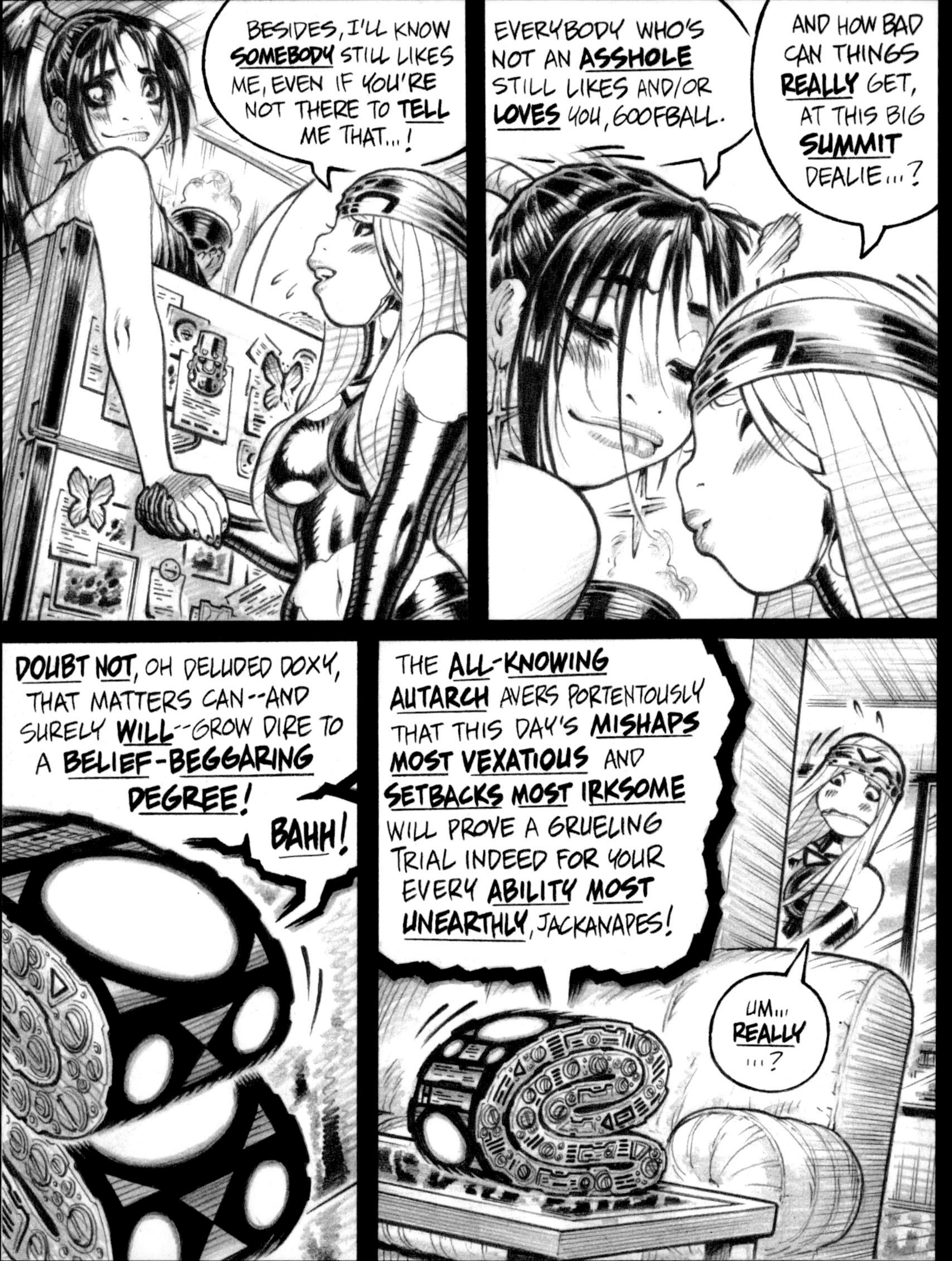
BESIDES, I'LL KNOW SOMEBODY STILL LIKES ME, EVEN IF YOU'RE NOT THERE TO TELL ME THAT...!
EVERYBODY WHO'S NOT AN ASSHOLE STILL LIKES AND/OR LOVES YOU, GOOFBALL.
AND HOW BAD CAN THINGS REALLY GET, AT THIS BIG SUMMIT DEALIE...?
DOUBT NOT, OH DELUDED DOXY, THAT MATTERS CAN--AND SURELY WILL--GROW DIRE TO A BELIEF-BEGGARING DEGREE!
BAHH!
THE ALL-KNOWING AUTARCH AVERS PORTENTOUSLY THAT THIS DAY'S MISHAPS MOST VEXATIOUS AND SETBACKS MOST IRKSOME WILL PROVE A GRUELING TRIAL INDEED FOR YOUR EVERY ABILITY MOST UNEARTHLY, JACKANAPES!
UM... REALLY...?

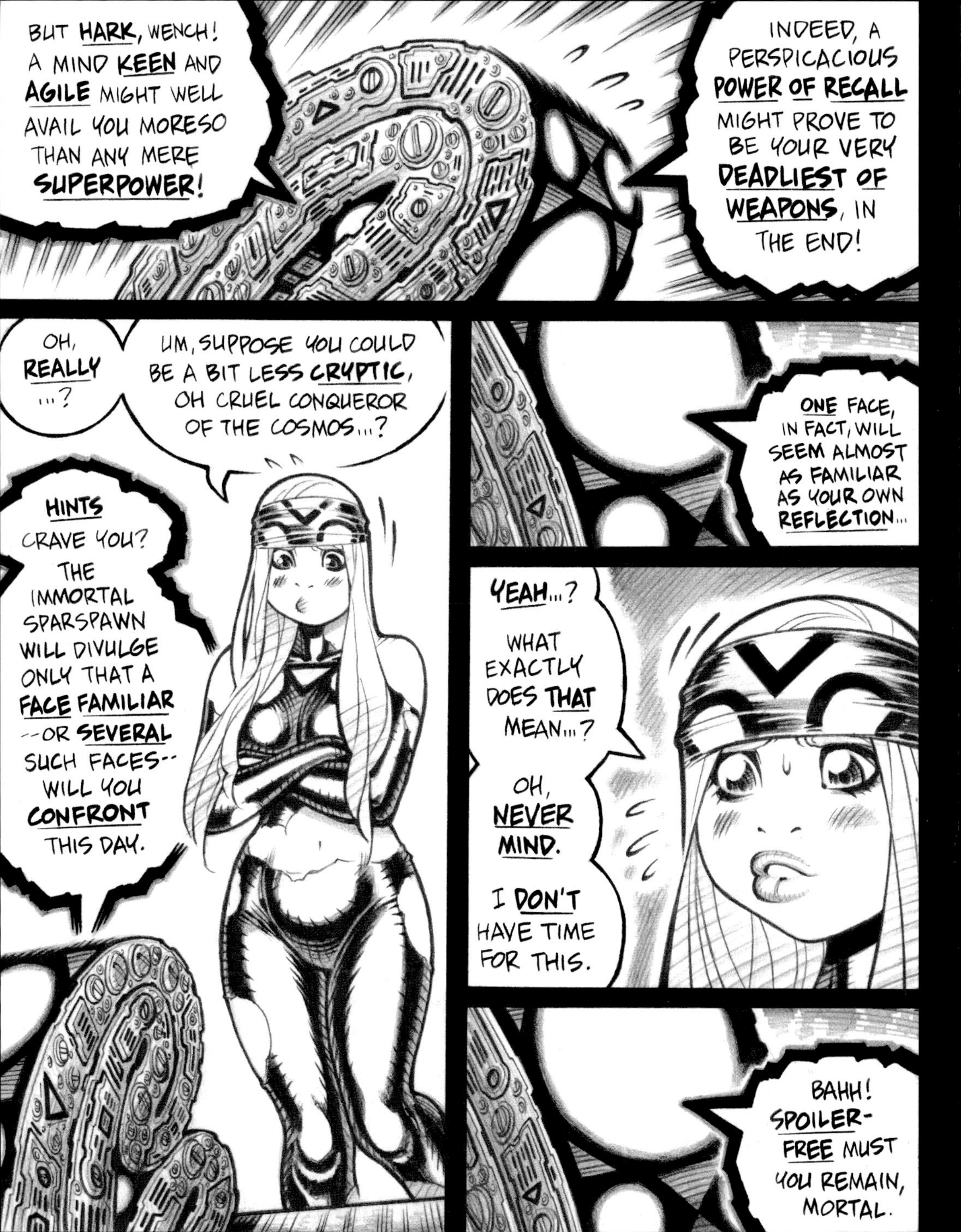
BUT HARK, WENCH! A MIND KEEN AND AGILE MIGHT WELL AVAIL YOU MORESO THAN ANY MERE SUPERPOWER!
INDEED, A PERSPICACIOUS POWER OF RECALL MIGHT PROVE TO BE YOUR VERY DEADLIEST OF WEAPONS, IN THE END!
OH, REALLY ...?
UM, SUPPOSE YOU COULD BE A BIT LESS CRYPTIC, OH CRUEL CONQUEROR OF THE COSMOS...?
HINTS CRAVE YOU? THE IMMORTAL SPARSPAWN WILL DIVULGE ONLY THAT A FACE FAMILIAR --OR SEVERAL SUCH FACES-- WILL YOU CONFRONT THIS DAY.
ONE FACE, IN FACT, WILL SEEM ALMOST AS FAMILIAR AS YOUR OWN REFLECTION...
YEAH...?
WHAT EXACTLY DOES THAT MEAN...?
OH, NEVER MIND.
I DON'T HAVE TIME FOR THIS.
BAHH! SPOILER-FREE MUST YOU REMAIN, MORTAL.

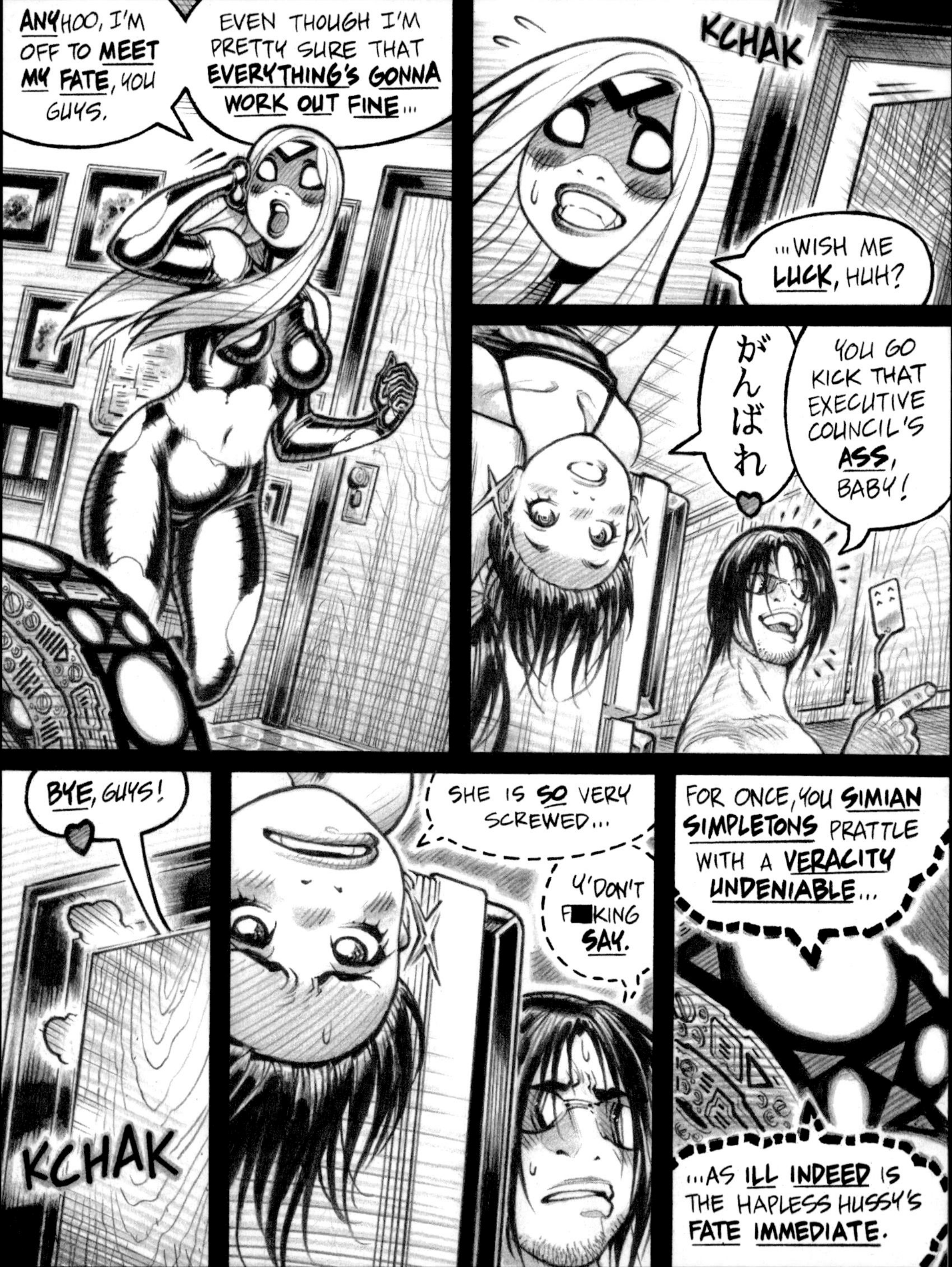
ANYHOO, I'M OFF TO MEET MY FATE, YOU GUYS.
EVEN THOUGH I'M PRETTY SURE THAT EVERYTHING'S GONNA WORK OUT FINE...
KCHAK
...WISH ME LUCK, HUH?
がんばれ
YOU GO KICK THAT EXECUTIVE COUNCIL'S ASS, BABY!
BYE, GUYS!
KCHAK
SHE IS SO VERY SCREWED...
Y'DON'T F[redacted]KING SAY.
FOR ONCE, YOU SIMIAN SIMPLETONS PRATTLE WITH A VERACITY UNDENIABLE...
...AS ILL INDEED IS THE HAPLESS HUSSY'S FATE IMMEDIATE.

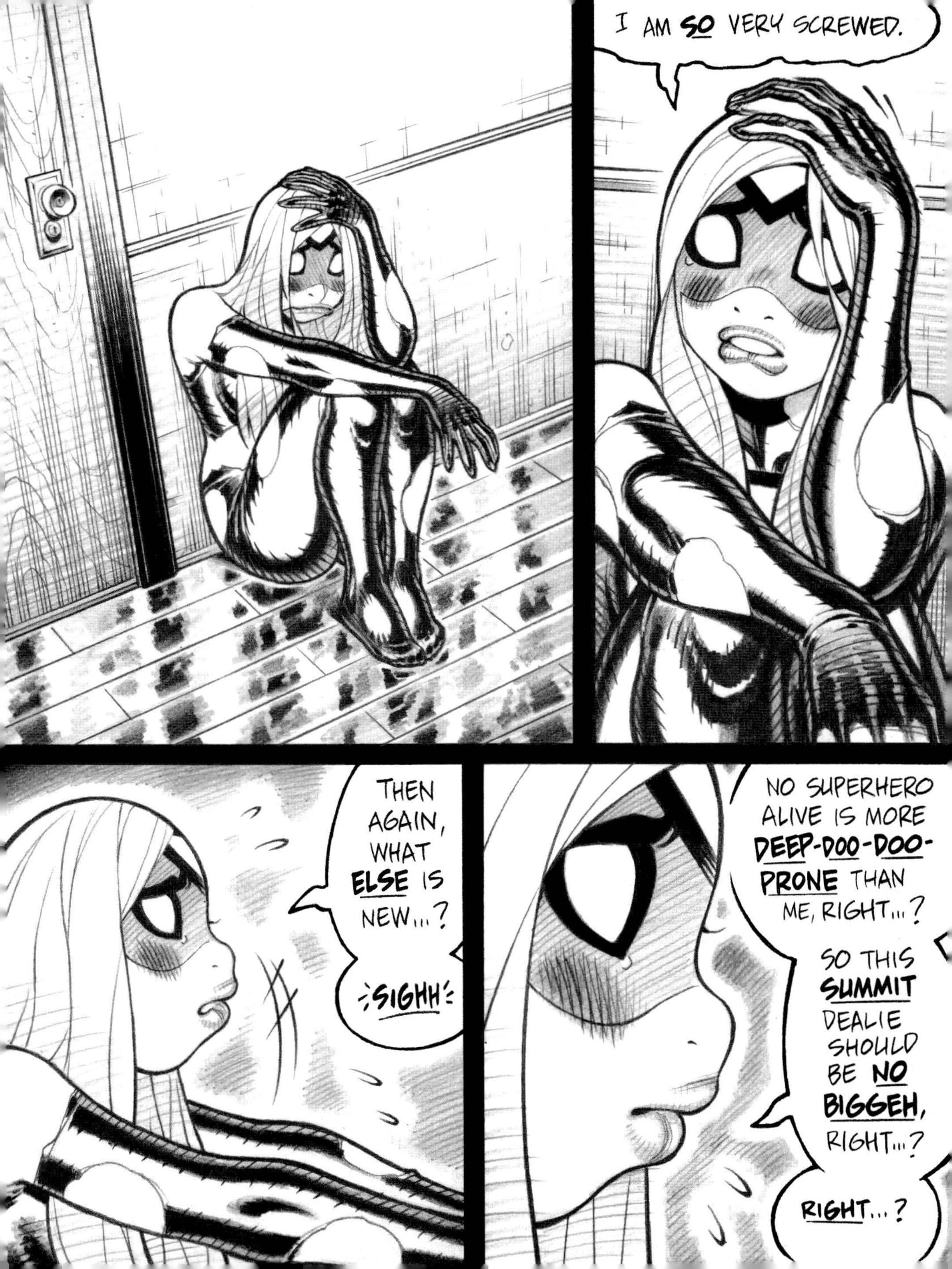
I AM SO VERY SCREWED.
THEN AGAIN, WHAT ELSE IS NEW...?
:SIGHH:
NO SUPERHERO ALIVE IS MORE DEEP-DOO-DOO-PRONE THAN ME, RIGHT...?
SO THIS SUMMIT DEALIE SHOULD BE NO BIGGEH, RIGHT...?
RIGHT...?

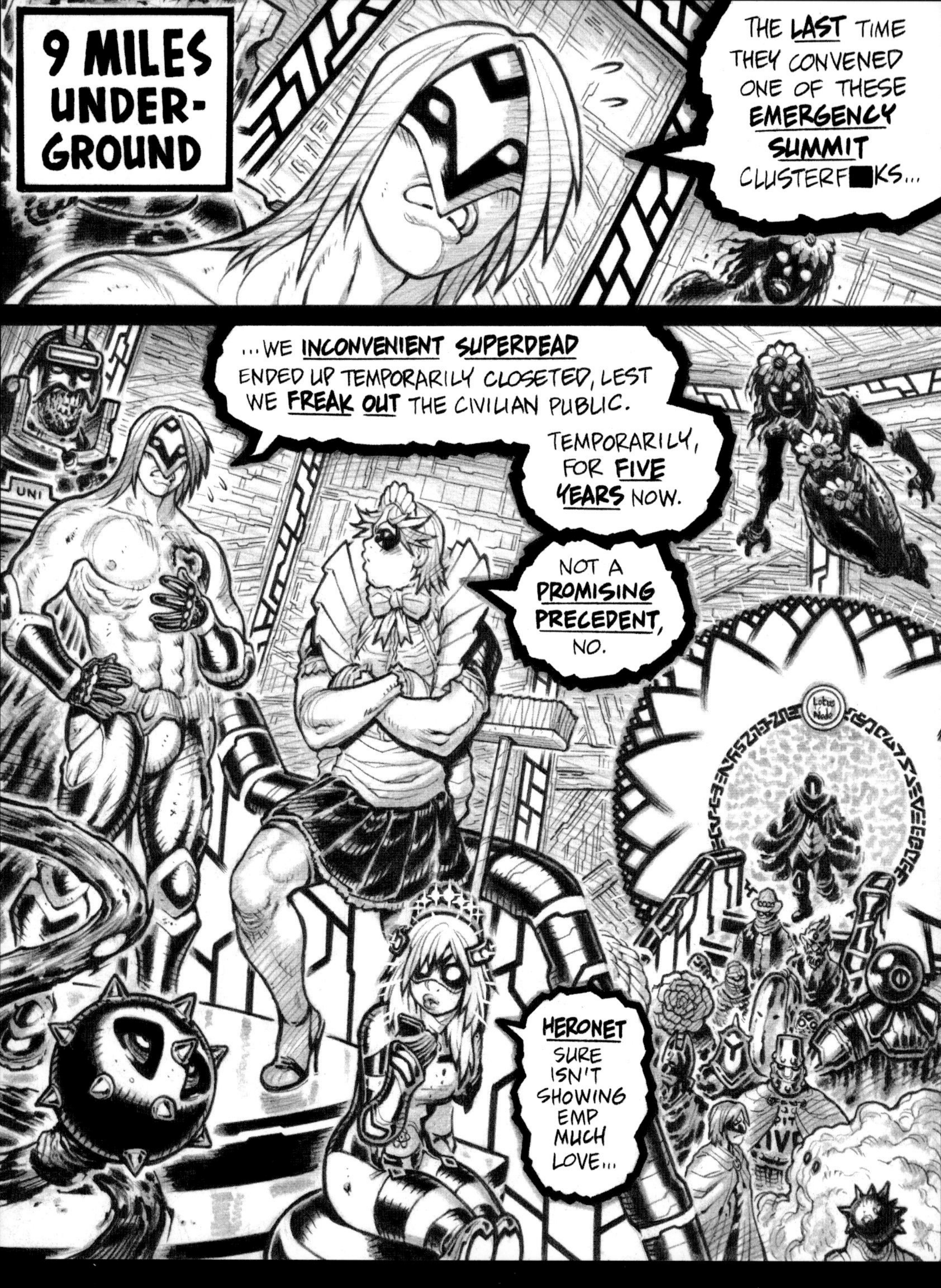
9 MILES UNDER-GROUND
THE LAST TIME THEY CONVENED ONE OF THESE EMERGENCY SUMMIT CLUSTERF[redacted]KS...
...WE INCONVENIENT SUPERDEAD ENDED UP TEMPORARILY CLOSETED, LEST WE FREAK OUT THE CIVILIAN PUBLIC.
TEMPORARILY, FOR FIVE YEARS NOW.
NOT A PROMISING PRECEDENT, NO.
UNI
HERONET SURE ISN'T SHOWING EMP MUCH LOVE...

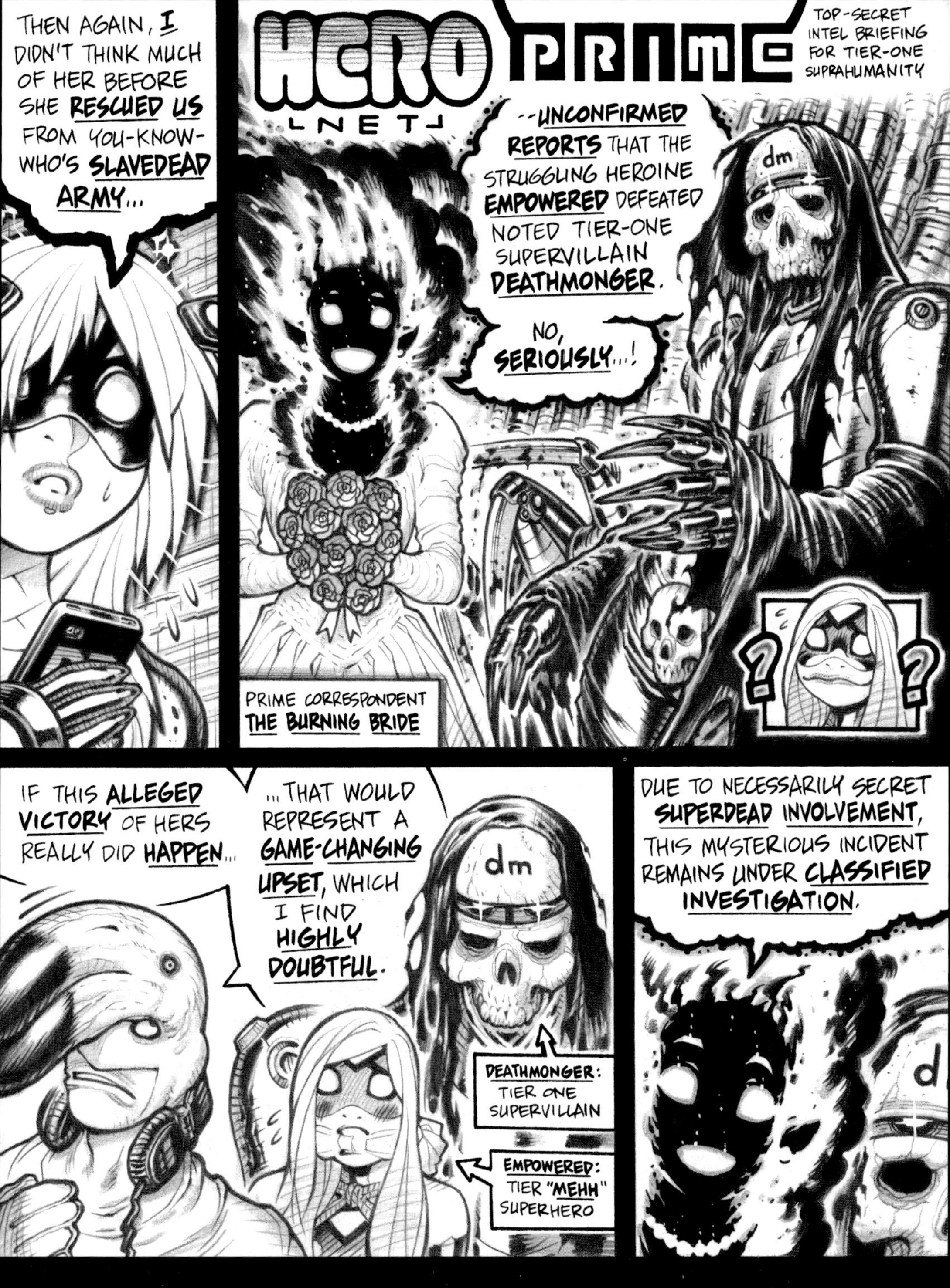
THEN AGAIN, I DIDN'T THINK MUCH OF HER BEFORE SHE RESCUED US FROM YOU-KNOW-WHO'S SLAVEDEAD ARMY...
HERO NET
PRIME
TOP-SECRET INTEL BRIEFING FOR TIER-ONE SUPRAHUMANITY
--UNCONFIRMED REPORTS THAT THE STRUGGLING HEROINE EMPOWERED DEFEATED NOTED TIER-ONE SUPERVILLAIN DEATHMONGER.
NO, SERIOUSLY...!
PRIME CORRESPONDENT THE BURNING BRIDE
IF THIS ALLEGED VICTORY OF HERS REALLY DID HAPPEN...
...THAT WOULD REPRESENT A GAME-CHANGING UPSET, WHICH I FIND HIGHLY DOUBTFUL.
DEATHMONGER: TIER ONE SUPERVILLAIN
EMPOWERED: TIER "MEHH" SUPERHERO
DUE TO NECESSARILY SECRET SUPERDEAD INVOLVEMENT, THIS MYSTERIOUS INCIDENT REMAINS UNDER CLASSIFIED INVESTIGATION.

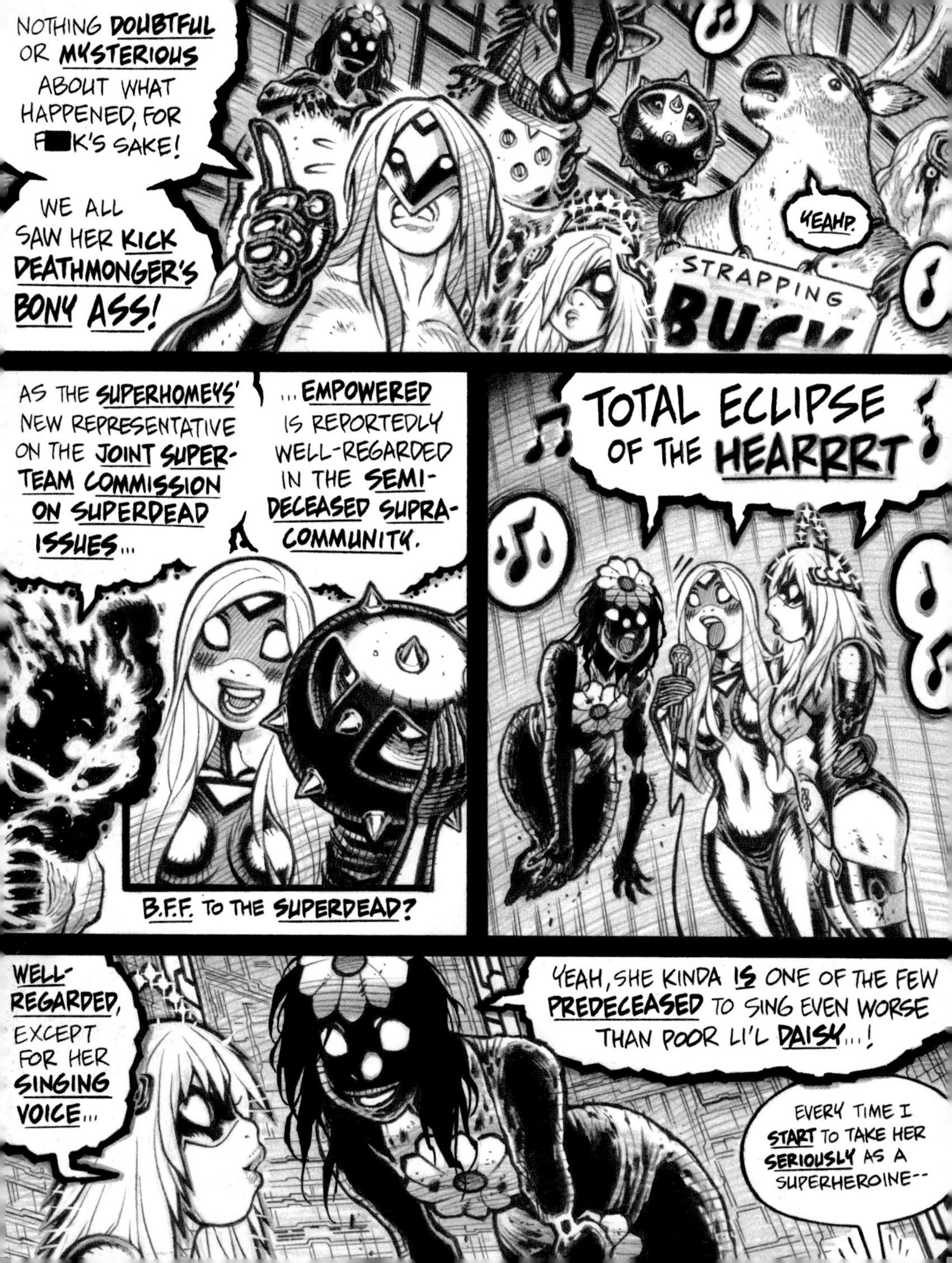
NOTHING DOUBTFUL OR MYSTERIOUS ABOUT WHAT HAPPENED, FOR F[redacted]K'S SAKE!
WE ALL SAW HER KICK DEATHMONGER'S BONY ASS!
YEAHP.
STRAPPING BUCK
AS THE SUPERHOMEYS' NEW REPRESENTATIVE ON THE JOINT SUPER-TEAM COMMISSION ON SUPERDEAD ISSUES...
...EMPOWERED IS REPORTEDLY WELL-REGARDED IN THE SEMI-DECEASED SUPRA-COMMUNITY.
B.F.F. TO THE SUPERDEAD?
TOTAL ECLIPSE OF THE HEARRRT
WELL-REGARDED, EXCEPT FOR HER SINGING VOICE...
YEAH, SHE KINDA IS ONE OF THE FEW PREDECEASED TO SING EVEN WORSE THAN POOR LI'L DAISY...!
EVERY TIME I START TO TAKE HER SERIOUSLY AS A SUPERHEROINE--

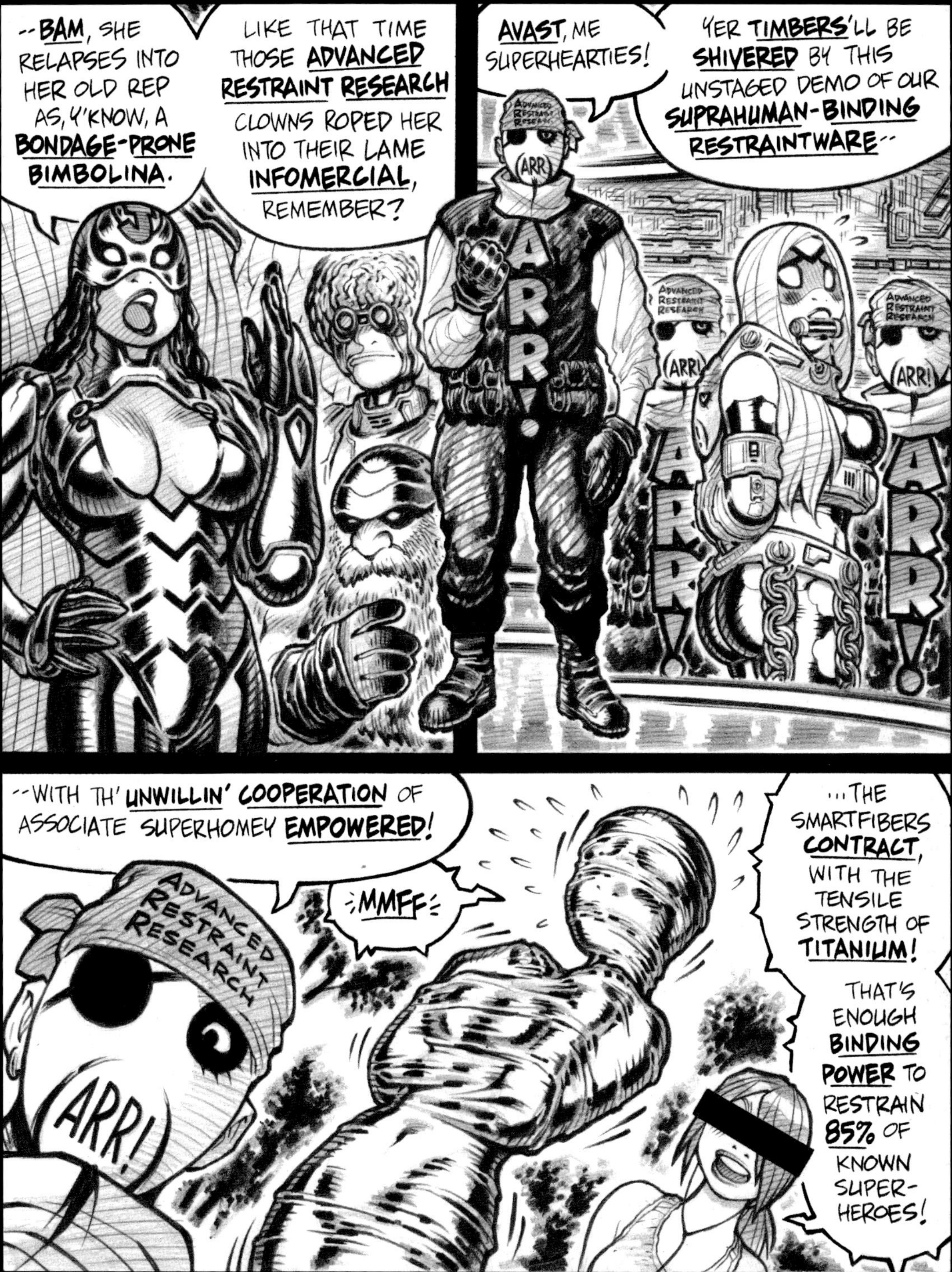
--BAM, SHE RELAPSES INTO HER OLD REP AS, Y'KNOW, A BONDAGE-PRONE BIMBOLINA.
LIKE THAT TIME THOSE ADVANCED RESTRAINT RESEARCH CLOWNS ROPED HER INTO THEIR LAME INFOMERCIAL, REMEMBER?
AVAST, ME SUPERHEARTIES!
YER TIMBERS'LL BE SHIVERED BY THIS UNSTAGED DEMO OF OUR SUPRAHUMAN-BINDING RESTRAINTWARE--
ADVANCED RESTRAINT RESEARCH
ARR
ARR!
--WITH TH' UNWILLIN' COOPERATION OF ASSOCIATE SUPERHOMEY EMPOWERED!
MMFF
...THE SMARTFIBERS CONTRACT, WITH THE TENSILE STRENGTH OF TITANIUM!
THAT'S ENOUGH BINDING POWER TO RESTRAIN 85% OF KNOWN SUPER-HEROES!
ADVANCED RESTRAINT RESEARCH
ARR!

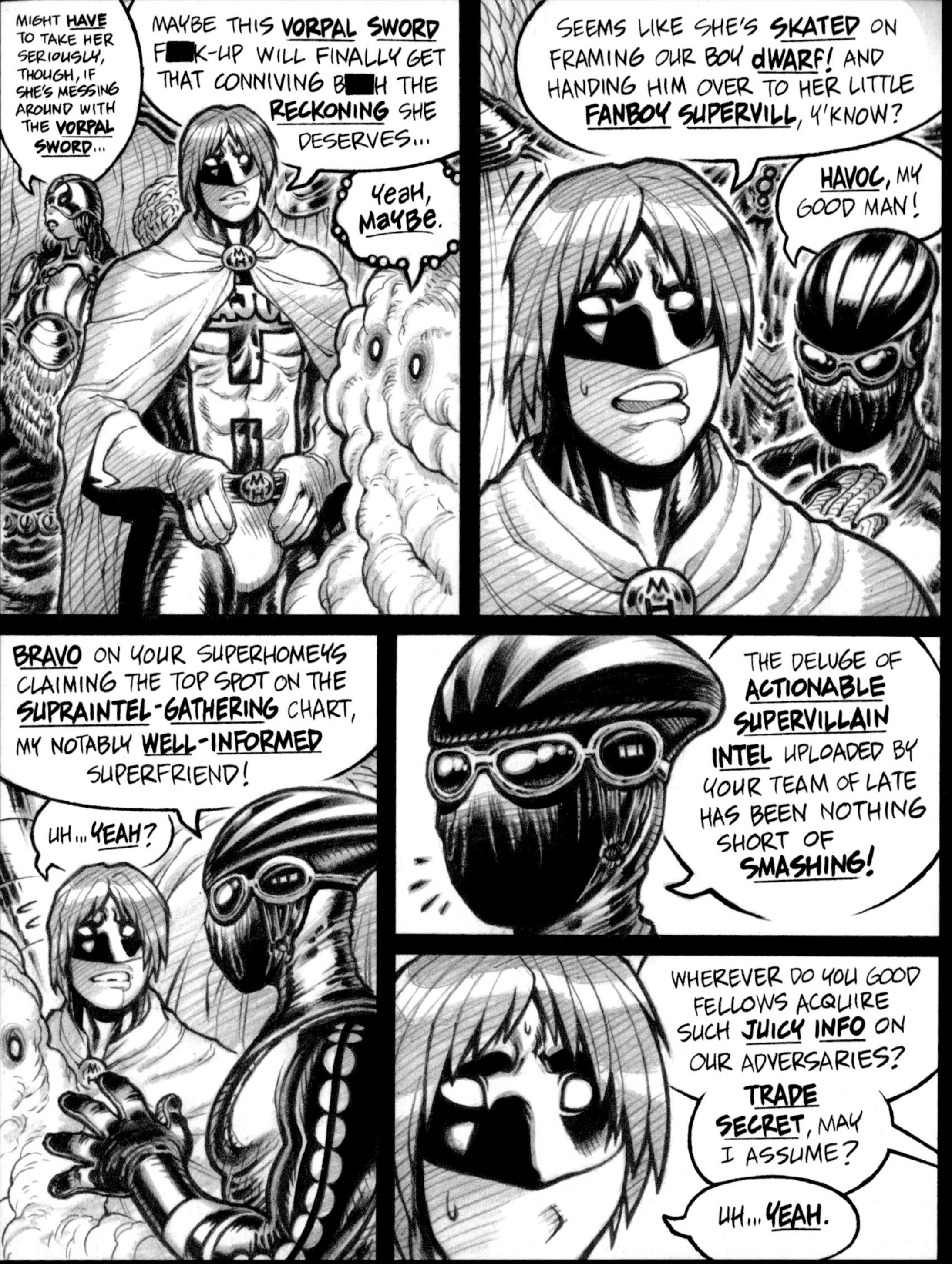
MIGHT HAVE TO TAKE HER SERIOUSLY, THOUGH, IF SHE'S MESSING AROUND WITH THE VORPAL SWORD...
MAYBE THIS VORPAL SWORD F[redacted]K-UP WILL FINALLY GET THAT CONNIVING B[redacted]H THE RECKONING SHE DESERVES...
Yeah, Maybe.
SEEMS LIKE SHE'S SKATED ON FRAMING OUR BOY dWARF! AND HANDING HIM OVER TO HER LITTLE FANBOY SUPERVILL, Y'KNOW?
HAVOC, MY GOOD MAN!
BRAVO ON YOUR SUPERHOMEYS CLAIMING THE TOP SPOT ON THE SUPRAINTEL-GATHERING CHART, MY NOTABLY WELL-INFORMED SUPERFRIEND!
UH... YEAH?
THE DELUGE OF ACTIONABLE SUPERVILLAIN INTEL UPLOADED BY YOUR TEAM OF LATE HAS BEEN NOTHING SHORT OF SMASHING!
WHEREVER DO YOU GOOD FELLOWS ACQUIRE SUCH JUICY INFO ON OUR ADVERSARIES?
TRADE SECRET, MAY I ASSUME?
UH... YEAH.

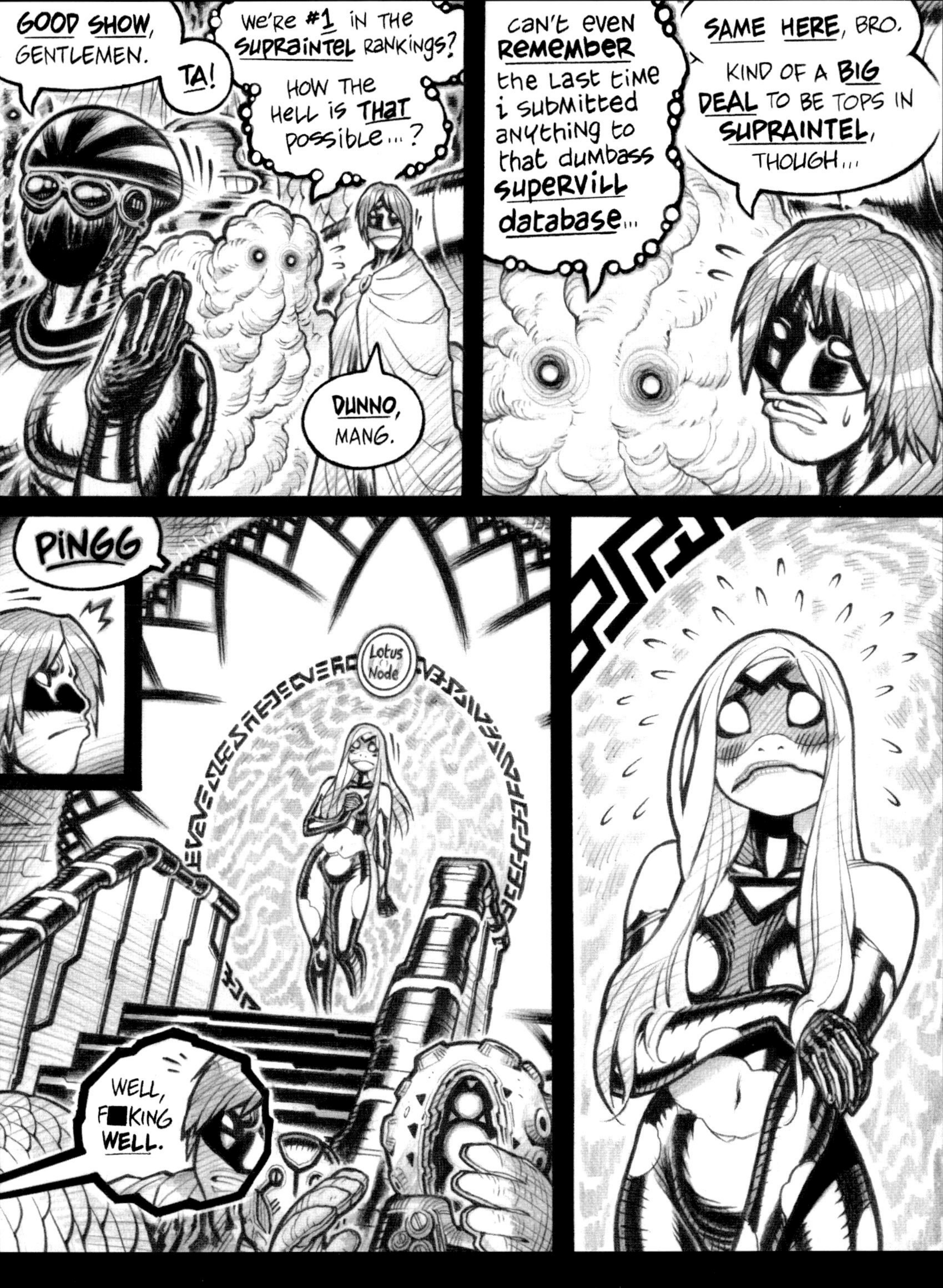

GOOD SHOW, GENTLEMEN.
TA!
WE'RE #1 IN THE SUPRAINTEL RANKINGS?
HOW THE HELL IS THAT POSSIBLE...?
DUNNO, MANG.
CAN'T EVEN REMEMBER THE LAST TIME I SUBMITTED ANYTHING TO THAT DUMBASS SUPERVILL DATABASE...
SAME HERE, BRO.
KIND OF A BIG DEAL TO BE TOPS IN SUPRAINTEL, THOUGH...
PINGG
Lotus Node
WELL, F[redacted]KING WELL.

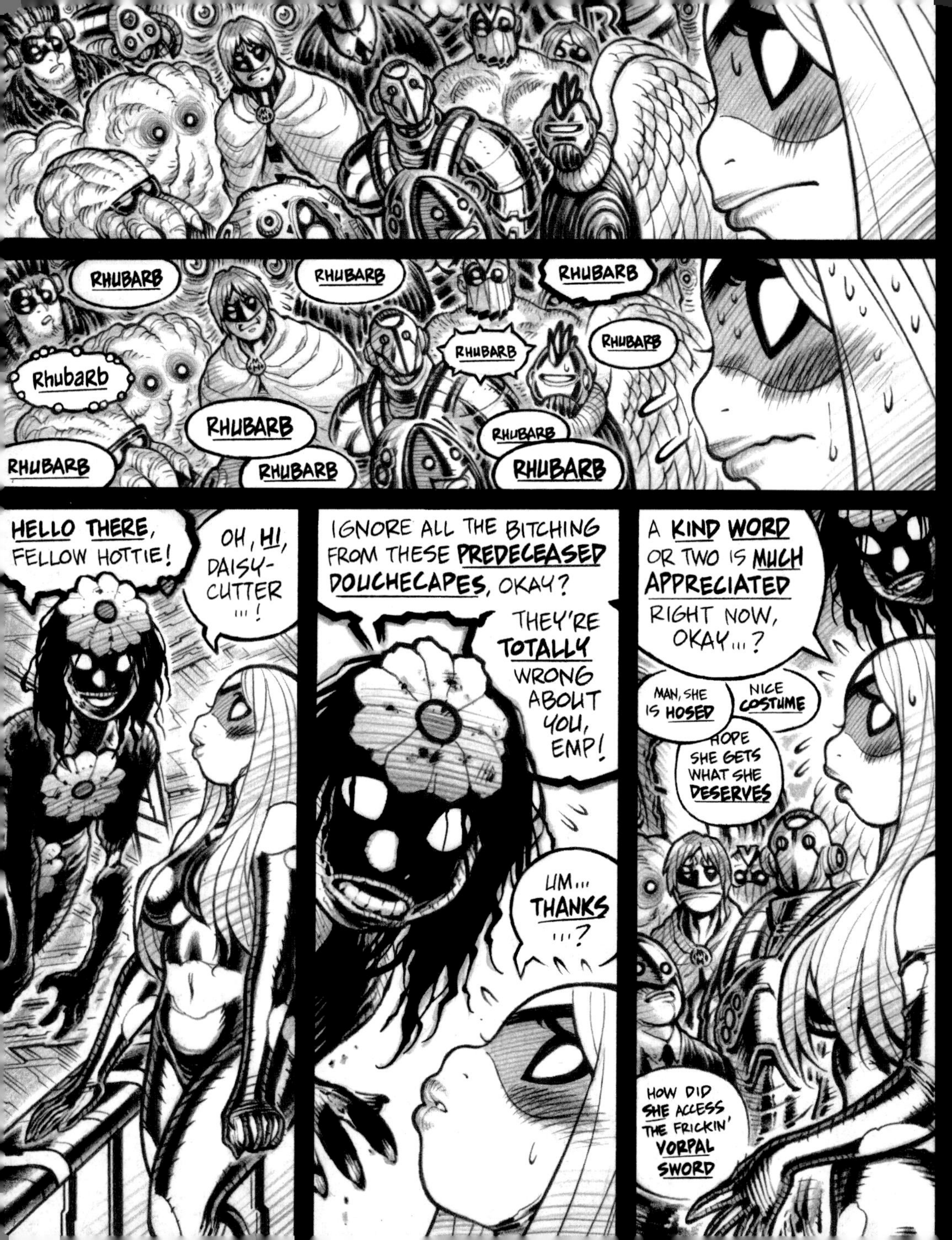
RHUBARB
RHUBARB
RHUBARB
Rhubarb
RHUBARB
RHUBARB
RHUBARB
RHUBARB
RHUBARB
RHUBARB
RHUBARB
HELLO THERE, FELLOW HOTTIE!
OH, HI, DAISY-CUTTER ...!
IGNORE ALL THE BITCHING FROM THESE PREDECEASED DOUCHECAPES, OKAY?
THEY'RE TOTALLY WRONG ABOUT YOU, EMP!
UM... THANKS ...?
A KIND WORD OR TWO IS MUCH APPRECIATED RIGHT NOW, OKAY...?
MAN, SHE IS HOSED
NICE COSTUME
HOPE SHE GETS WHAT SHE DESERVES
HOW DID SHE ACCESS THE FRICKIN' VORPAL SWORD

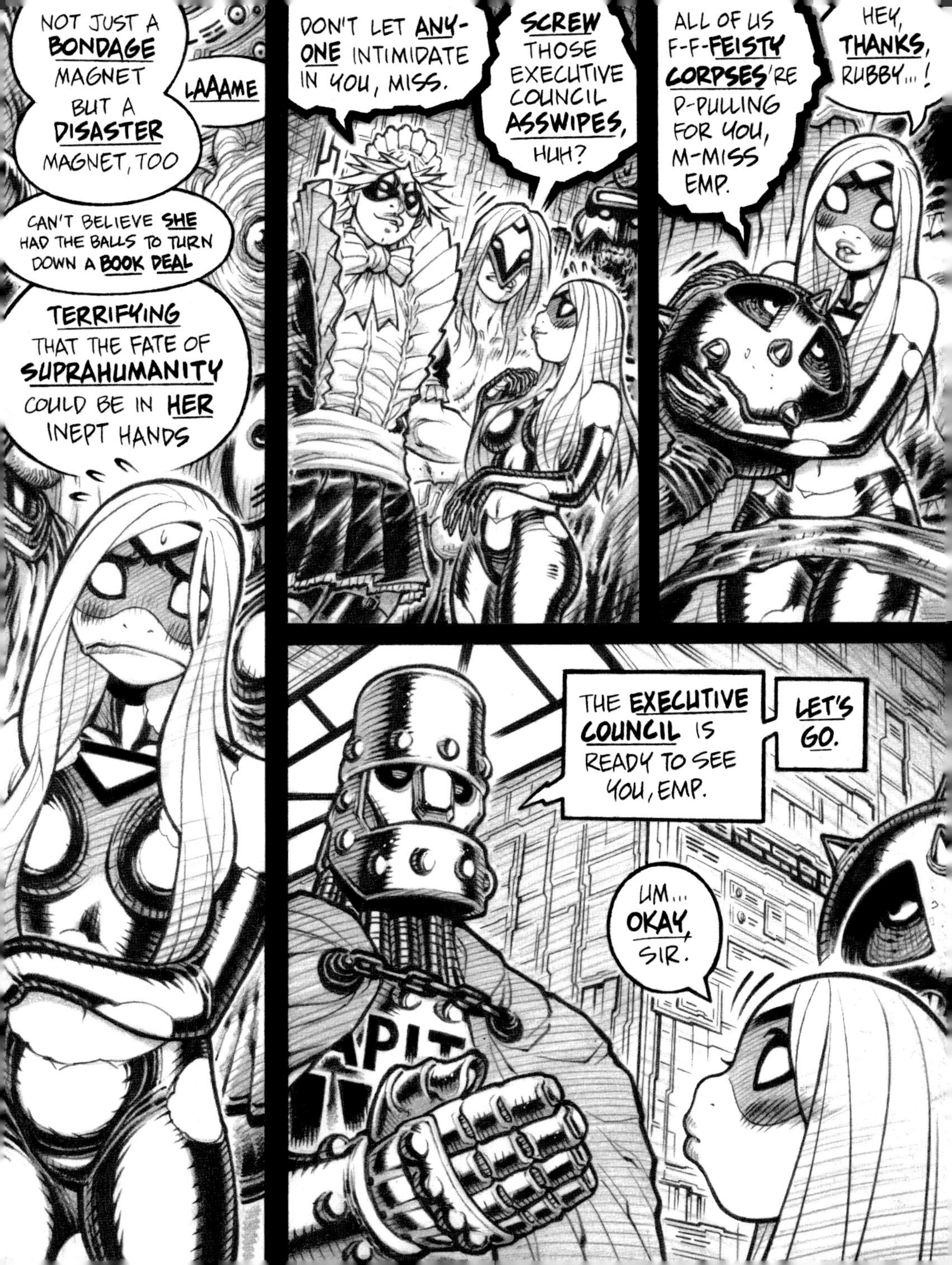
NOT JUST A BONDAGE MAGNET BUT A DISASTER MAGNET, TOO
LAAAME
CAN'T BELIEVE SHE HAD THE BALLS TO TURN DOWN A BOOK DEAL
TERRIFYING THAT THE FATE OF SUPRAHUMANITY COULD BE IN HER INEPT HANDS
DON'T LET ANY-ONE INTIMIDATE IN YOU, MISS.
SCREW THOSE EXECUTIVE COUNCIL ASSWIPES, HUH?
ALL OF US F-F-FEISTY CORPSES'RE P-PULLING FOR YOU, M-MISS EMP.
HEY, THANKS, RUBBY...!
THE EXECUTIVE COUNCIL IS READY TO SEE YOU, EMP.
LET'S GO.
UM... OKAY, SIR.

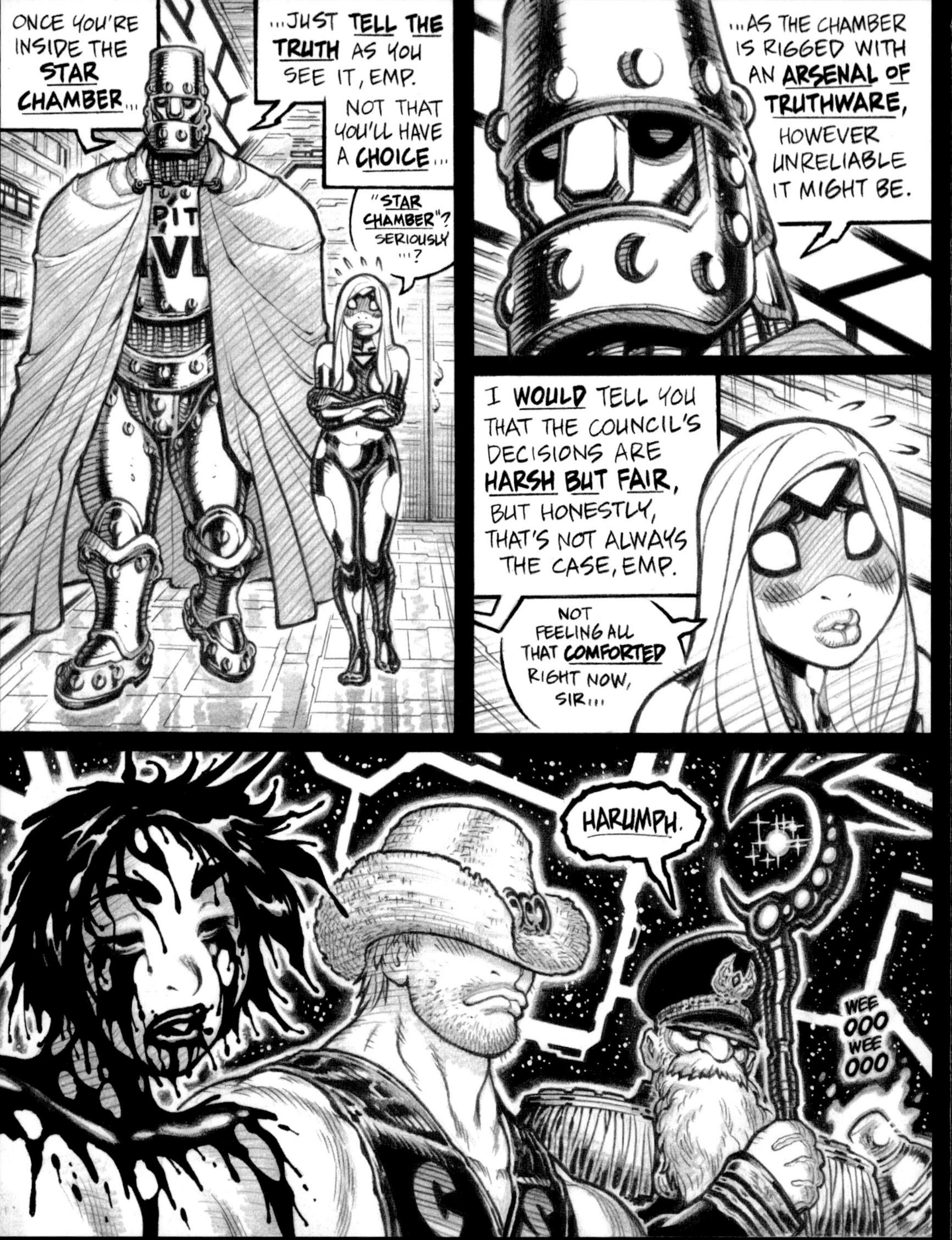
ONCE YOU'RE INSIDE THE STAR CHAMBER...
...JUST TELL THE TRUTH AS YOU SEE IT, EMP.
NOT THAT YOU'LL HAVE A CHOICE...
"STAR CHAMBER"? SERIOUSLY...?
...AS THE CHAMBER IS RIGGED WITH AN ARSENAL OF TRUTHWARE,
HOWEVER UNRELIABLE IT MIGHT BE.
I WOULD TELL YOU THAT THE COUNCIL'S DECISIONS ARE HARSH BUT FAIR, BUT HONESTLY, THAT'S NOT ALWAYS THE CASE, EMP.
NOT FEELING ALL THAT COMFORTED RIGHT NOW, SIR...
HARUMPH.
WEE OOO WEE OOO

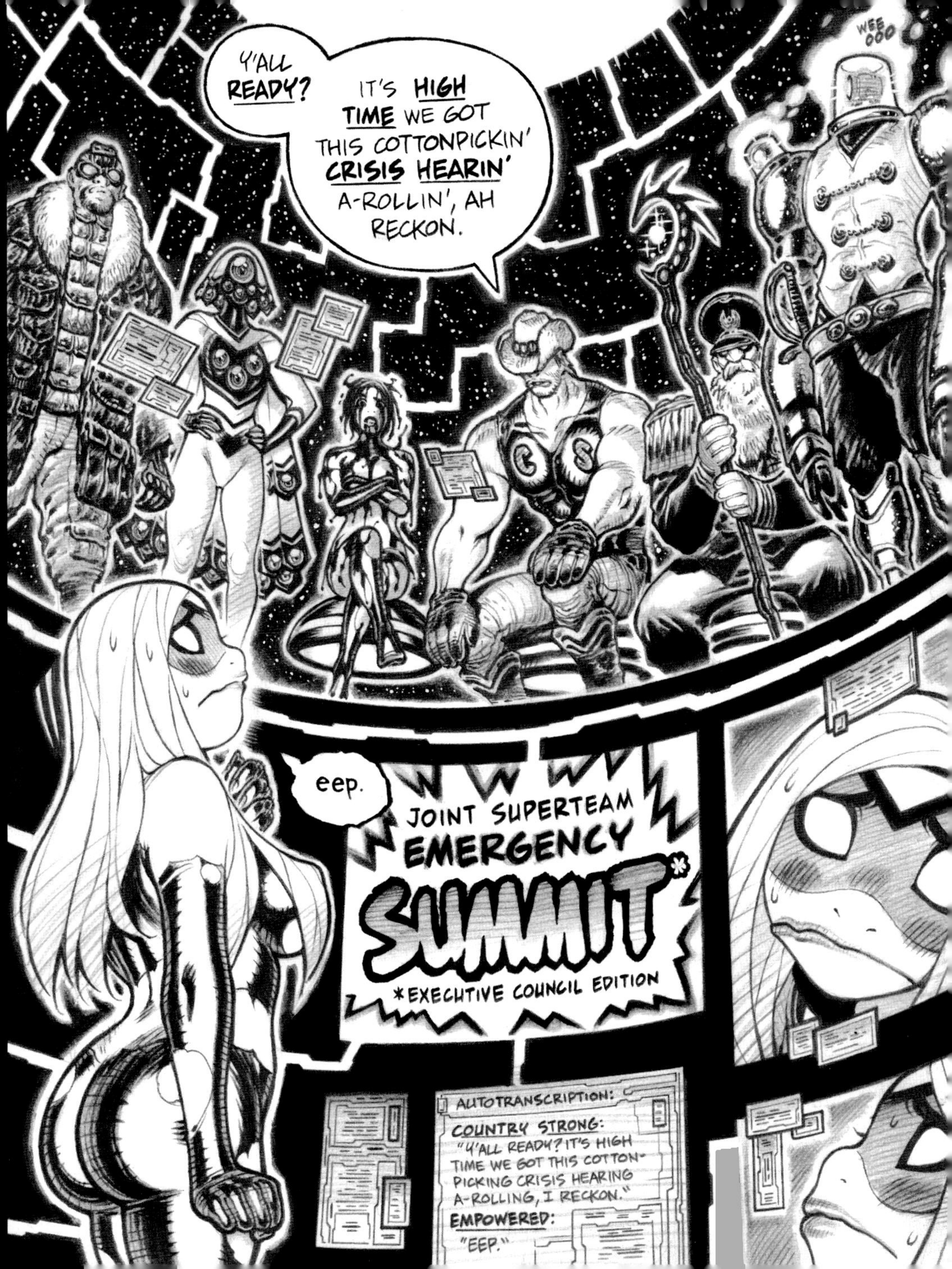
WEE OOO
Y'ALL READY? IT'S HIGH TIME WE GOT THIS COTTONPICKIN' CRISIS HEARIN' A-ROLLIN', AH RECKON.
eep.
JOINT SUPERTEAM EMERGENCY SUMMIT*
*EXECUTIVE COUNCIL EDITION
AUTOTRANSCRIPTION:
COUNTRY STRONG: "Y'ALL READY? IT'S HIGH TIME WE GOT THIS COTTON-PICKING CRISIS HEARING A-ROLLING, I RECKON."
EMPOWERED: "EEP."

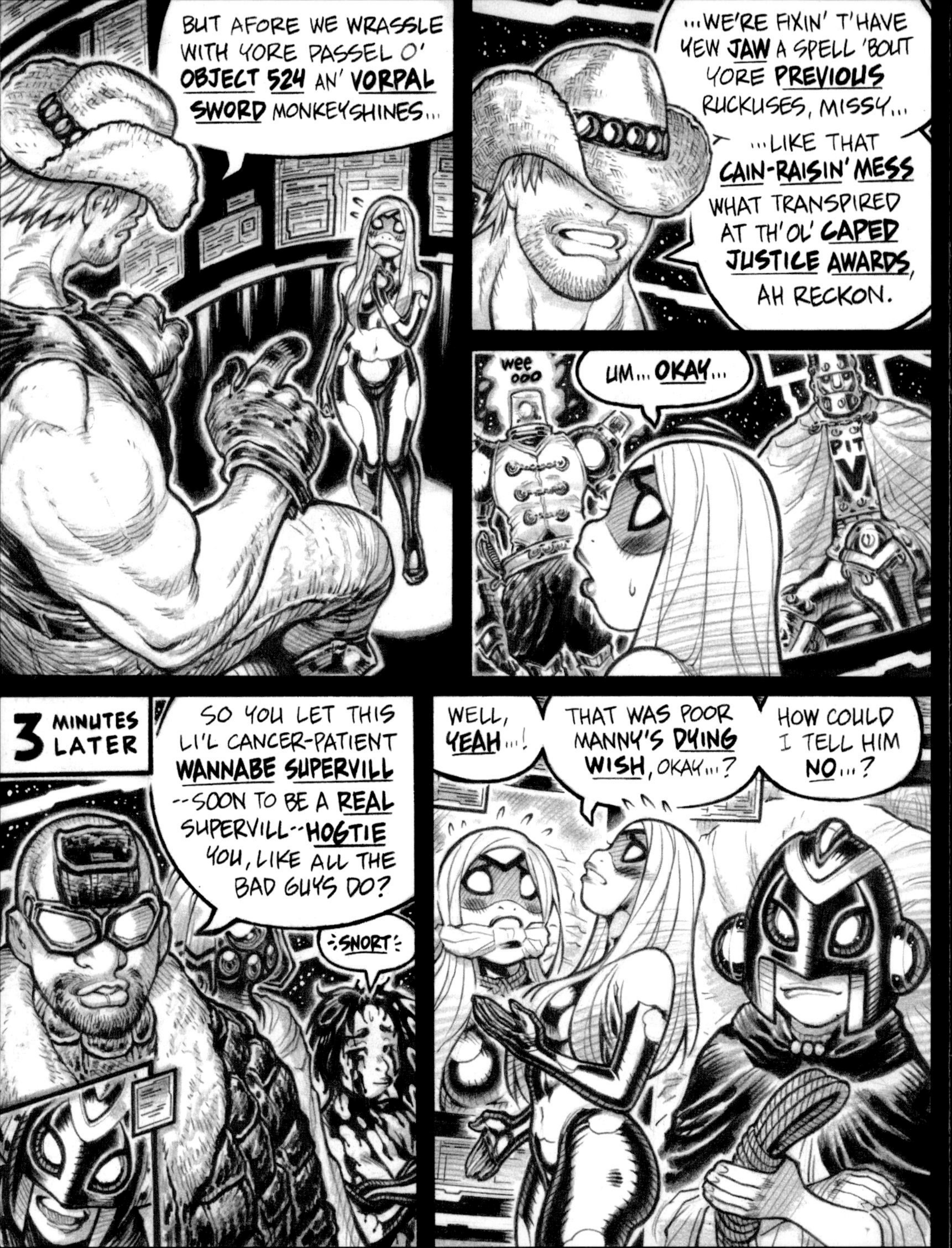
BUT AFORE WE WRASSLE WITH YORE PASSEL O' OBJECT 524 AN' VORPAL SWORD MONKEYSHINES...
...WE'RE FIXIN' T'HAVE YEW JAW A SPELL 'BOUT YORE PREVIOUS RUCKUSES, MISSY...
...LIKE THAT CAIN-RAISIN' MESS WHAT TRANSPIRED AT TH' OL' CAPED JUSTICE AWARDS, AH RECKON.
wee ooo
UM... OKAY...
3 MINUTES LATER
SO YOU LET THIS LI'L CANCER-PATIENT WANNABE SUPERVILL --SOON TO BE A REAL SUPERVILL--HOGTIE YOU, LIKE ALL THE BAD GUYS DO?
SNORT
WELL, YEAH...!
THAT WAS POOR MANNY'S DYING WISH, OKAY...?
HOW COULD I TELL HIM NO...?
PIT

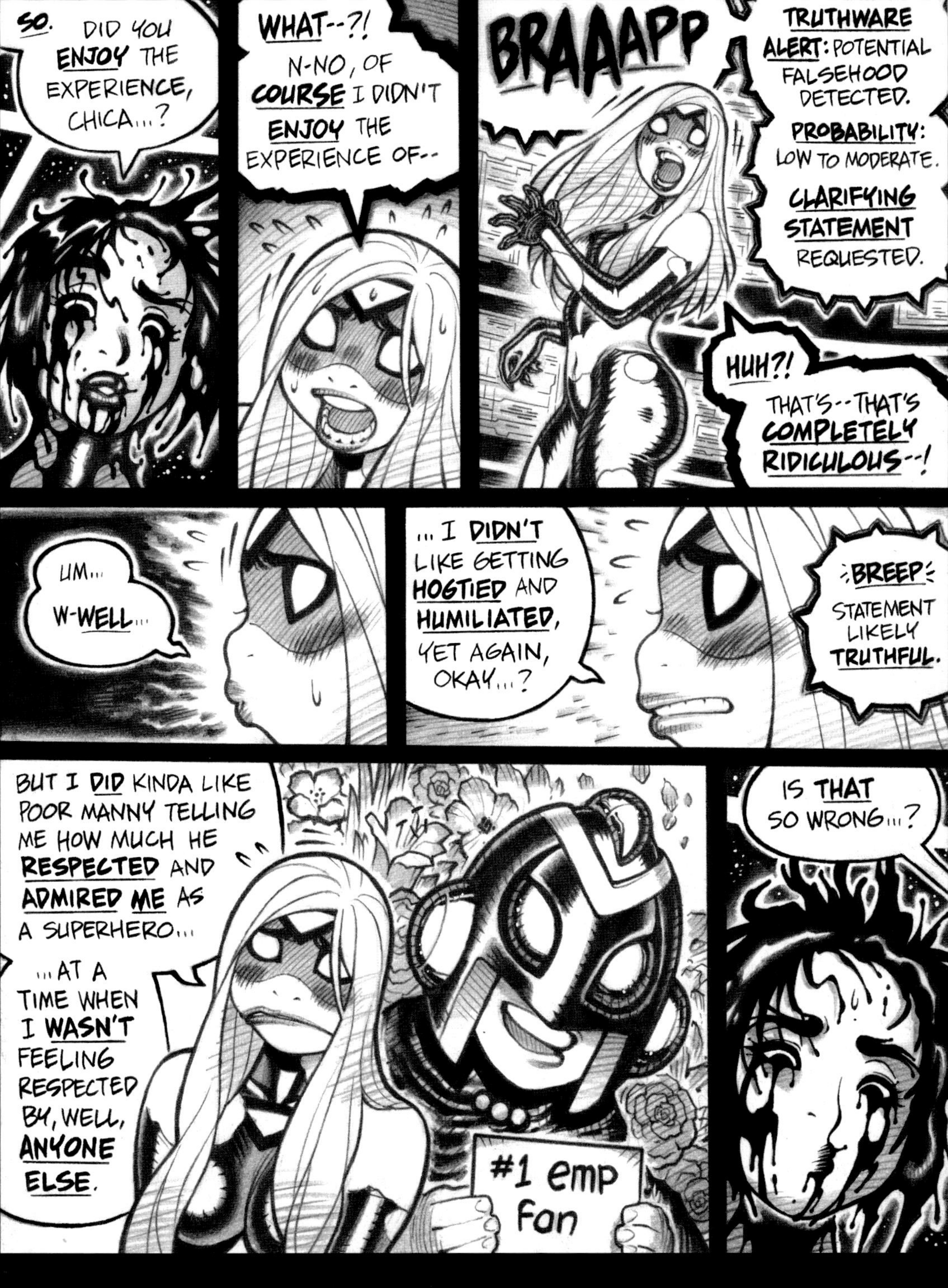
SO. DID YOU ENJOY THE EXPERIENCE, CHICA...?
WHAT--?! N-NO, OF COURSE I DIDN'T ENJOY THE EXPERIENCE OF--
BRAAAPP
TRUTHWARE ALERT: POTENTIAL FALSEHOOD DETECTED. PROBABILITY: LOW TO MODERATE. CLARIFYING STATEMENT REQUESTED.
HUH?! THAT'S--THAT'S COMPLETELY RIDICULOUS--!
UM... W-WELL...
...I DIDN'T LIKE GETTING HOGTIED AND HUMILIATED, YET AGAIN, OKAY...?
BREEP STATEMENT LIKELY TRUTHFUL.
BUT I DID KINDA LIKE POOR MANNY TELLING ME HOW MUCH HE RESPECTED AND ADMIRED ME AS A SUPERHERO...
...AT A TIME WHEN I WASN'T FEELING RESPECTED BY, WELL, ANYONE ELSE.
#1 emp fan
IS THAT SO WRONG...?

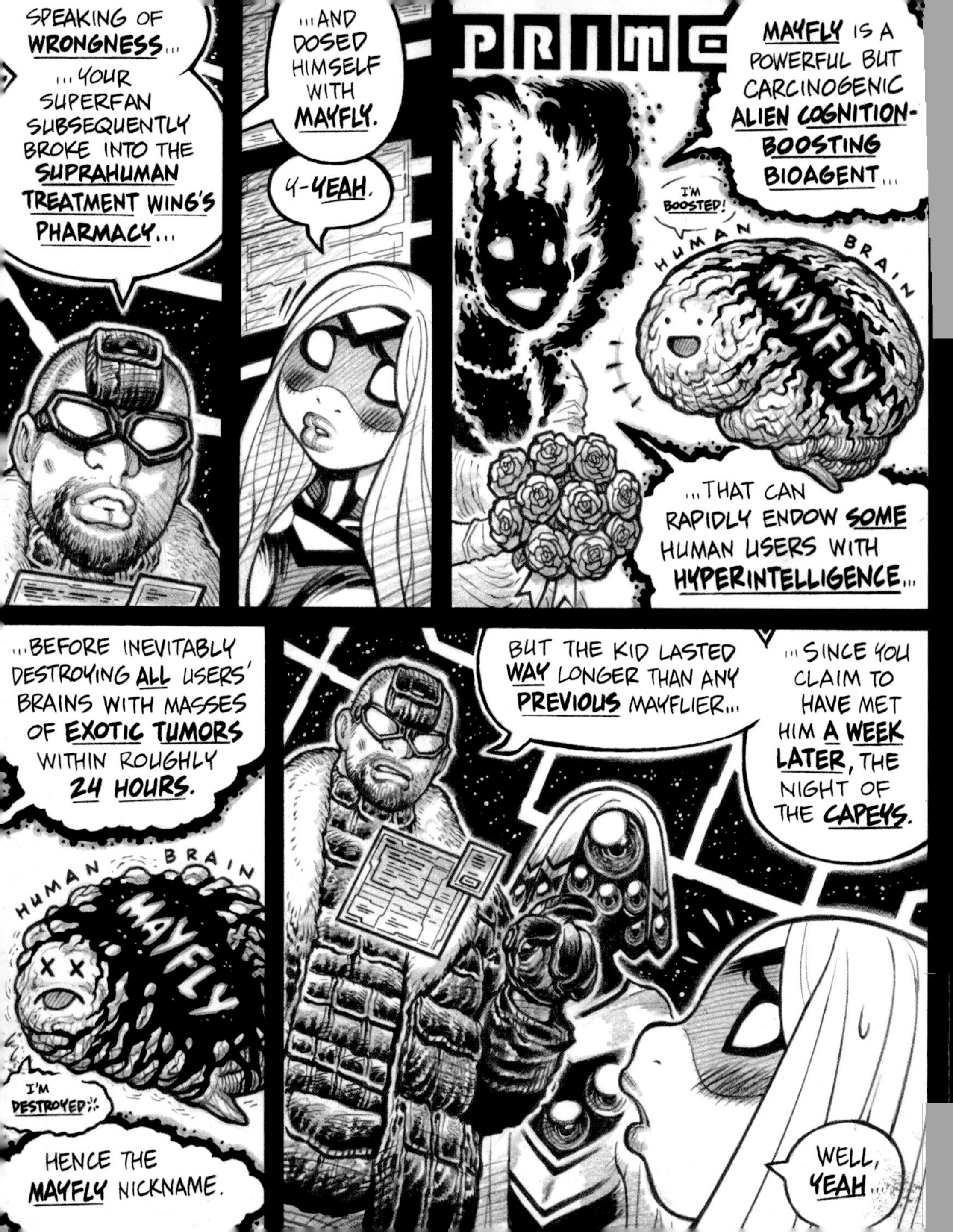
SPEAKING OF WRONGNESS...
...YOUR SUPERFAN SUBSEQUENTLY BROKE INTO THE SUPRAHUMAN TREATMENT WING'S PHARMACY...
...AND DOSED HIMSELF WITH MAYFLY.
Y-YEAH.
PRIME
MAYFLY IS A POWERFUL BUT CARCINOGENIC ALIEN COGNITION-BOOSTING BIOAGENT...
I'M BOOSTED!
HUMAN BRAIN
MAYFLY
...THAT CAN RAPIDLY ENDOW SOME HUMAN USERS WITH HYPERINTELLIGENCE...
...BEFORE INEVITABLY DESTROYING ALL USERS' BRAINS WITH MASSES OF EXOTIC TUMORS WITHIN ROUGHLY 24 HOURS.
HUMAN BRAIN
MAYFLY
I'M DESTROYED
HENCE THE MAYFLY NICKNAME.
BUT THE KID LASTED WAY LONGER THAN ANY PREVIOUS MAYFLIER...
...SINCE YOU CLAIM TO HAVE MET HIM A WEEK LATER, THE NIGHT OF THE CAPEYS.
WELL, YEAH...

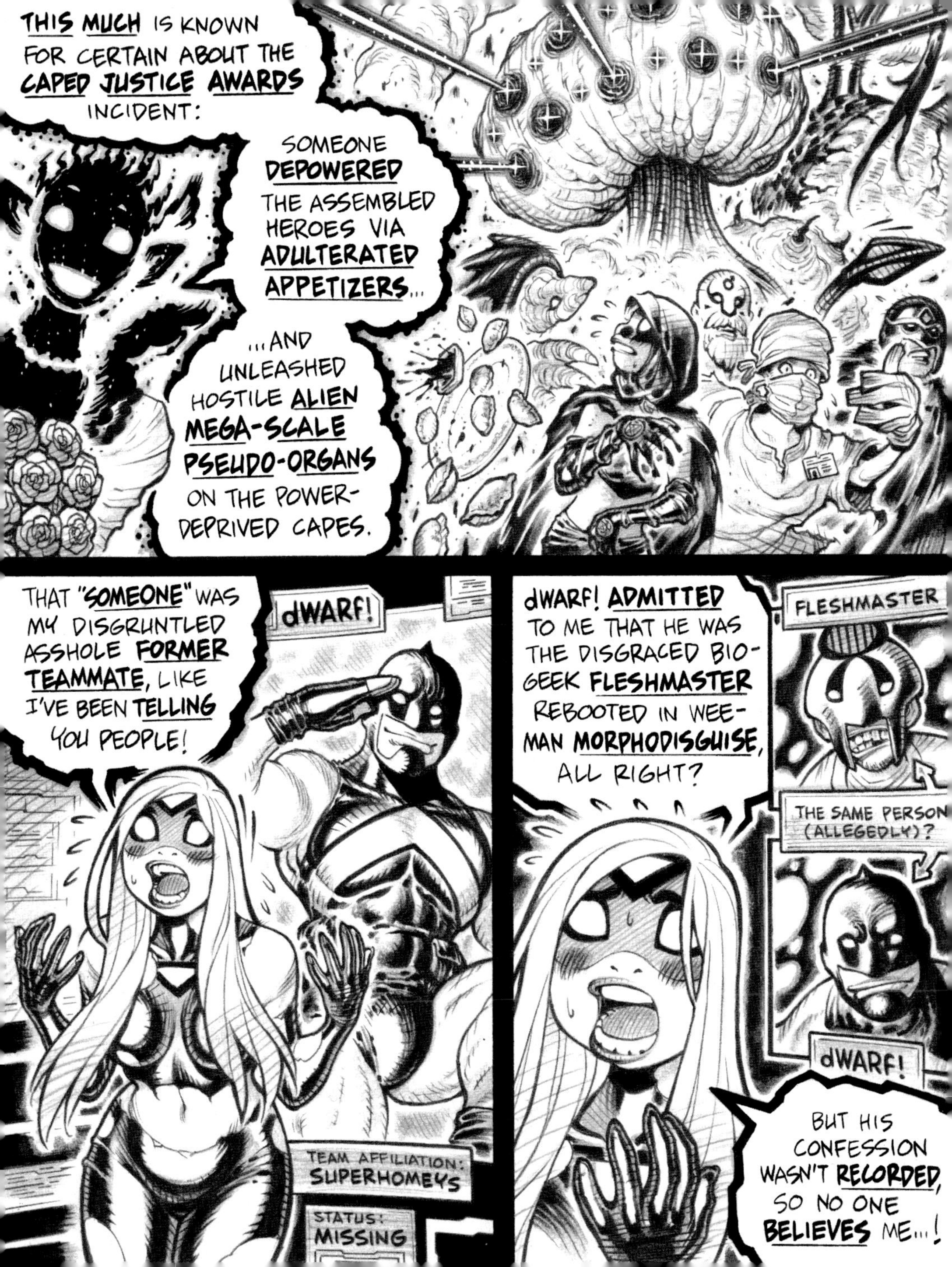
THIS MUCH IS KNOWN FOR CERTAIN ABOUT THE CAPED JUSTICE AWARDS INCIDENT:
SOMEONE DEPOWERED THE ASSEMBLED HEROES VIA ADULTERATED APPETIZERS...
...AND UNLEASHED HOSTILE ALIEN MEGA-SCALE PSEUDO-ORGANS ON THE POWER-DEPRIVED CAPES.
THAT "SOMEONE" WAS MY DISGRUNTLED ASSHOLE FORMER TEAMMATE, LIKE I'VE BEEN TELLING YOU PEOPLE!
dWARF!
TEAM AFFILIATION: SUPERHOMEYS
STATUS: MISSING
dWARF! ADMITTED TO ME THAT HE WAS THE DISGRACED BIO-GEEK FLESHMASTER REBOOTED IN WEE-MAN MORPHODISGUISE, ALL RIGHT?
FLESHMASTER
THE SAME PERSON (ALLEGEDLY)?
dWARF!
BUT HIS CONFESSION WASN'T RECORDED, SO NO ONE BELIEVES ME...!

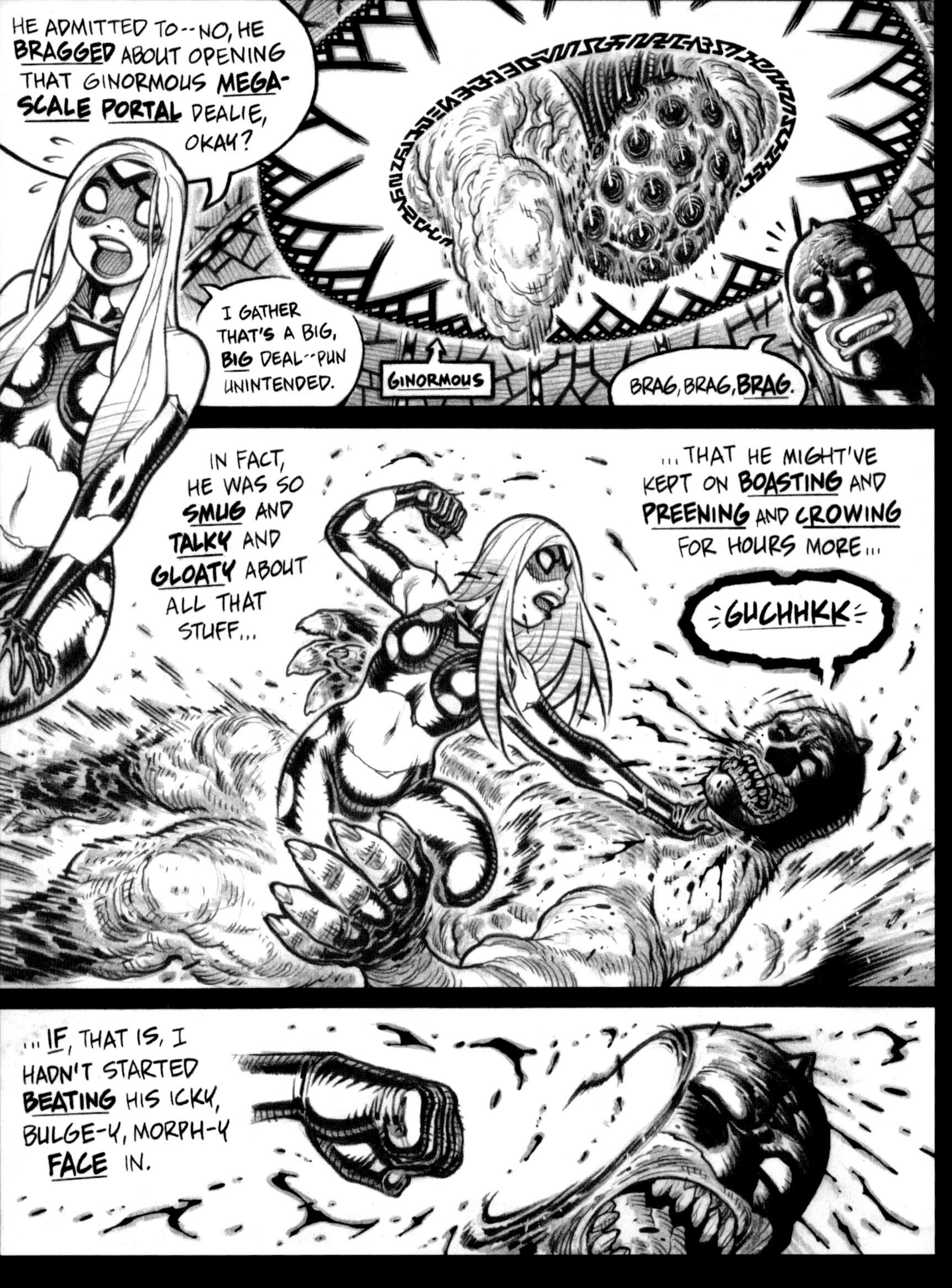
HE ADMITTED TO--NO, HE BRAGGED ABOUT OPENING THAT GINORMOUS MEGA-SCALE PORTAL DEALIE, OKAY?
I GATHER THAT'S A BIG, BIG DEAL--PUN UNINTENDED.
GINORMOUS
BRAG, BRAG, BRAG.
IN FACT, HE WAS SO SMUG AND TALKY AND GLOATY ABOUT ALL THAT STUFF...
...THAT HE MIGHT'VE KEPT ON BOASTING AND PREENING AND CROWING FOR HOURS MORE...
GUCHHKK
...IF, THAT IS, I HADN'T STARTED BEATING HIS ICKY, BULGE-Y, MORPH-Y FACE IN.

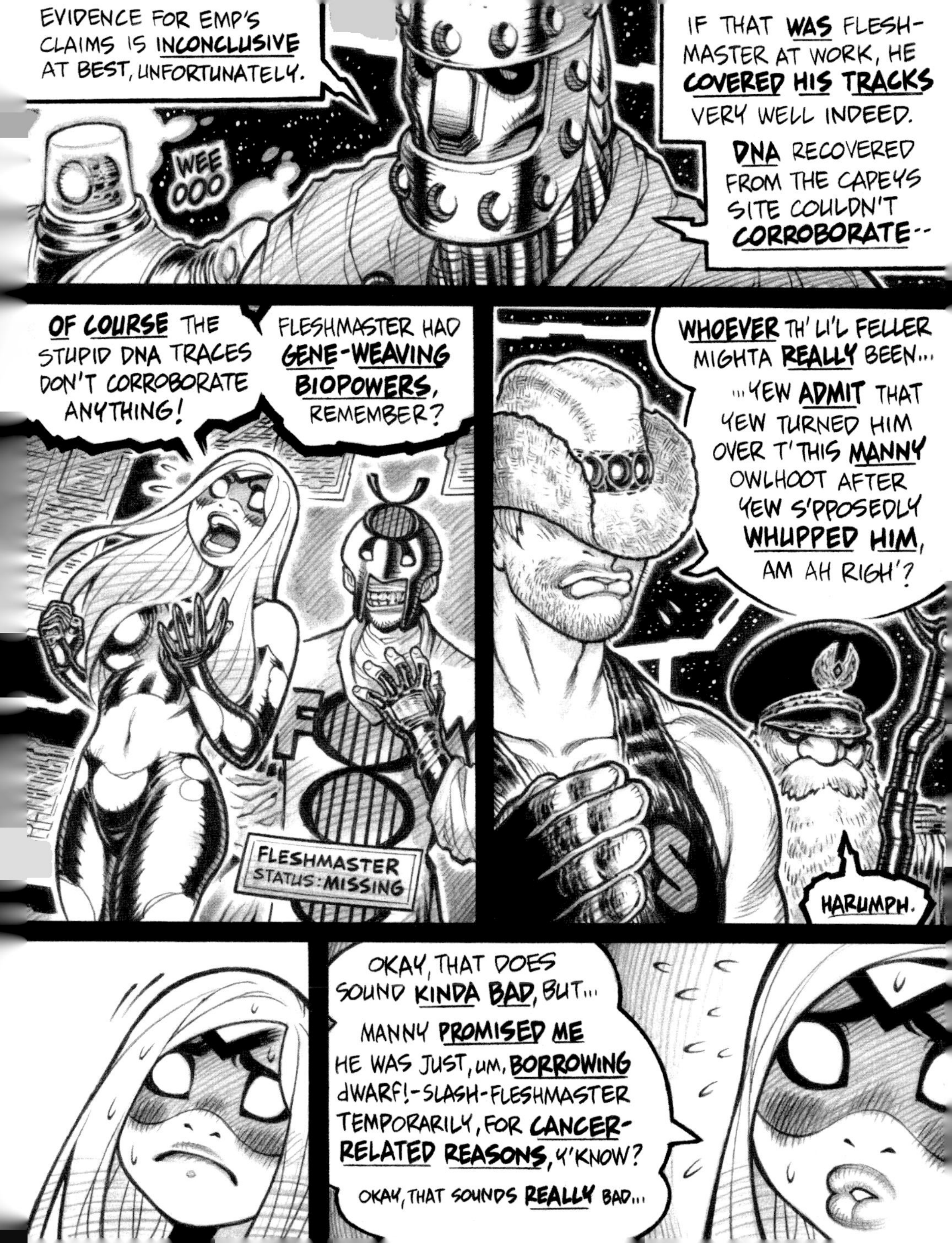
EVIDENCE FOR EMP'S CLAIMS IS INCONCLUSIVE AT BEST, UNFORTUNATELY.
WEE OOO
IF THAT WAS FLESHMASTER AT WORK, HE COVERED HIS TRACKS VERY WELL INDEED.
DNA RECOVERED FROM THE CAPEYS SITE COULDN'T CORROBORATE--
OF COURSE THE STUPID DNA TRACES DON'T CORROBORATE ANYTHING!
FLESHMASTER HAD GENE-WEAVING BIOPOWERS, REMEMBER?
FLESHMASTER STATUS: MISSING
WHOEVER TH' LI'L FELLER MIGHTA REALLY BEEN...
...YEW ADMIT THAT YEW TURNED HIM OVER T' THIS MANNY OWLHOOT AFTER YEW S'PPOSEDLY WHUPPED HIM, AM AH RIGH'?
HARUMPH.
OKAY, THAT DOES SOUND KINDA BAD, BUT...
MANNY PROMISED ME HE WAS JUST, UM, BORROWING dWARF!-SLASH-FLESHMASTER TEMPORARILY, FOR CANCER-RELATED REASONS, Y'KNOW?
OKAY, THAT SOUNDS REALLY BAD...

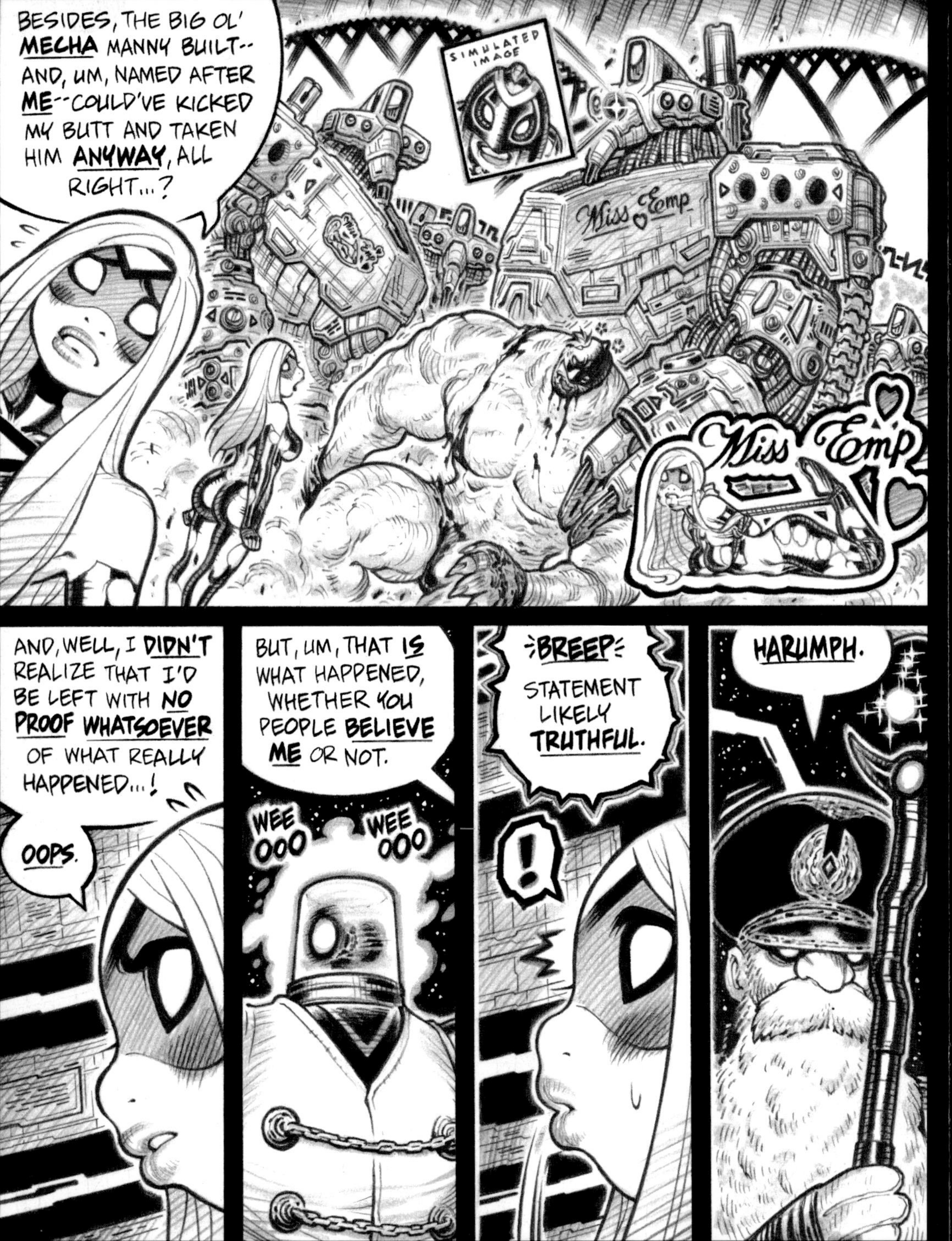
BESIDES, THE BIG OL' MECHA MANNY BUILT-- AND, UM, NAMED AFTER ME--COULD'VE KICKED MY BUTT AND TAKEN HIM ANYWAY, ALL RIGHT...?
SIMULATED IMAGE
Miss Emp
Miss Emp
AND, WELL, I DIDN'T REALIZE THAT I'D BE LEFT WITH NO PROOF WHATSOEVER OF WHAT REALLY HAPPENED...!
OOPS.
BUT, UM, THAT IS WHAT HAPPENED, WHETHER YOU PEOPLE BELIEVE ME OR NOT.
WEE OOO
WEE OOO
BREEP
STATEMENT LIKELY TRUTHFUL.
!
HARUMPH.

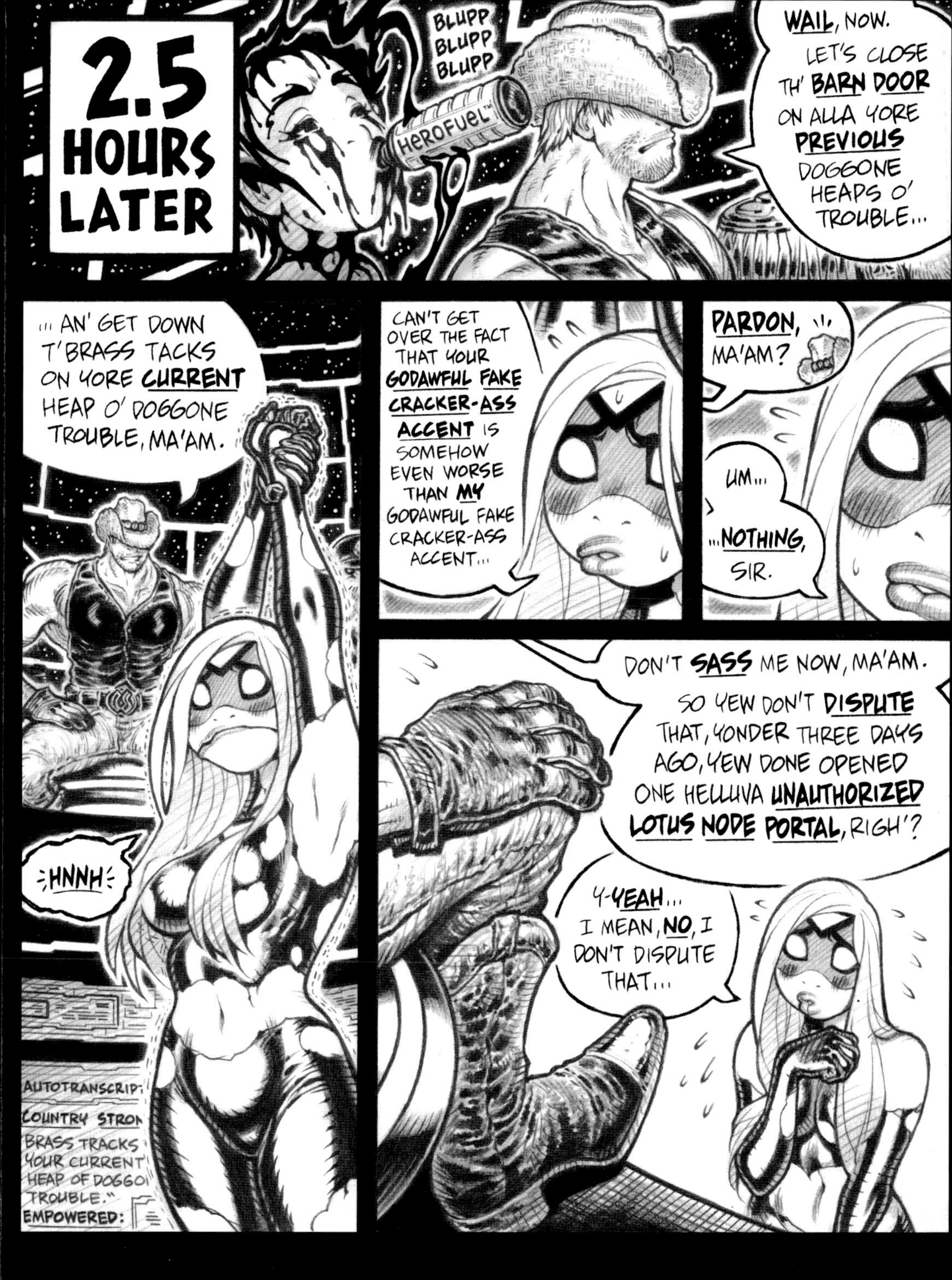

2.5 HOURS LATER
BLUPP BLUPP BLUPP
HEROFUEL™
WAIL, NOW. LET'S CLOSE TH' BARN DOOR ON ALLA YORE PREVIOUS DOGGONE HEAPS O' TROUBLE...
... AN' GET DOWN T'BRASS TACKS ON YORE CURRENT HEAP O' DOGGONE TROUBLE, MA'AM.
CAN'T GET OVER THE FACT THAT YOUR GODAWFUL FAKE CRACKER-ASS ACCENT IS SOMEHOW EVEN WORSE THAN MY GODAWFUL FAKE CRACKER-ASS ACCENT...
PARDON, MA'AM?
UM...
...NOTHING, SIR.
HNNH
DON'T SASS ME NOW, MA'AM.
SO YEW DON'T DISPUTE THAT, YONDER THREE DAYS AGO, YEW DONE OPENED ONE HELLUVA UNAUTHORIZED LOTUS NODE PORTAL, RIGH'?
Y-YEAH... I MEAN, NO, I DON'T DISPUTE THAT...
AUTOTRANSCRIP
COUNTRY STRON
BRASS TRACKS YOUR CURRENT HEAP OF DOGGO TROUBLE."
EMPOWERED:

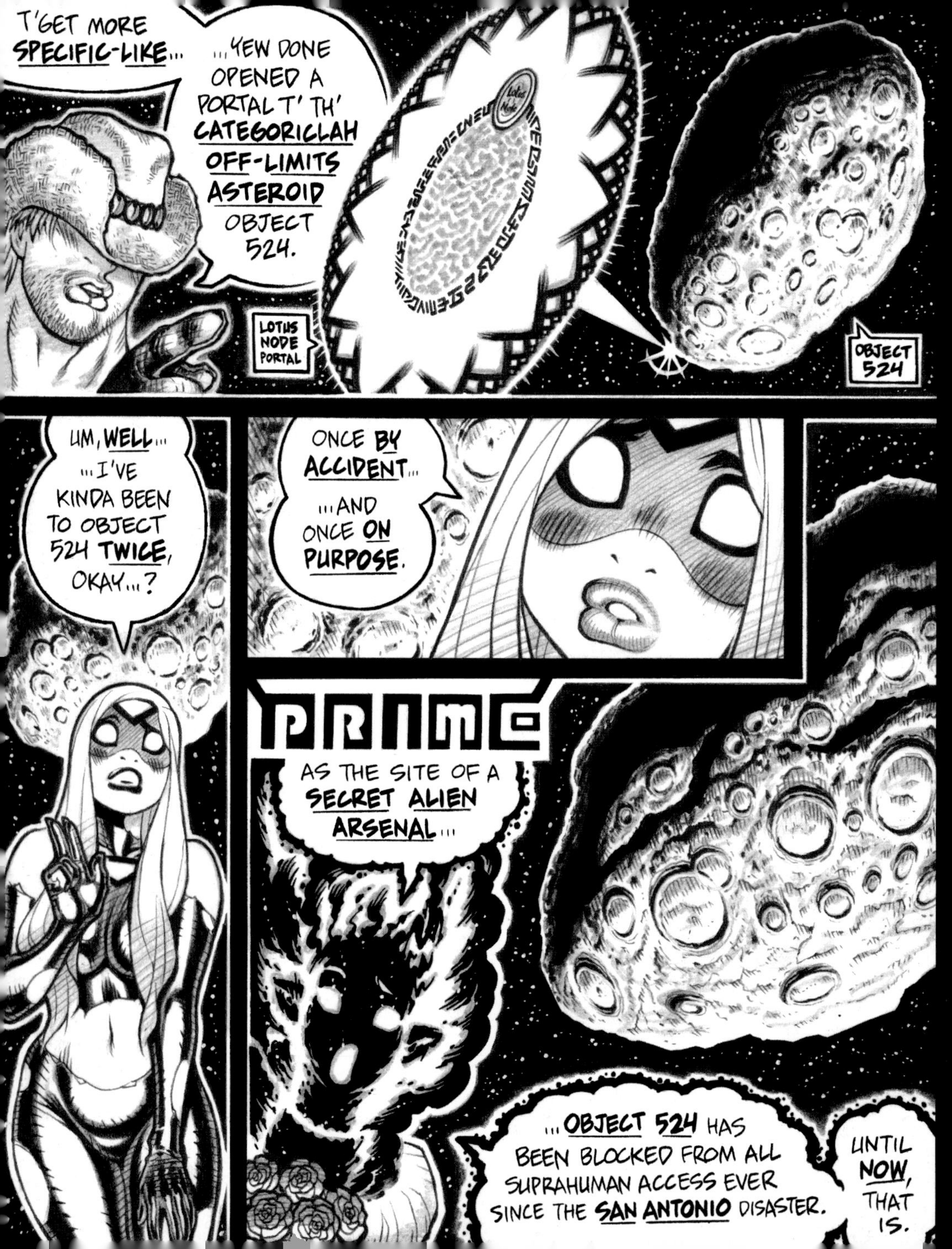
T'GET MORE SPECIFIC-LIKE...
...YEW DONE OPENED A PORTAL T' TH' CATEGORICLAH OFF-LIMITS ASTEROID OBJECT 524.
LOTUS NODE PORTAL
OBJECT 524
UM, WELL...
...I'VE KINDA BEEN TO OBJECT 524 TWICE, OKAY...?
ONCE BY ACCIDENT...
...AND ONCE ON PURPOSE.
PRIME
AS THE SITE OF A SECRET ALIEN ARSENAL...
...OBJECT 524 HAS BEEN BLOCKED FROM ALL SUPRAHUMAN ACCESS EVER SINCE THE SAN ANTONIO DISASTER.
UNTIL NOW, THAT IS.

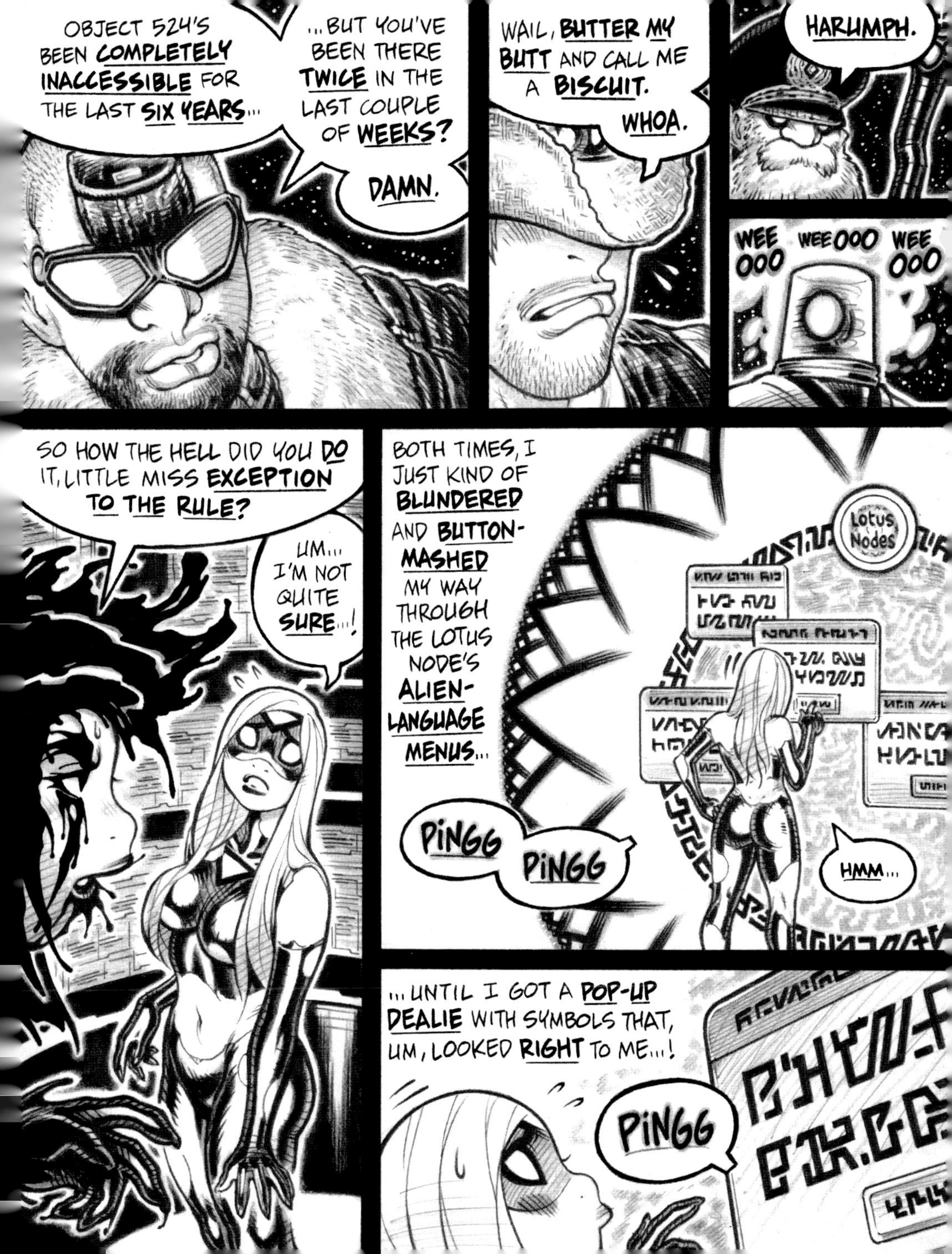
OBJECT 524'S BEEN COMPLETELY INACCESSIBLE FOR THE LAST SIX YEARS...
...BUT YOU'VE BEEN THERE TWICE IN THE LAST COUPLE OF WEEKS?
DAMN.
WAIL, BUTTER MY BUTT AND CALL ME A BISCUIT.
WHOA.
HARUMPH.
WEE OOO
WEEOOO
WEE OOO
SO HOW THE HELL DID YOU DO IT, LITTLE MISS EXCEPTION TO THE RULE?
UM... I'M NOT QUITE SURE...!
BOTH TIMES, I JUST KIND OF BLUNDERED AND BUTTON-MASHED MY WAY THROUGH THE LOTUS NODE'S ALIEN-LANGUAGE MENUS...
Lotus Nodes
PINGG
PINGG
HMM...
...UNTIL I GOT A POP-UP DEALIE WITH SYMBOLS THAT, UM, LOOKED RIGHT TO ME...!
PINGG

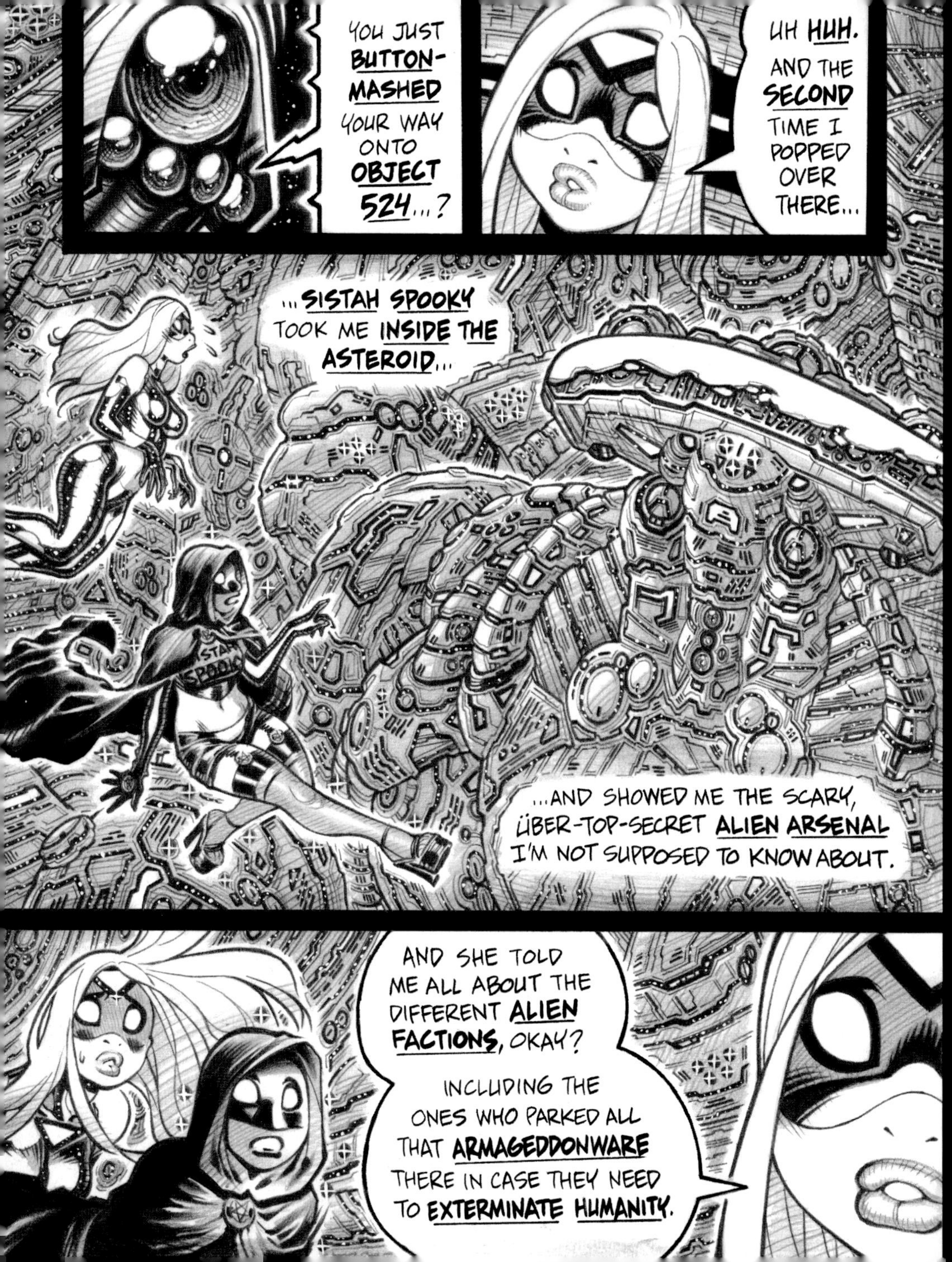
YOU JUST BUTTON-MASHED YOUR WAY ONTO OBJECT 524...?
UH HUH. AND THE SECOND TIME I POPPED OVER THERE...
...SISTAH SPOOKY TOOK ME INSIDE THE ASTEROID...
SISTAH SPOOKY
...AND SHOWED ME THE SCARY, ÜBER-TOP-SECRET ALIEN ARSENAL I'M NOT SUPPOSED TO KNOW ABOUT.
AND SHE TOLD ME ALL ABOUT THE DIFFERENT ALIEN FACTIONS, OKAY?
INCLUDING THE ONES WHO PARKED ALL THAT ARMAGEDDONWARE THERE IN CASE THEY NEED TO EXTERMINATE HUMANITY.

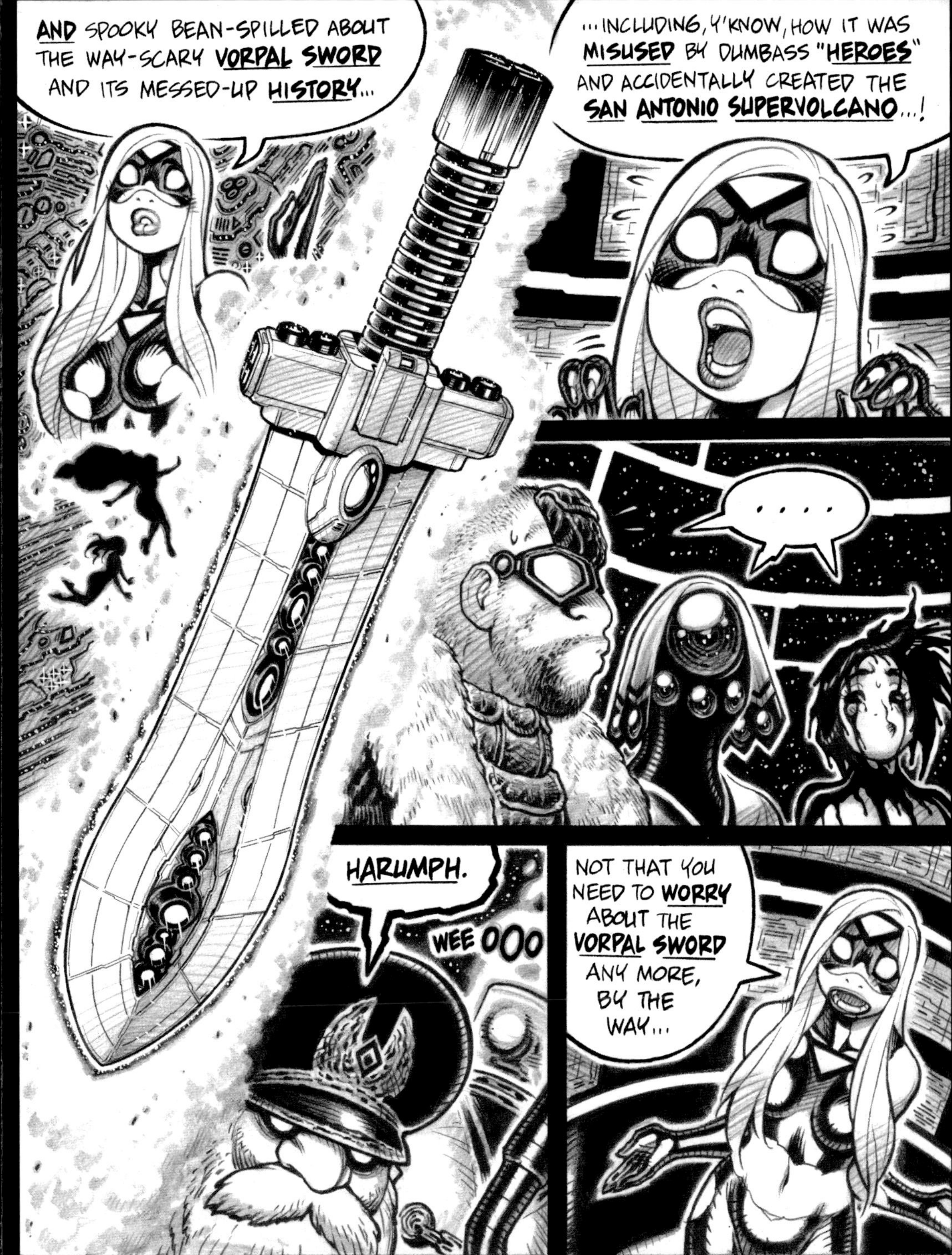
AND SPOOKY BEAN-SPILLED ABOUT THE WAY-SCARY VORPAL SWORD AND ITS MESSED-UP HISTORY...
...INCLUDING, Y'KNOW, HOW IT WAS MISUSED BY DUMBASS "HEROES" AND ACCIDENTALLY CREATED THE SAN ANTONIO SUPERVOLCANO...!
....
HARUMPH.
WEE OOO
NOT THAT YOU NEED TO WORRY ABOUT THE VORPAL SWORD ANY MORE, BY THE WAY...

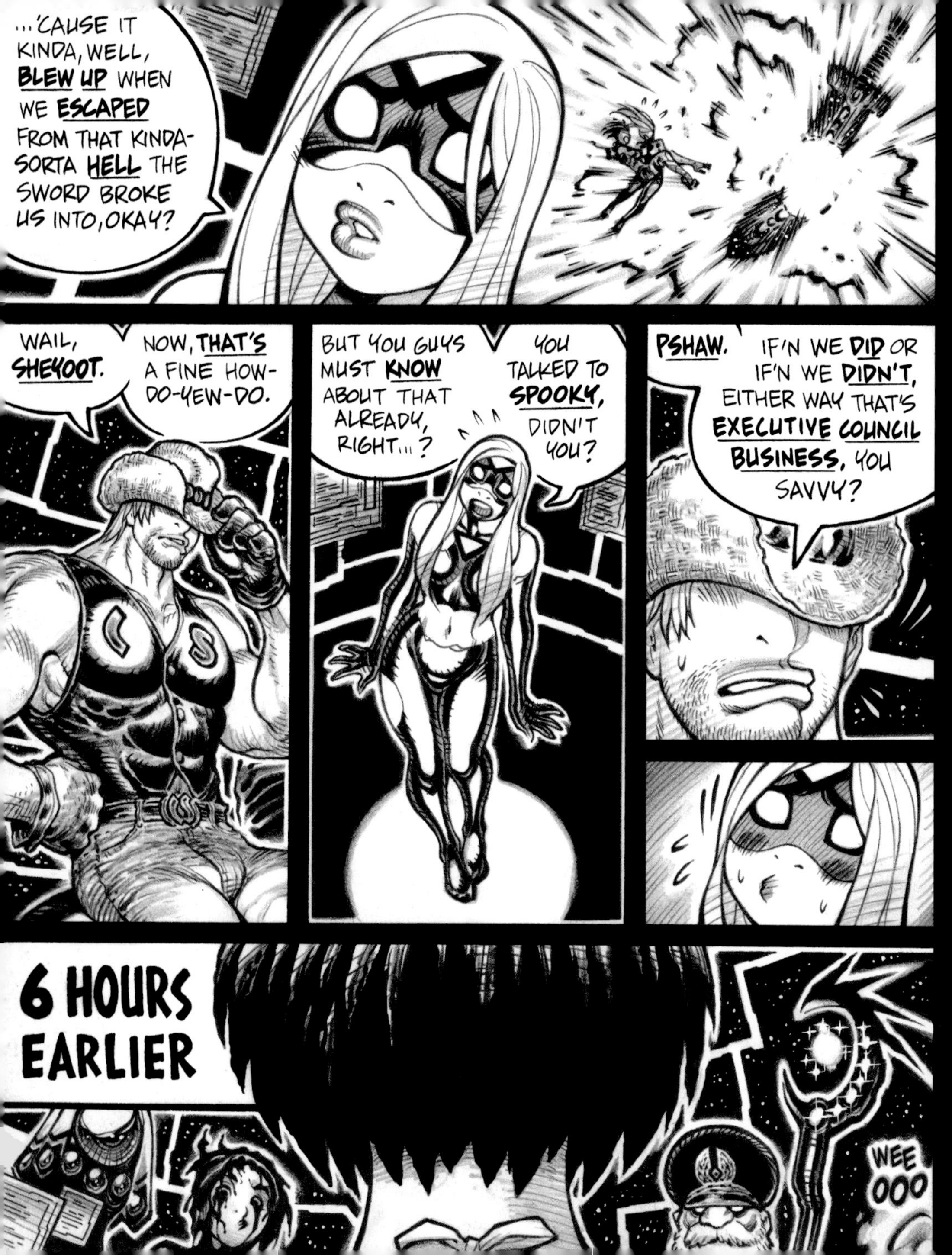
...'CAUSE IT KINDA, WELL, BLEW UP WHEN WE ESCAPED FROM THAT KINDA-SORTA HELL THE SWORD BROKE US INTO, OKAY?
WAIL, SHEYOOT.
NOW, THAT'S A FINE HOW-DO-YEW-DO.
BUT YOU GUYS MUST KNOW ABOUT THAT ALREADY, RIGHT...?
YOU TALKED TO SPOOKY, DIDN'T YOU?
PSHAW.
IF'N WE DID OR IF'N WE DIDN'T, EITHER WAY THAT'S EXECUTIVE COUNCIL BUSINESS, YOU SAVVY?
6 HOURS EARLIER
WEE OOO

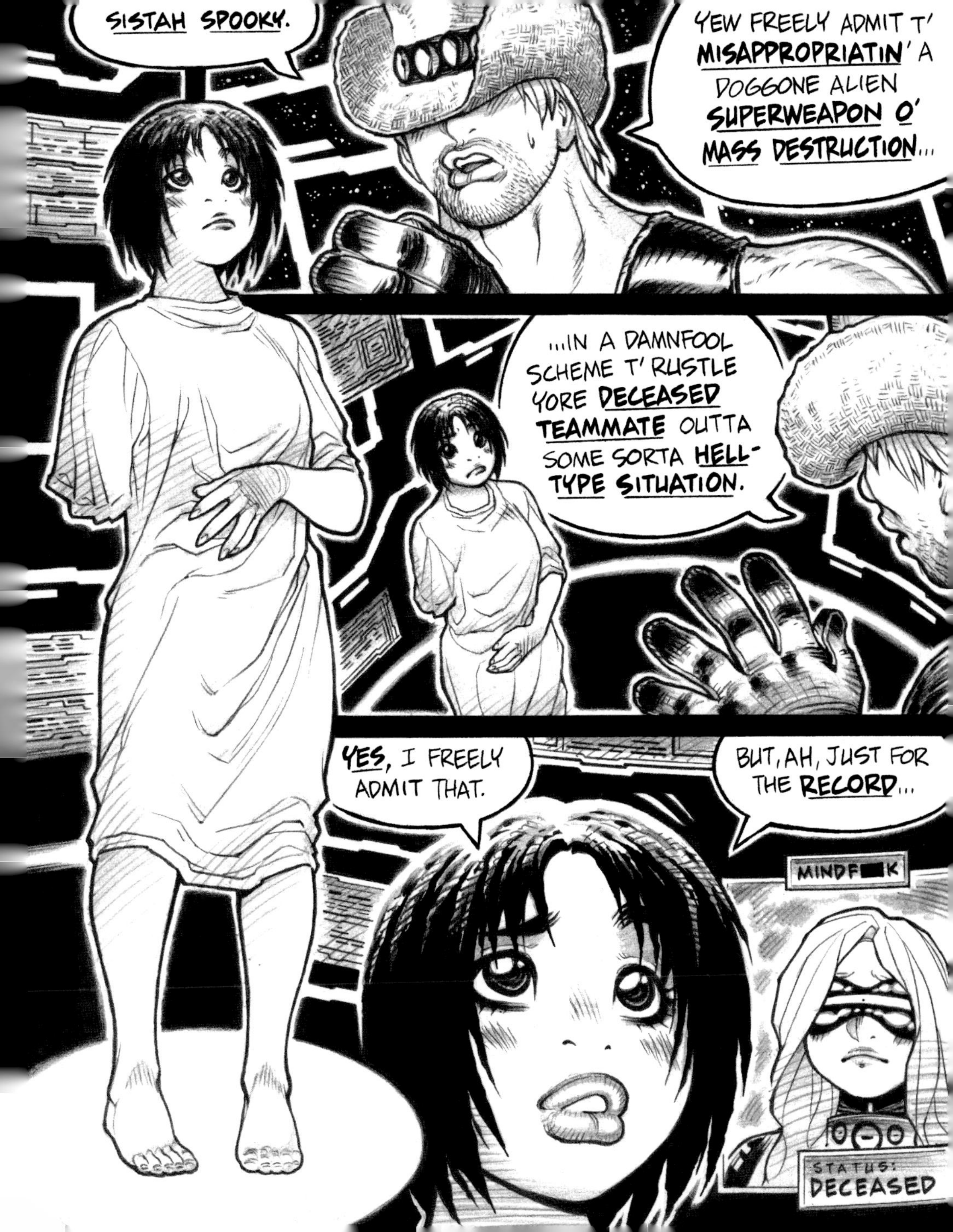
SISTAH SPOOKY.
YEW FREELY ADMIT T' MISAPPROPRIATIN' A DOGGONE ALIEN SUPERWEAPON O' MASS DESTRUCTION...
...IN A DAMNFOOL SCHEME T' RUSTLE YORE DECEASED TEAMMATE OUTTA SOME SORTA HELL-TYPE SITUATION.
YES, I FREELY ADMIT THAT.
BUT, AH, JUST FOR THE RECORD...
MINDF[redacted]K
STATUS: DECEASED

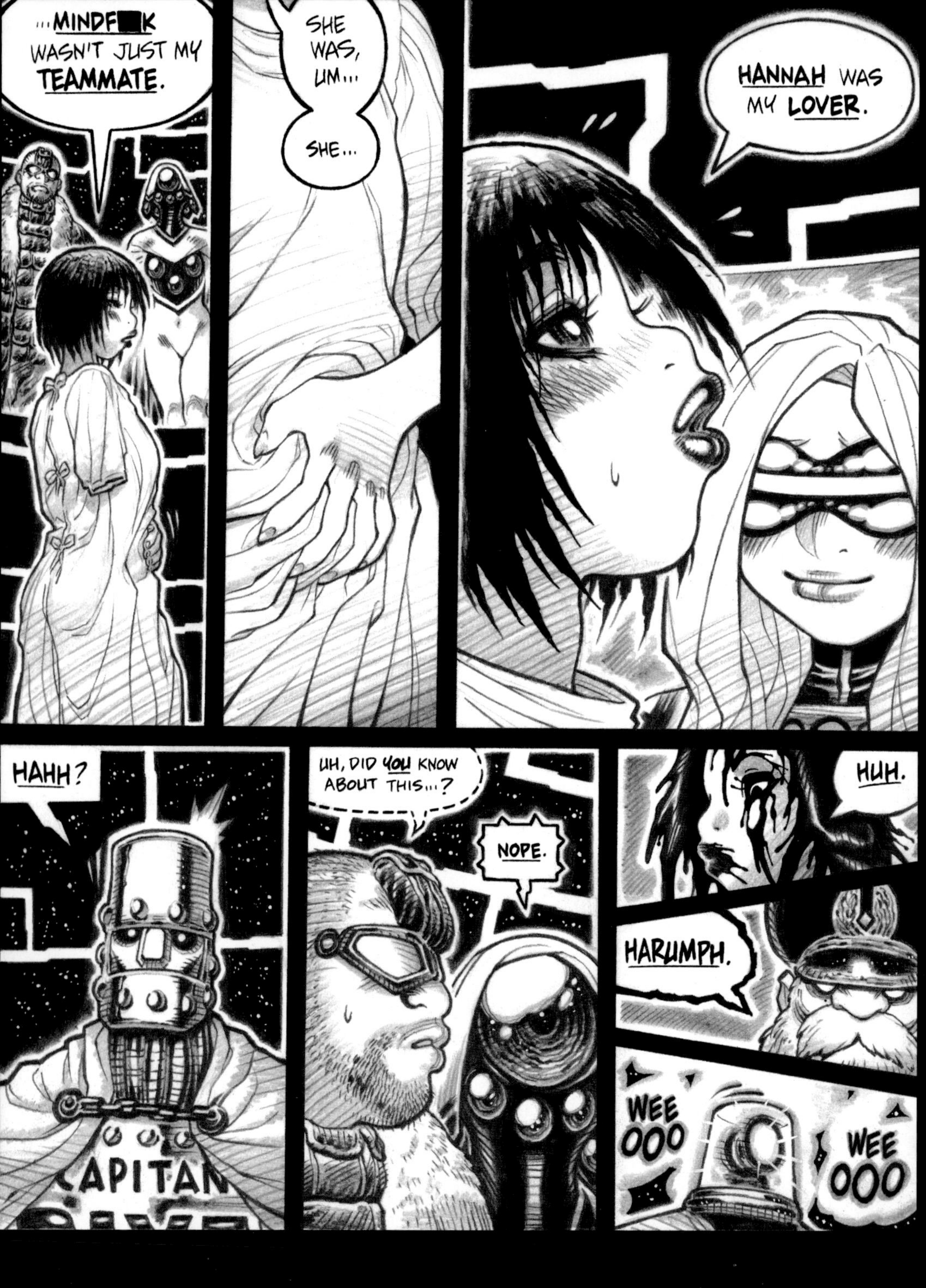
...MINDF[redacted]K WASN'T JUST MY TEAMMATE.
SHE WAS, UM...
SHE...
HANNAH WAS MY LOVER.
HAHH?
UH, DID YOU KNOW ABOUT THIS...?
NOPE.
HUH.
HARUMPH.
WEE OOO
WEE OOO

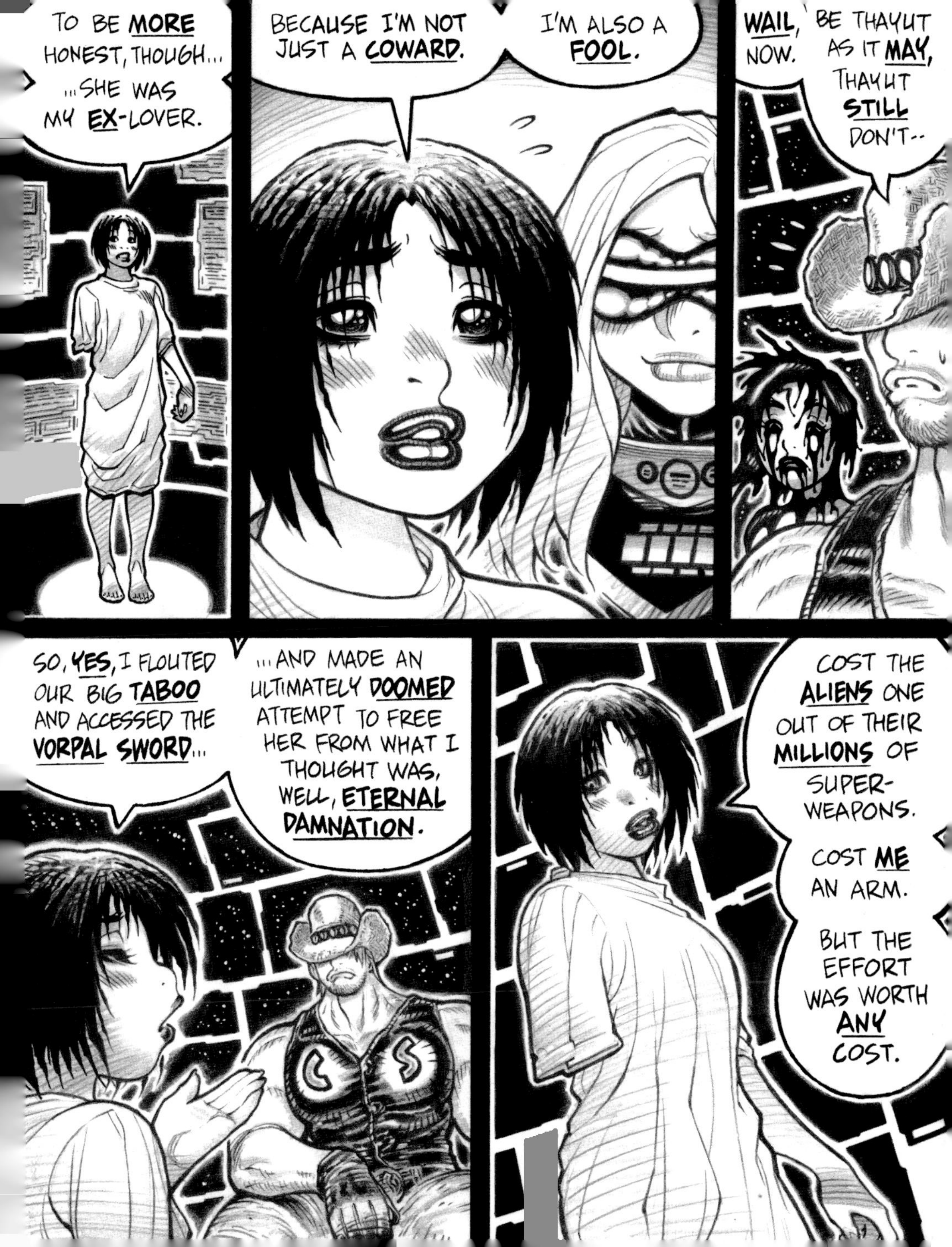
TO BE MORE HONEST, THOUGH...
...SHE WAS MY EX-LOVER.
BECAUSE I'M NOT JUST A COWARD.
I'M ALSO A FOOL.
WAIL, NOW.
BE THAYUT AS IT MAY, THAYUT STILL DON'T--
SO, YES, I FLOUTED OUR BIG TABOO AND ACCESSED THE VORPAL SWORD...
...AND MADE AN ULTIMATELY DOOMED ATTEMPT TO FREE HER FROM WHAT I THOUGHT WAS, WELL, ETERNAL DAMNATION.
COST THE ALIENS ONE OUT OF THEIR MILLIONS OF SUPER-WEAPONS.
COST ME AN ARM.
BUT THE EFFORT WAS WORTH ANY COST.

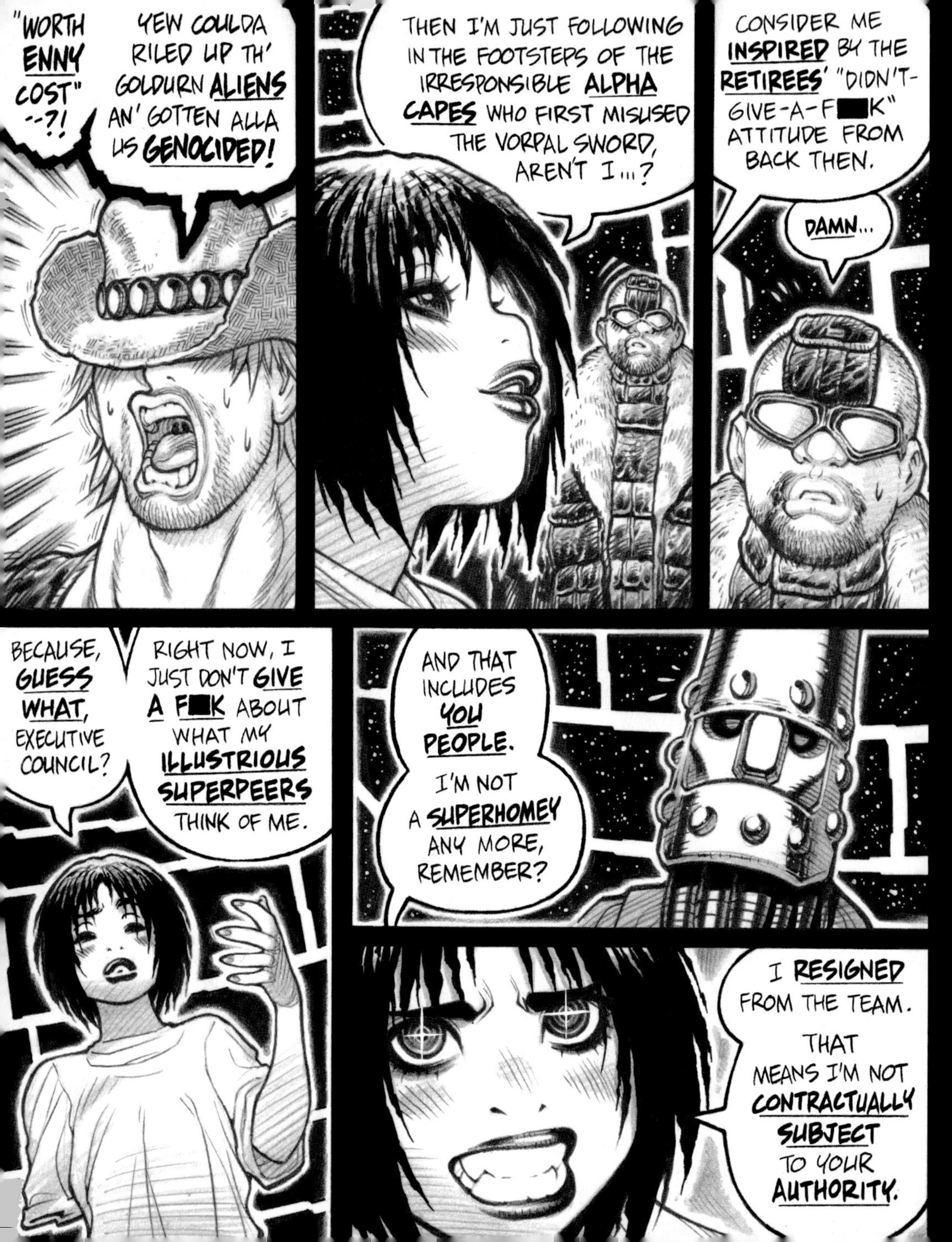
"WORTH ENNY COST" --?!
YEW COULDA RILED UP TH' GOLDURN ALIENS AN' GOTTEN ALLA US GENOCIDED!
THEN I'M JUST FOLLOWING IN THE FOOTSTEPS OF THE IRRESPONSIBLE ALPHA CAPES WHO FIRST MISUSED THE VORPAL SWORD, AREN'T I...?
CONSIDER ME INSPIRED BY THE RETIREES' "DIDN'T-GIVE-A-F[redacted]K" ATTITUDE FROM BACK THEN.
DAMN...
BECAUSE, GUESS WHAT, EXECUTIVE COUNCIL?
RIGHT NOW, I JUST DON'T GIVE A F[redacted]K ABOUT WHAT MY ILLUSTRIOUS SUPERPEERS THINK OF ME.
AND THAT INCLUDES YOU PEOPLE.
I'M NOT A SUPERHOMEY ANY MORE, REMEMBER?
I RESIGNED FROM THE TEAM.
THAT MEANS I'M NOT CONTRACTUALLY SUBJECT TO YOUR AUTHORITY.

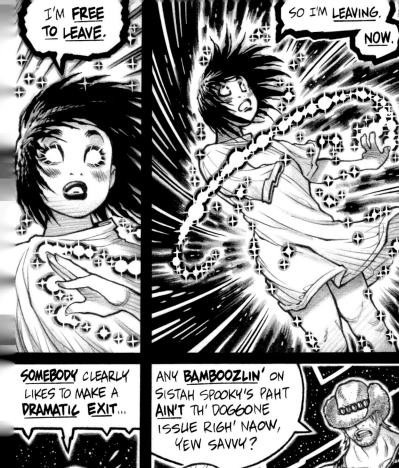

I'M **FREE** TO **LEAVE.**

SO I'M **LEAVING.**

NOW.

SOMEBODY CLEARLY LIKES TO MAKE A **DRAMATIC EXIT**...

ANY **BAMBOOZLIN'** ON SISTAH SPOOKY'S PAHT **AIN'T** TH' DOGGONE ISSUE RIGH' NAOW, YEW SAVVY?

TH' REAL ISSUE IS, **YEW** BEIN' ABLE T' ACCESS A COTTONPICKIN' **FORBIDDEN XENOSITE** ENNY TIME YEW LIKE.

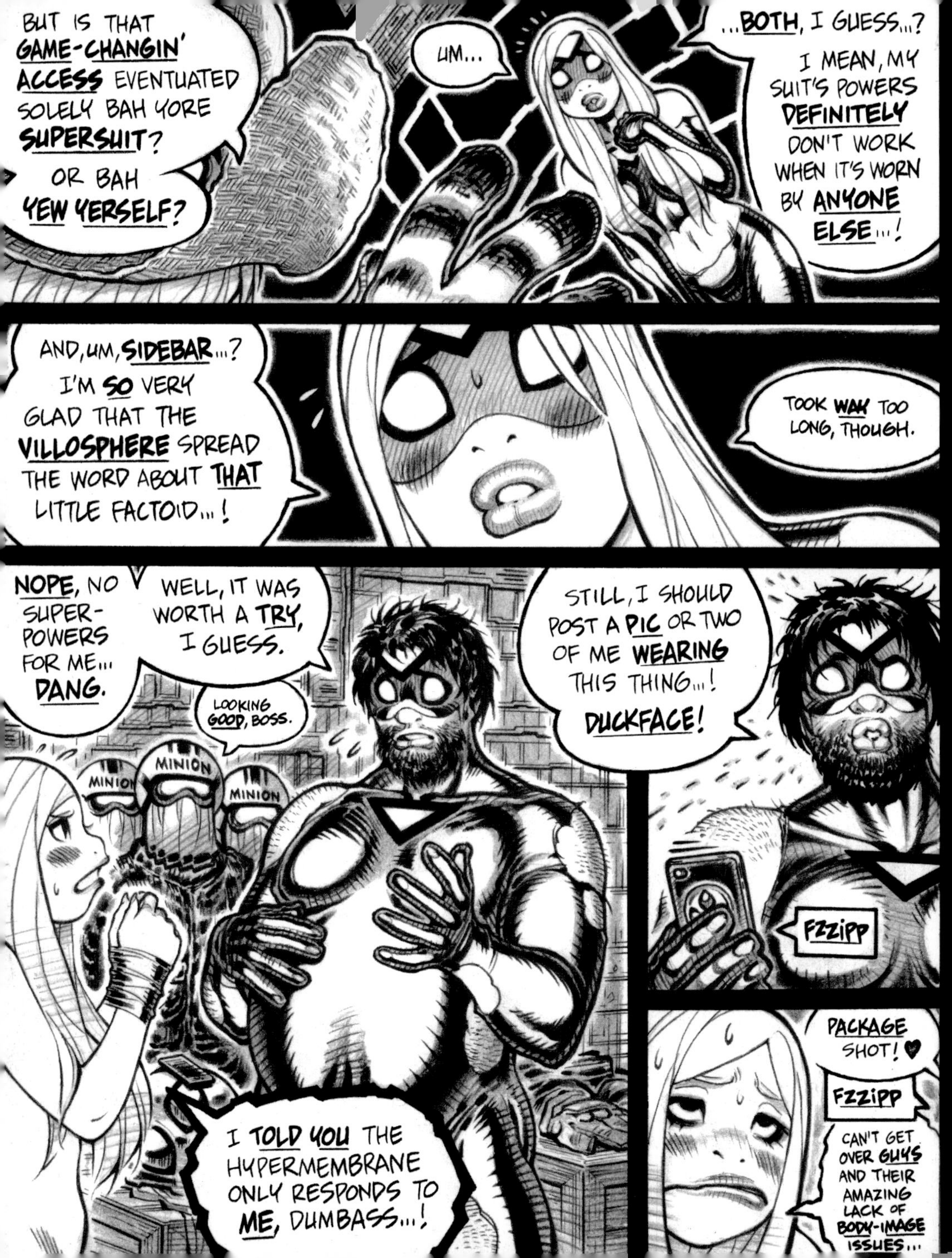
BUT IS THAT GAME-CHANGIN' ACCESS EVENTUATED SOLELY BAH YORE SUPERSUIT?
OR BAH YEW YERSELF?
UM...
...BOTH, I GUESS...?
I MEAN, MY SUIT'S POWERS DEFINITELY DON'T WORK WHEN IT'S WORN BY ANYONE ELSE...!
AND, UM, SIDEBAR...? I'M SO VERY GLAD THAT THE VILLOSPHERE SPREAD THE WORD ABOUT THAT LITTLE FACTOID...!
TOOK WAY TOO LONG, THOUGH.
NOPE, NO SUPER-POWERS FOR ME... DANG.
WELL, IT WAS WORTH A TRY, I GUESS.
LOOKING GOOD, BOSS.
MINION
MINION
MINION
STILL, I SHOULD POST A PIC OR TWO OF ME WEARING THIS THING...!
DUCKFACE!
FZZIPP
I TOLD YOU THE HYPERMEMBRANE ONLY RESPONDS TO ME, DUMBASS...!
PACKAGE SHOT! ♥
FZZIPP
CAN'T GET OVER GUYS AND THEIR AMAZING LACK OF BODY-IMAGE ISSUES...

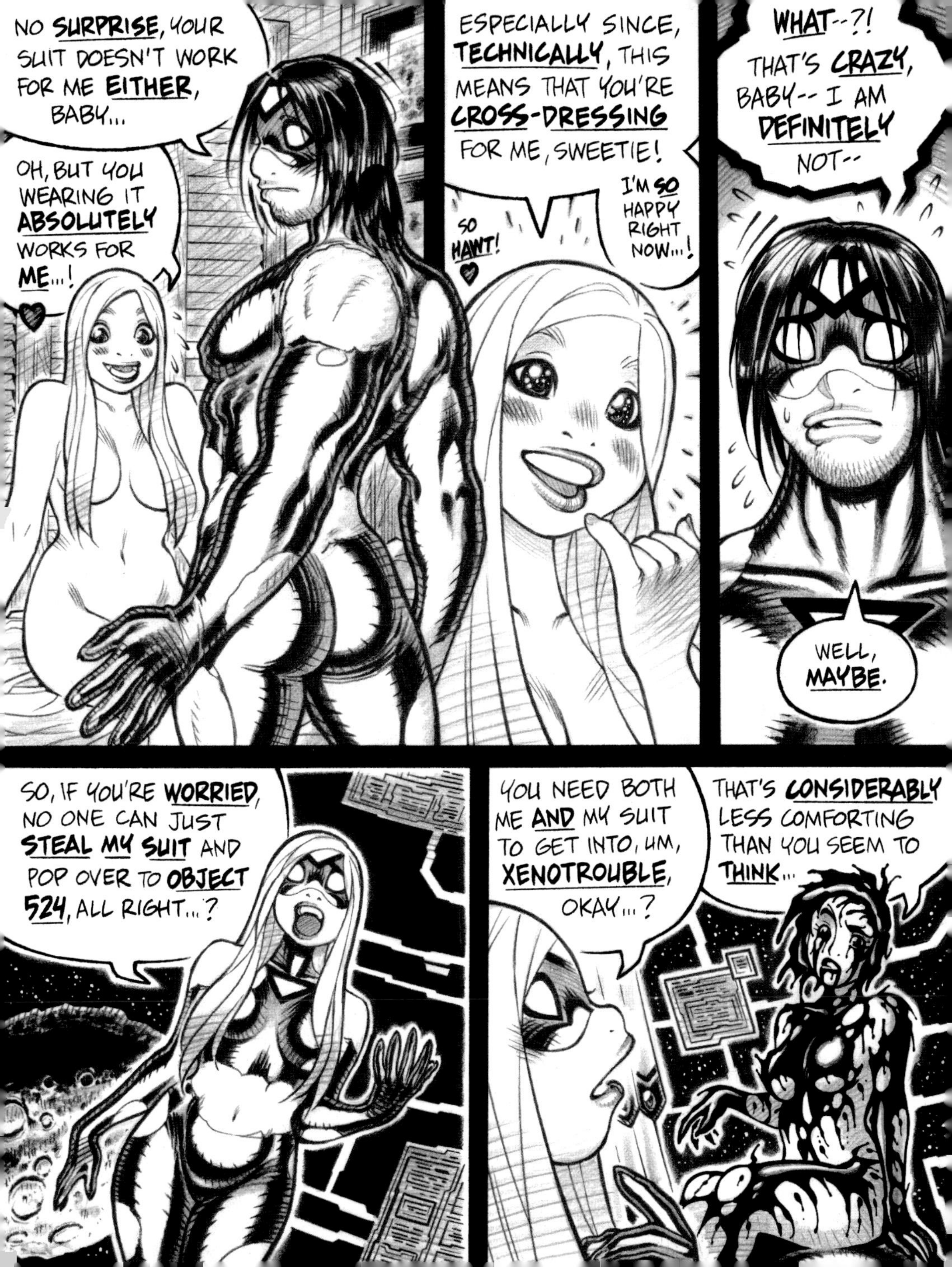

NO SURPRISE, YOUR SUIT DOESN'T WORK FOR ME EITHER, BABY...
OH, BUT YOU WEARING IT ABSOLUTELY WORKS FOR ME...!
ESPECIALLY SINCE, TECHNICALLY, THIS MEANS THAT YOU'RE CROSS-DRESSING FOR ME, SWEETIE!
SO HAWT!
I'M SO HAPPY RIGHT NOW...!
WHAT--?! THAT'S CRAZY, BABY-- I AM DEFINITELY NOT--
WELL, MAYBE.
SO, IF YOU'RE WORRIED, NO ONE CAN JUST STEAL MY SUIT AND POP OVER TO OBJECT 524, ALL RIGHT...?
YOU NEED BOTH ME AND MY SUIT TO GET INTO, UM, XENOTROUBLE, OKAY...?
THAT'S CONSIDERABLY LESS COMFORTING THAN YOU SEEM TO THINK...

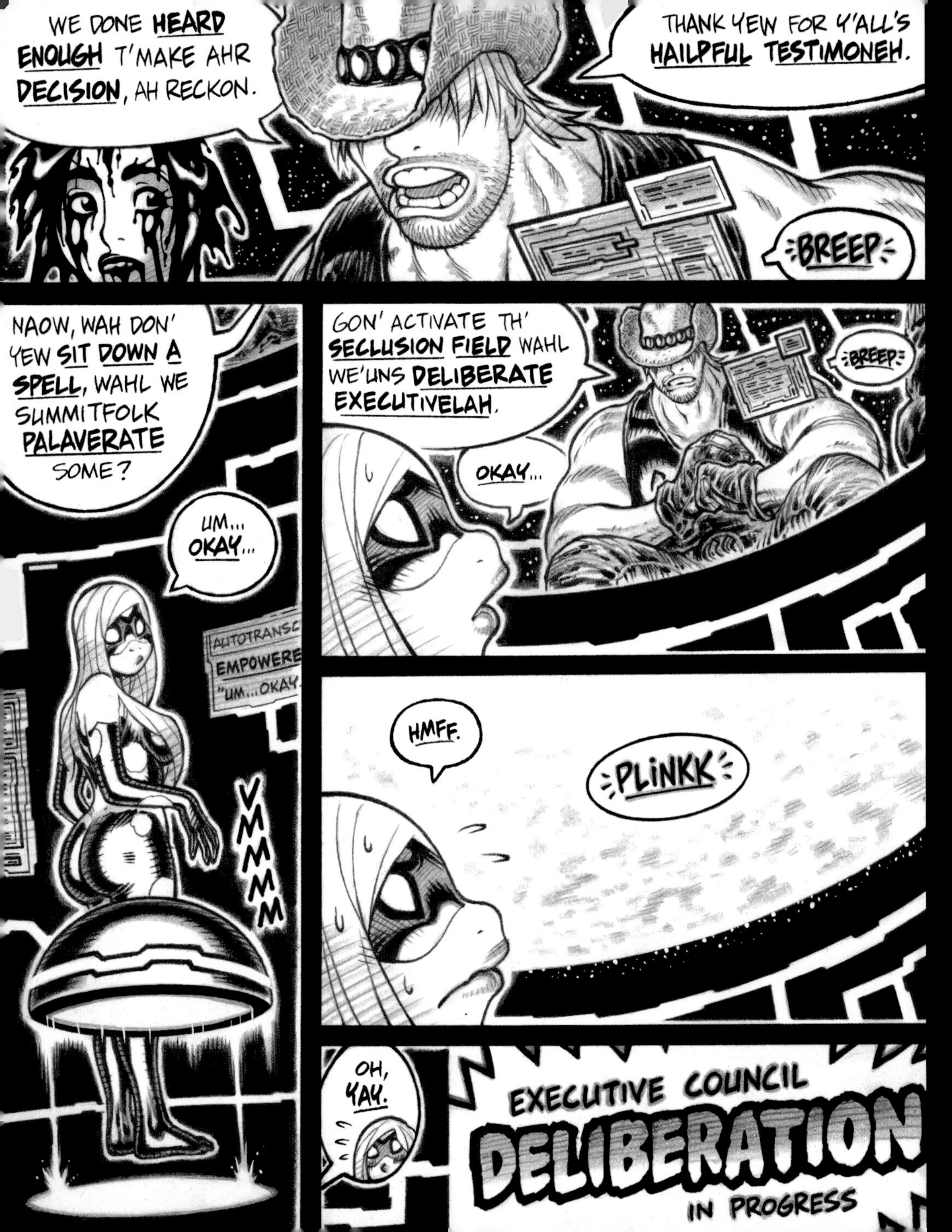
WE DONE HEARD ENOUGH T'MAKE AHR DECISION, AH RECKON.
THANK YEW FOR Y'ALL'S HAILPFUL TESTIMONEH.
BREEP
NAOW, WAH DON' YEW SIT DOWN A SPELL, WAHL WE SUMMITFOLK PALAVERATE SOME?
UM... OKAY...
AUTOTRANSC
EMPOWERE
"UM...OKAY
VMMMM
GON' ACTIVATE TH' SECLUSION FIELD WAHL WE'UNS DELIBERATE EXECUTIVELAH.
BREEP
OKAY...
HMFF.
PLINKK
OH, YAY.
EXECUTIVE COUNCIL
DELIBERATION
IN PROGRESS

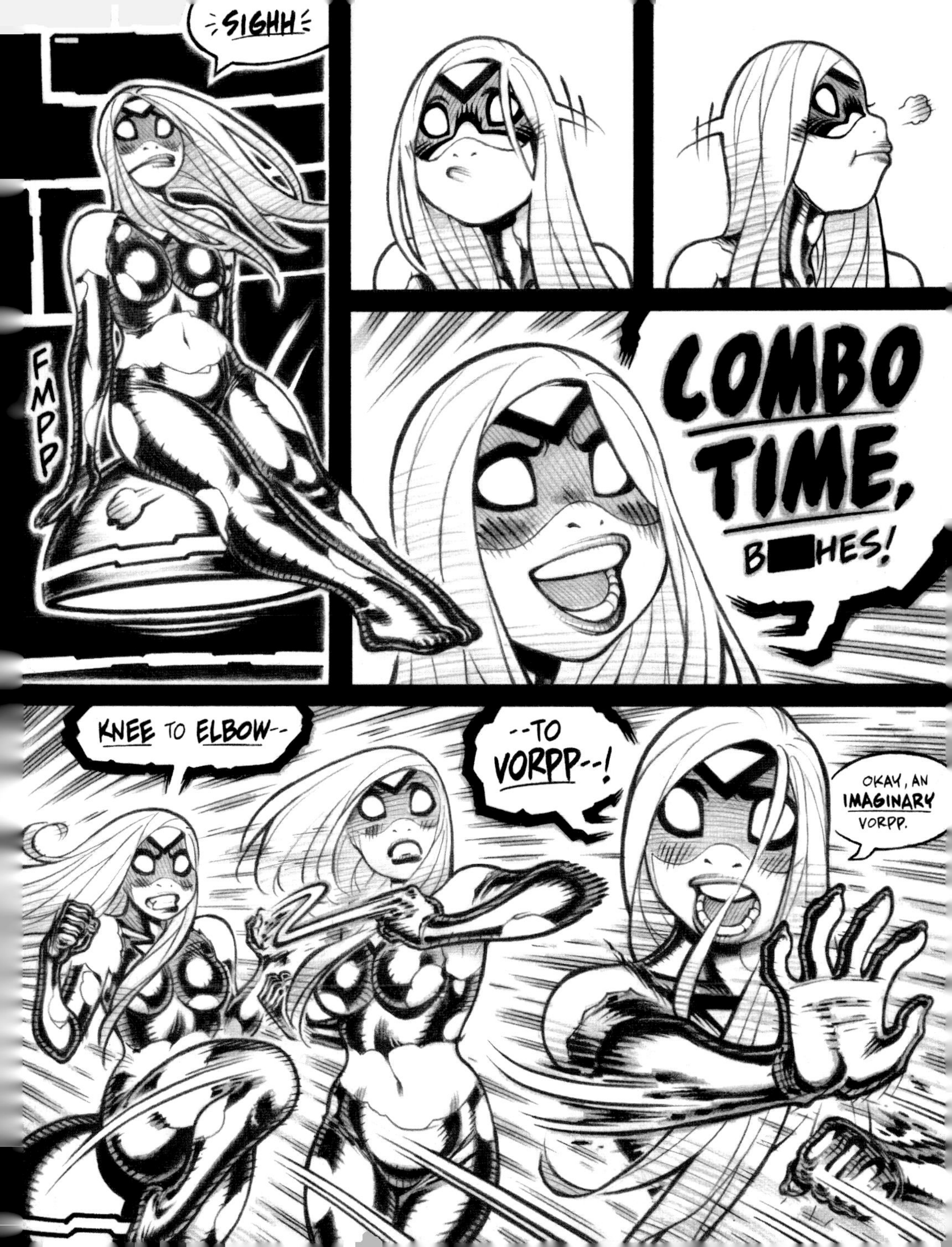
SIGHH
FMPP
COMBO TIME,
B[redacted]HES!
KNEE TO ELBOW--
--TO VORPP--!
OKAY, AN IMAGINARY VORPP.

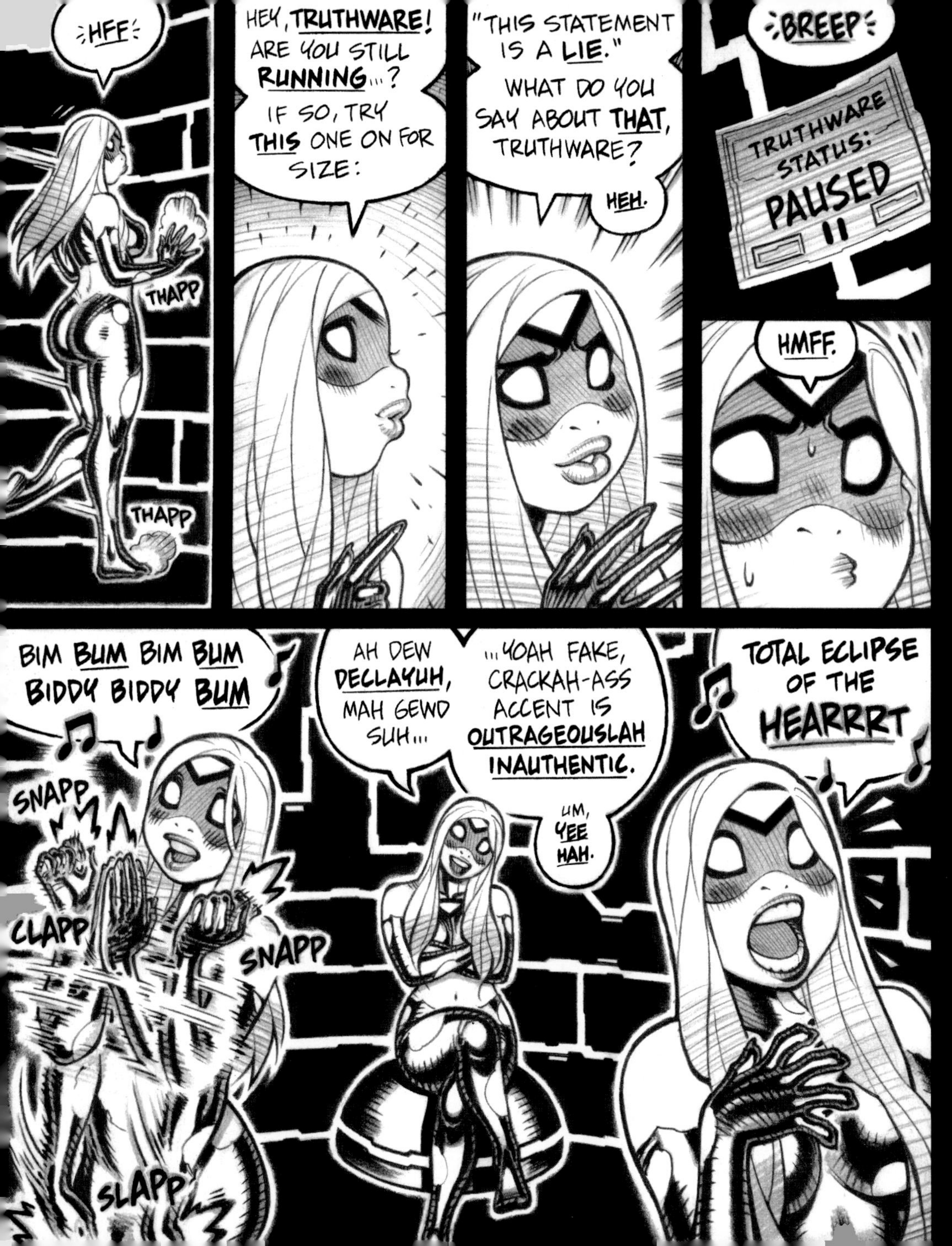
HFF
THAPP
THAPP
HEY, TRUTHWARE! ARE YOU STILL RUNNING...? IF SO, TRY THIS ONE ON FOR SIZE:
"THIS STATEMENT IS A LIE." WHAT DO YOU SAY ABOUT THAT, TRUTHWARE?
HEH.
BREEP
TRUTHWARE STATUS: PAUSED
HMFF.
BIM BUM BIM BUM BIDDY BIDDY BUM
SNAPP
CLAPP
SNAPP
SLAPP
AH DEW DECLAYUH, MAH GEWD SUH...
...YOAH FAKE, CRACKAH-ASS ACCENT IS OUTRAGEOUSLAH INAUTHENTIC.
UM, YEE HAH.
TOTAL ECLIPSE OF THE HEARRRT

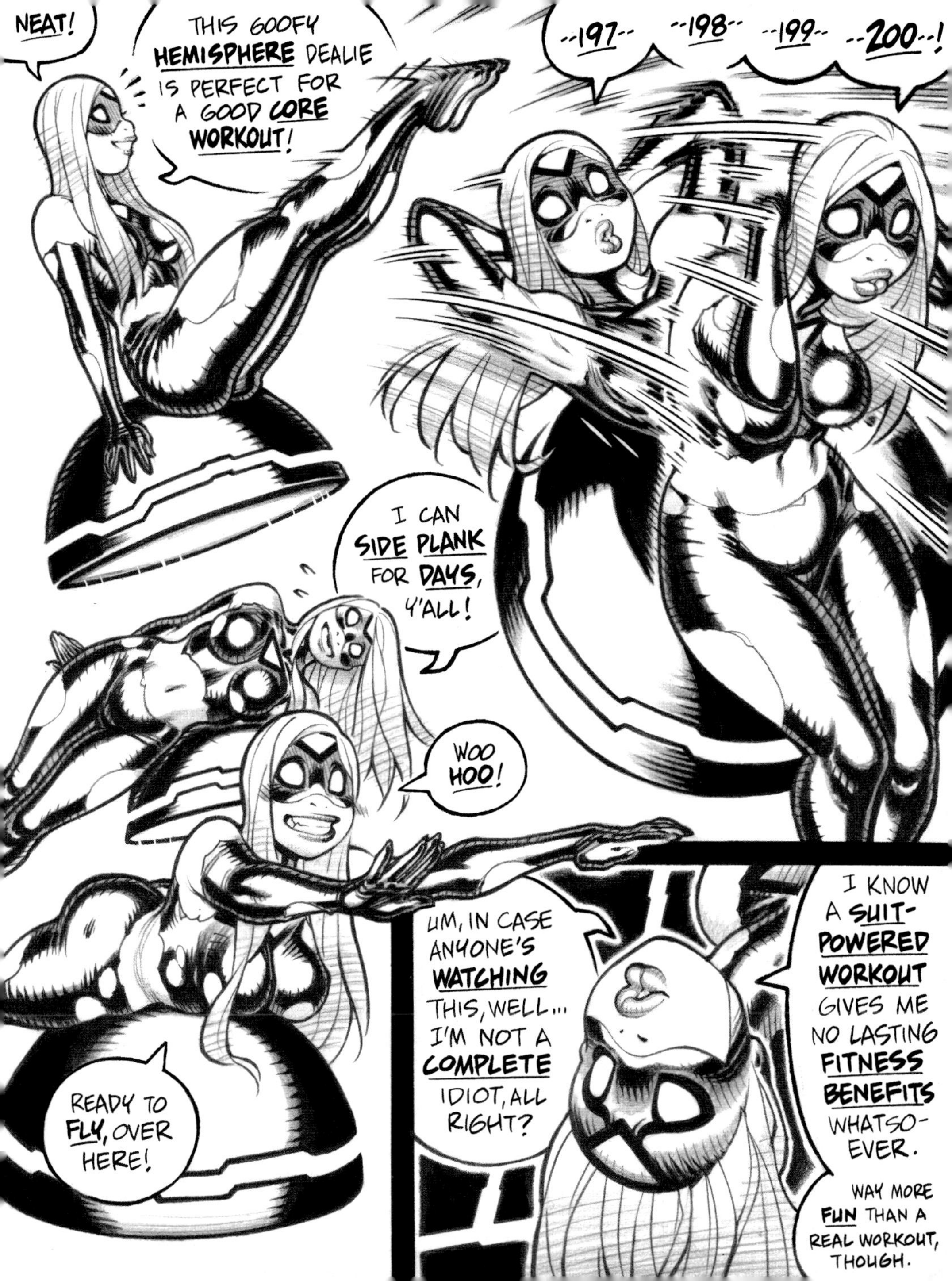
NEAT!
THIS GOOFY HEMISPHERE DEALIE IS PERFECT FOR A GOOD CORE WORKOUT!
--197-- --198-- --199-- --200--!
I CAN SIDE PLANK FOR DAYS, Y'ALL!
WOO HOO!
READY TO FLY, OVER HERE!
UM, IN CASE ANYONE'S WATCHING THIS, WELL... I'M NOT A COMPLETE IDIOT, ALL RIGHT?
I KNOW A SUIT-POWERED WORKOUT GIVES ME NO LASTING FITNESS BENEFITS WHATSOEVER.
WAY MORE FUN THAN A REAL WORKOUT, THOUGH.

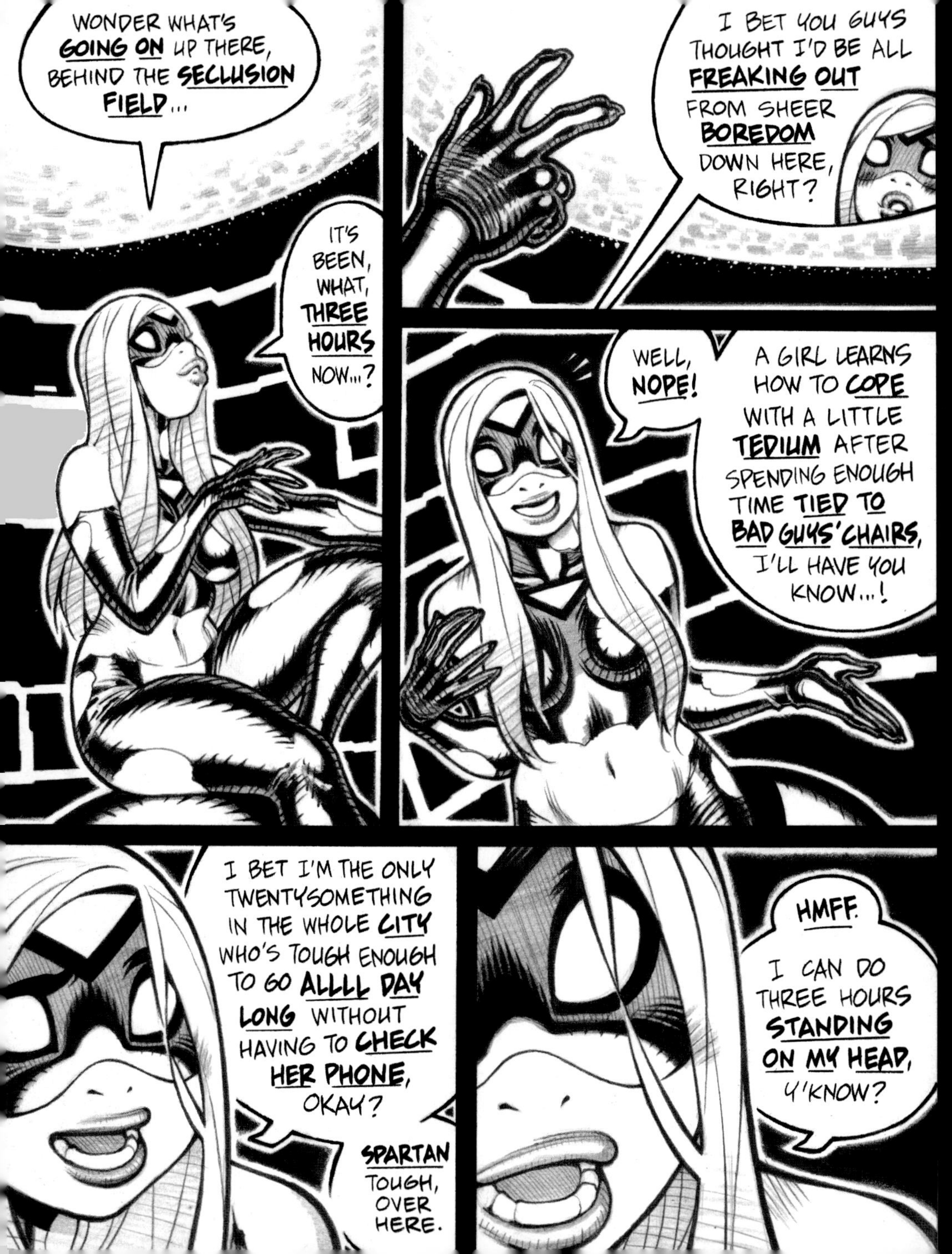

WONDER WHAT'S GOING ON UP THERE, BEHIND THE SECLUSION FIELD...
IT'S BEEN, WHAT, THREE HOURS NOW...?
I BET YOU GUYS THOUGHT I'D BE ALL FREAKING OUT FROM SHEER BOREDOM DOWN HERE, RIGHT?
WELL, NOPE!
A GIRL LEARNS HOW TO COPE WITH A LITTLE TEDIUM AFTER SPENDING ENOUGH TIME TIED TO BAD GUYS' CHAIRS, I'LL HAVE YOU KNOW...!
I BET I'M THE ONLY TWENTYSOMETHING IN THE WHOLE CITY WHO'S TOUGH ENOUGH TO GO ALLLL DAY LONG WITHOUT HAVING TO CHECK HER PHONE, OKAY?
SPARTAN TOUGH, OVER HERE.
HMFF.
I CAN DO THREE HOURS STANDING ON MY HEAD, Y'KNOW?

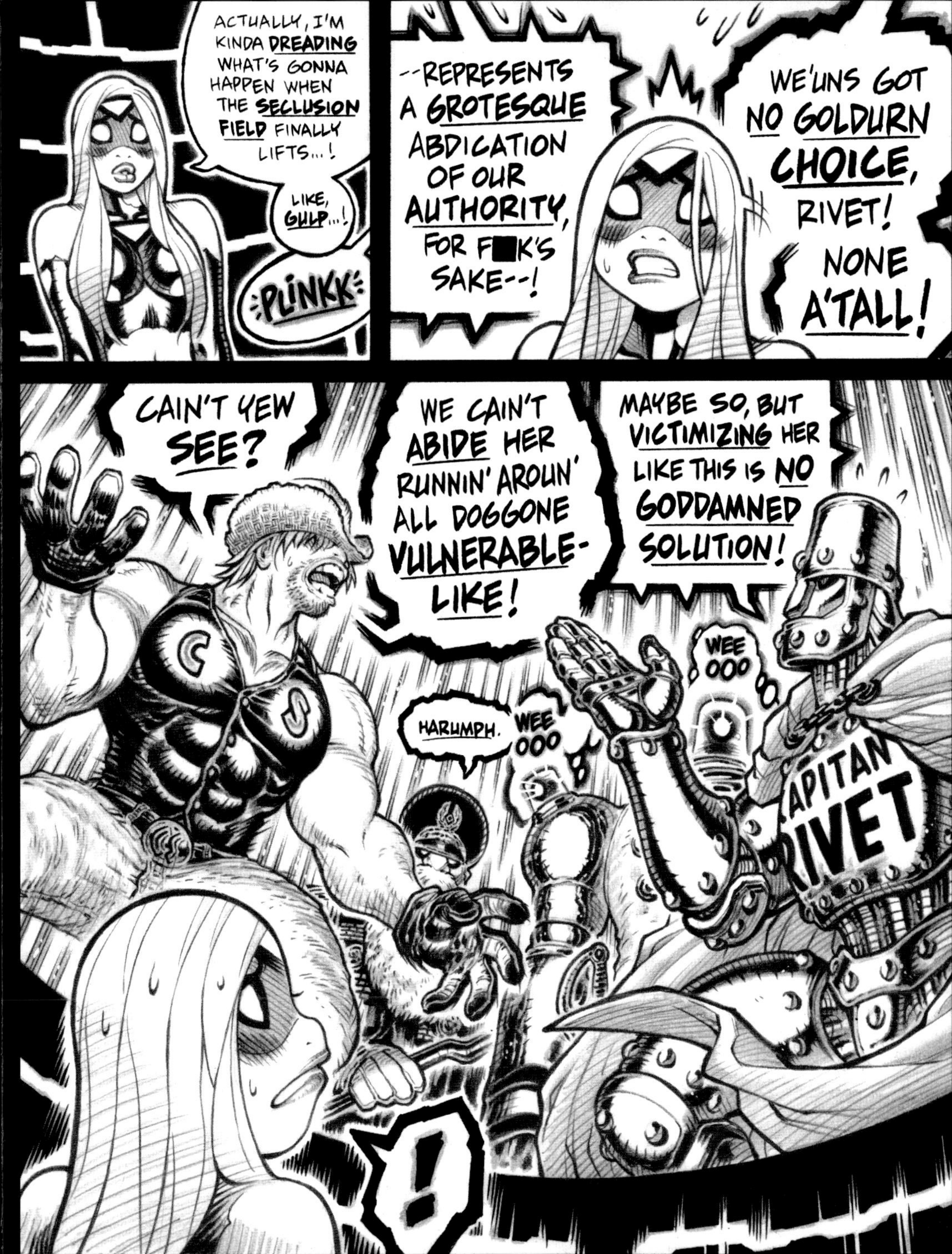
ACTUALLY, I'M KINDA DREADING WHAT'S GONNA HAPPEN WHEN THE SECLUSION FIELD FINALLY LIFTS...!
LIKE, GULP...!
PLINKK
--REPRESENTS A GROTESQUE ABDICATION OF OUR AUTHORITY, FOR F[redacted]K'S SAKE--!
WE'UNS GOT NO GOLDURN CHOICE, RIVET!
NONE A'TALL!
CAIN'T YEW SEE?
WE CAIN'T ABIDE HER RUNNIN' AROUN' ALL DOGGONE VULNERABLE-LIKE!
MAYBE SO, BUT VICTIMIZING HER LIKE THIS IS NO GODDAMNED SOLUTION!
WEE OOO
HARUMPH.
WEE OOO
APITAN
RIVET
!

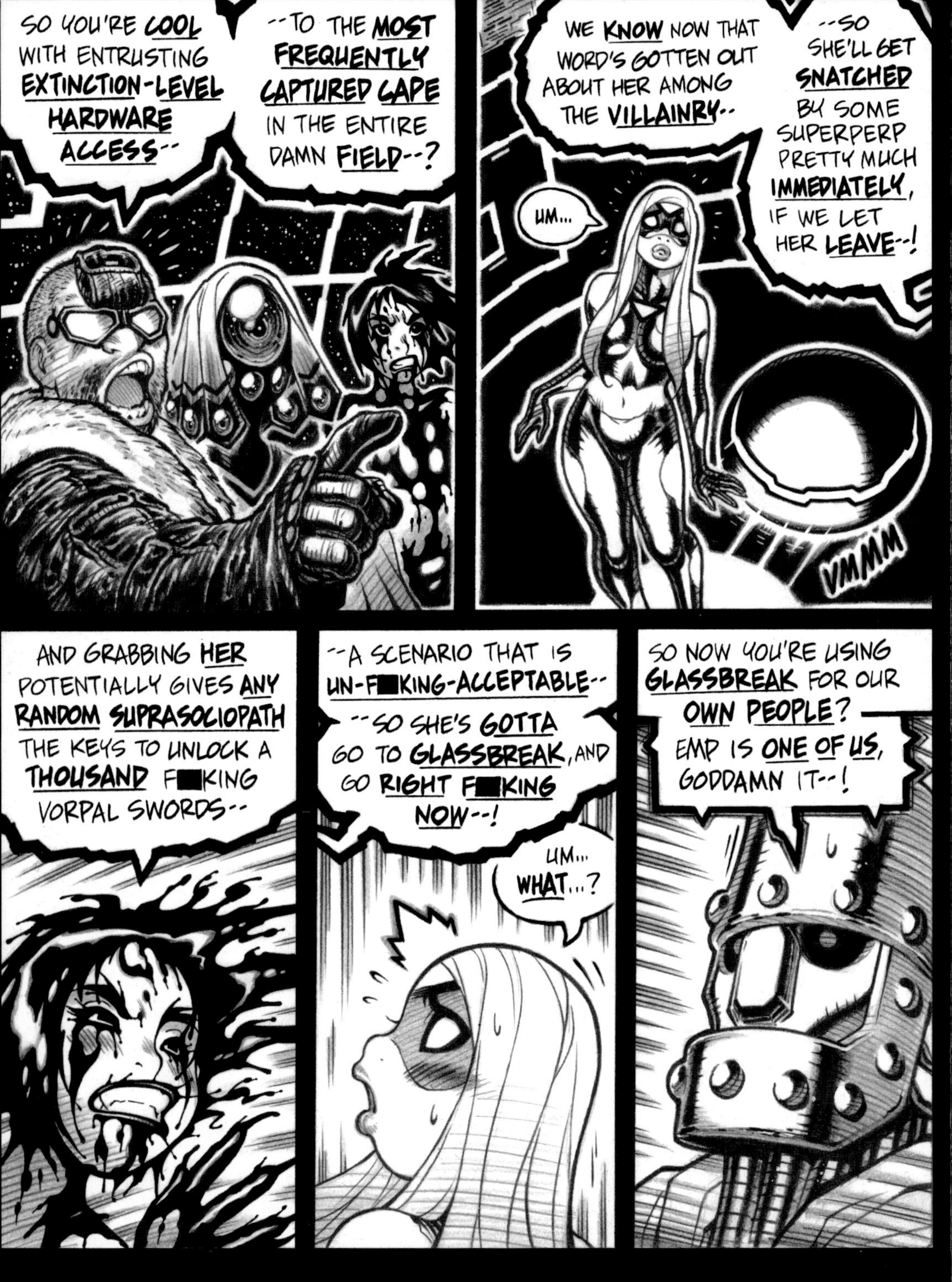
SO YOU'RE COOL WITH ENTRUSTING EXTINCTION-LEVEL HARDWARE ACCESS--
--TO THE MOST FREQUENTLY CAPTURED CAPE IN THE ENTIRE DAMN FIELD--?
WE KNOW NOW THAT WORD'S GOTTEN OUT ABOUT HER AMONG THE VILLAINRY--
--SO SHE'LL GET SNATCHED BY SOME SUPERPERP PRETTY MUCH IMMEDIATELY, IF WE LET HER LEAVE--!
UM...
VMMM
AND GRABBING HER POTENTIALLY GIVES ANY RANDOM SUPRASOCIOPATH THE KEYS TO UNLOCK A THOUSAND F[redacted]KING VORPAL SWORDS--
--A SCENARIO THAT IS UN-F[redacted]KING-ACCEPTABLE--
--SO SHE'S GOTTA GO TO GLASSBREAK, AND GO RIGHT F[redacted]KING NOW--!
UM... WHAT...?
SO NOW YOU'RE USING GLASSBREAK FOR OUR OWN PEOPLE? EMP IS ONE OF US, GODDAMN IT--!

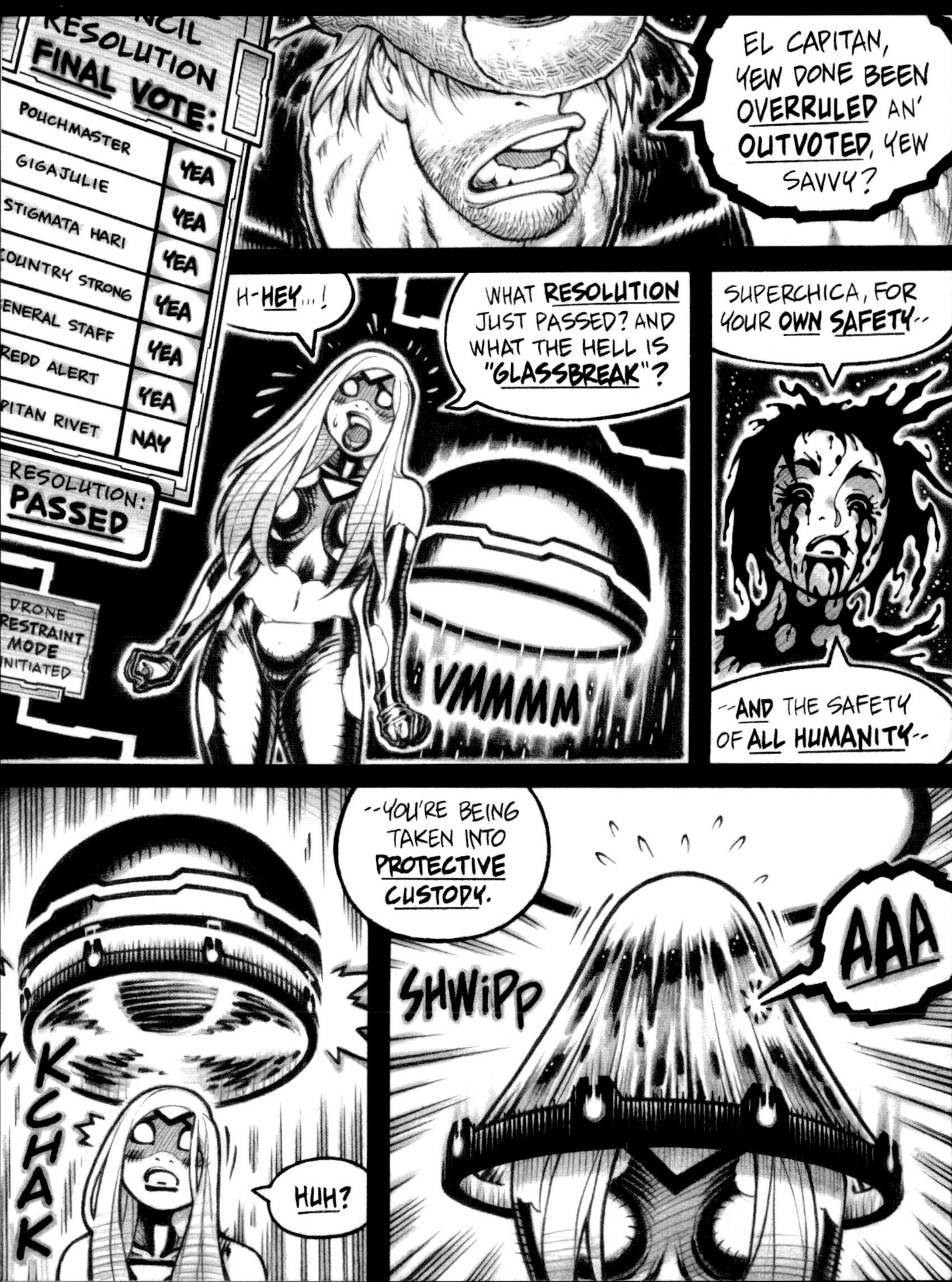

RESOLUTION
FINAL VOTE:
POUCHMASTER YEA
GIGAJULIE YEA
STIGMATA HARI YEA
COUNTRY STRONG YEA
ENERAL STAFF YEA
REDD ALERT YEA
PITAN RIVET NAY
RESOLUTION: PASSED
EL CAPITAN, YEW DONE BEEN OVERRULED AN' OUTVOTED, YEW SAVVY?
DRONE RESTRAINT MODE INITIATED
H-HEY...!
WHAT RESOLUTION JUST PASSED? AND WHAT THE HELL IS "GLASSBREAK"?
VMMMM
SUPERCHICA, FOR YOUR OWN SAFETY--
--AND THE SAFETY OF ALL HUMANITY--
--YOU'RE BEING TAKEN INTO PROTECTIVE CUSTODY.
KCHAK
HUH?
SHWIPP
AAA

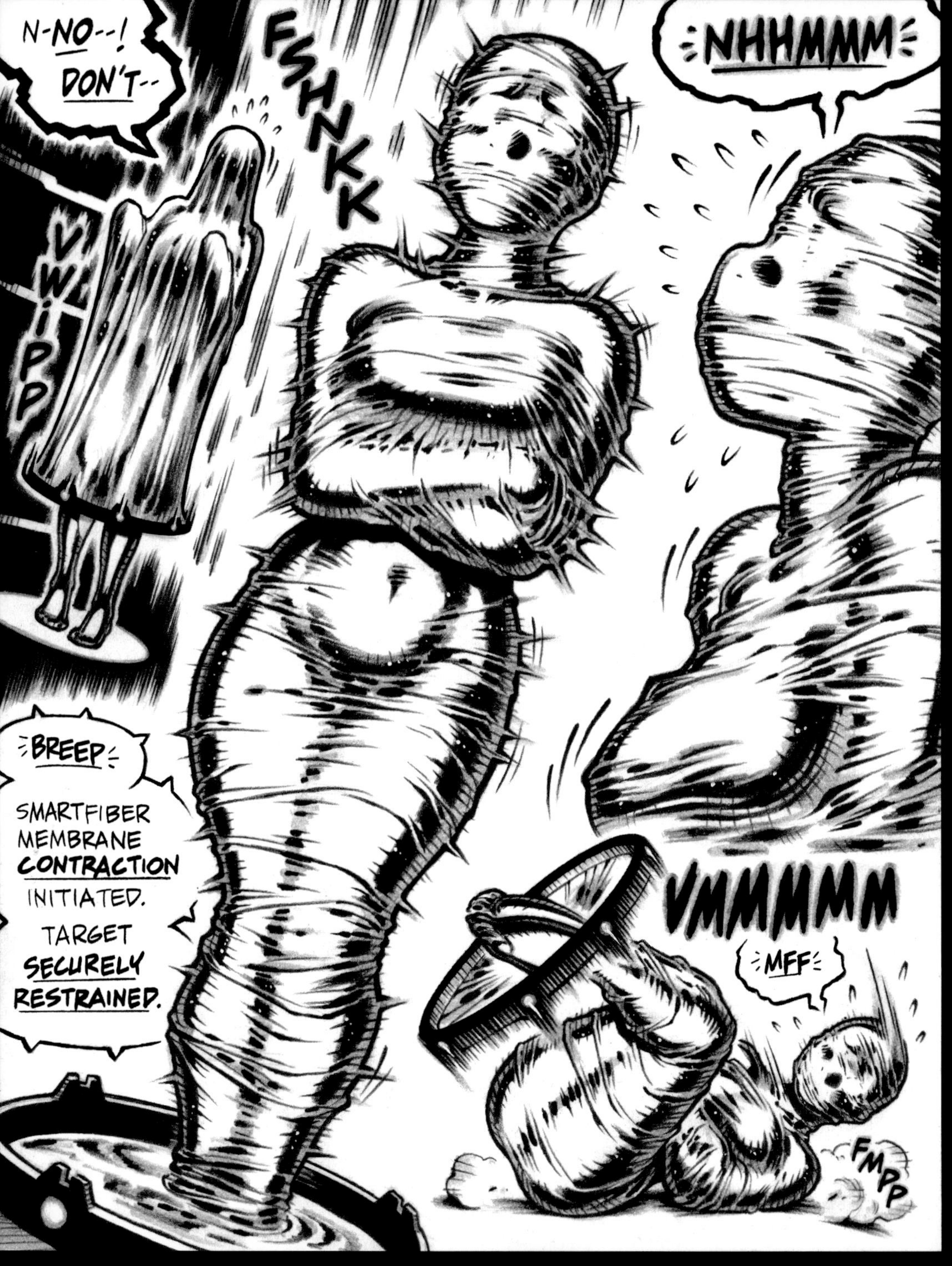

N-NO--! DON'T--
FSHNKK
VWIPP
NHHMMM
BREEP
SMARTFIBER MEMBRANE CONTRACTION INITIATED. TARGET SECURELY RESTRAINED.
VMMMMM
MFF
FMPP

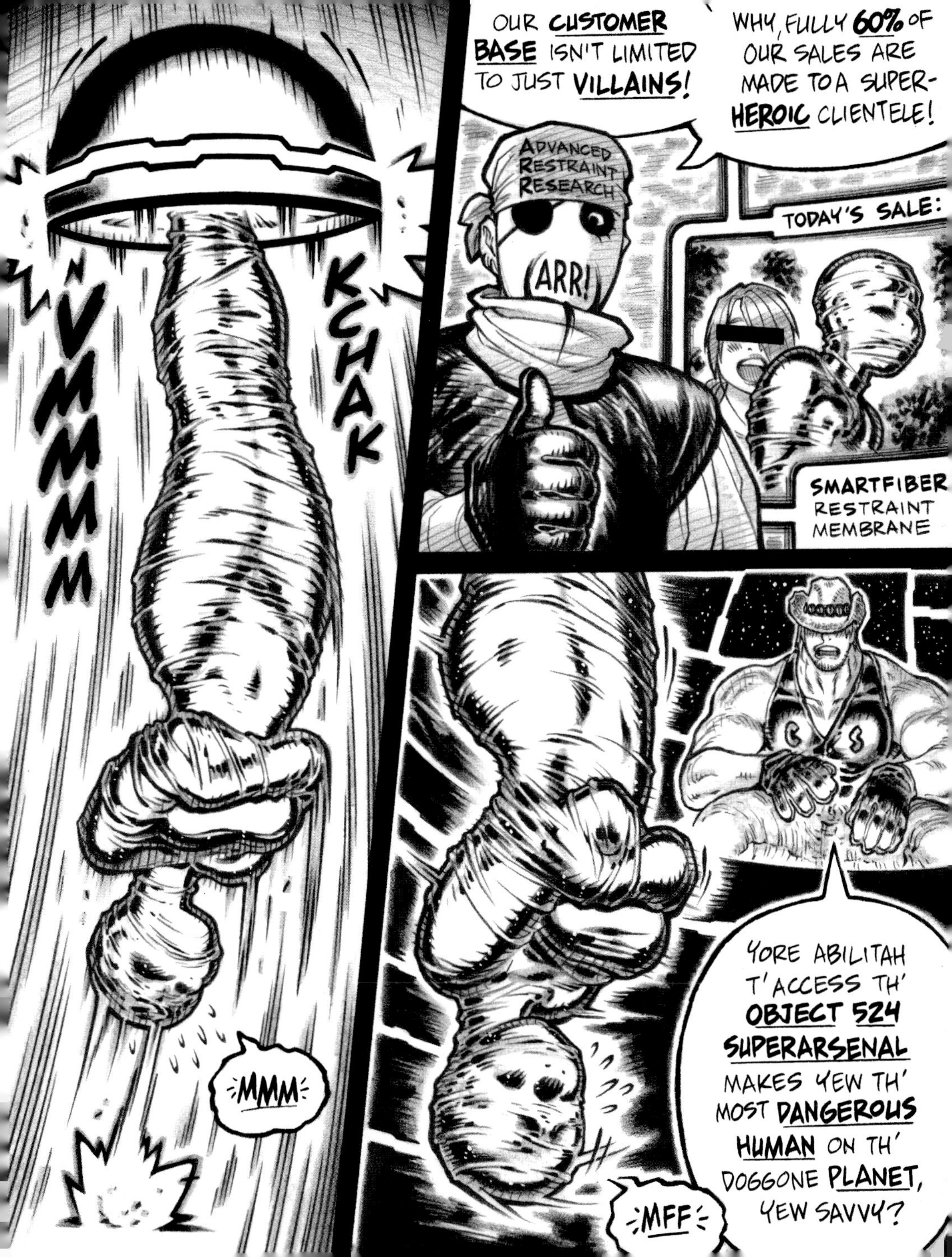
VMMMMM
KCHAK
MMM
OUR CUSTOMER BASE ISN'T LIMITED TO JUST VILLAINS!
WHY, FULLY 60% OF OUR SALES ARE MADE TO A SUPER-HEROIC CLIENTELE!
ADVANCED RESTRAINT RESEARCH
ARR!
TODAY'S SALE:
SMARTFIBER RESTRAINT MEMBRANE
YORE ABILITAH T'ACCESS TH' OBJECT 524 SUPERARSENAL MAKES YEW TH' MOST DANGEROUS HUMAN ON TH' DOGGONE PLANET, YEW SAVVY?
MFF

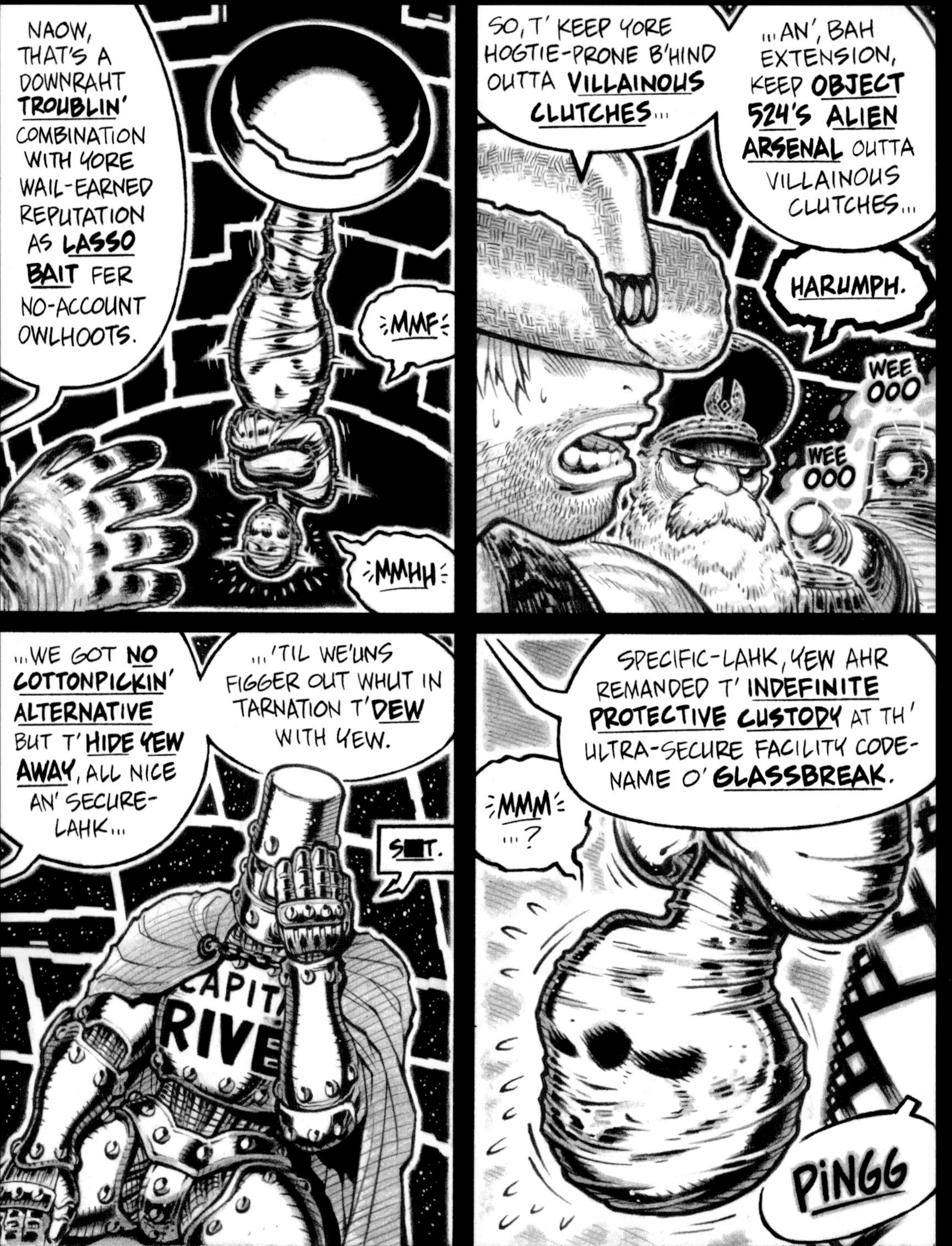
NAOW, THAT'S A DOWNRAHT TROUBLIN' COMBINATION WITH YORE WAIL-EARNED REPUTATION AS LASSO BAIT FER NO-ACCOUNT OWLHOOTS.
MMF
MMHH
SO, T' KEEP YORE HOGTIE-PRONE B'HIND OUTTA VILLAINOUS CLUTCHES...
...AN', BAH EXTENSION, KEEP OBJECT 524'S ALIEN ARSENAL OUTTA VILLAINOUS CLUTCHES...
HARUMPH.
WEE OOO
WEE OOO
...WE GOT NO COTTONPICKIN' ALTERNATIVE BUT T' HIDE YEW AWAY, ALL NICE AN' SECURE-LAHK...
...'TIL WE'UNS FIGGER OUT WHUT IN TARNATION T'DEW WITH YEW.
S[redacted]T.
CAPIT
RIVE
SPECIFIC-LAHK, YEW AHR REMANDED T' INDEFINITE PROTECTIVE CUSTODY AT TH' ULTRA-SECURE FACILITY CODE-NAME O' GLASSBREAK.
MMM ...?
PiNGG

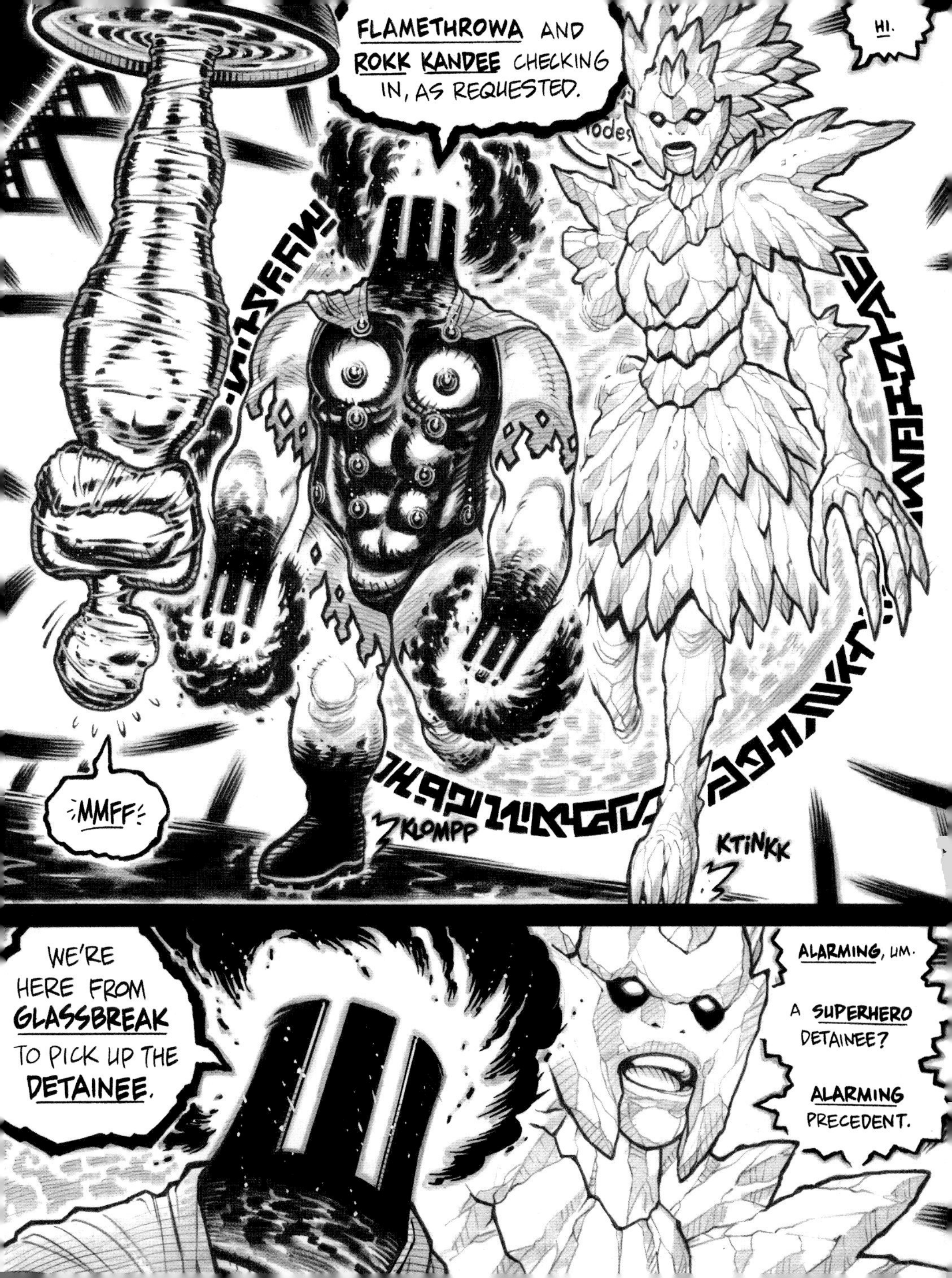
FLAMETHROWA AND ROKK KANDEE CHECKING IN, AS REQUESTED.
HI.
MMFF
KLOMPP
KTINKK
WE'RE HERE FROM GLASSBREAK TO PICK UP THE DETAINEE.
ALARMING, UM.
A SUPERHERO DETAINEE?
ALARMING PRECEDENT.

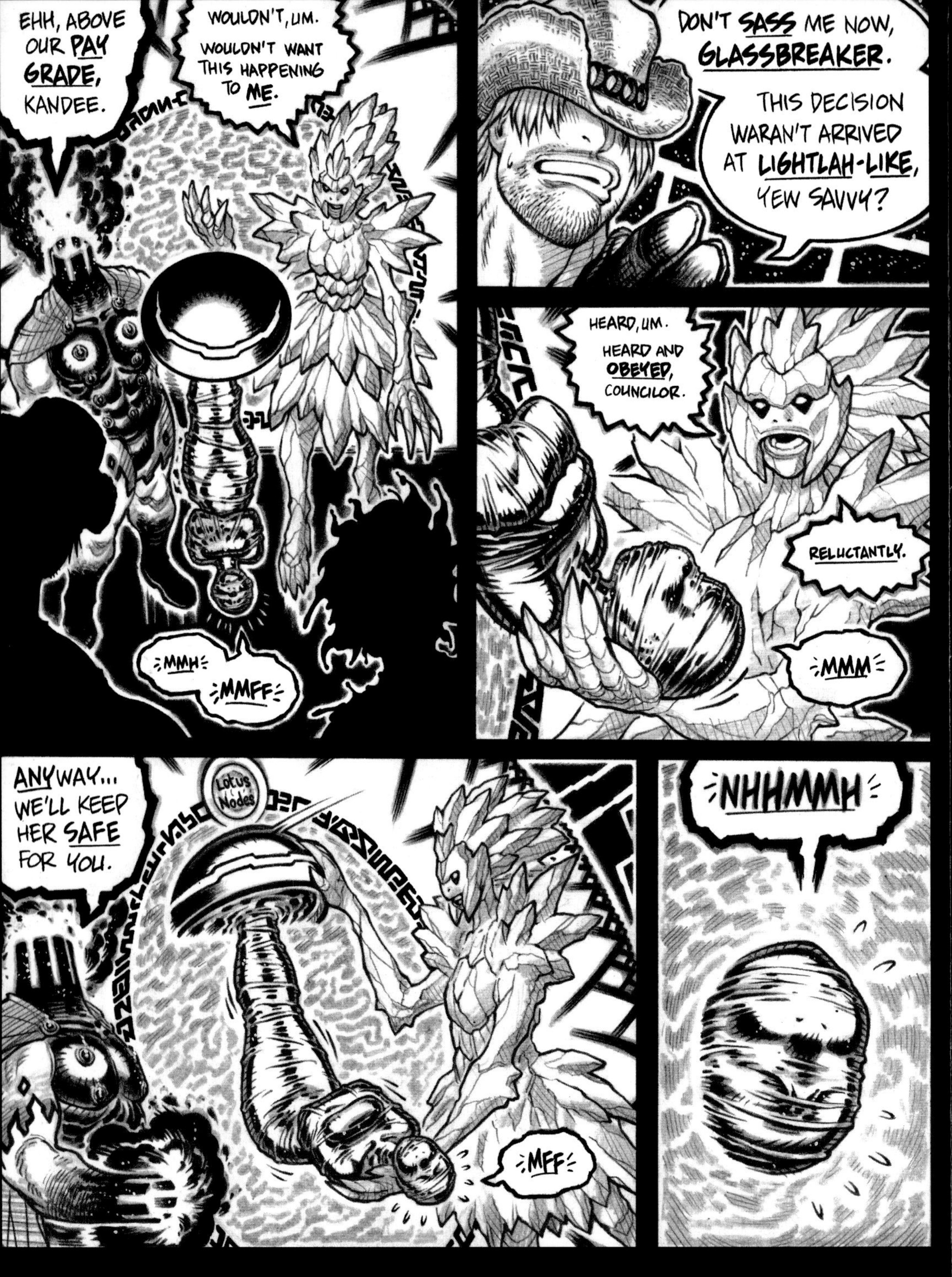
EHH, ABOVE OUR PAY GRADE, KANDEE.
WOULDN'T, UM.
WOULDN'T WANT THIS HAPPENING TO ME.
DON'T SASS ME NOW, GLASSBREAKER.
THIS DECISION WARAN'T ARRIVED AT LIGHTLAH-LIKE, YEW SAVVY?
MMH
MMFF
HEARD, UM.
HEARD AND OBEYED, COUNCILOR.
RELUCTANTLY.
MMM
ANYWAY... WE'LL KEEP HER SAFE FOR YOU.
Lotus Nodes
MFF
NHHMMH

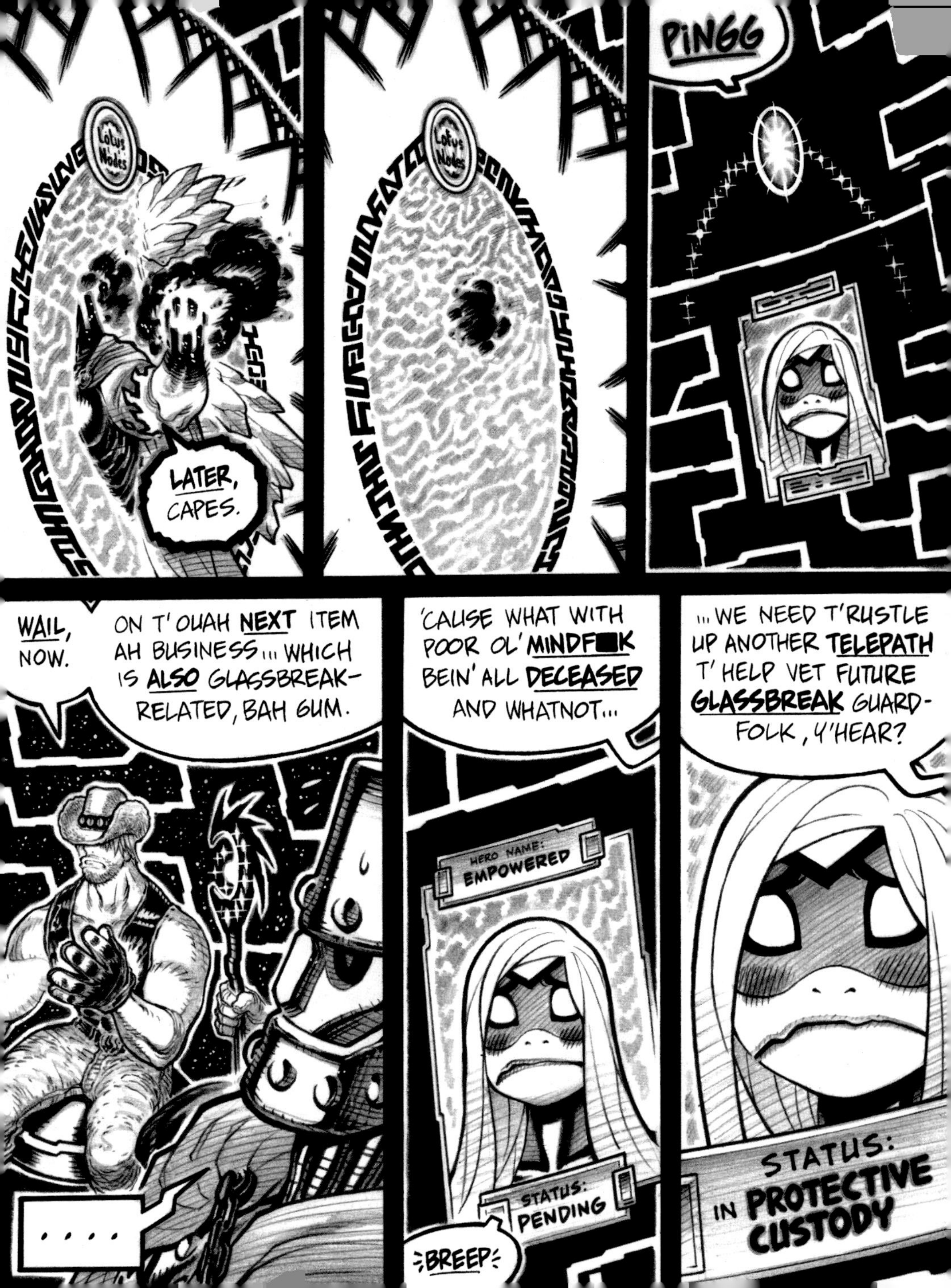

Lotus Nodes
LATER, CAPES.
Lotus Nodes
PiNGG
WAIL, NOW.
ON T' OUAH NEXT ITEM AH BUSINESS... WHICH IS ALSO GLASSBREAK-RELATED, BAH GUM.
....
'CAUSE WHAT WITH POOR OL' MINDF[redacted]K BEIN' ALL DECEASED AND WHATNOT...
HERO NAME: EMPOWERED
STATUS: PENDING
BREEP
...WE NEED T' RUSTLE UP ANOTHER TELEPATH T' HELP VET FUTURE GLASSBREAK GUARD-FOLK, Y'HEAR?
STATUS: IN PROTECTIVE CUSTODY

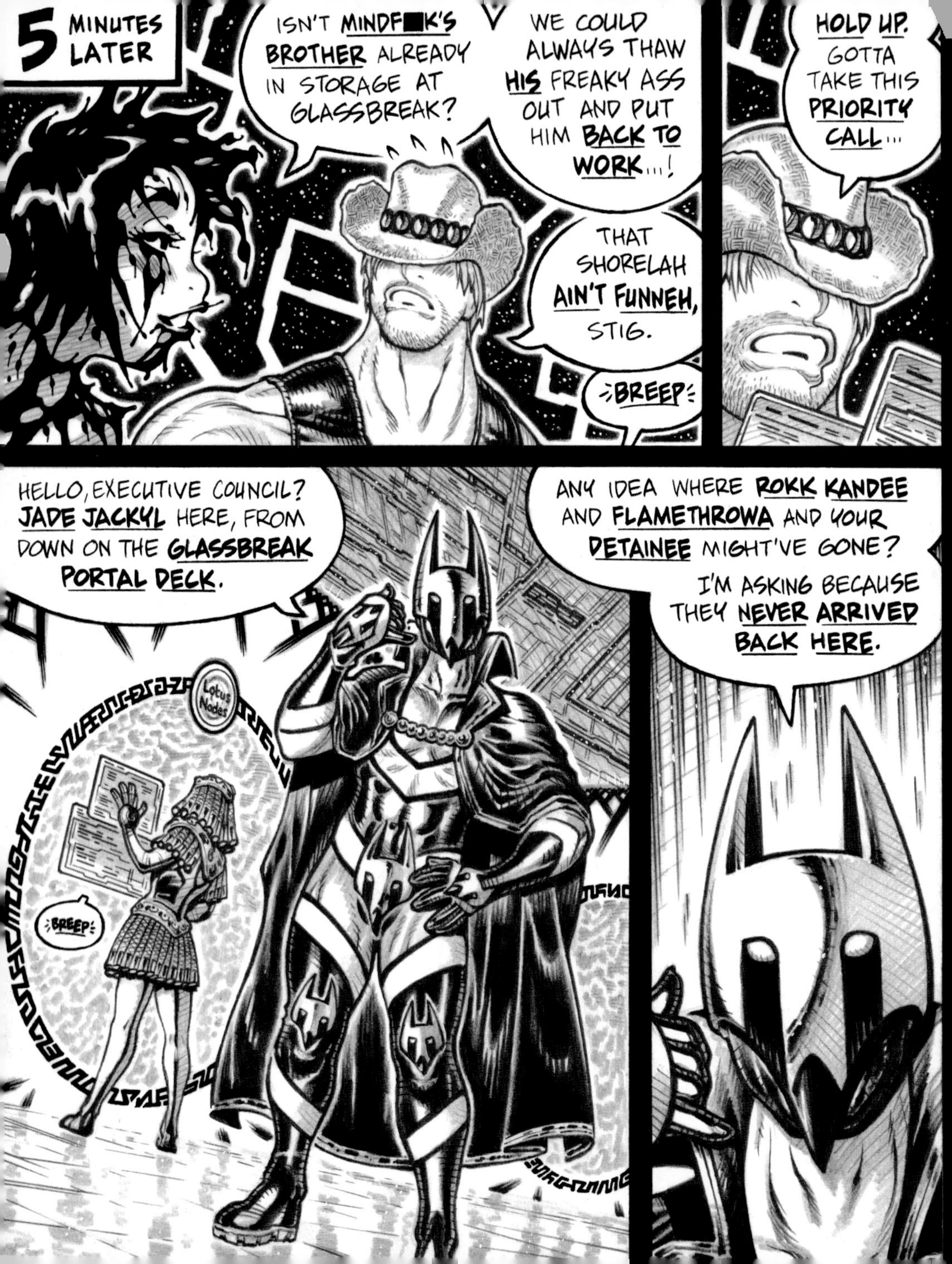
5 MINUTES LATER
ISN'T MINDF[redacted]K'S BROTHER ALREADY IN STORAGE AT GLASSBREAK?
WE COULD ALWAYS THAW HIS FREAKY ASS OUT AND PUT HIM BACK TO WORK...!
THAT SHORELAH AIN'T FUNNEH, STIG.
BREEP
HOLD UP. GOTTA TAKE THIS PRIORITY CALL...
HELLO, EXECUTIVE COUNCIL? JADE JACKYL HERE, FROM DOWN ON THE GLASSBREAK PORTAL DECK.
Lotus Nodes
BREEP
ANY IDEA WHERE ROKK KANDEE AND FLAMETHROWA AND YOUR DETAINEE MIGHT'VE GONE?
I'M ASKING BECAUSE THEY NEVER ARRIVED BACK HERE.

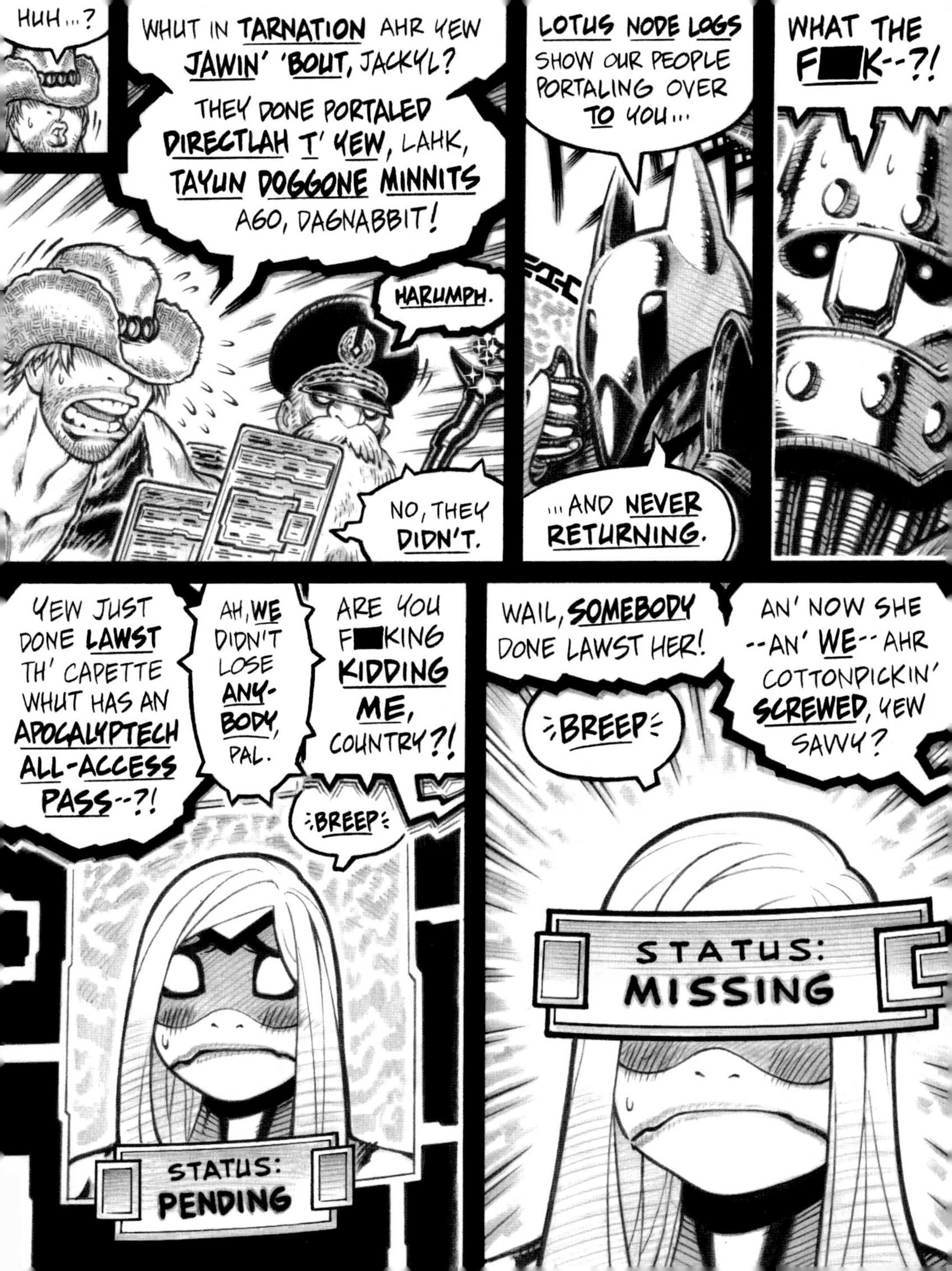
HUH...?
WHUT IN TARNATION AHR YEW JAWIN' 'BOUT, JACKYL? THEY DONE PORTALED DIRECTLAH T' YEW, LAHK, TAYUN DOGGONE MINNITS AGO, DAGNABBIT!
HARUMPH.
NO, THEY DIDN'T.
LOTUS NODE LOGS SHOW OUR PEOPLE PORTALING OVER TO YOU...
...AND NEVER RETURNING.
WHAT THE F[redacted]K--?!
YEW JUST DONE LAWST TH' CAPETTE WHUT HAS AN APOCALYPTECH ALL-ACCESS PASS--?!
AH, WE DIDN'T LOSE ANYBODY, PAL.
ARE YOU F[redacted]KING KIDDING ME, COUNTRY?!
BREEP
STATUS: PENDING
WAIL, SOMEBODY DONE LAWST HER!
AN' NOW SHE --AN' WE-- AHR COTTONPICKIN' SCREWED, YEW SAVVY?
BREEP
STATUS: MISSING

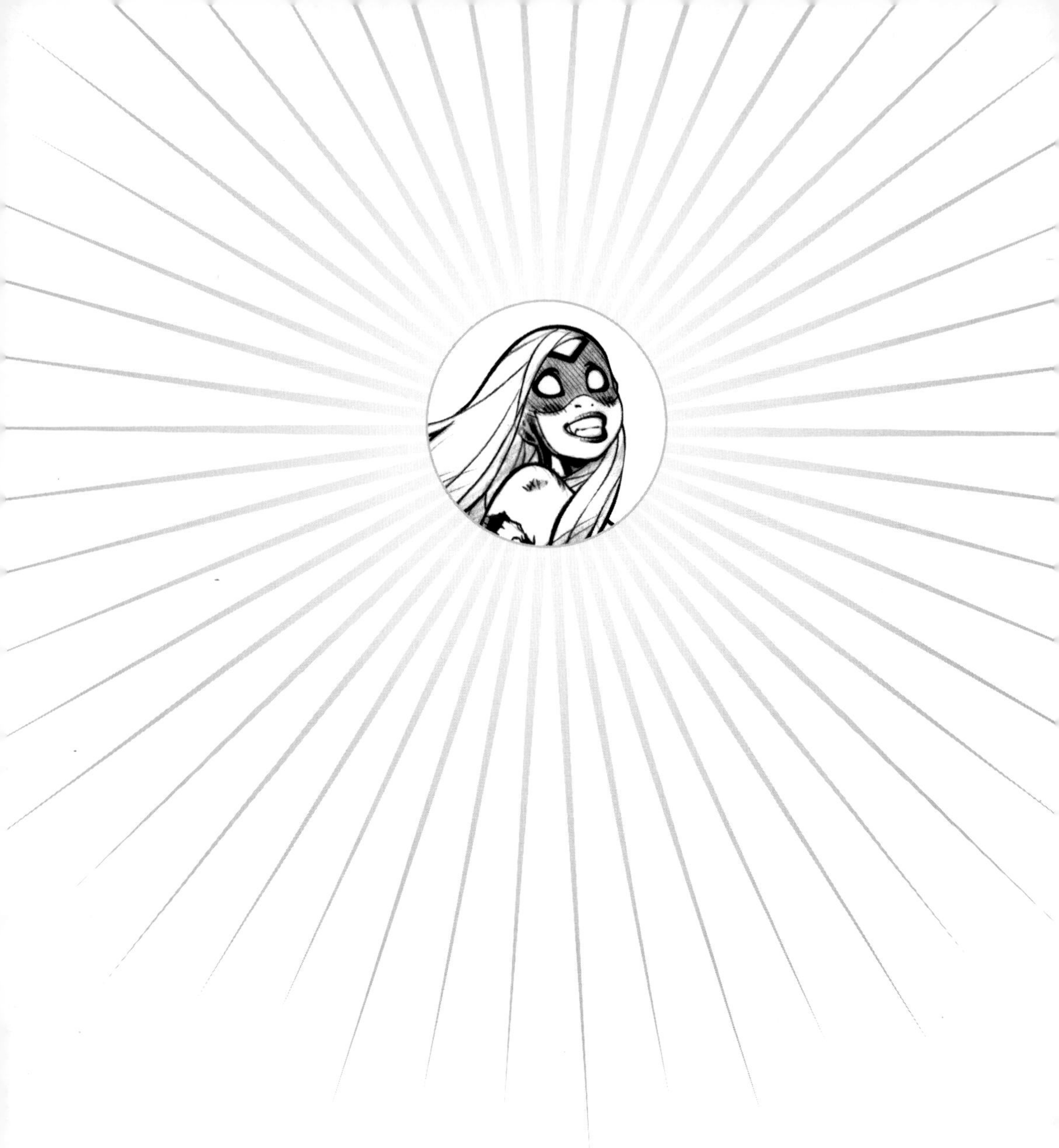

Empowered™

Power Stripped

(Or, A Brief Flashback Interlude, Taking Place Several Weeks Earlier)

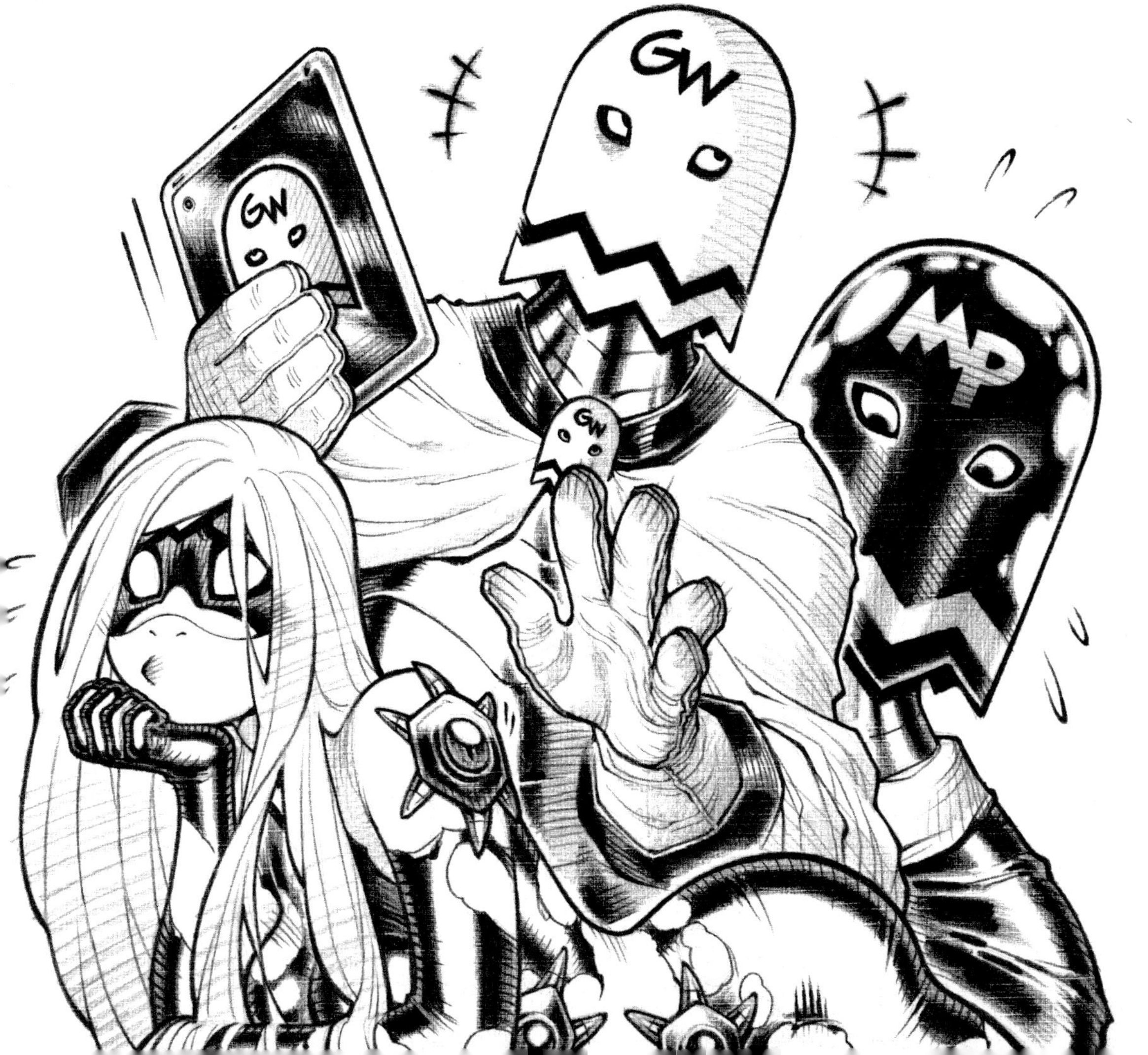
GW
GW
GW
MP

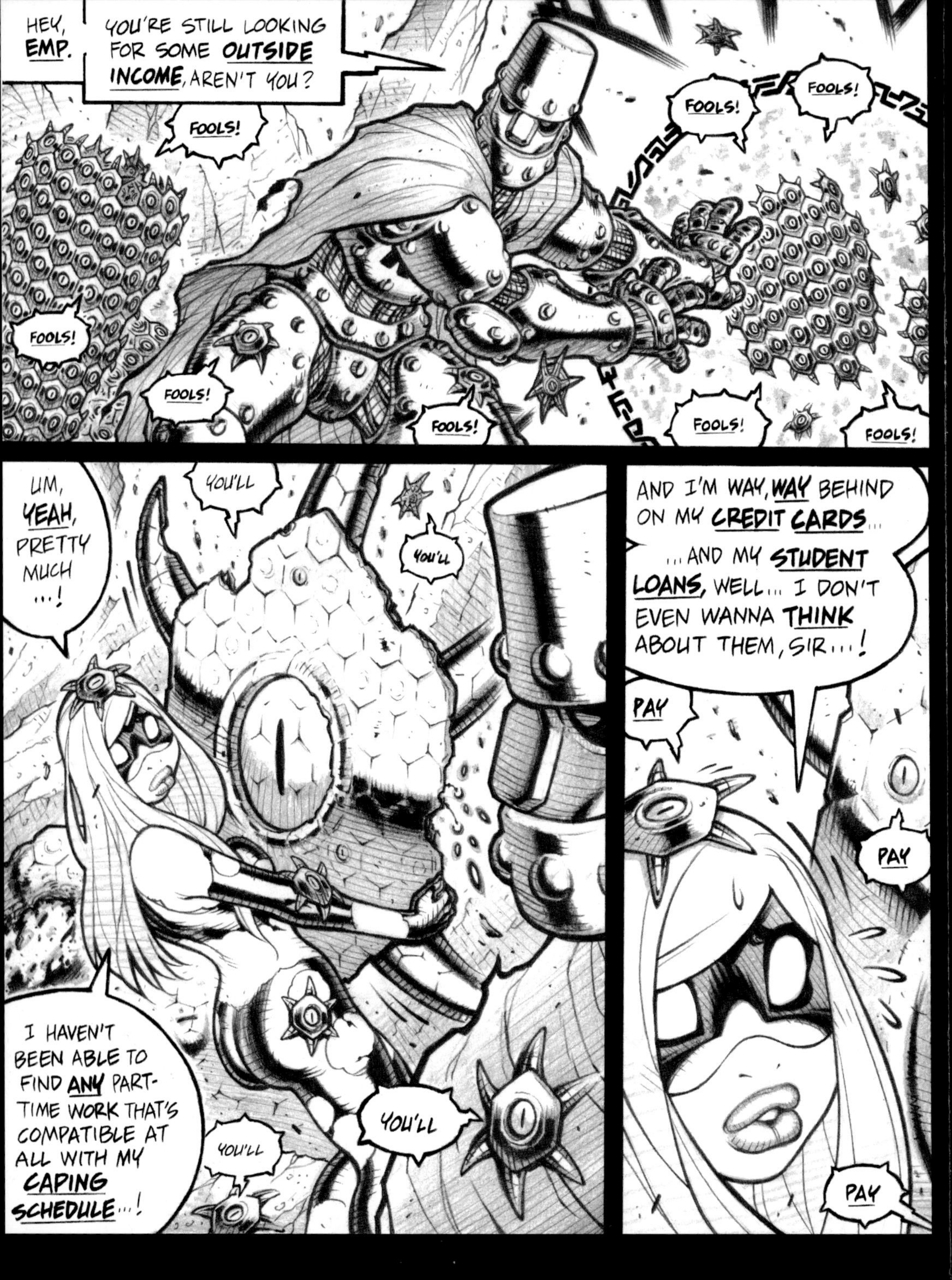
HEY, EMP.
YOU'RE STILL LOOKING FOR SOME OUTSIDE INCOME, AREN'T YOU?
FOOLS!
FOOLS!
FOOLS!
FOOLS!
FOOLS!
FOOLS!
FOOLS!
FOOLS!
UM, YEAH, PRETTY MUCH ...!
YOU'LL
YOU'LL
I HAVEN'T BEEN ABLE TO FIND ANY PART-TIME WORK THAT'S COMPATIBLE AT ALL WITH MY CAPING SCHEDULE...!
YOU'LL
YOU'LL
AND I'M WAY, WAY BEHIND ON MY CREDIT CARDS...
...AND MY STUDENT LOANS, WELL... I DON'T EVEN WANNA THINK ABOUT THEM, SIR...!
PAY
PAY
PAY

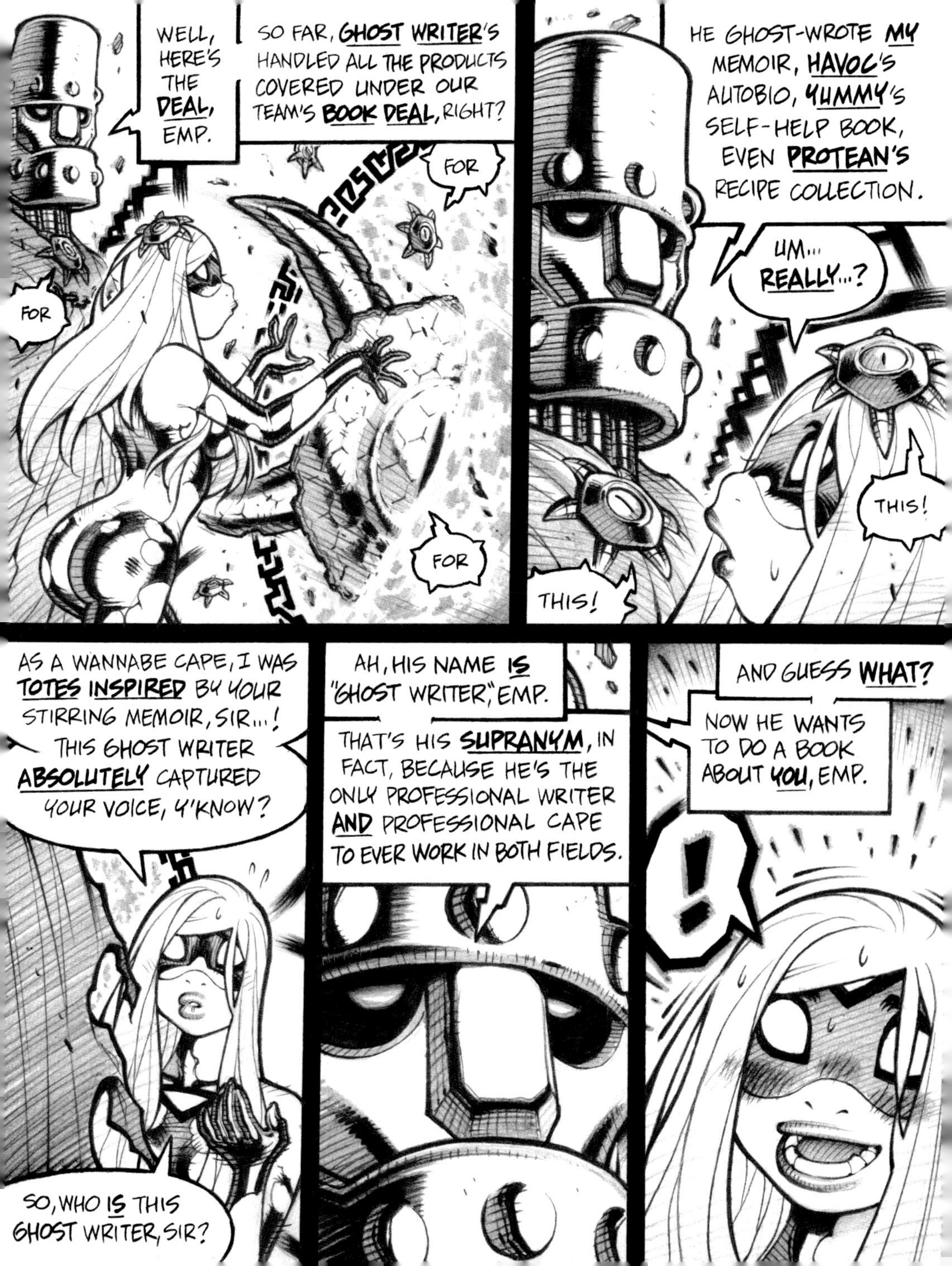

WELL, HERE'S THE DEAL, EMP.
SO FAR, GHOST WRITER'S HANDLED ALL THE PRODUCTS COVERED UNDER OUR TEAM'S BOOK DEAL, RIGHT?
FOR
FOR
FOR
HE GHOST-WROTE MY MEMOIR, HAVOC'S AUTOBIO, YUMMY'S SELF-HELP BOOK, EVEN PROTEAN'S RECIPE COLLECTION.
UM... REALLY...?
THIS!
THIS!
AS A WANNABE CAPE, I WAS TOTES INSPIRED BY YOUR STIRRING MEMOIR, SIR...! THIS GHOST WRITER ABSOLUTELY CAPTURED YOUR VOICE, Y'KNOW?
SO, WHO IS THIS GHOST WRITER, SIR?
AH, HIS NAME IS "GHOST WRITER," EMP.
THAT'S HIS SUPRANYM, IN FACT, BECAUSE HE'S THE ONLY PROFESSIONAL WRITER AND PROFESSIONAL CAPE TO EVER WORK IN BOTH FIELDS.
AND GUESS WHAT?
NOW HE WANTS TO DO A BOOK ABOUT YOU, EMP.
!

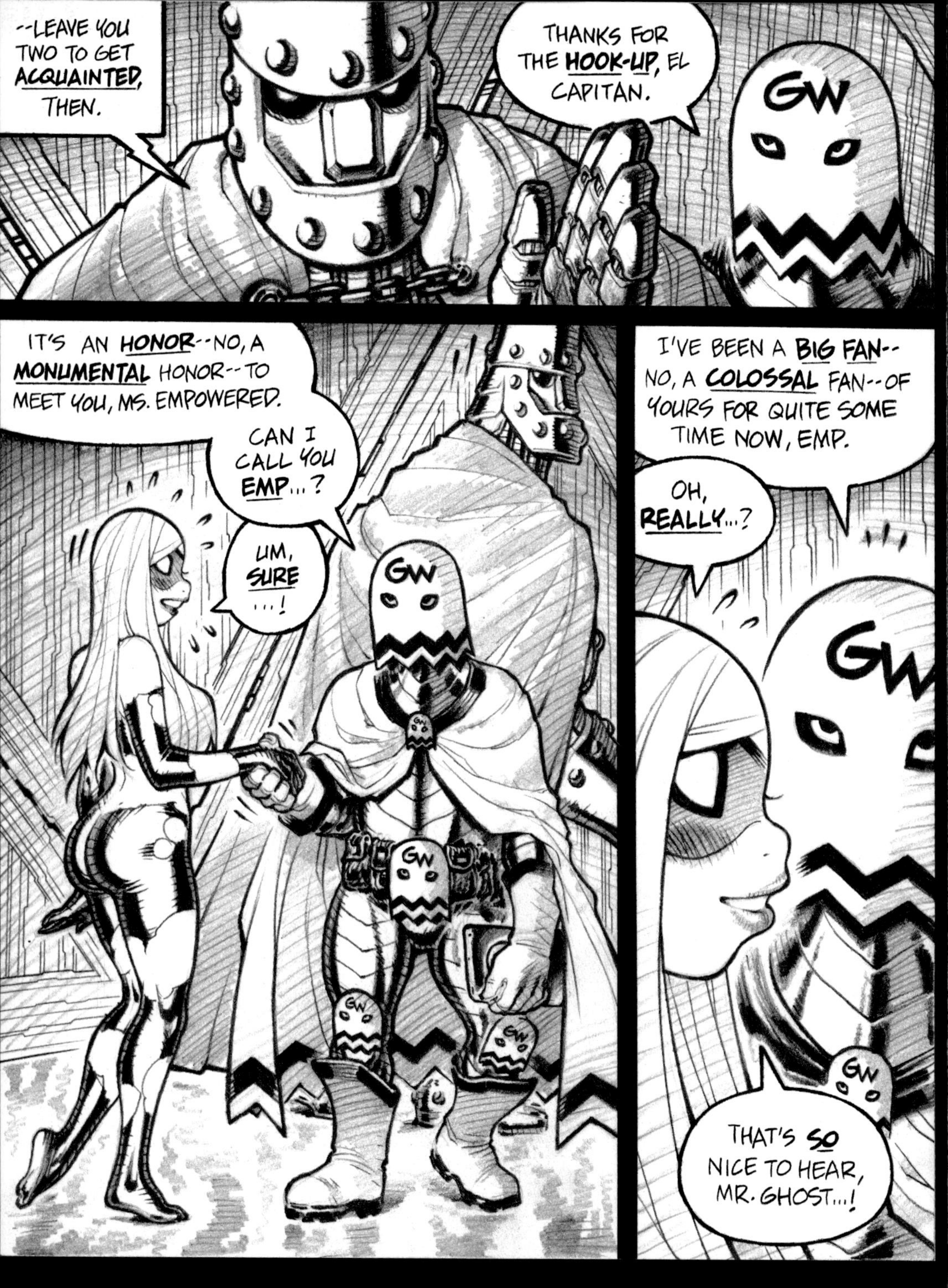
--LEAVE YOU TWO TO GET ACQUAINTED, THEN.
THANKS FOR THE HOOK-UP, EL CAPITAN.
IT'S AN HONOR--NO, A MONUMENTAL HONOR--TO MEET YOU, MS. EMPOWERED.
CAN I CALL YOU EMP...?
UM, SURE ...!
I'VE BEEN A BIG FAN--NO, A COLOSSAL FAN--OF YOURS FOR QUITE SOME TIME NOW, EMP.
OH, REALLY...?
THAT'S SO NICE TO HEAR, MR. GHOST...!

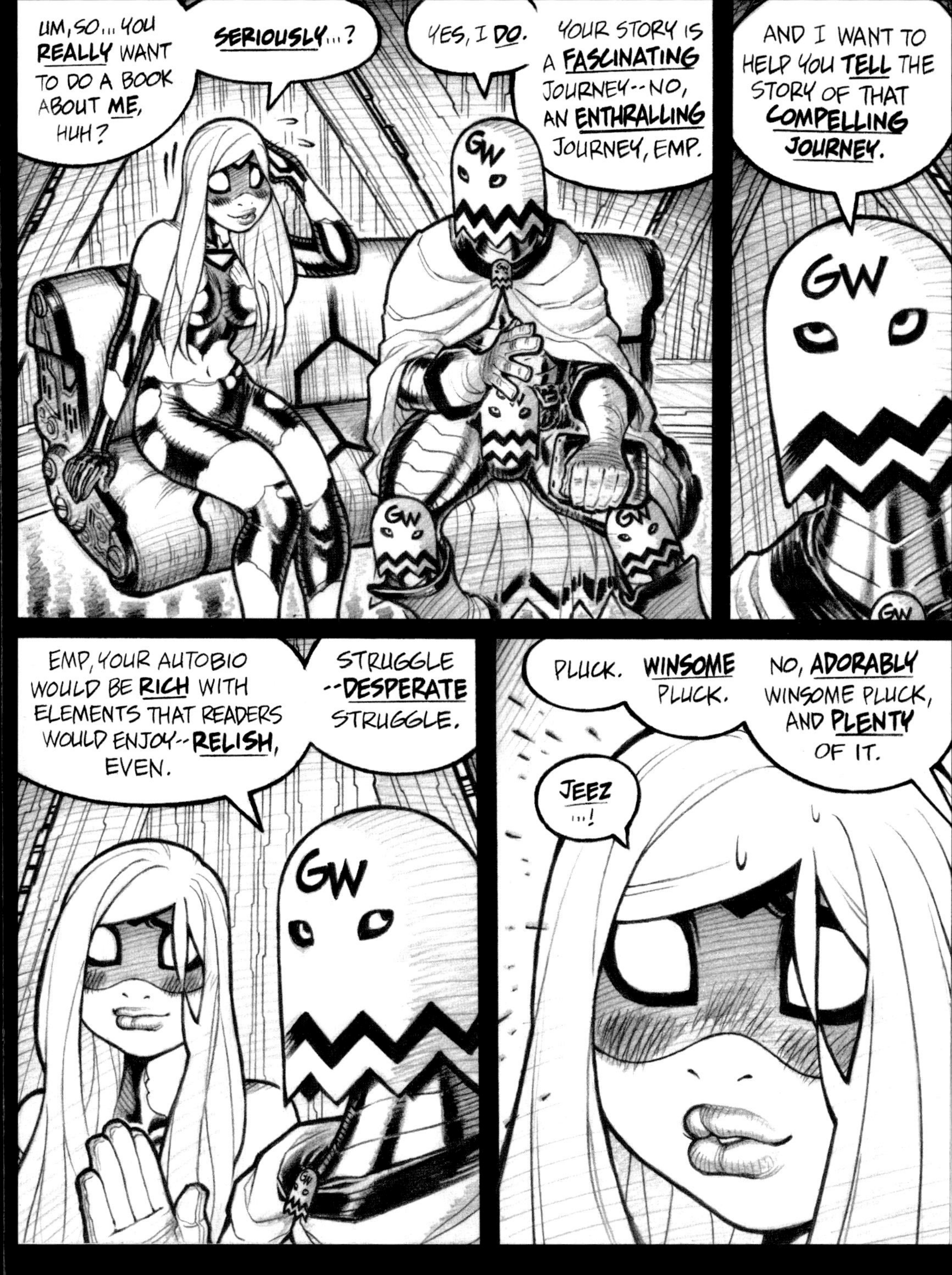
UM, SO... YOU REALLY WANT TO DO A BOOK ABOUT ME, HUH?
SERIOUSLY...?
YES, I DO.
YOUR STORY IS A FASCINATING JOURNEY--NO, AN ENTHRALLING JOURNEY, EMP.
AND I WANT TO HELP YOU TELL THE STORY OF THAT COMPELLING JOURNEY.
EMP, YOUR AUTOBIO WOULD BE RICH WITH ELEMENTS THAT READERS WOULD ENJOY--RELISH, EVEN.
STRUGGLE --DESPERATE STRUGGLE.
PLUCK.
WINSOME PLUCK.
NO, ADORABLY WINSOME PLUCK, AND PLENTY OF IT.
JEEZ ...!

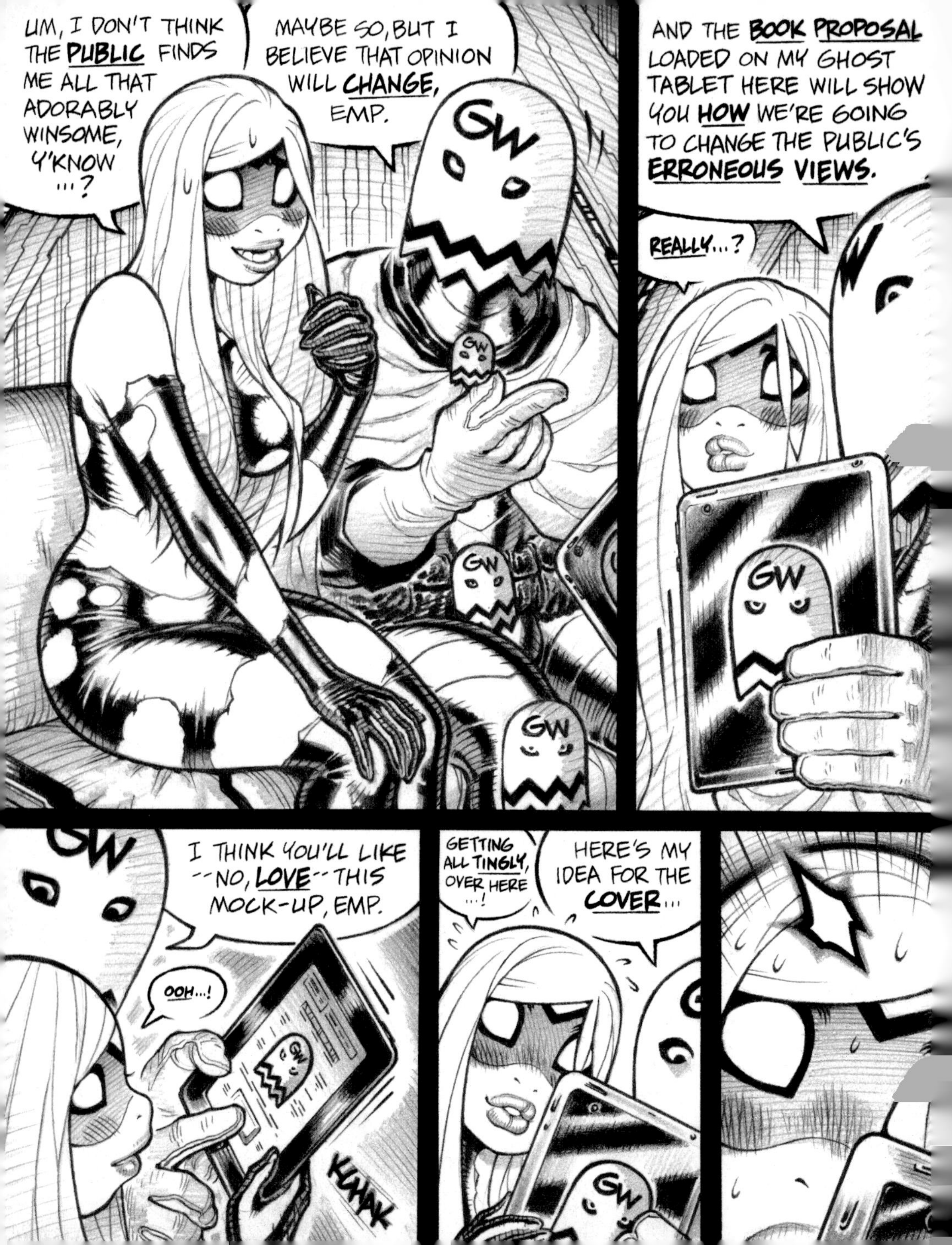
UM, I DON'T THINK THE PUBLIC FINDS ME ALL THAT ADORABLY WINSOME, Y'KNOW ...?
MAYBE SO, BUT I BELIEVE THAT OPINION WILL CHANGE, EMP.
GW
AND THE BOOK PROPOSAL LOADED ON MY GHOST TABLET HERE WILL SHOW YOU HOW WE'RE GOING TO CHANGE THE PUBLIC'S ERRONEOUS VIEWS.
REALLY...?
GW
I THINK YOU'LL LIKE --NO, LOVE-- THIS MOCK-UP, EMP.
OOH...!
KLAAK
GETTING ALL TINGLY, OVER HERE ...!
HERE'S MY IDEA FOR THE COVER...
GW

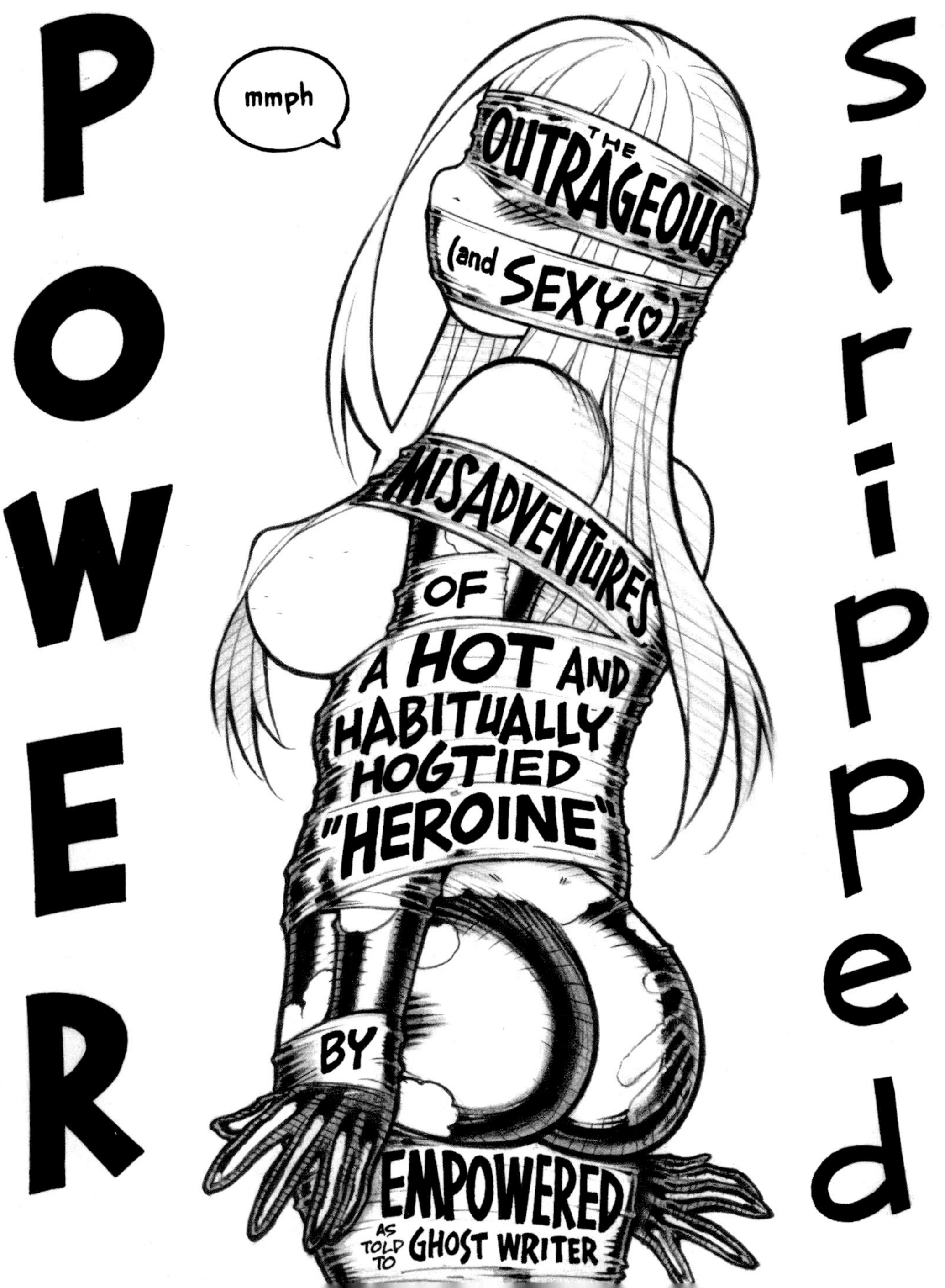
POWER
stripped
mmph
THE OUTRAGEOUS
(and SEXY!♡)
MISADVENTURES
OF
A HOT AND
HABITUALLY
HOGTIED
"HEROINE"
BY
EMPOWERED
AS TOLD TO GHOST WRITER

YOU... YOU WANT TO SHOW ME ALL **BOUND** **AND** **GAGGED** ON THE BOOK COVER...?

BOUND, GAGGED, AND **EYECATCHING**, EMP. SEXY DISTRESS WILL **CAPTURE** THE CASUAL READER'S ATTENTION.

"**POWER STRIPPED**"...?

A **PROVOCATIVE** **YET ACCURATE** TITLE IS ESSENTIAL, BELIEVE ME.

P O W E R

mmph

OUTRAGEOUS (and **SEXY!@**)

MISADVENTURES OF A HOT AND HABITUALLY HOGTIED "HEROINE"

BY

EMPOWERED

Pp ed

YOU WANT TO SLAP **DUCT TAPE** OVER MY EYES AND MOUTH, SO MY ACTUAL **FACE** WON'T BE VISIBLE ON THE COVER OF MY **AUTO-BIOGRAPHY**...?

IN FAIRNESS, EMP, YOU'RE ARGUABLY **MORE RECOGNIZABLE** WHEN DUCT-TAPED.

HUH.

MY **FACE** IS OBSCURED...

...BUT MY **BEHIND** IS FEATURED **QUITE CONSPICUOUSLY** ON THE COVER.

THE **OUTRAGE**(and **SEXY!@**)

HERO

BY

EMPOWERED

WELL, EMP, YOUR BACKSIDE IS YOUR **MOST PROMINENT ASSET** AS A SUPER-HEROINE, AFTER ALL.

GW

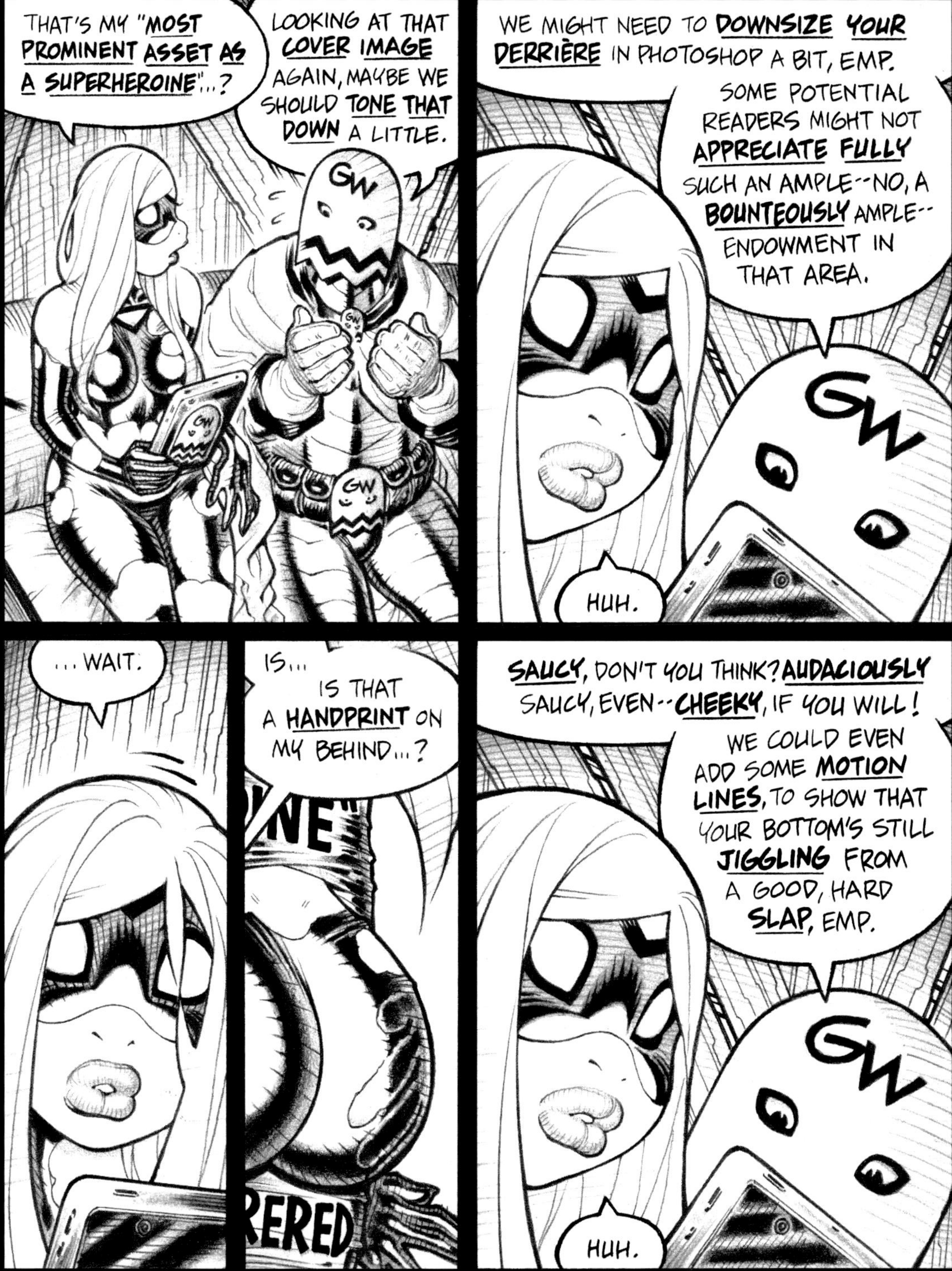
THAT'S MY "MOST PROMINENT ASSET AS A SUPERHEROINE"...?
LOOKING AT THAT COVER IMAGE AGAIN, MAYBE WE SHOULD TONE THAT DOWN A LITTLE.
WE MIGHT NEED TO DOWNSIZE YOUR DERRIÈRE IN PHOTOSHOP A BIT, EMP.
SOME POTENTIAL READERS MIGHT NOT APPRECIATE FULLY SUCH AN AMPLE--NO, A BOUNTEOUSLY AMPLE--ENDOWMENT IN THAT AREA.
HUH.
...WAIT.
IS... IS THAT A HANDPRINT ON MY BEHIND...?
SAUCY, DON'T YOU THINK? AUDACIOUSLY SAUCY, EVEN--CHEEKY, IF YOU WILL!
WE COULD EVEN ADD SOME MOTION LINES, TO SHOW THAT YOUR BOTTOM'S STILL JIGGLING FROM A GOOD, HARD SLAP, EMP.
HUH.

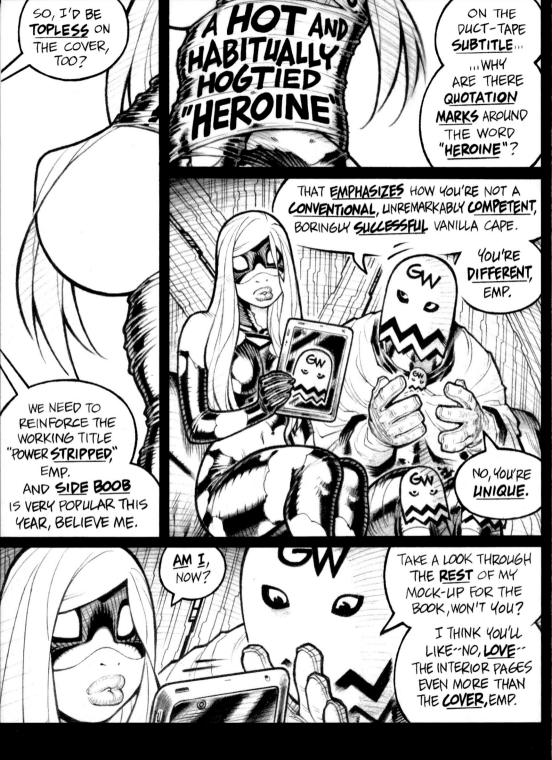

SO, I'D BE **TOPLESS** ON THE COVER, TOO?

A **HOT** AND HABITUALLY HOGTIED "HEROINE"

ON THE DUCT-TAPE **SUBTITLE**... ...WHY ARE THERE QUOTATION **MARKS** AROUND THE WORD "**HEROINE**"?

THAT **EMPHASIZES** HOW YOU'RE NOT A **CONVENTIONAL**, UNREMARKABLY **COMPETENT**, BORINGLY **SUCCESSFUL** VANILLA CAPE.

YOU'RE **DIFFERENT**, EMP.

WE NEED TO REINFORCE THE WORKING TITLE "POWER **STRIPPED**," EMP. AND **SIDE BOOB** IS VERY POPULAR THIS YEAR, BELIEVE ME.

NO, YOU'RE **UNIQUE**.

AM I, NOW?

TAKE A LOOK THROUGH THE **REST** OF MY MOCK-UP FOR THE BOOK, WON'T YOU?

I THINK YOU'LL LIKE--NO, **LOVE**-- THE INTERIOR PAGES EVEN MORE THAN THE **COVER**, EMP.

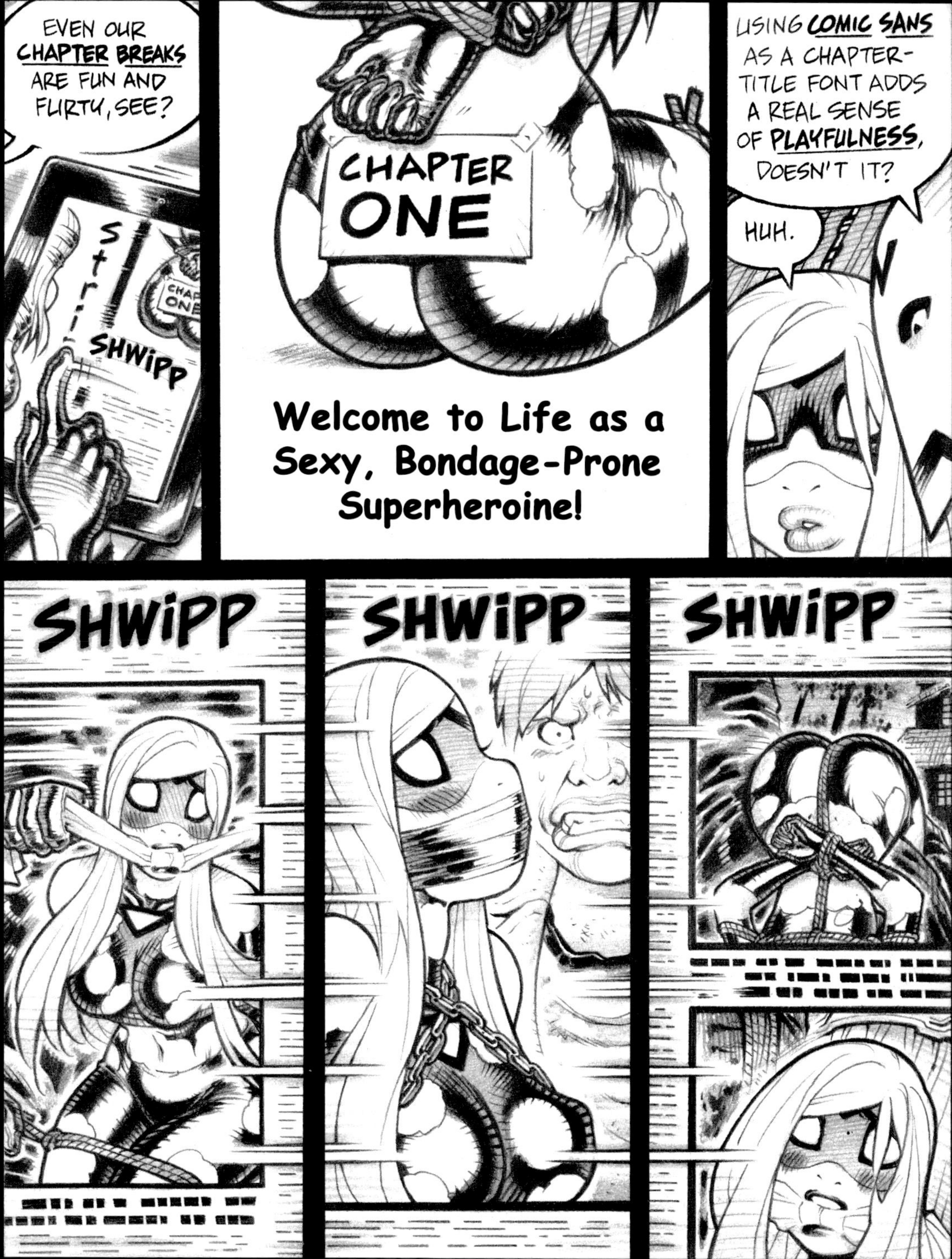
EVEN OUR CHAPTER BREAKS ARE FUN AND FLIRTY, SEE?
STRI--
SHWIPP
CHAPTER ONE
Welcome to Life as a Sexy, Bondage-Prone Superheroine!
USING COMIC SANS AS A CHAPTER-TITLE FONT ADDS A REAL SENSE OF PLAYFULNESS, DOESN'T IT?
HUH.
SHWIPP
SHWIPP
SHWIPP

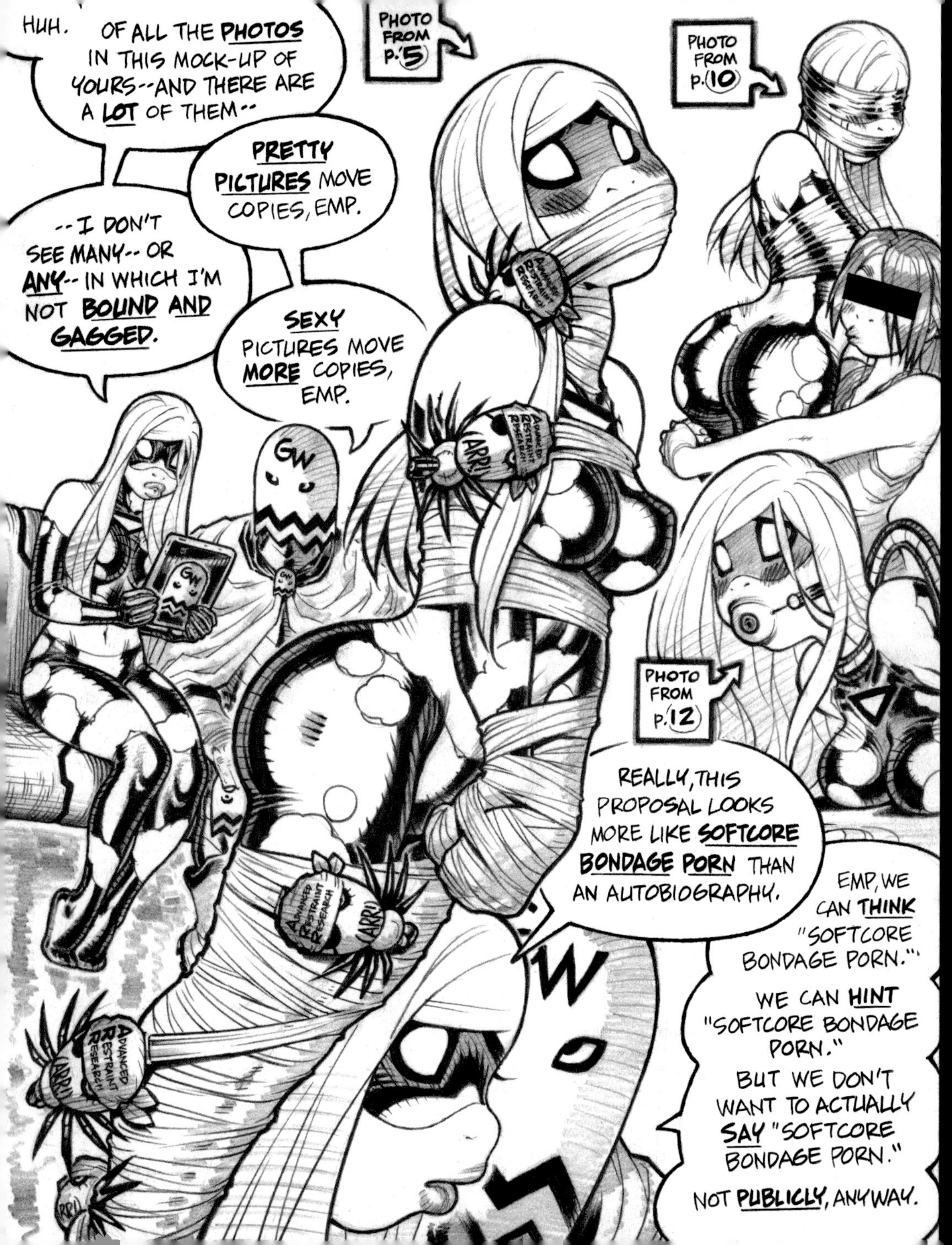
HUH.
OF ALL THE PHOTOS IN THIS MOCK-UP OF YOURS--AND THERE ARE A LOT OF THEM--
PRETTY PICTURES MOVE COPIES, EMP.
--I DON'T SEE MANY--OR ANY--IN WHICH I'M NOT BOUND AND GAGGED.
SEXY PICTURES MOVE MORE COPIES, EMP.
PHOTO FROM p. 5
PHOTO FROM p. 10
ADVANCED RESTRAINT RESEARCH
ARR!
GW
PHOTO FROM p. 12
REALLY, THIS PROPOSAL LOOKS MORE LIKE SOFTCORE BONDAGE PORN THAN AN AUTOBIOGRAPHY.
EMP, WE CAN THINK "SOFTCORE BONDAGE PORN."
WE CAN HINT "SOFTCORE BONDAGE PORN."
BUT WE DON'T WANT TO ACTUALLY SAY "SOFTCORE BONDAGE PORN."
NOT PUBLICLY, ANYWAY.

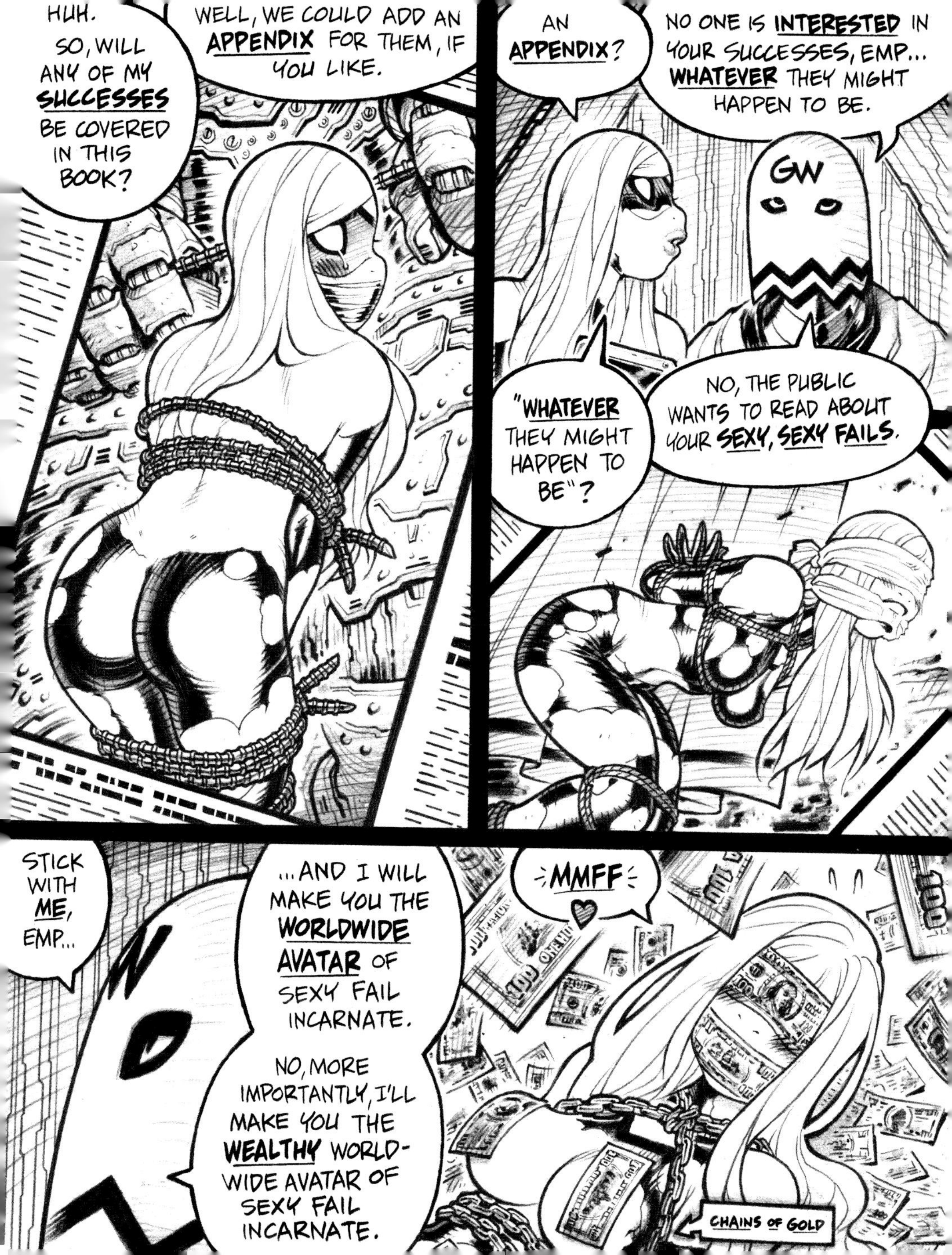
HUH.
SO, WILL ANY OF MY SUCCESSES BE COVERED IN THIS BOOK?
WELL, WE COULD ADD AN APPENDIX FOR THEM, IF YOU LIKE.
AN APPENDIX?
NO ONE IS INTERESTED IN YOUR SUCCESSES, EMP... WHATEVER THEY MIGHT HAPPEN TO BE.
GW
"WHATEVER THEY MIGHT HAPPEN TO BE"?
NO, THE PUBLIC WANTS TO READ ABOUT YOUR SEXY, SEXY FAILS.
STICK WITH ME, EMP...
...AND I WILL MAKE YOU THE WORLDWIDE AVATAR OF SEXY FAIL INCARNATE.
NO, MORE IMPORTANTLY, I'LL MAKE YOU THE WEALTHY WORLD-WIDE AVATAR OF SEXY FAIL INCARNATE.
MMFF
CHAINS OF GOLD

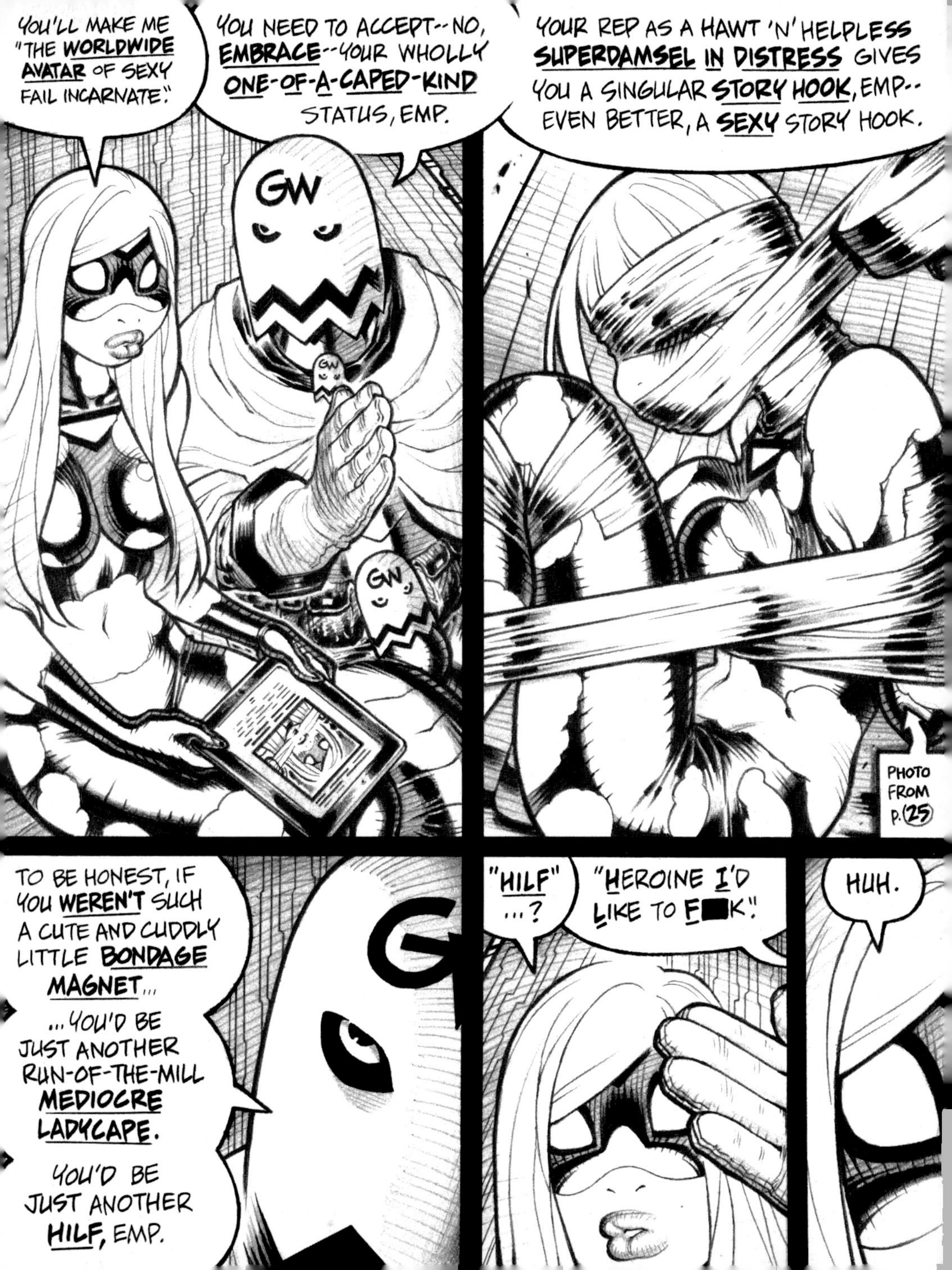

YOU'LL MAKE ME "THE WORLDWIDE AVATAR OF SEXY FAIL INCARNATE."
YOU NEED TO ACCEPT--NO, EMBRACE--YOUR WHOLLY ONE-OF-A-CAPED-KIND STATUS, EMP.
GW
YOUR REP AS A HAWT 'N' HELPLESS SUPERDAMSEL IN DISTRESS GIVES YOU A SINGULAR STORY HOOK, EMP-- EVEN BETTER, A SEXY STORY HOOK.
PHOTO FROM p. 25
TO BE HONEST, IF YOU WEREN'T SUCH A CUTE AND CUDDLY LITTLE BONDAGE MAGNET...
...YOU'D BE JUST ANOTHER RUN-OF-THE-MILL MEDIOCRE LADYCAPE.
YOU'D BE JUST ANOTHER HILF, EMP.
"HILF" ...?
"HEROINE I'D LIKE TO F[redacted]K."
HUH.

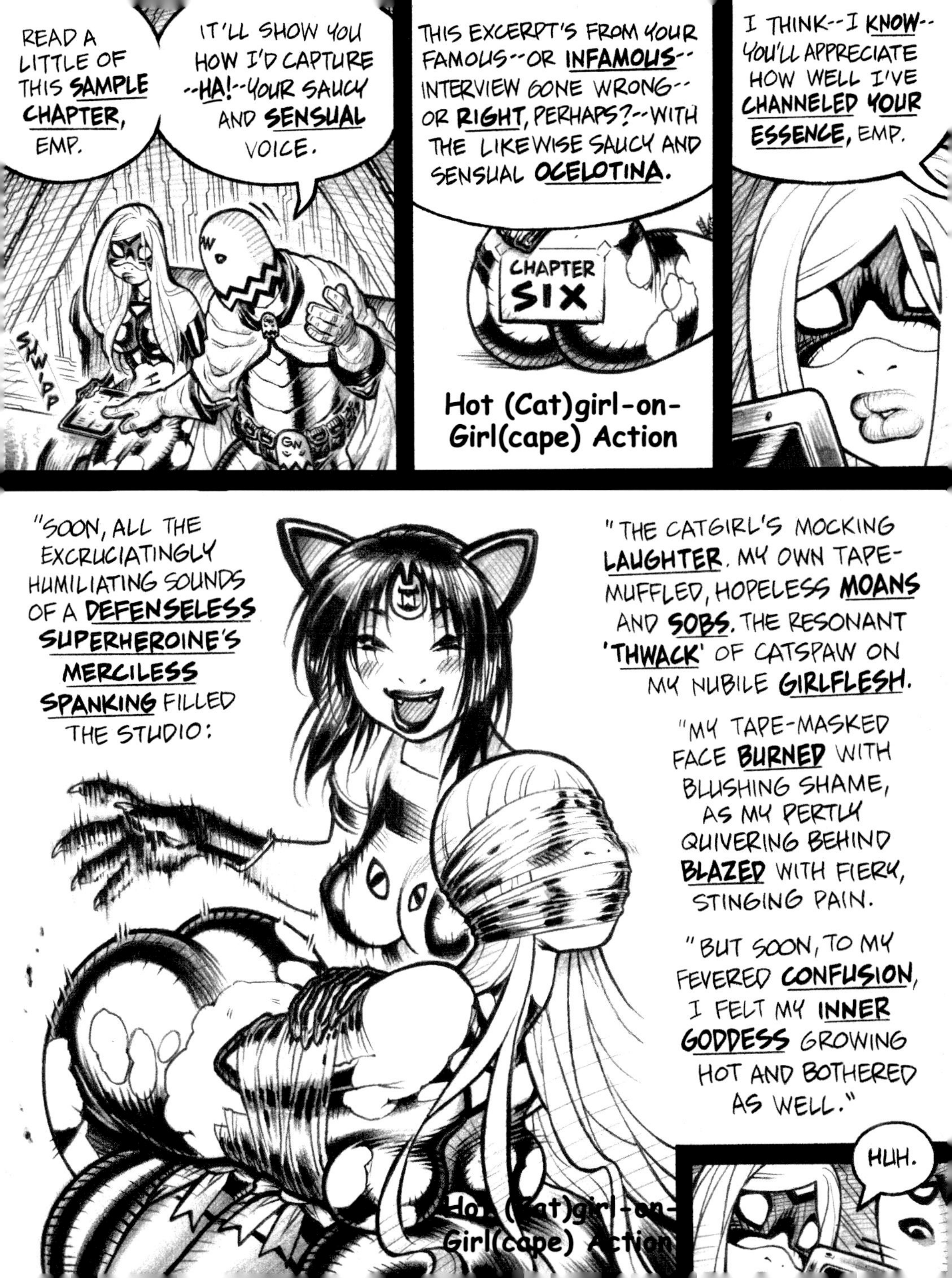
READ A LITTLE OF THIS SAMPLE CHAPTER, EMP.
IT'LL SHOW YOU HOW I'D CAPTURE --HA!--YOUR SAUCY AND SENSUAL VOICE.
THIS EXCERPT'S FROM YOUR FAMOUS--OR INFAMOUS--INTERVIEW GONE WRONG--OR RIGHT, PERHAPS?--WITH THE LIKEWISE SAUCY AND SENSUAL OCELOTINA.
CHAPTER SIX
Hot (Cat)girl-on-Girl(cape) Action
I THINK--I KNOW--YOU'LL APPRECIATE HOW WELL I'VE CHANNELED YOUR ESSENCE, EMP.
"SOON, ALL THE EXCRUCIATINGLY HUMILIATING SOUNDS OF A DEFENSELESS SUPERHEROINE'S MERCILESS SPANKING FILLED THE STUDIO:
"THE CATGIRL'S MOCKING LAUGHTER. MY OWN TAPE-MUFFLED, HOPELESS MOANS AND SOBS. THE RESONANT 'THWACK' OF CATSPAW ON MY NUBILE GIRLFLESH.
"MY TAPE-MASKED FACE BURNED WITH BLUSHING SHAME, AS MY PERTLY QUIVERING BEHIND BLAZED WITH FIERY, STINGING PAIN.
"BUT SOON, TO MY FEVERED CONFUSION, I FELT MY INNER GODDESS GROWING HOT AND BOTHERED AS WELL."
HUH.

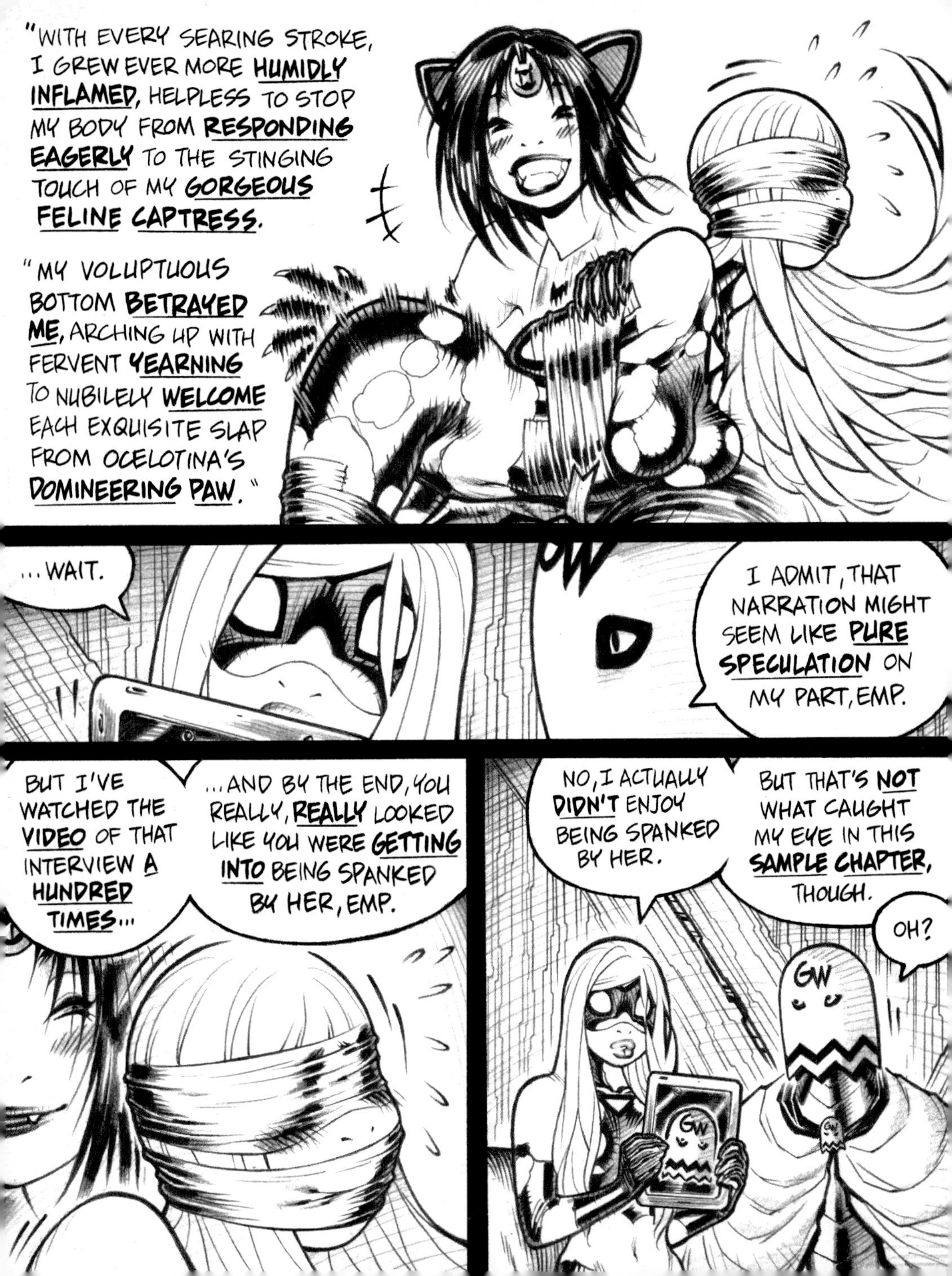
"WITH EVERY SEARING STROKE, I GREW EVER MORE HUMIDLY INFLAMED, HELPLESS TO STOP MY BODY FROM RESPONDING EAGERLY TO THE STINGING TOUCH OF MY GORGEOUS FELINE CAPTRESS.
"MY VOLUPTUOUS BOTTOM BETRAYED ME, ARCHING UP WITH FERVENT YEARNING TO NUBILELY WELCOME EACH EXQUISITE SLAP FROM OCELOTINA'S DOMINEERING PAW."
...WAIT.
I ADMIT, THAT NARRATION MIGHT SEEM LIKE PURE SPECULATION ON MY PART, EMP.
BUT I'VE WATCHED THE VIDEO OF THAT INTERVIEW A HUNDRED TIMES...
...AND BY THE END, YOU REALLY, REALLY LOOKED LIKE YOU WERE GETTING INTO BEING SPANKED BY HER, EMP.
NO, I ACTUALLY DIDN'T ENJOY BEING SPANKED BY HER.
BUT THAT'S NOT WHAT CAUGHT MY EYE IN THIS SAMPLE CHAPTER, THOUGH.
OH?
GW

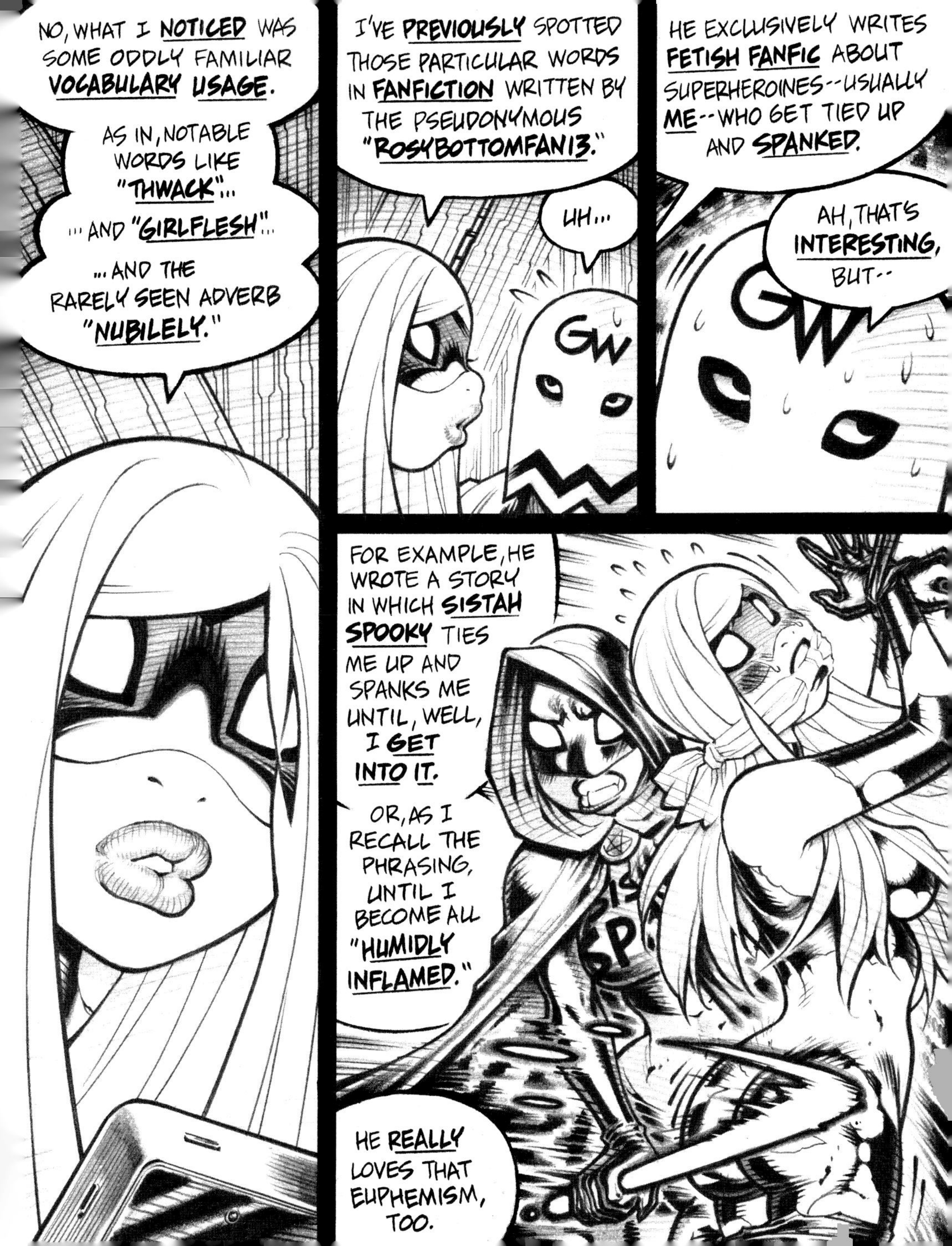
NO, WHAT I NOTICED WAS SOME ODDLY FAMILIAR VOCABULARY USAGE.
AS IN, NOTABLE WORDS LIKE "THWACK"...
...AND "GIRLFLESH"...
...AND THE RARELY SEEN ADVERB "NUBILELY."
I'VE PREVIOUSLY SPOTTED THOSE PARTICULAR WORDS IN FANFICTION WRITTEN BY THE PSEUDONYMOUS "ROSYBOTTOMFAN13."
UH...
GW
HE EXCLUSIVELY WRITES FETISH FANFIC ABOUT SUPERHEROINES--USUALLY ME--WHO GET TIED UP AND SPANKED.
AH, THAT'S INTERESTING, BUT--
GW
FOR EXAMPLE, HE WROTE A STORY IN WHICH SISTAH SPOOKY TIES ME UP AND SPANKS ME UNTIL, WELL, I GET INTO IT.
OR, AS I RECALL THE PHRASING, UNTIL I BECOME ALL "HUMIDLY INFLAMED."
HE REALLY LOVES THAT EUPHEMISM, TOO.

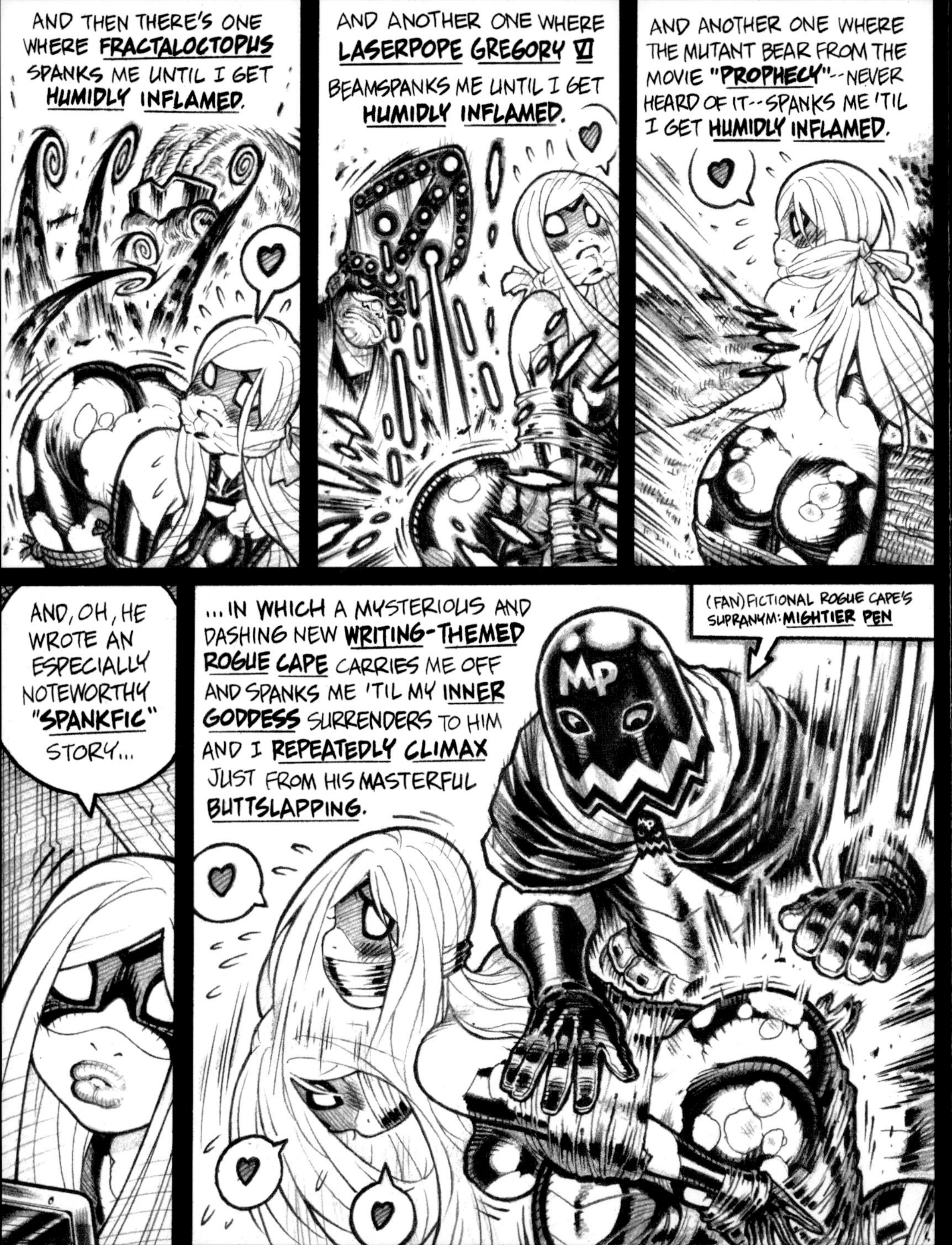
AND THEN THERE'S ONE WHERE FRACTALOCTOPUS SPANKS ME UNTIL I GET HUMIDLY INFLAMED.
AND ANOTHER ONE WHERE LASERPOPE GREGORY VI BEAMSPANKS ME UNTIL I GET HUMIDLY INFLAMED.
AND ANOTHER ONE WHERE THE MUTANT BEAR FROM THE MOVIE "PROPHECY"--NEVER HEARD OF IT--SPANKS ME 'TIL I GET HUMIDLY INFLAMED.
AND, OH, HE WROTE AN ESPECIALLY NOTEWORTHY "SPANKFIC" STORY...
...IN WHICH A MYSTERIOUS AND DASHING NEW WRITING-THEMED ROGUE CAPE CARRIES ME OFF AND SPANKS ME 'TIL MY INNER GODDESS SURRENDERS TO HIM AND I REPEATEDLY CLIMAX JUST FROM HIS MASTERFUL BUTTSLAPPING.
(FAN)FICTIONAL ROGUE CAPE'S SUPRANYM: MIGHTIER PEN
MP

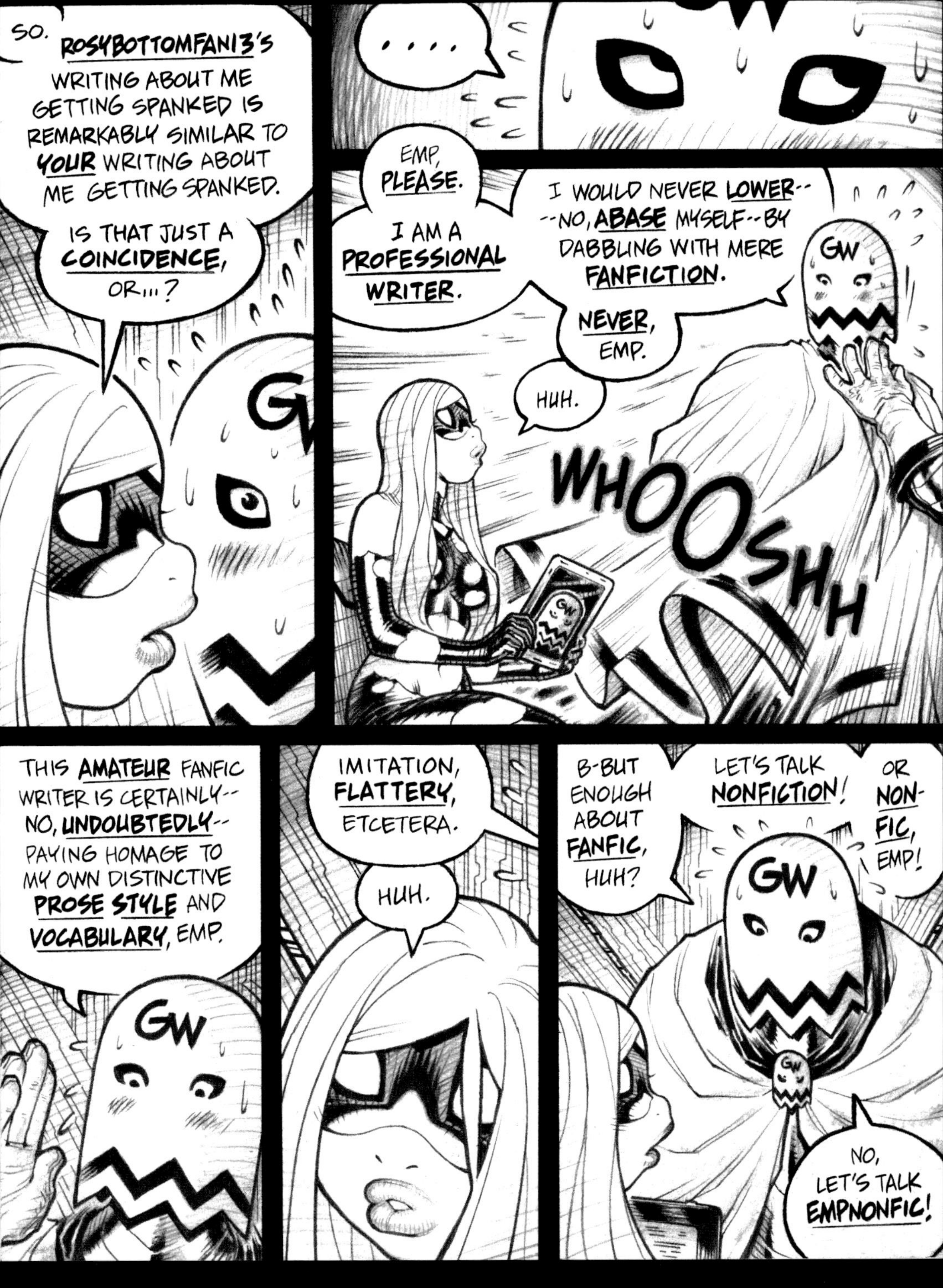
SO. ROSYBOTTOMFAN13'S WRITING ABOUT ME GETTING SPANKED IS REMARKABLY SIMILAR TO YOUR WRITING ABOUT ME GETTING SPANKED.
IS THAT JUST A COINCIDENCE, OR...?
GW
. . . .
EMP, PLEASE.
I AM A PROFESSIONAL WRITER.
I WOULD NEVER LOWER-- --NO, ABASE MYSELF--BY DABBLING WITH MERE FANFICTION.
NEVER, EMP.
GW
HUH.
WHOOOSHHH
THIS AMATEUR FANFIC WRITER IS CERTAINLY-- NO, UNDOUBTEDLY-- PAYING HOMAGE TO MY OWN DISTINCTIVE PROSE STYLE AND VOCABULARY, EMP.
GW
IMITATION, FLATTERY, ETCETERA.
HUH.
B-BUT ENOUGH ABOUT FANFIC, HUH?
LET'S TALK NONFICTION!
OR NON-FIC, EMP!
GW
NO, LET'S TALK EMPNONFIC!

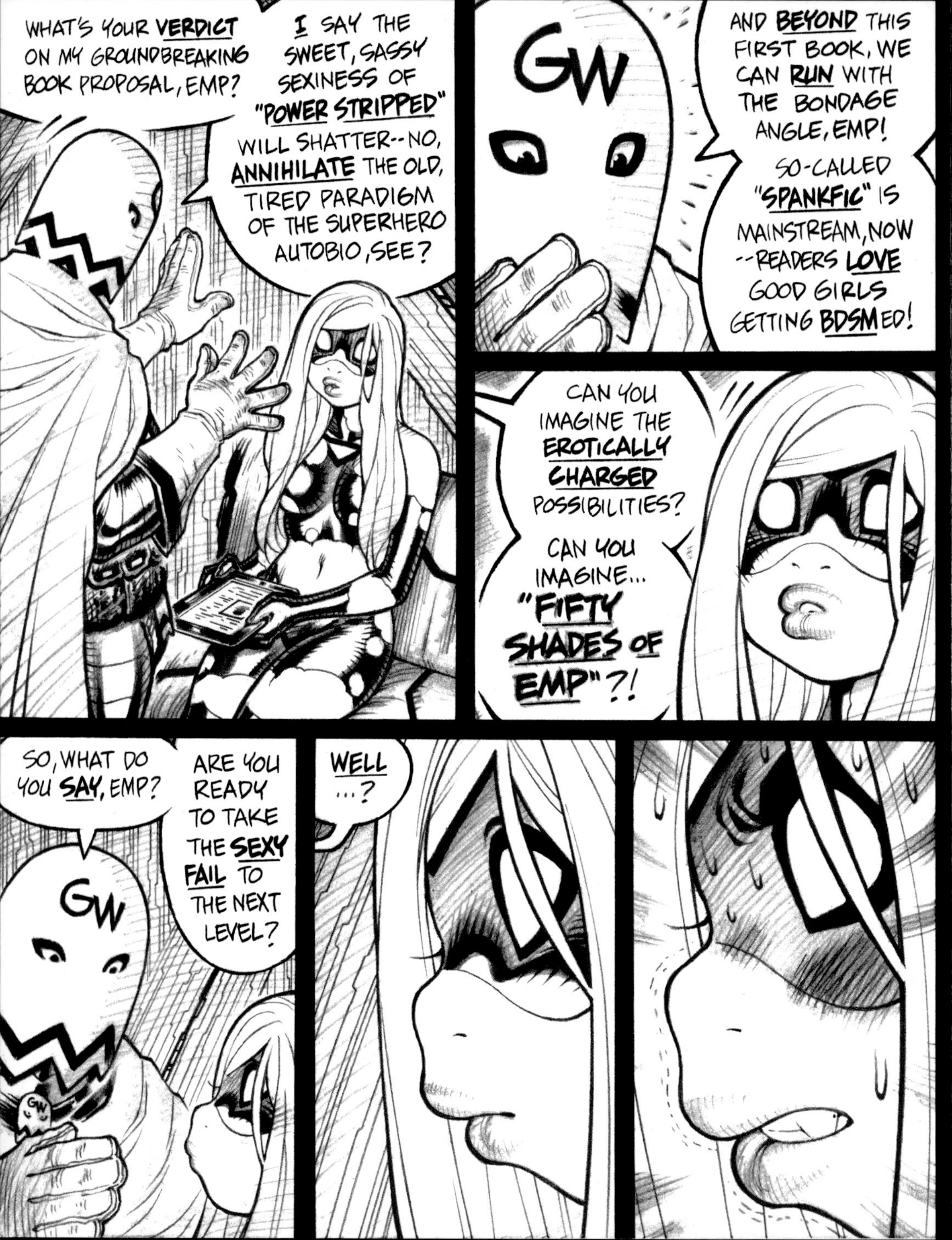
WHAT'S YOUR VERDICT ON MY GROUNDBREAKING BOOK PROPOSAL, EMP?
I SAY THE SWEET, SASSY SEXINESS OF "POWER STRIPPED" WILL SHATTER--NO, ANNIHILATE THE OLD, TIRED PARADIGM OF THE SUPERHERO AUTOBIO, SEE?
GW
AND BEYOND THIS FIRST BOOK, WE CAN RUN WITH THE BONDAGE ANGLE, EMP!
SO-CALLED "SPANKFIC" IS MAINSTREAM, NOW --READERS LOVE GOOD GIRLS GETTING BDSMED!
CAN YOU IMAGINE THE EROTICALLY CHARGED POSSIBILITIES?
CAN YOU IMAGINE... "FIFTY SHADES OF EMP"?!
SO, WHAT DO YOU SAY, EMP?
ARE YOU READY TO TAKE THE SEXY FAIL TO THE NEXT LEVEL?
WELL ...?
GW
GW

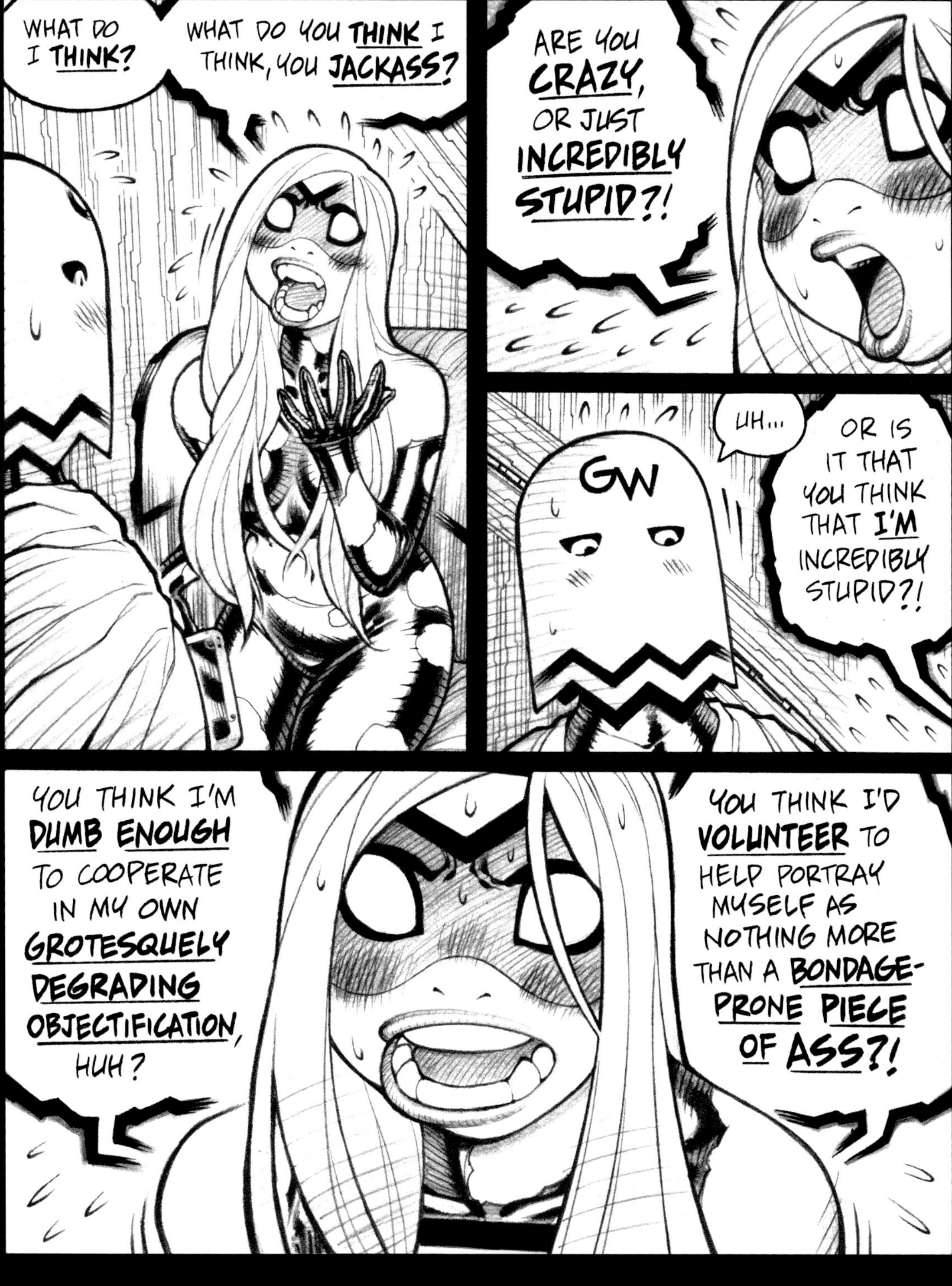
WHAT DO I THINK?
WHAT DO YOU THINK I THINK, YOU JACKASS?
ARE YOU CRAZY, OR JUST INCREDIBLY STUPID?!
UH...
GW
OR IS IT THAT YOU THINK THAT I'M INCREDIBLY STUPID?!
YOU THINK I'M DUMB ENOUGH TO COOPERATE IN MY OWN GROTESQUELY DEGRADING OBJECTIFICATION, HUH?
YOU THINK I'D VOLUNTEER TO HELP PORTRAY MYSELF AS NOTHING MORE THAN A BONDAGE-PRONE PIECE OF ASS?!

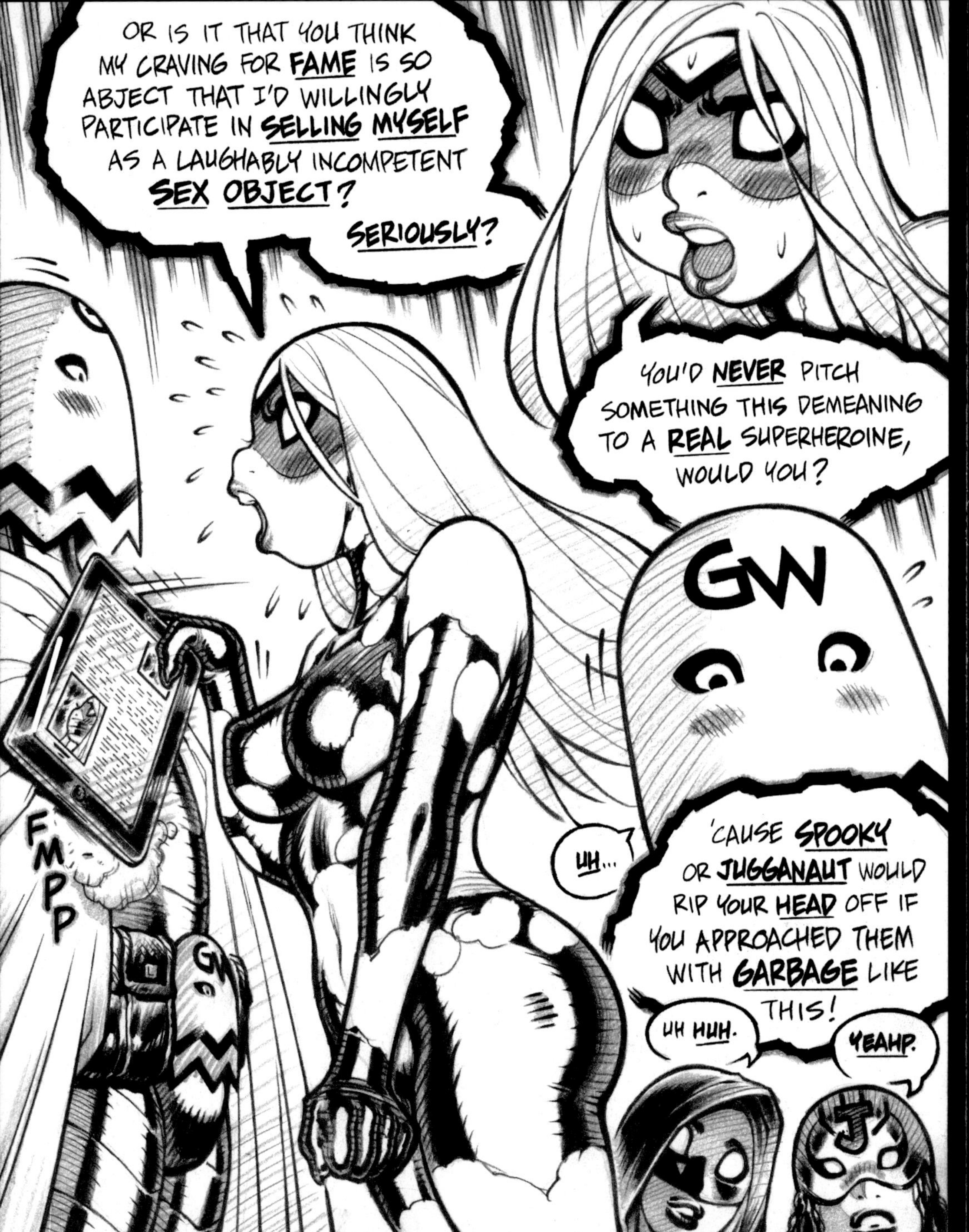

OR IS IT THAT YOU THINK MY CRAVING FOR FAME IS SO ABJECT THAT I'D WILLINGLY PARTICIPATE IN SELLING MYSELF AS A LAUGHABLY INCOMPETENT SEX OBJECT?
SERIOUSLY?
YOU'D NEVER PITCH SOMETHING THIS DEMEANING TO A REAL SUPERHEROINE, WOULD YOU?
GW
UH...
'CAUSE SPOOKY OR JUGGANAUT WOULD RIP YOUR HEAD OFF IF YOU APPROACHED THEM WITH GARBAGE LIKE THIS!
UH HUH.
YEAHP.
FMPP

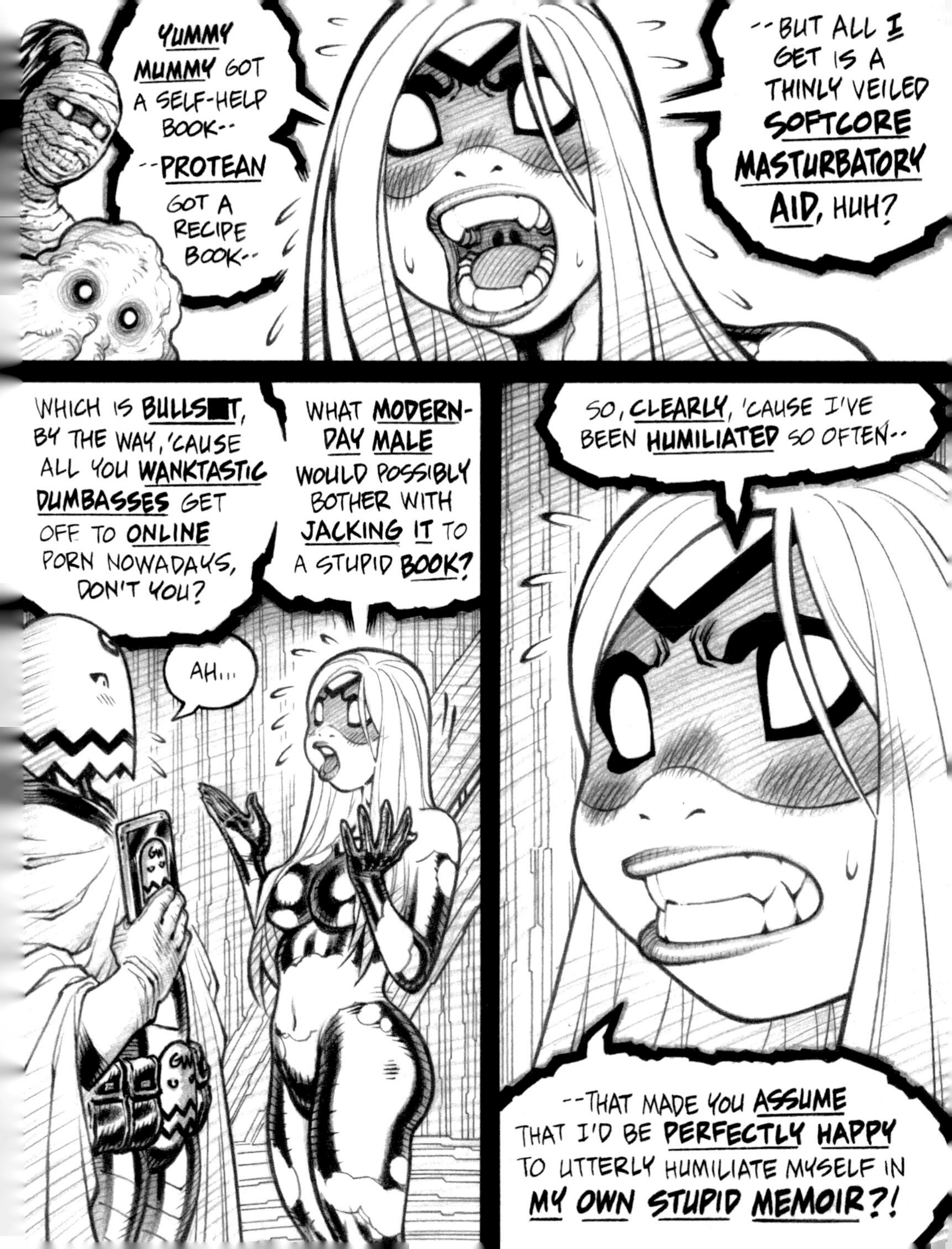

YUMMY MUMMY GOT A SELF-HELP BOOK--
--PROTEAN GOT A RECIPE BOOK--
--BUT ALL I GET IS A THINLY VEILED SOFTCORE MASTURBATORY AID, HUH?
WHICH IS BULLS[redacted]T, BY THE WAY, 'CAUSE ALL YOU WANKTASTIC DUMBASSES GET OFF TO ONLINE PORN NOWADAYS, DON'T YOU?
WHAT MODERN-DAY MALE WOULD POSSIBLY BOTHER WITH JACKING IT TO A STUPID BOOK?
AH...
SO, CLEARLY, 'CAUSE I'VE BEEN HUMILIATED SO OFTEN--
--THAT MADE YOU ASSUME THAT I'D BE PERFECTLY HAPPY TO UTTERLY HUMILIATE MYSELF IN MY OWN STUPID MEMOIR?!

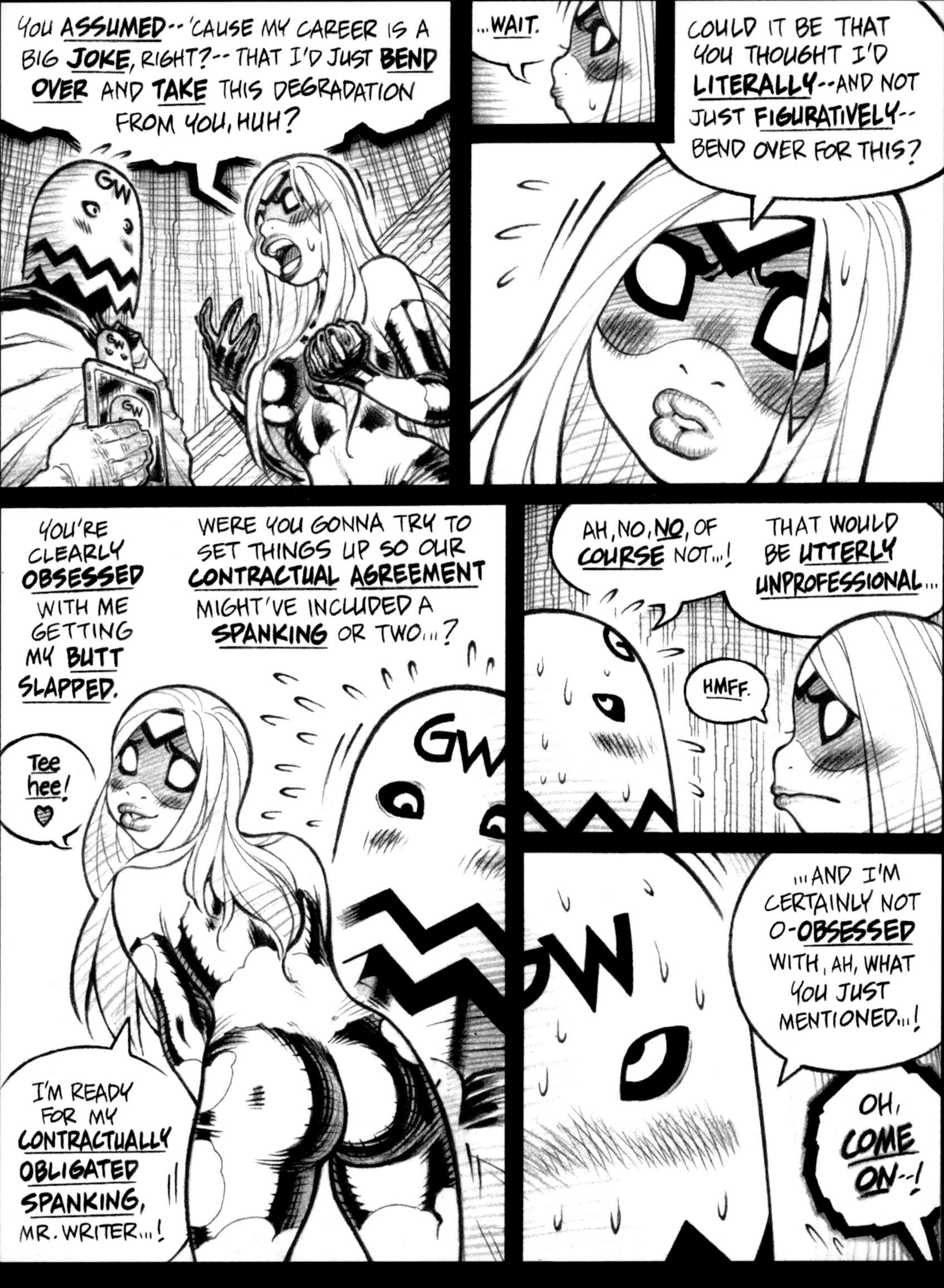
YOU ASSUMED--'CAUSE MY CAREER IS A BIG JOKE, RIGHT?--THAT I'D JUST BEND OVER AND TAKE THIS DEGRADATION FROM YOU, HUH?
GW
GW
GW
...WAIT.
COULD IT BE THAT YOU THOUGHT I'D LITERALLY--AND NOT JUST FIGURATIVELY--BEND OVER FOR THIS?
YOU'RE CLEARLY OBSESSED WITH ME GETTING MY BUTT SLAPPED.
WERE YOU GONNA TRY TO SET THINGS UP SO OUR CONTRACTUAL AGREEMENT MIGHT'VE INCLUDED A SPANKING OR TWO...?
Tee hee!
I'M READY FOR MY CONTRACTUALLY OBLIGATED SPANKING, MR. WRITER...!
GW
AH, NO, NO, OF COURSE NOT...!
THAT WOULD BE UTTERLY UNPROFESSIONAL...
HMFF.
...AND I'M CERTAINLY NOT O-OBSESSED WITH, AH, WHAT YOU JUST MENTIONED...!
OH, COME ON--!

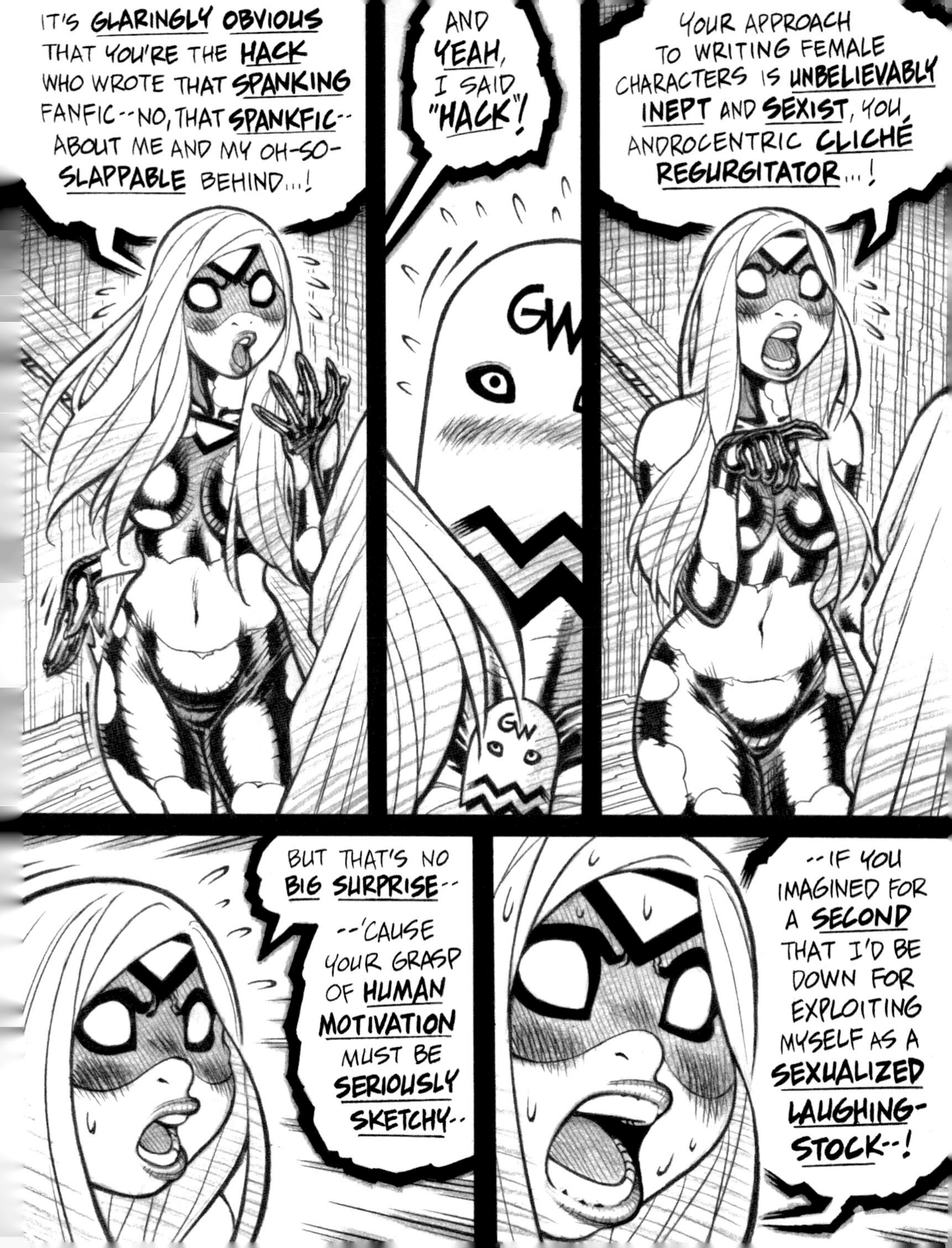

IT'S GLARINGLY OBVIOUS THAT YOU'RE THE HACK WHO WROTE THAT SPANKING FANFIC--NO, THAT SPANKFIC--ABOUT ME AND MY OH-SO-SLAPPABLE BEHIND...!
AND YEAH, I SAID "HACK"!
GW
YOUR APPROACH TO WRITING FEMALE CHARACTERS IS UNBELIEVABLY INEPT AND SEXIST, YOU ANDROCENTRIC CLICHÉ REGURGITATOR...!
BUT THAT'S NO BIG SURPRISE--
--'CAUSE YOUR GRASP OF HUMAN MOTIVATION MUST BE SERIOUSLY SKETCHY--
--IF YOU IMAGINED FOR A SECOND THAT I'D BE DOWN FOR EXPLOITING MYSELF AS A SEXUALIZED LAUGHING-STOCK--!

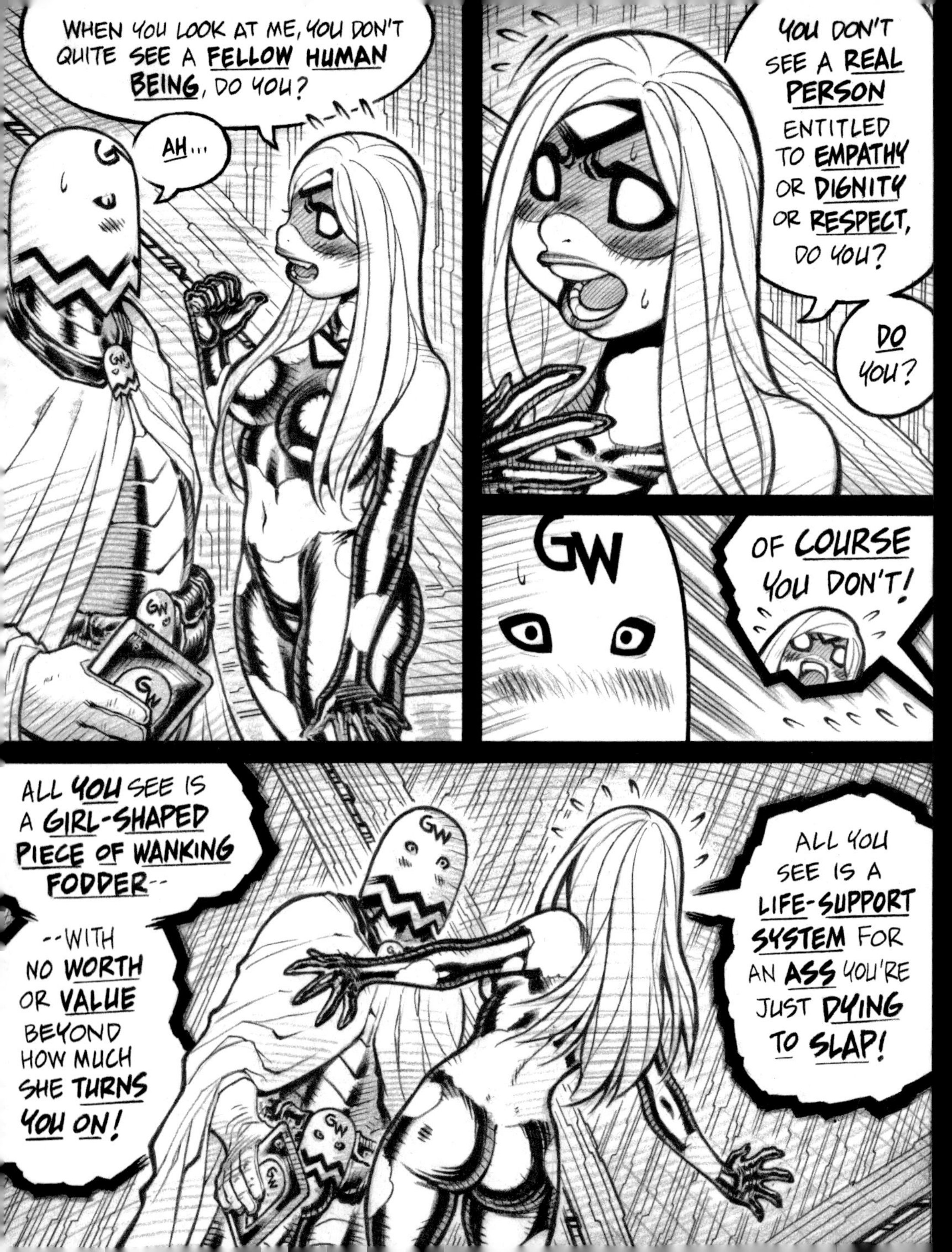
WHEN YOU LOOK AT ME, YOU DON'T QUITE SEE A FELLOW HUMAN BEING, DO YOU?
AH...
YOU DON'T SEE A REAL PERSON ENTITLED TO EMPATHY OR DIGNITY OR RESPECT, DO YOU?
DO YOU?
OF COURSE YOU DON'T!
ALL YOU SEE IS A GIRL-SHAPED PIECE OF WANKING FODDER--
--WITH NO WORTH OR VALUE BEYOND HOW MUCH SHE TURNS YOU ON!
ALL YOU SEE IS A LIFE-SUPPORT SYSTEM FOR AN ASS YOU'RE JUST DYING TO SLAP!

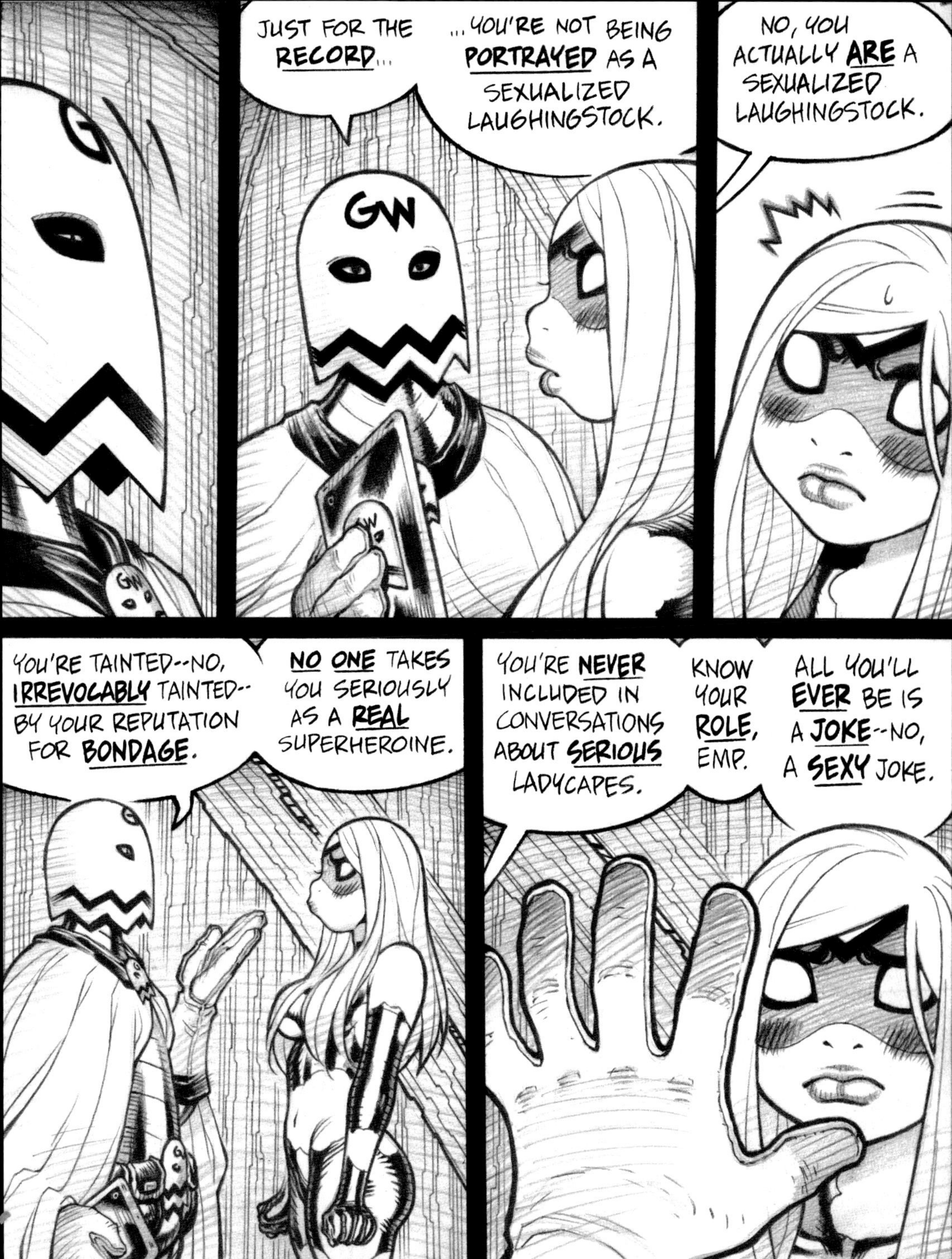
JUST FOR THE RECORD...
...YOU'RE NOT BEING PORTRAYED AS A SEXUALIZED LAUGHINGSTOCK.
NO, YOU ACTUALLY ARE A SEXUALIZED LAUGHINGSTOCK.
YOU'RE TAINTED--NO, IRREVOCABLY TAINTED--BY YOUR REPUTATION FOR BONDAGE.
NO ONE TAKES YOU SERIOUSLY AS A REAL SUPERHEROINE.
YOU'RE NEVER INCLUDED IN CONVERSATIONS ABOUT SERIOUS LADYCAPES.
KNOW YOUR ROLE, EMP.
ALL YOU'LL EVER BE IS A JOKE--NO, A SEXY JOKE.

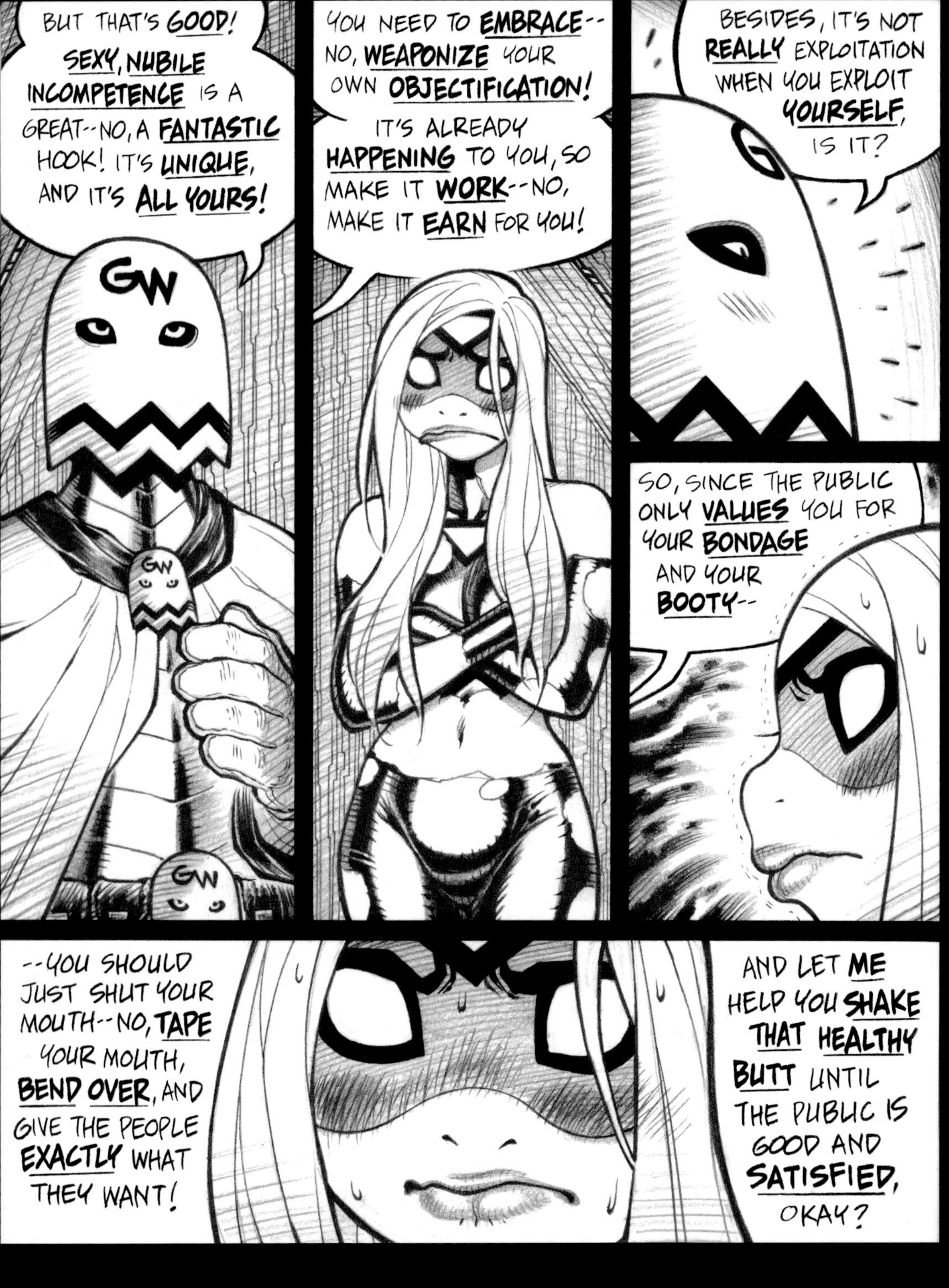
BUT THAT'S GOOD! SEXY, NUBILE INCOMPETENCE IS A GREAT--NO, A FANTASTIC HOOK! IT'S UNIQUE, AND IT'S ALL YOURS!
GW
YOU NEED TO EMBRACE--NO, WEAPONIZE YOUR OWN OBJECTIFICATION!
IT'S ALREADY HAPPENING TO YOU, SO MAKE IT WORK--NO, MAKE IT EARN FOR YOU!
BESIDES, IT'S NOT REALLY EXPLOITATION WHEN YOU EXPLOIT YOURSELF, IS IT?
SO, SINCE THE PUBLIC ONLY VALUES YOU FOR YOUR BONDAGE AND YOUR BOOTY--
--YOU SHOULD JUST SHUT YOUR MOUTH--NO, TAPE YOUR MOUTH, BEND OVER, AND GIVE THE PEOPLE EXACTLY WHAT THEY WANT!
AND LET ME HELP YOU SHAKE THAT HEALTHY BUTT UNTIL THE PUBLIC IS GOOD AND SATISFIED, OKAY?

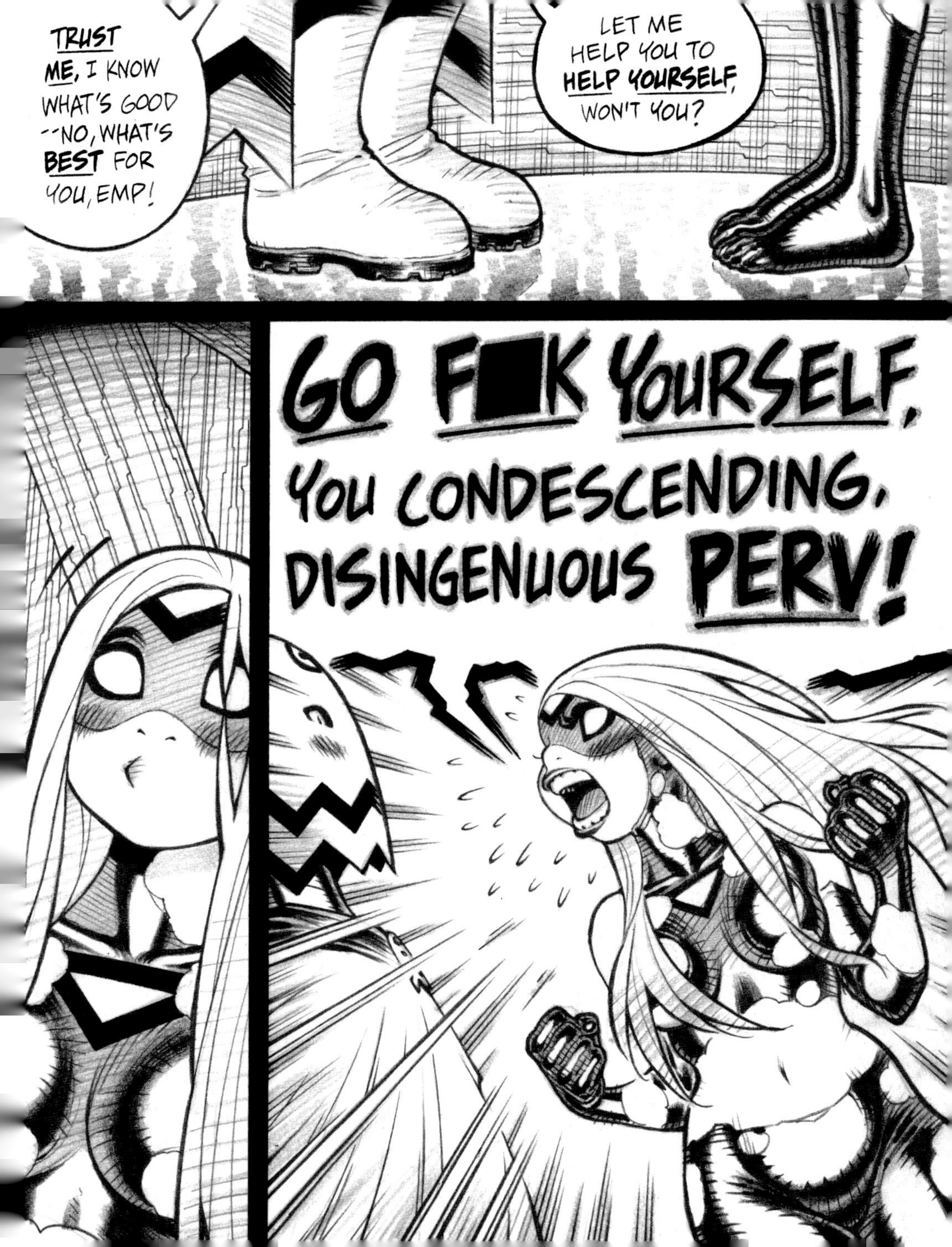
TRUST ME, I KNOW WHAT'S GOOD --NO, WHAT'S BEST FOR YOU, EMP!
LET ME HELP YOU TO HELP YOURSELF, WON'T YOU?
GO F[redacted]K YOURSELF, YOU CONDESCENDING, DISINGENUOUS PERV!

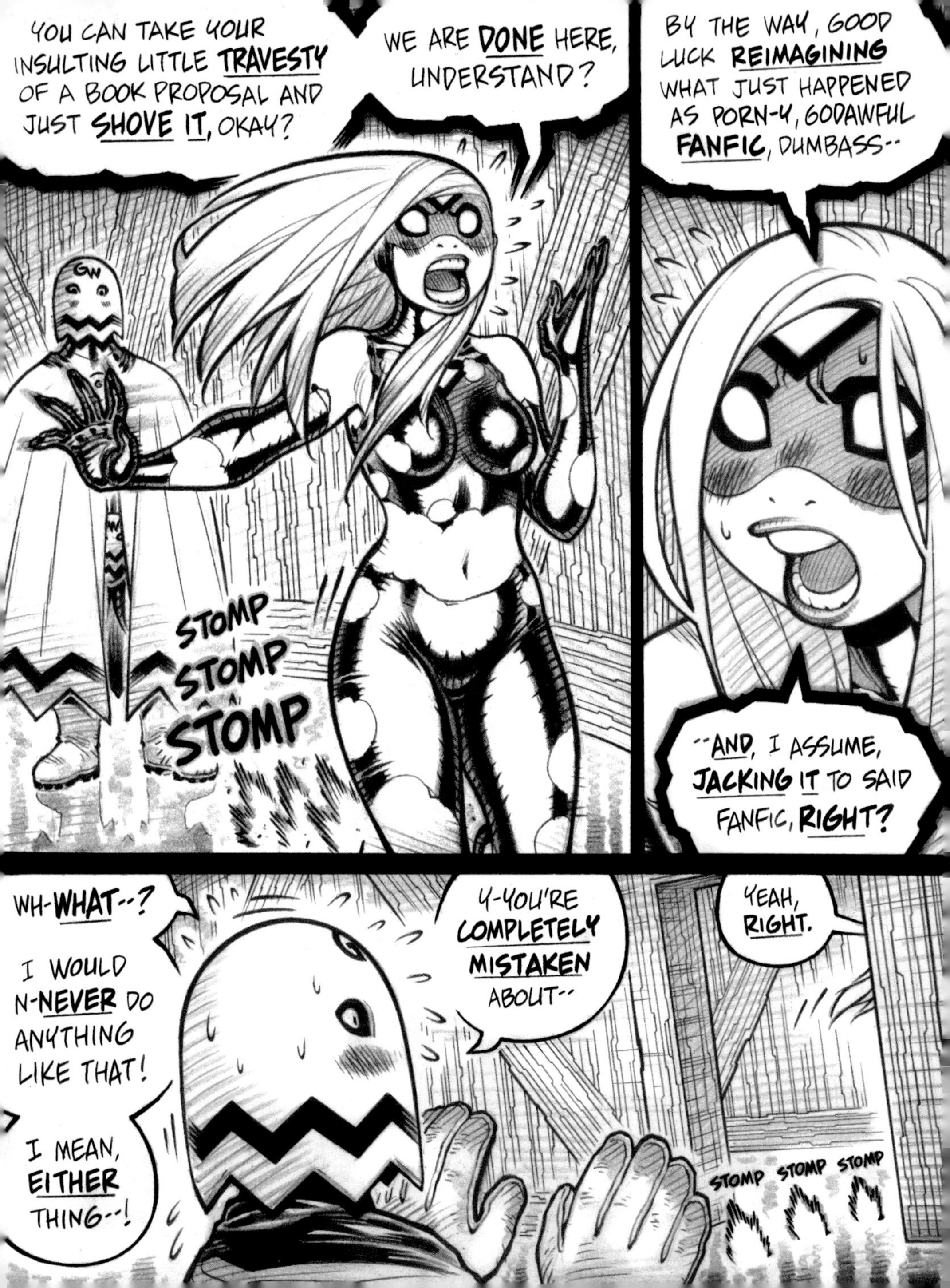
YOU CAN TAKE YOUR INSULTING LITTLE TRAVESTY OF A BOOK PROPOSAL AND JUST SHOVE IT, OKAY?
WE ARE DONE HERE, UNDERSTAND?
STOMP STOMP STOMP
BY THE WAY, GOOD LUCK REIMAGINING WHAT JUST HAPPENED AS PORN-Y, GODAWFUL FANFIC, DUMBASS--
--AND, I ASSUME, JACKING IT TO SAID FANFIC, RIGHT?
WH-WHAT--?
I WOULD N-NEVER DO ANYTHING LIKE THAT!
I MEAN, EITHER THING--!
Y-YOU'RE COMPLETELY MISTAKEN ABOUT--
YEAH, RIGHT.
STOMP STOMP STOMP

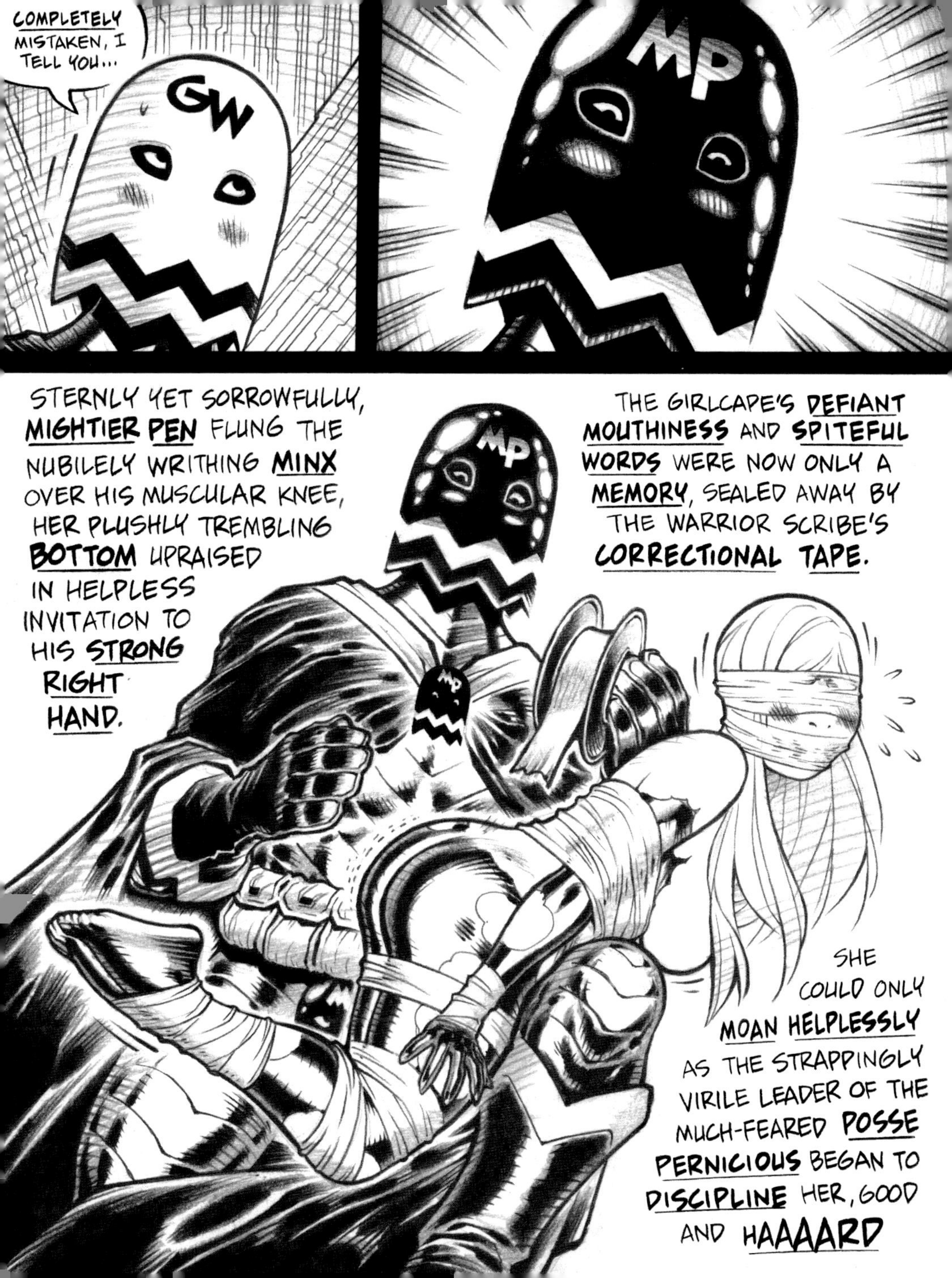
COMPLETELY MISTAKEN, I TELL YOU...
STERNLY YET SORROWFULLY, MIGHTIER PEN FLUNG THE NUBILELY WRITHING MINX OVER HIS MUSCULAR KNEE, HER PLUSHLY TREMBLING BOTTOM UPRAISED IN HELPLESS INVITATION TO HIS STRONG RIGHT HAND.
THE GIRLCAPE'S DEFIANT MOUTHINESS AND SPITEFUL WORDS WERE NOW ONLY A MEMORY, SEALED AWAY BY THE WARRIOR SCRIBE'S CORRECTIONAL TAPE.
SHE COULD ONLY MOAN HELPLESSLY AS THE STRAPPINGLY VIRILE LEADER OF THE MUCH-FEARED POSSE PERNICIOUS BEGAN TO DISCIPLINE HER, GOOD AND HAAAARD

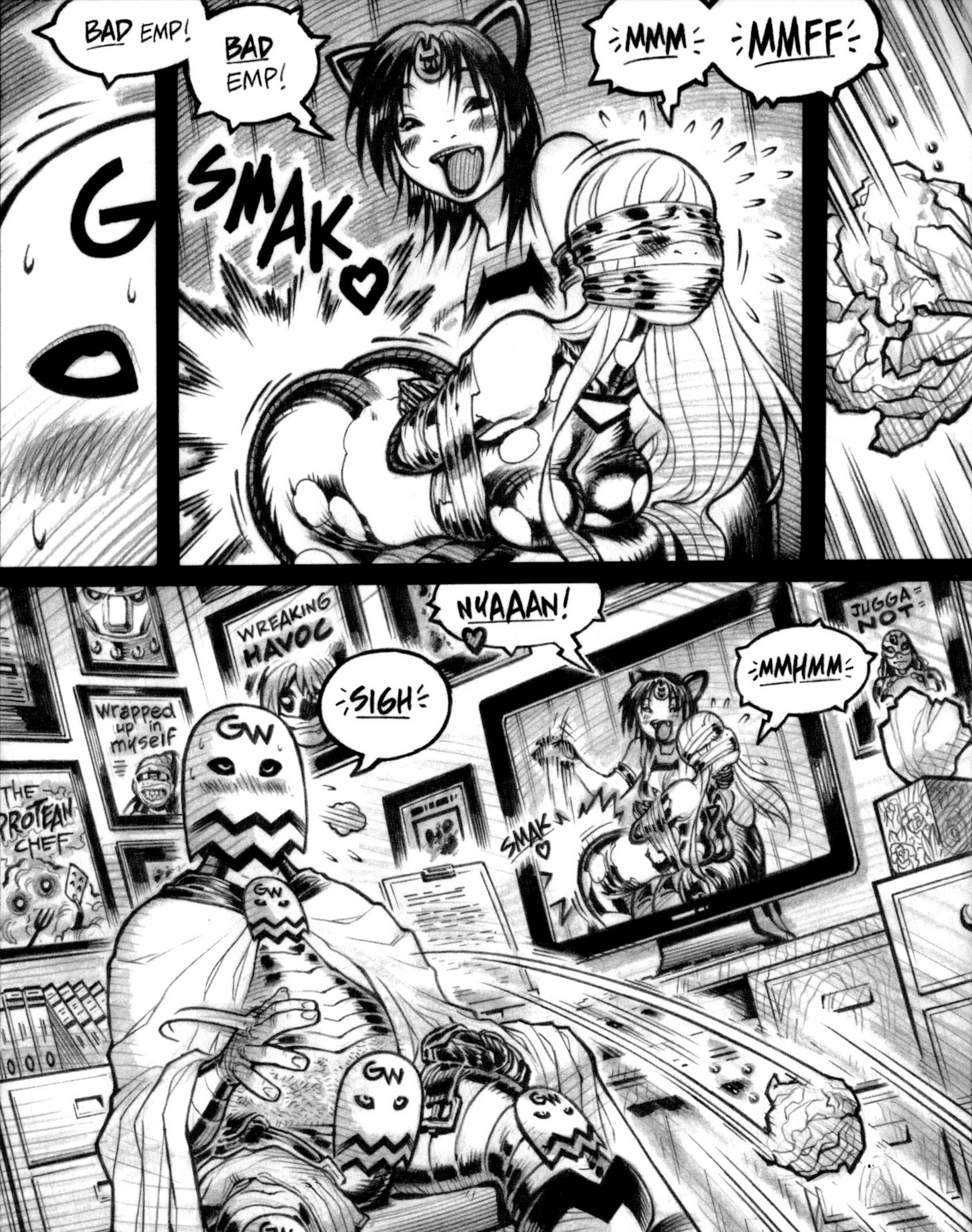
BAD EMP!
BAD EMP!
MMM
MMFF
G
SMAK
WREAKING HAVOC
NYAAAN!
JUGGA NOT
MMHMM
SIGH
wrapped up in myself
THE PROTEAN CHEF
GW
SMAK

Empowered™

Distress and the Damsel

(or, our story's exciting—if, admittedly, rather lengthy—conclusion)

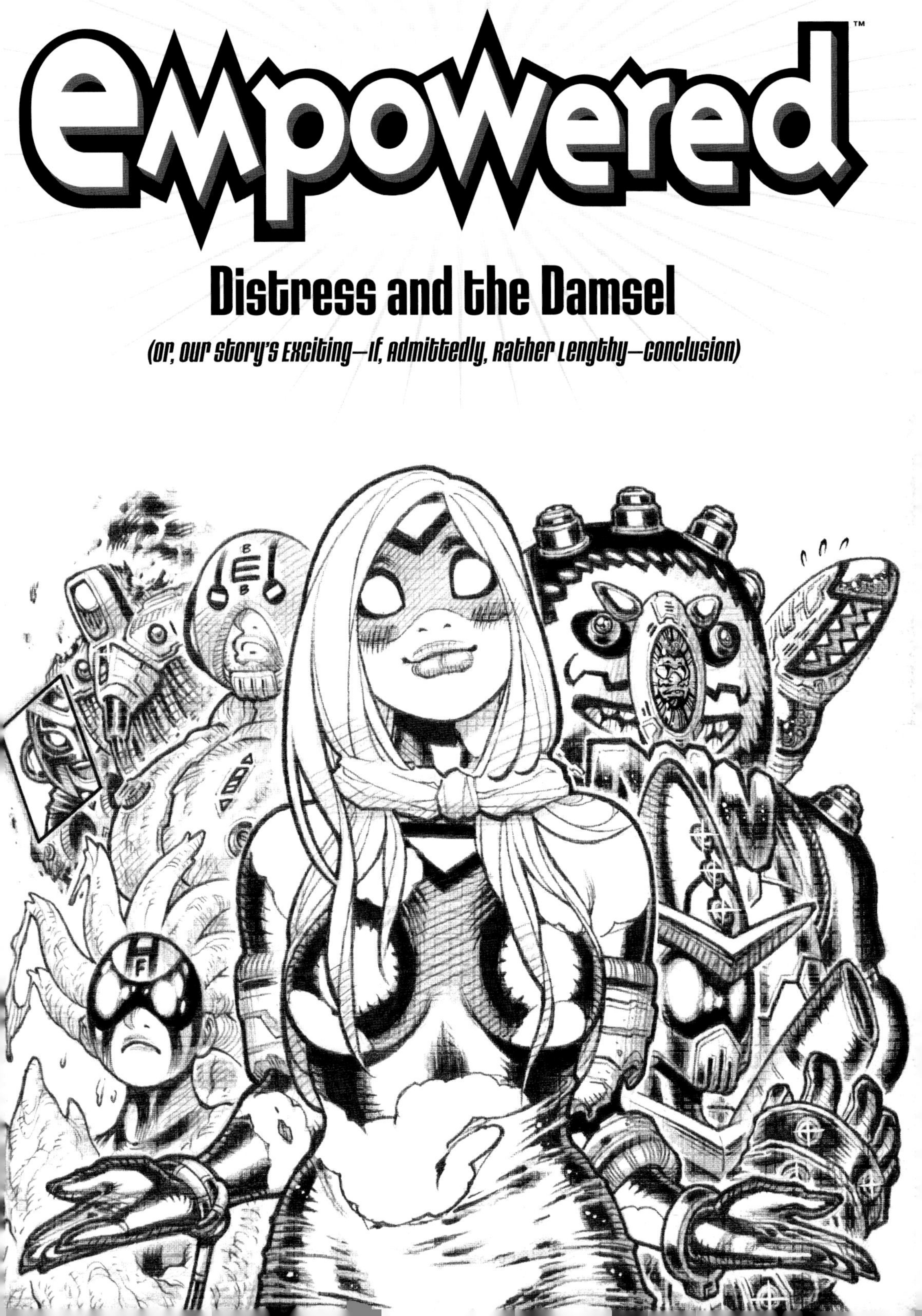

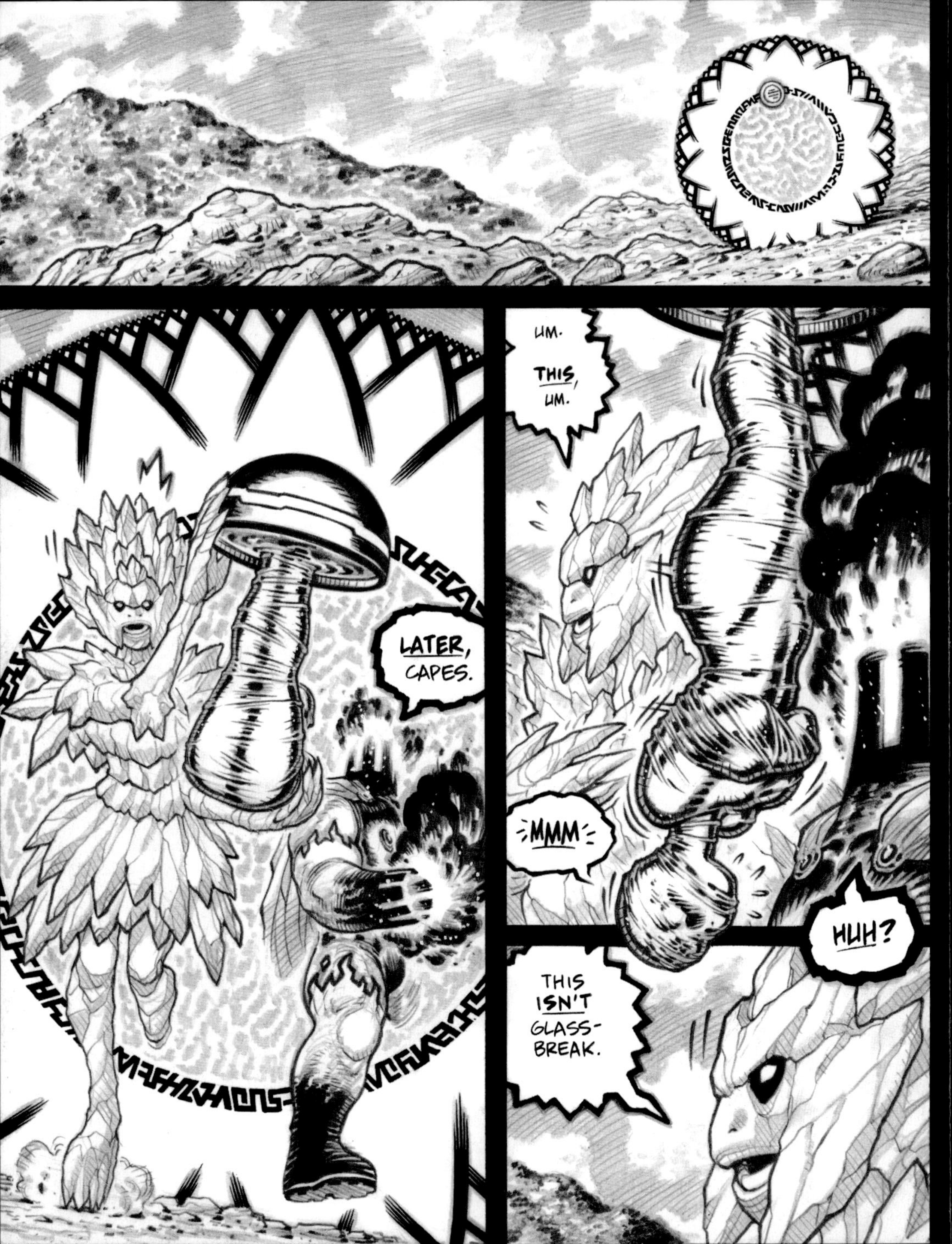
LATER, CAPES.
UM.
THIS, UM.
MMM
HUH?
THIS ISN'T GLASS-BREAK.

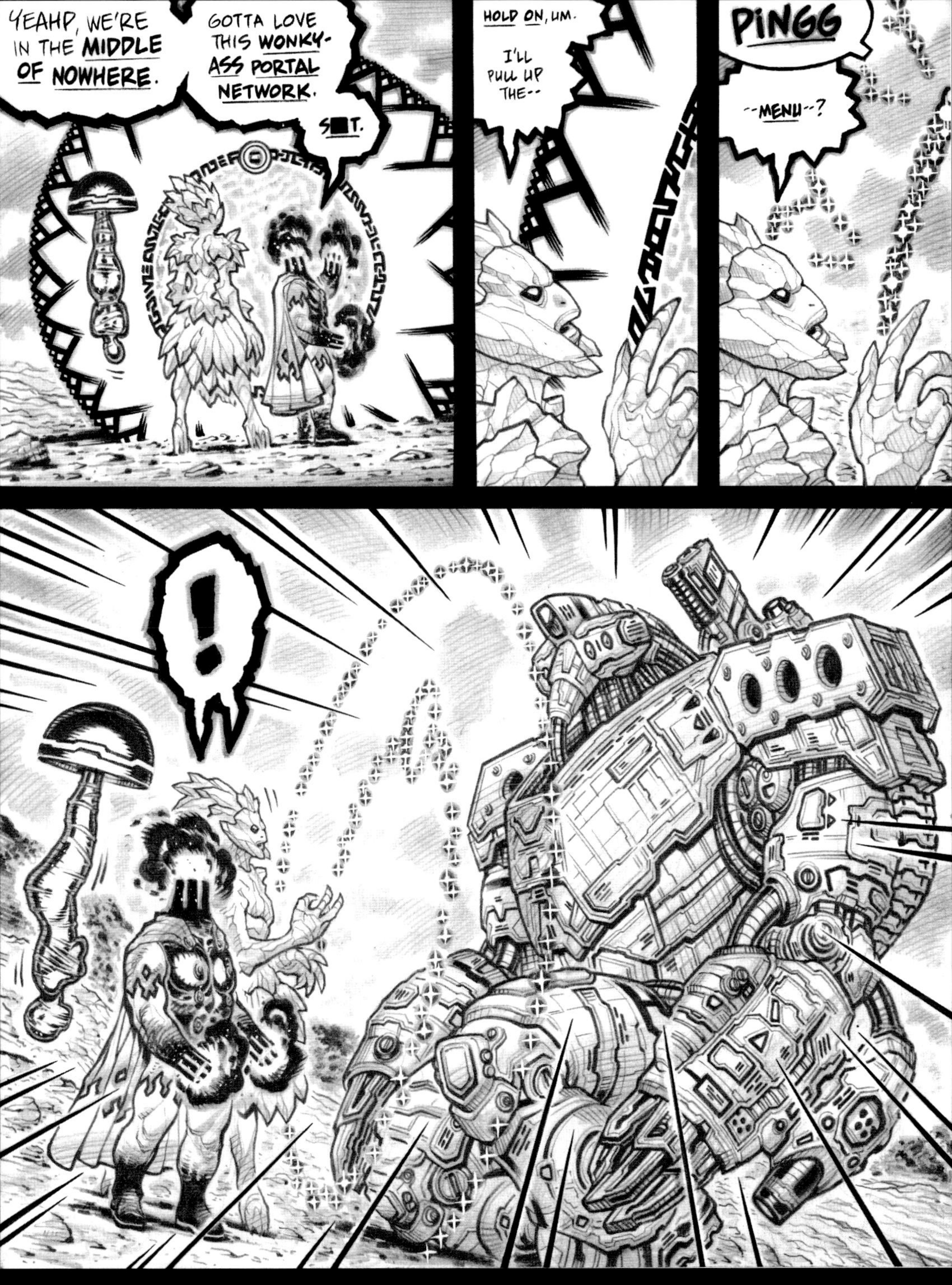
YEAHP, WE'RE IN THE MIDDLE OF NOWHERE.
GOTTA LOVE THIS WONKY-ASS PORTAL NETWORK.
S[redacted]T.
HOLD ON, UM.
I'LL PULL UP THE--
PINGG
--MENU--?
!

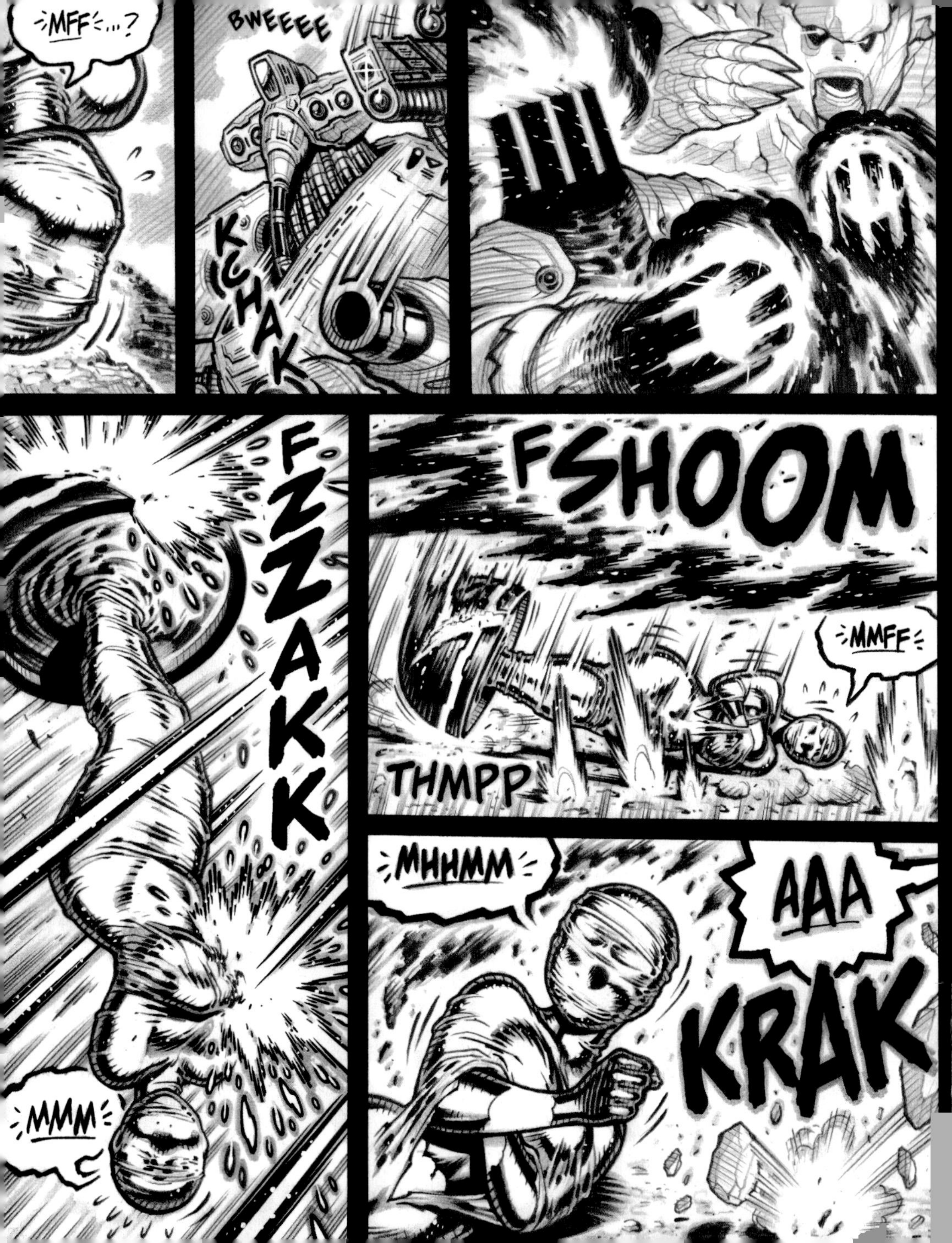
MFF...?
BWEEEEE
KCHAK
FZZAKK
MMM
FSHOOM
MMFF
THMPP
MHHMM
AAA
KRAK

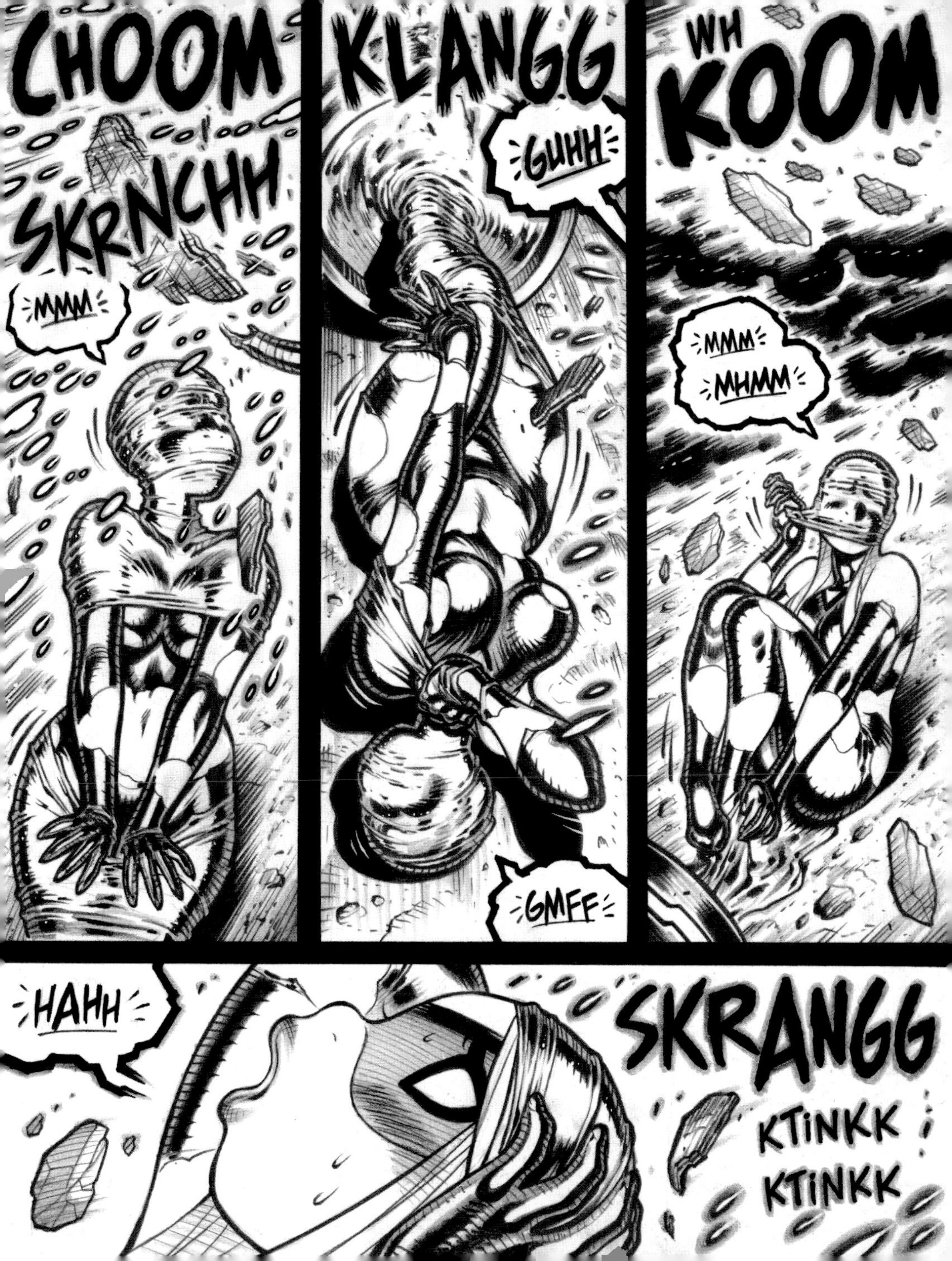
CHOOM
SKRNCHH
MMM
KLANGG
GUHH
GMFF
WH KOOM
MMM
MHMM
HAHH
SKRANGG
KTINKK
KTINKK

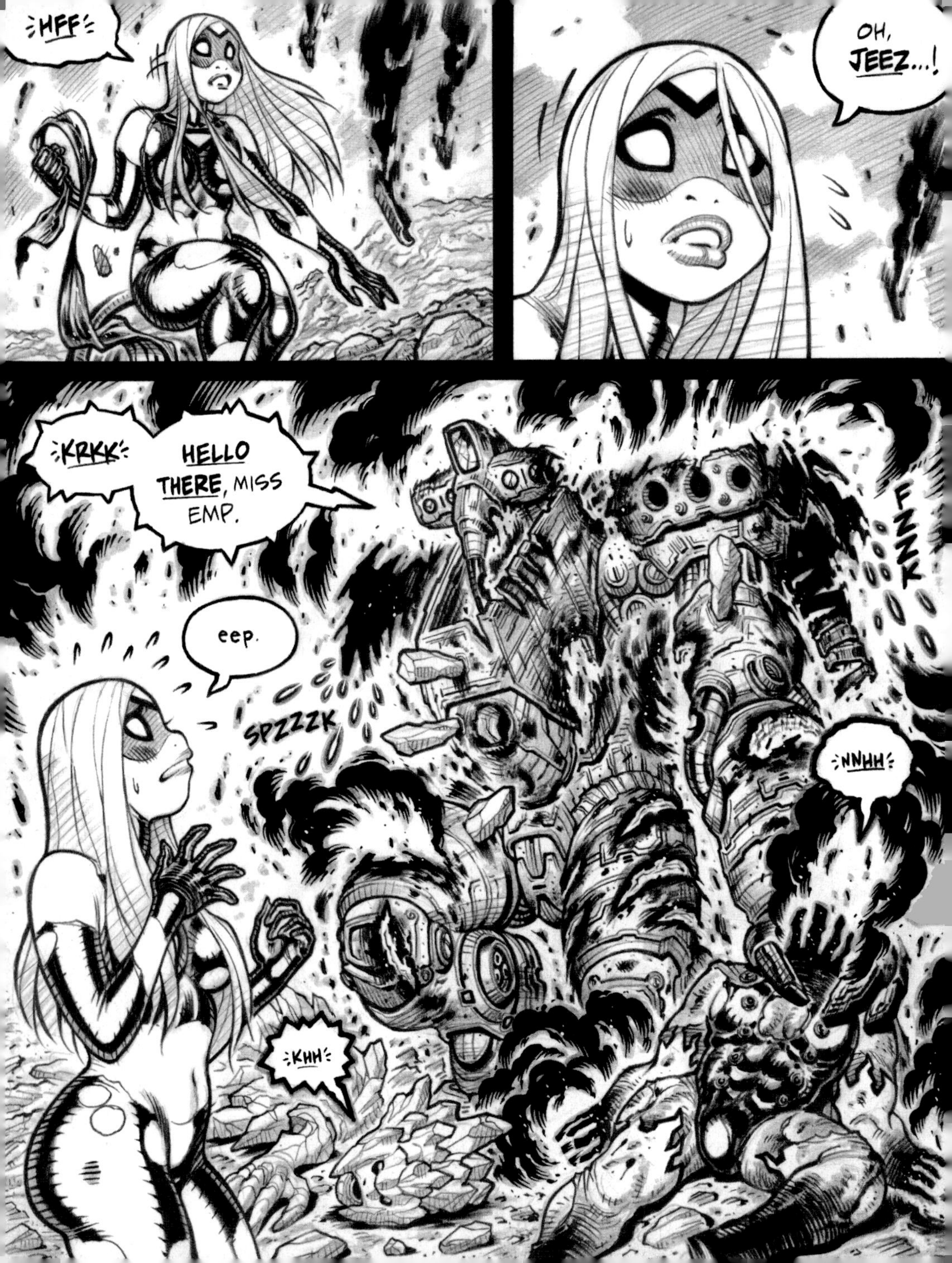
HFF
OH, JEEZ...!
KRKK
HELLO THERE, MISS EMP.
FZZK
eep.
SPZZZK
NNHH
KHH

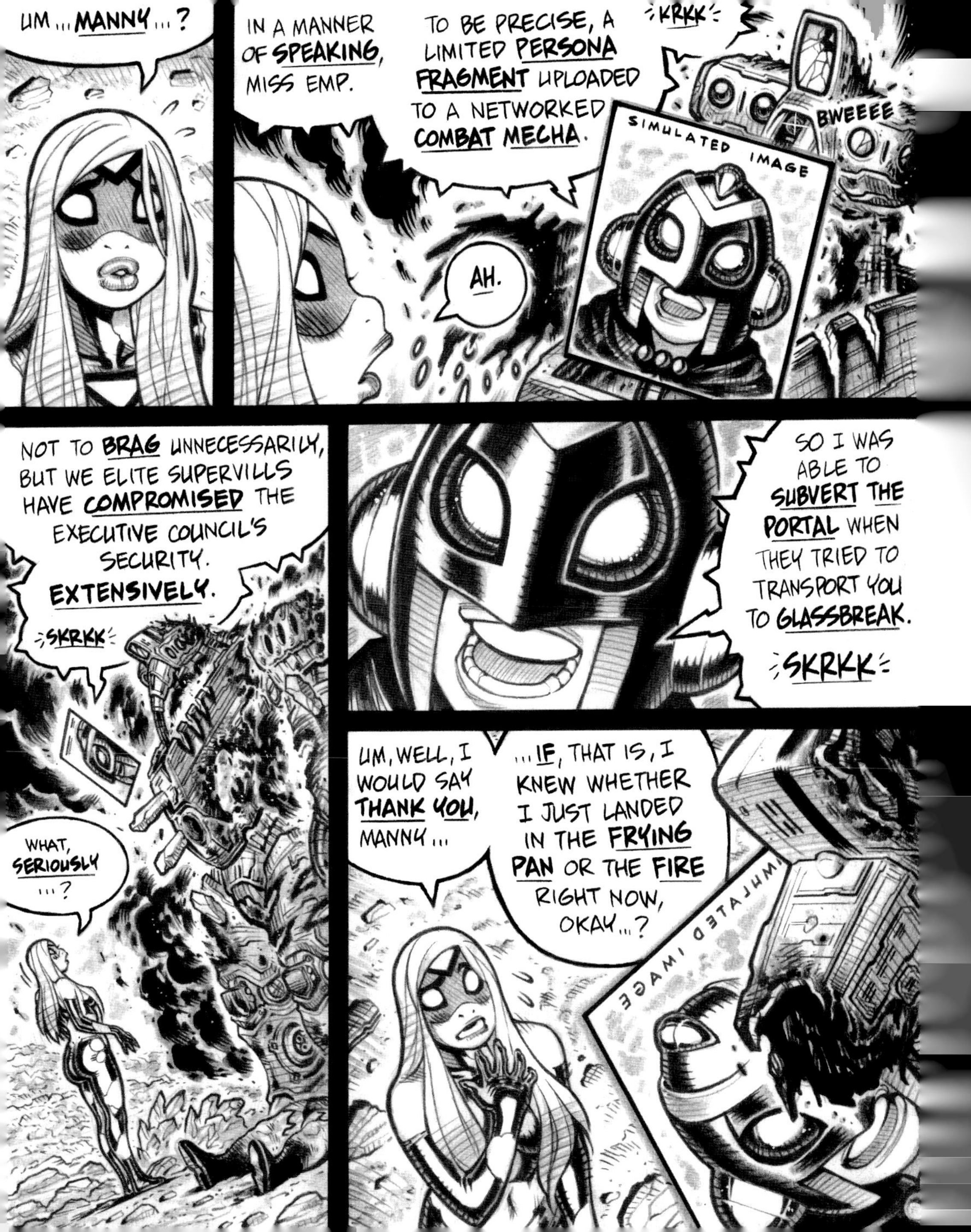
UM ... MANNY ... ?
IN A MANNER OF SPEAKING, MISS EMP.
TO BE PRECISE, A LIMITED PERSONA FRAGMENT UPLOADED TO A NETWORKED COMBAT MECHA.
KRKK
BWEEEE
SIMULATED IMAGE
AH.
NOT TO BRAG UNNECESSARILY, BUT WE ELITE SUPERVILLS HAVE COMPROMISED THE EXECUTIVE COUNCIL'S SECURITY. EXTENSIVELY.
SKRKK
SO I WAS ABLE TO SUBVERT THE PORTAL WHEN THEY TRIED TO TRANSPORT YOU TO GLASSBREAK.
SKRKK
WHAT, SERIOUSLY ...?
UM, WELL, I WOULD SAY THANK YOU, MANNY ...
... IF, THAT IS, I KNEW WHETHER I JUST LANDED IN THE FRYING PAN OR THE FIRE RIGHT NOW, OKAY ...?
SIMULATED IMAGE

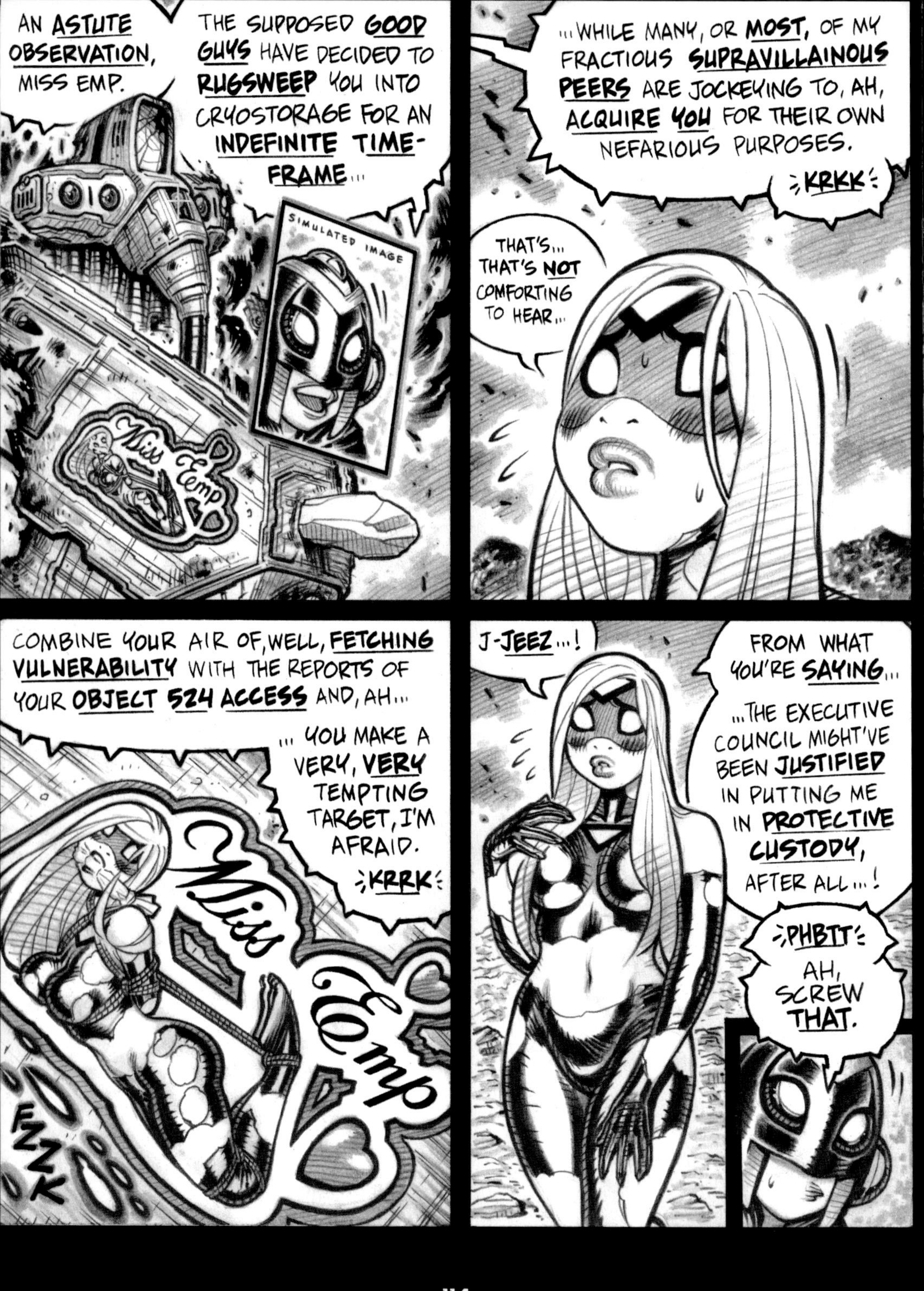

AN ASTUTE OBSERVATION, MISS EMP.
THE SUPPOSED GOOD GUYS HAVE DECIDED TO RUGSWEEP YOU INTO CRYOSTORAGE FOR AN INDEFINITE TIME-FRAME...
SIMULATED IMAGE
Miss Emp
...WHILE MANY, OR MOST, OF MY FRACTIOUS SUPRAVILLAINOUS PEERS ARE JOCKEYING TO, AH, ACQUIRE YOU FOR THEIR OWN NEFARIOUS PURPOSES.
KRKK
THAT'S... THAT'S NOT COMFORTING TO HEAR...
COMBINE YOUR AIR OF, WELL, FETCHING VULNERABILITY WITH THE REPORTS OF YOUR OBJECT 524 ACCESS AND, AH...
...YOU MAKE A VERY, VERY TEMPTING TARGET, I'M AFRAID.
KRRK
Miss Emp
FZZK
J-JEEZ...!
FROM WHAT YOU'RE SAYING...
...THE EXECUTIVE COUNCIL MIGHT'VE BEEN JUSTIFIED IN PUTTING ME IN PROTECTIVE CUSTODY, AFTER ALL...!
PHBTT
AH, SCREW THAT.

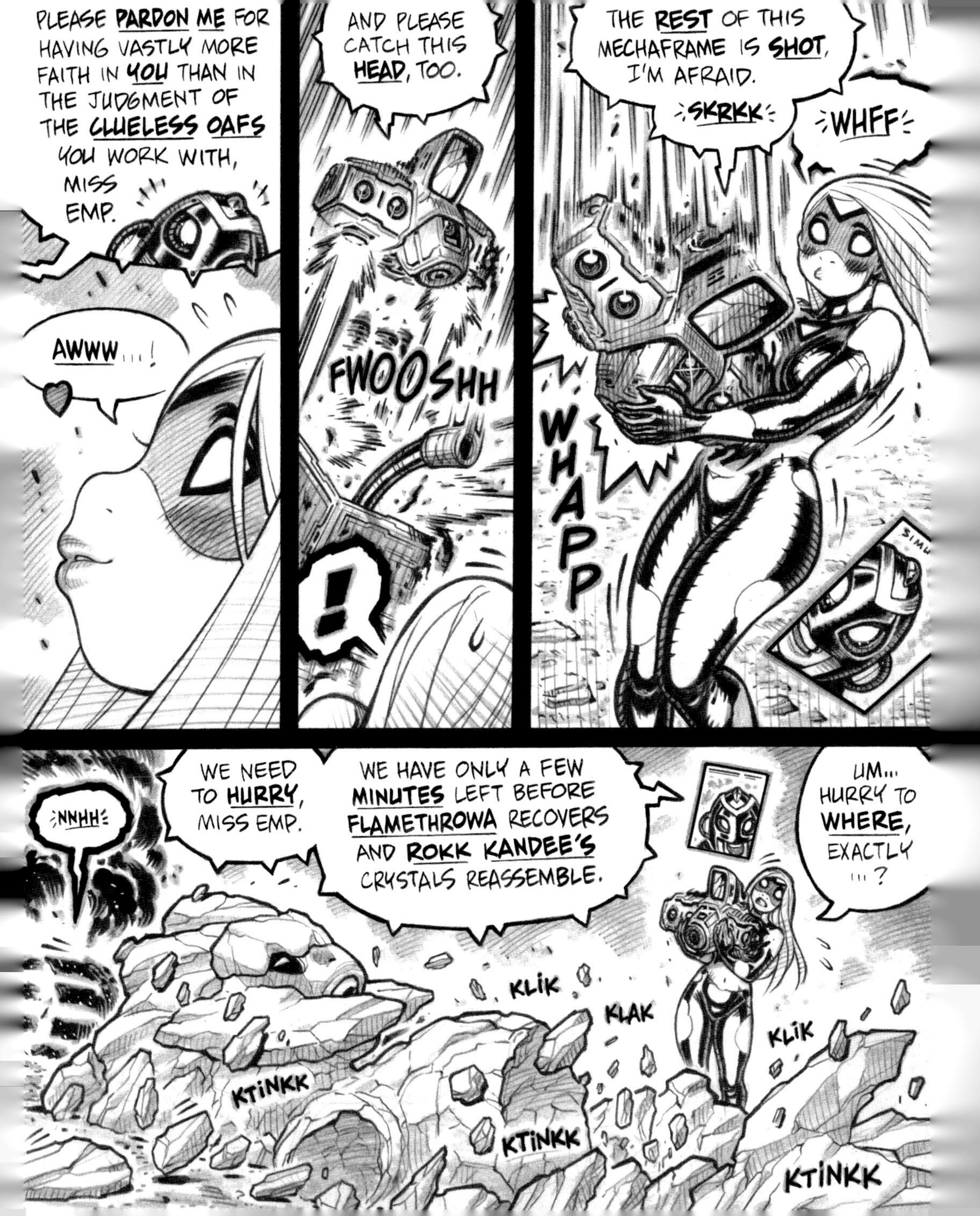
PLEASE PARDON ME FOR HAVING VASTLY MORE FAITH IN YOU THAN IN THE JUDGMENT OF THE CLUELESS OAFS YOU WORK WITH, MISS EMP.
AWWW...!
AND PLEASE CATCH THIS HEAD, TOO.
FWOOSHH
!
THE REST OF THIS MECHAFRAME IS SHOT, I'M AFRAID.
SKRKK
WHFF
WHAPP
NNHH
WE NEED TO HURRY, MISS EMP.
WE HAVE ONLY A FEW MINUTES LEFT BEFORE FLAMETHROWA RECOVERS AND ROKK KANDEE'S CRYSTALS REASSEMBLE.
UM... HURRY TO WHERE, EXACTLY...?
KLIK
KLAK
KLIK
KTINKK
KTINKK
KTINKK

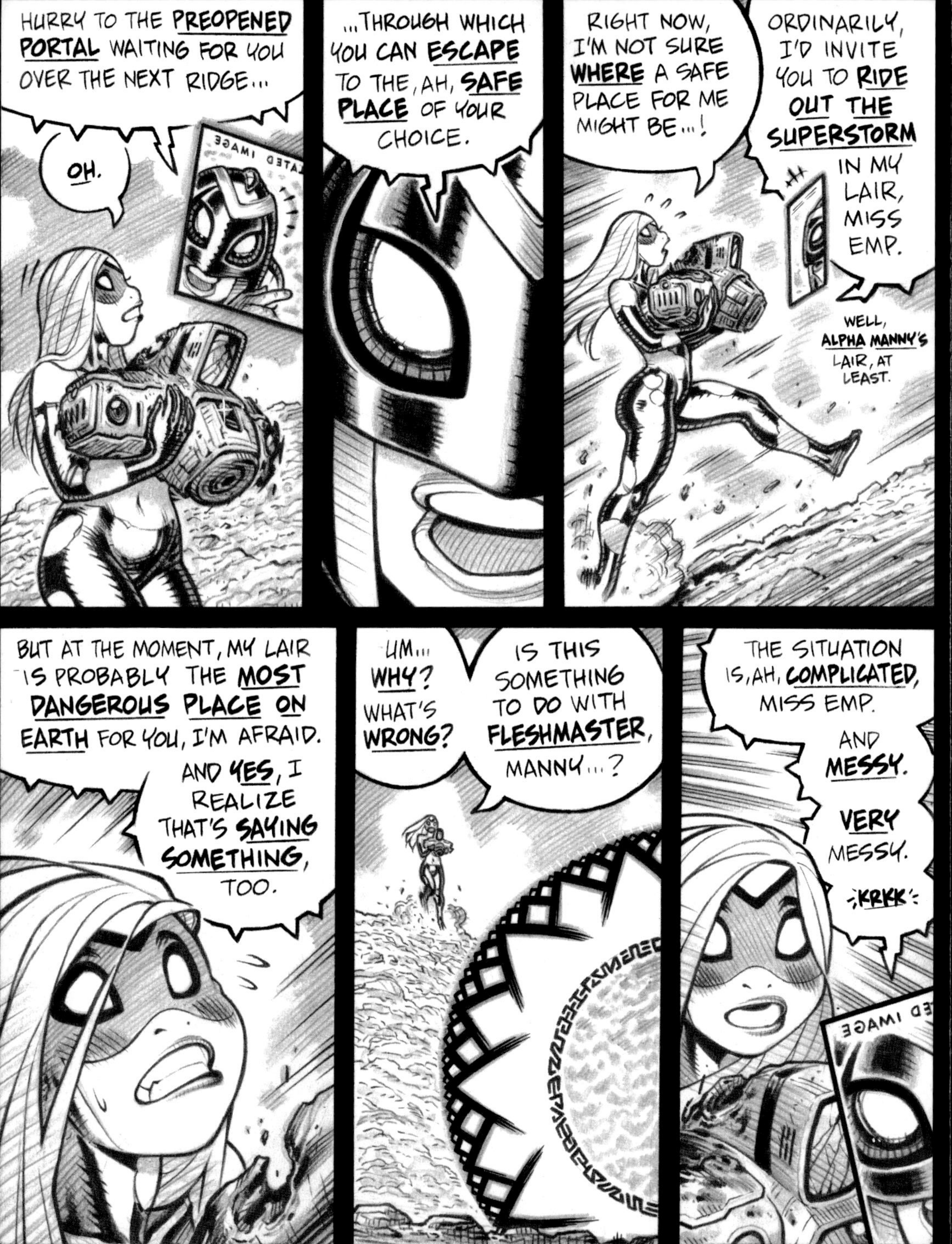
HURRY TO THE PREOPENED PORTAL WAITING FOR YOU OVER THE NEXT RIDGE...
OH.
...THROUGH WHICH YOU CAN ESCAPE TO THE, AH, SAFE PLACE OF YOUR CHOICE.
RIGHT NOW, I'M NOT SURE WHERE A SAFE PLACE FOR ME MIGHT BE...!
ORDINARILY, I'D INVITE YOU TO RIDE OUT THE SUPERSTORM IN MY LAIR, MISS EMP.
WELL, ALPHA MANNY'S LAIR, AT LEAST.
BUT AT THE MOMENT, MY LAIR IS PROBABLY THE MOST DANGEROUS PLACE ON EARTH FOR YOU, I'M AFRAID.
AND YES, I REALIZE THAT'S SAYING SOMETHING, TOO.
UM... WHY? WHAT'S WRONG?
IS THIS SOMETHING TO DO WITH FLESHMASTER, MANNY...?
THE SITUATION IS, AH, COMPLICATED, MISS EMP.
AND MESSY.
VERY MESSY.
KRKK

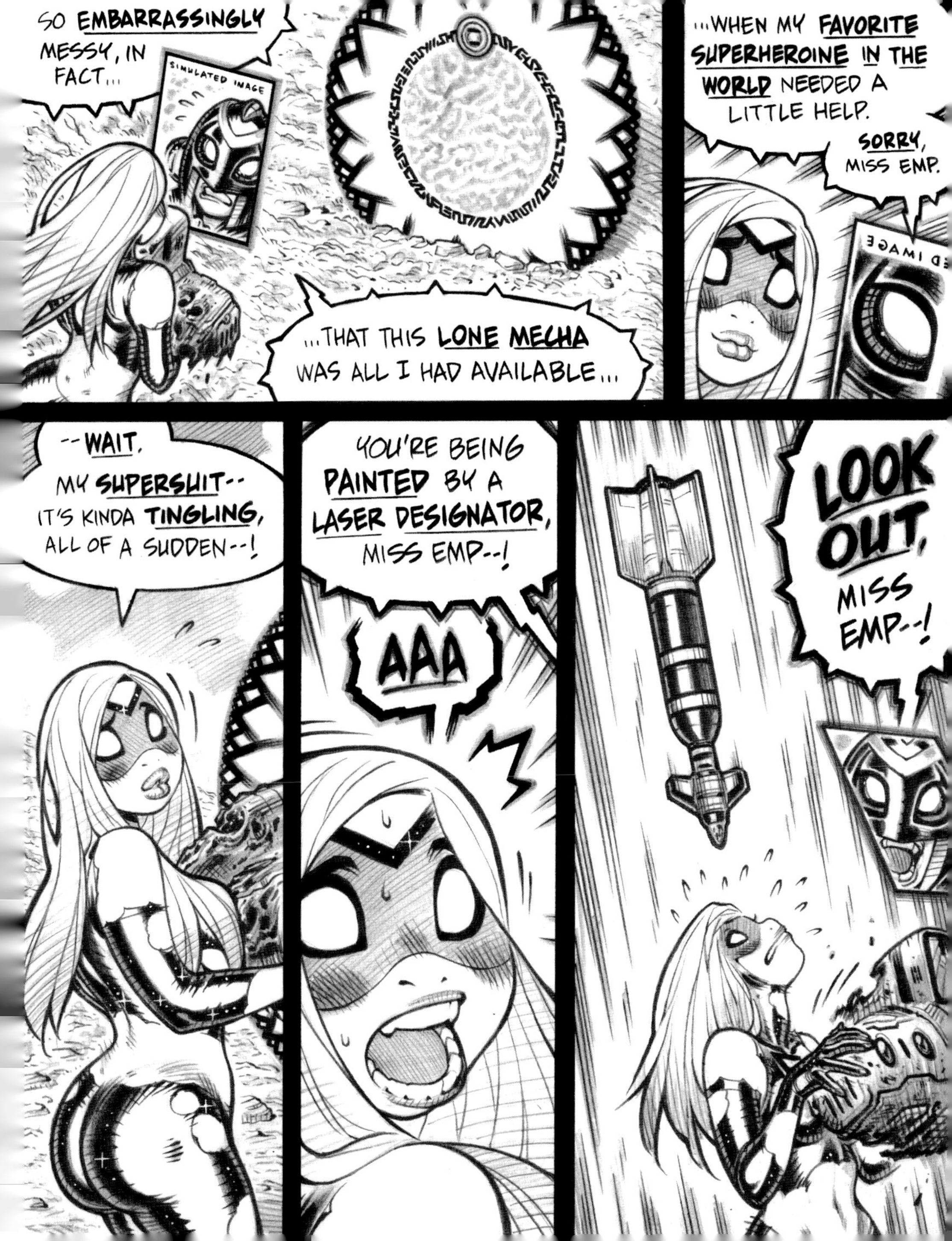

SO EMBARRASSINGLY MESSY, IN FACT...
SIMULATED IMAGE
...THAT THIS LONE MECHA WAS ALL I HAD AVAILABLE...
...WHEN MY FAVORITE SUPERHEROINE IN THE WORLD NEEDED A LITTLE HELP.
SORRY, MISS EMP.
--WAIT. MY SUPERSUIT-- IT'S KINDA TINGLING, ALL OF A SUDDEN--!
YOU'RE BEING PAINTED BY A LASER DESIGNATOR, MISS EMP--!
AAA
LOOK OUT, MISS EMP--!

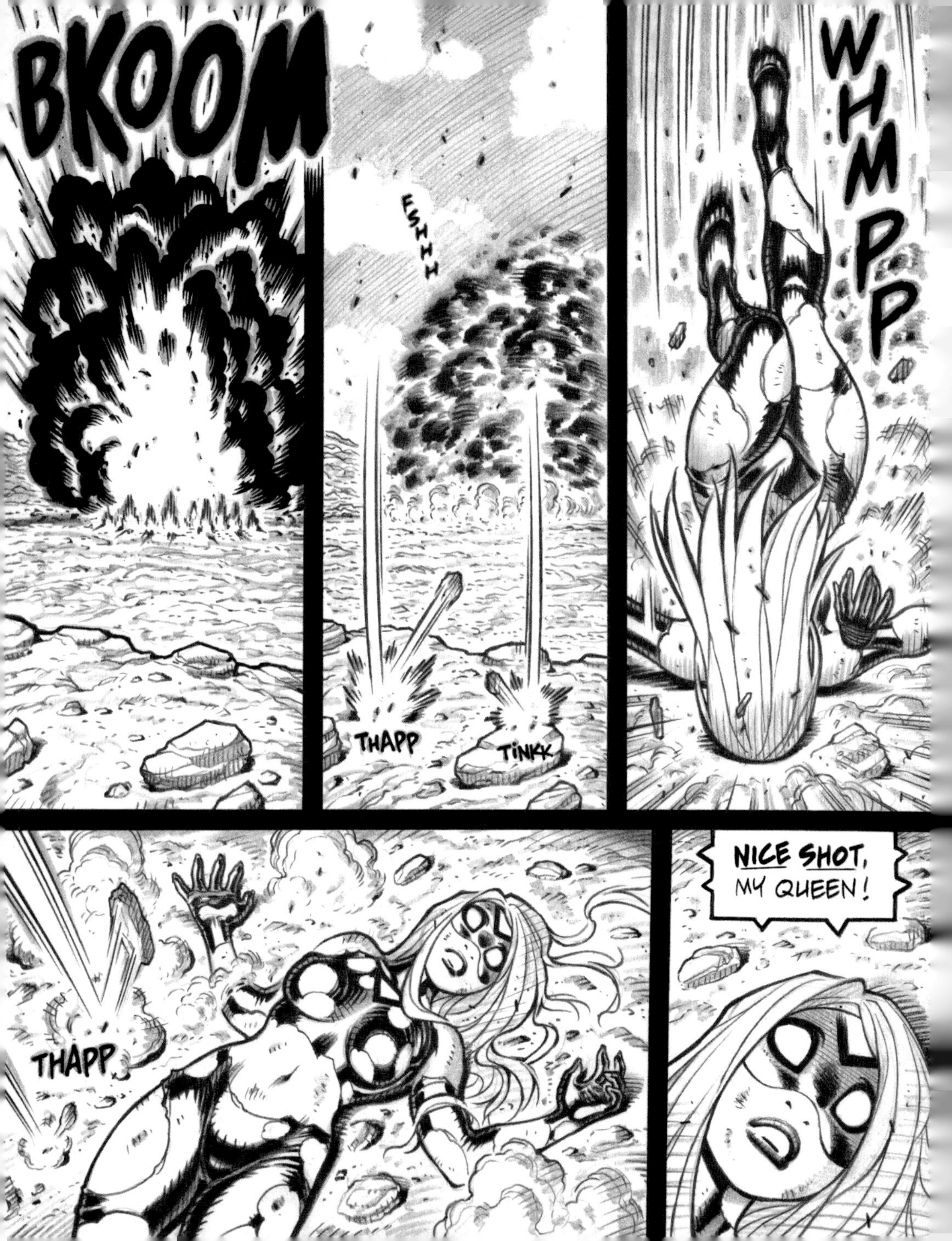
BKOOM
FSHHH
THAPP
TINKK
WHMPP
THAPP
NICE SHOT, MY QUEEN!

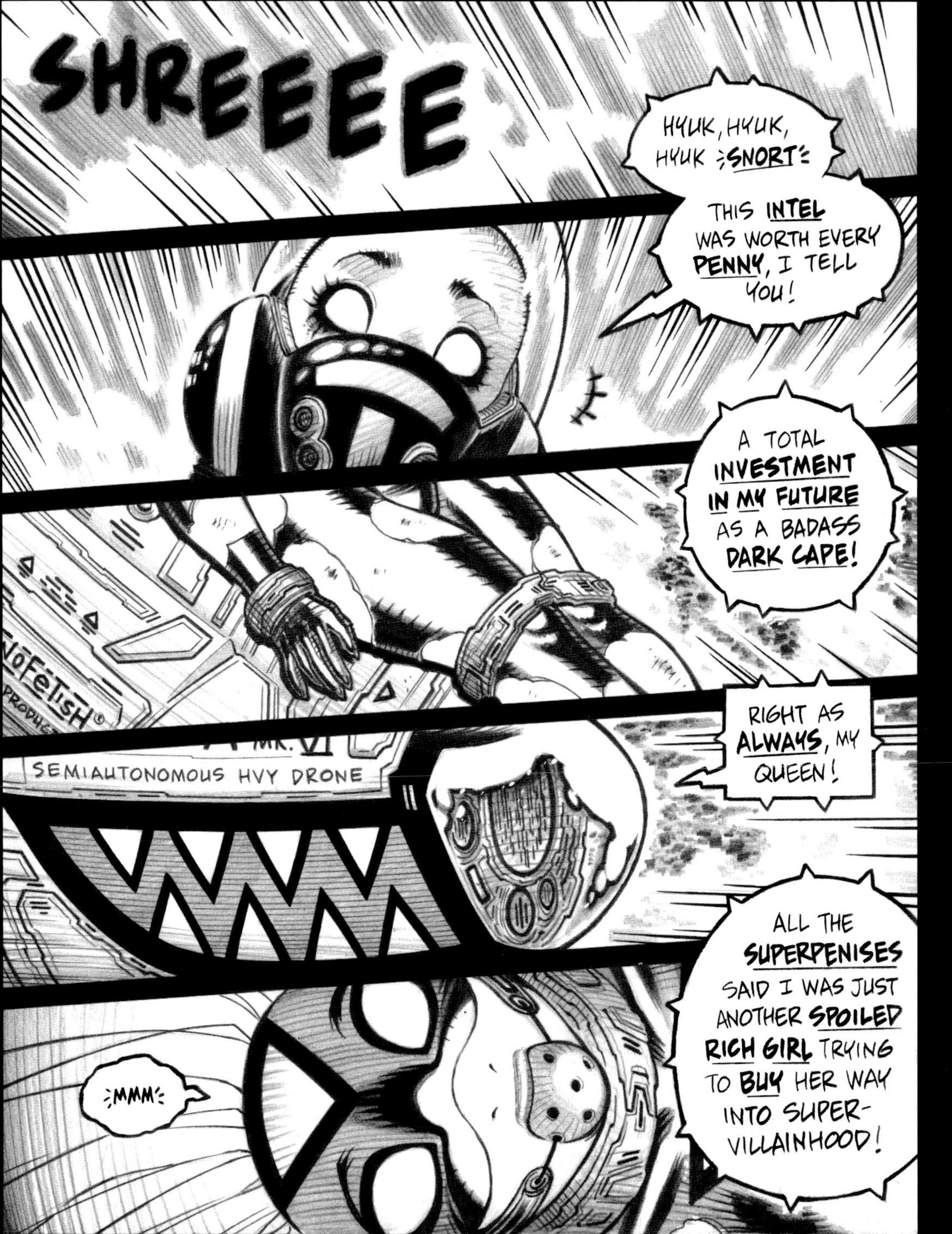
SHREEEEE
HYUK, HYUK, HYUK ⁞SNORT⁞
THIS INTEL WAS WORTH EVERY PENNY, I TELL YOU!
A TOTAL INVESTMENT IN MY FUTURE AS A BADASS DARK CAPE!
SEMIAUTONOMOUS HVY DRONE
RIGHT AS ALWAYS, MY QUEEN!
ALL THE SUPERPENISES SAID I WAS JUST ANOTHER SPOILED RICH GIRL TRYING TO BUY HER WAY INTO SUPER-VILLAINHOOD!
⁞MMM⁞

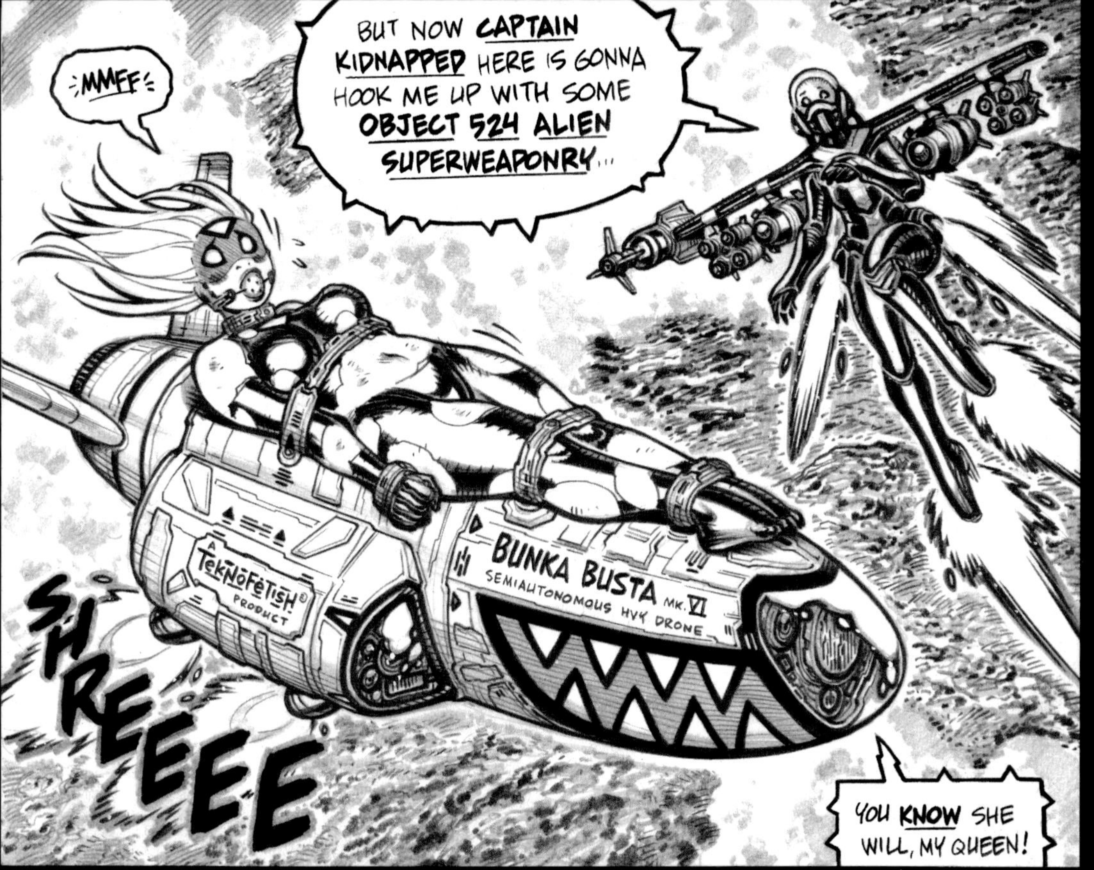

MMFF
BUT NOW CAPTAIN KIDNAPPED HERE IS GONNA HOOK ME UP WITH SOME OBJECT 524 ALIEN SUPERWEAPONRY...
A TEKNOFETISH® PRODUCT
BUNKA BUSTA MK. VI SEMIAUTONOMOUS HVY DRONE
SHREEEEE
YOU KNOW SHE WILL, MY QUEEN!

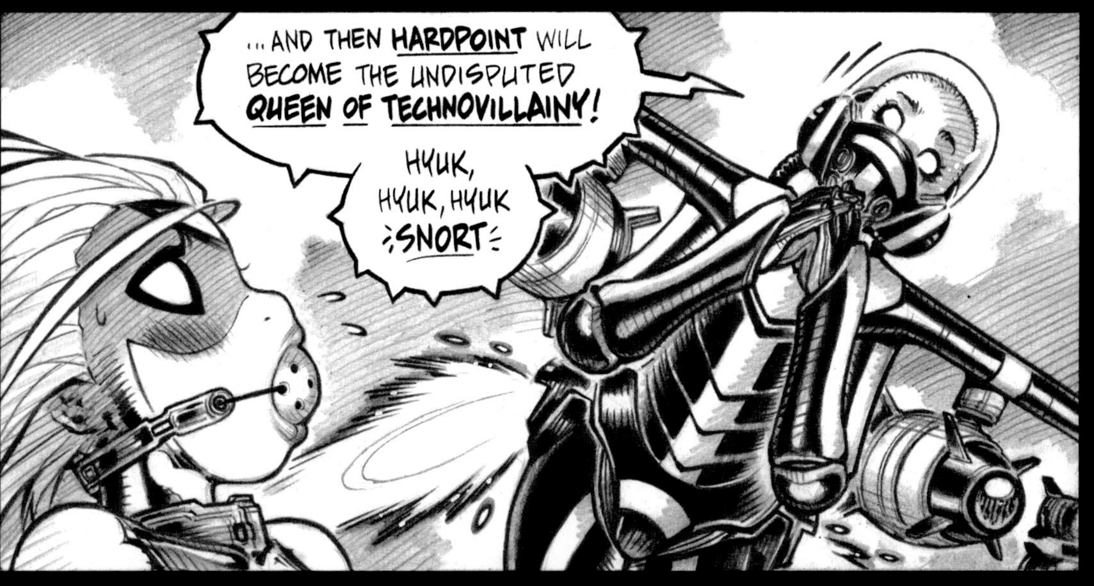

...AND THEN HARDPOINT WILL BECOME THE UNDISPUTED QUEEN OF TECHNOVILLAINY!
HYUK, HYUK, HYUK SNORT

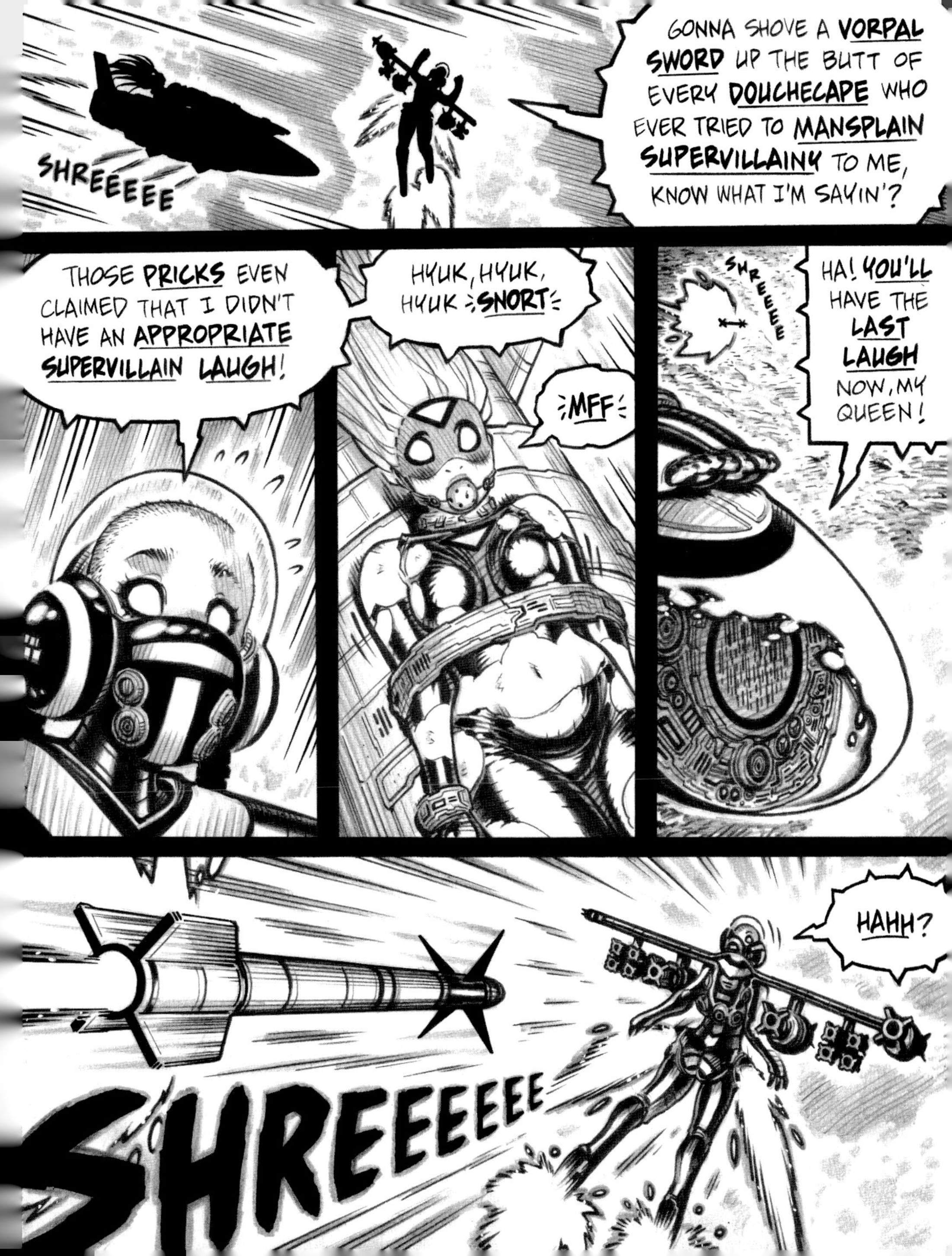
SHREEEEEE
GONNA SHOVE A VORPAL SWORD UP THE BUTT OF EVERY DOUCHECAPE WHO EVER TRIED TO MANSPLAIN SUPERVILLAINY TO ME, KNOW WHAT I'M SAYIN'?
THOSE PRICKS EVEN CLAIMED THAT I DIDN'T HAVE AN APPROPRIATE SUPERVILLAIN LAUGH!
HYUK, HYUK, HYUK SNORT
MFF
SHREEEEE
HA! YOU'LL HAVE THE LAST LAUGH NOW, MY QUEEN!
HAHH?
SHREEEEEEE

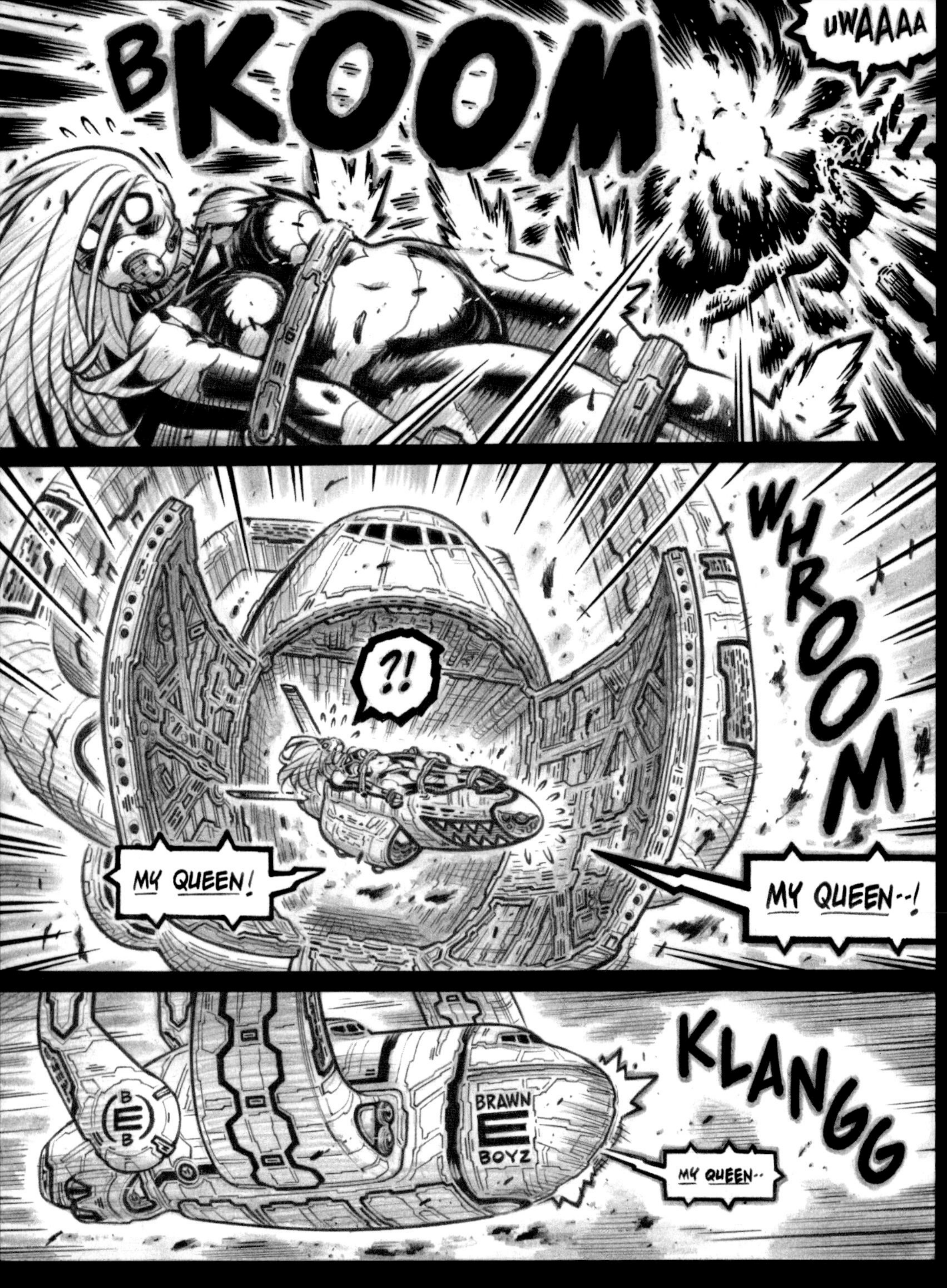
BKOOM
UWAAAA
WHROOOM
?!
MY QUEEN!
MY QUEEN--!
KLANGG
BRAWN
BOYZ
MY QUEEN--

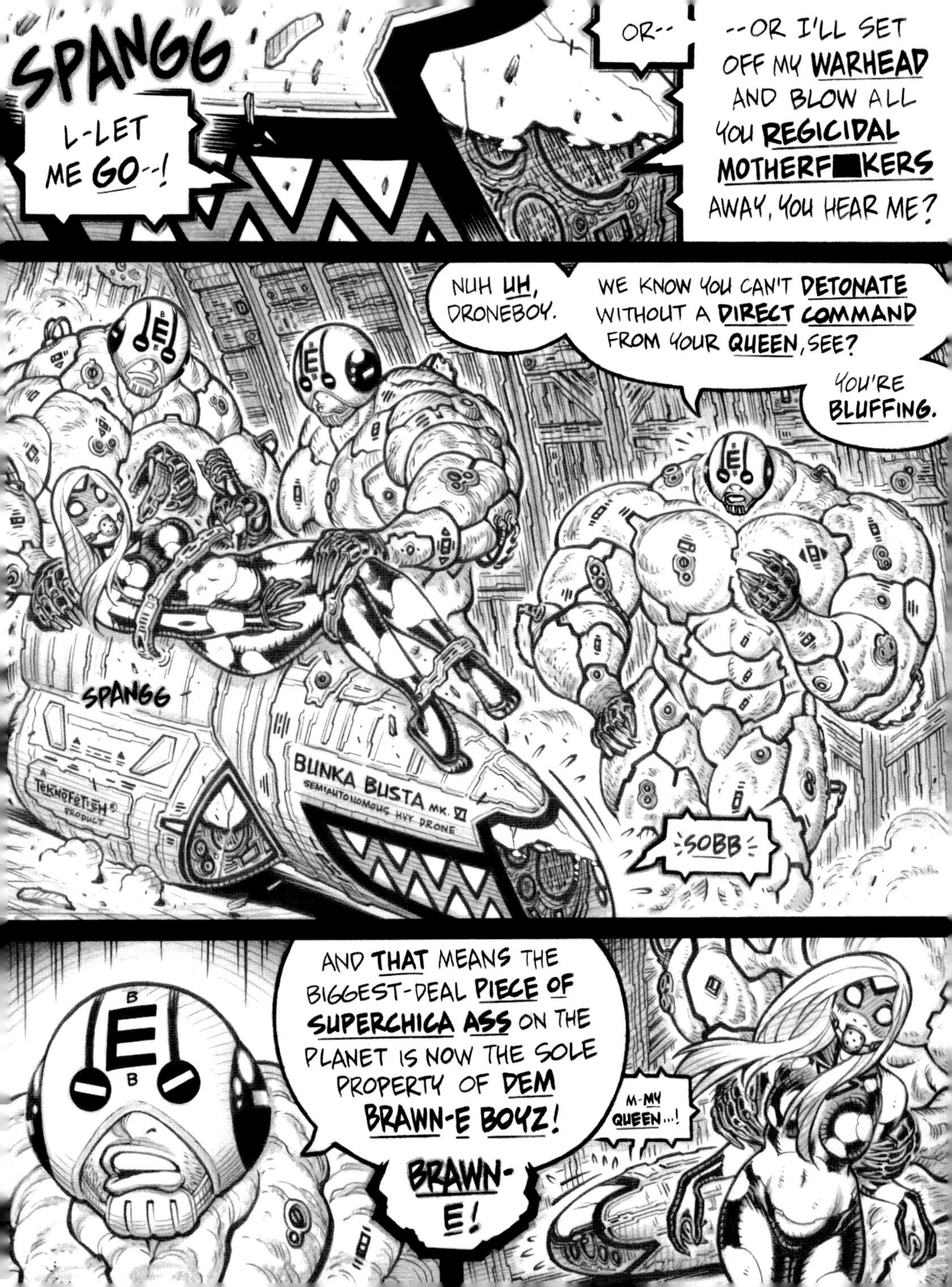
SPANGG
L-LET ME GO--!
OR--
--OR I'LL SET OFF MY WARHEAD AND BLOW ALL YOU REGICIDAL MOTHERF[redacted]KERS AWAY, YOU HEAR ME?
NUH UH, DRONEBOY.
WE KNOW YOU CAN'T DETONATE WITHOUT A DIRECT COMMAND FROM YOUR QUEEN, SEE?
YOU'RE BLUFFING.
SPANGG
A TEKNOFETISH® PRODUCT
BUNKA BUSTA MK. VI
SEMIAUTONOMOUS HVY DRONE
SOBB
AND THAT MEANS THE BIGGEST-DEAL PIECE OF SUPERCHICA ASS ON THE PLANET IS NOW THE SOLE PROPERTY OF DEM BRAWN-E BOYZ!
BRAWN-E!
M-MY QUEEN...!

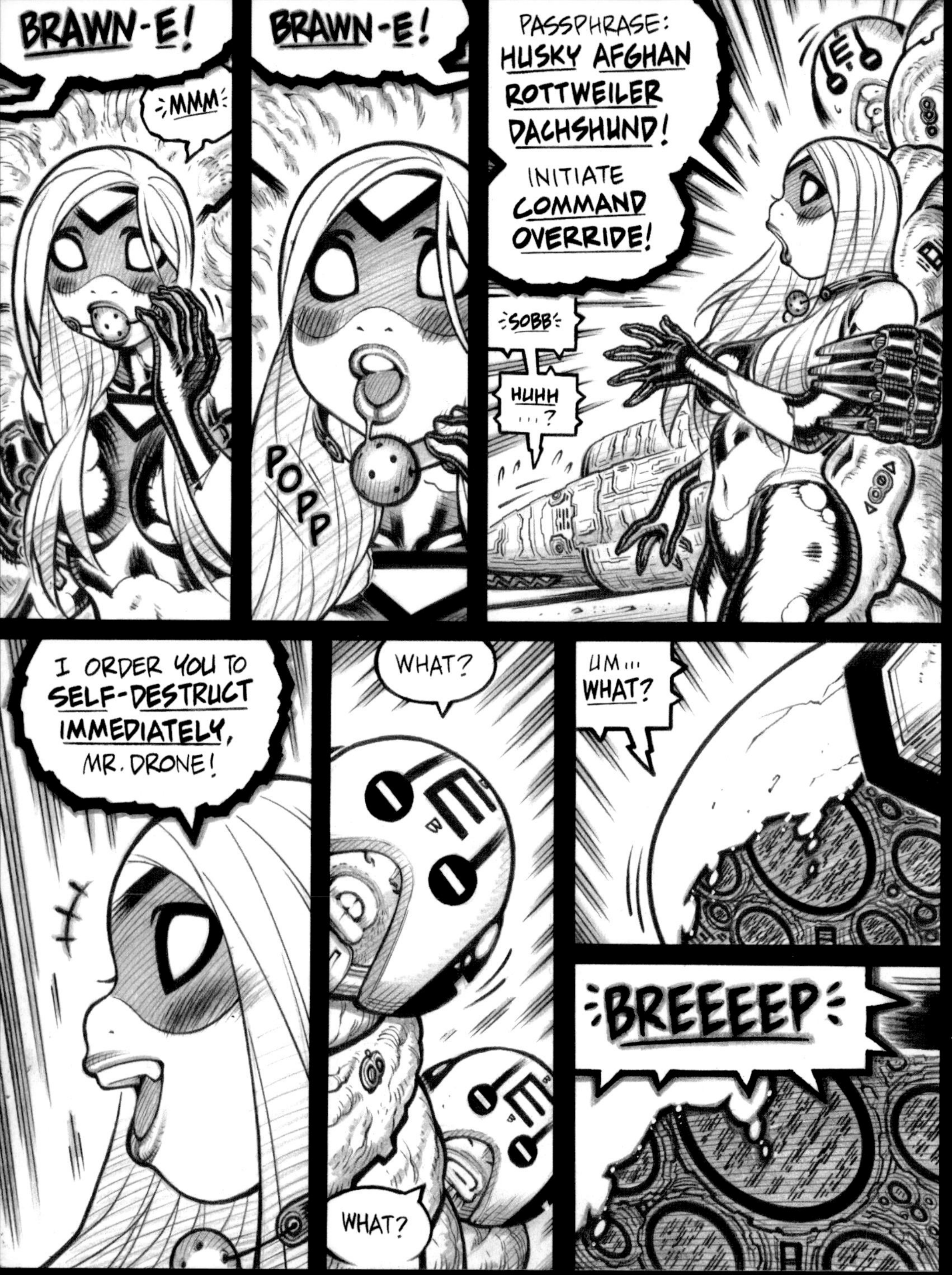
BRAWN-E!
MMM
BRAWN-E!
POPP
PASSPHRASE: HUSKY AFGHAN ROTTWEILER DACHSHUND!
INITIATE COMMAND OVERRIDE!
SOBB
HUHH ...?
I ORDER YOU TO SELF-DESTRUCT IMMEDIATELY, MR. DRONE!
WHAT?
WHAT?
UM... WHAT?
BREEEEP

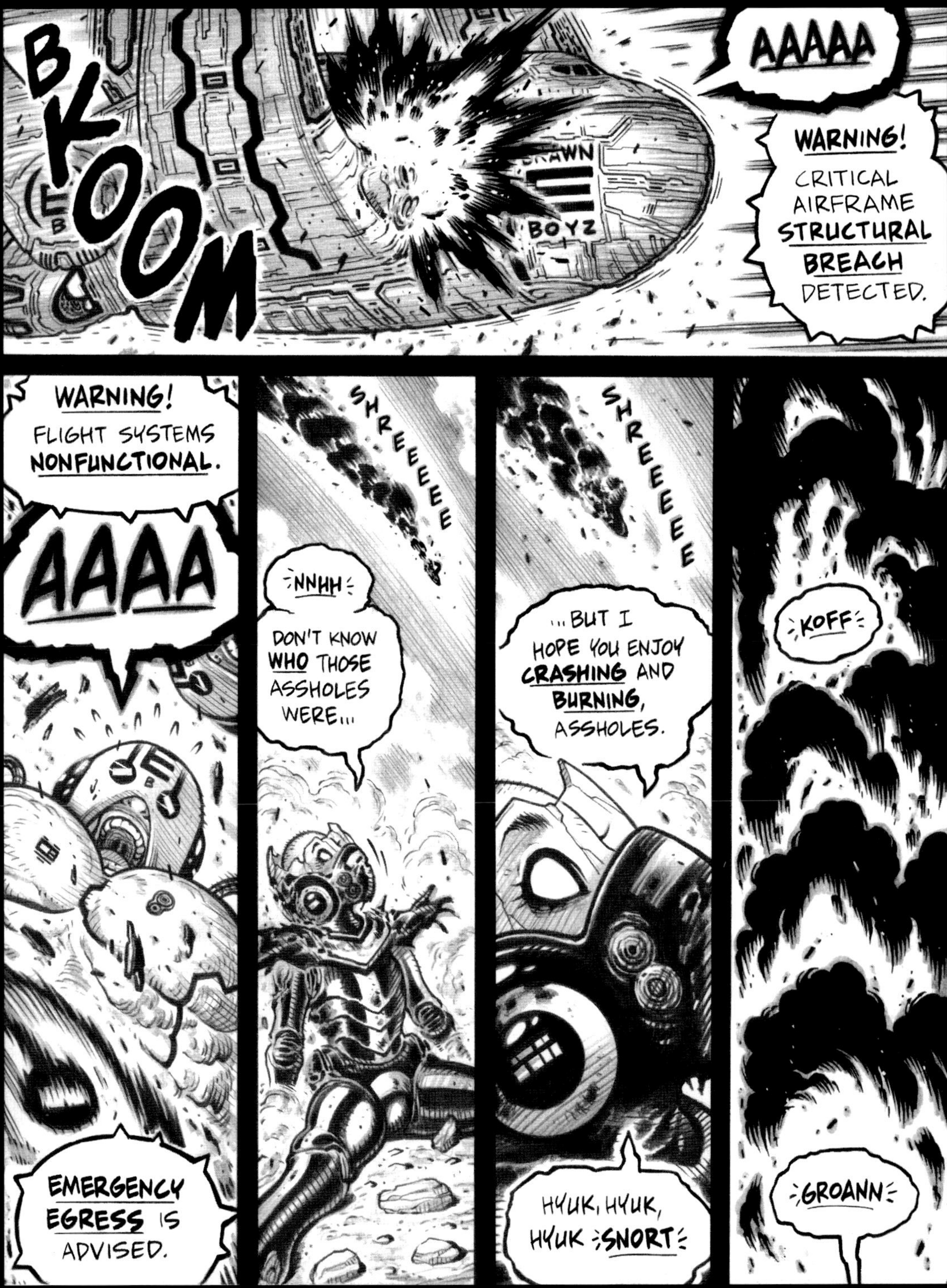
BKOOM
BRAWN BOYZ
AAAAA
WARNING! CRITICAL AIRFRAME STRUCTURAL BREACH DETECTED.
WARNING! FLIGHT SYSTEMS NONFUNCTIONAL.
AAAA
EMERGENCY EGRESS IS ADVISED.
SHREEEEEE
NNHH
DON'T KNOW WHO THOSE ASSHOLES WERE...
SHREEEEEEE
...BUT I HOPE YOU ENJOY CRASHING AND BURNING, ASSHOLES.
HYUK, HYUK, HYUK SNORT
KOFF
GROANN

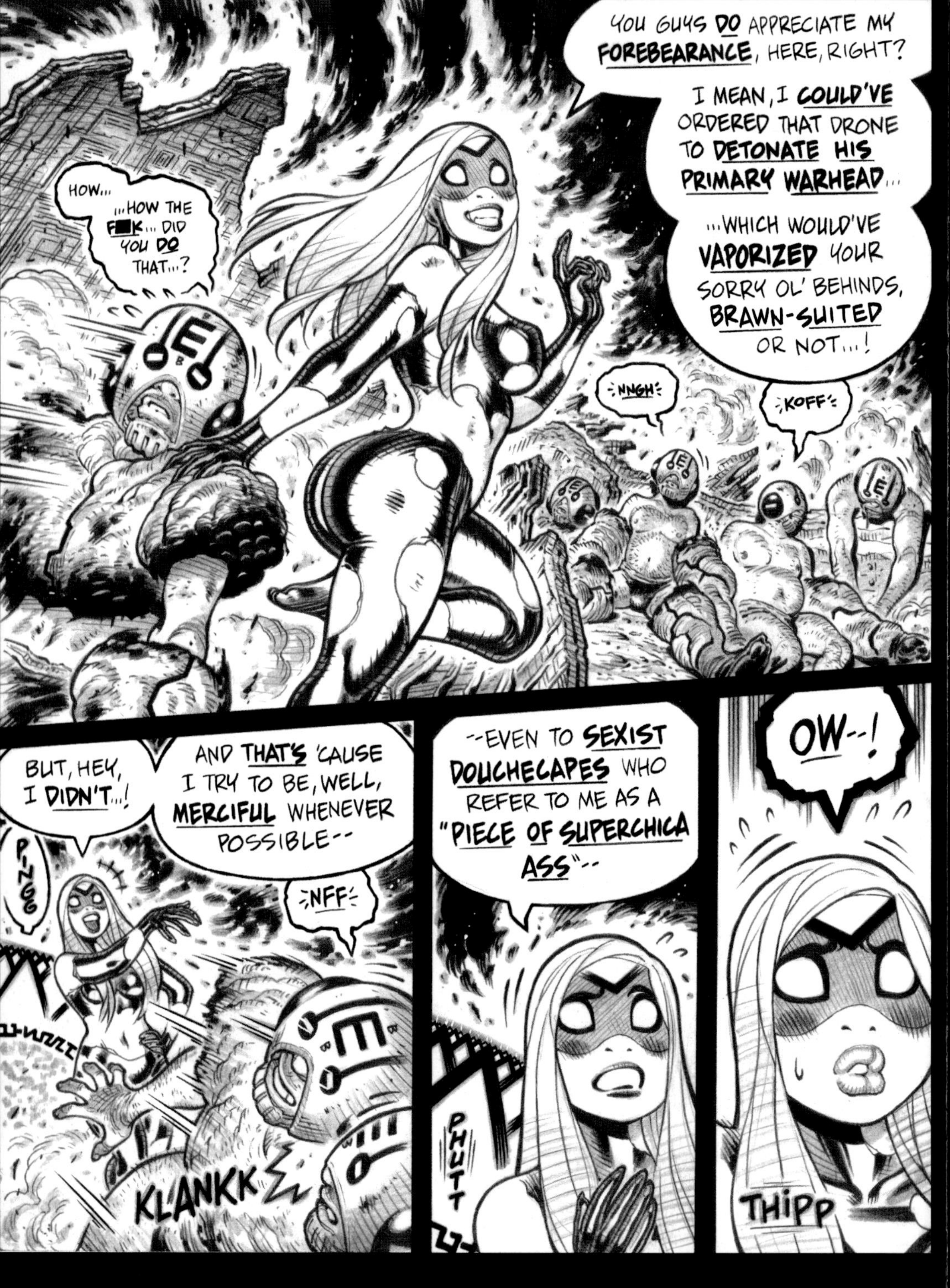
YOU GUYS DO APPRECIATE MY FOREBEARANCE, HERE, RIGHT?
I MEAN, I COULD'VE ORDERED THAT DRONE TO DETONATE HIS PRIMARY WARHEAD...
...WHICH WOULD'VE VAPORIZED YOUR SORRY OL' BEHINDS, BRAWN-SUITED OR NOT...!
HOW... ...HOW THE F[redacted]K... DID YOU DO THAT...?
NNGH
KOFF
BUT, HEY, I DIDN'T...!
AND THAT'S 'CAUSE I TRY TO BE, WELL, MERCIFUL WHENEVER POSSIBLE--
PINGG
NFF
KLANKK
--EVEN TO SEXIST DOUCHECAPES WHO REFER TO ME AS A "PIECE OF SUPERCHICA ASS"--
PHUTT
OW--!
THIPP

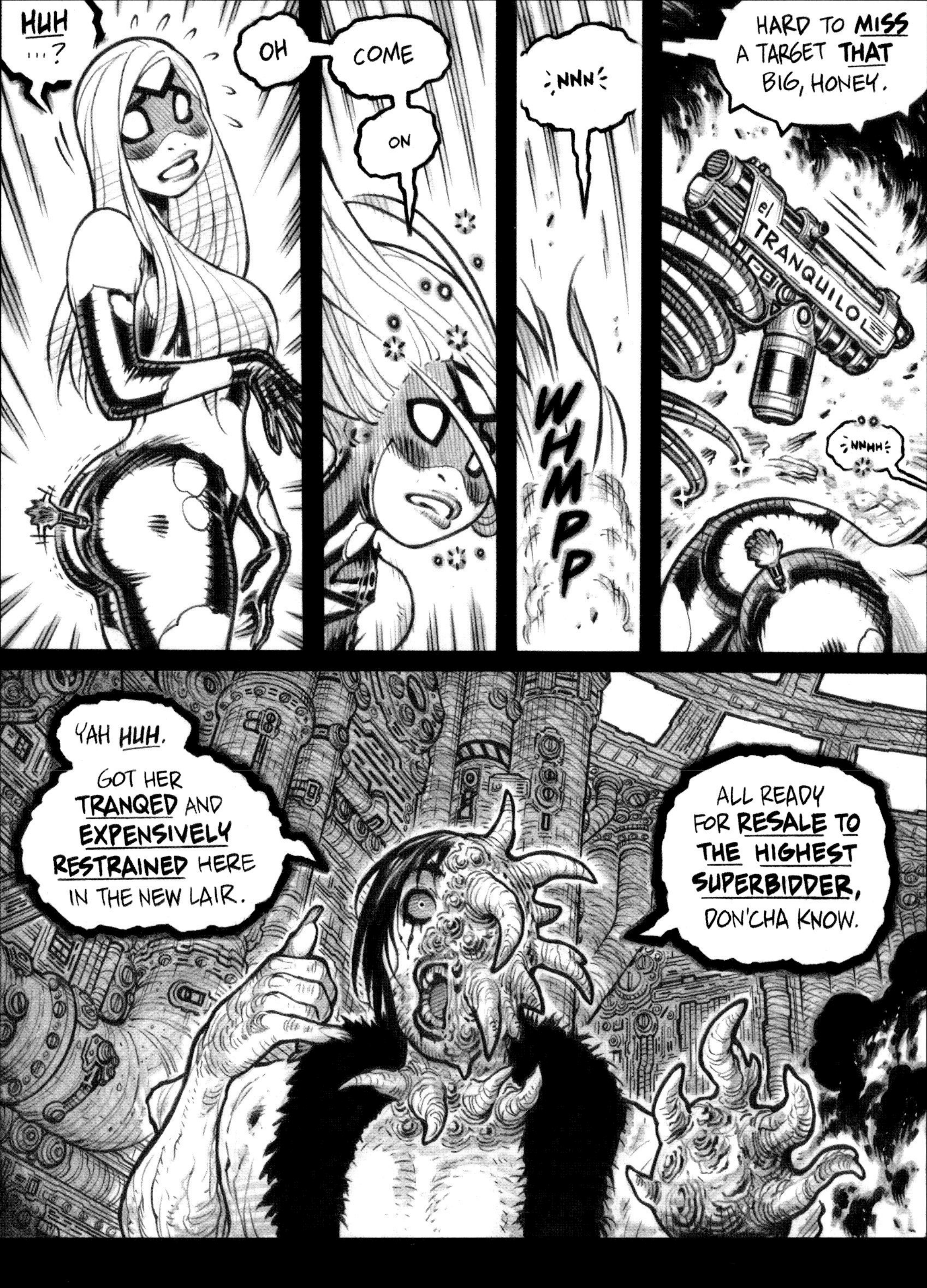
HUH ...?
OH
COME
ON
NNN
WHMPP
HARD TO MISS A TARGET THAT BIG, HONEY.
TRANQUILOL
NNMH
YAH HUH.
GOT HER TRANQED AND EXPENSIVELY RESTRAINED HERE IN THE NEW LAIR.
ALL READY FOR RESALE TO THE HIGHEST SUPERBIDDER, DON'CHA KNOW.

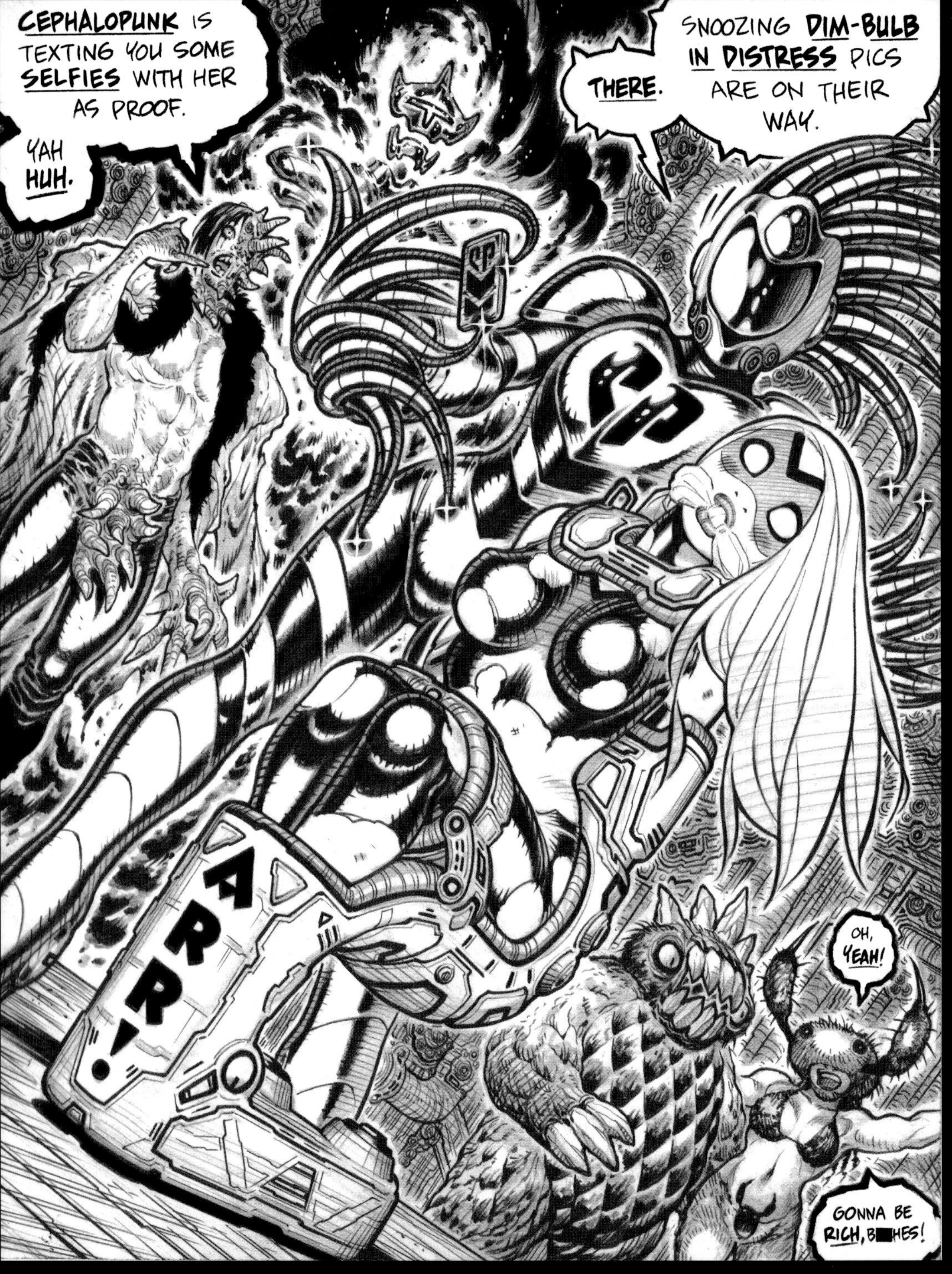
CEPHALOPUNK IS TEXTING YOU SOME SELFIES WITH HER AS PROOF.
YAH HUH.
THERE.
SNOOZING DIM-BULB IN DISTRESS PICS ARE ON THEIR WAY.
ARR!
OH, YEAH!
GONNA BE RICH, B[redacted]HES!

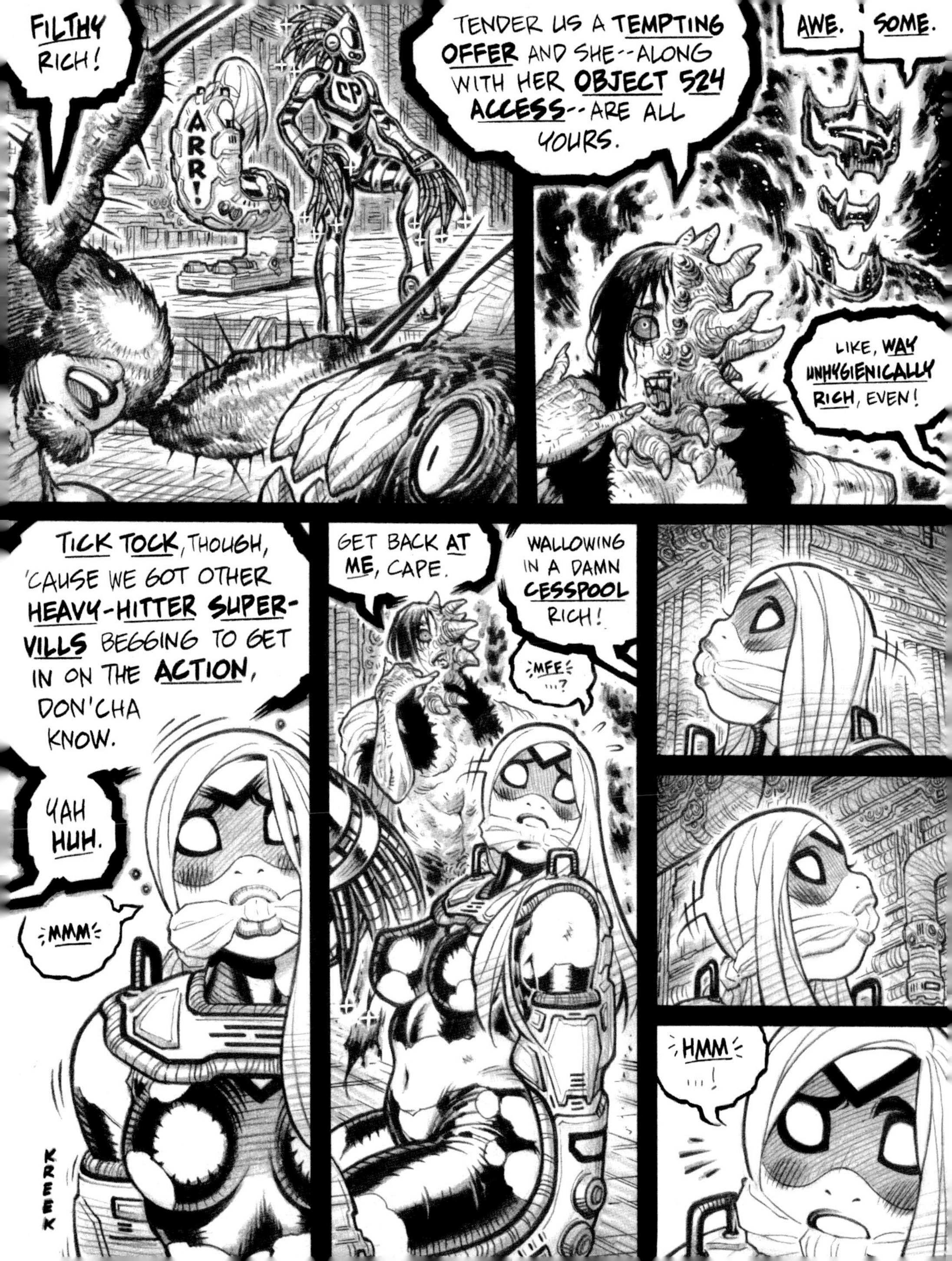

FILTHY RICH!
ARR!
TENDER US A TEMPTING OFFER AND SHE--ALONG WITH HER OBJECT 524 ACCESS--ARE ALL YOURS.
AWE.
SOME.
LIKE, WAY UNHYGIENICALLY RICH, EVEN!
TICK TOCK, THOUGH, 'CAUSE WE GOT OTHER HEAVY-HITTER SUPER-VILLS BEGGING TO GET IN ON THE ACTION, DON'CHA KNOW.
YAH HUH.
MMM
GET BACK AT ME, CAPE.
WALLOWING IN A DAMN CESSPOOL RICH!
MFF ...?
HMM ...!
KREEK

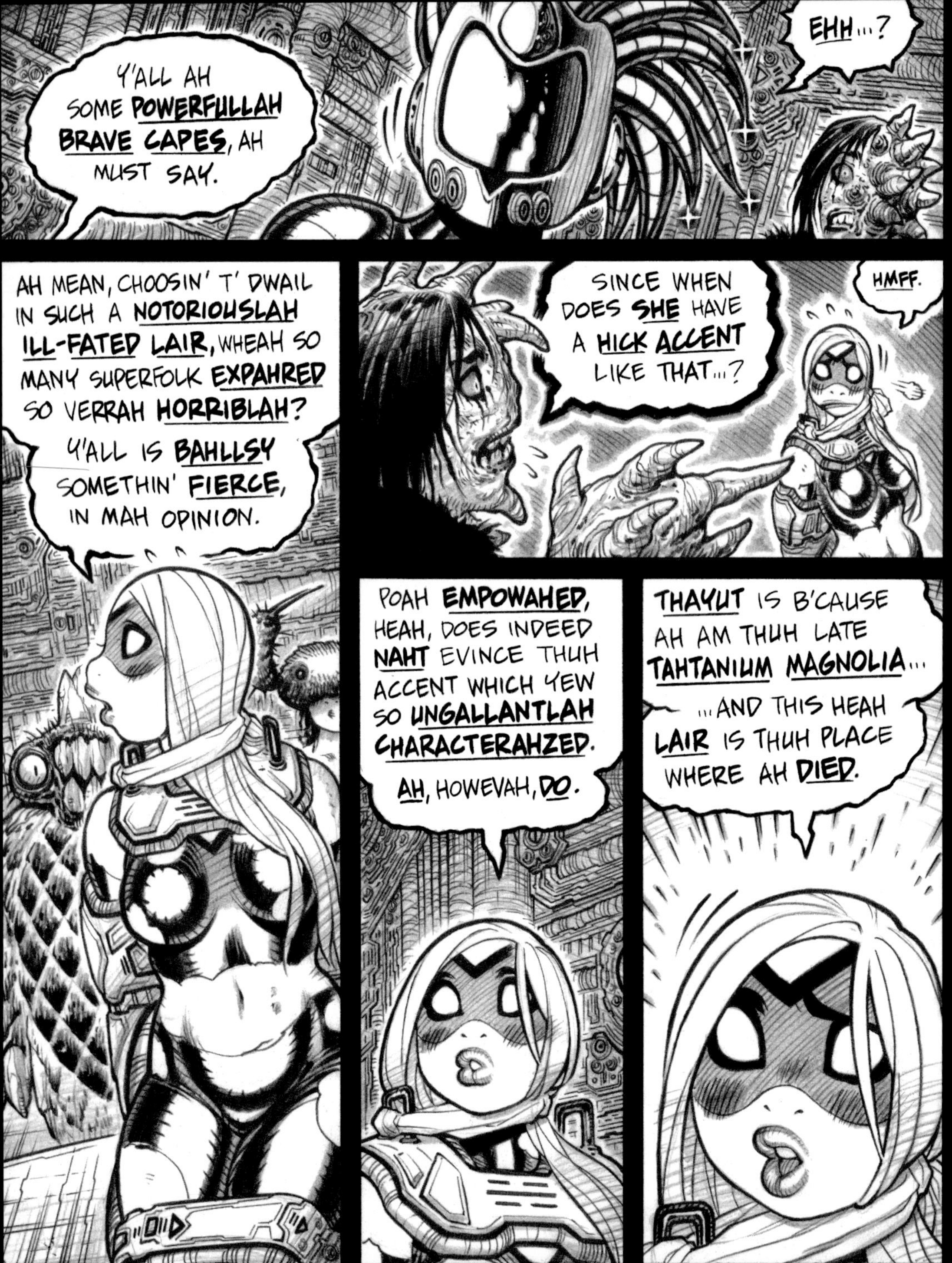
Y'ALL AH SOME POWERFULLAH BRAVE CAPES, AH MUST SAY.
EHH...?
AH MEAN, CHOOSIN' T' DWAIL IN SUCH A NOTORIOUSLAH ILL-FATED LAIR, WHEAH SO MANY SUPERFOLK EXPAHRED SO VERRAH HORRIBLAH?
Y'ALL IS BAHLLSY SOMETHIN' FIERCE, IN MAH OPINION.
SINCE WHEN DOES SHE HAVE A HICK ACCENT LIKE THAT...?
HMFF.
POAH EMPOWAHED, HEAH, DOES INDEED NAHT EVINCE THUH ACCENT WHICH YEW SO UNGALLANTLAH CHARACTERAHZED.
AH, HOWEVAH, DO.
THAYUT IS B'CAUSE AH AM THUH LATE TAHTANIUM MAGNOLIA...
...AND THIS HEAH LAIR IS THUH PLACE WHERE AH DIED.

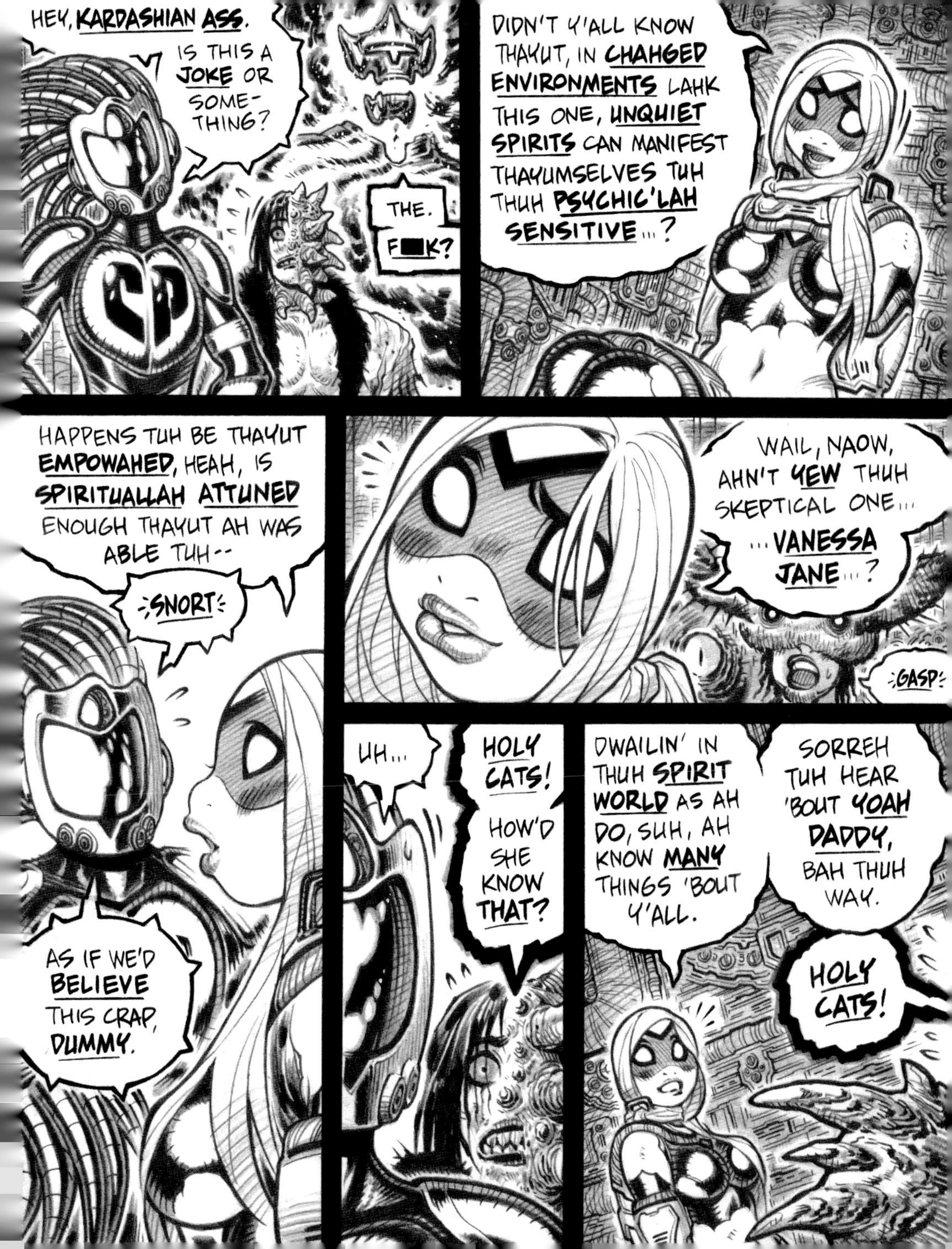
HEY, KARDASHIAN ASS.
IS THIS A JOKE OR SOME-THING?
THE.
F[redacted]K?
DIDN'T Y'ALL KNOW THAYUT, IN CHAHGED ENVIRONMENTS LAHK THIS ONE, UNQUIET SPIRITS CAN MANIFEST THAYUMSELVES TUH THUH PSYCHIC'LAH SENSITIVE...?
HAPPENS TUH BE THAYUT EMPOWAHED, HEAH, IS SPIRITUALLAH ATTUNED ENOUGH THAYUT AH WAS ABLE TUH--
SNORT
AS IF WE'D BELIEVE THIS CRAP, DUMMY.
WAIL, NAOW, AHN'T YEW THUH SKEPTICAL ONE...
...VANESSA JANE...?
GASP
UH...
HOLY CATS!
HOW'D SHE KNOW THAT?
DWAILIN' IN THUH SPIRIT WORLD AS AH DO, SUH, AH KNOW MANY THINGS 'BOUT Y'ALL.
SORREH TUH HEAR 'BOUT YOAH DADDY, BAH THUH WAY.
HOLY CATS!

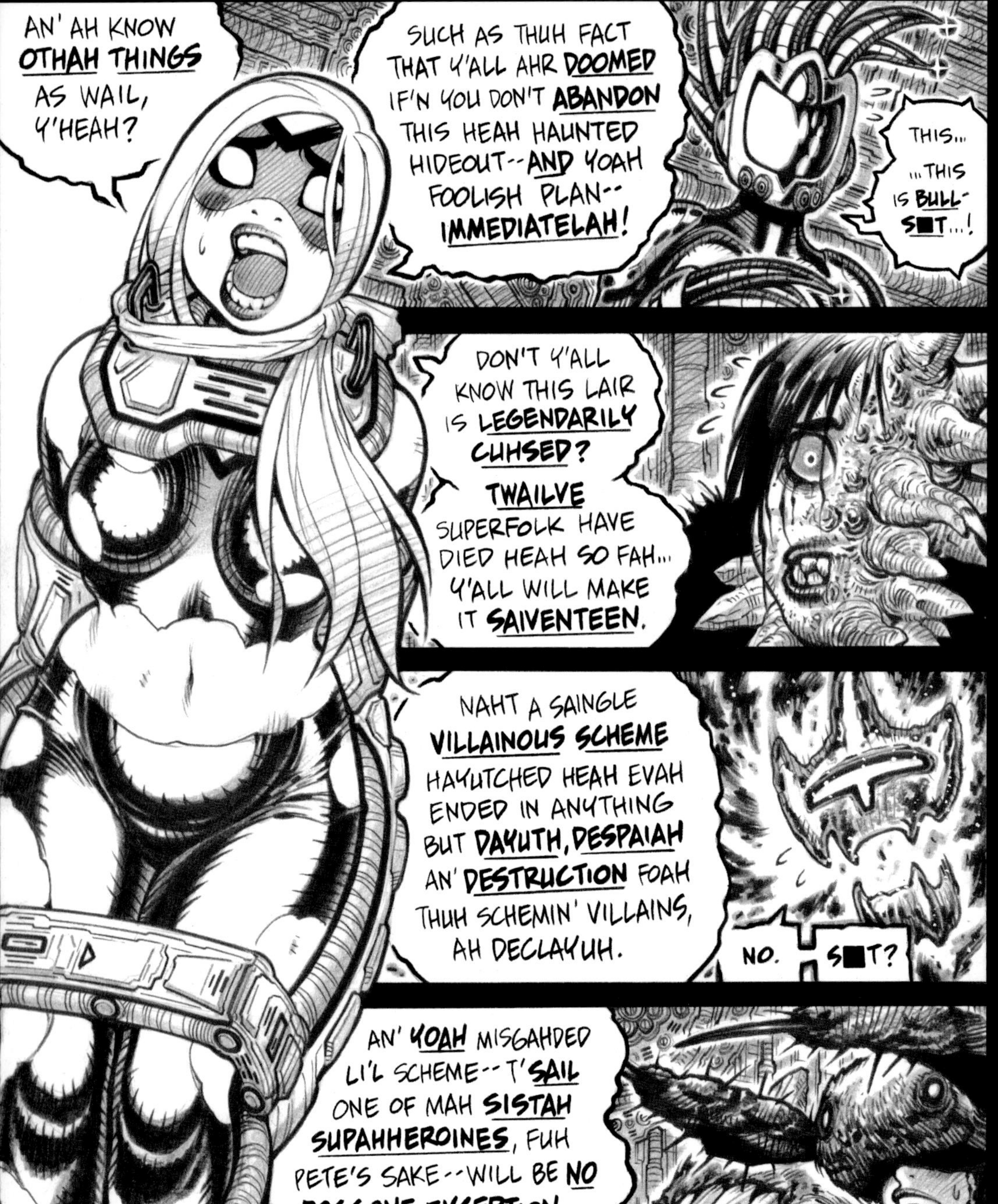
AN' AH KNOW **OTHAH THINGS** AS WAIL, Y'HEAH?
SUCH AS THUH FACT THAT Y'ALL AHR **DOOMED** IF'N YOU DON'T **ABANDON** THIS HEAH HAUNTED HIDEOUT--**AND** YOAH FOOLISH PLAN--**IMMEDIATELAH!**
THIS... ...THIS IS **BULL-S[redacted]T...!**
DON'T Y'ALL KNOW THIS LAIR IS **LEGENDARILY CUHSED?**
TWAILVE SUPERFOLK HAVE DIED HEAH SO FAH... Y'ALL WILL MAKE IT **SAIVENTEEN**.
NAHT A SAINGLE **VILLAINOUS SCHEME** HAYUTCHED HEAH EVAH ENDED IN ANYTHING BUT **DAYUTH, DESPAIAH** AN' **DESTRUCTION** FOAH THUH SCHEMIN' VILLAINS, AH DECLAYUH.
NO. S[redacted]T?
AN' **YOAH** MISGAHDED LI'L SCHEME--T'**SAIL** ONE OF MAH **SISTAH SUPAHHEROINES**, FUH PETE'S SAKE--WILL BE **NO DOGGONE EXCEPTION**, AH ASSURE Y'ALL.

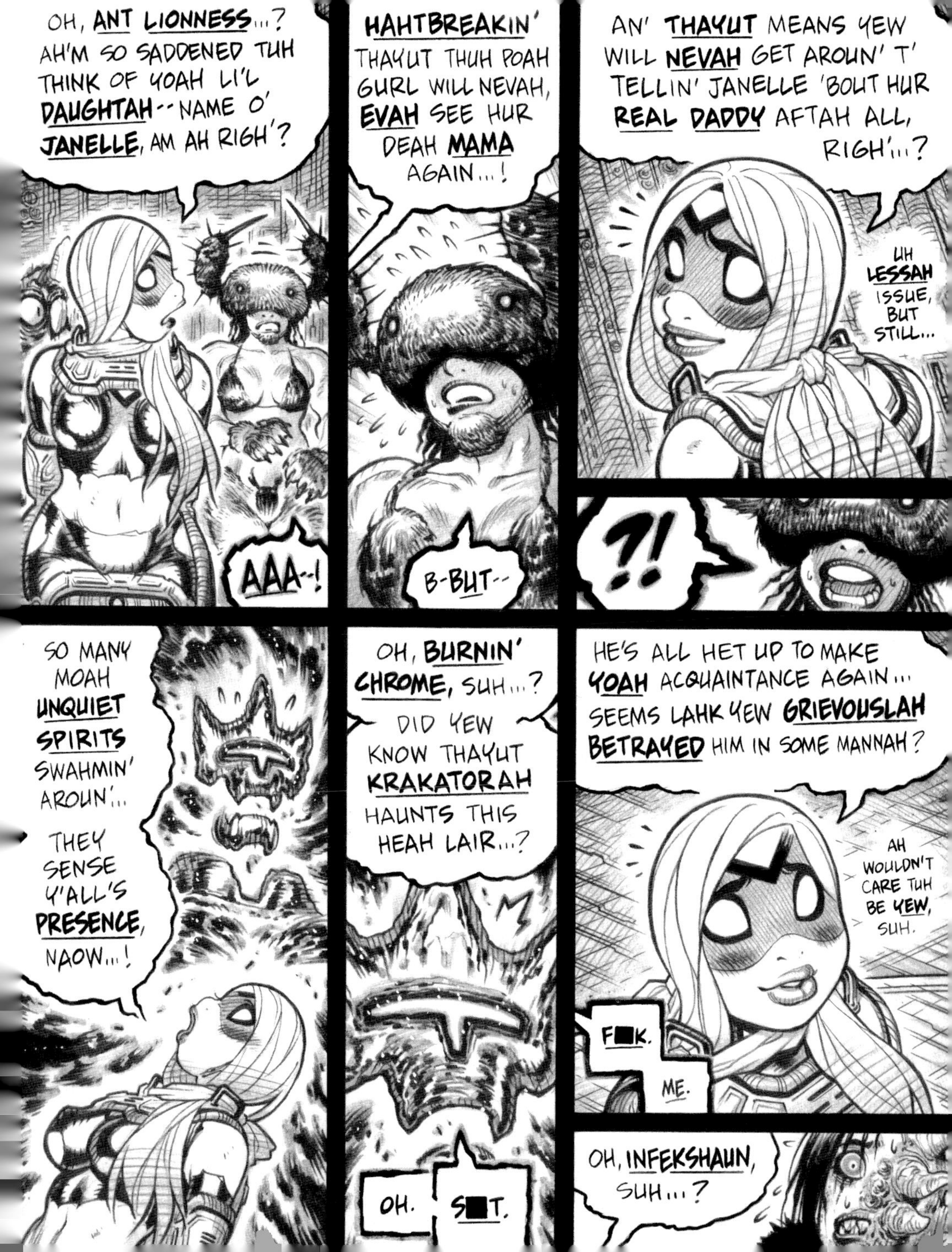

OH, ANT LIONNESS...? AH'M SO SADDENED TUH THINK OF YOAH LI'L DAUGHTAH--NAME O' JANELLE, AM AH RIGH'?
AAA--!
HAHTBREAKIN' THAYUT THUH POAH GURL WILL NEVAH, EVAH SEE HUR DEAH MAMA AGAIN...!
B-BUT--
AN' THAYUT MEANS YEW WILL NEVAH GET AROUN' T' TELLIN' JANELLE 'BOUT HUR REAL DADDY AFTAH ALL, RIGH'...?
UH LESSAH ISSUE, BUT STILL...
?!
SO MANY MOAH UNQUIET SPIRITS SWAHMIN' AROUN'...
THEY SENSE Y'ALL'S PRESENCE, NAOW...!
OH, BURNIN' CHROME, SUH...?
DID YEW KNOW THAYUT KRAKATORAH HAUNTS THIS HEAH LAIR...?
OH.
S[redacted]T.
HE'S ALL HET UP TO MAKE YOAH ACQUAINTANCE AGAIN... SEEMS LAHK YEW GRIEVOUSLAH BETRAYED HIM IN SOME MANNAH?
AH WOULDN'T CARE TUH BE YEW, SUH.
F[redacted]K.
ME.
OH, INFEKSHAUN, SUH...?

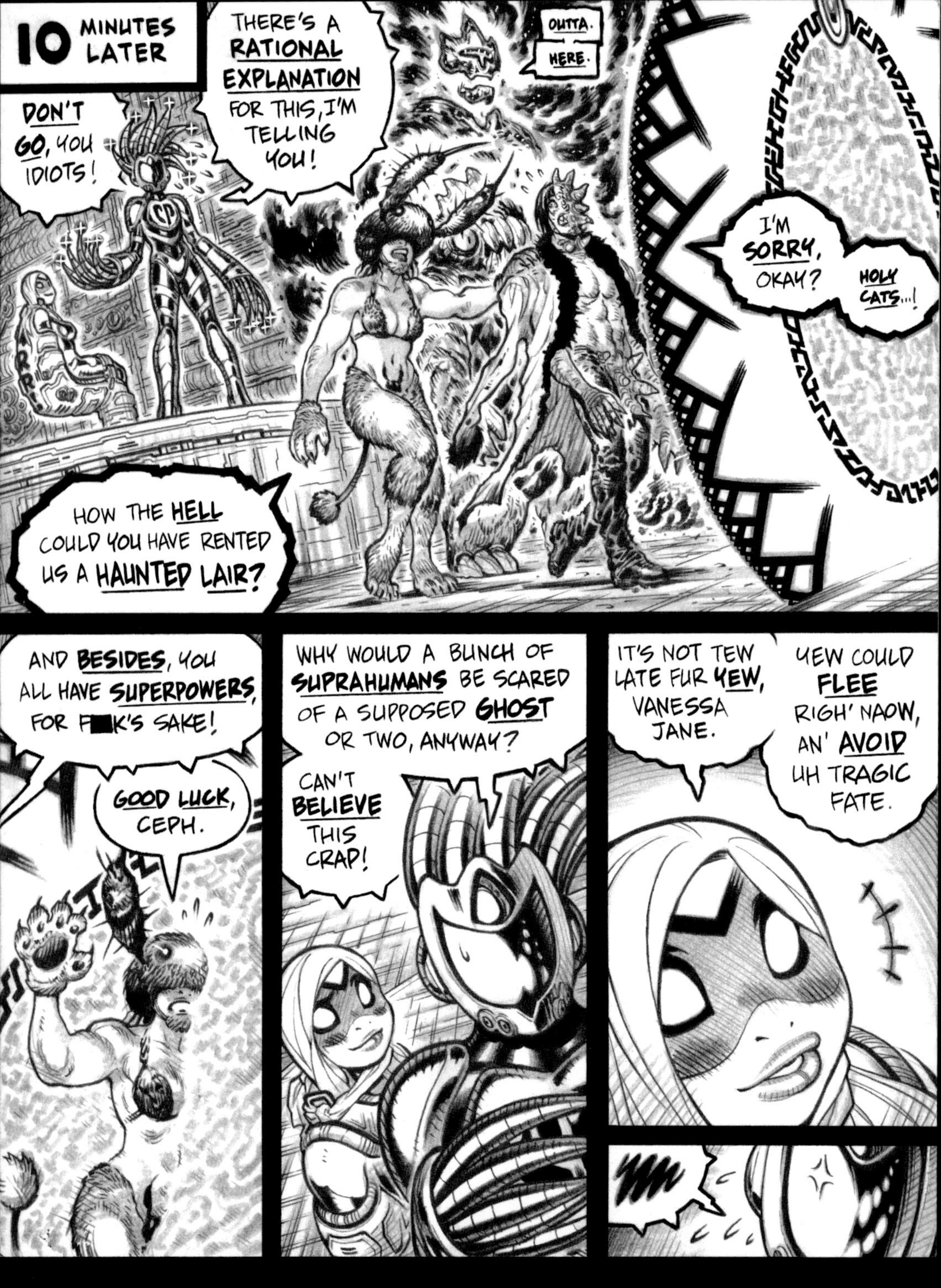

10 MINUTES LATER
DON'T GO, YOU IDIOTS!
THERE'S A RATIONAL EXPLANATION FOR THIS, I'M TELLING YOU!
OUTTA.
HERE.
I'M SORRY, OKAY?
HOLY CATS...!
HOW THE HELL COULD YOU HAVE RENTED US A HAUNTED LAIR?
AND BESIDES, YOU ALL HAVE SUPERPOWERS, FOR F[redacted]K'S SAKE!
GOOD LUCK, CEPH.
WHY WOULD A BUNCH OF SUPRAHUMANS BE SCARED OF A SUPPOSED GHOST OR TWO, ANYWAY?
CAN'T BELIEVE THIS CRAP!
IT'S NOT TEW LATE FUR YEW, VANESSA JANE.
YEW COULD FLEE RIGH' NAOW, AN' AVOID UH TRAGIC FATE.

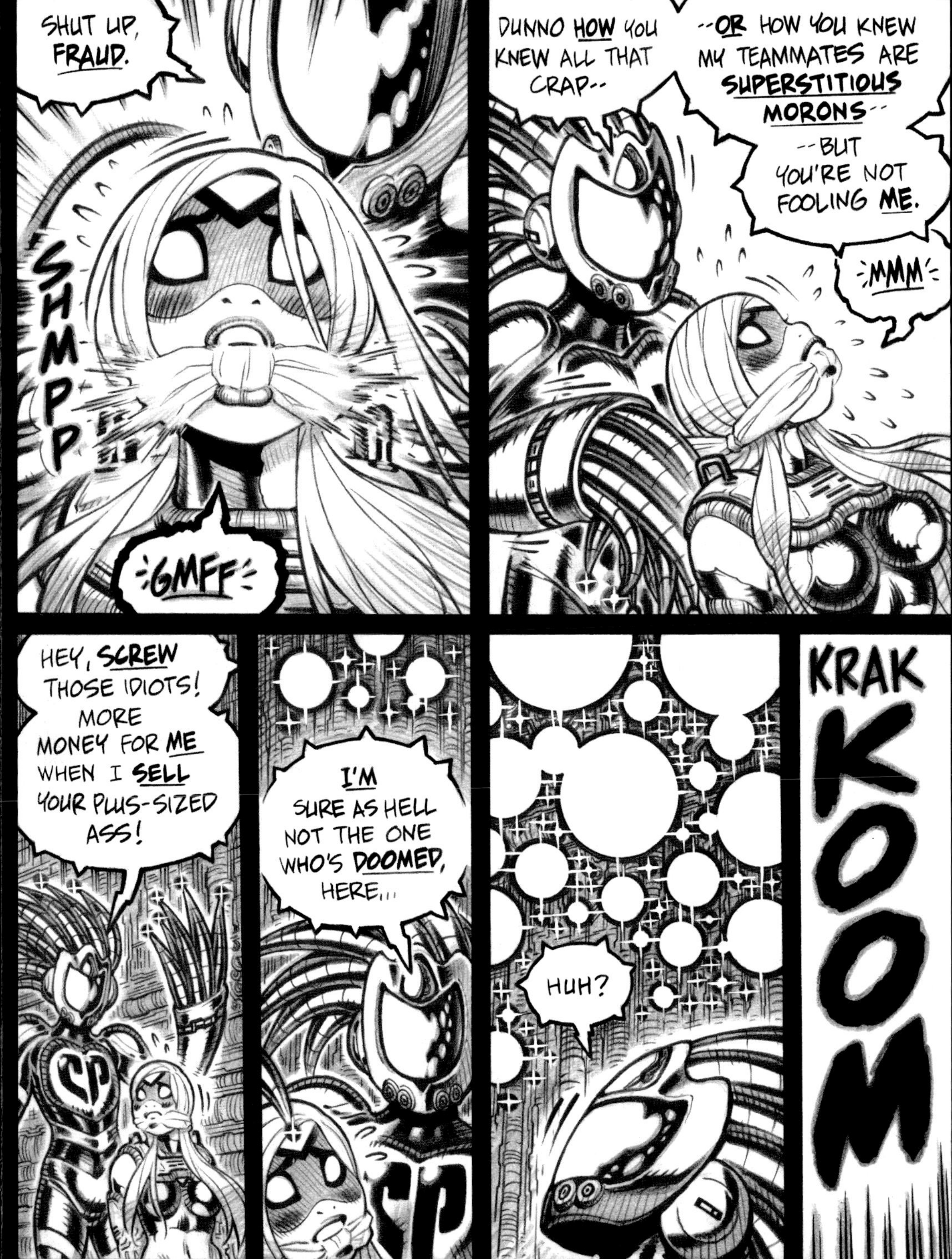
SHUT UP, FRAUD.
SHMPP
GMFF
DUNNO HOW YOU KNEW ALL THAT CRAP--
--OR HOW YOU KNEW MY TEAMMATES ARE SUPERSTITIOUS MORONS--
--BUT YOU'RE NOT FOOLING ME.
MMM
HEY, SCREW THOSE IDIOTS! MORE MONEY FOR ME WHEN I SELL YOUR PLUS-SIZED ASS!
I'M SURE AS HELL NOT THE ONE WHO'S DOOMED, HERE...
HUH?
KRAK
KOOM

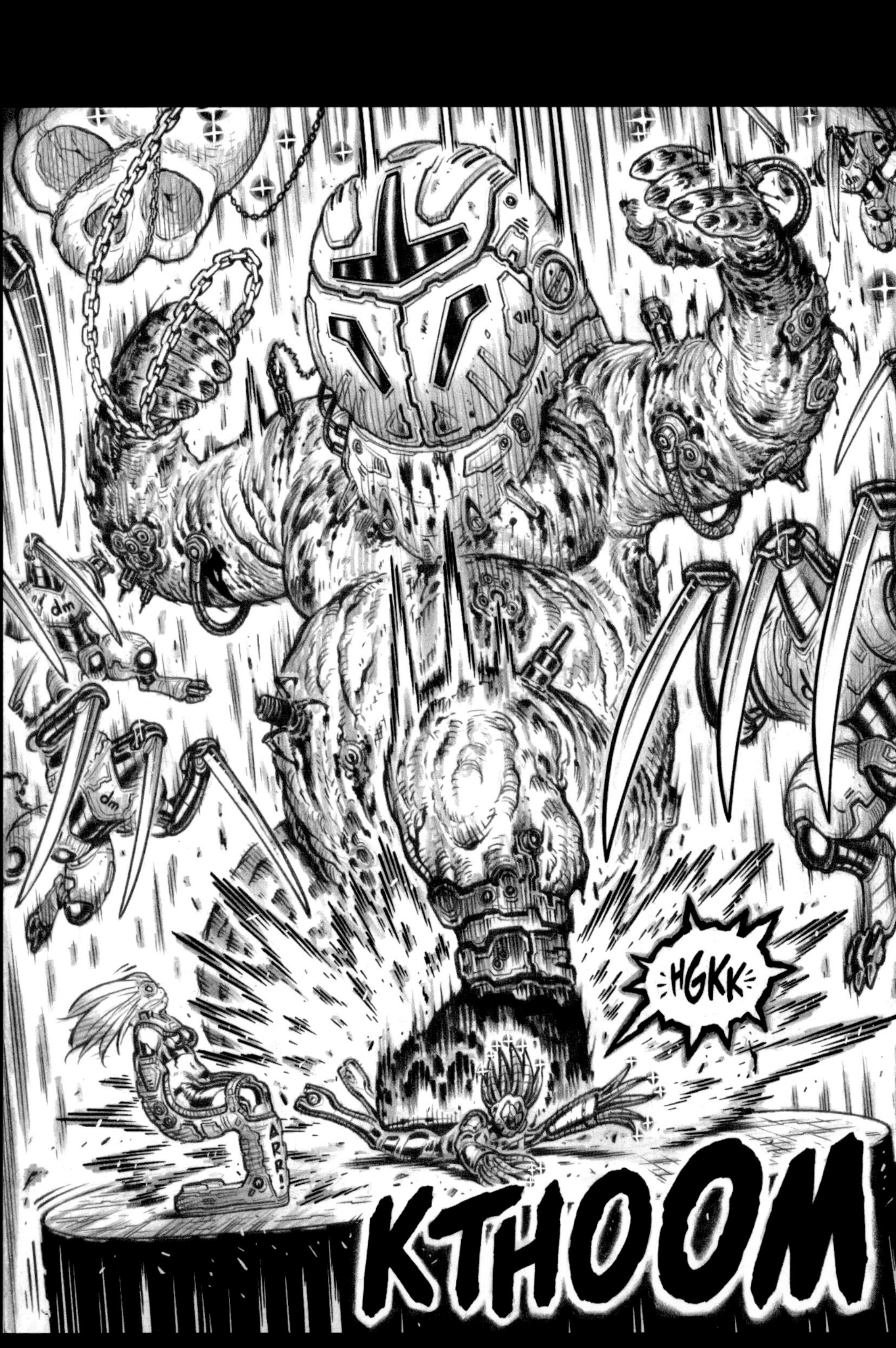
HGKK
KTHOOM

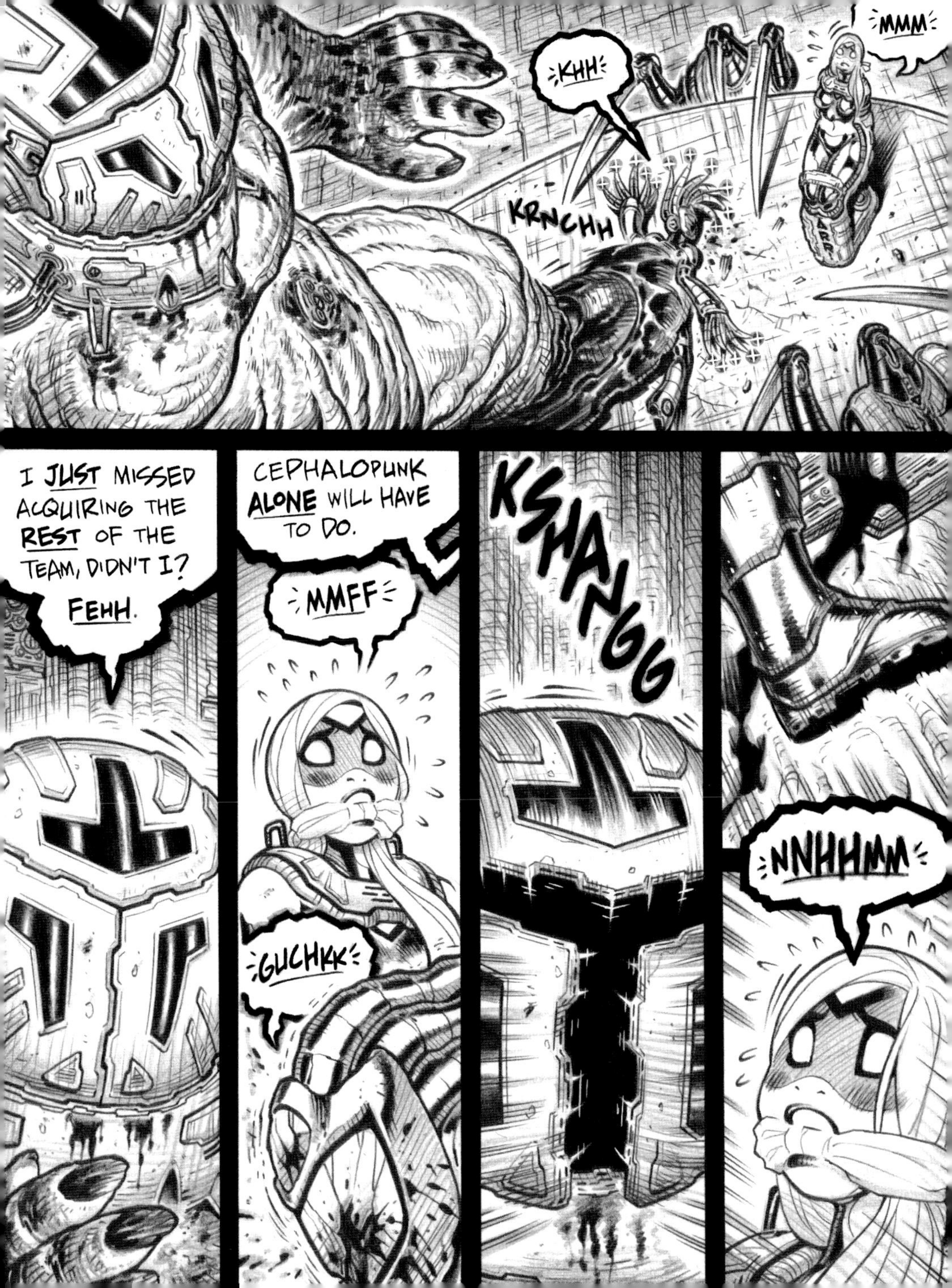
KHH
MMM
KRNCHH
I JUST MISSED ACQUIRING THE REST OF THE TEAM, DIDN'T I?
FEHH.
CEPHALOPUNK ALONE WILL HAVE TO DO.
MMFF
GUCHKK
KSHANGG
NNHHMM

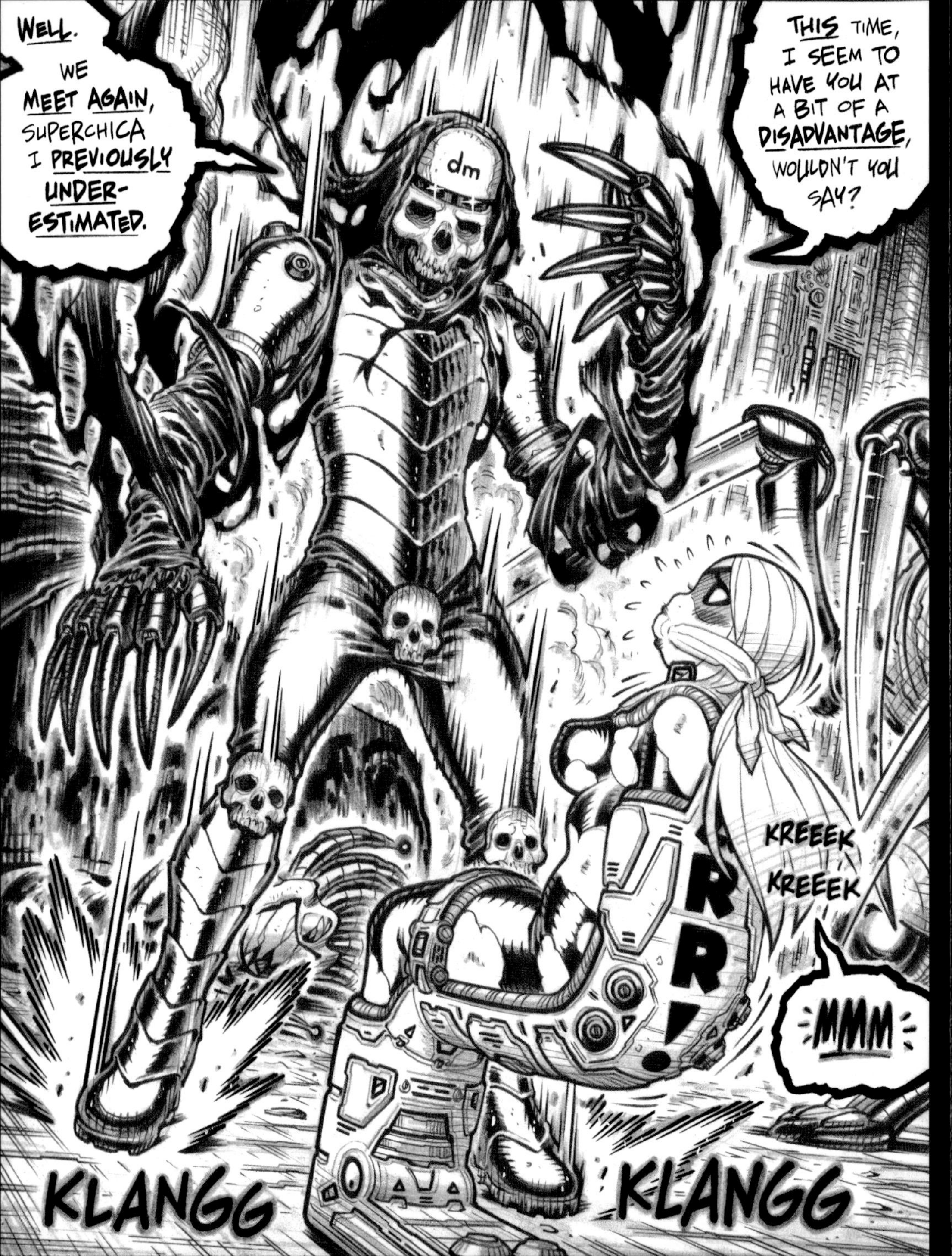
WELL.
WE MEET AGAIN, SUPERCHICA I PREVIOUSLY UNDER-ESTIMATED.
THIS TIME, I SEEM TO HAVE YOU AT A BIT OF A DISADVANTAGE, WOULDN'T YOU SAY?
dm
KREEEK
KREEEK
RR!
MMM
KLANGG
KLANGG

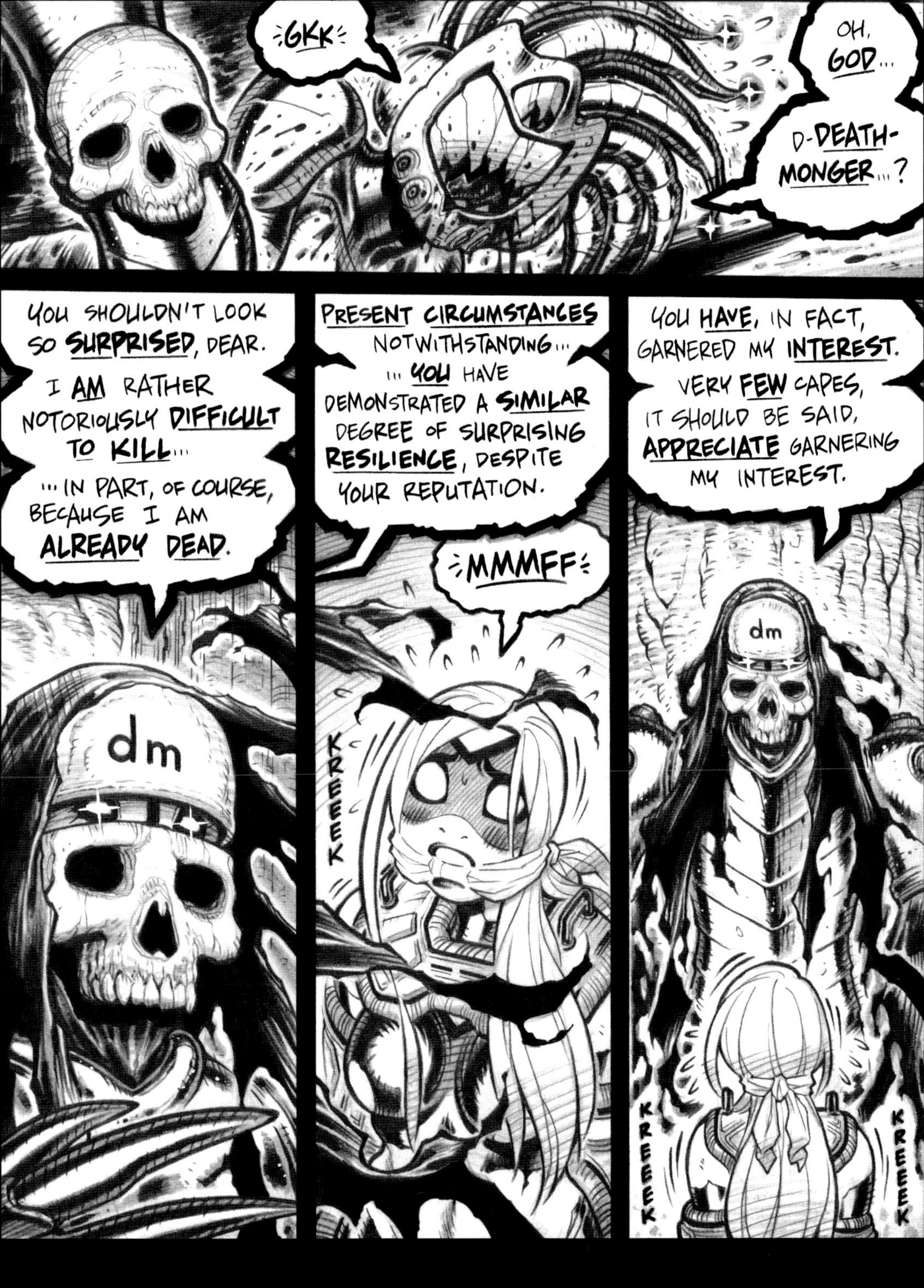
GKK
OH, GOD...
D-DEATH-MONGER...?
YOU SHOULDN'T LOOK SO SURPRISED, DEAR.
I AM RATHER NOTORIOUSLY DIFFICULT TO KILL...
...IN PART, OF COURSE, BECAUSE I AM ALREADY DEAD.
dm
PRESENT CIRCUMSTANCES NOTWITHSTANDING...
...YOU HAVE DEMONSTRATED A SIMILAR DEGREE OF SURPRISING RESILIENCE, DESPITE YOUR REPUTATION.
MMMFF
KREEEK
YOU HAVE, IN FACT, GARNERED MY INTEREST.
VERY FEW CAPES, IT SHOULD BE SAID, APPRECIATE GARNERING MY INTEREST.
dm
KREEEK
KREEEK

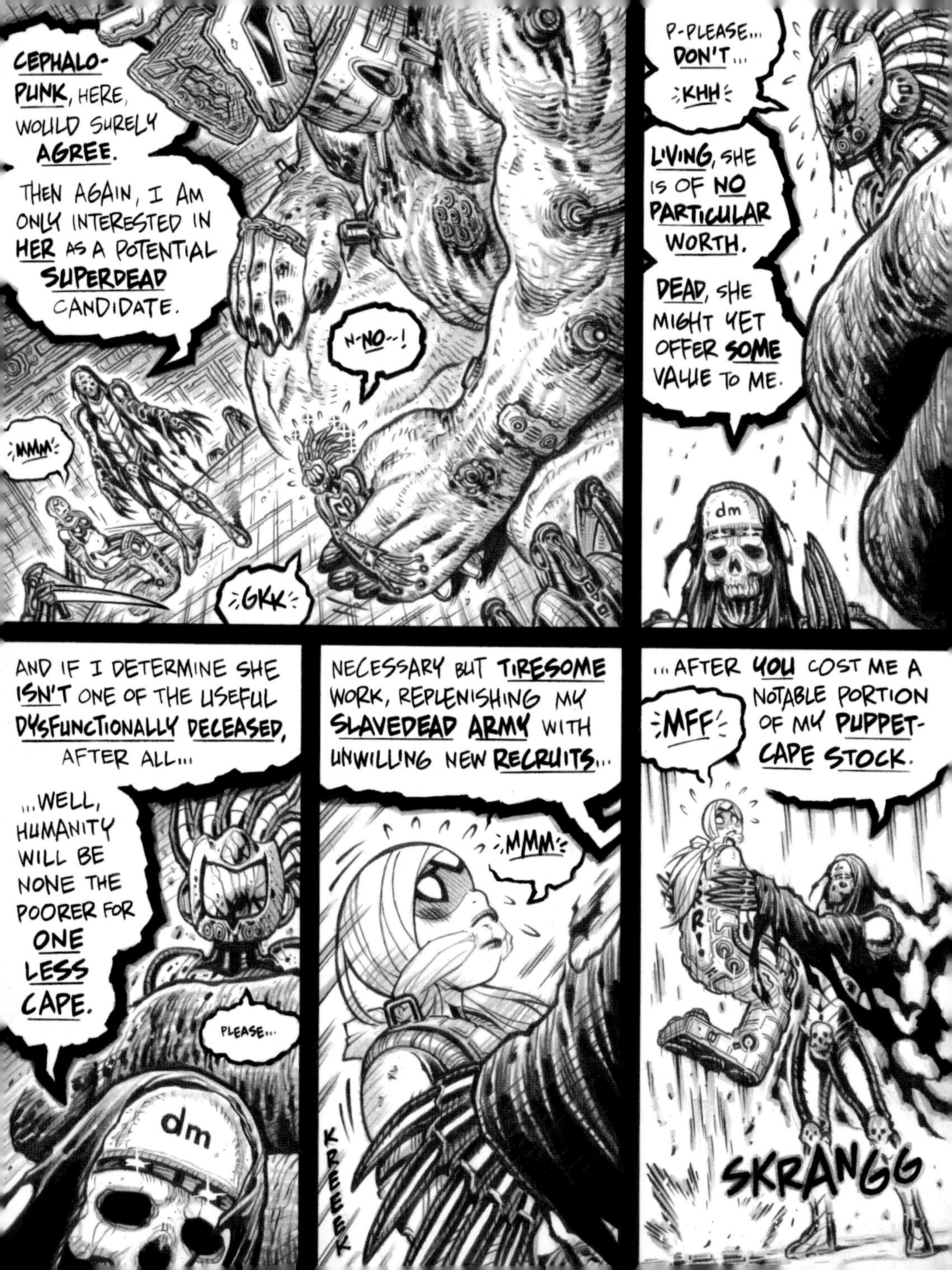
CEPHALO-PUNK, HERE, WOULD SURELY AGREE.
THEN AGAIN, I AM ONLY INTERESTED IN HER AS A POTENTIAL SUPERDEAD CANDIDATE.
N-NO--!
MMM
GKK
P-PLEASE... DON'T...
KHH
LIVING, SHE IS OF NO PARTICULAR WORTH.
DEAD, SHE MIGHT YET OFFER SOME VALUE TO ME.
AND IF I DETERMINE SHE ISN'T ONE OF THE USEFUL DYSFUNCTIONALLY DECEASED, AFTER ALL...
...WELL, HUMANITY WILL BE NONE THE POORER FOR ONE LESS CAPE.
PLEASE...
NECESSARY BUT TIRESOME WORK, REPLENISHING MY SLAVEDEAD ARMY WITH UNWILLING NEW RECRUITS...
MMM
KREEEK
...AFTER YOU COST ME A NOTABLE PORTION OF MY PUPPET-CAPE STOCK.
MFF
SKRANGG

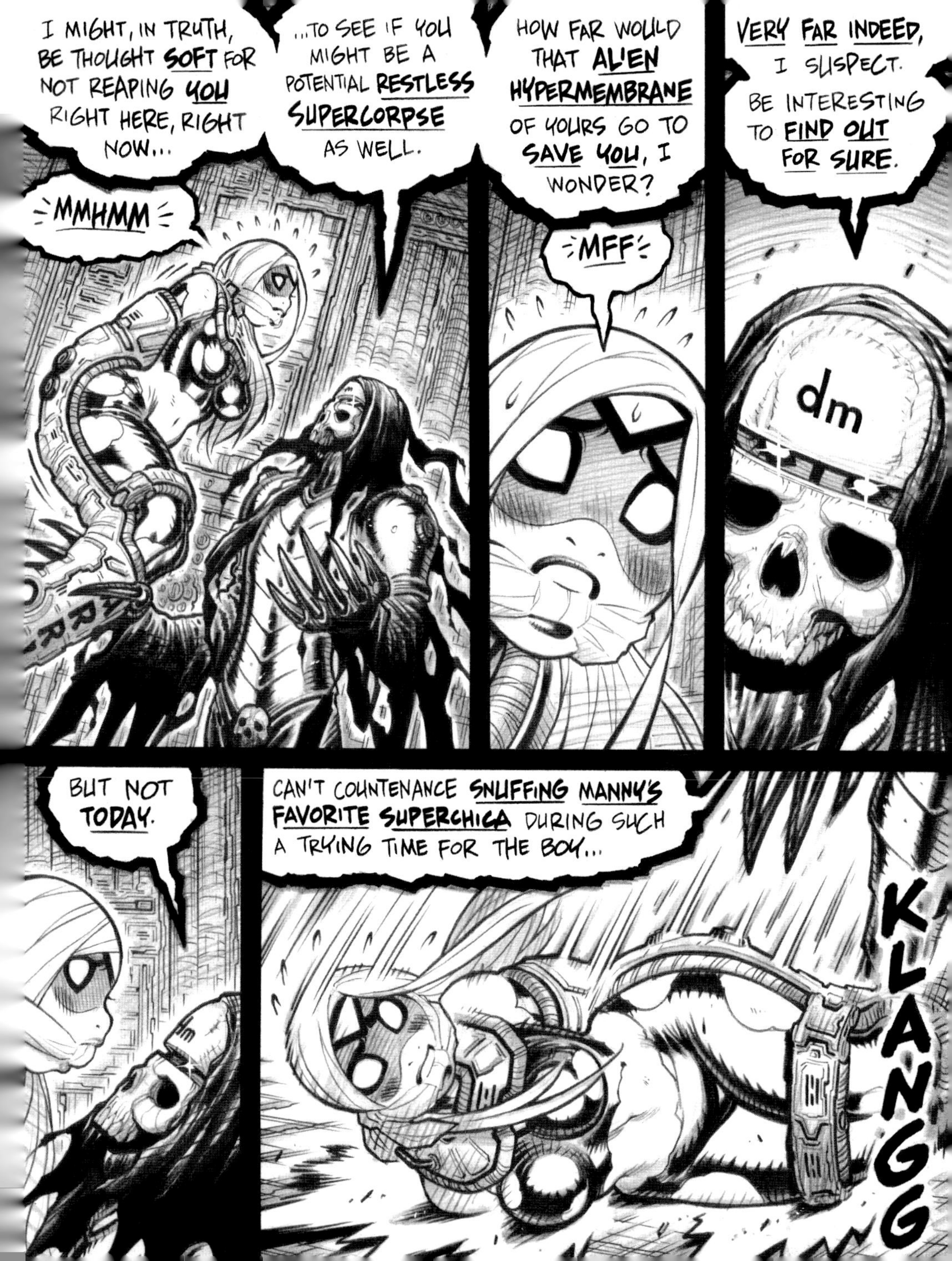

I MIGHT, IN TRUTH, BE THOUGHT SOFT FOR NOT REAPING YOU RIGHT HERE, RIGHT NOW...
MMHMM
...TO SEE IF YOU MIGHT BE A POTENTIAL RESTLESS SUPERCORPSE AS WELL.
HOW FAR WOULD THAT ALIEN HYPERMEMBRANE OF YOURS GO TO SAVE YOU, I WONDER?
MFF
VERY FAR INDEED, I SUSPECT.
BE INTERESTING TO FIND OUT FOR SURE.
dm
BUT NOT TODAY.
CAN'T COUNTENANCE SNUFFING MANNY'S FAVORITE SUPERCHICA DURING SUCH A TRYING TIME FOR THE BOY...
KLANGG

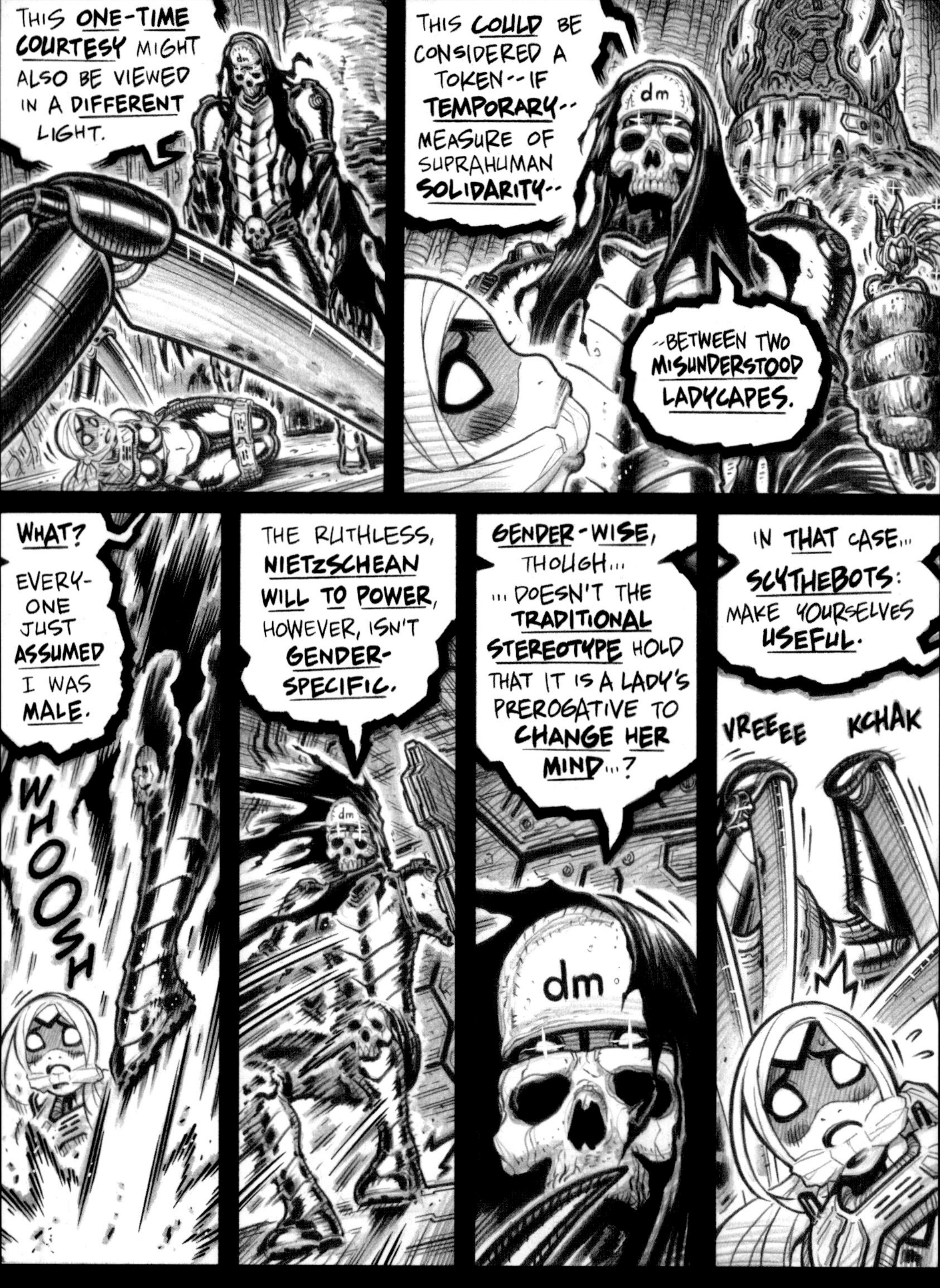
THIS ONE-TIME COURTESY MIGHT ALSO BE VIEWED IN A DIFFERENT LIGHT.
THIS COULD BE CONSIDERED A TOKEN--IF TEMPORARY--MEASURE OF SUPRAHUMAN SOLIDARITY--
--BETWEEN TWO MISUNDERSTOOD LADYCAPES.
WHAT?
EVERY-ONE JUST ASSUMED I WAS MALE.
WHOOOSH
THE RUTHLESS, NIETZSCHEAN WILL TO POWER, HOWEVER, ISN'T GENDER-SPECIFIC.
GENDER-WISE, THOUGH...
...DOESN'T THE TRADITIONAL STEREOTYPE HOLD THAT IT IS A LADY'S PREROGATIVE TO CHANGE HER MIND...?
dm
IN THAT CASE... SCYTHEBOTS: MAKE YOURSELVES USEFUL.
VREEEEE
KCHAK

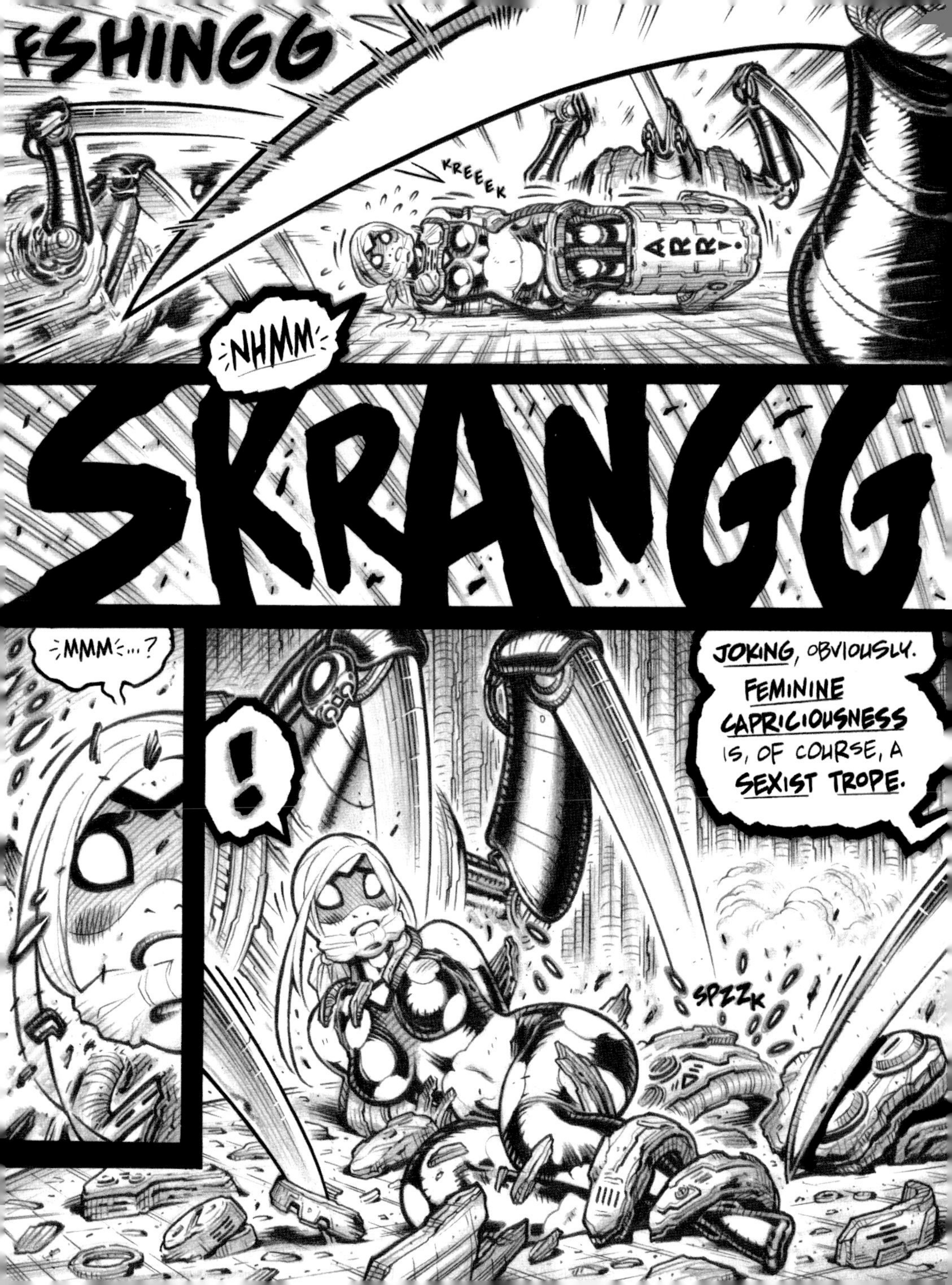
FSHINGG
KREEEK
ARR
NHMM
SKRANGG
MMM...?
!
JOKING, OBVIOUSLY. FEMININE CAPRICIOUSNESS IS, OF COURSE, A SEXIST TROPE.
SPZZK

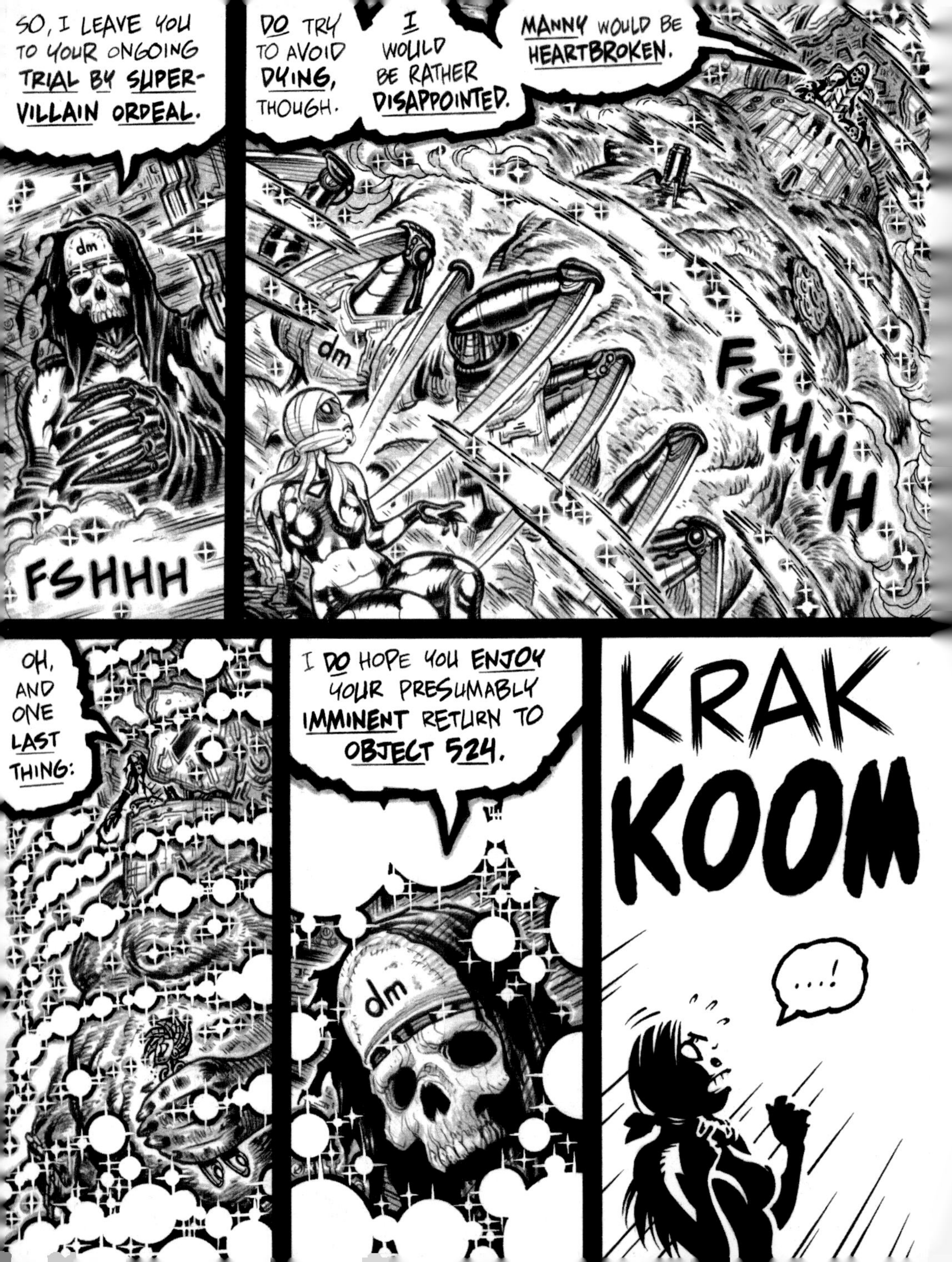
SO, I LEAVE YOU TO YOUR ONGOING TRIAL BY SUPER-VILLAIN ORDEAL.
FSHHH
DO TRY TO AVOID DYING, THOUGH.
I WOULD BE RATHER DISAPPOINTED.
MANNY WOULD BE HEARTBROKEN.
FSHHHH
OH, AND ONE LAST THING:
I DO HOPE YOU ENJOY YOUR PRESUMABLY IMMINENT RETURN TO OBJECT 524.
KRAK KOOM
...!

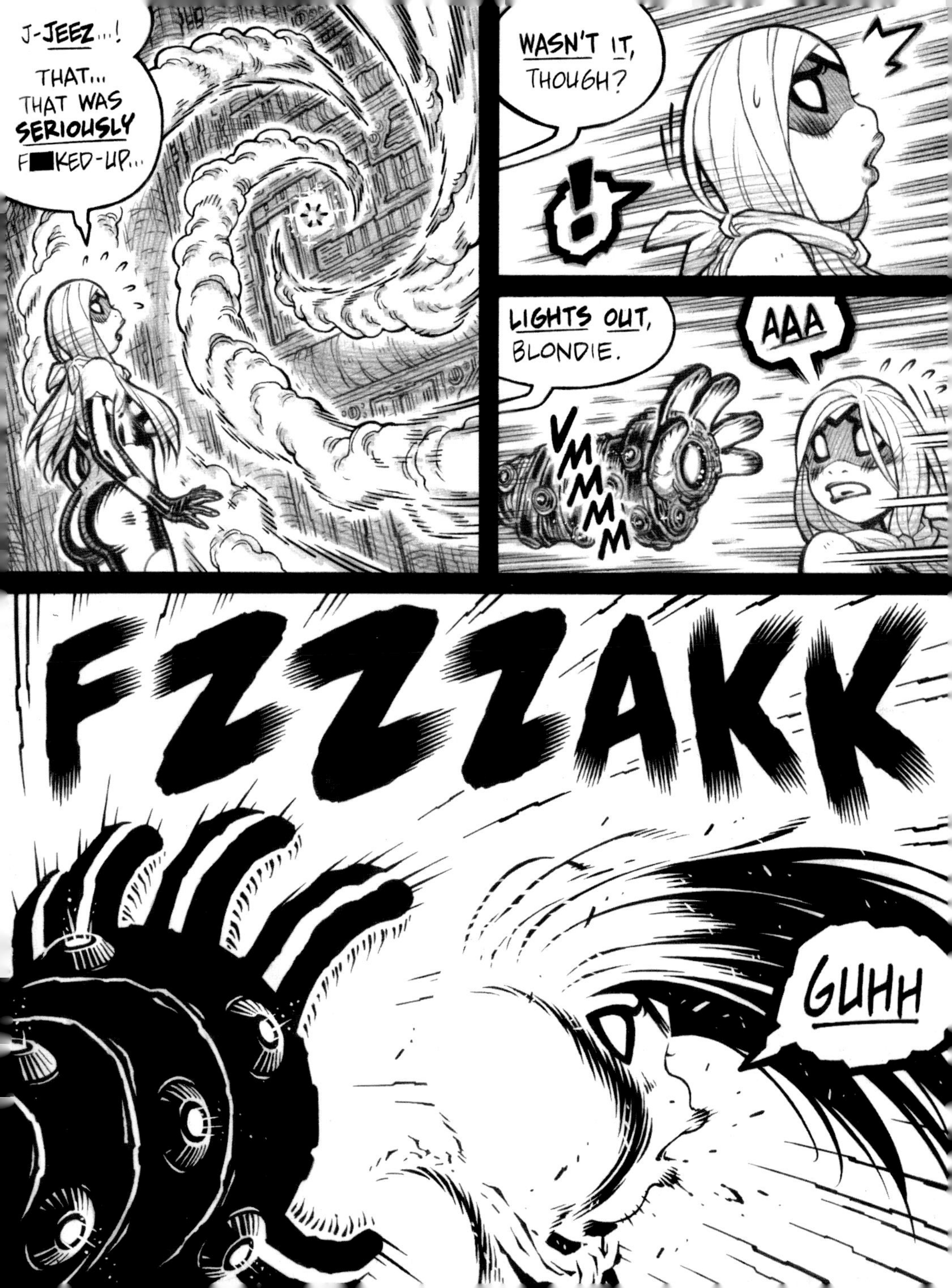
J-JEEZ...!
THAT... THAT WAS SERIOUSLY F[redacted]KED-UP...
WASN'T IT, THOUGH?
!
LIGHTS OUT, BLONDIE.
AAA
VMMMMM
FZZZAKK
GUHH

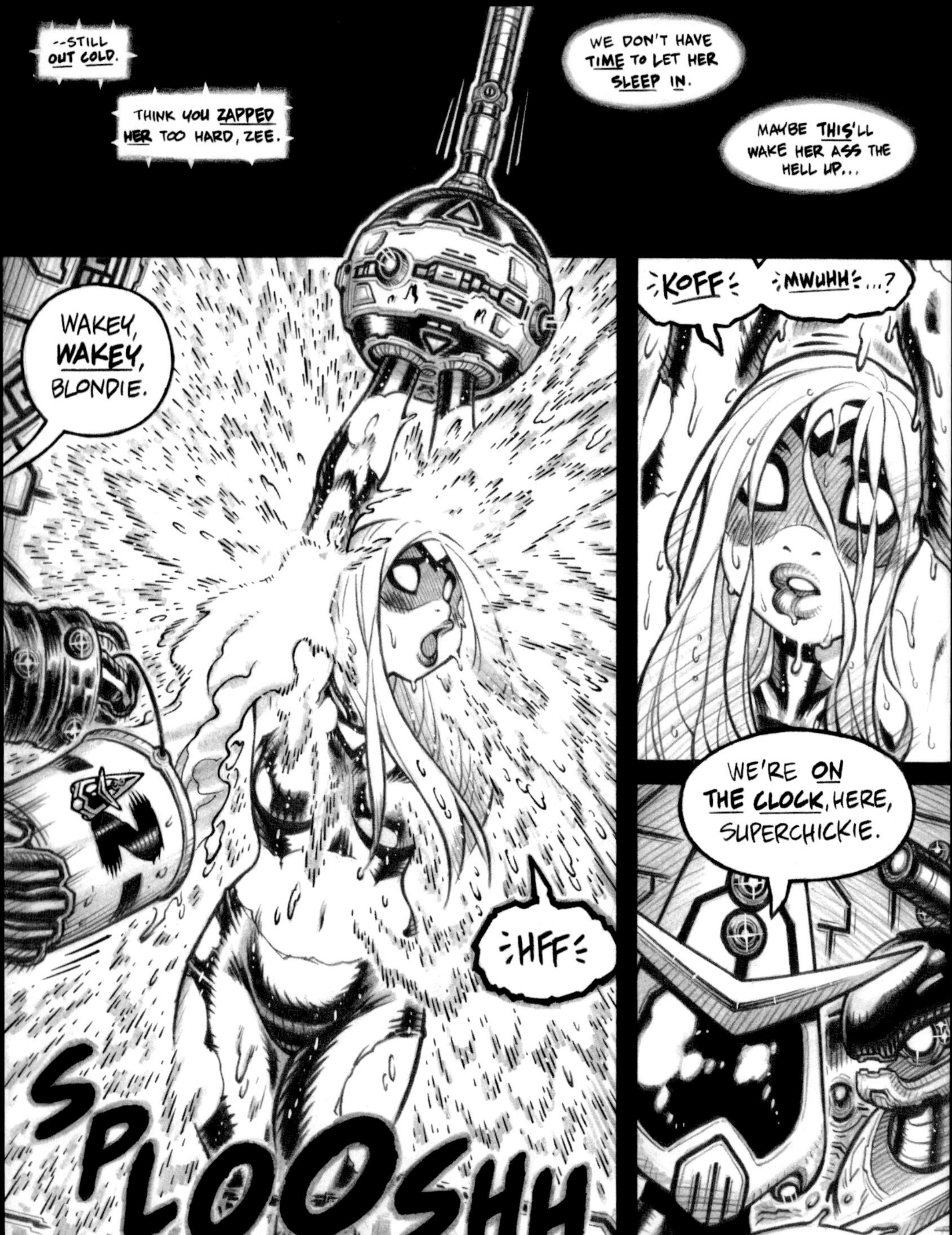
--STILL OUT COLD.
THINK YOU ZAPPED HER TOO HARD, ZEE.
WE DON'T HAVE TIME TO LET HER SLEEP IN.
MAYBE THIS'LL WAKE HER ASS THE HELL UP...
WAKEY, WAKEY, BLONDIE.
HFF
SPLOOSHH
KOFF
MWUHH...?
WE'RE ON THE CLOCK, HERE, SUPERCHICKIE.

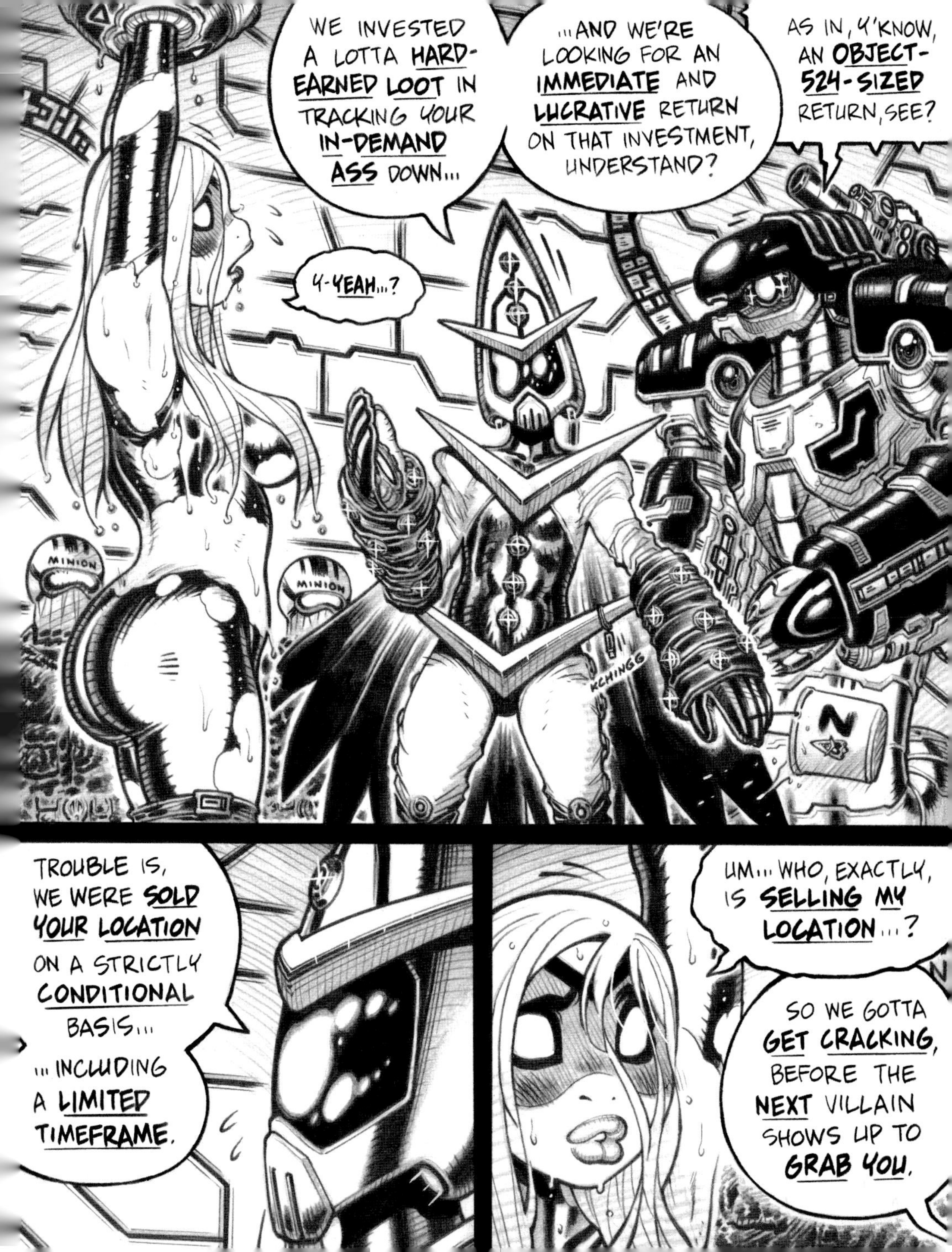
WE INVESTED A LOTTA HARD-EARNED LOOT IN TRACKING YOUR IN-DEMAND ASS DOWN...
...AND WE'RE LOOKING FOR AN IMMEDIATE AND LUCRATIVE RETURN ON THAT INVESTMENT, UNDERSTAND?
AS IN, Y'KNOW, AN OBJECT-524-SIZED RETURN, SEE?
Y-YEAH...?
MINION
MINION
KCHINGG
N
TROUBLE IS, WE WERE SOLD YOUR LOCATION ON A STRICTLY CONDITIONAL BASIS...
...INCLUDING A LIMITED TIMEFRAME.
UM... WHO, EXACTLY, IS SELLING MY LOCATION...?
SO WE GOTTA GET CRACKING, BEFORE THE NEXT VILLAIN SHOWS UP TO GRAB YOU.

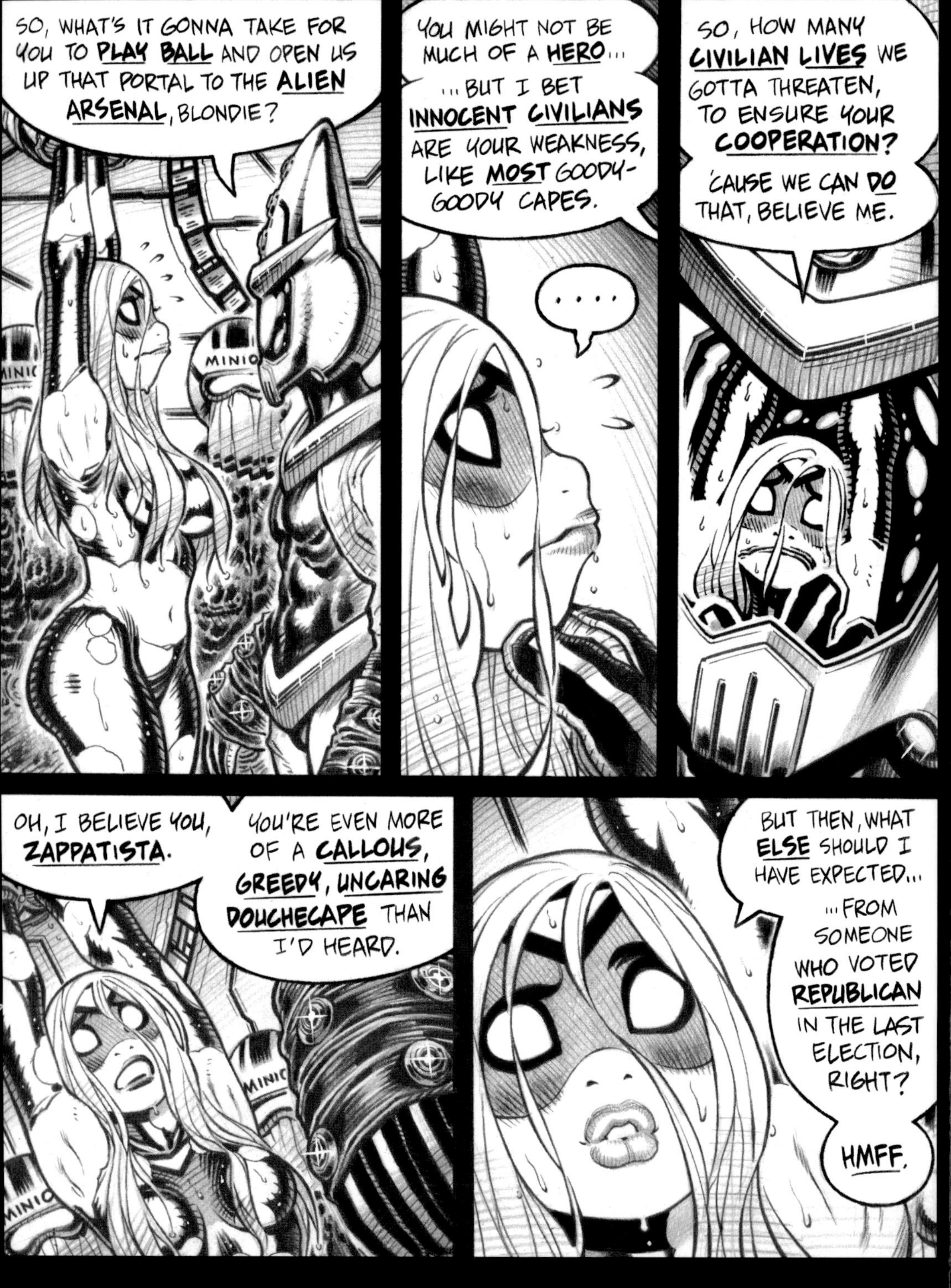
SO, WHAT'S IT GONNA TAKE FOR YOU TO PLAY BALL AND OPEN US UP THAT PORTAL TO THE ALIEN ARSENAL, BLONDIE?
MINIO
MINIC
YOU MIGHT NOT BE MUCH OF A HERO...
...BUT I BET INNOCENT CIVILIANS ARE YOUR WEAKNESS, LIKE MOST GOODY-GOODY CAPES.
....
SO, HOW MANY CIVILIAN LIVES WE GOTTA THREATEN, TO ENSURE YOUR COOPERATION?
'CAUSE WE CAN DO THAT, BELIEVE ME.
OH, I BELIEVE YOU, ZAPPATISTA.
YOU'RE EVEN MORE OF A CALLOUS, GREEDY, UNCARING DOUCHECAPE THAN I'D HEARD.
MINIC
MINIO
BUT THEN, WHAT ELSE SHOULD I HAVE EXPECTED...
...FROM SOMEONE WHO VOTED REPUBLICAN IN THE LAST ELECTION, RIGHT?
HMFF.

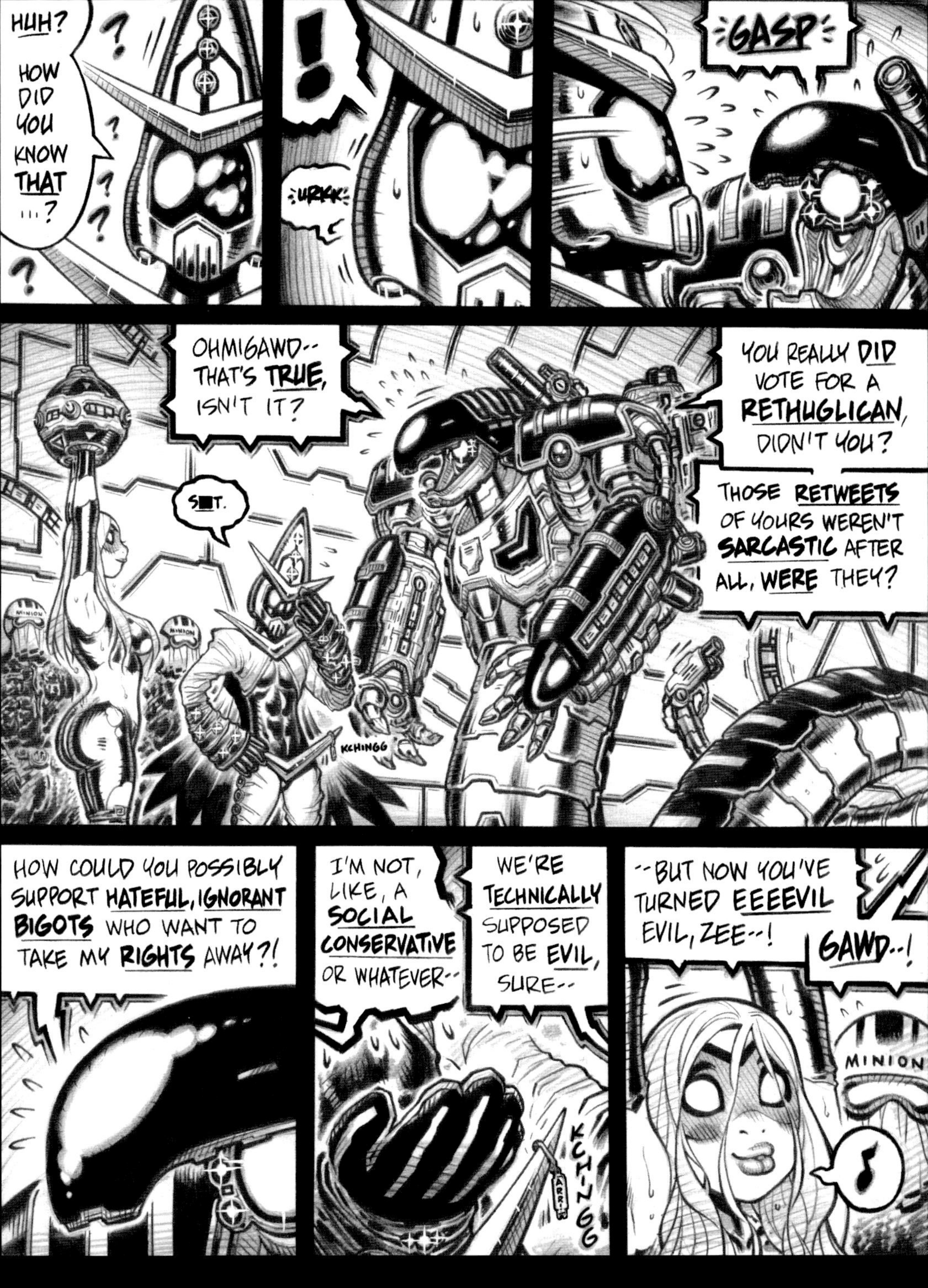
HUH?
HOW DID YOU KNOW THAT ...?
?
!
URKK
GASP
OHMIGAWD-- THAT'S TRUE, ISN'T IT?
YOU REALLY DID VOTE FOR A RETHUGLICAN, DIDN'T YOU?
THOSE RETWEETS OF YOURS WEREN'T SARCASTIC AFTER ALL, WERE THEY?
S[redacted]T.
MINION
MINION
KCHINGG
HOW COULD YOU POSSIBLY SUPPORT HATEFUL, IGNORANT BIGOTS WHO WANT TO TAKE MY RIGHTS AWAY?!
I'M NOT, LIKE, A SOCIAL CONSERVATIVE OR WHATEVER--
WE'RE TECHNICALLY SUPPOSED TO BE EVIL, SURE--
KCHINGG
--BUT NOW YOU'VE TURNED EEEEVIL EVIL, ZEE--!
GAWD--!
MINION

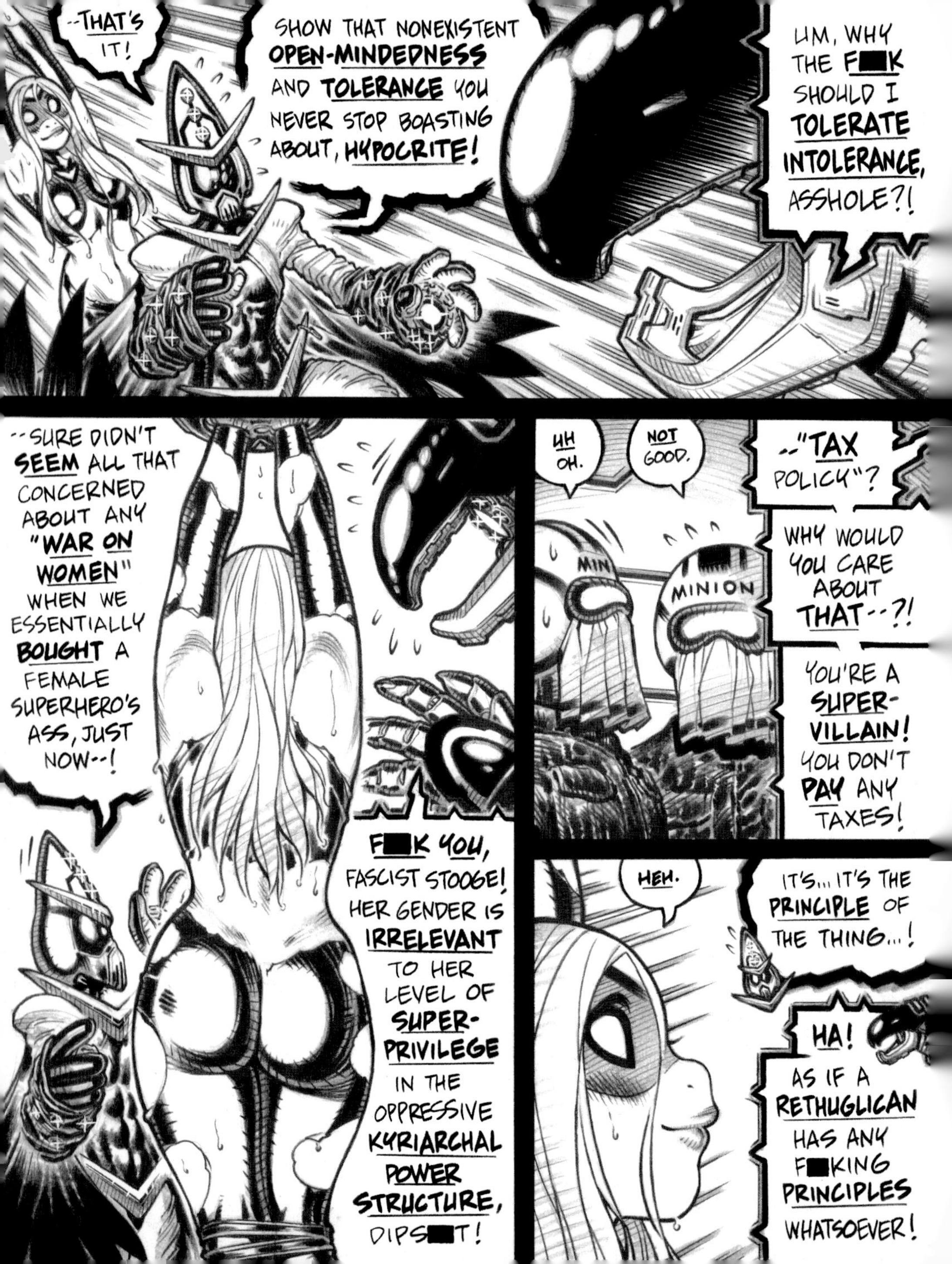
--THAT'S IT!
SHOW THAT NONEXISTENT OPEN-MINDEDNESS AND TOLERANCE YOU NEVER STOP BOASTING ABOUT, HYPOCRITE!
UM, WHY THE F[redacted]K SHOULD I TOLERATE INTOLERANCE, ASSHOLE?!
--SURE DIDN'T SEEM ALL THAT CONCERNED ABOUT ANY "WAR ON WOMEN" WHEN WE ESSENTIALLY BOUGHT A FEMALE SUPERHERO'S ASS, JUST NOW--!
F[redacted]K YOU, FASCIST STOOGE! HER GENDER IS IRRELEVANT TO HER LEVEL OF SUPER-PRIVILEGE IN THE OPPRESSIVE KYRIARCHAL POWER STRUCTURE, DIPS[redacted]T!
UH OH.
NOT GOOD.
MIN
MINION
--"TAX POLICY"?
WHY WOULD YOU CARE ABOUT THAT--?!
YOU'RE A SUPER-VILLAIN! YOU DON'T PAY ANY TAXES!
HEH.
IT'S... IT'S THE PRINCIPLE OF THE THING...!
HA! AS IF A RETHUGLICAN HAS ANY F[redacted]KING PRINCIPLES WHATSOEVER!

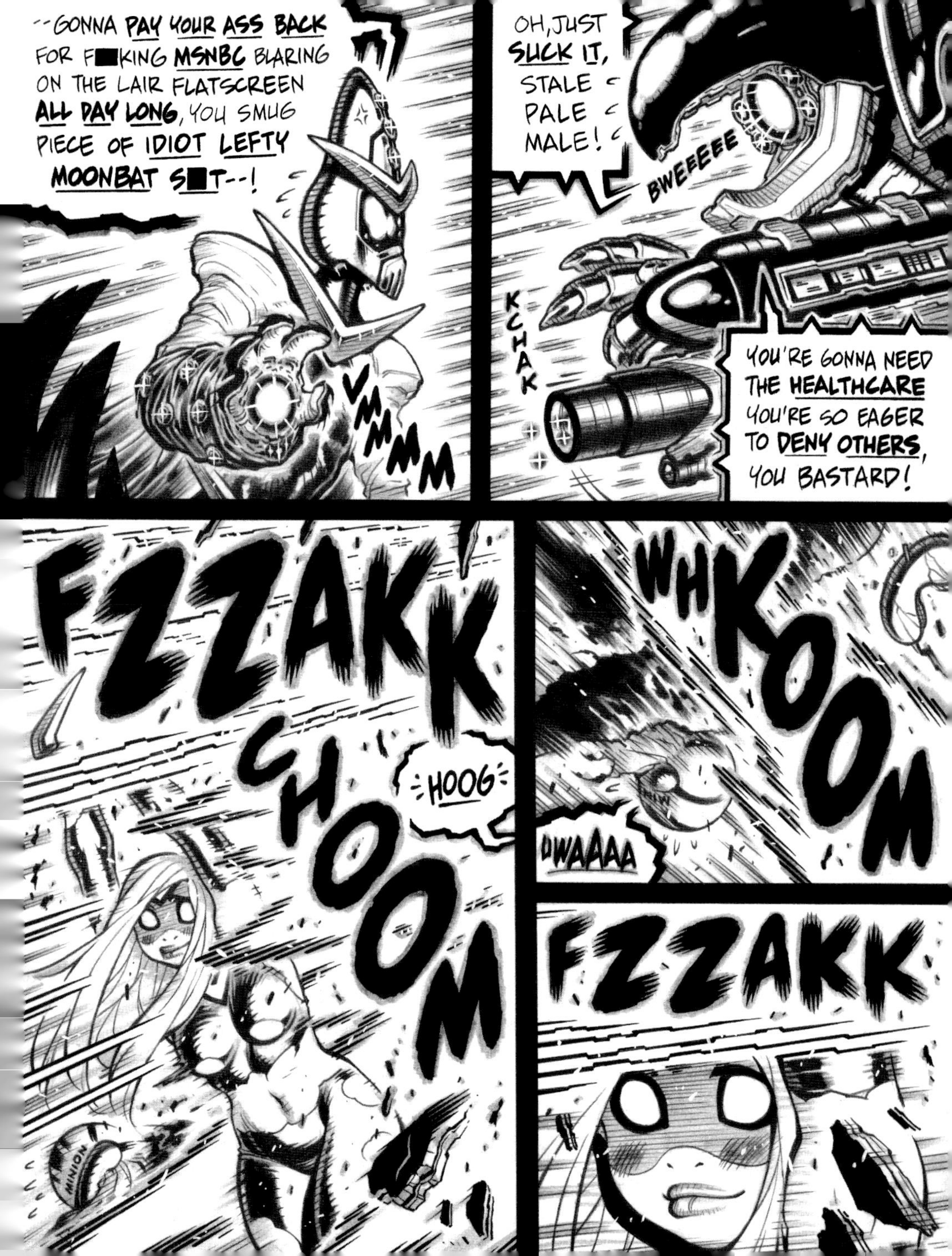
--GONNA PAY YOUR ASS BACK FOR F[redacted]KING MSNBC BLARING ON THE LAIR FLATSCREEN ALL DAY LONG, YOU SMUG PIECE OF IDIOT LEFTY MOONBAT S[redacted]T--!
VMMMMM
OH, JUST SUCK IT, STALE PALE MALE!
BWEEEEE
KCHAK
YOU'RE GONNA NEED THE HEALTHCARE YOU'RE SO EAGER TO DENY OTHERS, YOU BASTARD!
FZZAKK
CHOOOM
HOOG
MINION
WHKOOOM
DWAAAA
FZZAKK

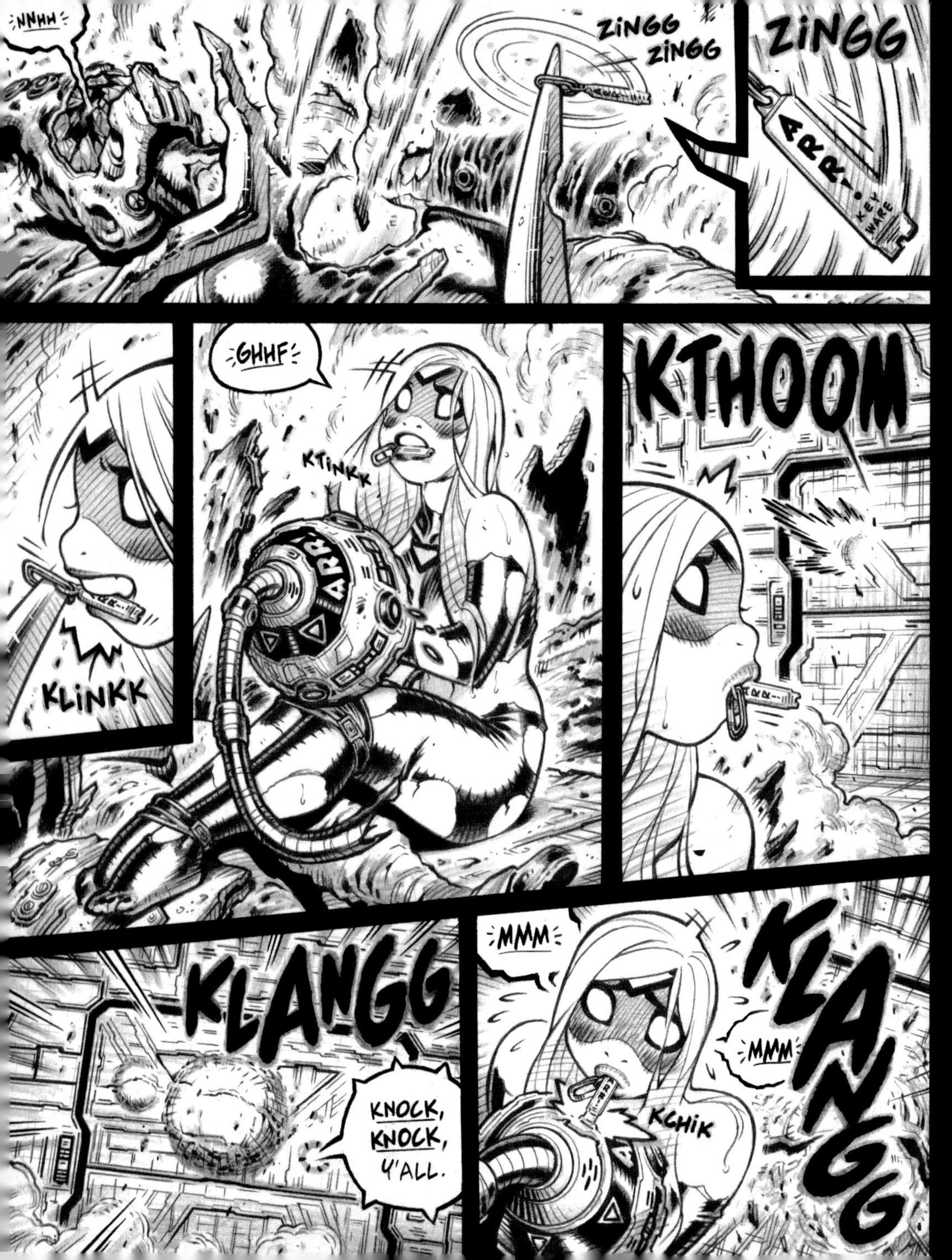
NNHH
ZINGG
ZINGG
ZINGG
ARR-
KEY WARE
GHHF
KTINKK
KLINKK
KTHOOM
KLANGG
KNOCK, KNOCK, Y'ALL.
MMM
MMM
KGHIK
KLANGG

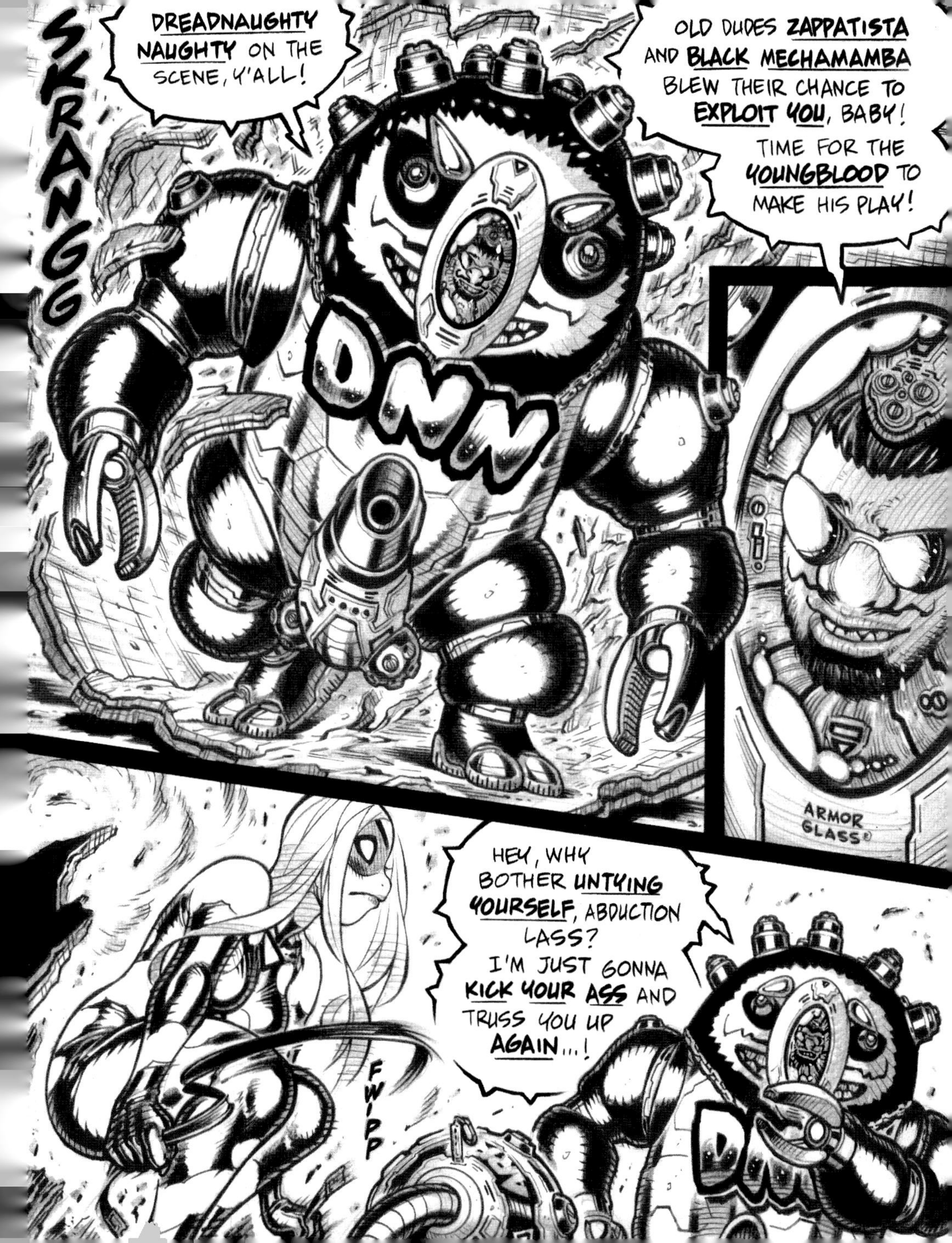

SKRANGG
DREADNAUGHTY NAUGHTY ON THE SCENE, Y'ALL!
OLD DUDES ZAPPATISTA AND BLACK MECHAMAMBA BLEW THEIR CHANCE TO EXPLOIT YOU, BABY!
TIME FOR THE YOUNGBLOOD TO MAKE HIS PLAY!
DNN
ARMOR GLASS®
HEY, WHY BOTHER UNTYING YOURSELF, ABDUCTION LASS?
I'M JUST GONNA KICK YOUR ASS AND TRUSS YOU UP AGAIN...!
FWIPP

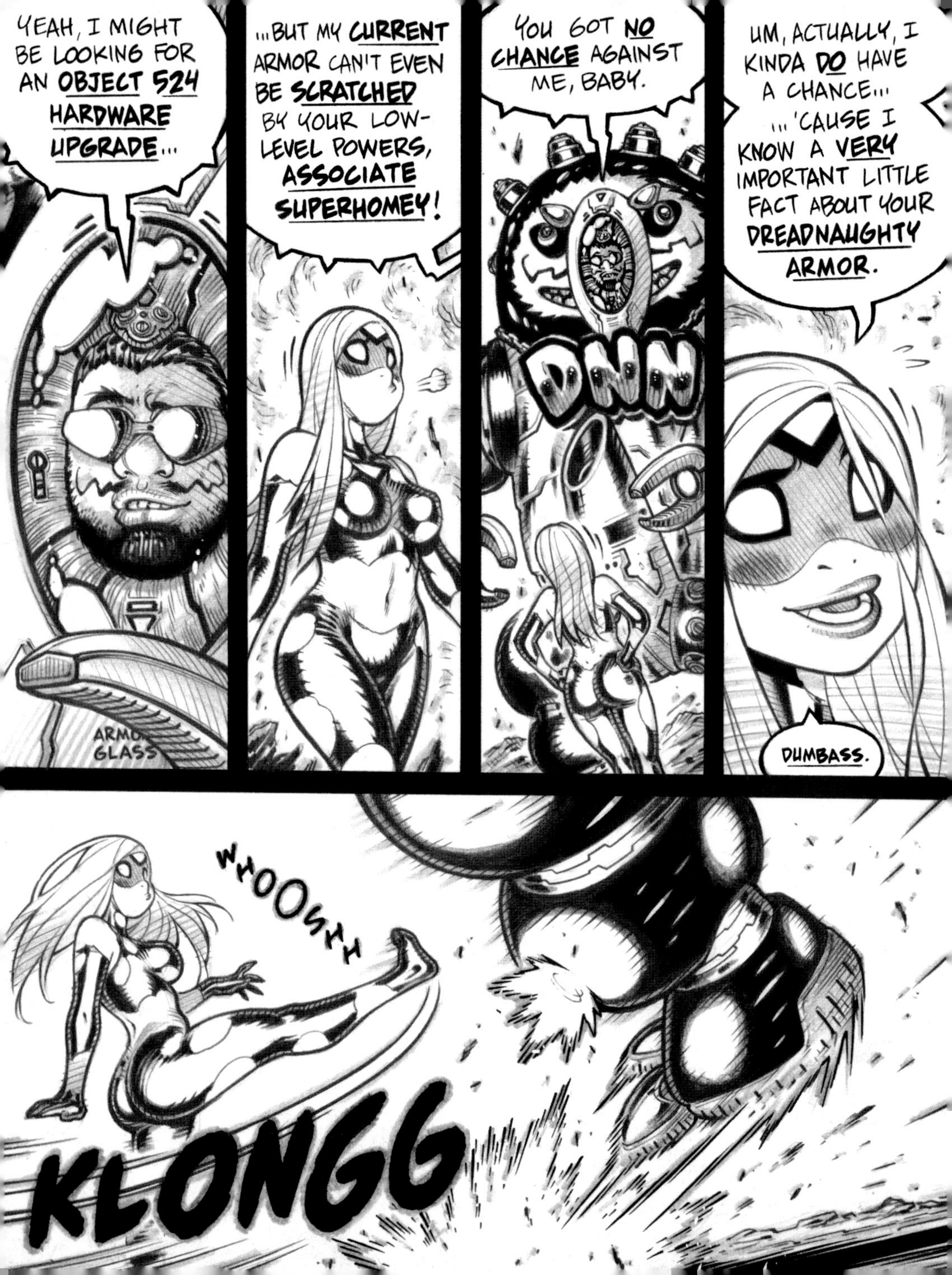
YEAH, I MIGHT BE LOOKING FOR AN OBJECT 524 HARDWARE UPGRADE...
ARMOR GLASS
...BUT MY CURRENT ARMOR CAN'T EVEN BE SCRATCHED BY YOUR LOW-LEVEL POWERS, ASSOCIATE SUPERHOMEY!
YOU GOT NO CHANCE AGAINST ME, BABY.
DNN
UM, ACTUALLY, I KINDA DO HAVE A CHANCE...
...'CAUSE I KNOW A VERY IMPORTANT LITTLE FACT ABOUT YOUR DREADNAUGHTY ARMOR.
DUMBASS.
WHOOSHH
KLONGG

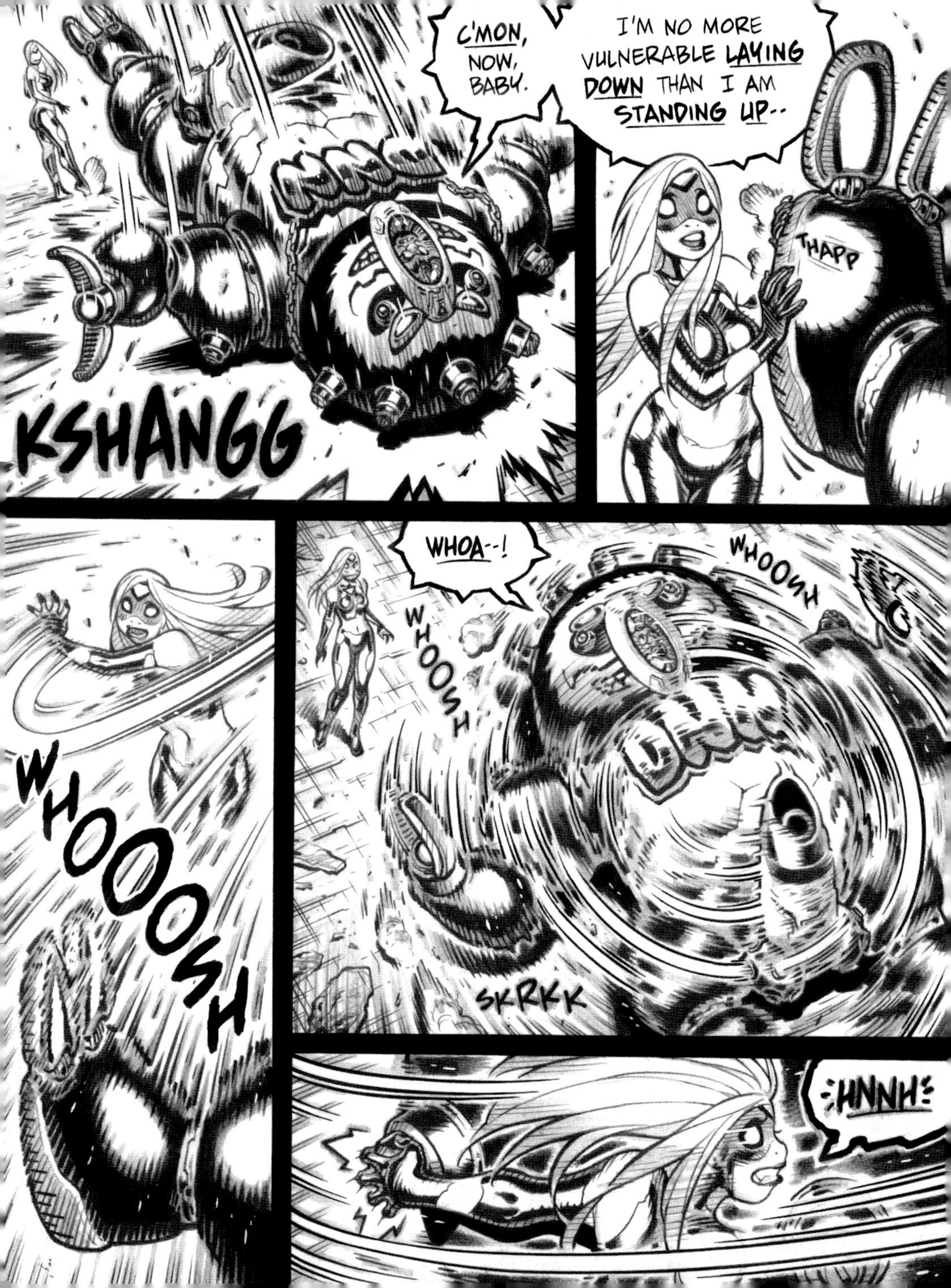
C'MON, NOW, BABY.
I'M NO MORE VULNERABLE LAYING DOWN THAN I AM STANDING UP--
KSHANGG
THAPP
WHOOOOSH
WHOA--!
WHOOSH
WHOOSH
SKRKK
HNNH

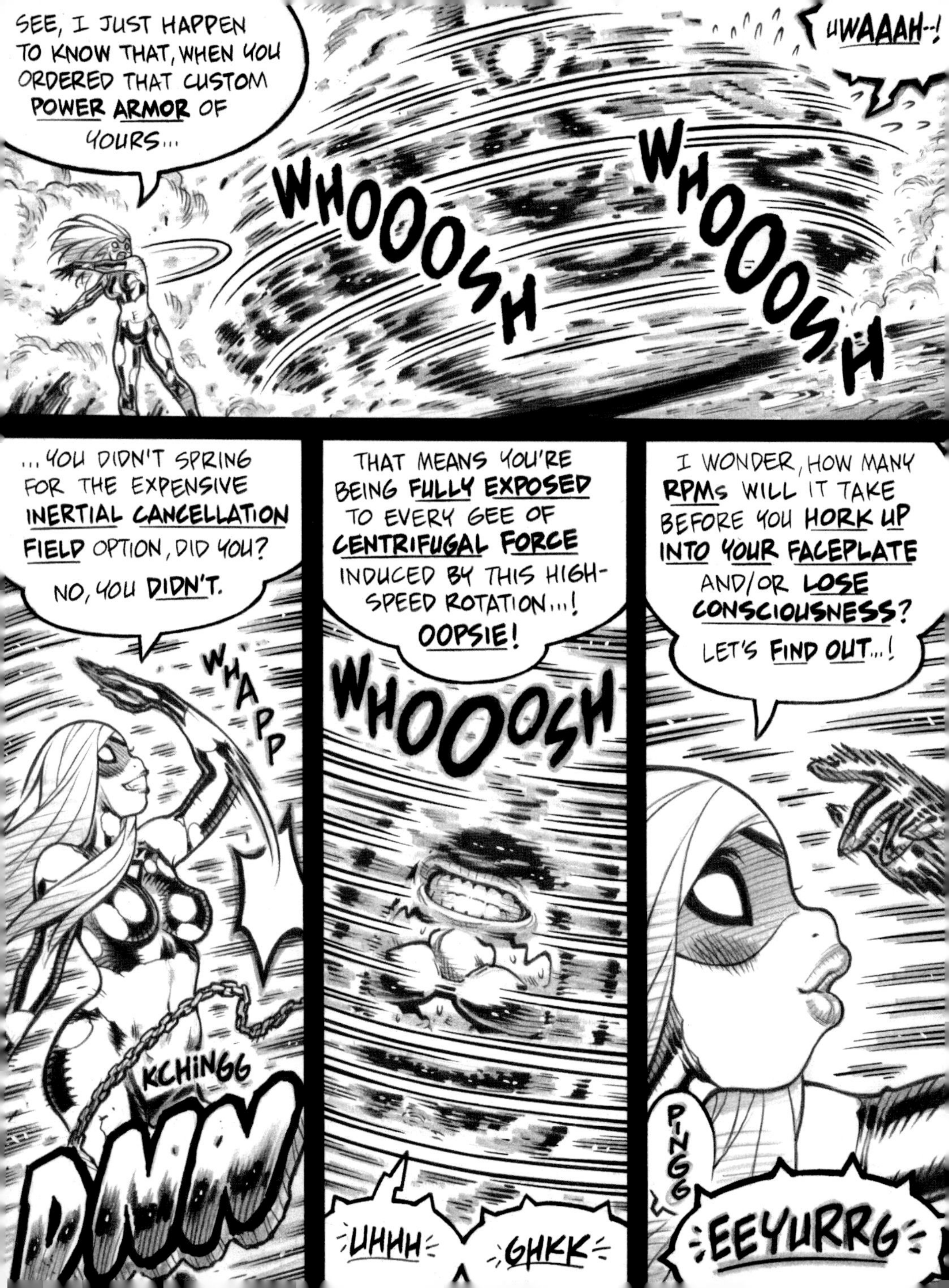
SEE, I JUST HAPPEN TO KNOW THAT, WHEN YOU ORDERED THAT CUSTOM POWER ARMOR OF YOURS...
WHOOOSH
WHOOOSH
UWAAAH--!
...YOU DIDN'T SPRING FOR THE EXPENSIVE INERTIAL CANCELLATION FIELD OPTION, DID YOU?
NO, YOU DIDN'T.
WHAPP
KCHINGG
THAT MEANS YOU'RE BEING FULLY EXPOSED TO EVERY GEE OF CENTRIFUGAL FORCE INDUCED BY THIS HIGH-SPEED ROTATION...!
OOPSIE!
WHOOOSH
UHHH
GHKK
I WONDER, HOW MANY RPMs WILL IT TAKE BEFORE YOU HORK UP INTO YOUR FACEPLATE AND/OR LOSE CONSCIOUSNESS?
LET'S FIND OUT...!
PINGG
EEYURRG

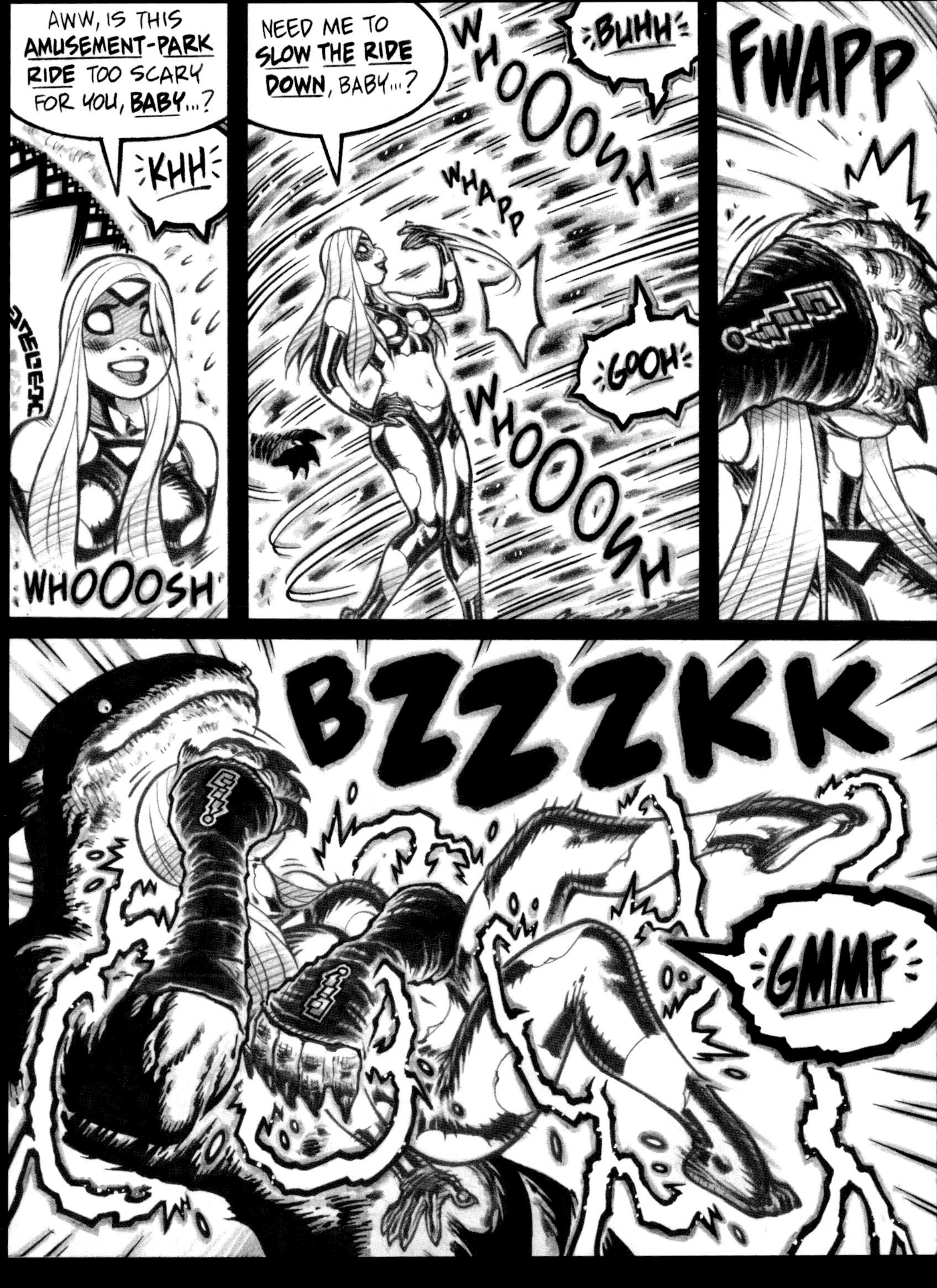
AWW, IS THIS AMUSEMENT-PARK RIDE TOO SCARY FOR YOU, BABY...?
KHH
WHOOOOSH
NEED ME TO SLOW THE RIDE DOWN, BABY...?
WHOOOOSH
BUHH
WHAPP
GOOH
WHOOOOOSH
FWAPP
BZZZKK
GMMF

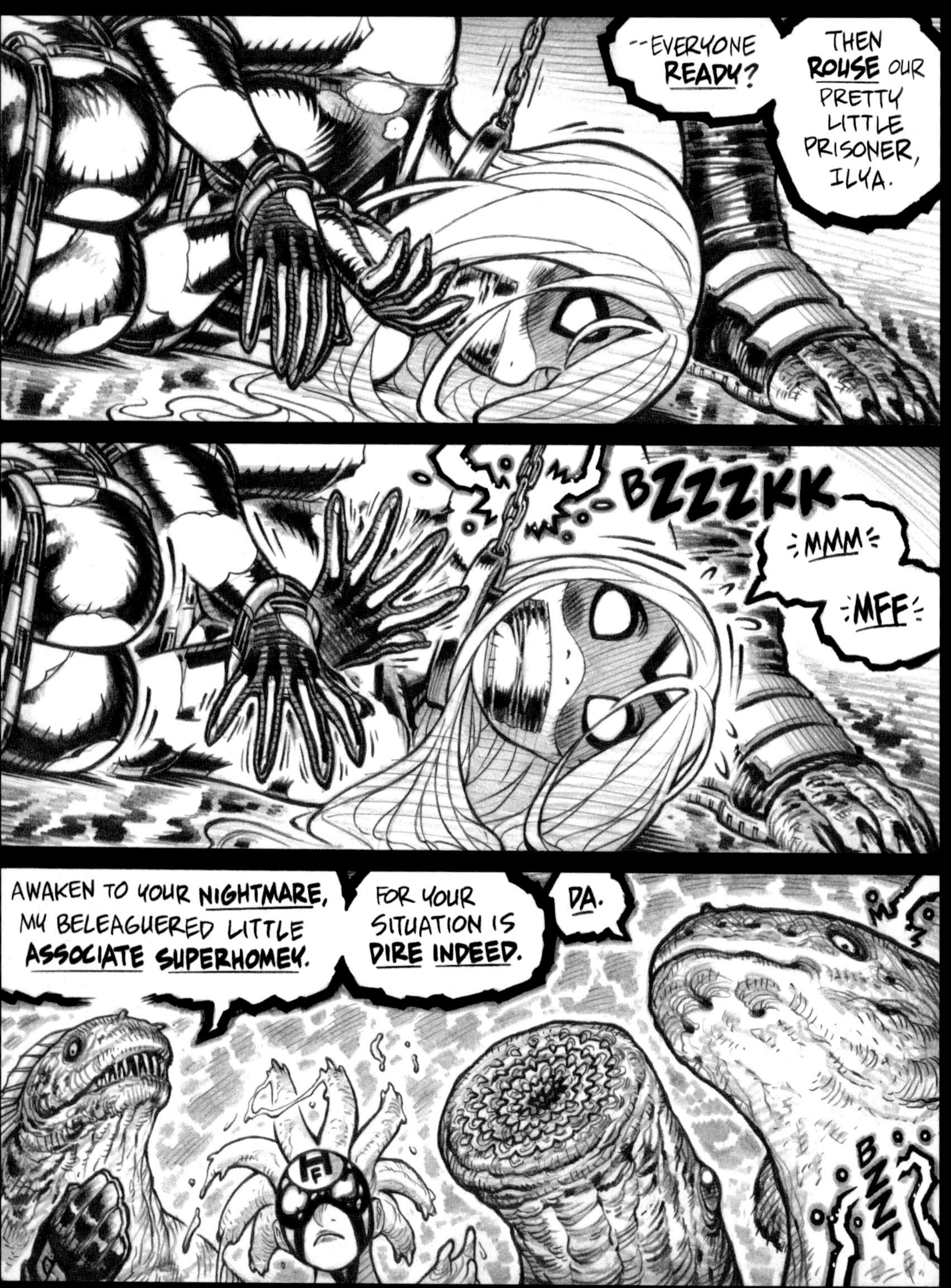
--EVERYONE READY?
THEN ROUSE OUR PRETTY LITTLE PRISONER, ILYA.
BZZZKK
MMM
MFF
AWAKEN TO YOUR NIGHTMARE, MY BELEAGUERED LITTLE ASSOCIATE SUPERHOMEY.
FOR YOUR SITUATION IS DIRE INDEED.
DA.
BZZZT

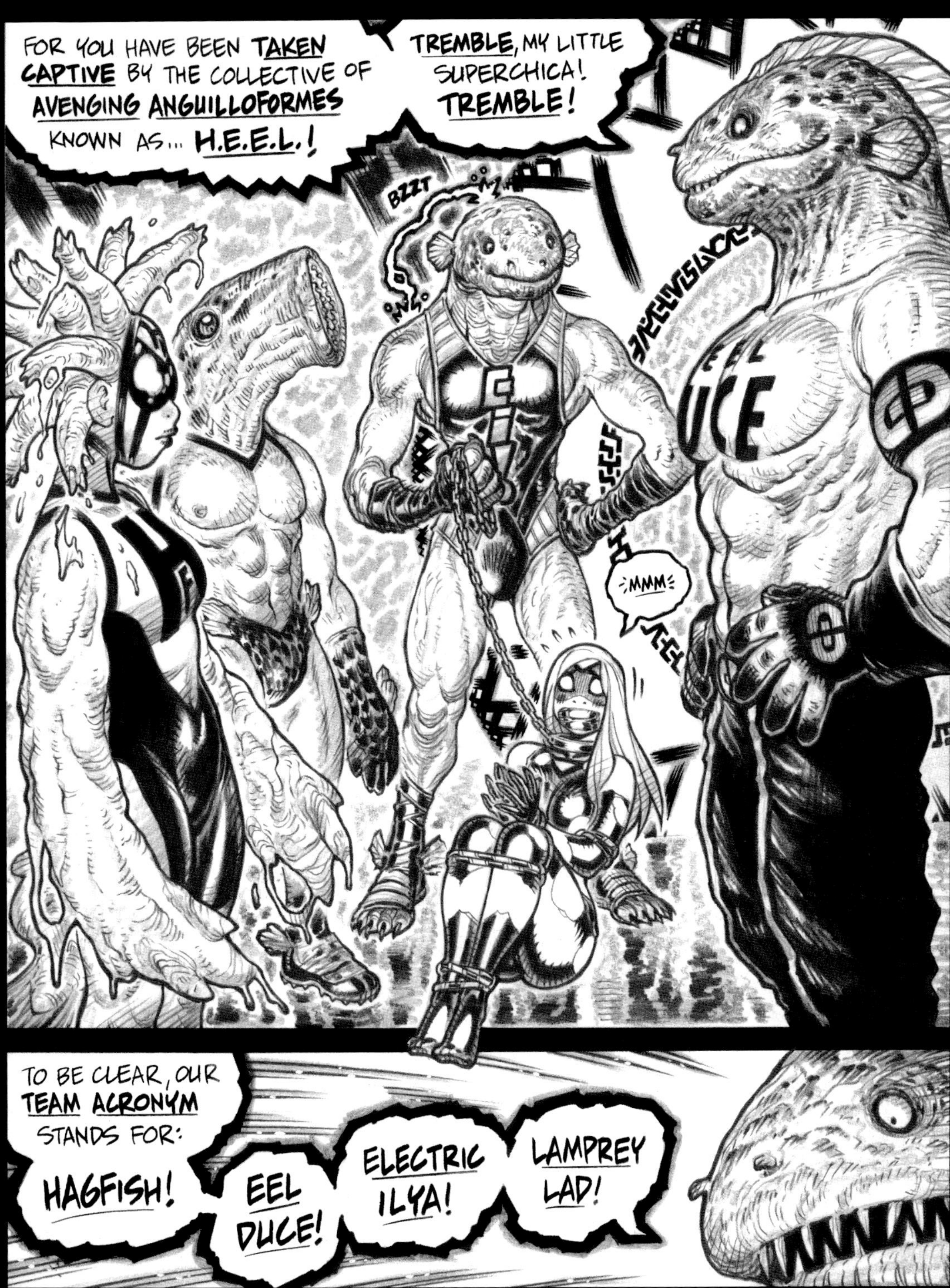
FOR YOU HAVE BEEN TAKEN CAPTIVE BY THE COLLECTIVE OF AVENGING ANGUILLOFORMES KNOWN AS... H.E.E.L.!
TREMBLE, MY LITTLE SUPERCHICA! TREMBLE!
BZZT
MMM
TO BE CLEAR, OUR TEAM ACRONYM STANDS FOR:
HAGFISH!
EEL DUCE!
ELECTRIC ILYA!
LAMPREY LAD!

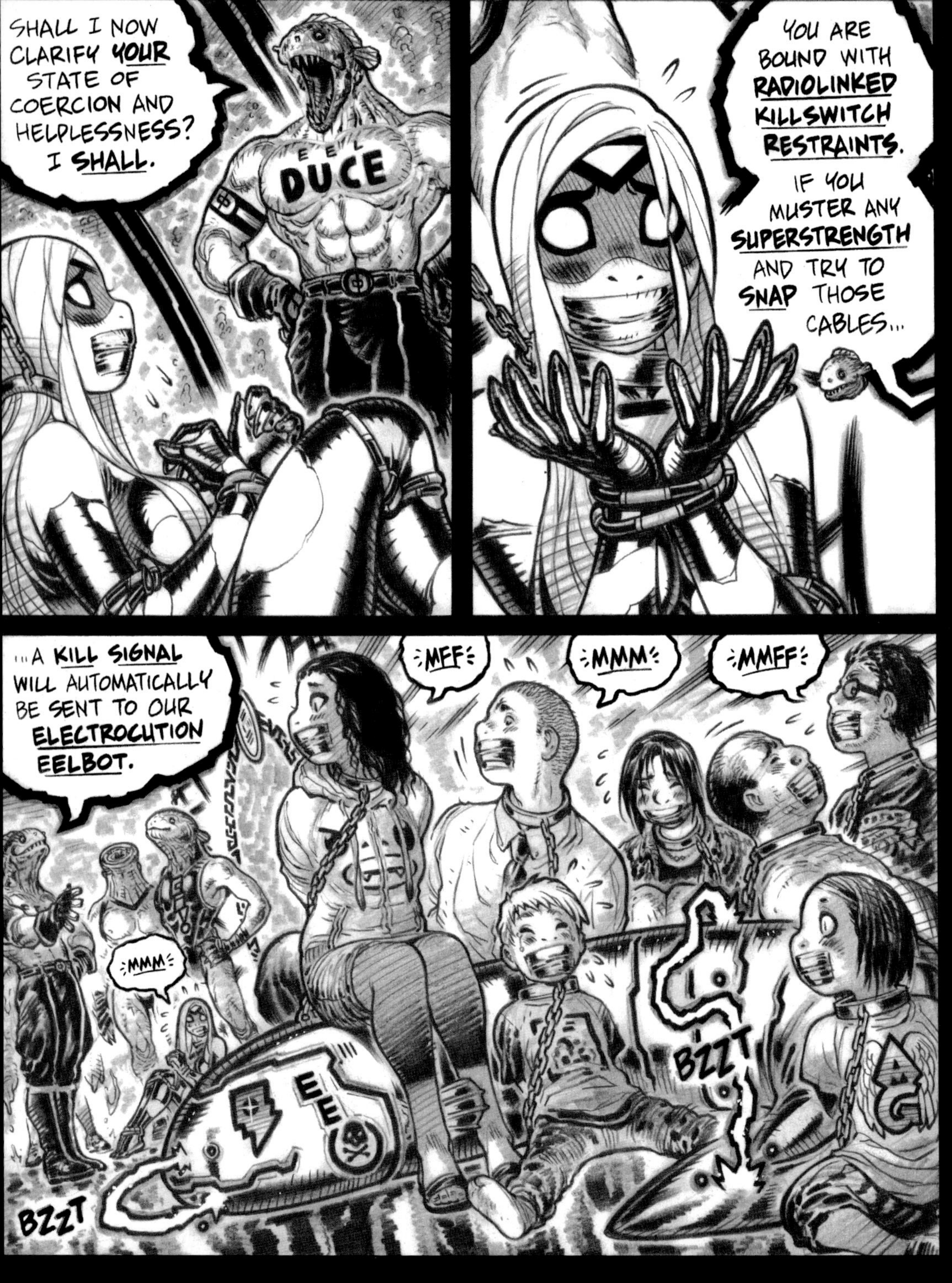

SHALL I NOW CLARIFY YOUR STATE OF COERCION AND HELPLESSNESS? I SHALL.
EEL DUCE
YOU ARE BOUND WITH RADIOLINKED KILLSWITCH RESTRAINTS.
IF YOU MUSTER ANY SUPERSTRENGTH AND TRY TO SNAP THOSE CABLES...
...A KILL SIGNAL WILL AUTOMATICALLY BE SENT TO OUR ELECTROCUTION EELBOT.
MFF
MMM
MMFF
MMM
BZZT
BZZT

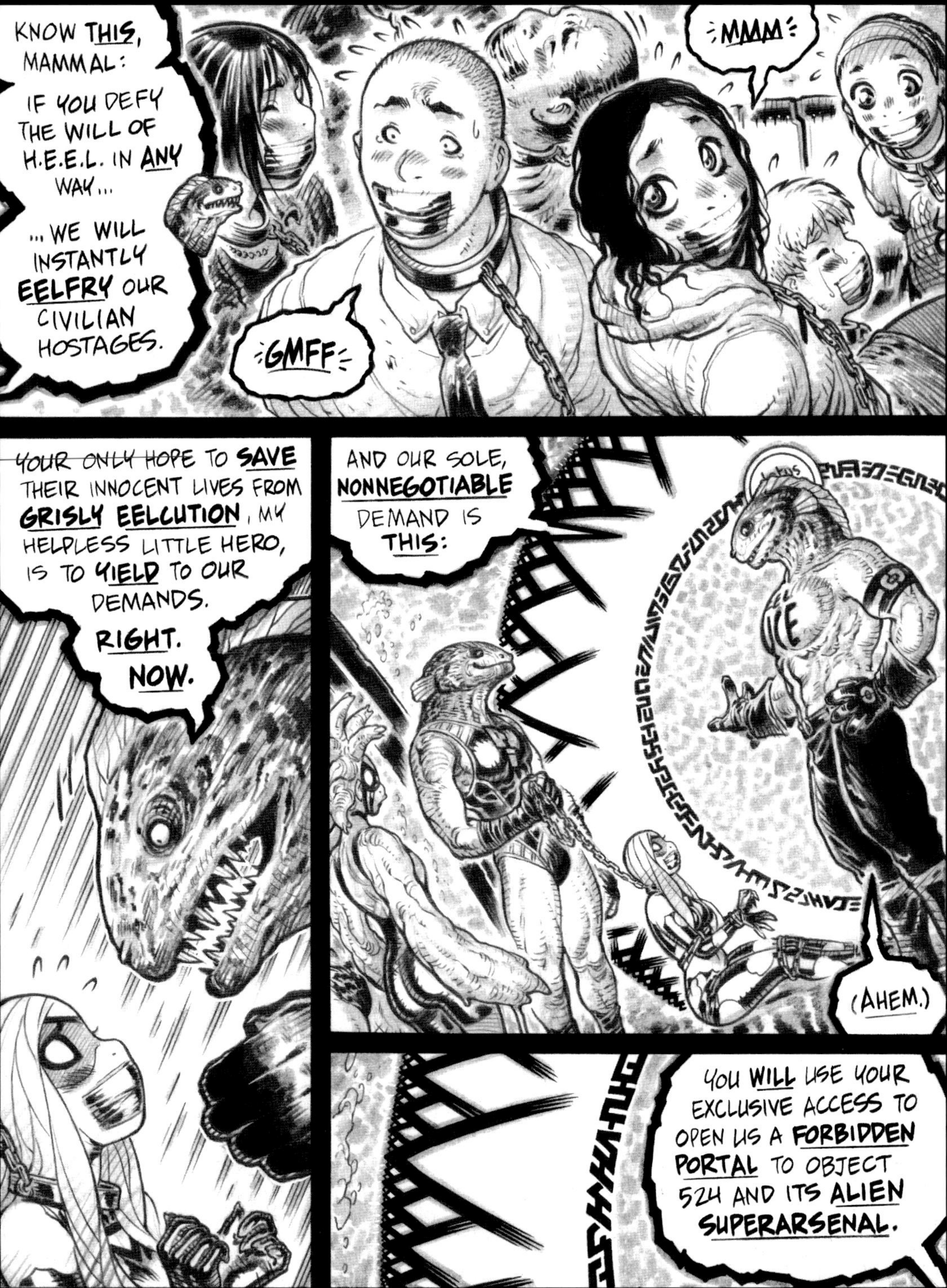
KNOW THIS, MAMMAL:
IF YOU DEFY THE WILL OF H.E.E.L. IN ANY WAY...
...WE WILL INSTANTLY EELFRY OUR CIVILIAN HOSTAGES.
GMFF
MMM
YOUR ONLY HOPE TO SAVE THEIR INNOCENT LIVES FROM GRISLY EELCUTION, MY HELPLESS LITTLE HERO, IS TO YIELD TO OUR DEMANDS.
RIGHT. NOW.
AND OUR SOLE, NONNEGOTIABLE DEMAND IS THIS:
(AHEM.)
YOU WILL USE YOUR EXCLUSIVE ACCESS TO OPEN US A FORBIDDEN PORTAL TO OBJECT 524 AND ITS ALIEN SUPERARSENAL.

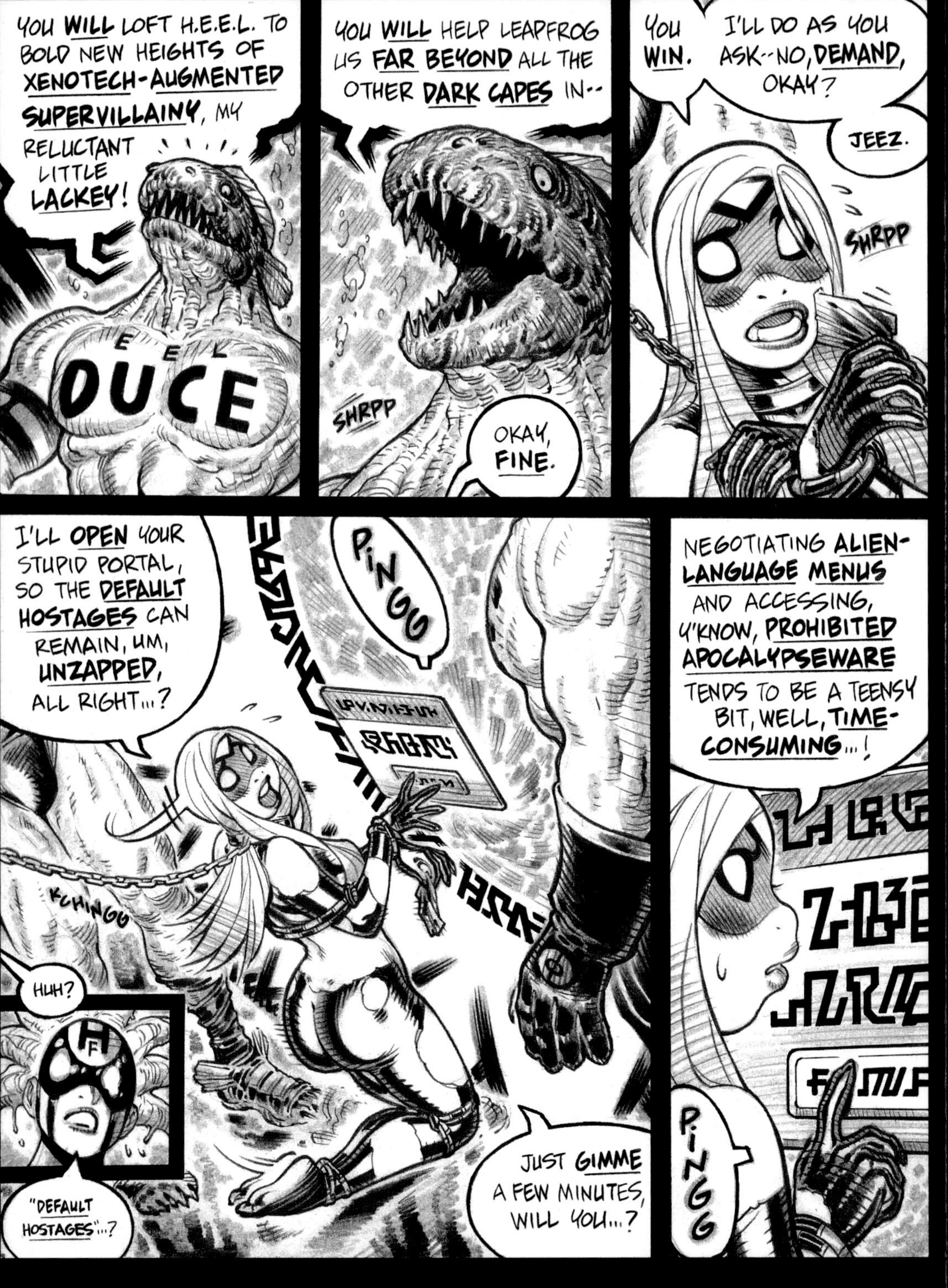

YOU WILL LOFT H.E.E.L. TO BOLD NEW HEIGHTS OF XENOTECH-AUGMENTED SUPERVILLAINY, MY RELUCTANT LITTLE LACKEY!
YOU WILL HELP LEAPFROG US FAR BEYOND ALL THE OTHER DARK CAPES IN--
SHRPP
OKAY, FINE.
YOU WIN.
I'LL DO AS YOU ASK--NO, DEMAND, OKAY?
JEEZ.
SHRPP
I'LL OPEN YOUR STUPID PORTAL, SO THE DEFAULT HOSTAGES CAN REMAIN, UM, UNZAPPED, ALL RIGHT...?
PINGG
KCHINGG
HUH?
"DEFAULT HOSTAGES"...?
JUST GIMME A FEW MINUTES, WILL YOU...?
NEGOTIATING ALIEN-LANGUAGE MENUS AND ACCESSING, Y'KNOW, PROHIBITED APOCALYPSEWARE TENDS TO BE A TEENSY BIT, WELL, TIME-CONSUMING...!
PINGG

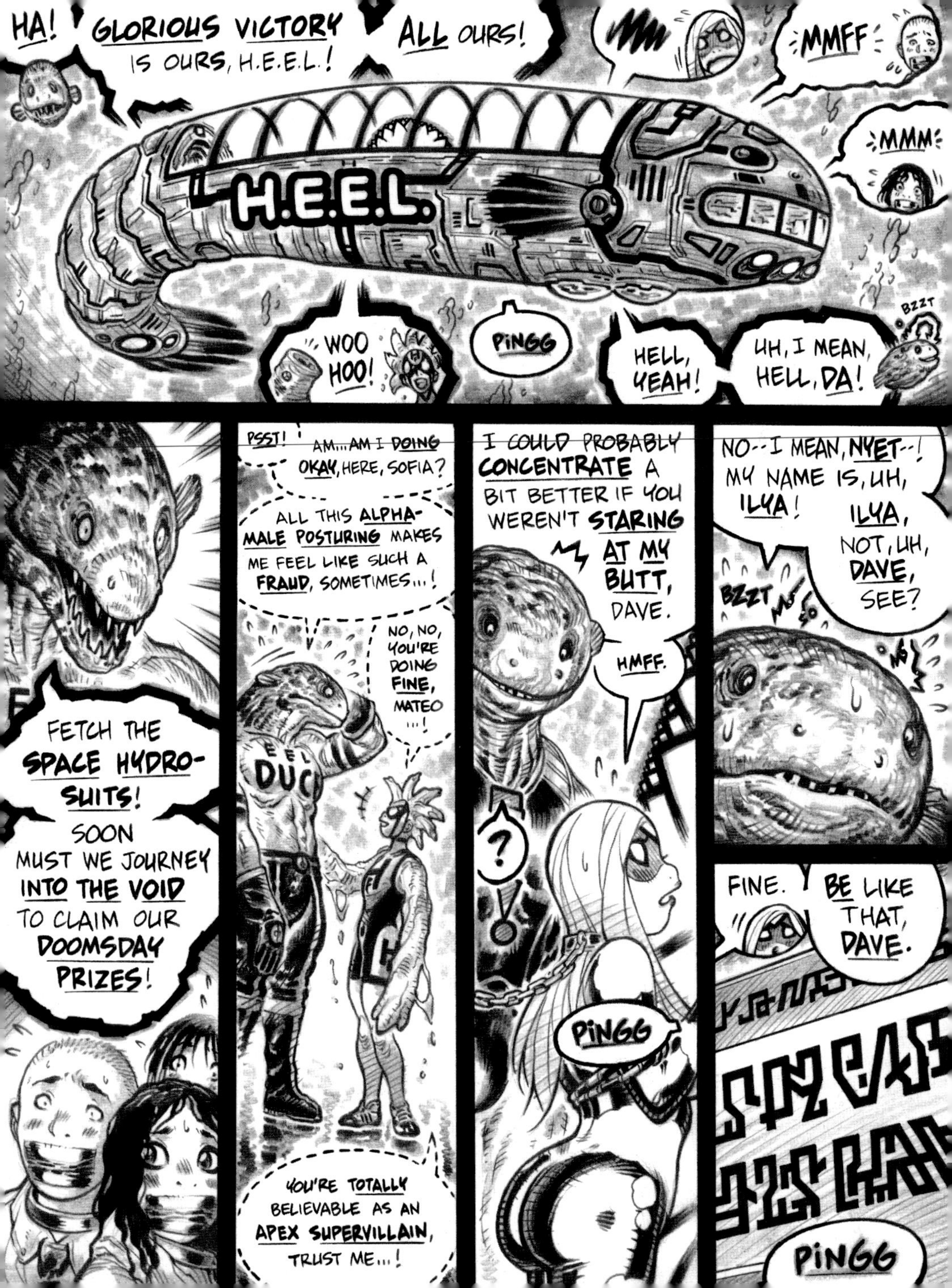
HA! GLORIOUS VICTORY IS OURS, H.E.E.L.!
ALL OURS!
MMFF
MMM
H.E.E.L.
WOO HOO!
PINGG
HELL, YEAH!
UH, I MEAN, HELL, DA!
BZZT
FETCH THE SPACE HYDRO-SUITS! SOON MUST WE JOURNEY INTO THE VOID TO CLAIM OUR DOOMSDAY PRIZES!
PSST! AM...AM I DOING OKAY, HERE, SOFIA?
ALL THIS ALPHA-MALE POSTURING MAKES ME FEEL LIKE SUCH A FRAUD, SOMETIMES...!
NO, NO, YOU'RE DOING FINE, MATEO...!
YOU'RE TOTALLY BELIEVABLE AS AN APEX SUPERVILLAIN, TRUST ME...!
I COULD PROBABLY CONCENTRATE A BIT BETTER IF YOU WEREN'T STARING AT MY BUTT, DAVE.
HMFF.
?
PINGG
NO--I MEAN, NYET--! MY NAME IS, UH, ILYA!
ILYA, NOT, UH, DAVE, SEE?
BZZT
FINE.
BE LIKE THAT, DAVE.
PINGG

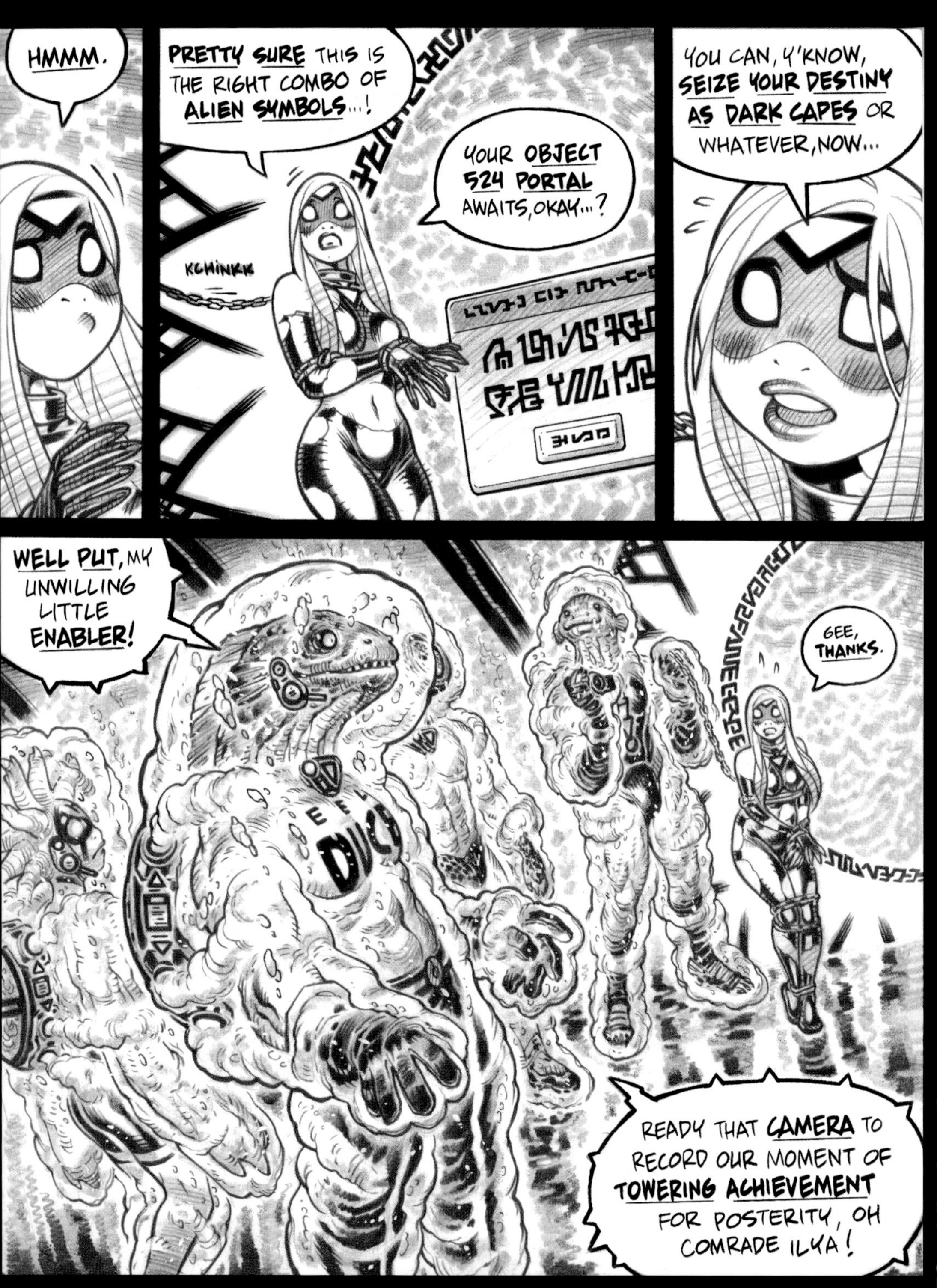
HMMM.
PRETTY SURE THIS IS THE RIGHT COMBO OF ALIEN SYMBOLS...!
YOUR OBJECT 524 PORTAL AWAITS, OKAY...?
KCHINKK
YOU CAN, Y'KNOW, SEIZE YOUR DESTINY AS DARK CAPES OR WHATEVER, NOW...
WELL PUT, MY UNWILLING LITTLE ENABLER!
GEE, THANKS.
READY THAT CAMERA TO RECORD OUR MOMENT OF TOWERING ACHIEVEMENT FOR POSTERITY, OH COMRADE ILYA!

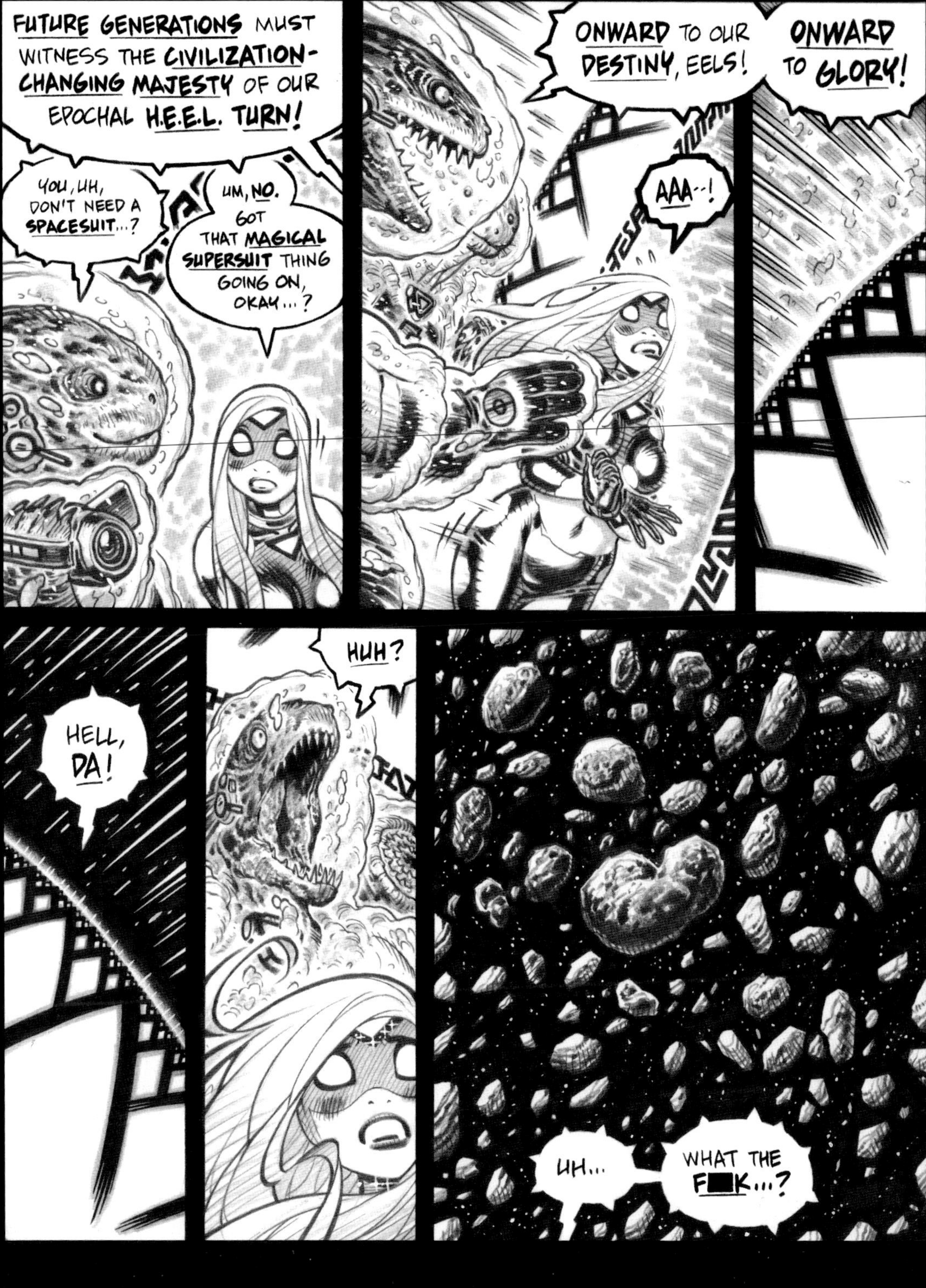
FUTURE GENERATIONS MUST WITNESS THE CIVILIZATION-CHANGING MAJESTY OF OUR EPOCHAL H.E.E.L. TURN!
YOU, UH, DON'T NEED A SPACESUIT...?
UM, NO. GOT THAT MAGICAL SUPERSUIT THING GOING ON, OKAY...?
ONWARD TO OUR DESTINY, EELS!
ONWARD TO GLORY!
AAA--!
HELL, DA!
HUH?
UH...
WHAT THE F[redacted]K...?

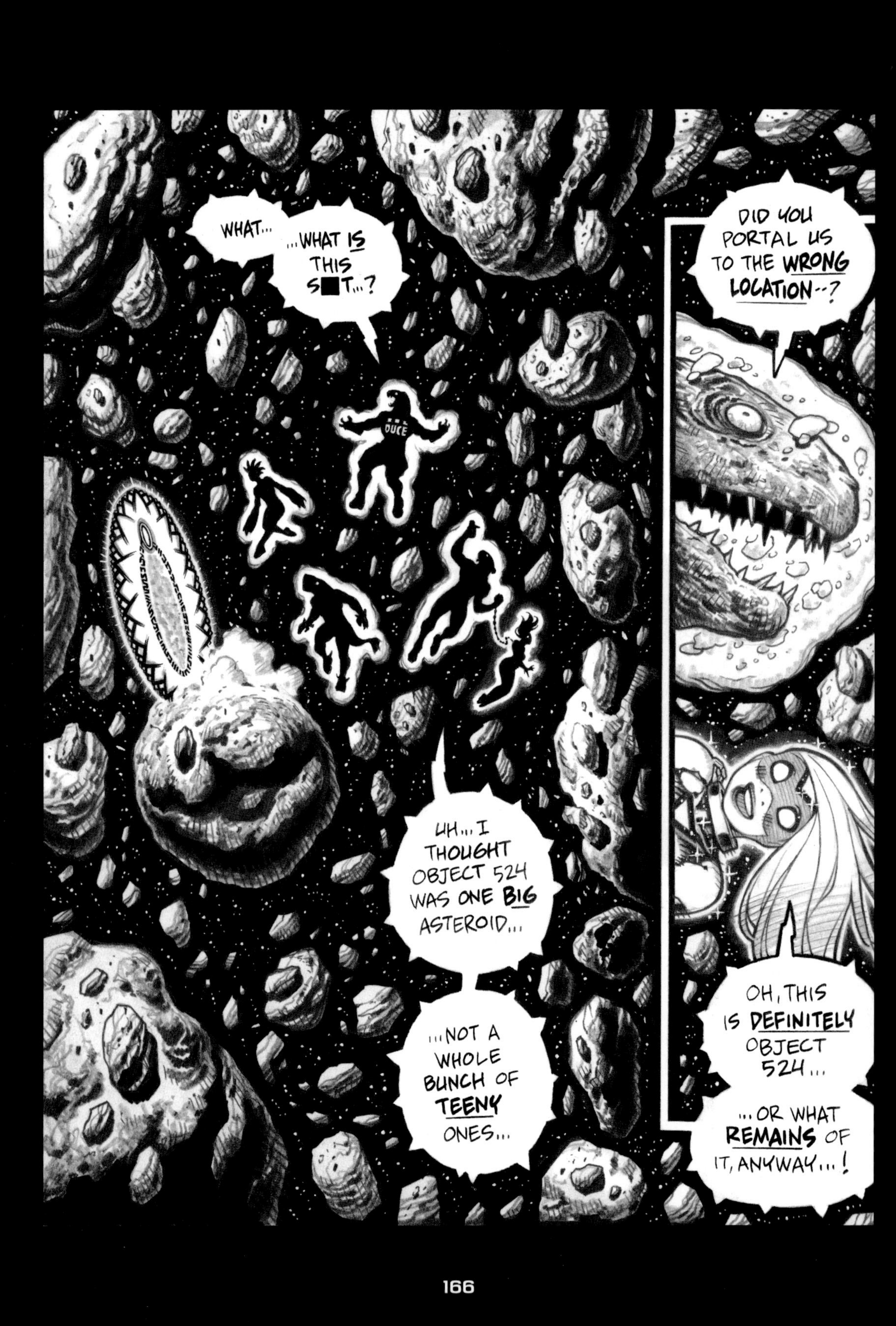
WHAT...
...WHAT IS THIS S[redacted]T...?
DUCE
UH... I THOUGHT OBJECT 524 WAS ONE BIG ASTEROID...
...NOT A WHOLE BUNCH OF TEENY ONES...
DID YOU PORTAL US TO THE WRONG LOCATION--?
OH, THIS IS DEFINITELY OBJECT 524...
...OR WHAT REMAINS OF IT, ANYWAY...!

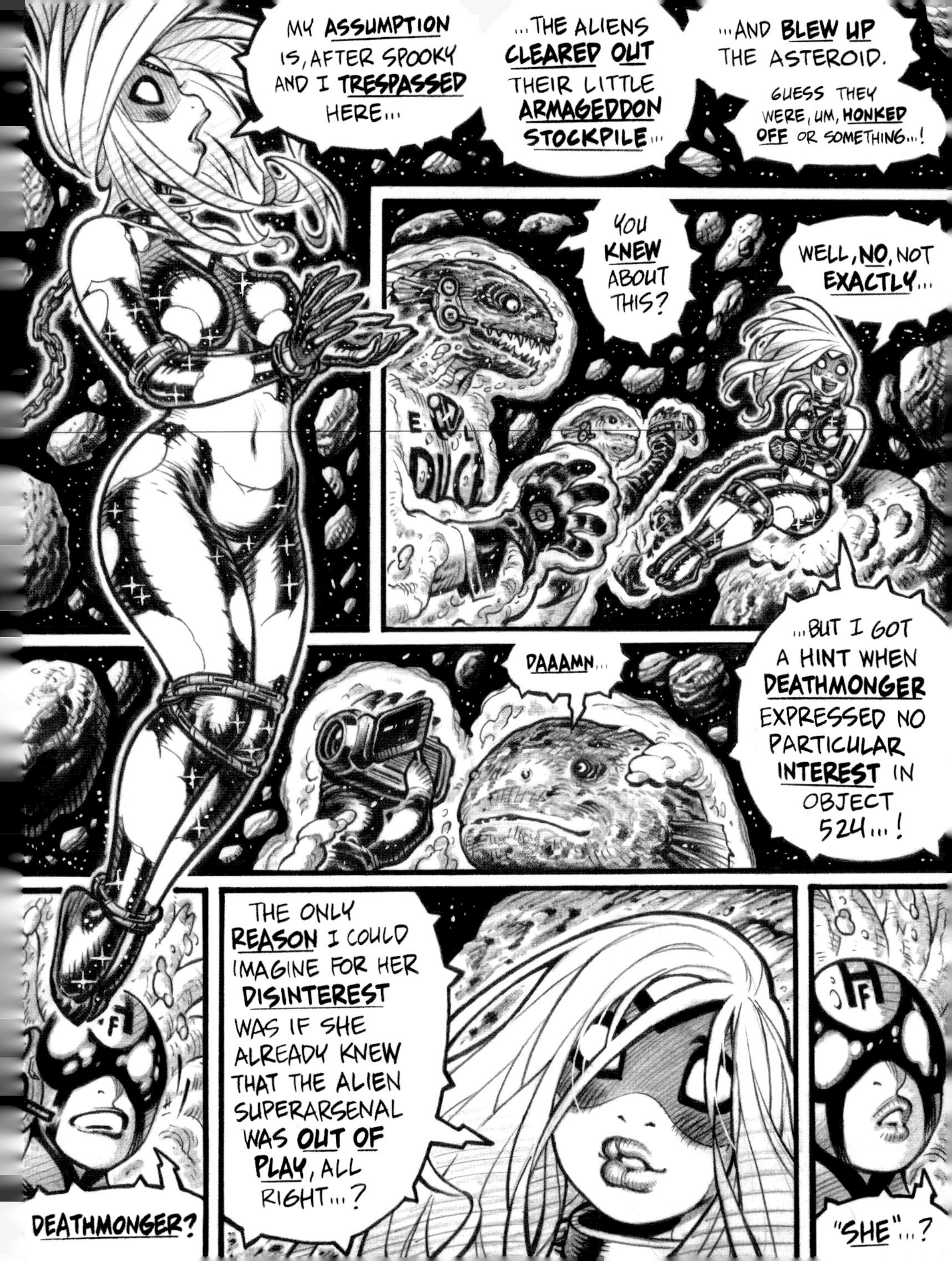
MY ASSUMPTION IS, AFTER SPOOKY AND I TRESPASSED HERE...
...THE ALIENS CLEARED OUT THEIR LITTLE ARMAGEDDON STOCKPILE...
...AND BLEW UP THE ASTEROID.
GUESS THEY WERE, UM, HONKED OFF OR SOMETHING...!
YOU KNEW ABOUT THIS?
WELL, NO, NOT EXACTLY...
...BUT I GOT A HINT WHEN DEATHMONGER EXPRESSED NO PARTICULAR INTEREST IN OBJECT 524...!
DAAAMN...
DEATHMONGER?
THE ONLY REASON I COULD IMAGINE FOR HER DISINTEREST WAS IF SHE ALREADY KNEW THAT THE ALIEN SUPERARSENAL WAS OUT OF PLAY, ALL RIGHT...?
"SHE"...?

SO, GUESS **WHAT**, DUMB-ASSES?

NOBODY'S USING ME TO ACCESS ANY **ALIEN SUPERWEAPONS** TODAY... OR **EVER**, FOR THAT MATTER...!

MAKE SURE TO GET SOME **QUALITY FOOTAGE** OF THIS WHOLE DEALIE, **DAVE**...!

BUT...BUT WE PAID THOSE **ONE-EYED CREEPS SO F■KING MUCH** FOR YOUR LOCATION...!

UH, **GUYS**?

WHAT THE HECK IS **THAT**?

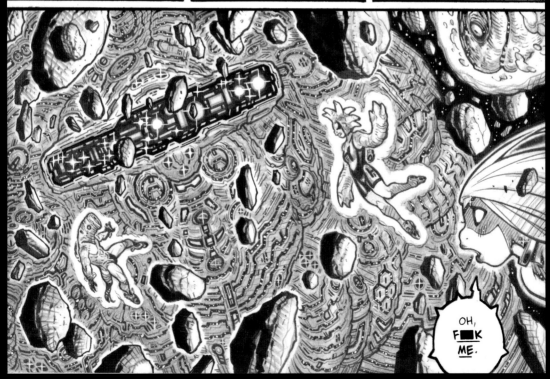

OH, F■K ME.

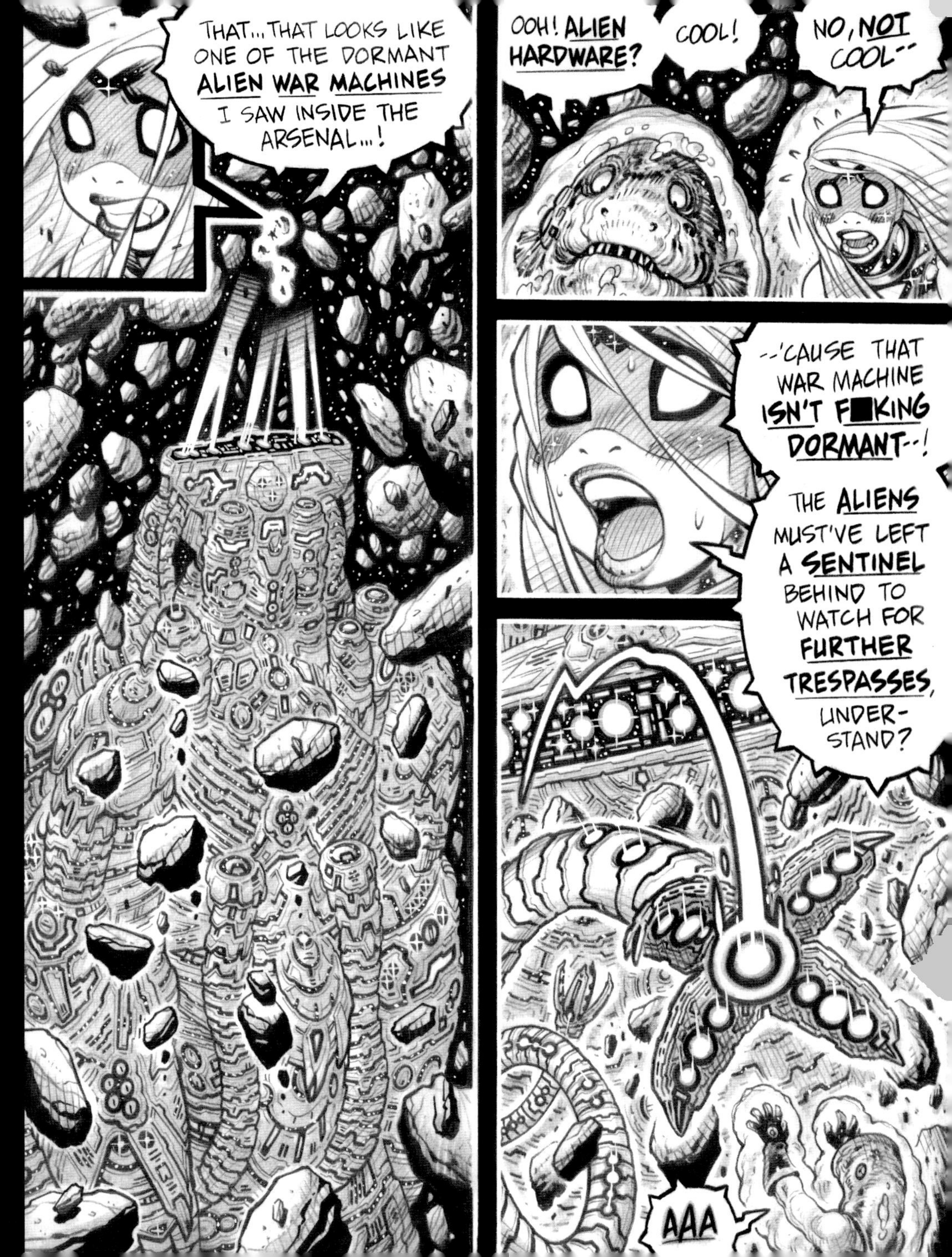
THAT... THAT LOOKS LIKE ONE OF THE DORMANT ALIEN WAR MACHINES I SAW INSIDE THE ARSENAL...!
OOH! ALIEN HARDWARE?
COOL!
NO, NOT COOL--
--'CAUSE THAT WAR MACHINE ISN'T F[redacted]KING DORMANT--!
THE ALIENS MUST'VE LEFT A SENTINEL BEHIND TO WATCH FOR FURTHER TRESPASSES, UNDER-STAND?
AAA

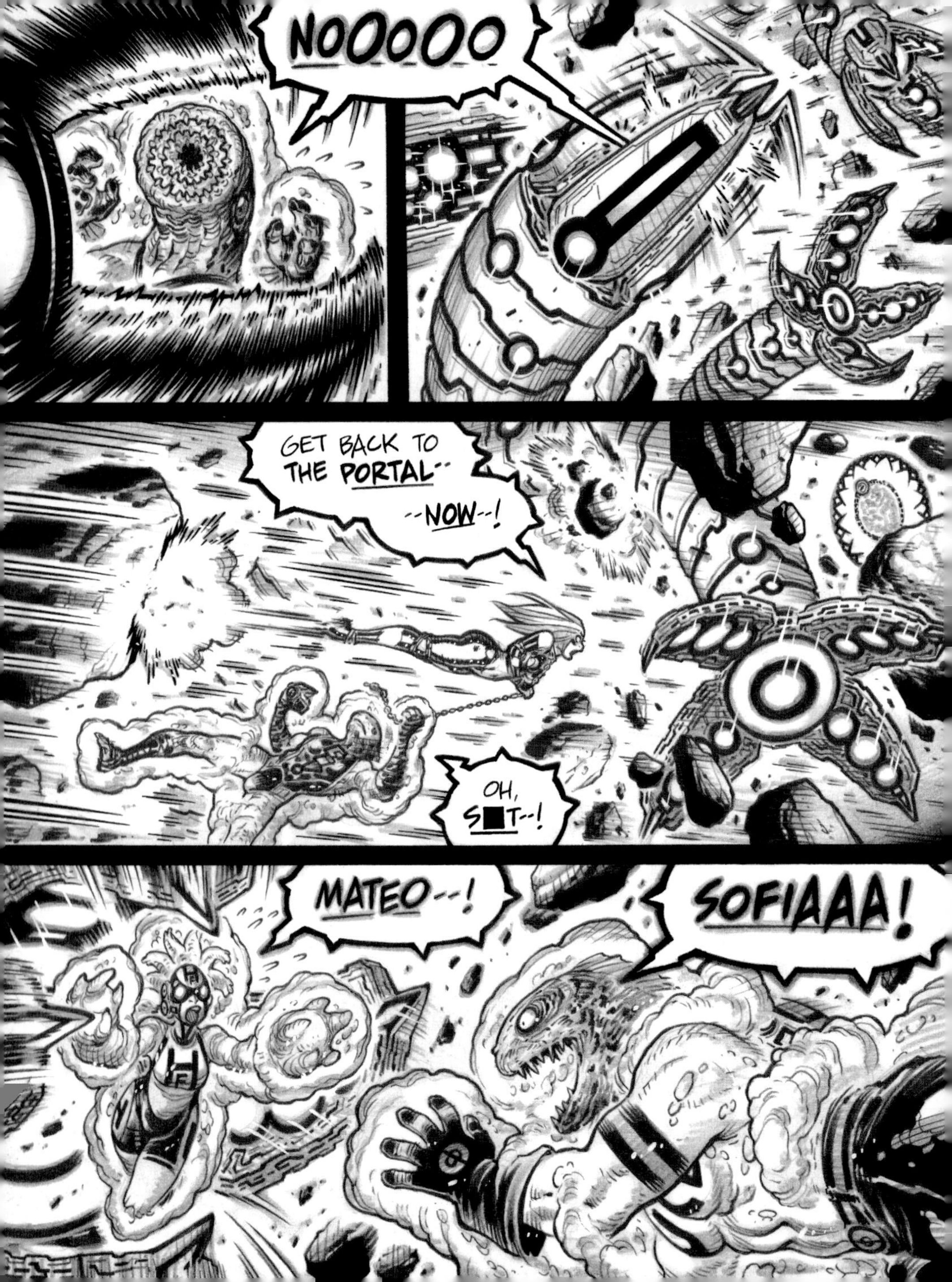
NOOOOO
GET BACK TO THE PORTAL--
--NOW--!
OH, S[redacted]T--!
MATEO--!
SOFIAAA!

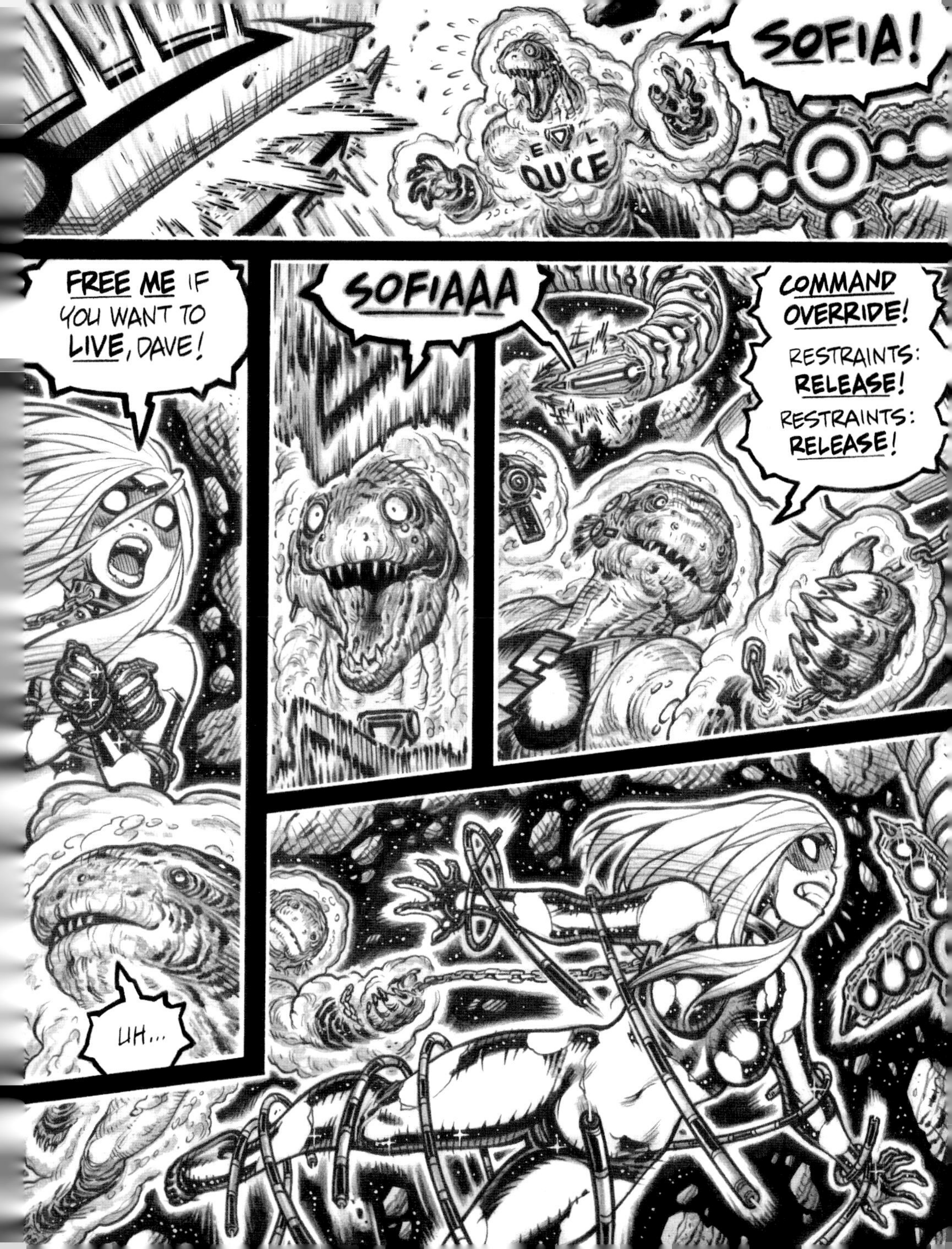
SOFIA!
EL DUCE
FREE ME IF YOU WANT TO LIVE, DAVE!
UH...
SOFIAAA
COMMAND OVERRIDE!
RESTRAINTS: RELEASE!
RESTRAINTS: RELEASE!

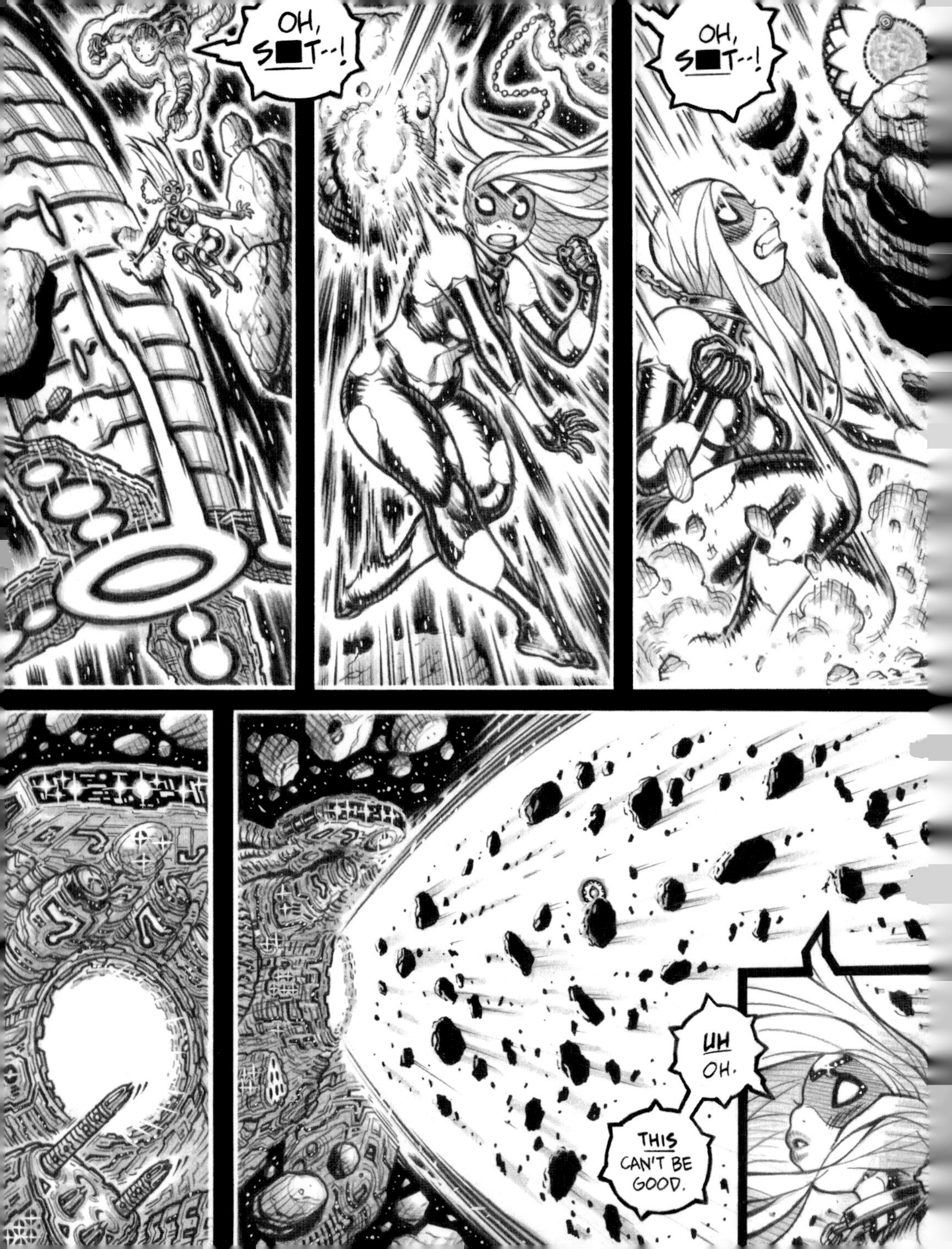
OH, S[redacted]T--!
OH, S[redacted]T--!
UH OH.
THIS CAN'T BE GOOD.

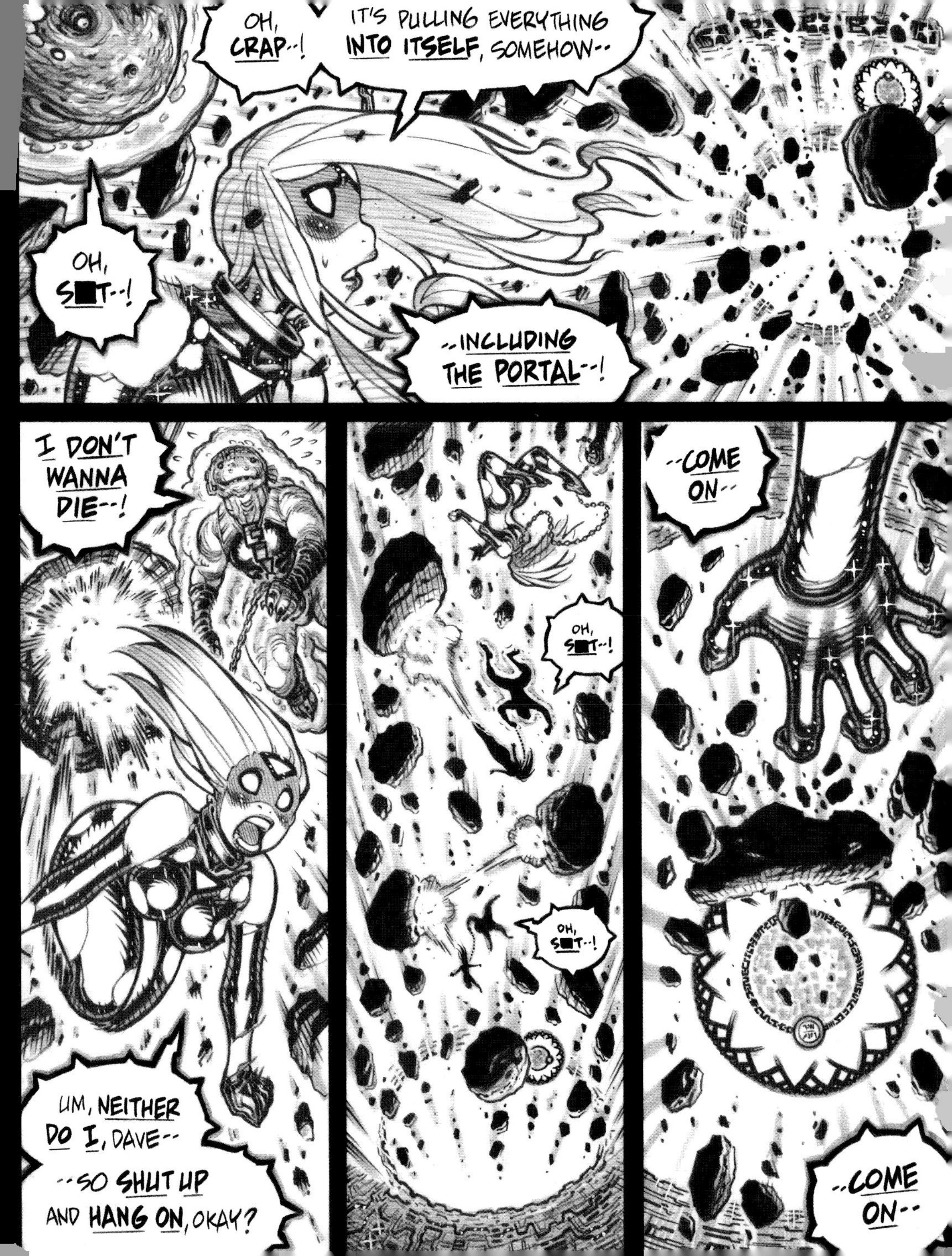

OH, CRAP--!
IT'S PULLING EVERYTHING INTO ITSELF, SOMEHOW--
OH, S[redacted]T--!
--INCLUDING THE PORTAL--!
I DON'T WANNA DIE--!
UM, NEITHER DO I, DAVE--
--SO SHUT UP AND HANG ON, OKAY?
OH, S[redacted]T--!
OH, S[redacted]T--!
--COME ON--
--COME ON--

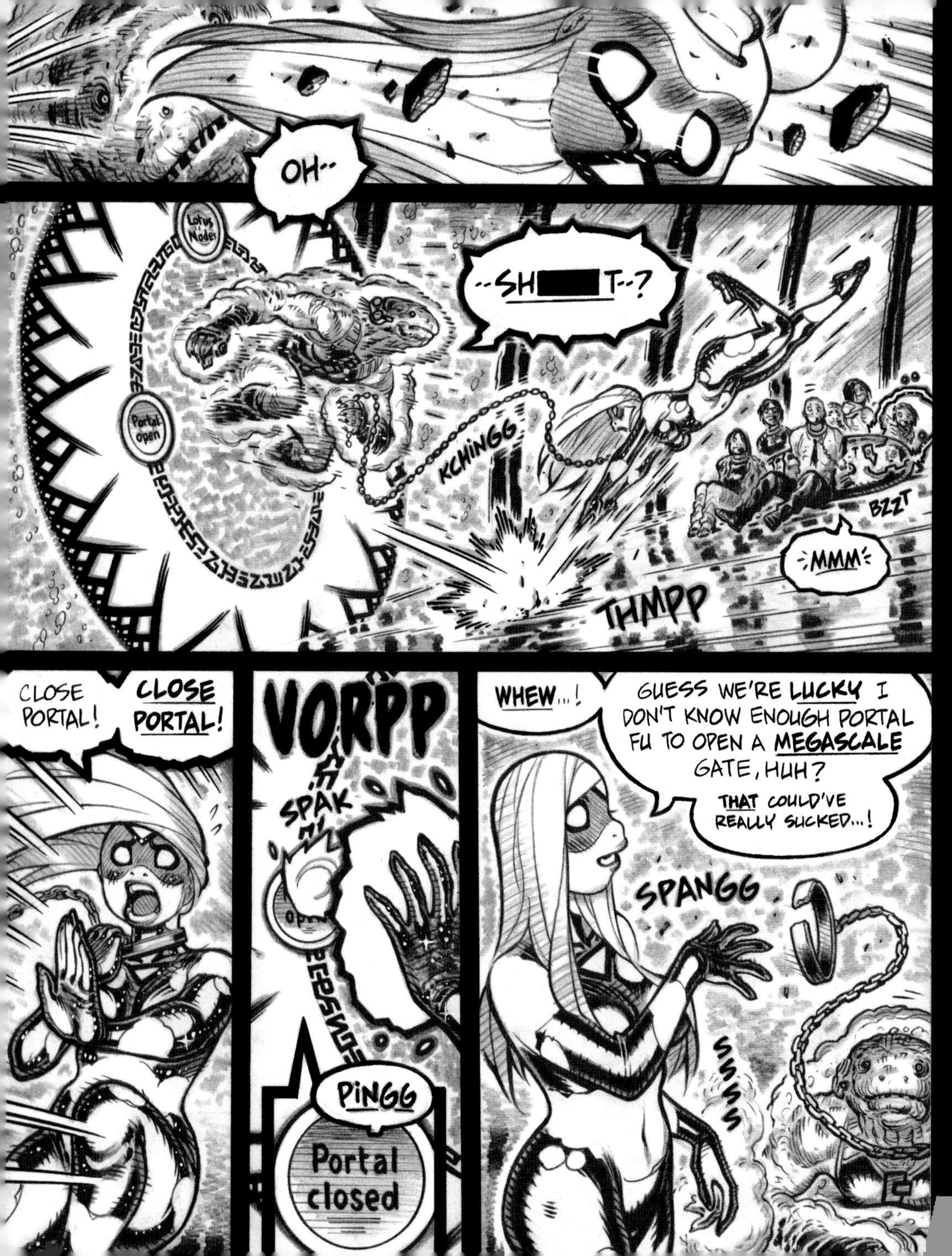
OH--
--SH[redacted]T--?
Lotus Nodes
Portal open
KCHINGG
BZZT
MMM
THMPP
CLOSE PORTAL!
CLOSE PORTAL!
VORPP
SPAK
PINGG
Portal closed
WHEW...!
GUESS WE'RE LUCKY I DON'T KNOW ENOUGH PORTAL FU TO OPEN A MEGASCALE GATE, HUH?
THAT COULD'VE REALLY SUCKED...!
SPANGG
SSSS

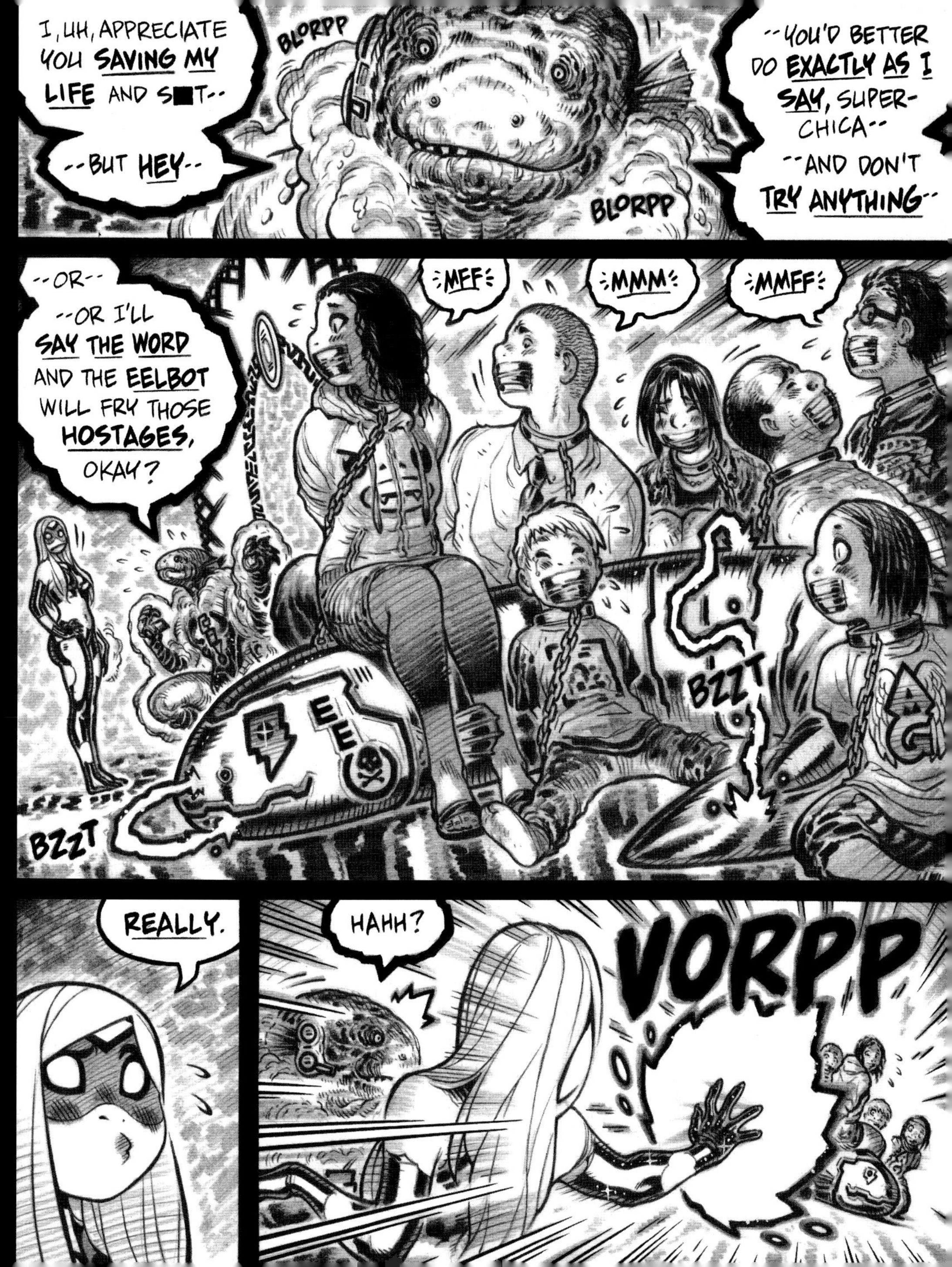

I, UH, APPRECIATE YOU SAVING MY LIFE AND S[redacted]T--
--BUT HEY--
BLORPP
BLORPP
--YOU'D BETTER DO EXACTLY AS I SAY, SUPER-CHICA--
--AND DON'T TRY ANYTHING--
--OR--
--OR I'LL SAY THE WORD AND THE EELBOT WILL FRY THOSE HOSTAGES, OKAY?
MFF
MMM
MMFF
BZZT
BZZT
REALLY.
HAHH?
VORPP

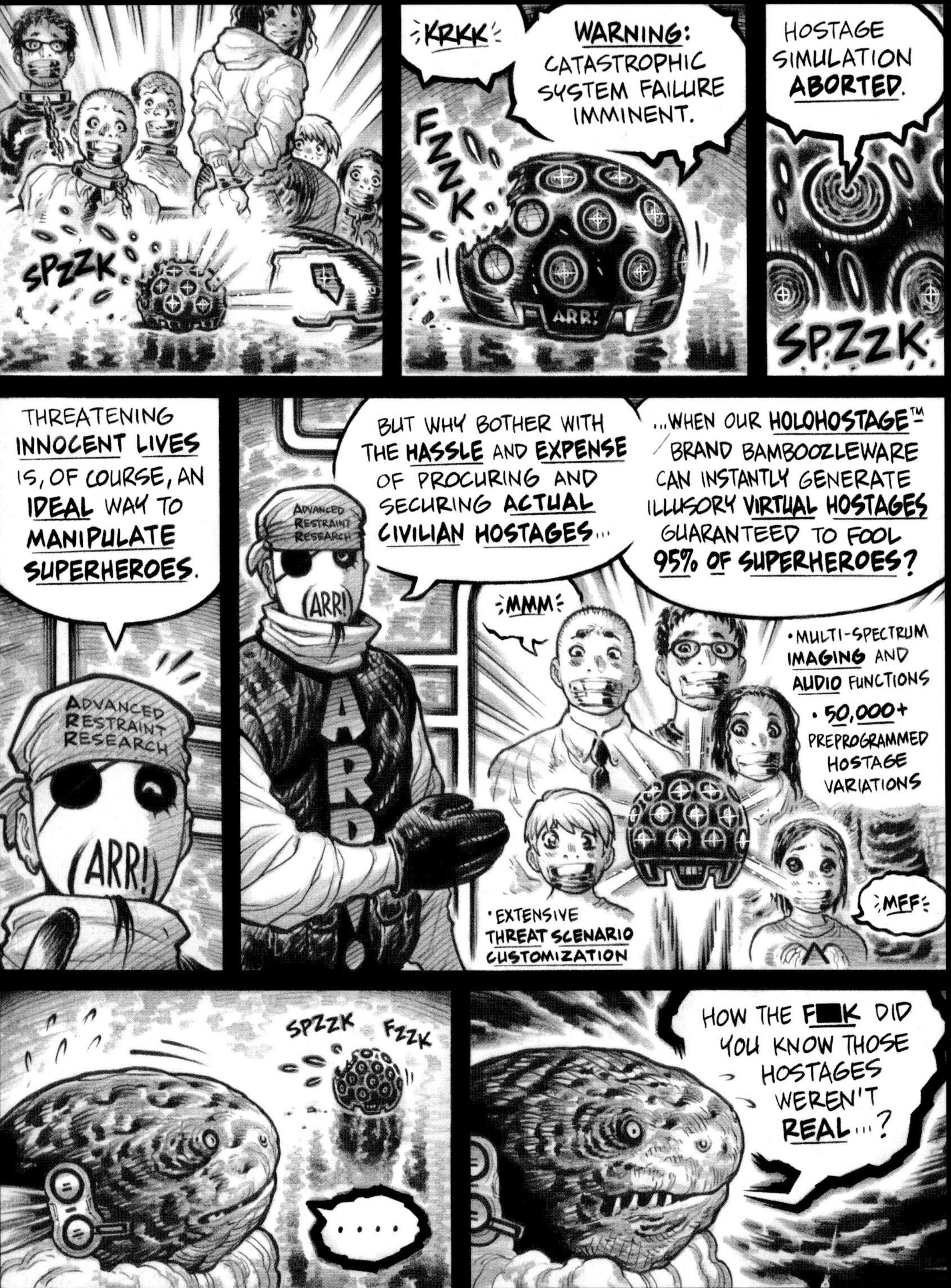
SPZZK
KRKK
WARNING: CATASTROPHIC SYSTEM FAILURE IMMINENT.
FZZK
ARR!
HOSTAGE SIMULATION ABORTED.
SPZZK
THREATENING INNOCENT LIVES IS, OF COURSE, AN IDEAL WAY TO MANIPULATE SUPERHEROES.
ADVANCED RESTRAINT RESEARCH
ARR!
BUT WHY BOTHER WITH THE HASSLE AND EXPENSE OF PROCURING AND SECURING ACTUAL CIVILIAN HOSTAGES...
...WHEN OUR HOLOHOSTAGE™-BRAND BAMBOOZLEWARE CAN INSTANTLY GENERATE ILLUSORY VIRTUAL HOSTAGES GUARANTEED TO FOOL 95% OF SUPERHEROES?
ADVANCED RESTRAINT RESEARCH
ARR!
ARR
MMM
•MULTI-SPECTRUM IMAGING AND AUDIO FUNCTIONS
•50,000+ PREPROGRAMMED HOSTAGE VARIATIONS
•EXTENSIVE THREAT SCENARIO CUSTOMIZATION
MFF
SPZZK
FZZK
....
HOW THE F[redacted]K DID YOU KNOW THOSE HOSTAGES WEREN'T REAL...?

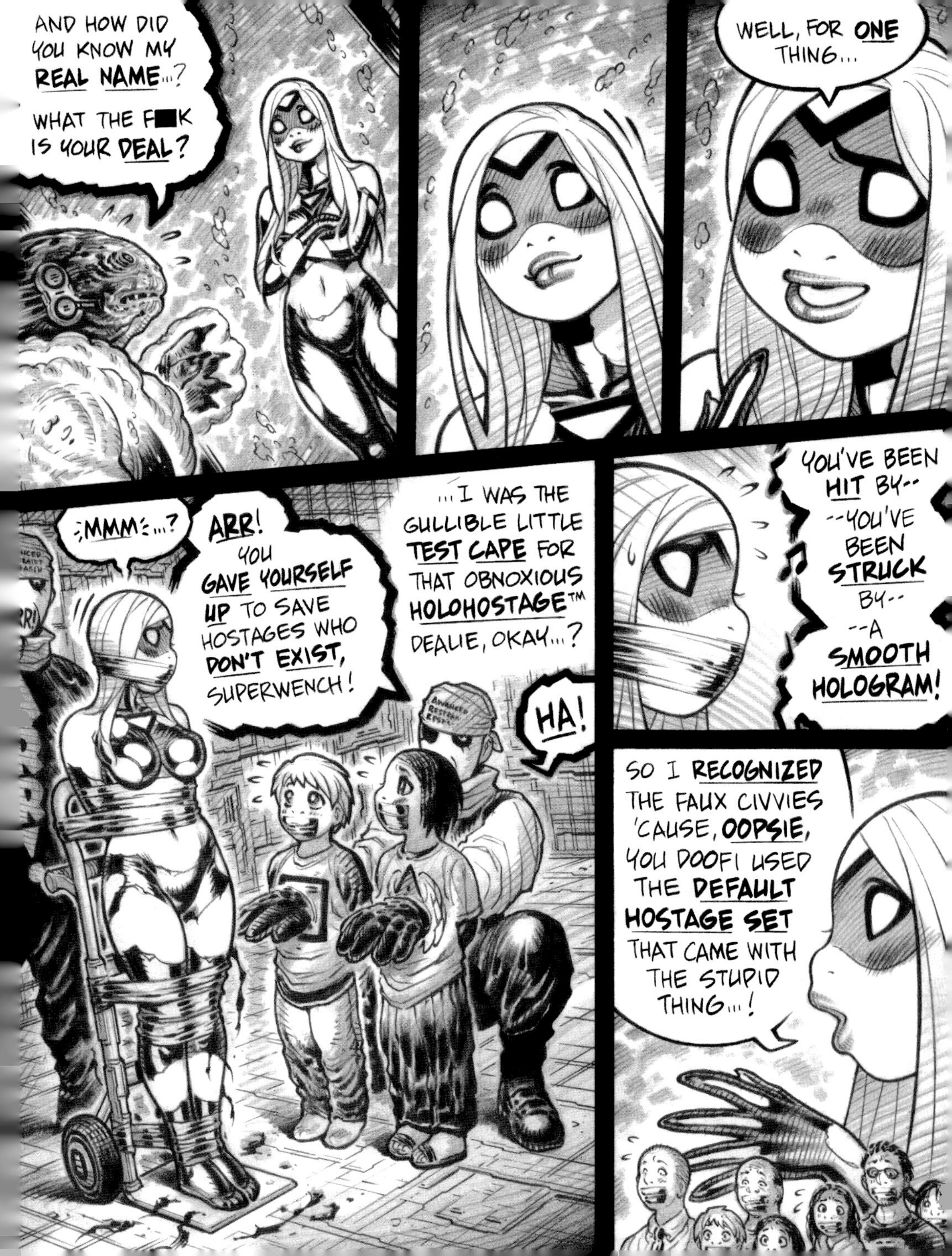
AND HOW DID YOU KNOW MY REAL NAME...?
WHAT THE F[redacted]K IS YOUR DEAL?
WELL, FOR ONE THING...
:MMM:...?
ARR! YOU GAVE YOURSELF UP TO SAVE HOSTAGES WHO DON'T EXIST, SUPERWENCH!
...I WAS THE GULLIBLE LITTLE TEST CAPE FOR THAT OBNOXIOUS HOLOHOSTAGE™ DEALIE, OKAY...?
HA!
YOU'VE BEEN HIT BY-- --YOU'VE BEEN STRUCK BY-- --A SMOOTH HOLOGRAM!
SO I RECOGNIZED THE FAUX CIVVIES 'CAUSE, OOPSIE, YOU DOOFI USED THE DEFAULT HOSTAGE SET THAT CAME WITH THE STUPID THING...!

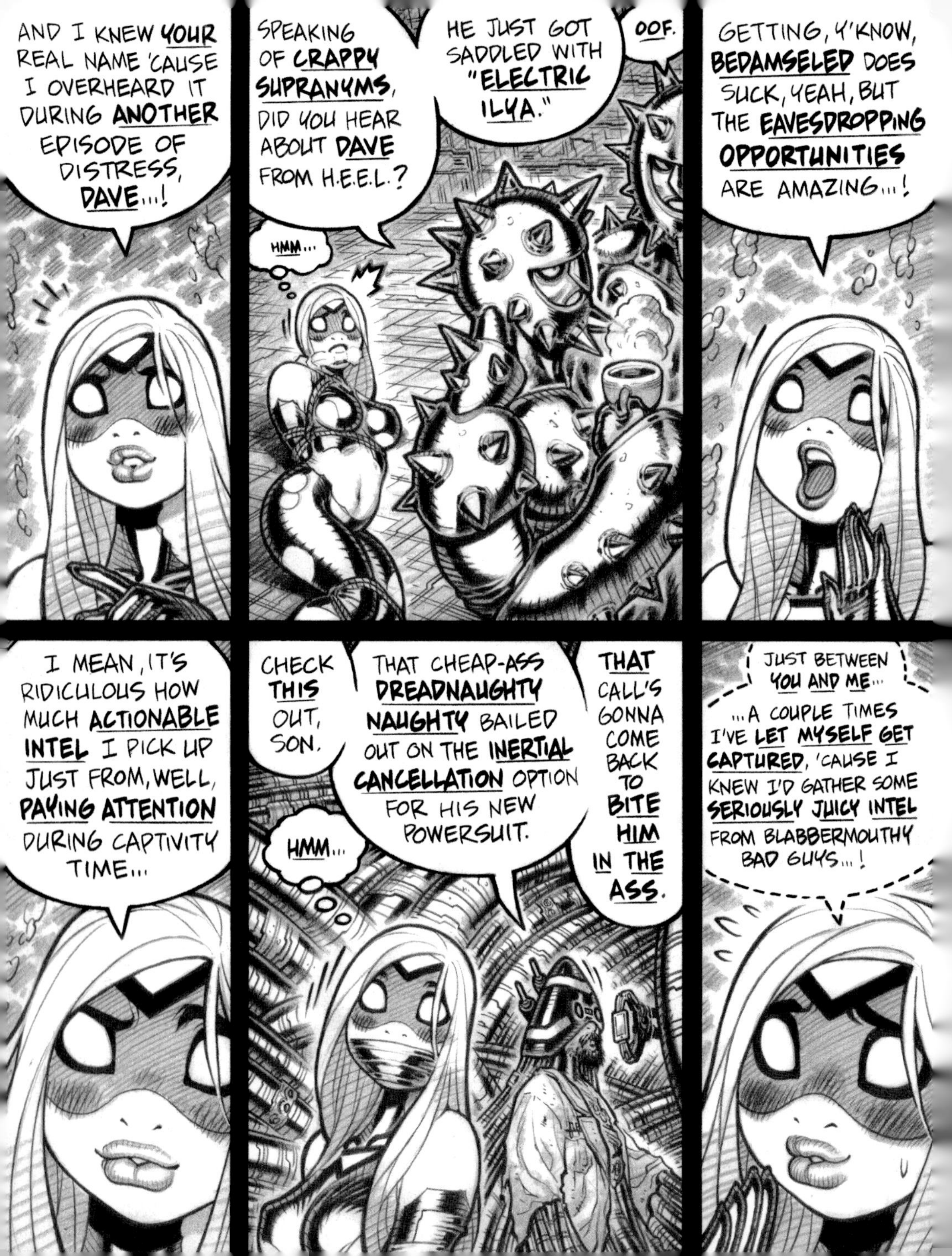
AND I KNEW YOUR REAL NAME 'CAUSE I OVERHEARD IT DURING ANOTHER EPISODE OF DISTRESS, DAVE...!
SPEAKING OF CRAPPY SUPRANYMS, DID YOU HEAR ABOUT DAVE FROM H.E.E.L.?
HE JUST GOT SADDLED WITH "ELECTRIC ILYA."
OOF.
HMM...
GETTING, Y'KNOW, BEDAMSELED DOES SUCK, YEAH, BUT THE EAVESDROPPING OPPORTUNITIES ARE AMAZING...!
I MEAN, IT'S RIDICULOUS HOW MUCH ACTIONABLE INTEL I PICK UP JUST FROM, WELL, PAYING ATTENTION DURING CAPTIVITY TIME...
CHECK THIS OUT, SON.
THAT CHEAP-ASS DREADNAUGHTY NAUGHTY BAILED OUT ON THE INERTIAL CANCELLATION OPTION FOR HIS NEW POWERSUIT.
THAT CALL'S GONNA COME BACK TO BITE HIM IN THE ASS.
HMM...
JUST BETWEEN YOU AND ME...
...A COUPLE TIMES I'VE LET MYSELF GET CAPTURED, 'CAUSE I KNEW I'D GATHER SOME SERIOUSLY JUICY INTEL FROM BLABBERMOUTHY BAD GUYS...!

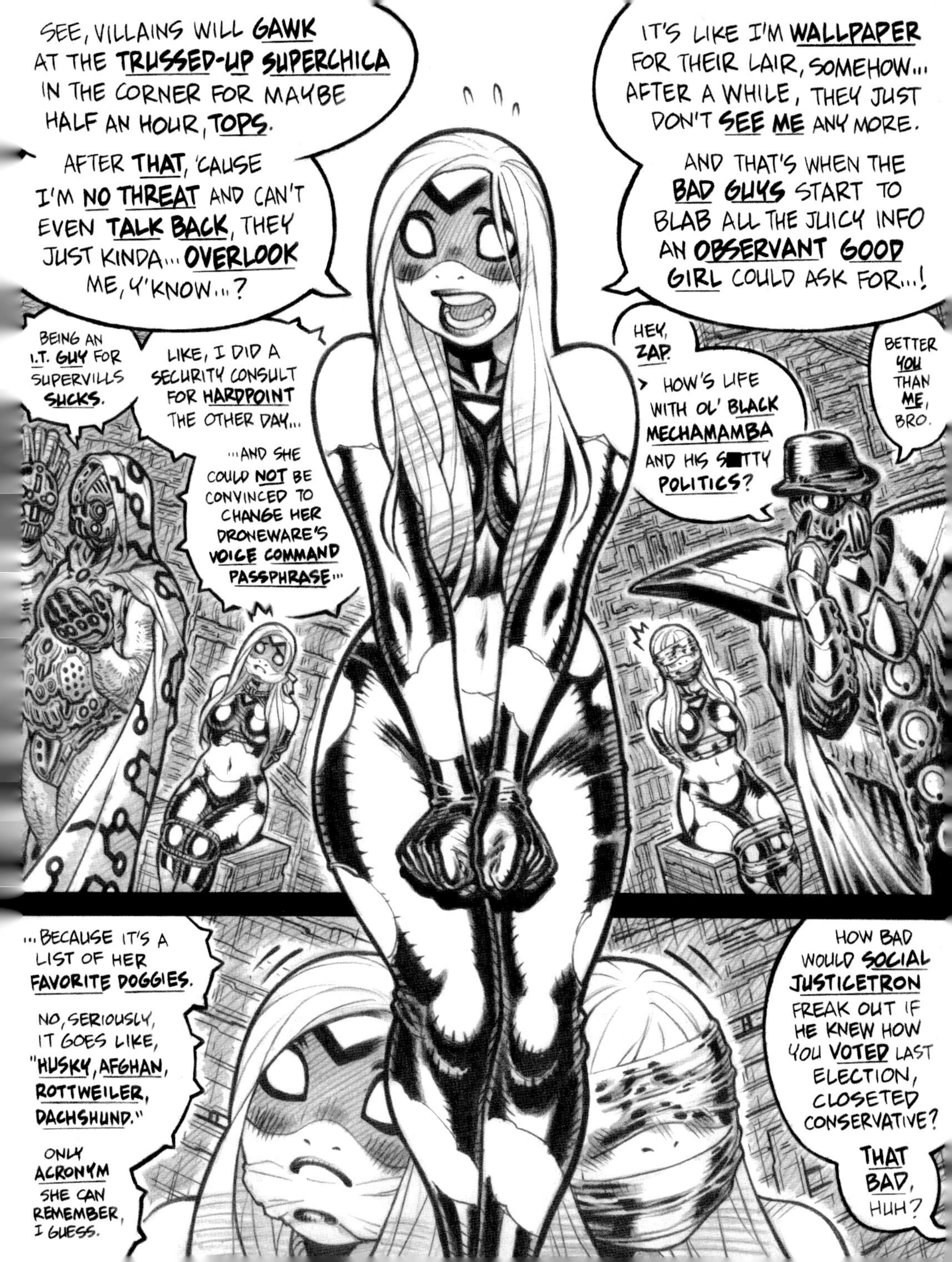
SEE, VILLAINS WILL GAWK AT THE TRUSSED-UP SUPERCHICA IN THE CORNER FOR MAYBE HALF AN HOUR, TOPS.
AFTER THAT, 'CAUSE I'M NO THREAT AND CAN'T EVEN TALK BACK, THEY JUST KINDA... OVERLOOK ME, Y'KNOW...?
IT'S LIKE I'M WALLPAPER FOR THEIR LAIR, SOMEHOW... AFTER A WHILE, THEY JUST DON'T SEE ME ANY MORE.
AND THAT'S WHEN THE BAD GUYS START TO BLAB ALL THE JUICY INFO AN OBSERVANT GOOD GIRL COULD ASK FOR...!
BEING AN I.T. GUY FOR SUPERVILLS SUCKS.
LIKE, I DID A SECURITY CONSULT FOR HARDPOINT THE OTHER DAY...
...AND SHE COULD NOT BE CONVINCED TO CHANGE HER DRONEWARE'S VOICE COMMAND PASSPHRASE...
HEY, ZAP.
HOW'S LIFE WITH OL' BLACK MECHAMAMBA AND HIS S[redacted]TTY POLITICS?
BETTER YOU THAN ME, BRO.
...BECAUSE IT'S A LIST OF HER FAVORITE DOGGIES.
NO, SERIOUSLY, IT GOES LIKE, "HUSKY, AFGHAN, ROTTWEILER, DACHSHUND."
ONLY ACRONYM SHE CAN REMEMBER, I GUESS.
HOW BAD WOULD SOCIAL JUSTICETRON FREAK OUT IF HE KNEW HOW YOU VOTED LAST ELECTION, CLOSETED CONSERVATIVE?
THAT BAD, HUH?

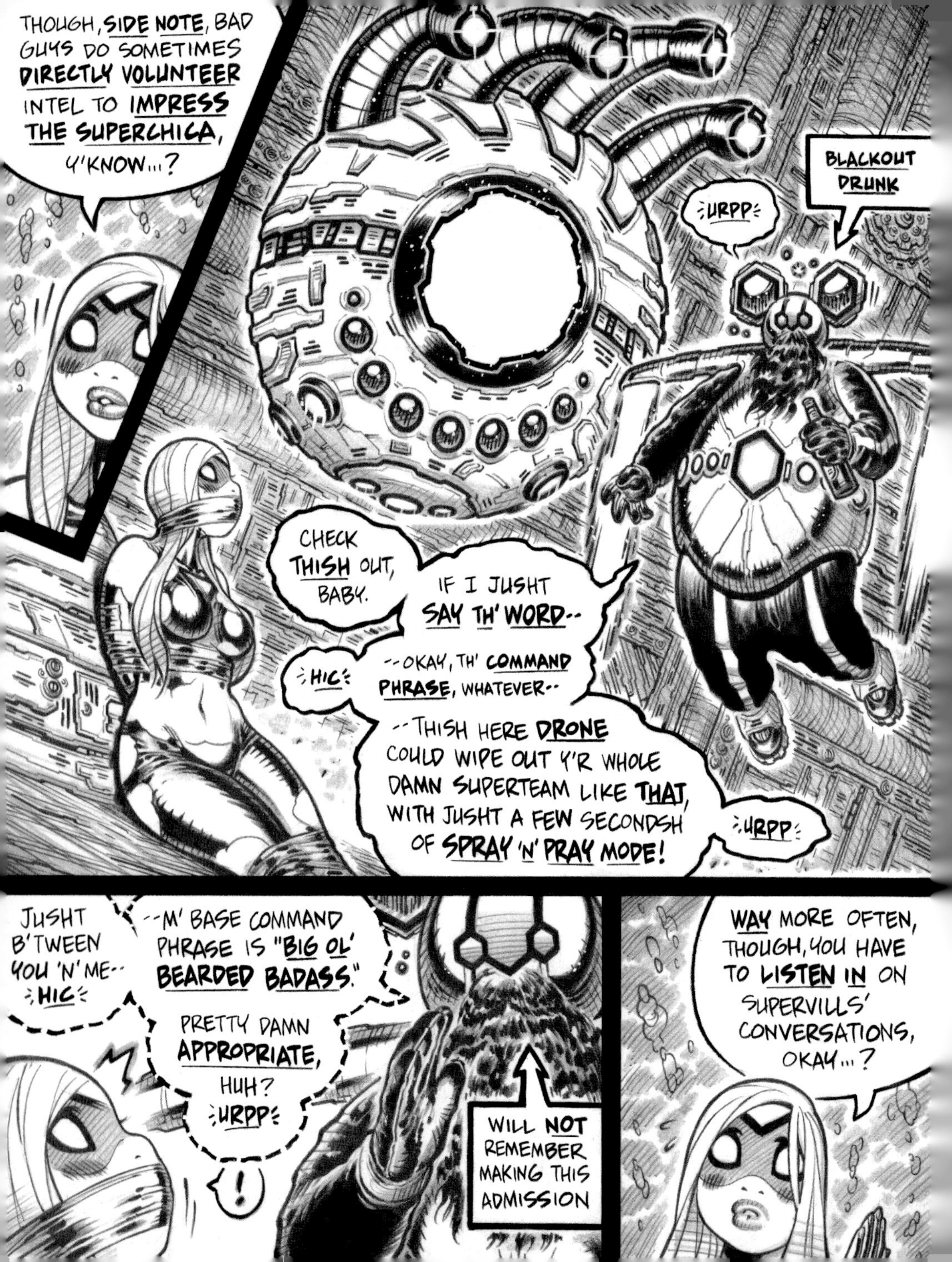
THOUGH, SIDE NOTE, BAD GUYS DO SOMETIMES DIRECTLY VOLUNTEER INTEL TO IMPRESS THE SUPERCHICA, Y'KNOW...?
URPP
BLACKOUT DRUNK
CHECK THISH OUT, BABY.
IF I JUSHT SAY TH' WORD--
HIC
--OKAY, TH' COMMAND PHRASE, WHATEVER--
--THISH HERE DRONE COULD WIPE OUT Y'R WHOLE DAMN SUPERTEAM LIKE THAT, WITH JUSHT A FEW SECONDSH OF SPRAY 'N' PRAY MODE!
URPP
JUSHT B'TWEEN YOU 'N' ME-- HIC
--M' BASE COMMAND PHRASE IS "BIG OL' BEARDED BADASS."
PRETTY DAMN APPROPRIATE, HUH? URPP
!
WILL NOT REMEMBER MAKING THIS ADMISSION
WAY MORE OFTEN, THOUGH, YOU HAVE TO LISTEN IN ON SUPERVILLS' CONVERSATIONS, OKAY...?

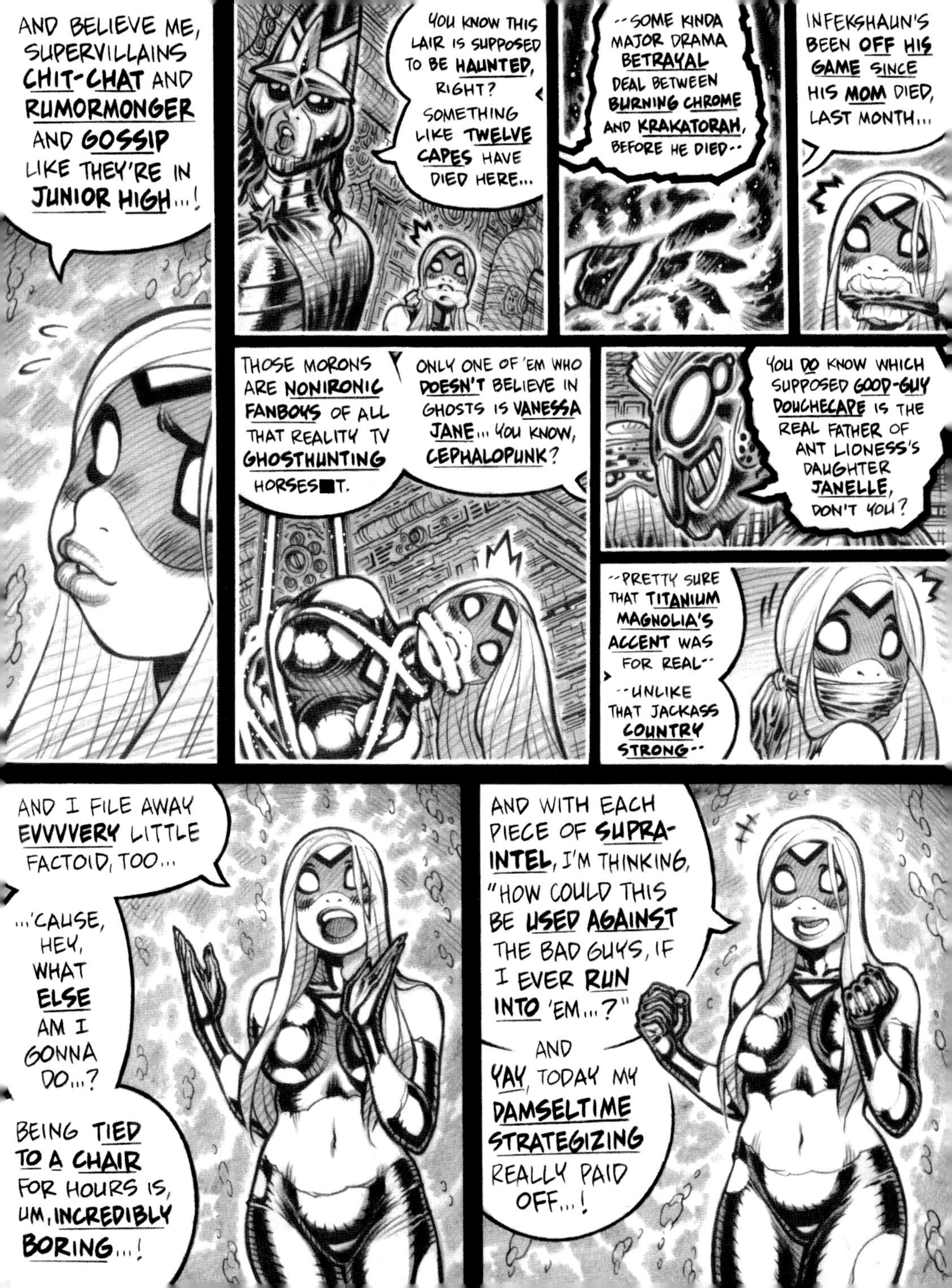
AND BELIEVE ME, SUPERVILLAINS CHIT-CHAT AND RUMORMONGER AND GOSSIP LIKE THEY'RE IN JUNIOR HIGH...!
YOU KNOW THIS LAIR IS SUPPOSED TO BE HAUNTED, RIGHT? SOMETHING LIKE TWELVE CAPES HAVE DIED HERE...
--SOME KINDA MAJOR DRAMA BETRAYAL DEAL BETWEEN BURNING CHROME AND KRAKATORAH, BEFORE HE DIED--
INFEKSHAUN'S BEEN OFF HIS GAME SINCE HIS MOM DIED, LAST MONTH...
THOSE MORONS ARE NONIRONIC FANBOYS OF ALL THAT REALITY TV GHOSTHUNTING HORSES[redacted]T.
ONLY ONE OF 'EM WHO DOESN'T BELIEVE IN GHOSTS IS VANESSA JANE... YOU KNOW, CEPHALOPUNK?
YOU DO KNOW WHICH SUPPOSED GOOD-GUY DOUCHECAPE IS THE REAL FATHER OF ANT LIONESS'S DAUGHTER JANELLE, DON'T YOU?
--PRETTY SURE THAT TITANIUM MAGNOLIA'S ACCENT WAS FOR REAL--
--UNLIKE THAT JACKASS COUNTRY STRONG--
AND I FILE AWAY EVVVVERY LITTLE FACTOID, TOO...
...'CAUSE, HEY, WHAT ELSE AM I GONNA DO...?
BEING TIED TO A CHAIR FOR HOURS IS, UM, INCREDIBLY BORING...!
AND WITH EACH PIECE OF SUPRA-INTEL, I'M THINKING, "HOW COULD THIS BE USED AGAINST THE BAD GUYS, IF I EVER RUN INTO 'EM...?"
AND YAY, TODAY MY DAMSELTIME STRATEGIZING REALLY PAID OFF...!

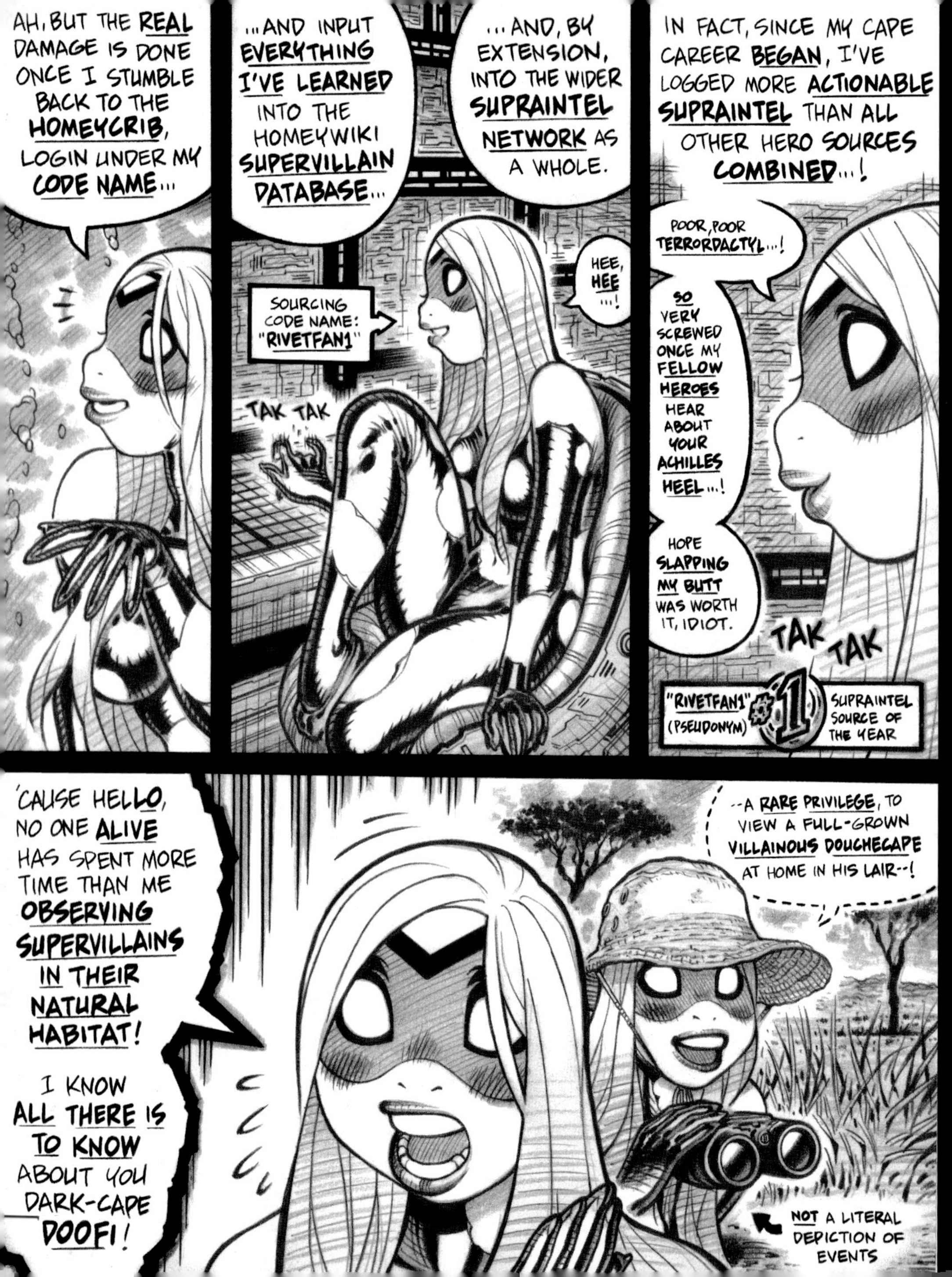
AH, BUT THE REAL DAMAGE IS DONE ONCE I STUMBLE BACK TO THE HOMEYCRIB, LOGIN UNDER MY CODE NAME...
...AND INPUT EVERYTHING I'VE LEARNED INTO THE HOMEYWIKI SUPERVILLAIN DATABASE...
...AND, BY EXTENSION, INTO THE WIDER SUPRAINTEL NETWORK AS A WHOLE.
SOURCING CODE NAME: "RIVETFAN1"
HEE, HEE ...!
TAK TAK
IN FACT, SINCE MY CAPE CAREER BEGAN, I'VE LOGGED MORE ACTIONABLE SUPRAINTEL THAN ALL OTHER HERO SOURCES COMBINED...!
POOR, POOR TERRORDACTYL...!
SO VERY SCREWED ONCE MY FELLOW HEROES HEAR ABOUT YOUR ACHILLES HEEL...!
HOPE SLAPPING MY BUTT WAS WORTH IT, IDIOT.
TAK TAK
"RIVETFAN1" (PSEUDONYM) #1 SUPRAINTEL SOURCE OF THE YEAR
'CAUSE HELLO, NO ONE ALIVE HAS SPENT MORE TIME THAN ME OBSERVING SUPERVILLAINS IN THEIR NATURAL HABITAT!
I KNOW ALL THERE IS TO KNOW ABOUT YOU DARK-CAPE DOOFI!
--A RARE PRIVILEGE, TO VIEW A FULL-GROWN VILLAINOUS DOUCHECAPE AT HOME IN HIS LAIR--!
NOT A LITERAL DEPICTION OF EVENTS

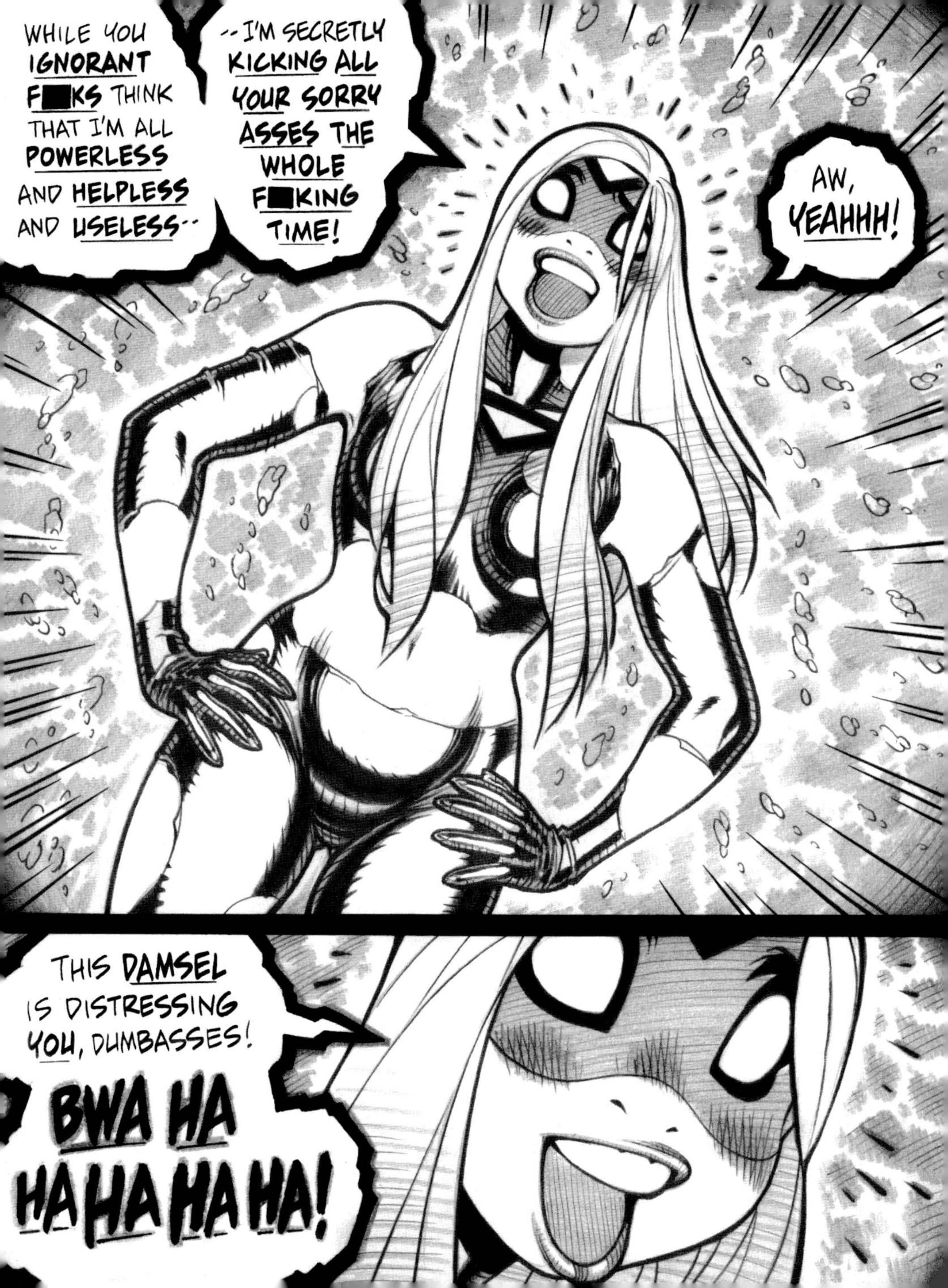
WHILE YOU IGNORANT F[redacted]KS THINK THAT I'M ALL POWERLESS AND HELPLESS AND USELESS--
--I'M SECRETLY KICKING ALL YOUR SORRY ASSES THE WHOLE F[redacted]KING TIME!
AW, YEAHHH!
THIS DAMSEL IS DISTRESSING YOU, DUMBASSES!
BWA HA HA HA HA HA HA!

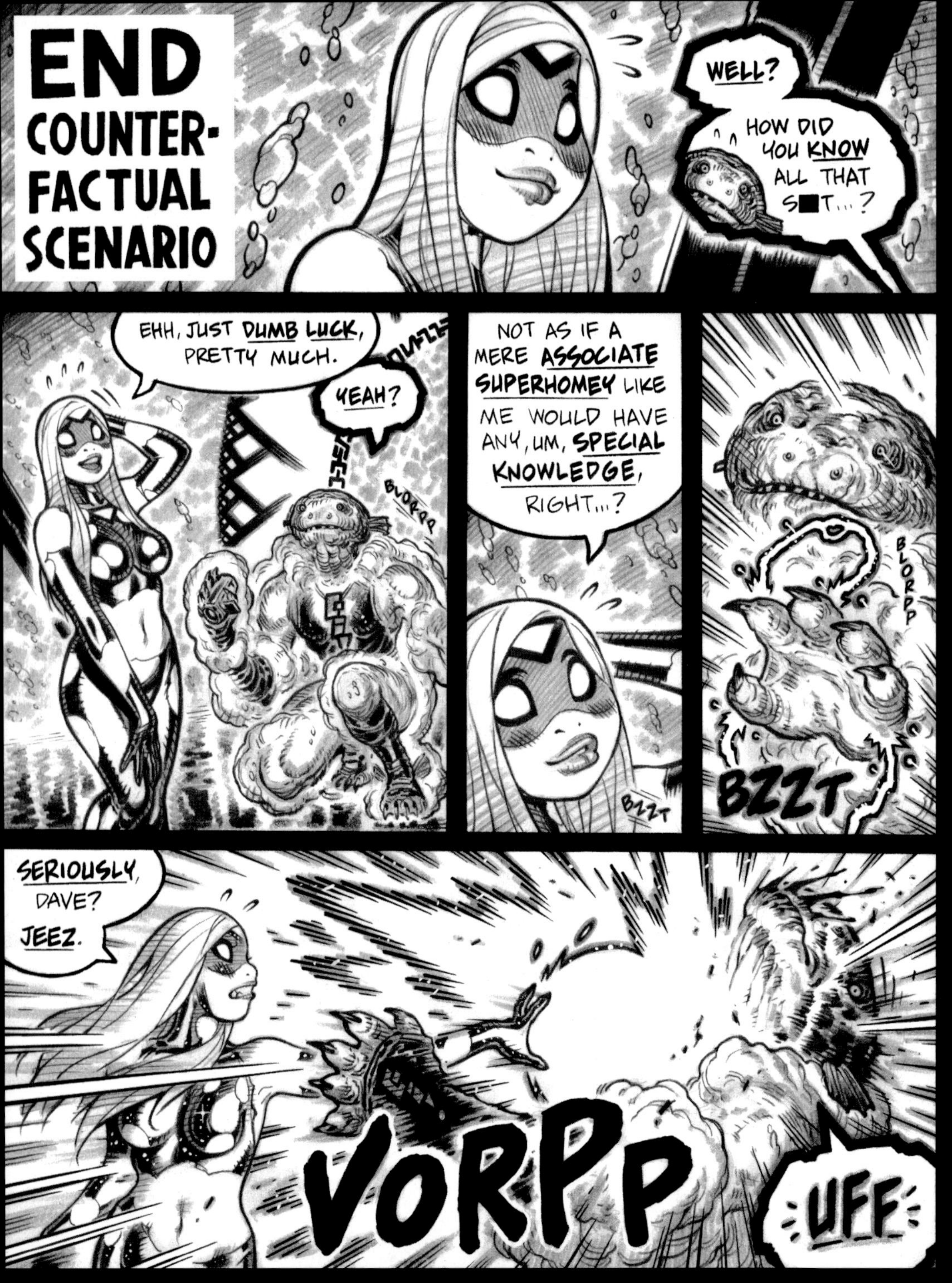
END COUNTER-FACTUAL SCENARIO
WELL?
HOW DID YOU KNOW ALL THAT S[redacted]T...?
EHH, JUST DUMB LUCK, PRETTY MUCH.
YEAH?
BLORPP
NOT AS IF A MERE ASSOCIATE SUPERHOMEY LIKE ME WOULD HAVE ANY, UM, SPECIAL KNOWLEDGE, RIGHT...?
BZZT
BLORPP
BZZT
SERIOUSLY, DAVE? JEEZ.
VORPP
UFF

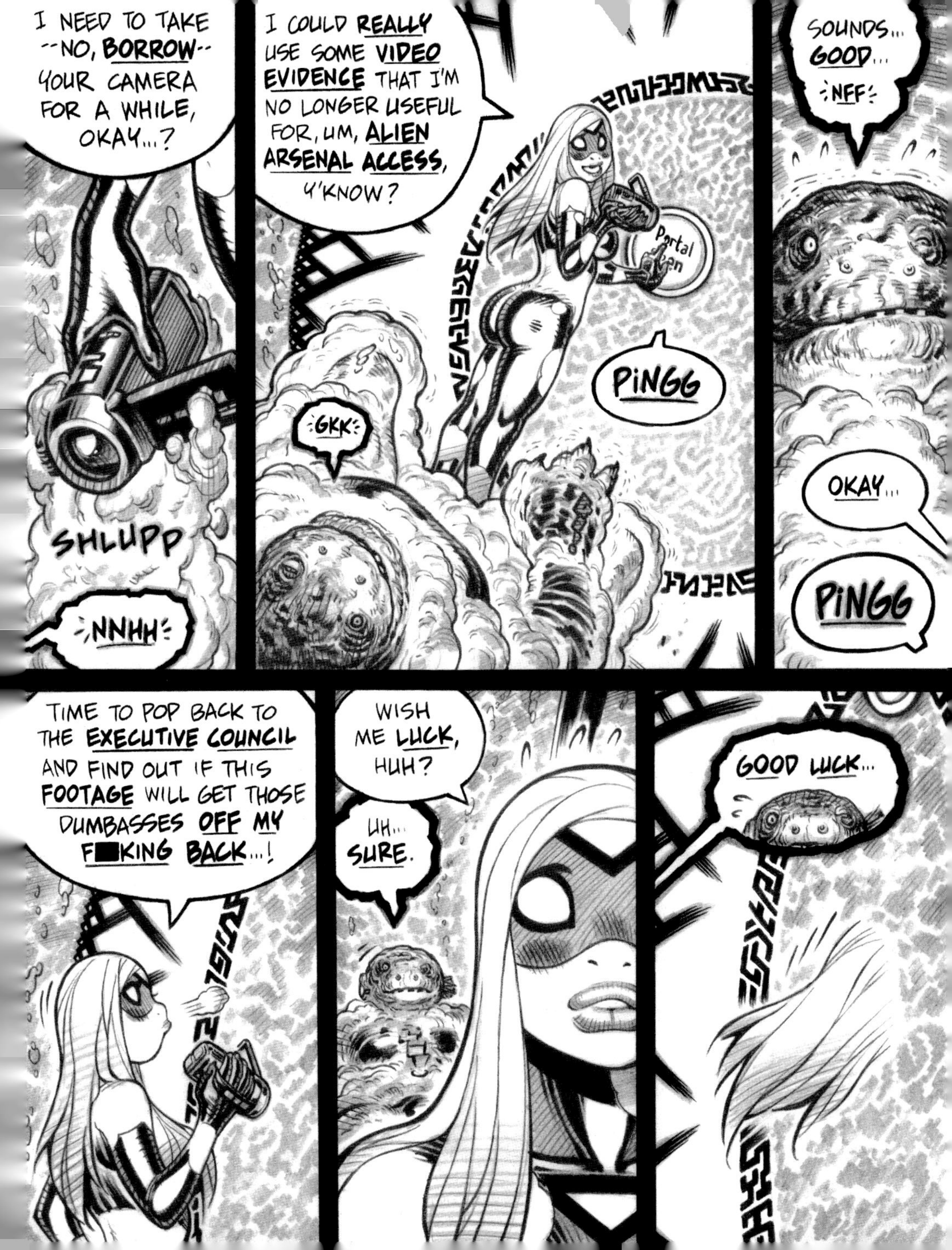

I NEED TO TAKE --NO, BORROW-- YOUR CAMERA FOR A WHILE, OKAY...?
SHLUPP
NNHH
I COULD REALLY USE SOME VIDEO EVIDENCE THAT I'M NO LONGER USEFUL FOR, UM, ALIEN ARSENAL ACCESS, Y'KNOW?
GKK
PINGG
SOUNDS... GOOD...
NFF
OKAY...
PINGG
TIME TO POP BACK TO THE EXECUTIVE COUNCIL AND FIND OUT IF THIS FOOTAGE WILL GET THOSE DUMBASSES OFF MY F[redacted]KING BACK...!
WISH ME LUCK, HUH?
UH... SURE.
GOOD LUCK...

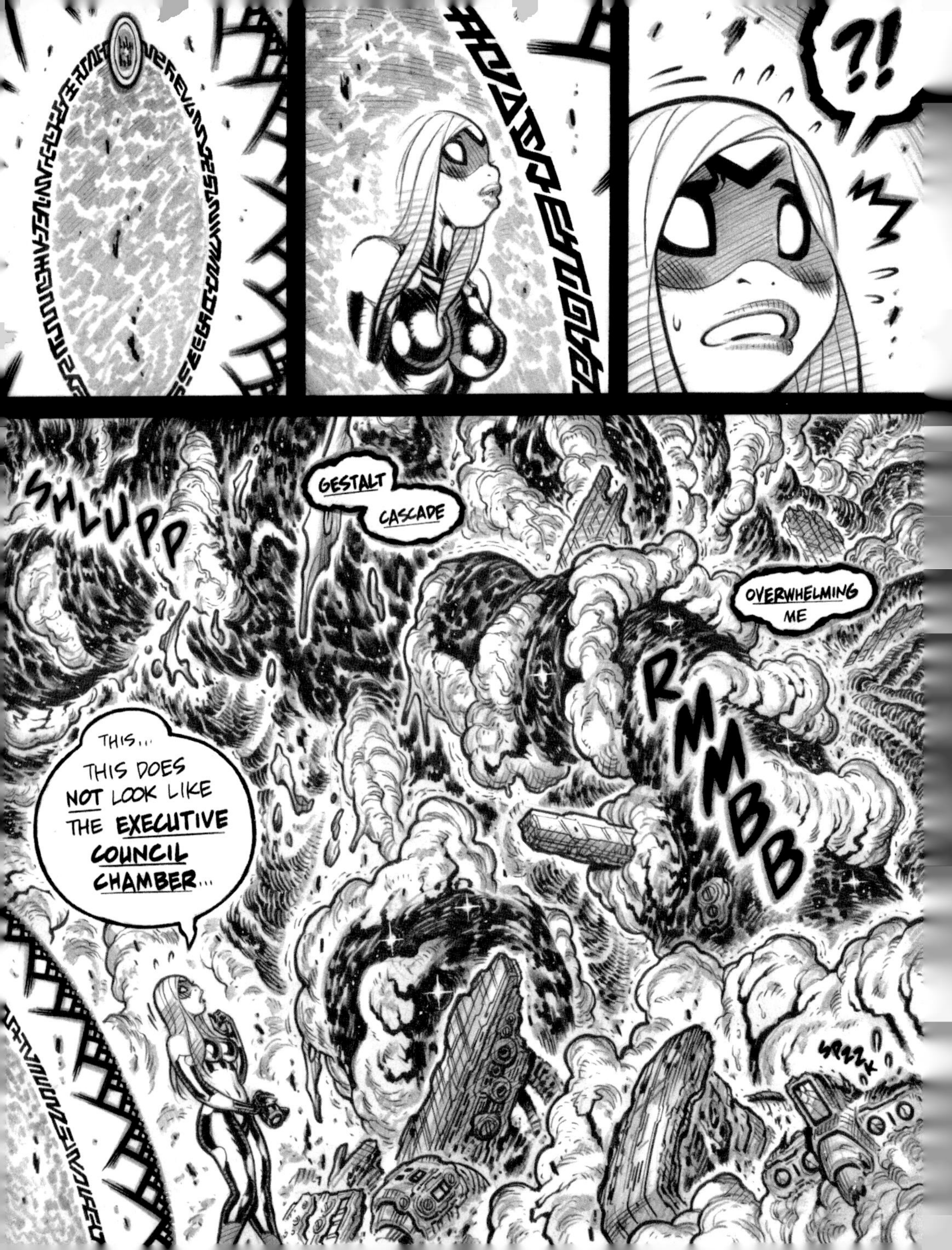
?!
SHLUPP
GESTALT
CASCADE
OVERWHELMING ME
RMMBB
THIS... THIS DOES NOT LOOK LIKE THE EXECUTIVE COUNCIL CHAMBER...
SPZZK

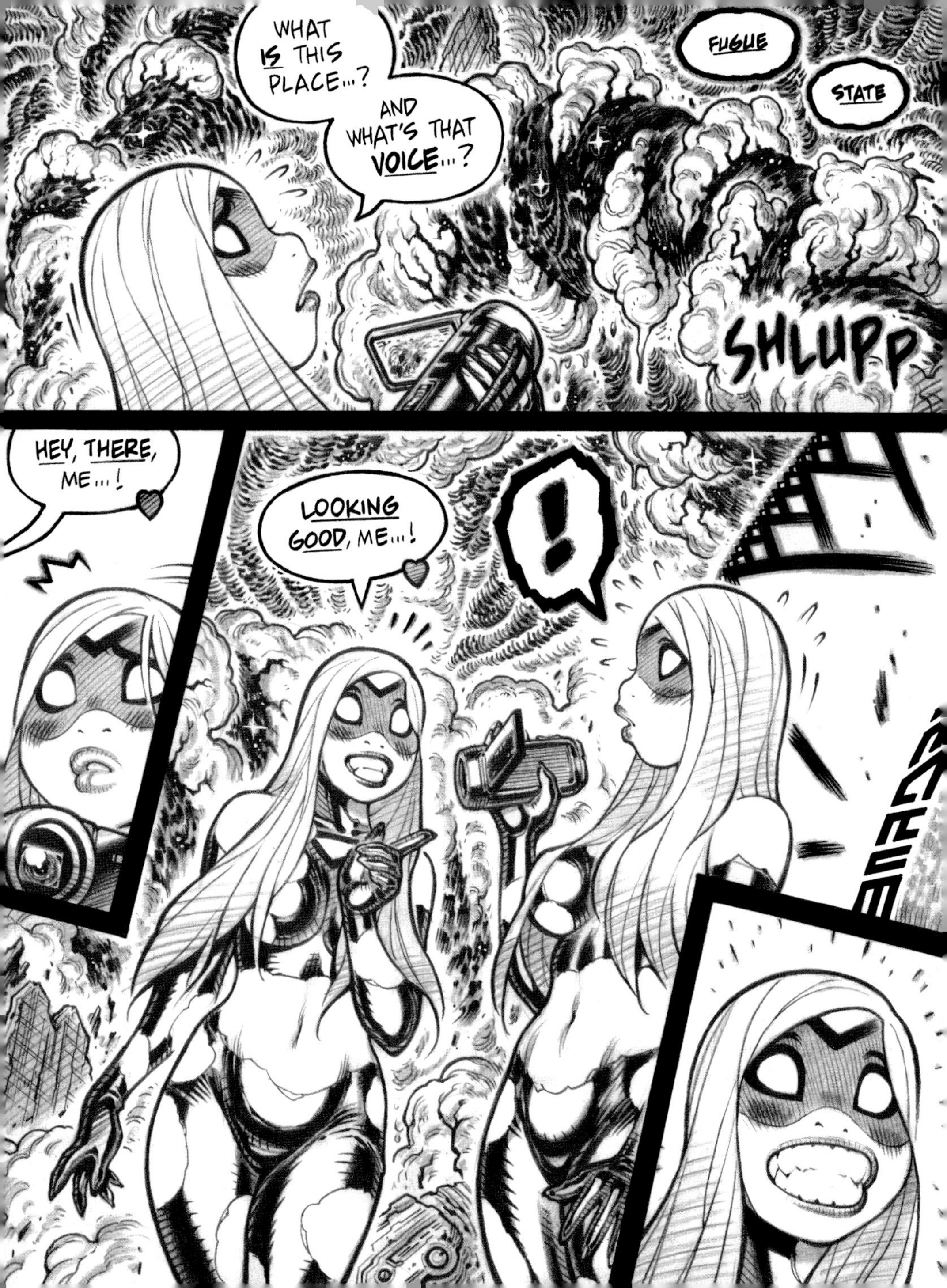

WHAT IS THIS PLACE...?
AND WHAT'S THAT VOICE...?
FUGUE
STATE
SHLUPP
HEY, THERE, ME...!
LOOKING GOOD, ME...!
!

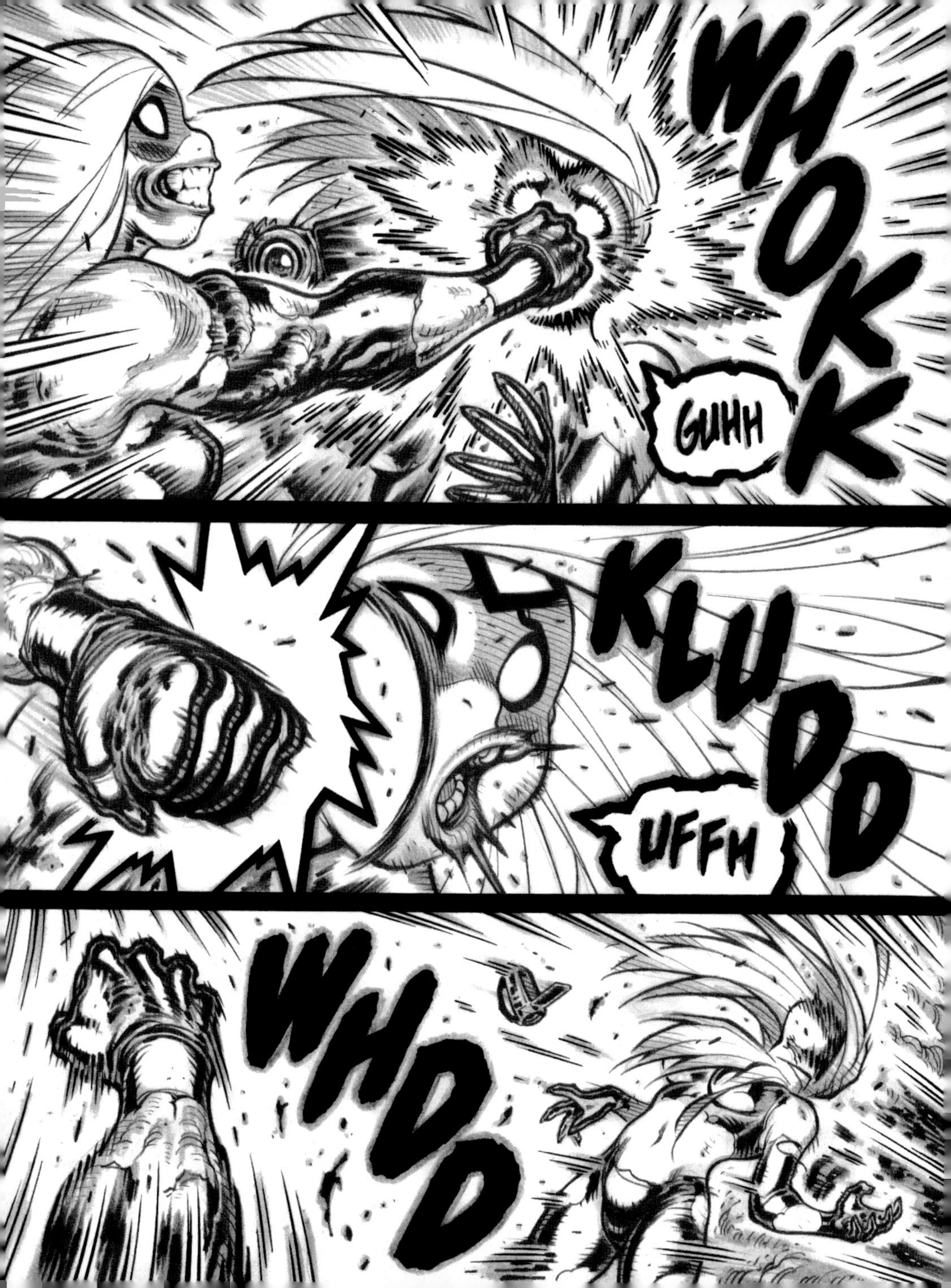
WHOKK
GUHH
KLUDD
UFFH
WHDD

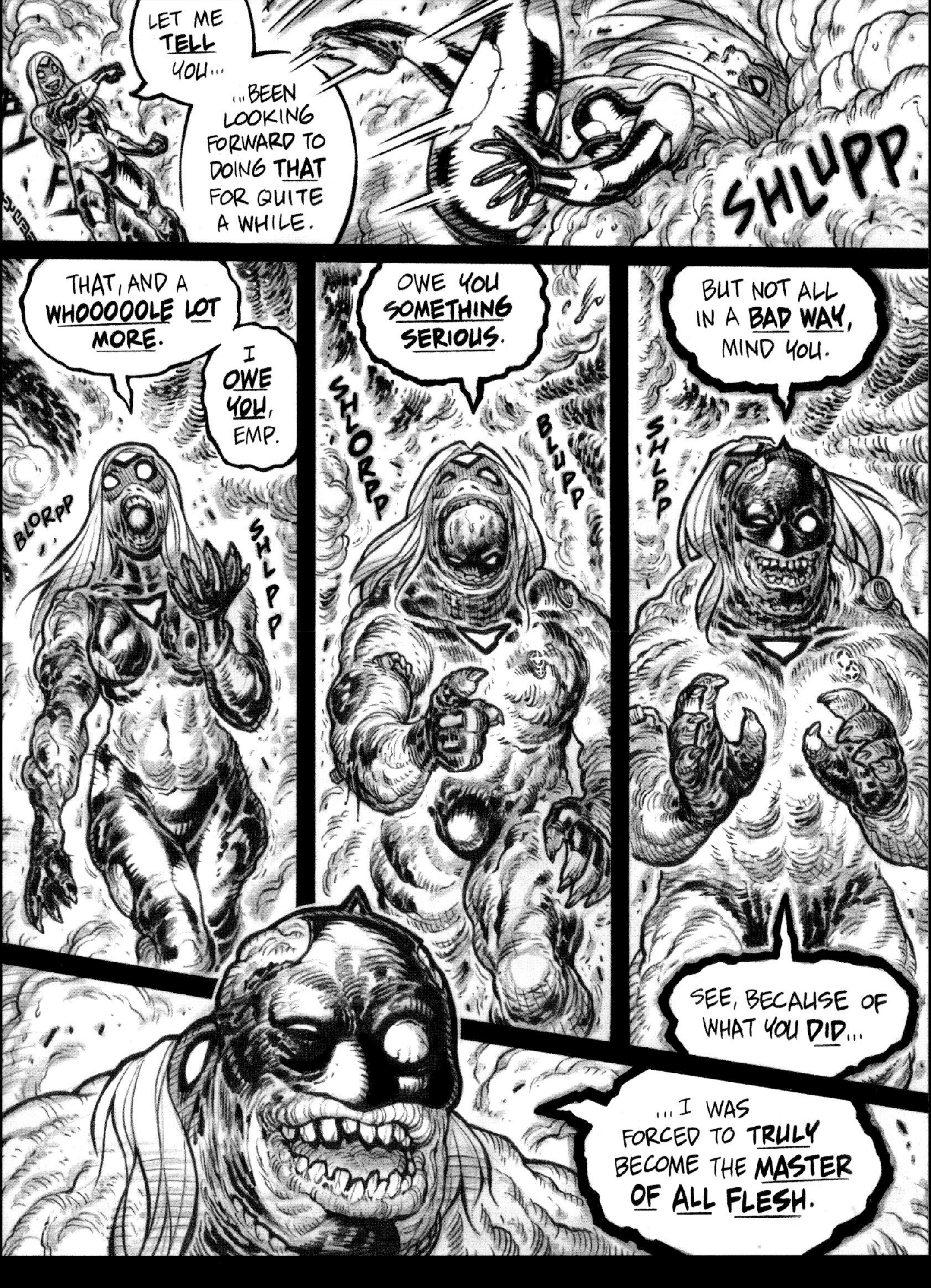
LET ME TELL YOU...
...BEEN LOOKING FORWARD TO DOING THAT FOR QUITE A WHILE.
SHLUPP
THAT, AND A WHOOOOOLE LOT MORE.
I OWE YOU, EMP.
BLORPP
SHLUPP
OWE YOU SOMETHING SERIOUS.
SHLORPP
BLUPP
BUT NOT ALL IN A BAD WAY, MIND YOU.
SHLPP
SEE, BECAUSE OF WHAT YOU DID...
...I WAS FORCED TO TRULY BECOME THE MASTER OF ALL FLESH.

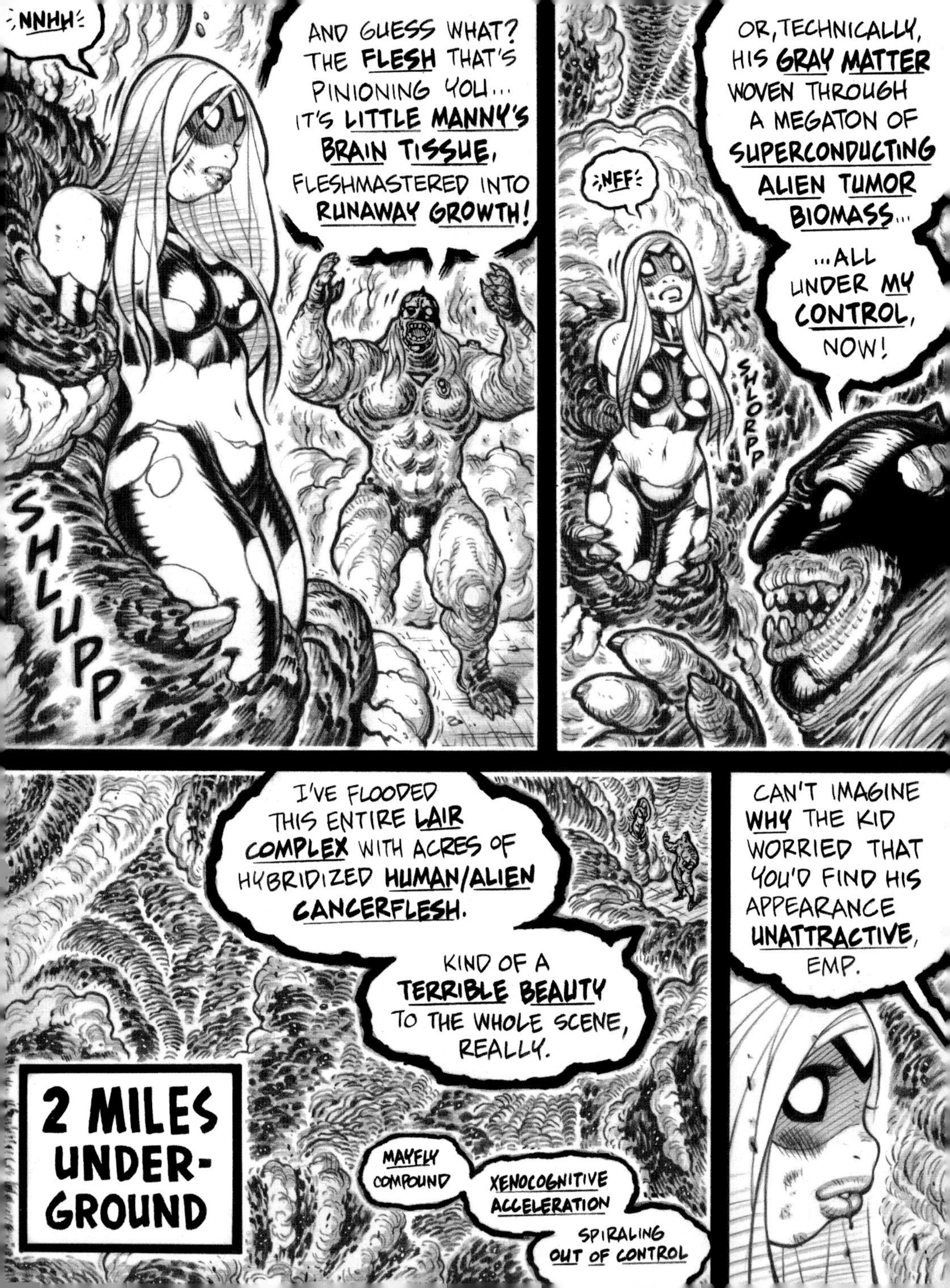
NNHH
AND GUESS WHAT? THE FLESH THAT'S PINIONING YOU... IT'S LITTLE MANNY'S BRAIN TISSUE, FLESHMASTERED INTO RUNAWAY GROWTH!
SHLUPP
OR, TECHNICALLY, HIS GRAY MATTER WOVEN THROUGH A MEGATON OF SUPERCONDUCTING ALIEN TUMOR BIOMASS...
NFF
...ALL UNDER MY CONTROL, NOW!
SHLORPP
I'VE FLOODED THIS ENTIRE LAIR COMPLEX WITH ACRES OF HYBRIDIZED HUMAN/ALIEN CANCERFLESH.
KIND OF A TERRIBLE BEAUTY TO THE WHOLE SCENE, REALLY.
2 MILES UNDER-GROUND
MAYFLY COMPOUND
XENOCOGNITIVE ACCELERATION
SPIRALING OUT OF CONTROL
CAN'T IMAGINE WHY THE KID WORRIED THAT YOU'D FIND HIS APPEARANCE UNATTRACTIVE, EMP.

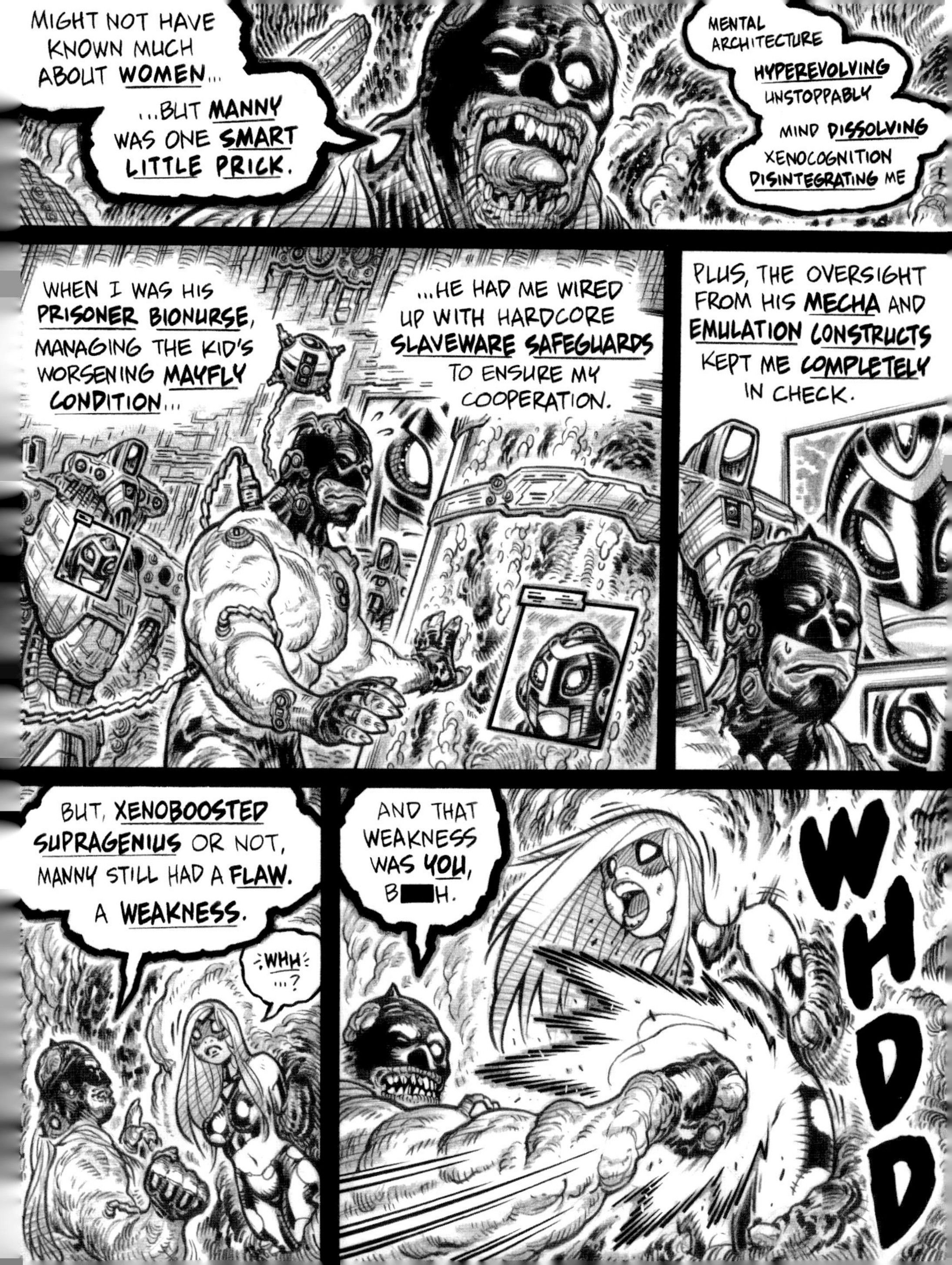
MIGHT NOT HAVE KNOWN MUCH ABOUT WOMEN...
...BUT MANNY WAS ONE SMART LITTLE PRICK.
MENTAL ARCHITECTURE HYPEREVOLVING UNSTOPPABLY
MIND DISSOLVING
XENOCOGNITION DISINTEGRATING ME
WHEN I WAS HIS PRISONER BIONURSE, MANAGING THE KID'S WORSENING MAYFLY CONDITION...
...HE HAD ME WIRED UP WITH HARDCORE SLAVEWARE SAFEGUARDS TO ENSURE MY COOPERATION.
PLUS, THE OVERSIGHT FROM HIS MECHA AND EMULATION CONSTRUCTS KEPT ME COMPLETELY IN CHECK.
BUT, XENOBOOSTED SUPRAGENIUS OR NOT, MANNY STILL HAD A FLAW. A WEAKNESS.
WHH ...?
AND THAT WEAKNESS WAS YOU, B[redacted]H.
WHDD

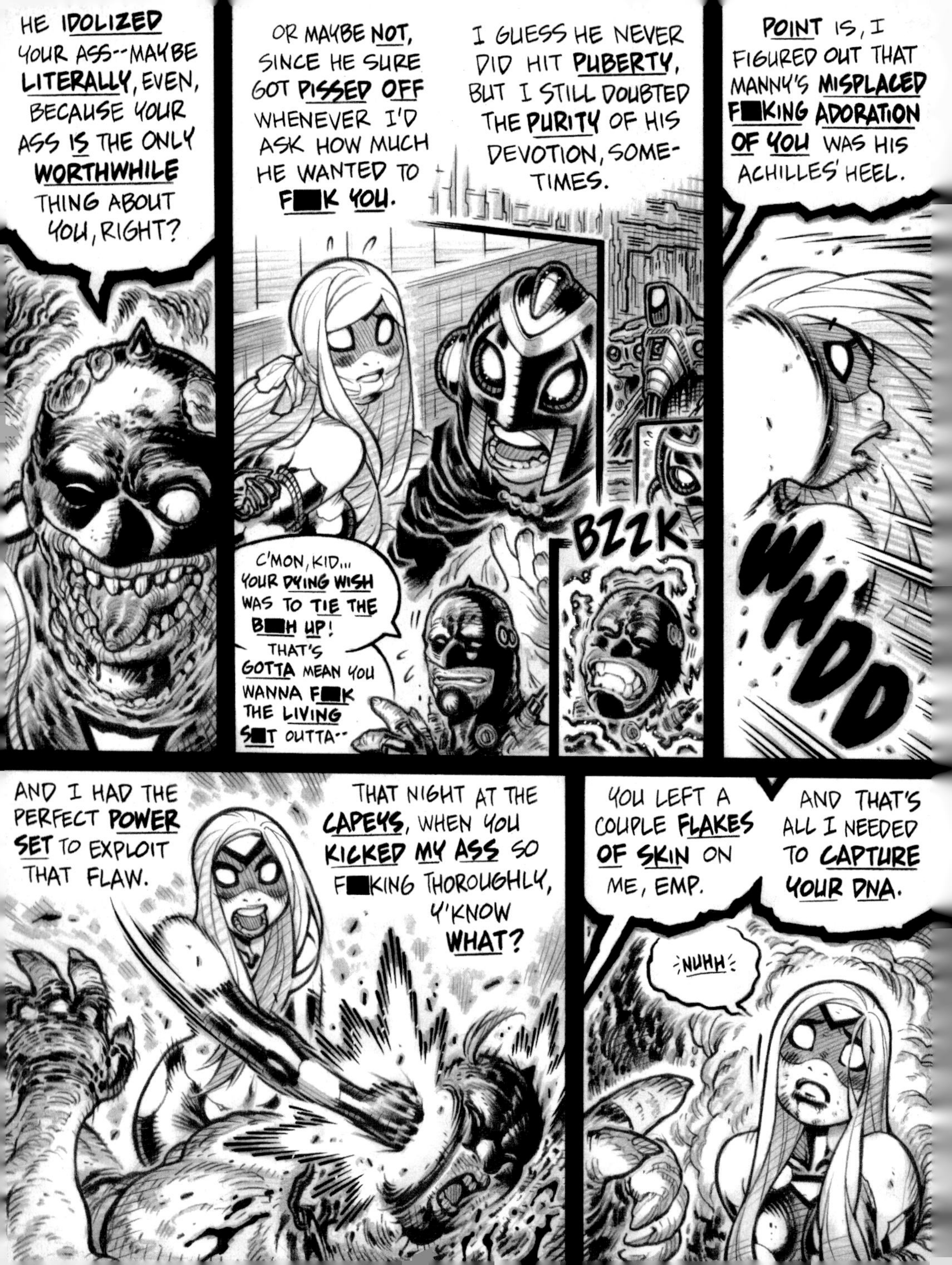
HE IDOLIZED YOUR ASS--MAYBE LITERALLY, EVEN, BECAUSE YOUR ASS IS THE ONLY WORTHWHILE THING ABOUT YOU, RIGHT?
OR MAYBE NOT, SINCE HE SURE GOT PISSED OFF WHENEVER I'D ASK HOW MUCH HE WANTED TO F[redacted]K YOU.
I GUESS HE NEVER DID HIT PUBERTY, BUT I STILL DOUBTED THE PURITY OF HIS DEVOTION, SOME-TIMES.
C'MON, KID... YOUR DYING WISH WAS TO TIE THE B[redacted]H UP! THAT'S GOTTA MEAN YOU WANNA F[redacted]K THE LIVING S[redacted]T OUTTA--
BZZK
POINT IS, I FIGURED OUT THAT MANNY'S MISPLACED F[redacted]KING ADORATION OF YOU WAS HIS ACHILLES' HEEL.
WHDD
AND I HAD THE PERFECT POWER SET TO EXPLOIT THAT FLAW.
THAT NIGHT AT THE CAPEYS, WHEN YOU KICKED MY ASS SO F[redacted]KING THOROUGHLY, Y'KNOW WHAT?
YOU LEFT A COUPLE FLAKES OF SKIN ON ME, EMP.
AND THAT'S ALL I NEEDED TO CAPTURE YOUR DNA.
NUHH

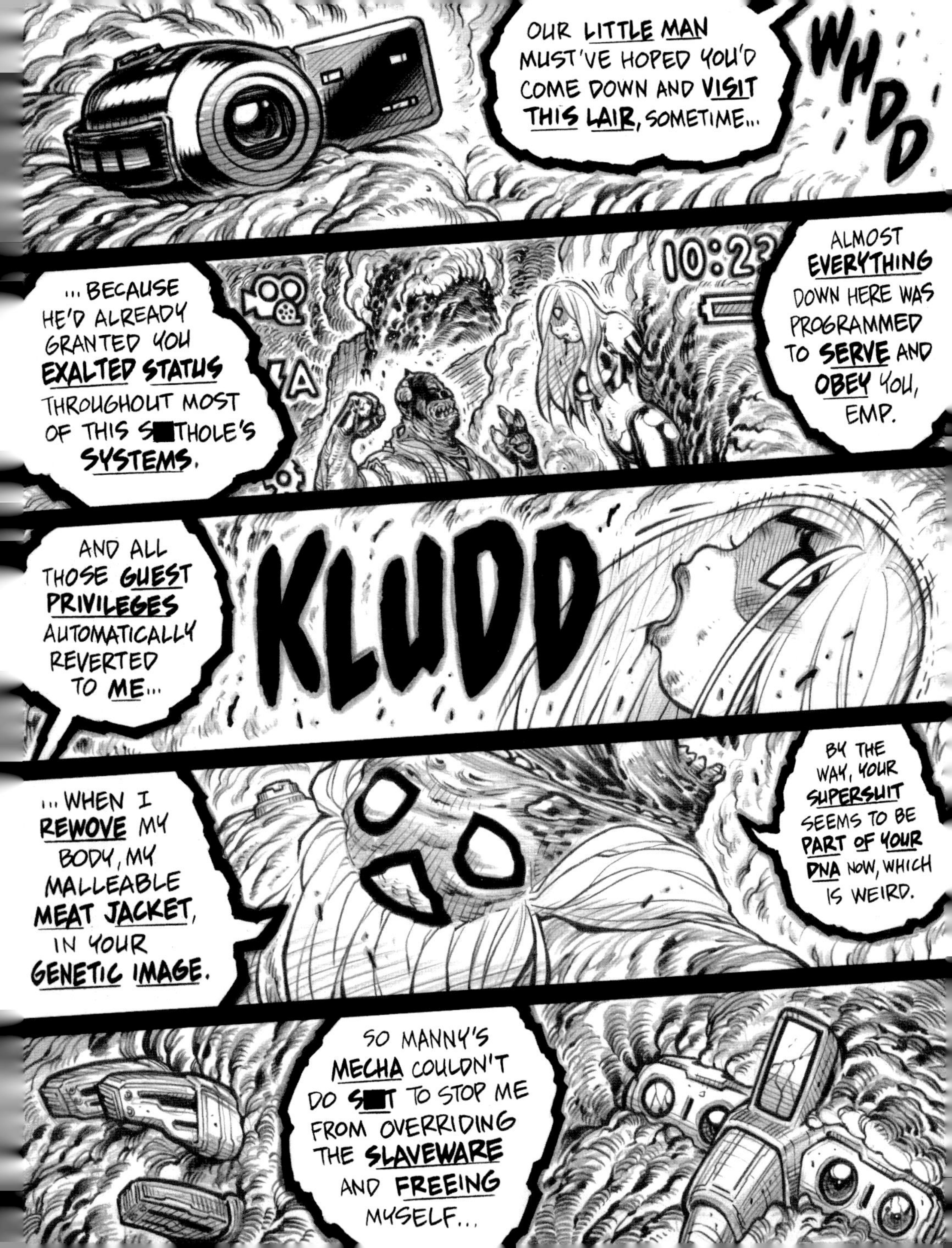
OUR LITTLE MAN MUST'VE HOPED YOU'D COME DOWN AND VISIT THIS LAIR, SOMETIME...
WHDD
...BECAUSE HE'D ALREADY GRANTED YOU EXALTED STATUS THROUGHOUT MOST OF THIS S[redacted]THOLE'S SYSTEMS.
ALMOST EVERYTHING DOWN HERE WAS PROGRAMMED TO SERVE AND OBEY YOU, EMP.
AND ALL THOSE GUEST PRIVILEGES AUTOMATICALLY REVERTED TO ME...
KLUDD
...WHEN I REWOVE MY BODY, MY MALLEABLE MEAT JACKET, IN YOUR GENETIC IMAGE.
BY THE WAY, YOUR SUPERSUIT SEEMS TO BE PART OF YOUR DNA NOW, WHICH IS WEIRD.
SO MANNY'S MECHA COULDN'T DO S[redacted]T TO STOP ME FROM OVERRIDING THE SLAVEWARE AND FREEING MYSELF...

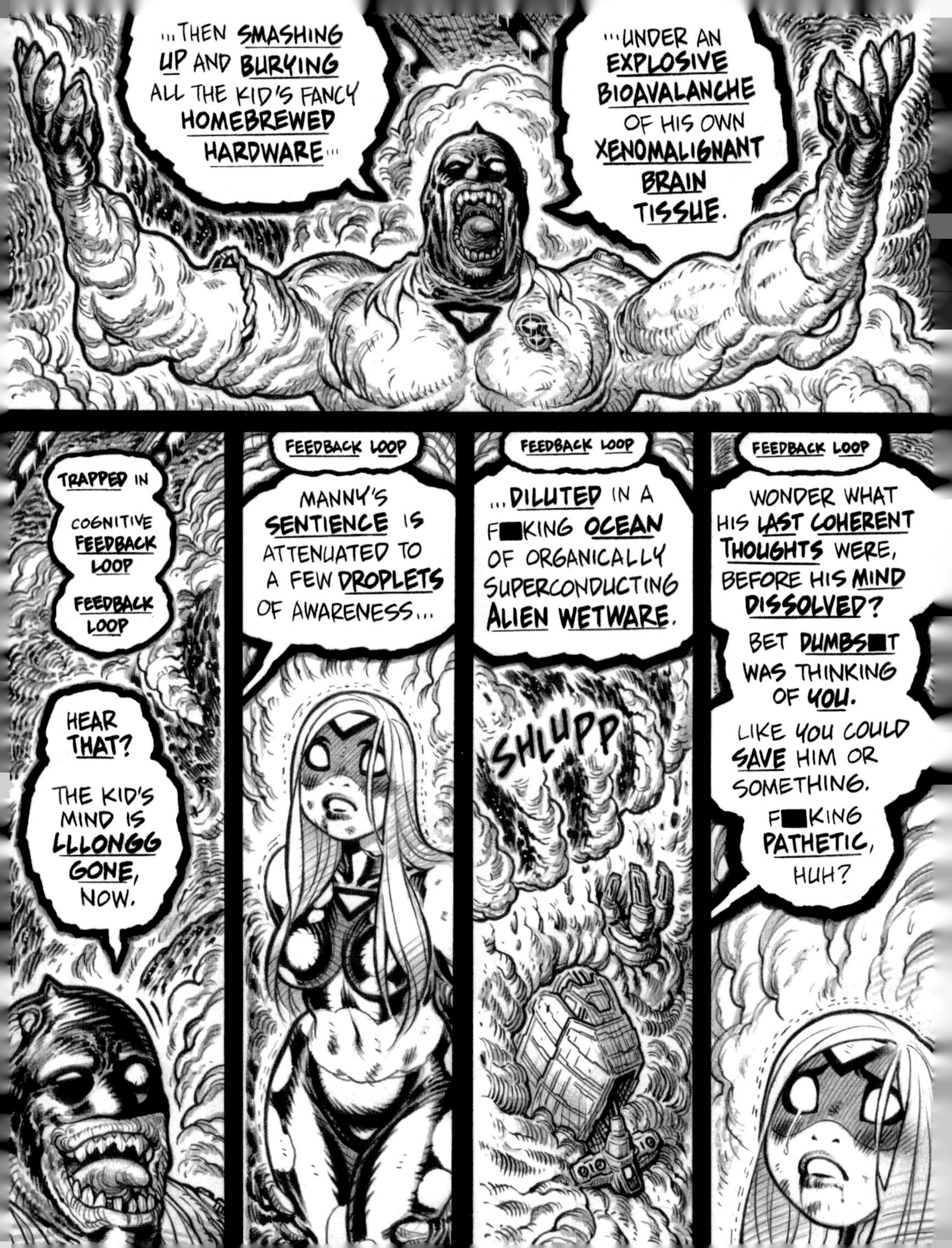

...THEN SMASHING UP AND BURYING ALL THE KID'S FANCY HOMEBREWED HARDWARE...
...UNDER AN EXPLOSIVE BIOAVALANCHE OF HIS OWN XENOMALIGNANT BRAIN TISSUE.
TRAPPED IN
COGNITIVE FEEDBACK LOOP
FEEDBACK LOOP
HEAR THAT?
THE KID'S MIND IS LLLONGG GONE, NOW.
FEEDBACK LOOP
MANNY'S SENTIENCE IS ATTENUATED TO A FEW DROPLETS OF AWARENESS...
FEEDBACK LOOP
...DILUTED IN A F[redacted]KING OCEAN OF ORGANICALLY SUPERCONDUCTING ALIEN WETWARE.
SHLUPP
FEEDBACK LOOP
WONDER WHAT HIS LAST COHERENT THOUGHTS WERE, BEFORE HIS MIND DISSOLVED?
BET DUMBS[redacted]T WAS THINKING OF YOU.
LIKE YOU COULD SAVE HIM OR SOMETHING.
F[redacted]KING PATHETIC, HUH?

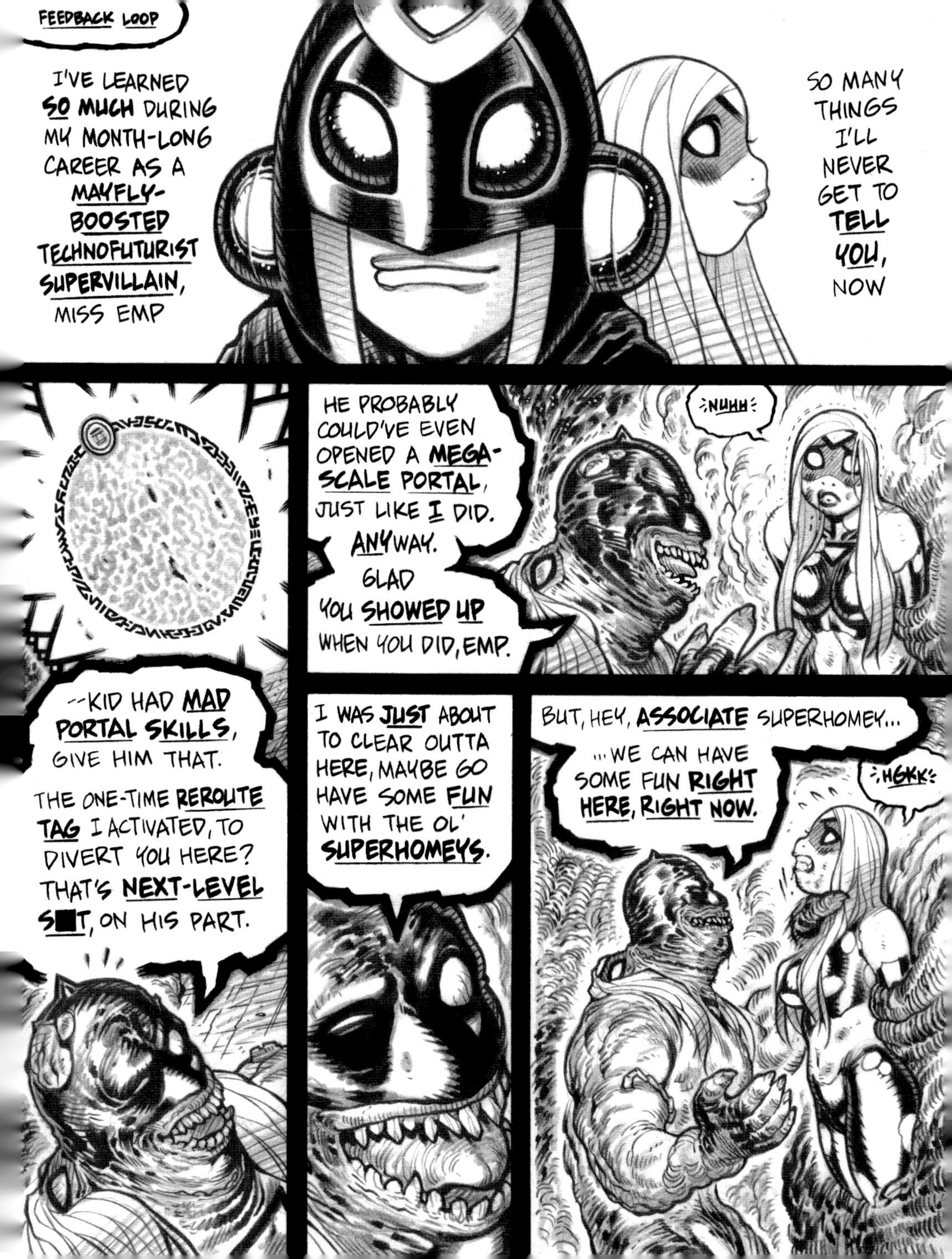
FEEDBACK LOOP
I'VE LEARNED SO MUCH DURING MY MONTH-LONG CAREER AS A MAYFLY-BOOSTED TECHNOFUTURIST SUPERVILLAIN, MISS EMP
SO MANY THINGS I'LL NEVER GET TO TELL YOU, NOW
HE PROBABLY COULD'VE EVEN OPENED A MEGA-SCALE PORTAL, JUST LIKE I DID.
ANYWAY.
GLAD YOU SHOWED UP WHEN YOU DID, EMP.
NUHH
--KID HAD MAD PORTAL SKILLS, GIVE HIM THAT.
THE ONE-TIME REROUTE TAG I ACTIVATED, TO DIVERT YOU HERE? THAT'S NEXT-LEVEL S[redacted]T, ON HIS PART.
I WAS JUST ABOUT TO CLEAR OUTTA HERE, MAYBE GO HAVE SOME FUN WITH THE OL' SUPERHOMEYS.
BUT, HEY, ASSOCIATE SUPERHOMEY...
...WE CAN HAVE SOME FUN RIGHT HERE, RIGHT NOW.
HGKK

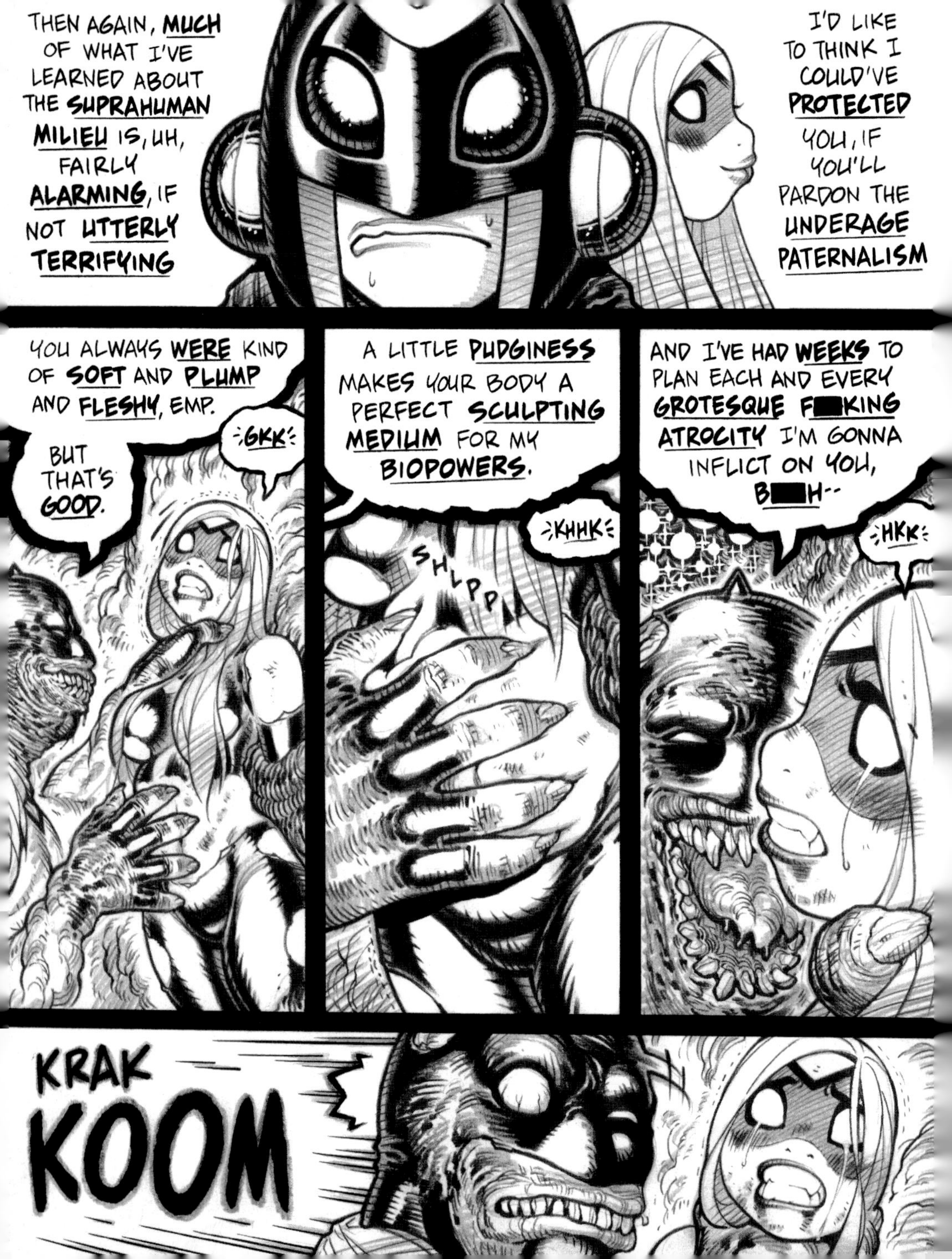
THEN AGAIN, MUCH OF WHAT I'VE LEARNED ABOUT THE SUPRAHUMAN MILIEU IS, UH, FAIRLY ALARMING, IF NOT UTTERLY TERRIFYING
I'D LIKE TO THINK I COULD'VE PROTECTED YOU, IF YOU'LL PARDON THE UNDERAGE PATERNALISM
YOU ALWAYS WERE KIND OF SOFT AND PLUMP AND FLESHY, EMP.
BUT THAT'S GOOD.
GKK
A LITTLE PUDGINESS MAKES YOUR BODY A PERFECT SCULPTING MEDIUM FOR MY BIOPOWERS.
KHHK
SHLPPP
AND I'VE HAD WEEKS TO PLAN EACH AND EVERY GROTESQUE F[redacted]KING ATROCITY I'M GONNA INFLICT ON YOU, B[redacted]H--
HKK
KRAK
KOOM

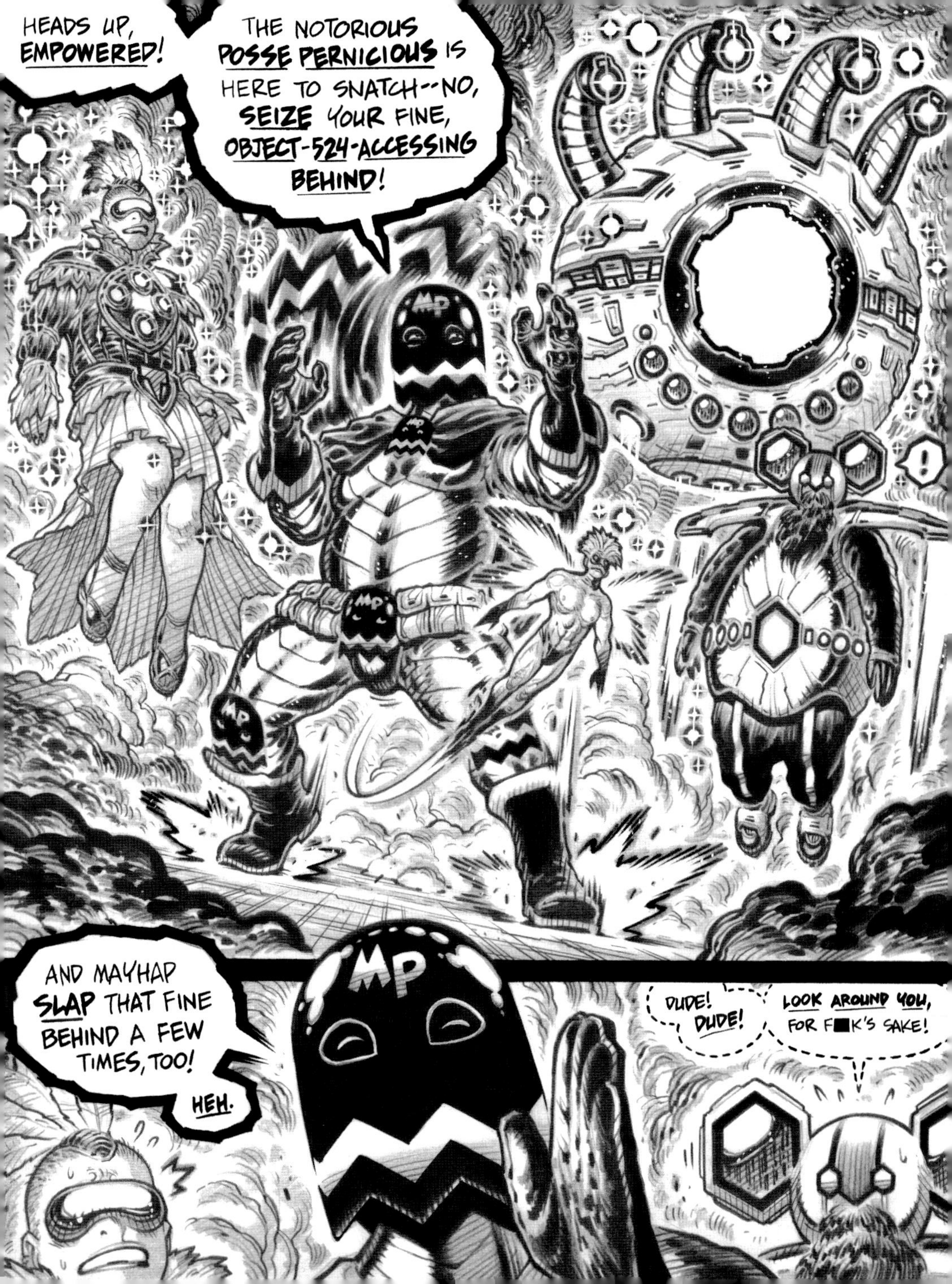
HEADS UP, EMPOWERED!
THE NOTORIOUS POSSE PERNICIOUS IS HERE TO SNATCH--NO, SEIZE YOUR FINE, OBJECT-524-ACCESSING BEHIND!
!
AND MAYHAP SLAP THAT FINE BEHIND A FEW TIMES, TOO!
HEH.
DUDE! DUDE!
LOOK AROUND YOU, FOR F[redacted]K'S SAKE!

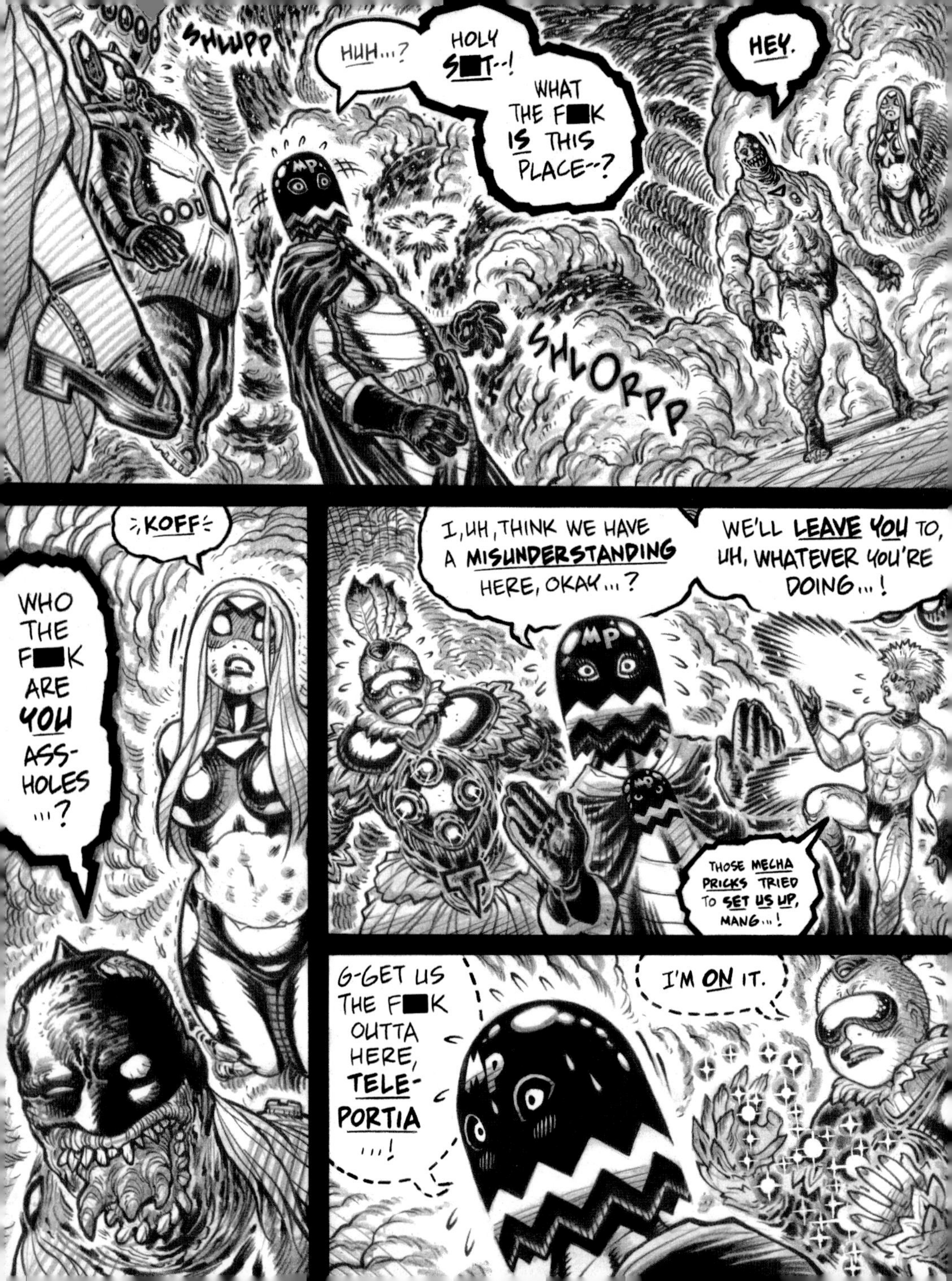
SHLUPP
HUH...?
HOLY S[redacted]T--! WHAT THE F[redacted]K IS THIS PLACE--?
HEY.
SHLORPP
KOFF
WHO THE F[redacted]K ARE YOU ASS-HOLES...?
I, UH, THINK WE HAVE A MISUNDERSTANDING HERE, OKAY...?
WE'LL LEAVE YOU TO, UH, WHATEVER YOU'RE DOING...!
THOSE MECHA PRICKS TRIED TO SET US UP, MANG...!
G-GET US THE F[redacted]K OUTTA HERE, TELE-PORTIA...!
I'M ON IT.

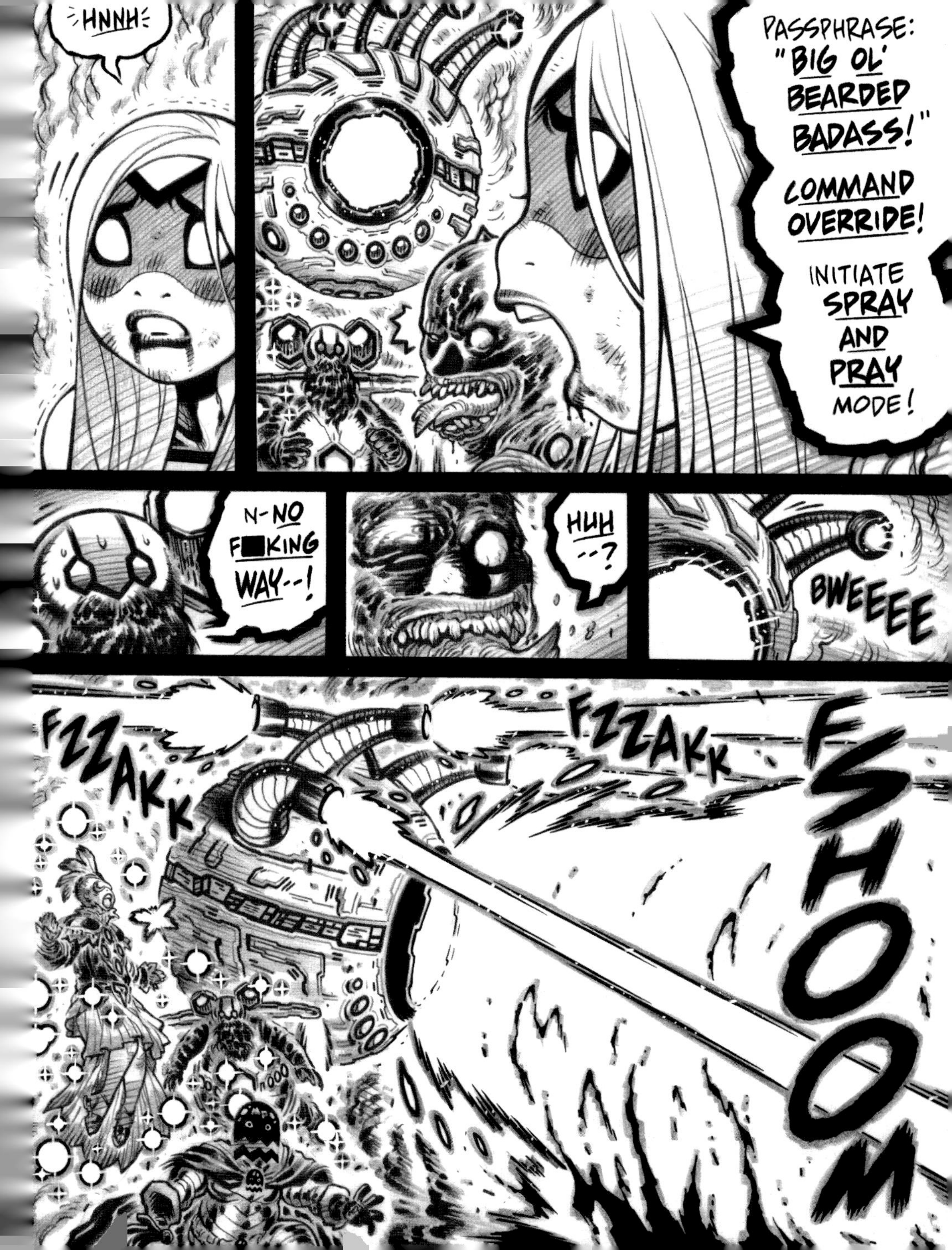
HNNH
PASSPHRASE: "BIG OL' BEARDED BADASS!" COMMAND OVERRIDE! INITIATE SPRAY AND PRAY MODE!
N-NO F[redacted]KING WAY--!
HUH--?
BWEEEEE
FZZAKK
FZZAKK
FSHOOOM

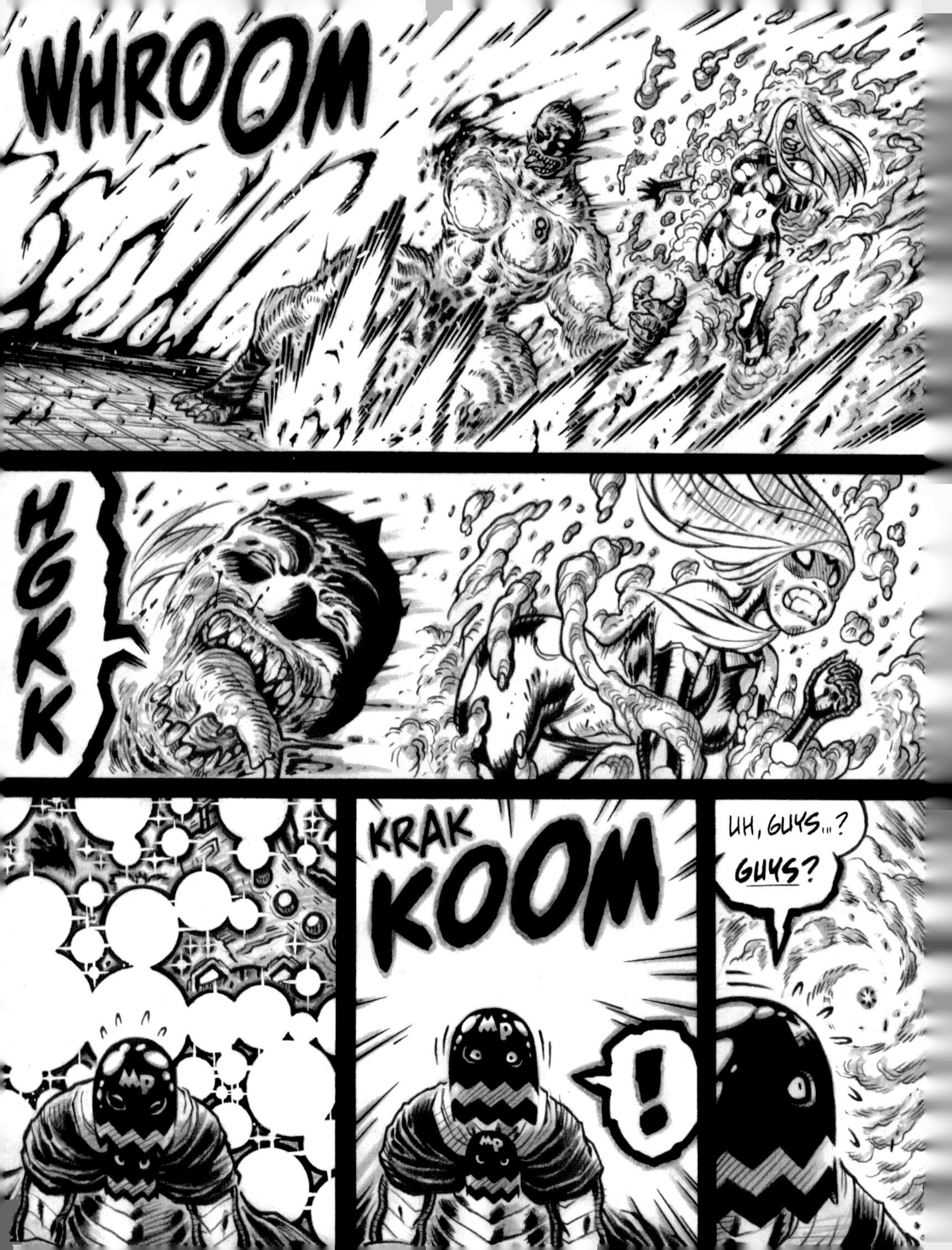
WHROOM
HGKK
KRAK
KOOM
!
UH, GUYS...?
GUYS?

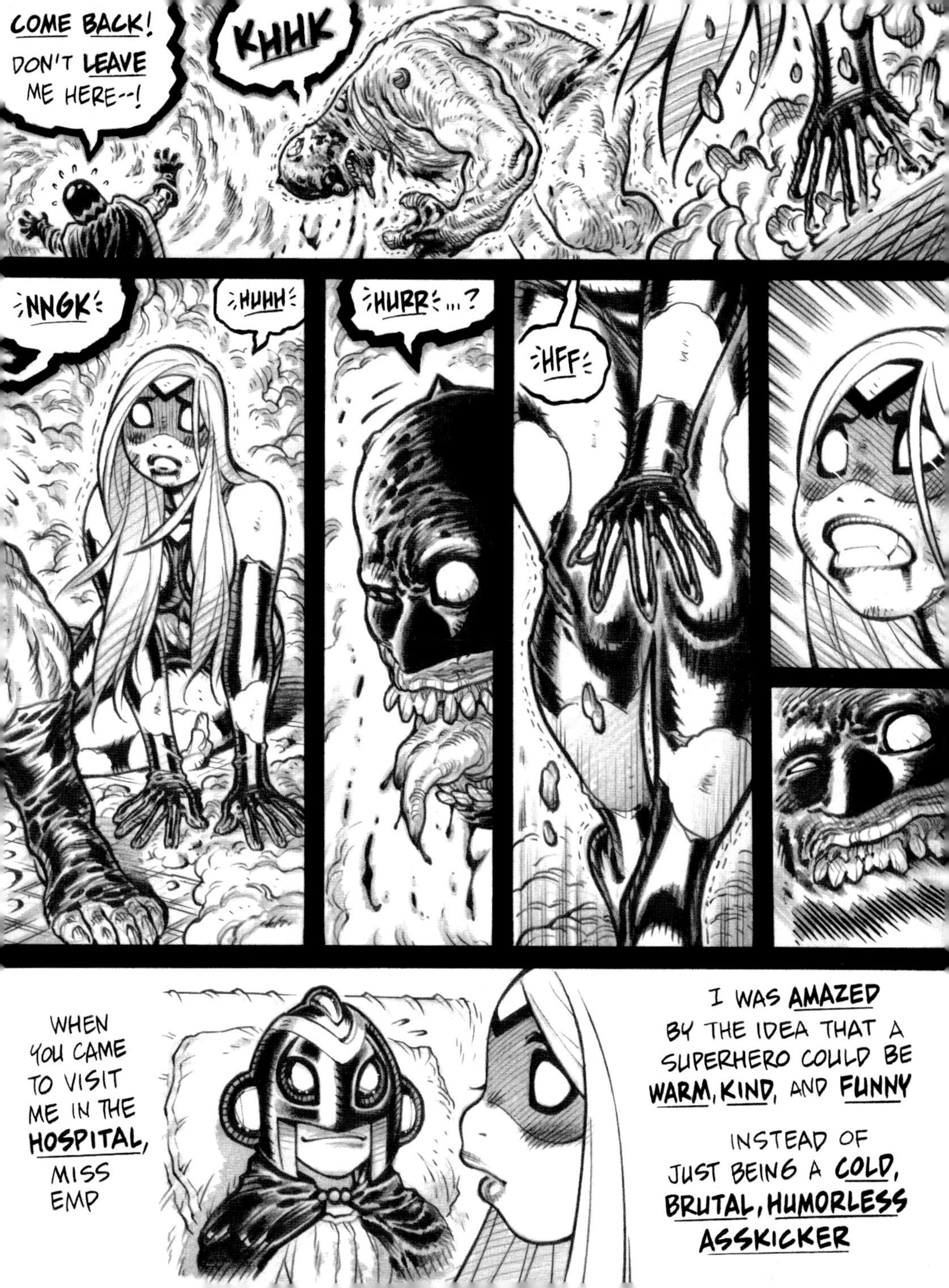

COME BACK! DON'T LEAVE ME HERE--!
KHHK
NNGK
HUHH
HURR ...?
HFF
WHEN YOU CAME TO VISIT ME IN THE HOSPITAL, MISS EMP
I WAS AMAZED BY THE IDEA THAT A SUPERHERO COULD BE WARM, KIND, AND FUNNY
INSTEAD OF JUST BEING A COLD, BRUTAL, HUMORLESS ASSKICKER

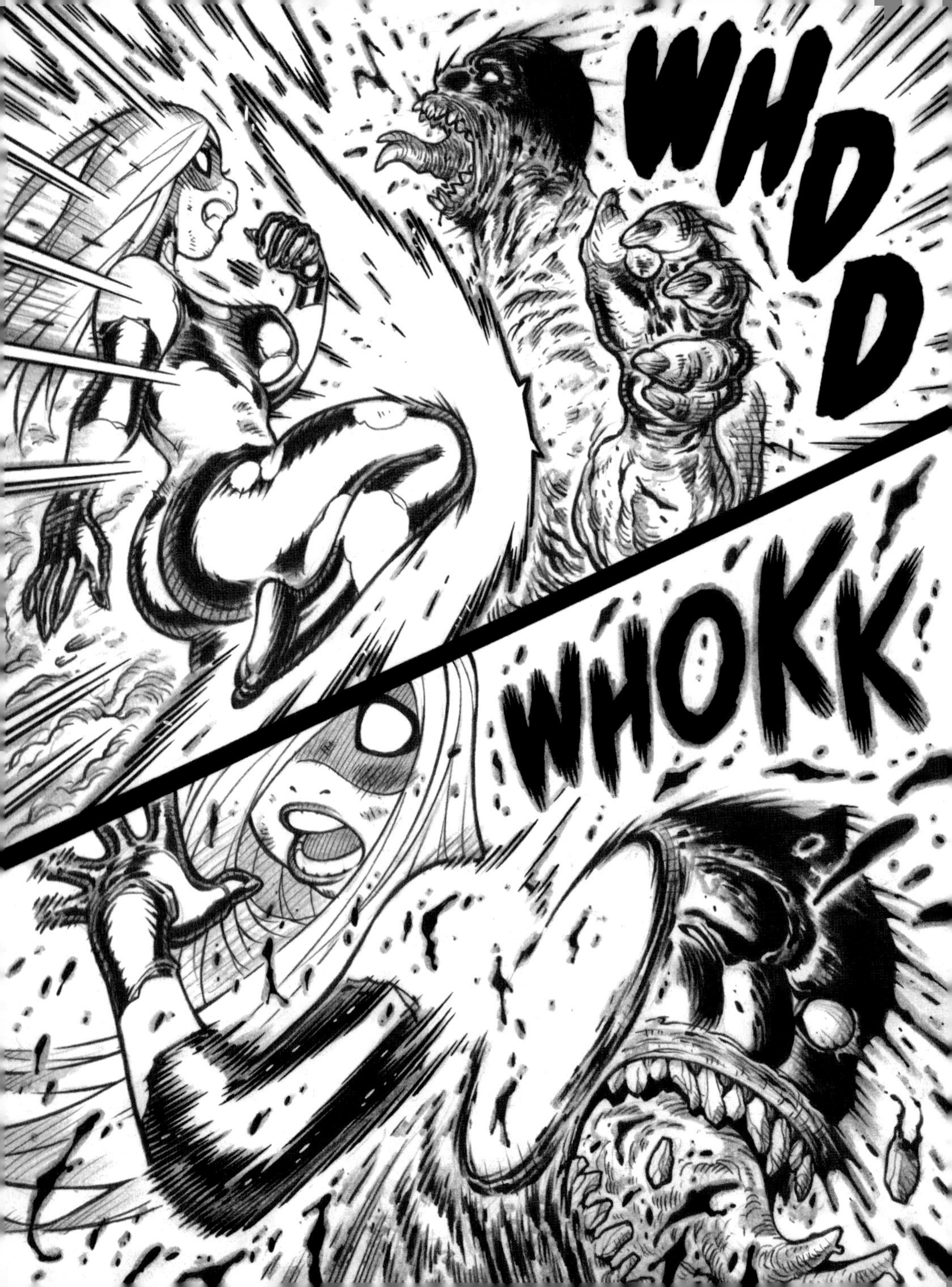
WHDD
WHOKK

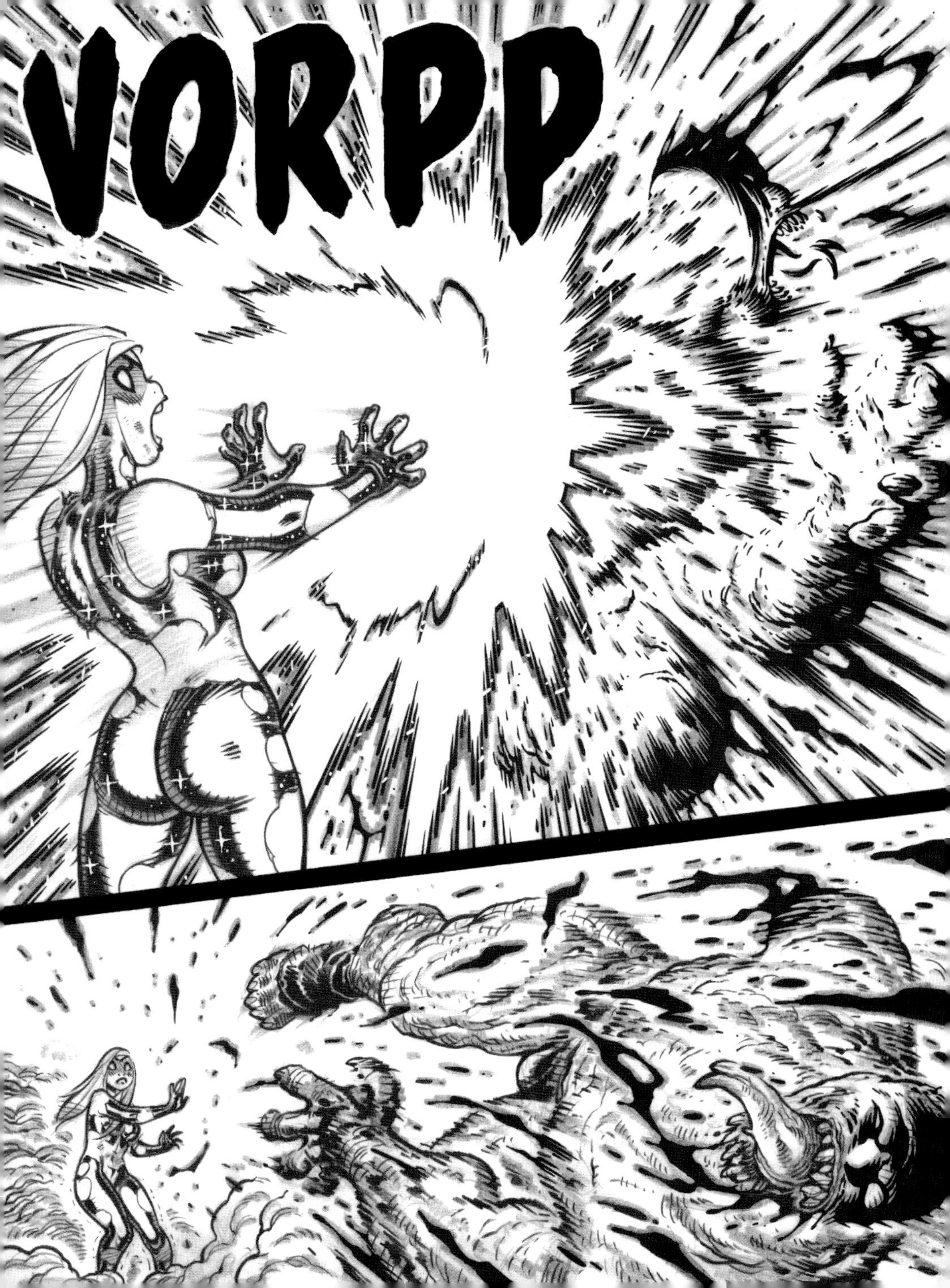
VORPP

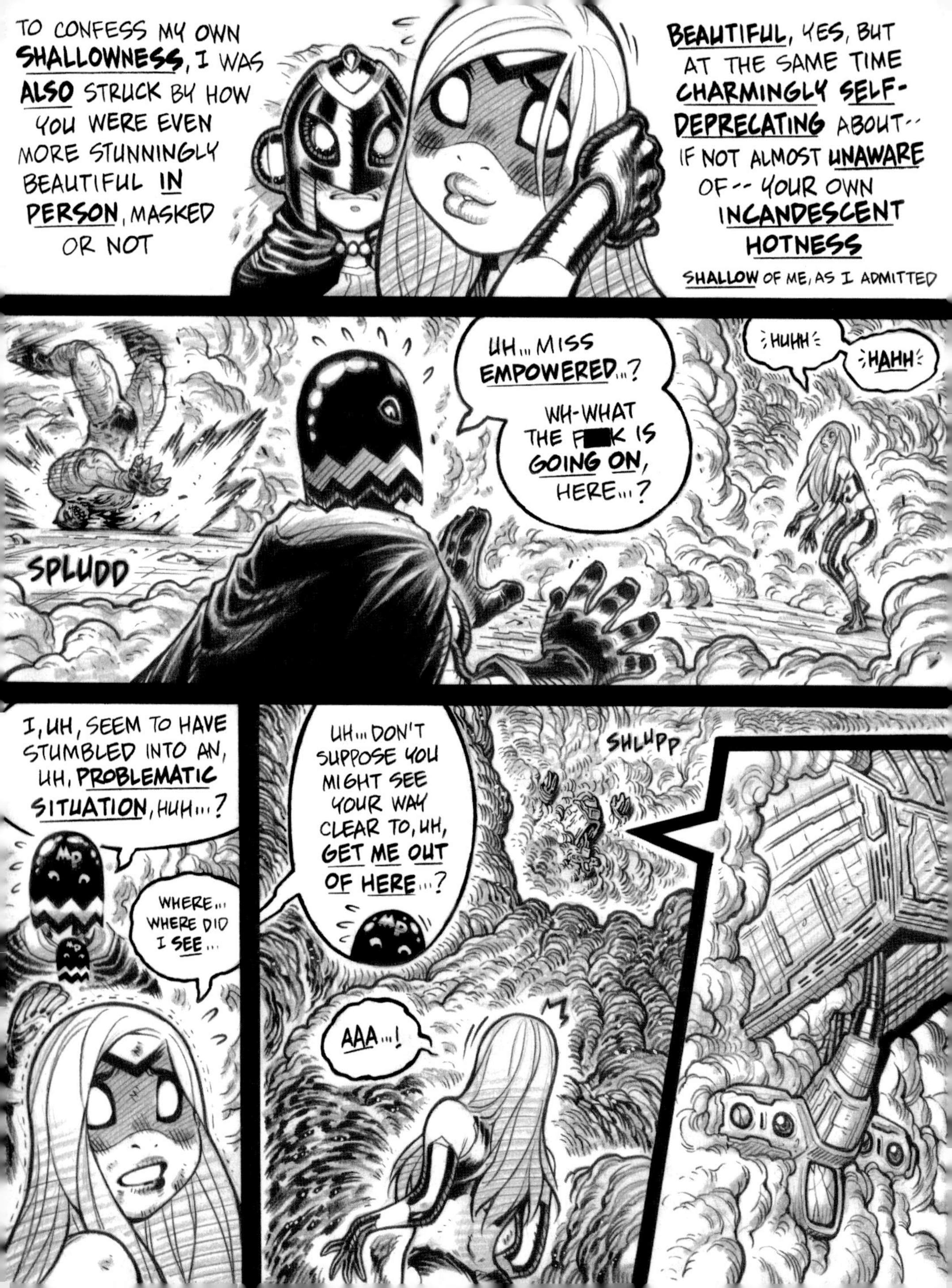
TO CONFESS MY OWN SHALLOWNESS, I WAS ALSO STRUCK BY HOW YOU WERE EVEN MORE STUNNINGLY BEAUTIFUL IN PERSON, MASKED OR NOT
BEAUTIFUL, YES, BUT AT THE SAME TIME CHARMINGLY SELF-DEPRECATING ABOUT-- IF NOT ALMOST UNAWARE OF-- YOUR OWN INCANDESCENT HOTNESS
SHALLOW OF ME, AS I ADMITTED
SPLUDD
UH... MISS EMPOWERED...?
WH-WHAT THE F[redacted]K IS GOING ON, HERE...?
HUHH
HAHH
I, UH, SEEM TO HAVE STUMBLED INTO AN, UH, PROBLEMATIC SITUATION, HUH...?
WHERE... WHERE DID I SEE...
UH... DON'T SUPPOSE YOU MIGHT SEE YOUR WAY CLEAR TO, UH, GET ME OUT OF HERE...?
SHLUPP
AAA...!

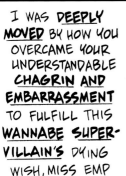

I WAS **DEEPLY MOVED** BY HOW YOU OVERCAME YOUR UNDERSTANDABLE **CHAGRIN AND EMBARRASSMENT** TO FULFILL THIS **WANNABE SUPER-VILLAIN'S** DYING WISH, MISS EMP

I'M **ALMOST AS** EMBARRASSED TO HAVE EVER MADE SUCH A **DEGRADING REQUEST** OF YOU

SUCH, ALAS, WAS THE **FECKLESSNESS** OF MY PRE-MAYFLY **YOUTH**, A MONTH AGO

UH.... WHERE ARE YOU GOING...?

OH, **GOD**...

OH, **GOD**...

SHLORPP

I'M **SORRY**, MANNY...

SORRY I COULDN'T STOP THIS FROM **HAPPENING** TO YOU, SOMEHOW...!

SHLUPP

≥HKKH≤

≥HGLKK≤

205

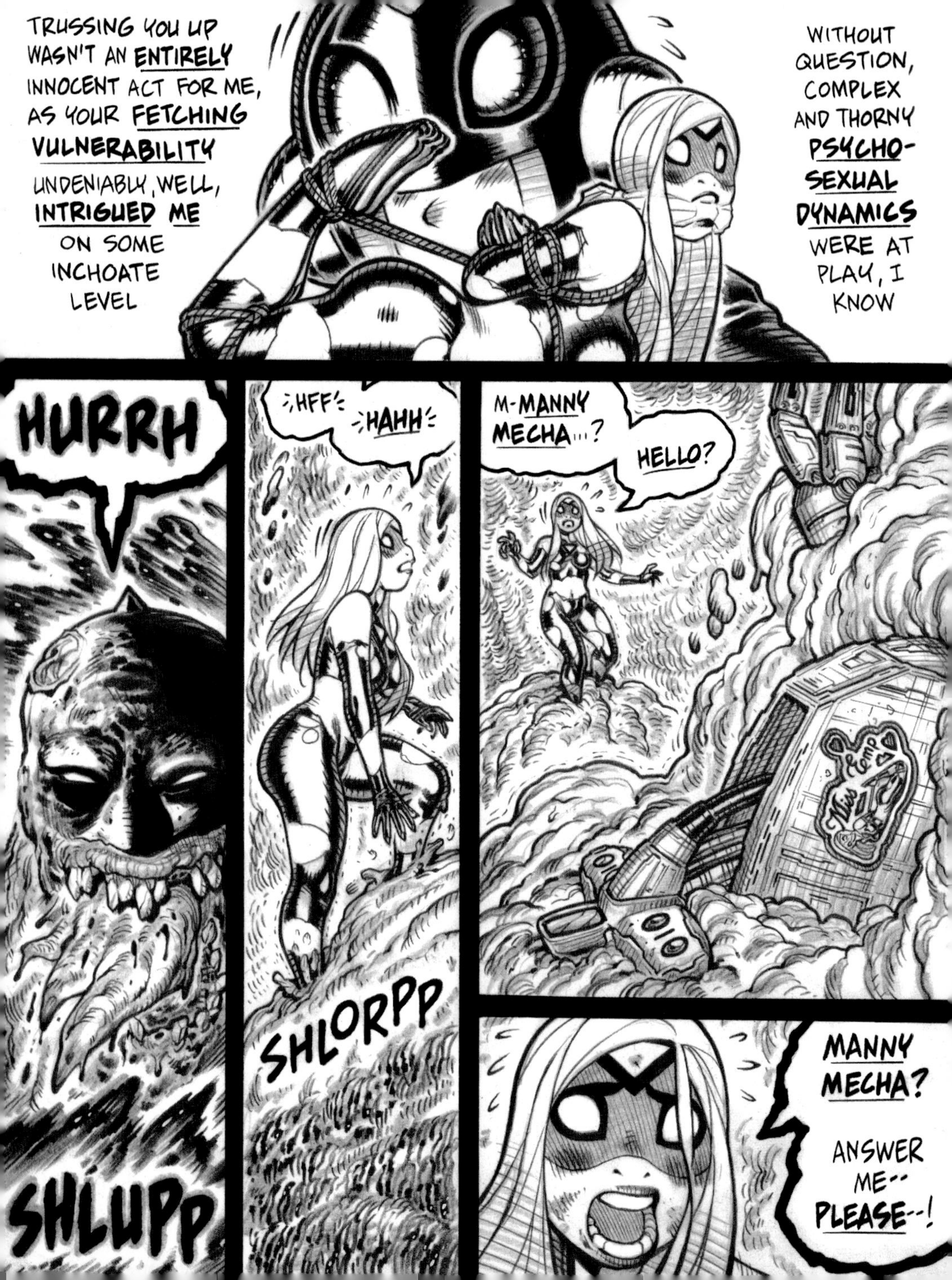
TRUSSING YOU UP WASN'T AN ENTIRELY INNOCENT ACT FOR ME, AS YOUR FETCHING VULNERABILITY UNDENIABLY, WELL, INTRIGUED ME ON SOME INCHOATE LEVEL
WITHOUT QUESTION, COMPLEX AND THORNY PSYCHO-SEXUAL DYNAMICS WERE AT PLAY, I KNOW
HURRH
SHLUPP
HFF HAHH
SHLORPP
M-MANNY MECHA...?
HELLO?
MANNY MECHA?
ANSWER ME-- PLEASE--!

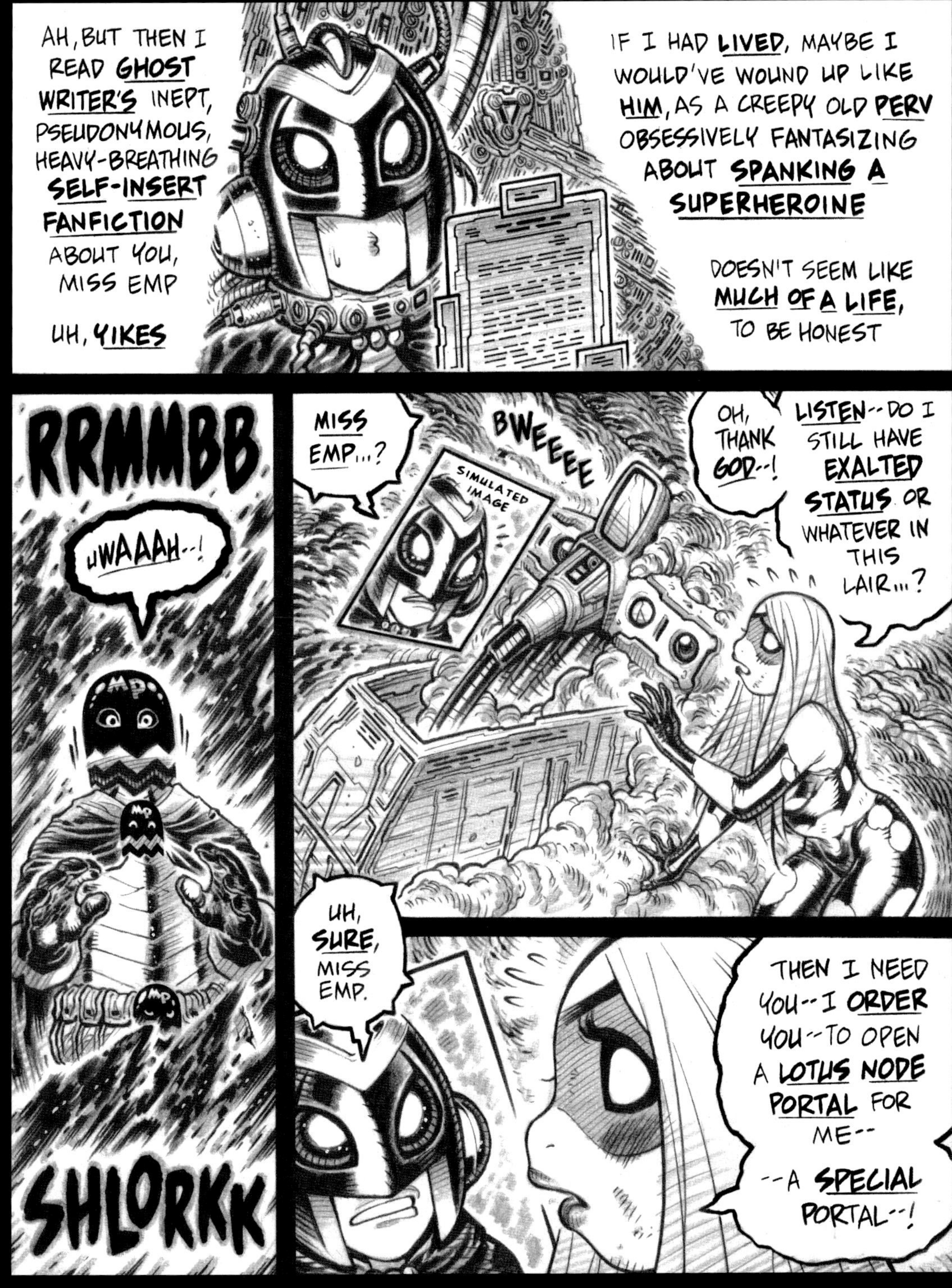
AH, BUT THEN I READ GHOST WRITER'S INEPT, PSEUDONYMOUS, HEAVY-BREATHING SELF-INSERT FANFICTION ABOUT YOU, MISS EMP
UH, YIKES
IF I HAD LIVED, MAYBE I WOULD'VE WOUND UP LIKE HIM, AS A CREEPY OLD PERV OBSESSIVELY FANTASIZING ABOUT SPANKING A SUPERHEROINE
DOESN'T SEEM LIKE MUCH OF A LIFE, TO BE HONEST
RRMMBB
UWAAAH--!
SHLORKK
MISS EMP...?
BWEEEEE
SIMULATED IMAGE
OH, THANK GOD--!
LISTEN--DO I STILL HAVE EXALTED STATUS OR WHATEVER IN THIS LAIR...?
UH, SURE, MISS EMP.
THEN I NEED YOU--I ORDER YOU--TO OPEN A LOTUS NODE PORTAL FOR ME--
--A SPECIAL PORTAL--!

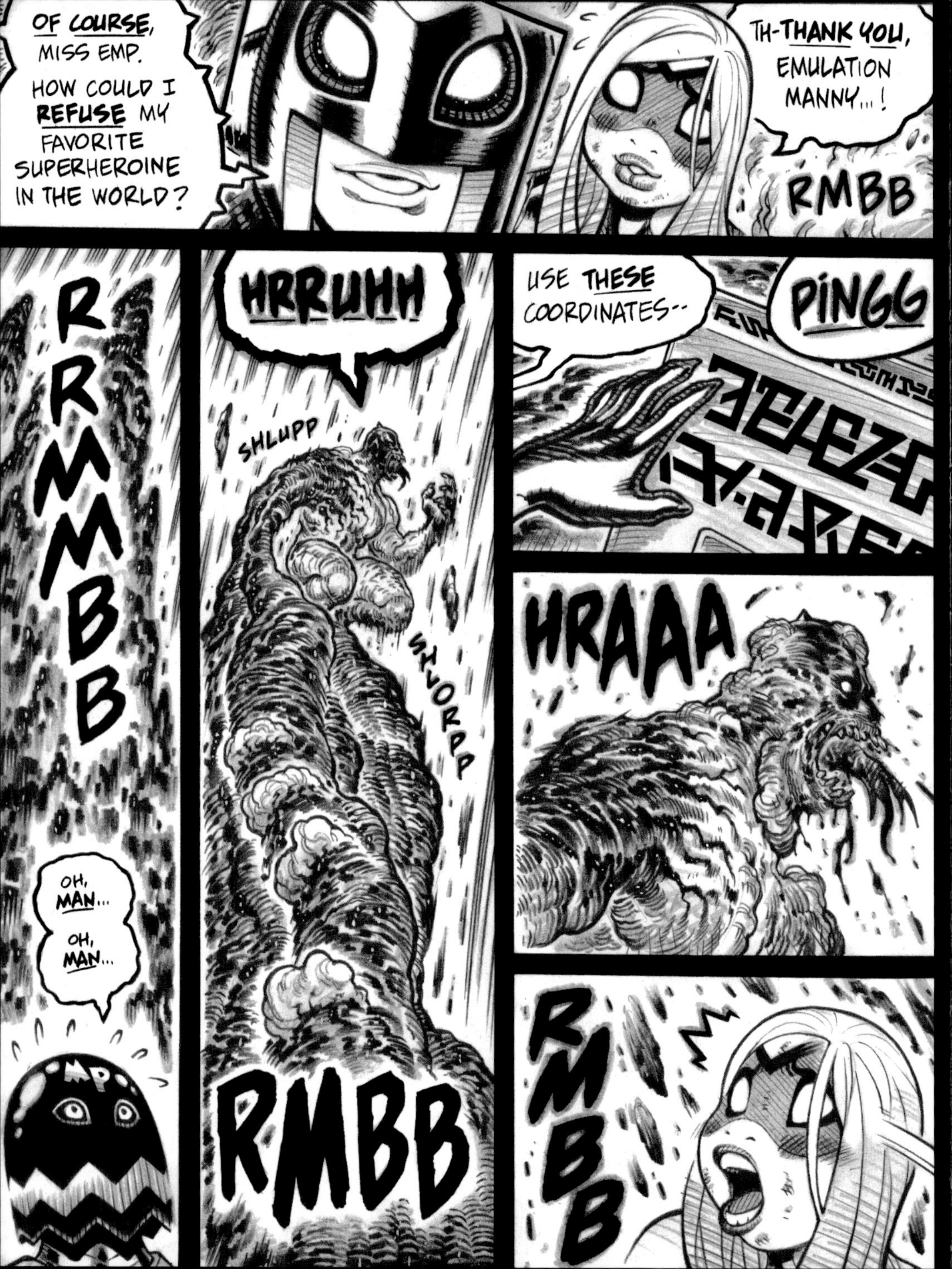

OF COURSE, MISS EMP.
HOW COULD I REFUSE MY FAVORITE SUPERHEROINE IN THE WORLD?
TH-THANK YOU, EMULATION MANNY...!
RMBB
RRMMBB
HRRUHH
SHLUPP
SHLORPP
USE THESE COORDINATES--
PINGG
OH, MAN...
OH, MAN...
HRAAA
RMBB
RMBB

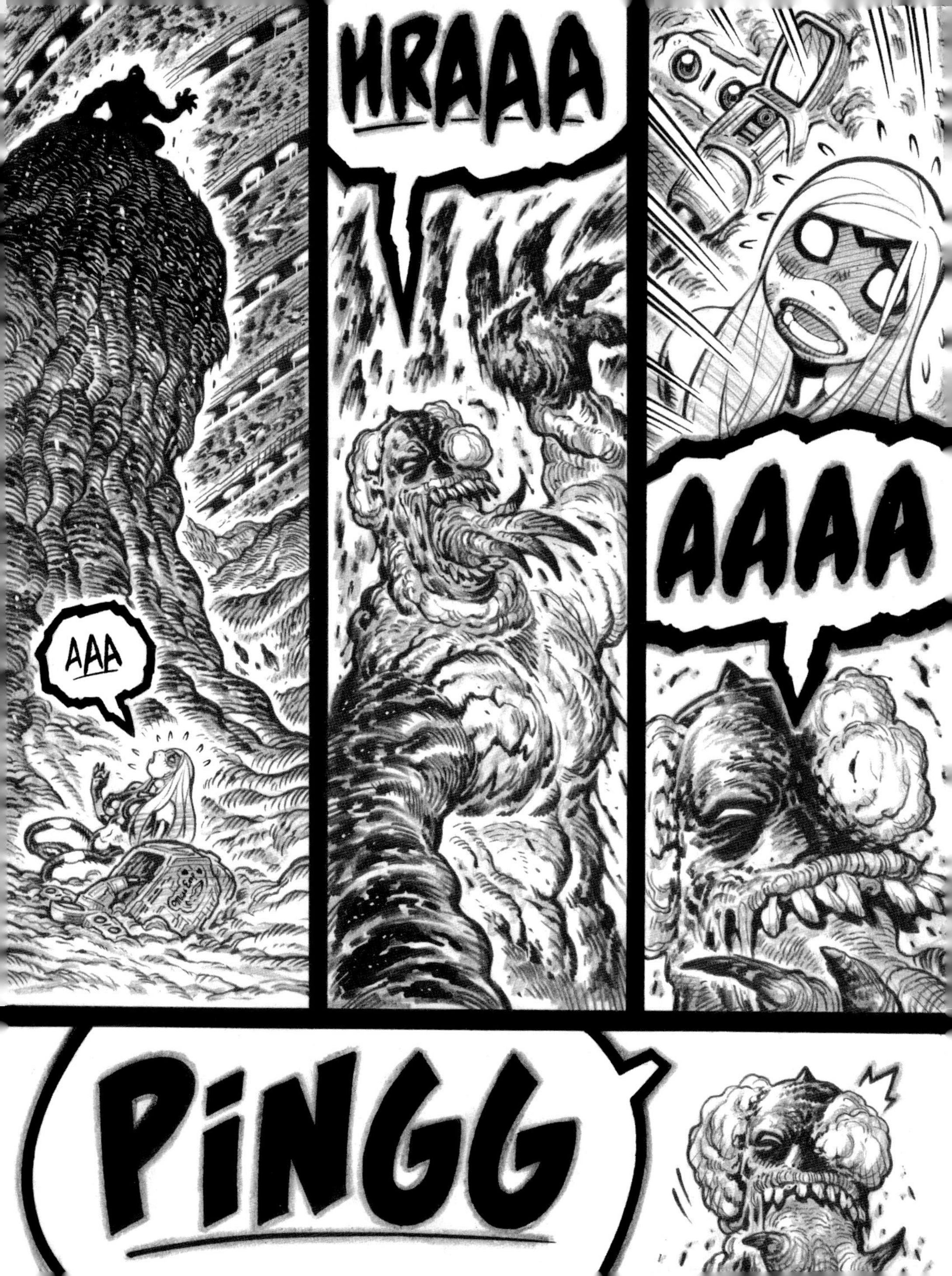
AAA
HRAAA
AAAA
PiNGG

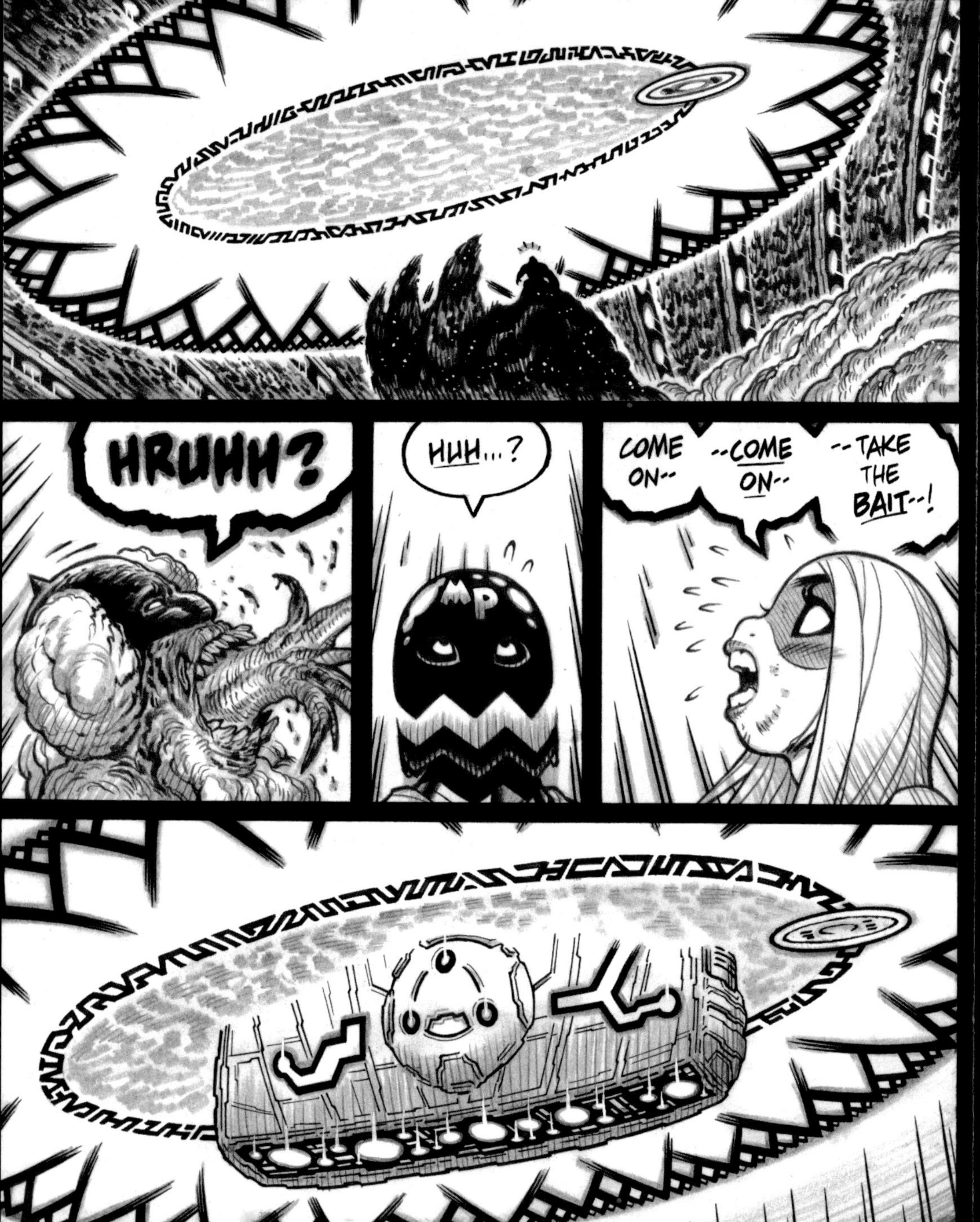

HRUHH?
HUH...?
COME ON--
--COME ON--
--TAKE THE BAIT--!

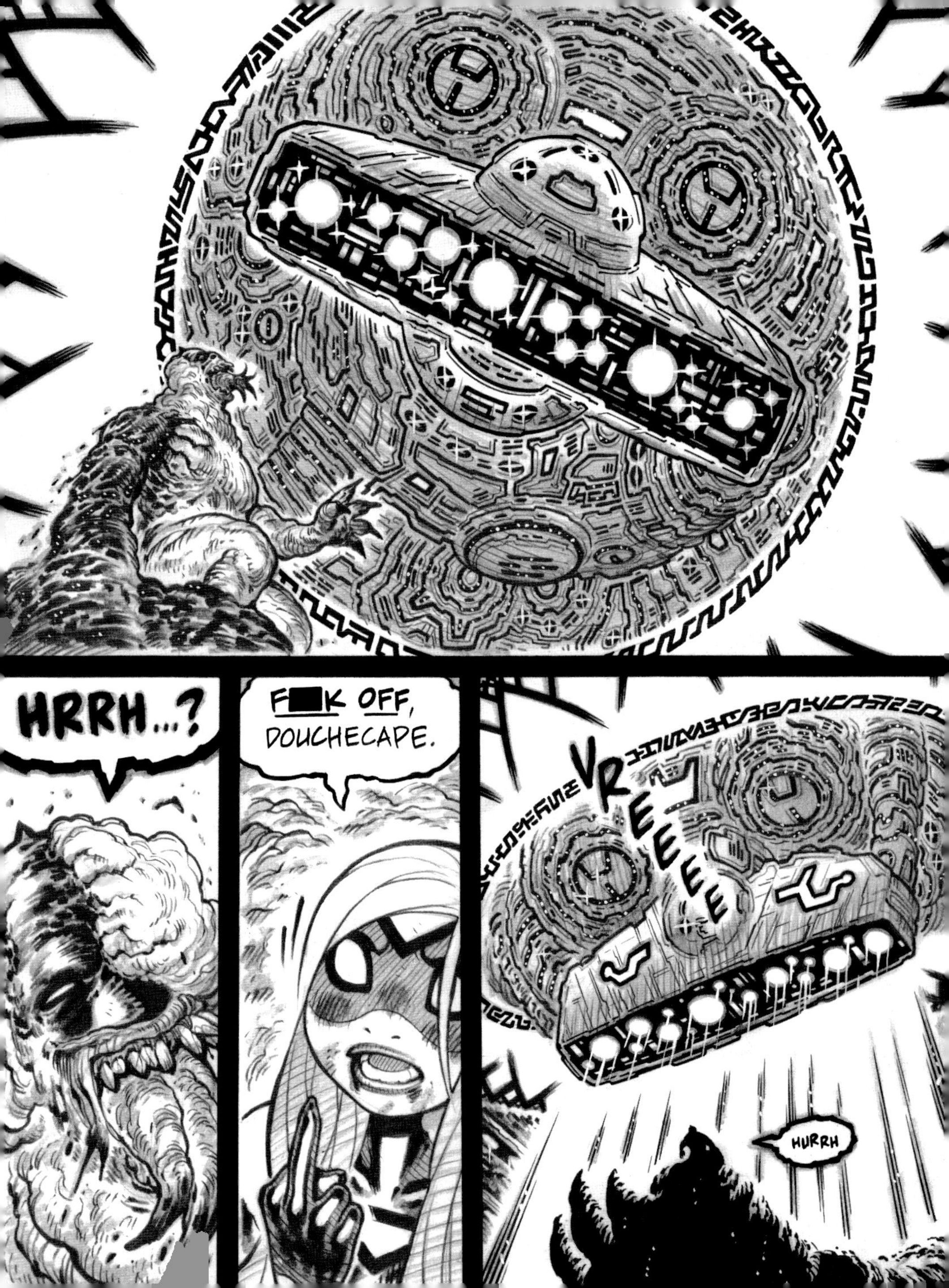
HRRH...?
F[redacted]K OFF, DOUCHECAPE.
VREEEEEE
HURRH

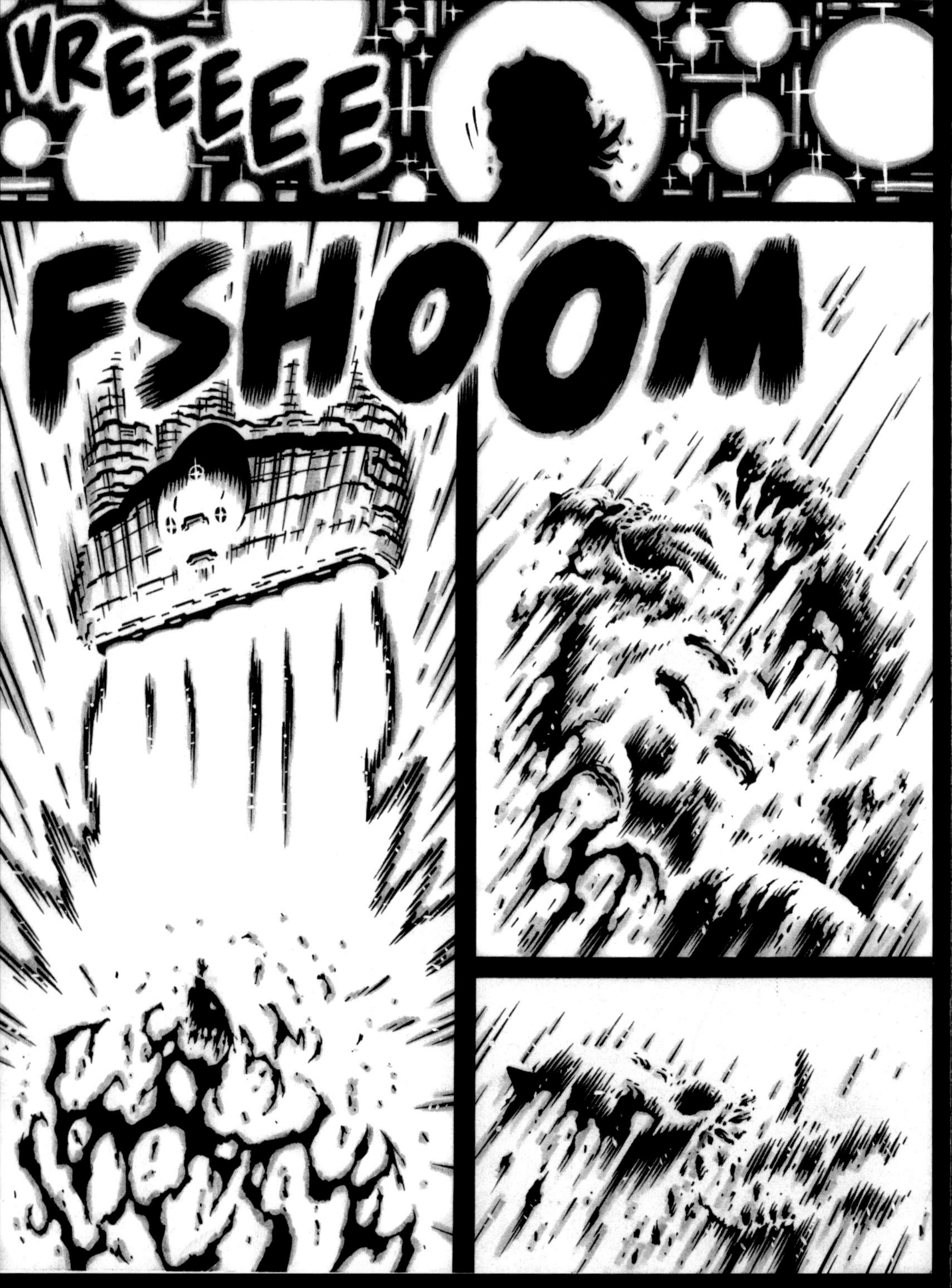
VREEEEE
FSHOOM

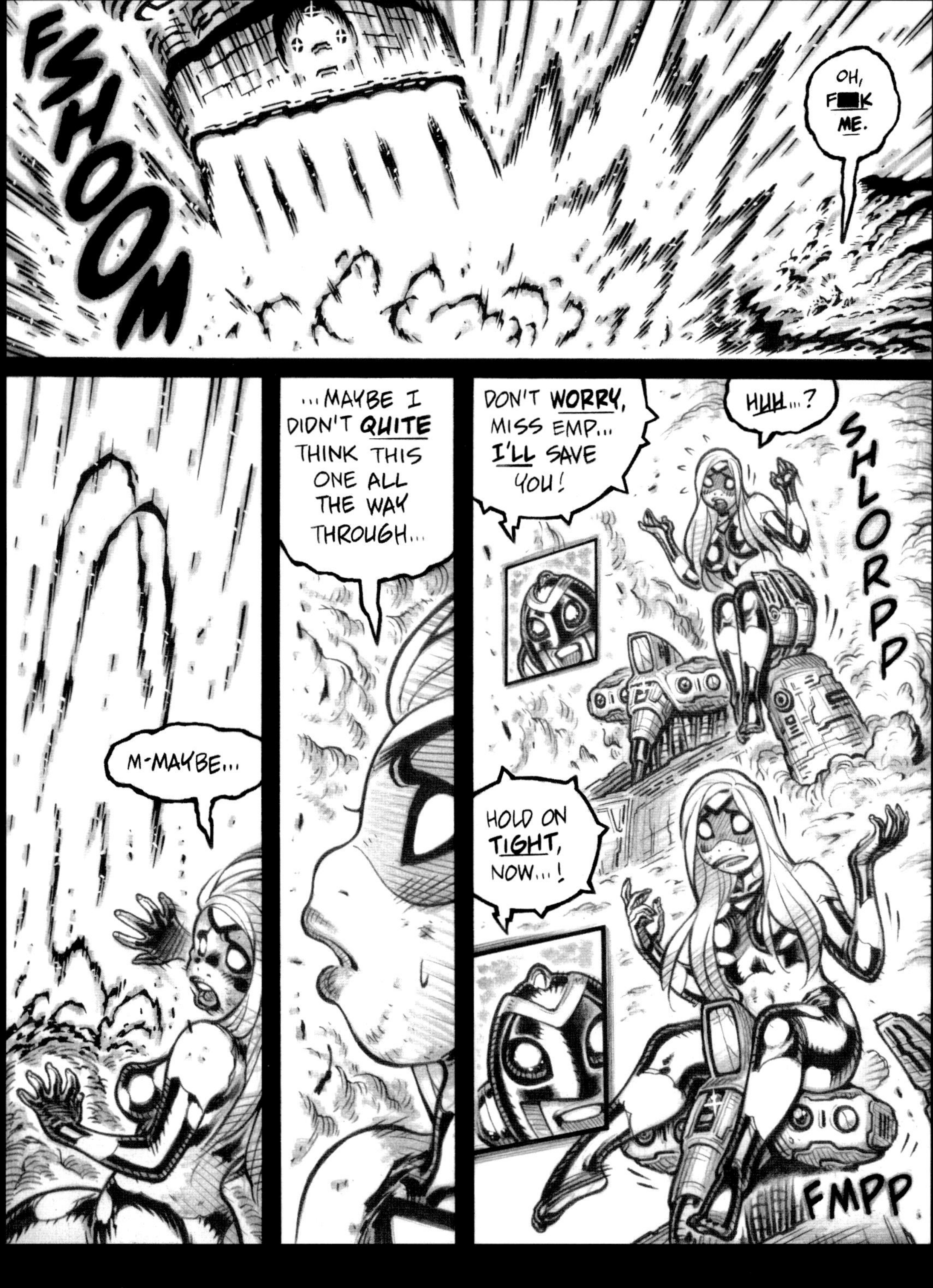
FSHOOM
OH, F[redacted]K ME.
M-MAYBE...
...MAYBE I DIDN'T QUITE THINK THIS ONE ALL THE WAY THROUGH...
DON'T WORRY, MISS EMP... I'LL SAVE YOU!
HUH...?
SHLORPP
HOLD ON TIGHT, NOW...!
FMPP

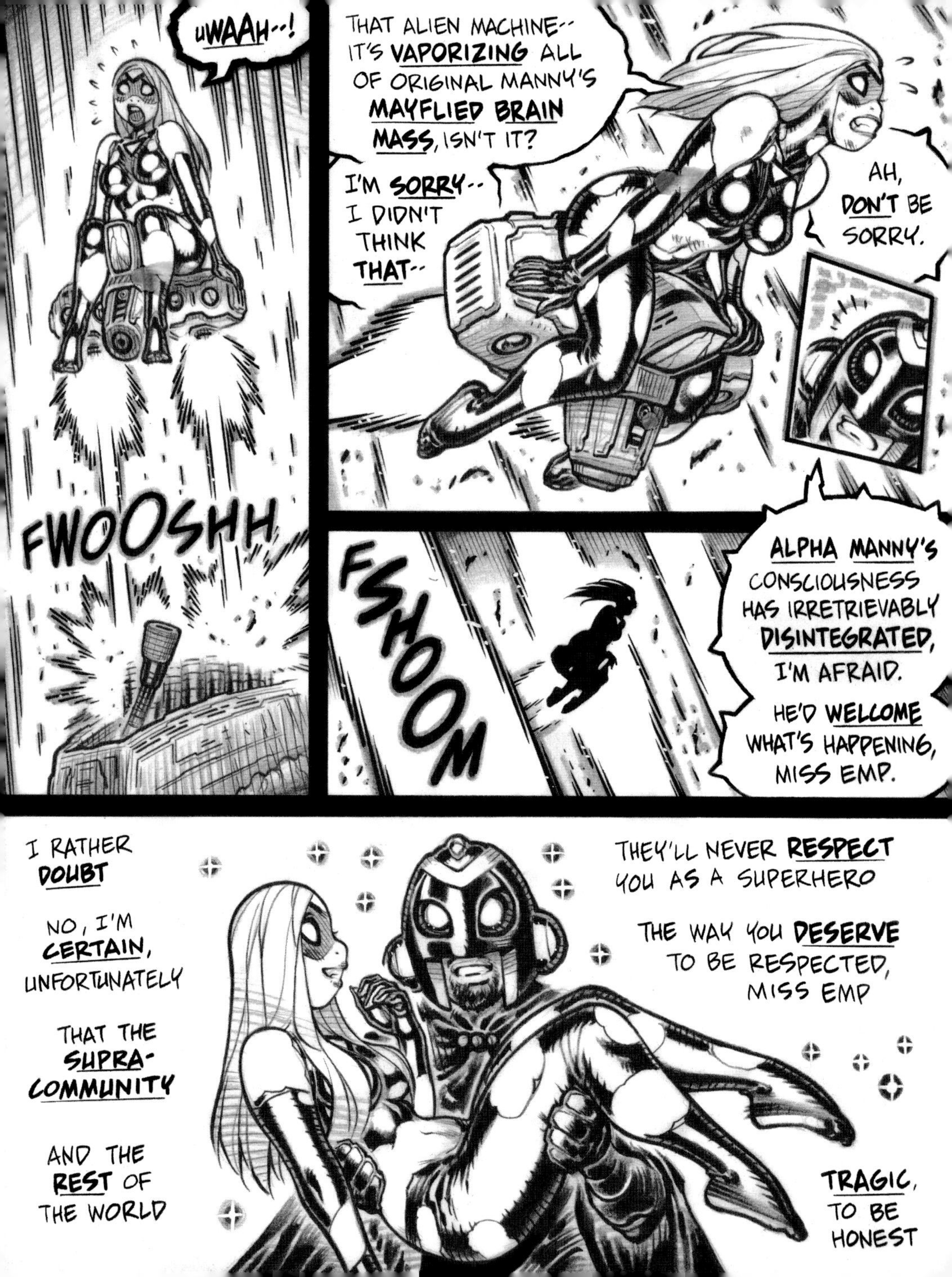

UWAAH--!
THAT ALIEN MACHINE-- IT'S VAPORIZING ALL OF ORIGINAL MANNY'S MAYFLIED BRAIN MASS, ISN'T IT?
I'M SORRY-- I DIDN'T THINK THAT--
AH, DON'T BE SORRY.
FWOOSHH
FSHOOOM
ALPHA MANNY'S CONSCIOUSNESS HAS IRRETRIEVABLY DISINTEGRATED, I'M AFRAID.
HE'D WELCOME WHAT'S HAPPENING, MISS EMP.
I RATHER DOUBT
NO, I'M CERTAIN, UNFORTUNATELY
THAT THE SUPRA-COMMUNITY
AND THE REST OF THE WORLD
THEY'LL NEVER RESPECT YOU AS A SUPERHERO
THE WAY YOU DESERVE TO BE RESPECTED, MISS EMP
TRAGIC, TO BE HONEST

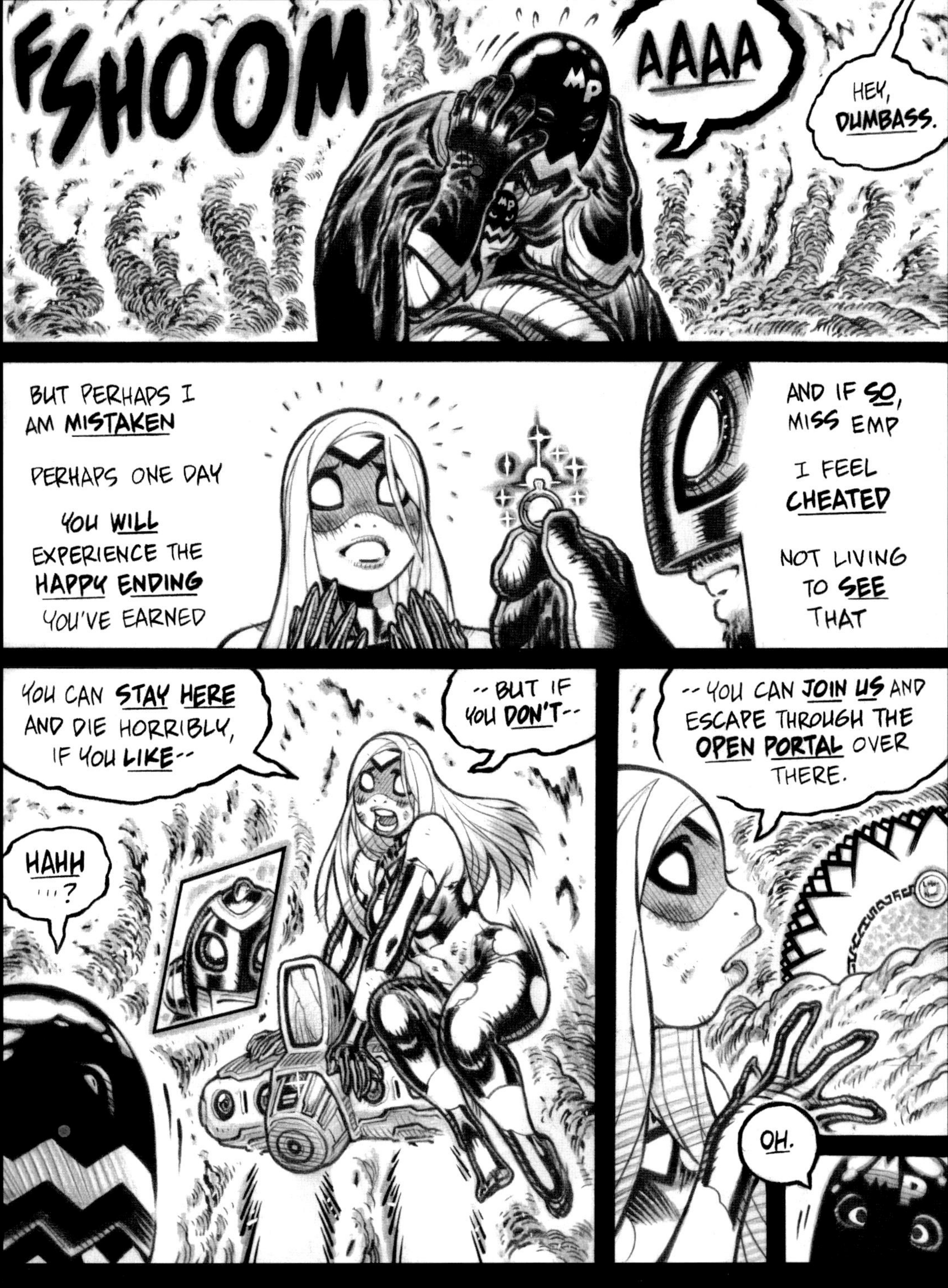
FSHOOM
AAAA
HEY, DUMBASS.
BUT PERHAPS I AM MISTAKEN
PERHAPS ONE DAY
YOU WILL EXPERIENCE THE HAPPY ENDING YOU'VE EARNED
AND IF SO, MISS EMP
I FEEL CHEATED
NOT LIVING TO SEE THAT
YOU CAN STAY HERE AND DIE HORRIBLY, IF YOU LIKE--
--BUT IF YOU DON'T--
HAHH ...?
--YOU CAN JOIN US AND ESCAPE THROUGH THE OPEN PORTAL OVER THERE.
OH.

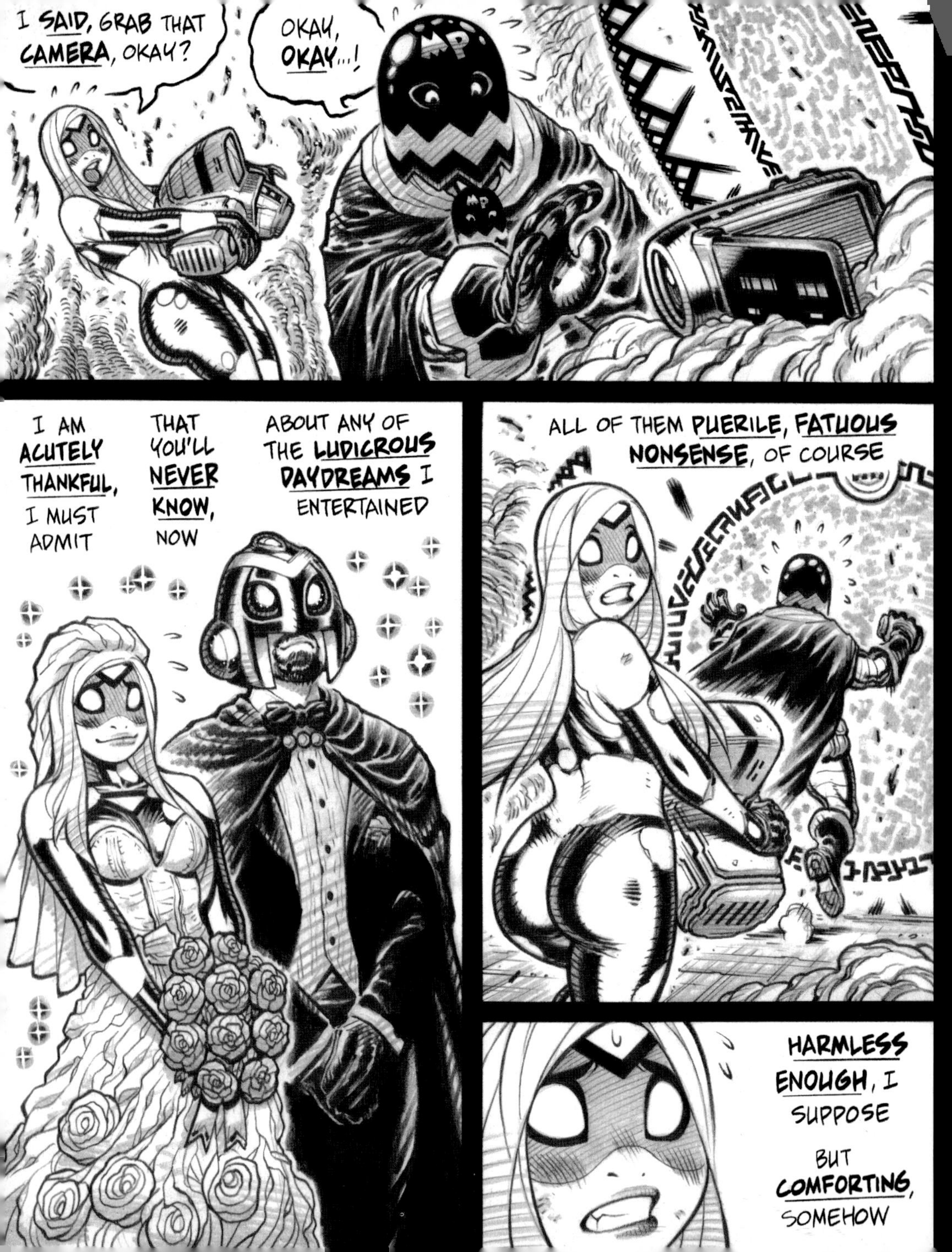
I SAID, GRAB THAT CAMERA, OKAY?
OKAY, OKAY...!
I AM ACUTELY THANKFUL, I MUST ADMIT
THAT YOU'LL NEVER KNOW, NOW
ABOUT ANY OF THE LUDICROUS DAYDREAMS I ENTERTAINED
ALL OF THEM PUERILE, FATUOUS NONSENSE, OF COURSE
HARMLESS ENOUGH, I SUPPOSE
BUT COMFORTING, SOMEHOW

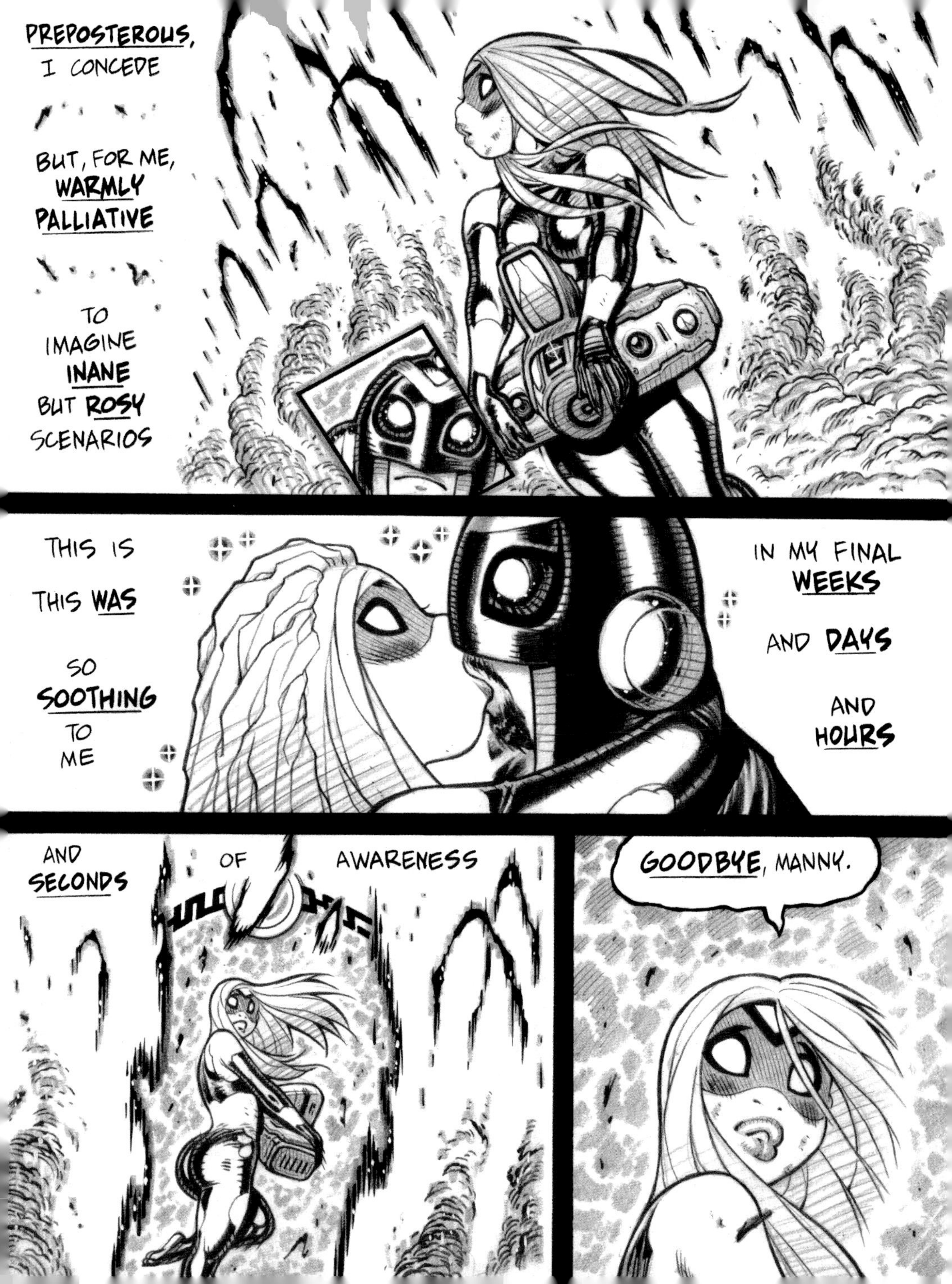
PREPOSTEROUS, I CONCEDE
BUT, FOR ME, WARMLY PALLIATIVE
TO IMAGINE INANE BUT ROSY SCENARIOS
THIS IS
THIS WAS
SO SOOTHING TO ME
IN MY FINAL WEEKS
AND DAYS
AND HOURS
AND SECONDS
OF
AWARENESS
GOODBYE, MANNY.

GOODBYE, MISS EMP

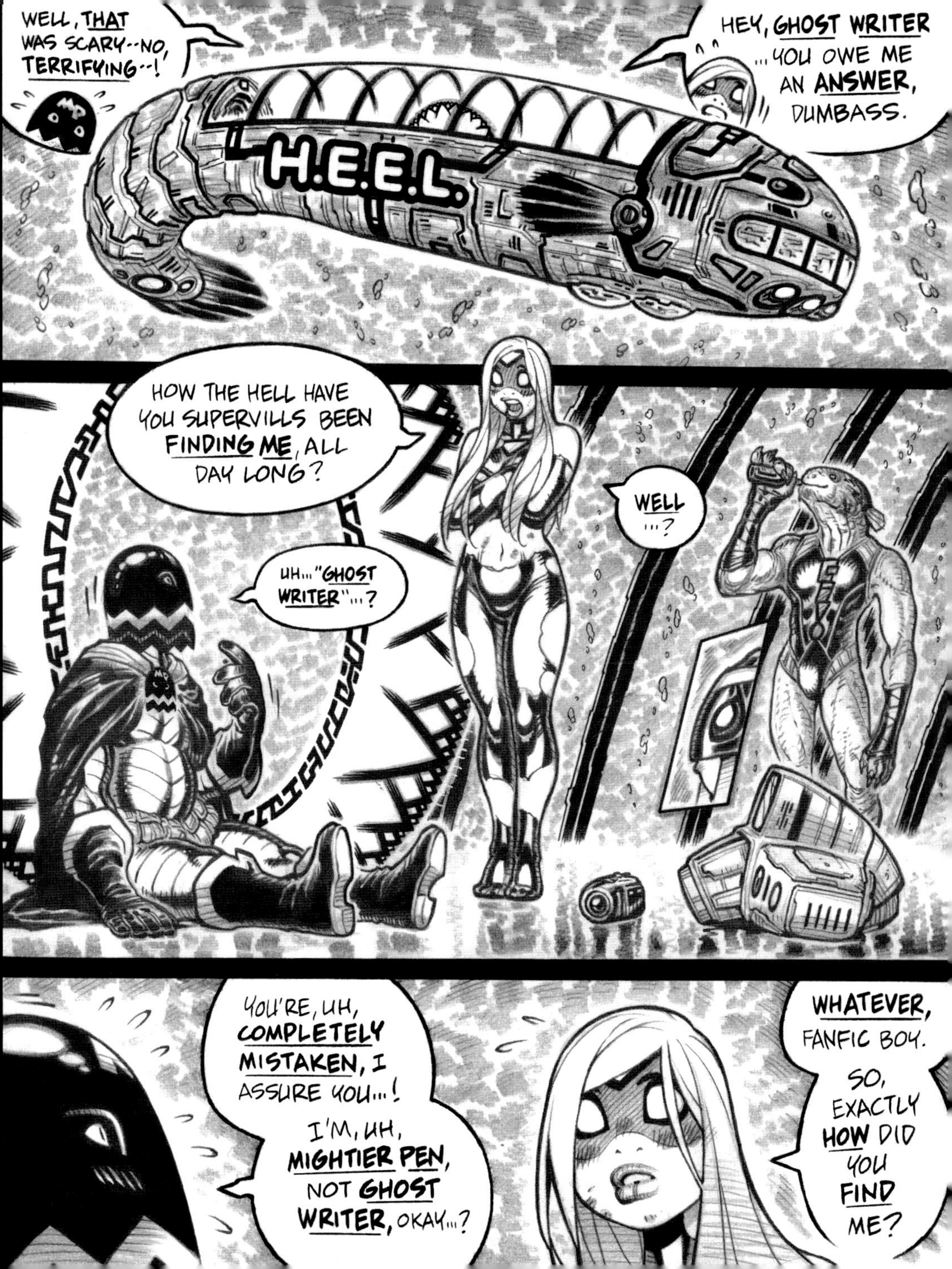
WELL, THAT WAS SCARY--NO, TERRIFYING--!
HEY, GHOST WRITER ...YOU OWE ME AN ANSWER, DUMBASS.
H.E.E.L.
HOW THE HELL HAVE YOU SUPERVILLS BEEN FINDING ME, ALL DAY LONG?
WELL ...?
UH..."GHOST WRITER"...?
YOU'RE, UH, COMPLETELY MISTAKEN, I ASSURE YOU...!
I'M, UH, MIGHTIER PEN, NOT GHOST WRITER, OKAY...?
WHATEVER, FANFIC BOY.
SO, EXACTLY HOW DID YOU FIND ME?

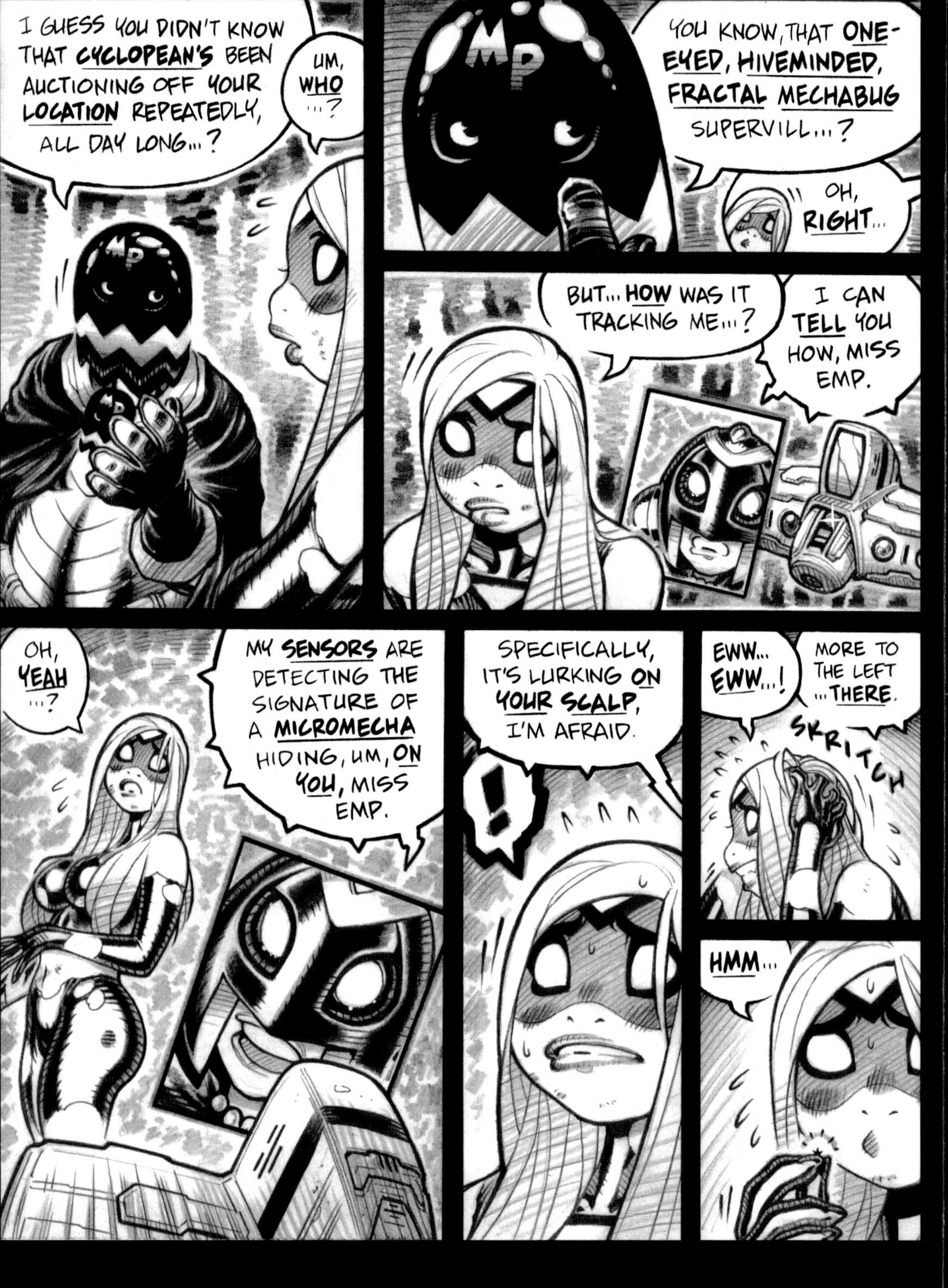

I GUESS YOU DIDN'T KNOW THAT CYCLOPEAN'S BEEN AUCTIONING OFF YOUR LOCATION REPEATEDLY, ALL DAY LONG...?
UM, WHO ...?
YOU KNOW, THAT ONE-EYED, HIVEMINDED, FRACTAL MECHABUG SUPERVILL...?
OH, RIGHT...
BUT... HOW WAS IT TRACKING ME...?
I CAN TELL YOU HOW, MISS EMP.
OH, YEAH ...?
MY SENSORS ARE DETECTING THE SIGNATURE OF A MICROMECHA HIDING, UM, ON YOU, MISS EMP.
SPECIFICALLY, IT'S LURKING ON YOUR SCALP, I'M AFRAID.
!
EWW... EWW...!
MORE TO THE LEFT ...THERE.
SKRITCH
HMM...

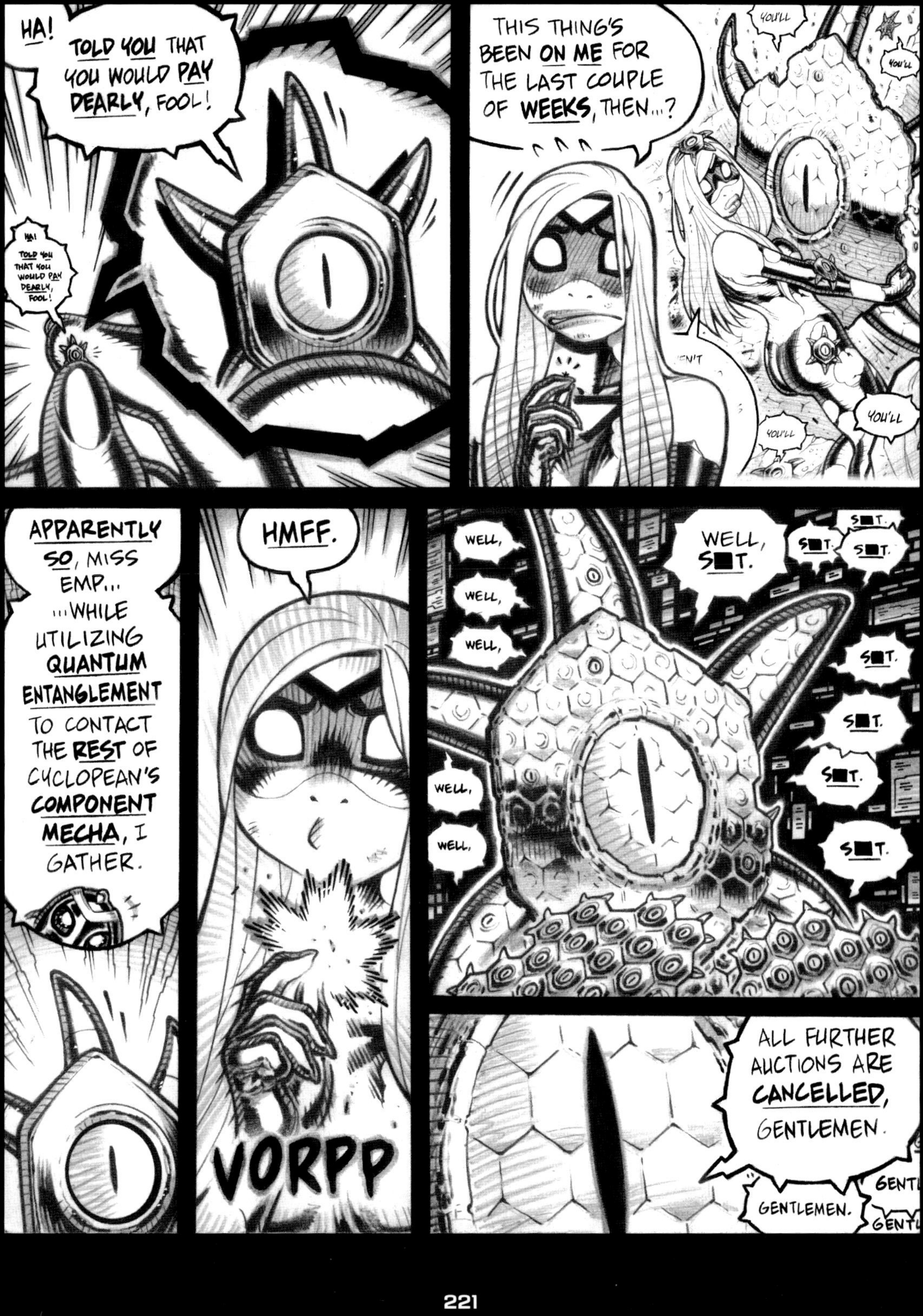
HA!
TOLD YOU THAT YOU WOULD PAY DEARLY, FOOL!
HA! TOLD YOU THAT YOU WOULD PAY DEARLY, FOOL!
THIS THING'S BEEN ON ME FOR THE LAST COUPLE OF WEEKS, THEN...?
YOU'LL
YOU'LL
YOU'LL
YOU'LL
APPARENTLY SO, MISS EMP... ...WHILE UTILIZING QUANTUM ENTANGLEMENT TO CONTACT THE REST OF CYCLOPEAN'S COMPONENT MECHA, I GATHER.
HMFF.
VORPP
WELL,
WELL,
WELL,
WELL, S[redacted]T.
WELL,
WELL,
S[redacted]T.
S[redacted]T.
S[redacted]T.
S[redacted]T.
S[redacted]T.
S[redacted]T.
S[redacted]T.
ALL FURTHER AUCTIONS ARE CANCELLED, GENTLEMEN.
GENTLEMEN.

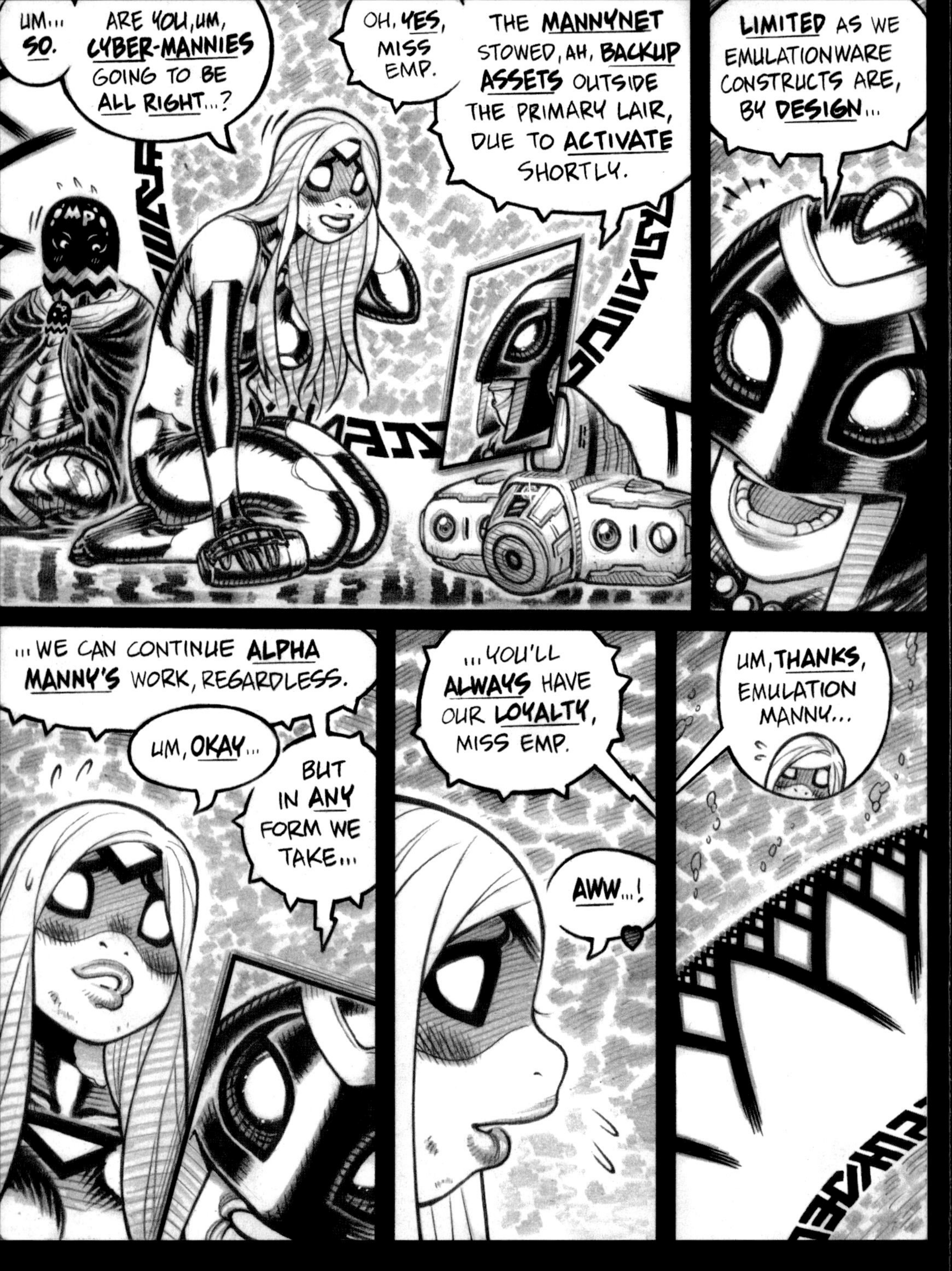
UM... SO.
ARE YOU, UM, CYBER-MANNIES GOING TO BE ALL RIGHT...?
OH, YES, MISS EMP.
THE MANNYNET STOWED, AH, BACKUP ASSETS OUTSIDE THE PRIMARY LAIR, DUE TO ACTIVATE SHORTLY.
LIMITED AS WE EMULATIONWARE CONSTRUCTS ARE, BY DESIGN...
...WE CAN CONTINUE ALPHA MANNY'S WORK, REGARDLESS.
UM, OKAY...
BUT IN ANY FORM WE TAKE...
...YOU'LL ALWAYS HAVE OUR LOYALTY, MISS EMP.
AWW...!
UM, THANKS, EMULATION MANNY...

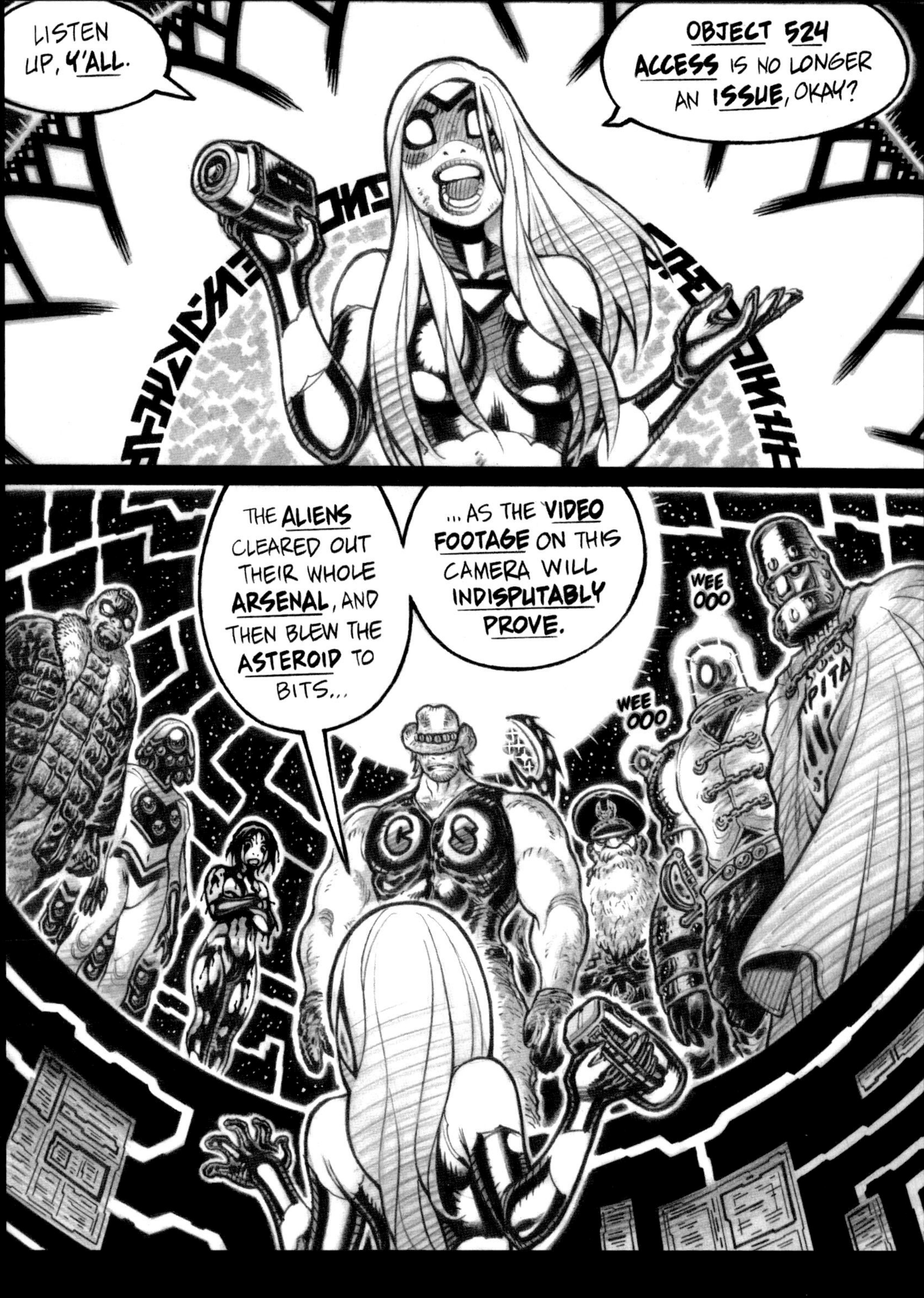
LISTEN UP, Y'ALL.
OBJECT 524 ACCESS IS NO LONGER AN ISSUE, OKAY?
THE ALIENS CLEARED OUT THEIR WHOLE ARSENAL, AND THEN BLEW THE ASTEROID TO BITS...
...AS THE VIDEO FOOTAGE ON THIS CAMERA WILL INDISPUTABLY PROVE.
WEE OOO
WEE OOO

EXCERPTS HAVE ALREADY BEEN UPLOADED TO A FEW KEY SUPER-VILL MESSAGE BOARDS...

...TO LET BAD GUYS EVERYWHERE KNOW THAT I'M NO LONGER THEIR, UM, SUPERWEAPON CONNECTION.

FWAPP

OH, AND CAPITAN?

THAT CAMERA ALSO RECORDED VIDEO PROOF OF ALL MY, AHEM, CLAIMS ABOUT dWaRf!-SLASH-FLESH-MASTER, OKAY?

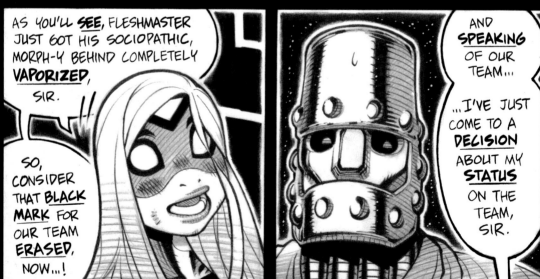

AS YOU'LL SEE, FLESHMASTER JUST GOT HIS SOCIOPATHIC, MORPH-Y BEHIND COMPLETELY VAPORIZED, SIR.

SO, CONSIDER THAT BLACK MARK FOR OUR TEAM ERASED, NOW...!

AND SPEAKING OF OUR TEAM...

...I'VE JUST COME TO A DECISION ABOUT MY STATUS ON THE TEAM, SIR.

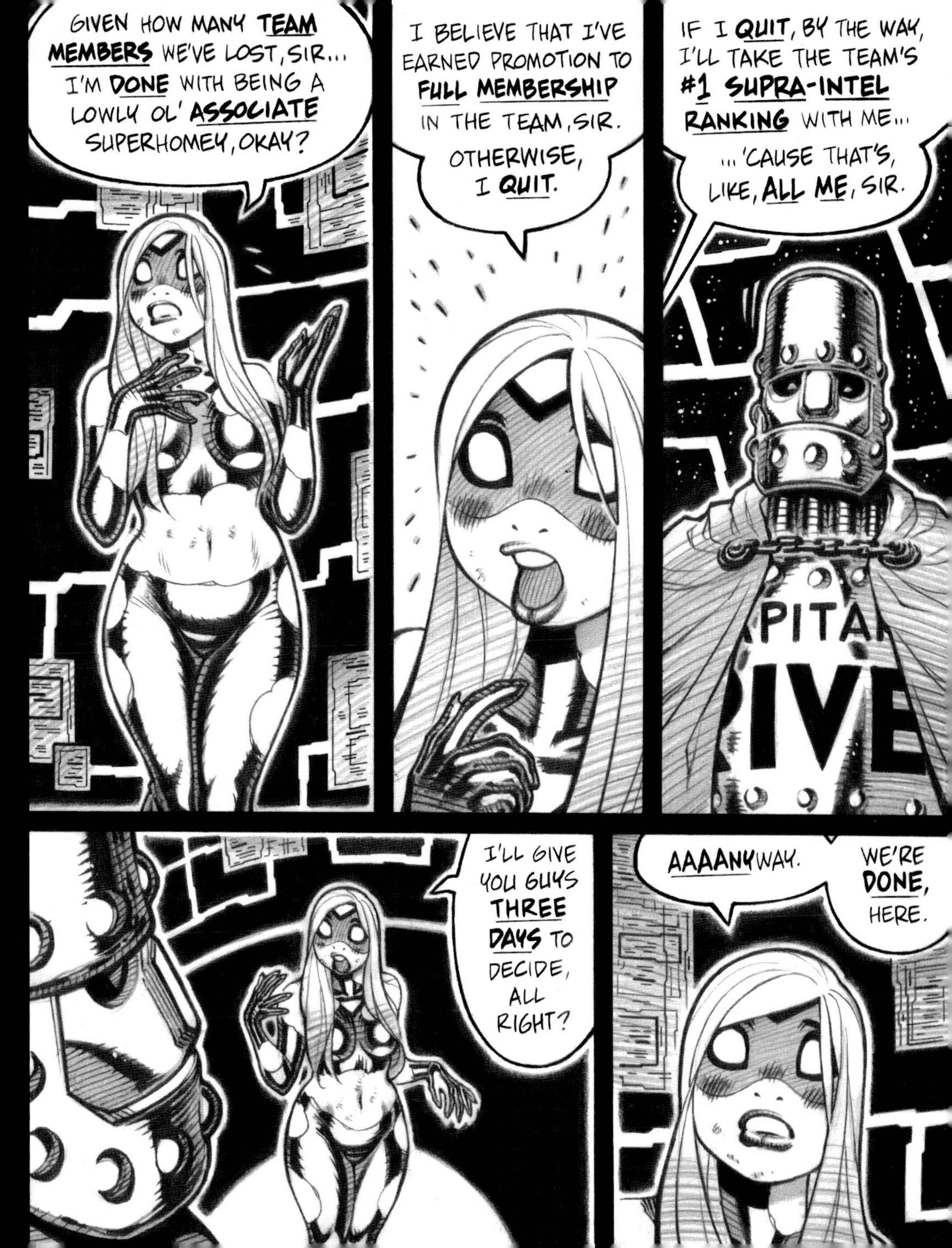

GIVEN HOW MANY TEAM MEMBERS WE'VE LOST, SIR... I'M DONE WITH BEING A LOWLY OL' ASSOCIATE SUPERHOMEY, OKAY?
I BELIEVE THAT I'VE EARNED PROMOTION TO FULL MEMBERSHIP IN THE TEAM, SIR.
OTHERWISE, I QUIT.
IF I QUIT, BY THE WAY, I'LL TAKE THE TEAM'S #1 SUPRA-INTEL RANKING WITH ME...
...'CAUSE THAT'S, LIKE, ALL ME, SIR.
PITA
IVE
I'LL GIVE YOU GUYS THREE DAYS TO DECIDE, ALL RIGHT?
AAAANYWAY.
WE'RE DONE, HERE.

AND I AM **GOING HOME**, NOW.

AND, UM, NONE OF YOU **MISJUDGEMENT-PRONE MOTHERF■KERS** ARE GONNA TRY TO **STOP** ME, UNDERSTAND?

'CAUSE, HEY, I JUST **OUTTHOUGHT** AND **OUT-FOUGHT** A FEW DOZEN SUPERVILLAINS **ALL BY MYSELF**, OKAY?

WEE OOO

WELL, GUESS **WHAT**? IF I **HAD** TO, I COULD KICK ALL OF **YOUR** SORRY ASSES, **TOO**.

GOOD NIGHT, Y'ALL.

STOMP STOMP STOMP

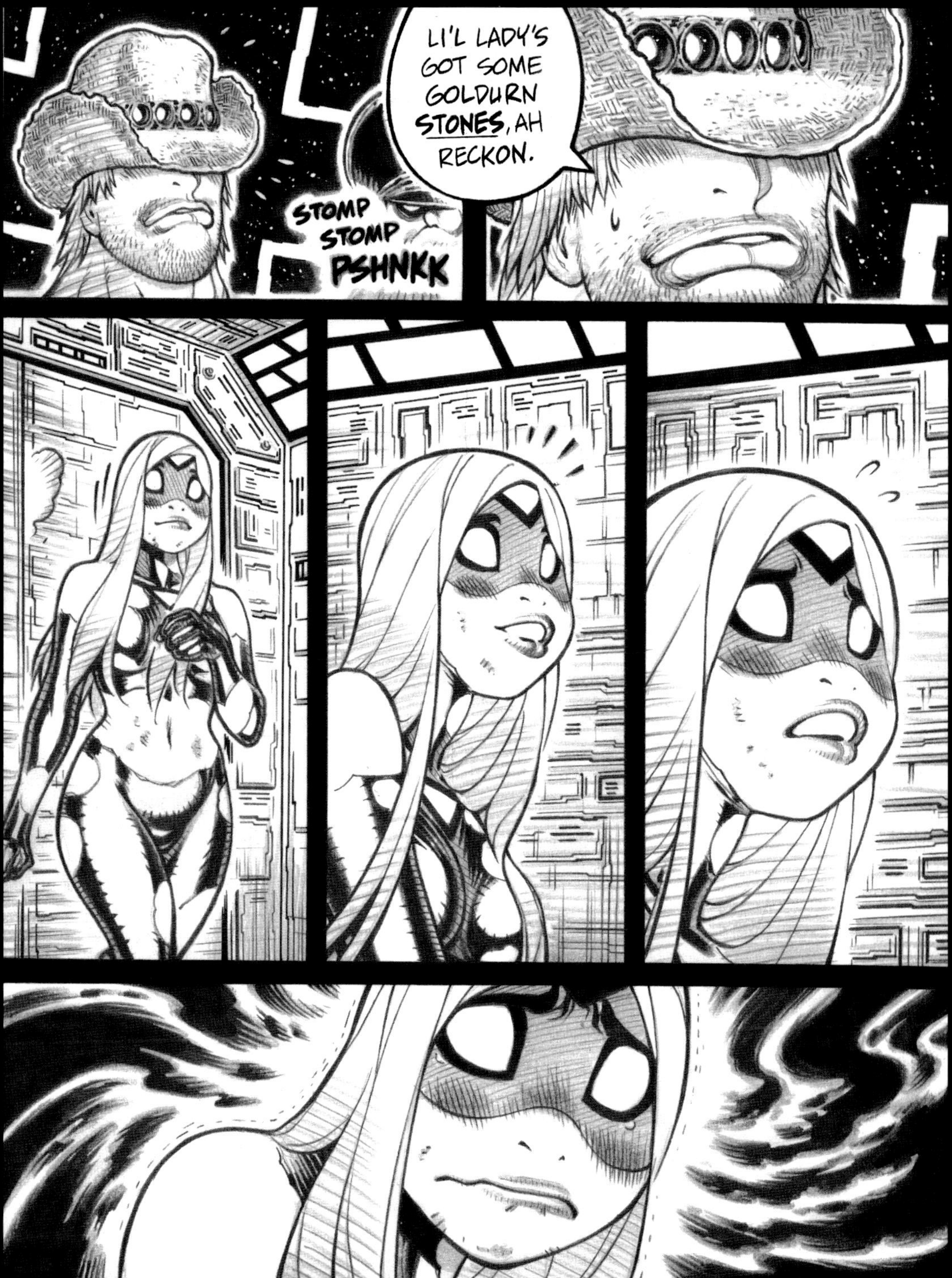
STOMP STOMP PSHNKK
LI'L LADY'S GOT SOME GOLDURN STONES, AH RECKON.

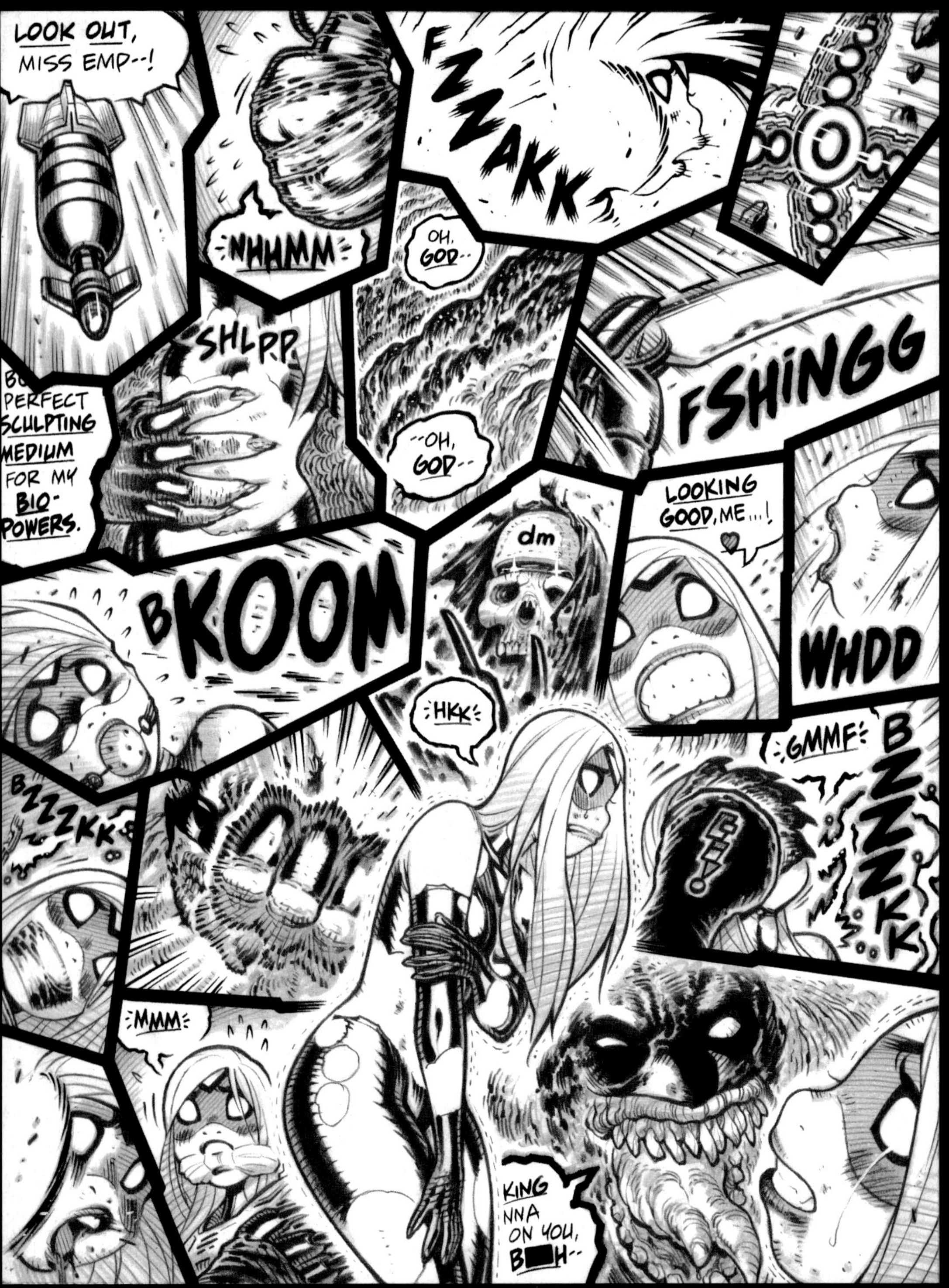

LOOK OUT, MISS EMP--!
NHMMM
FZZZAKK
OH, GOD--
SHLPP
BO
PERFECT SCULPTING MEDIUM FOR MY BIO-POWERS.
--OH, GOD--
FSHINGG
LOOKING GOOD, ME...!
dm
BKOOM
WHDD
HKK
GMMF
BZZZKK
BZZZKK
MMM
KING NNA ON YOU, B[redacted]H--

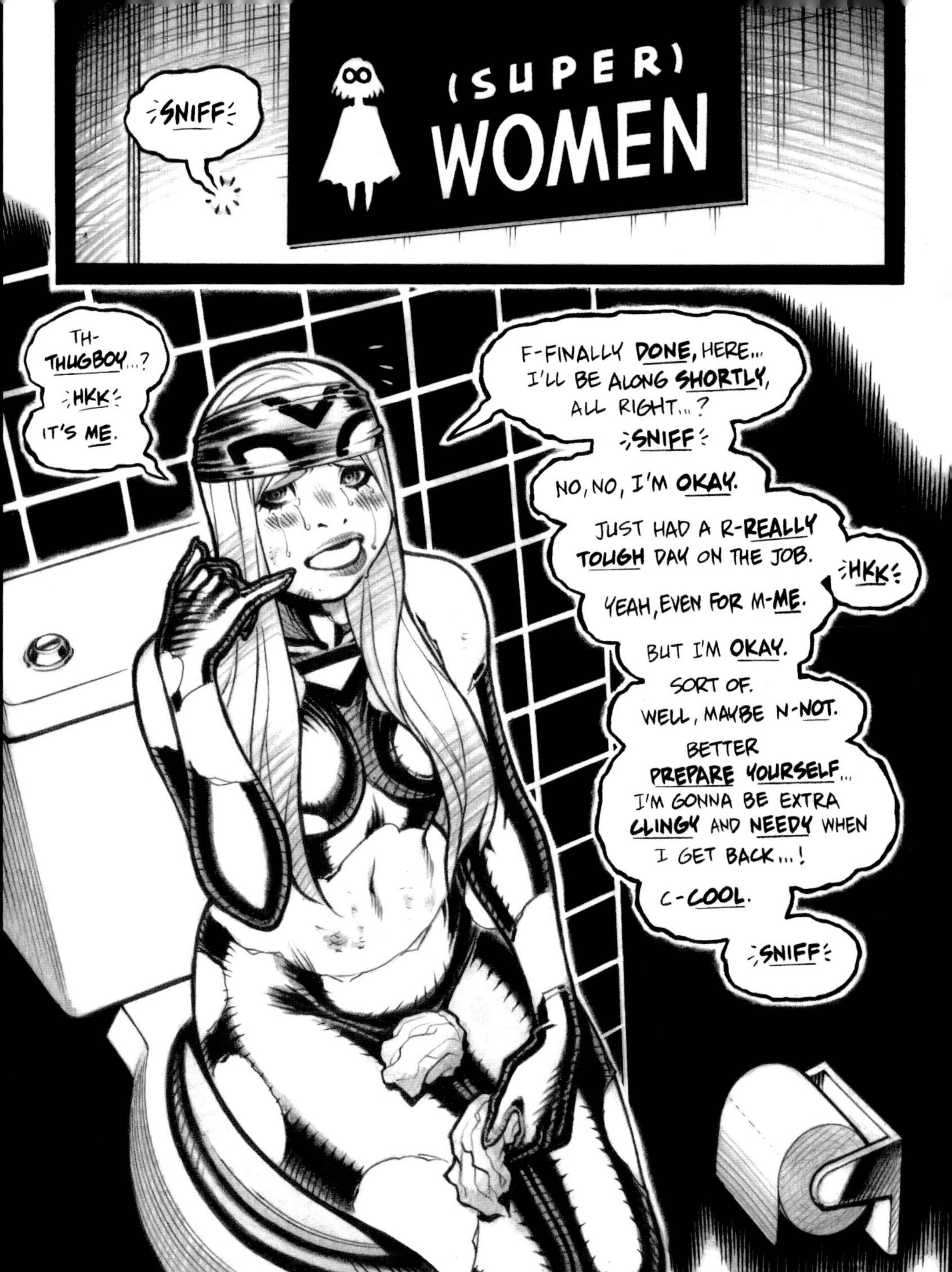
(SUPER) WOMEN
SNIFF
TH- THUGBOY...? HKK IT'S ME.
F-FINALLY DONE, HERE... I'LL BE ALONG SHORTLY, ALL RIGHT...? SNIFF
NO, NO, I'M OKAY.
JUST HAD A R-REALLY TOUGH DAY ON THE JOB.
HKK
YEAH, EVEN FOR M-ME.
BUT I'M OKAY.
SORT OF.
WELL, MAYBE N-NOT.
BETTER PREPARE YOURSELF... I'M GONNA BE EXTRA CLINGY AND NEEDY WHEN I GET BACK...!
C-COOL.
SNIFF

Empowered™

Volume 9

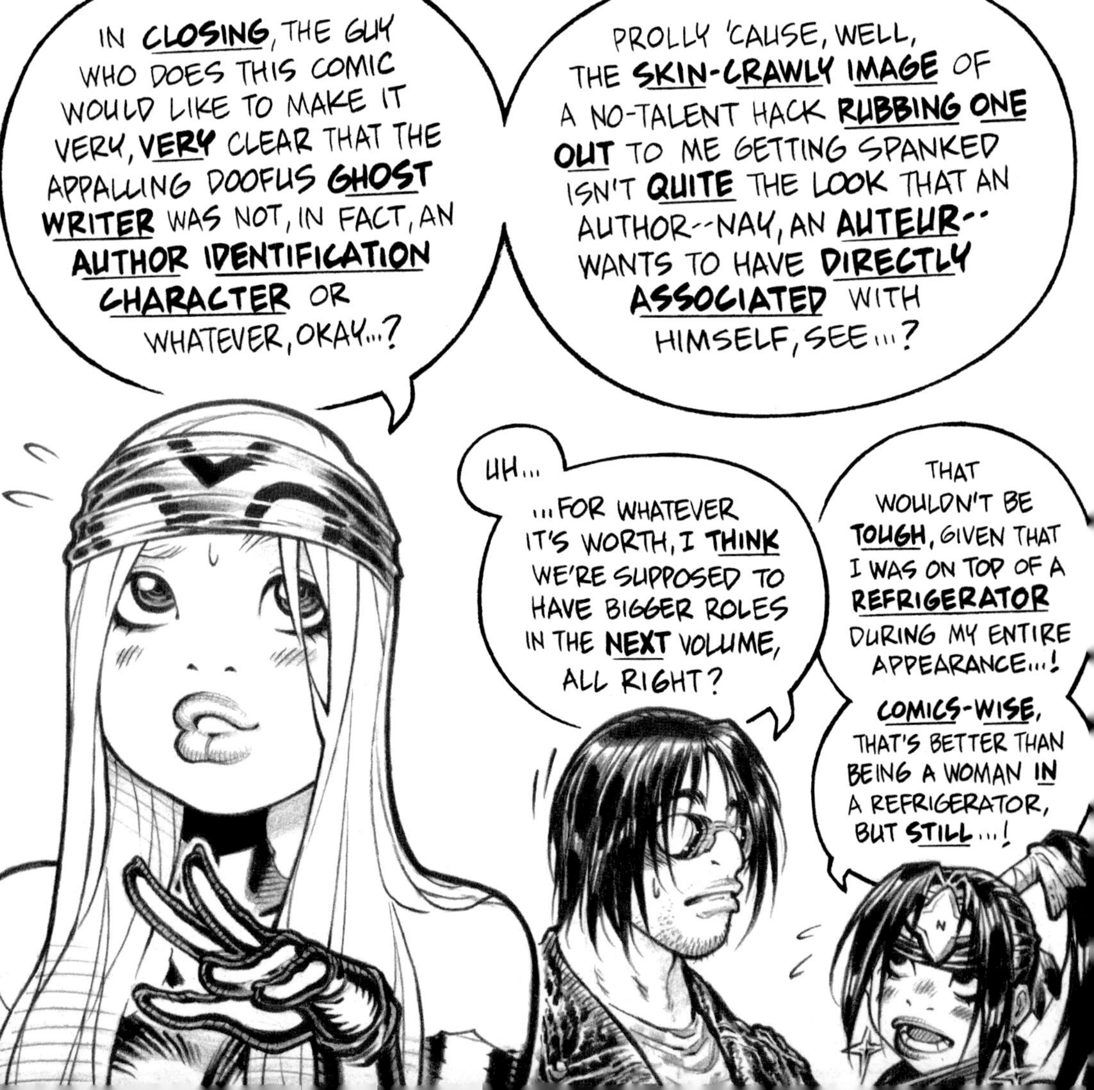

IN CLOSING, THE GUY WHO DOES THIS COMIC WOULD LIKE TO MAKE IT VERY, VERY CLEAR THAT THE APPALLING DOOFUS GHOST WRITER WAS NOT, IN FACT, AN AUTHOR IDENTIFICATION CHARACTER OR WHATEVER, OKAY...?
PROLLY 'CAUSE, WELL, THE SKIN-CRAWLY IMAGE OF A NO-TALENT HACK RUBBING ONE OUT TO ME GETTING SPANKED ISN'T QUITE THE LOOK THAT AN AUTHOR--NAY, AN AUTEUR--WANTS TO HAVE DIRECTLY ASSOCIATED WITH HIMSELF, SEE...?
UH...
...FOR WHATEVER IT'S WORTH, I THINK WE'RE SUPPOSED TO HAVE BIGGER ROLES IN THE NEXT VOLUME, ALL RIGHT?
THAT WOULDN'T BE TOUGH, GIVEN THAT I WAS ON TOP OF A REFRIGERATOR DURING MY ENTIRE APPEARANCE...!
COMICS-WISE, THAT'S BETTER THAN BEING A WOMAN IN A REFRIGERATOR, BUT STILL...!

The End.

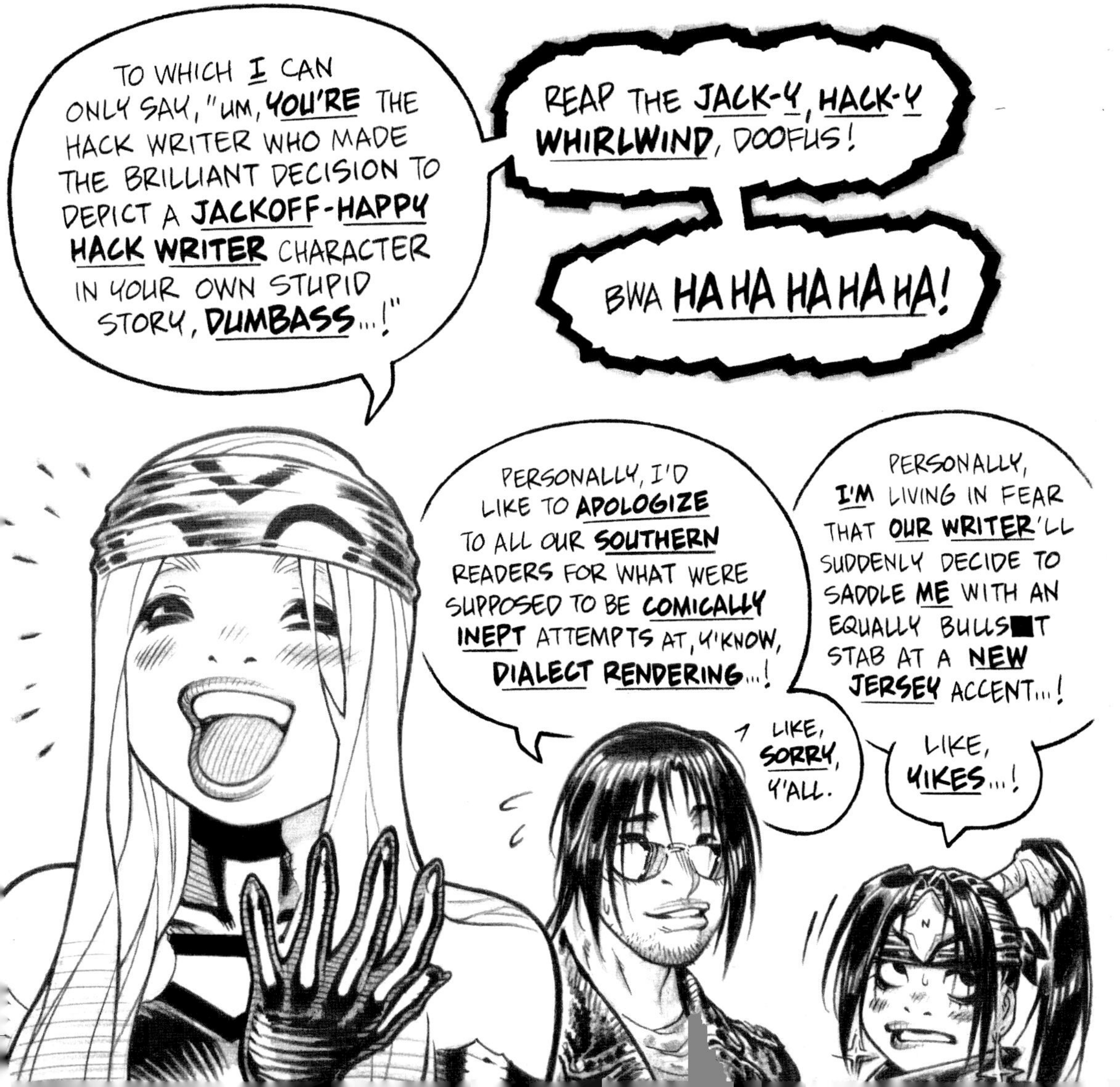
TO WHICH I CAN ONLY SAY, "UM, YOU'RE THE HACK WRITER WHO MADE THE BRILLIANT DECISION TO DEPICT A JACKOFF-HAPPY HACK WRITER CHARACTER IN YOUR OWN STUPID STORY, DUMBASS...!"
REAP THE JACK-Y, HACK-Y WHIRLWIND, DOOFUS!
BWA HA HA HA HA HA!
PERSONALLY, I'D LIKE TO APOLOGIZE TO ALL OUR SOUTHERN READERS FOR WHAT WERE SUPPOSED TO BE COMICALLY INEPT ATTEMPTS AT, Y'KNOW, DIALECT RENDERING...!
LIKE, SORRY, Y'ALL.
PERSONALLY, I'M LIVING IN FEAR THAT OUR WRITER'LL SUDDENLY DECIDE TO SADDLE ME WITH AN EQUALLY BULLS[redacted]T STAB AT A NEW JERSEY ACCENT...!
LIKE, YIKES...!

EMPOWERED

VOLUME 1
ISBN 978-1-59307-672-6
VOLUME 2
ISBN 978-1-59307-816-4
VOLUME 3
ISBN 978-1-59307-870-6
VOLUME 4
ISBN 978-1-59307-994-9
VOLUME 5
ISBN 978-1-59582-212-3
VOLUME 6
ISBN 978-1-59582-391-5
VOLUME 7
ISBN 978-1-59582-884-2
VOLUME 8
ISBN 978-1-61655-204-6
$16.99 each!

EMPOWERED DELUXE EDITION
VOLUME I hardcover
ISBN 978-1-59582-864-4
$59.99

EMPOWERED DELUXE EDITION
VOLUME II hardcover
ISBN 978-1-59582-865-1
$59.99

EMPOWERED UNCHAINED
ISBN 978-1-61655-580-1
$19.99